INSIDE DREAMWEA

BY
Sean Nicholson

New Riders

201 West 103rd Street, Indianapolis, Indiana 46290

Inside Dreamweaver UltraDev 4

Copyright © 2002 by New Riders Publishing

All rights reserved. No part of this book shall be reproduced, stored in a retrieval system, or transmitted by any means—electronic, mechanical, photocopying, recording, or otherwise—without written permission from the publisher. No patent liability is assumed with respect to the use of the information contained herein. Although every precaution has been taken in the preparation of this book, the publisher and author(s) assume no responsibility for errors or omissions. Neither is any liability assumed for damages resulting from the use of the information contained herein.

International Standard Book Number: 0-7357-1107-0

Library of Congress Catalog Card Number: 00-111654

Printed in the United States of America

First Printing: August 2001

05 04 03 02 01   7 6 5 4 3 2 1

Interpretation of the printing code: The rightmost double-digit number is the year of the book's printing; the rightmost single-digit number is the number of the book's printing. For example, the printing code 01-1 shows that the first printing of the book occurred in 2001.

Trademarks

All terms mentioned in this book that are known to be trademarks or service marks have been appropriately capitalized. New Riders Publishing cannot attest to the accuracy of this information. Use of a term in this book should not be regarded as affecting the validity of any trademark or service mark.

Warning and Disclaimer

Every effort has been made to make this book as complete and as accurate as possible, but no warranty of fitness is implied. The information provided is on an "as is" basis. The authors and the publisher shall have neither liability nor responsibility to any person or entity with respect to any loss or damages arising from the information contained in this book or from the use of the programs accompanying it.

Publisher
David Dwyer

Associate Publisher
Al Valvano

Executive Editor
Steve Weiss

Product Marketing Manager
Kathy Malmloff

Managing Editor
Sarah Kearns

Acquisitions Editor
Theresa Gheen

Development Editor
Grant Munroe

Project Editor
Michael Thurston

Copy Editor
Daryl Kessler

Technical Editors
David Alcala
Tom Steeper

Cover Designers
Doug Clarke
Aren Howell

Compositor
Marcia Deboy

Proofreader
Sharon Provart

Indexer
Lisa Stumpf

Contents at a Glance

Introduction xix

Part I Preparing to Go "Dynamic"

1. Introducing Dreamweaver UltraDev 4 5
2. Setting Up Your UltraDev Workstation as a Test Server 25
3. Developing Databases for the Web 53

Part II Building a Solid Foundation

4. Building an UltraDev Site from the Ground Up 79
5. The Dreamweaver in Dreamweaver UltraDev4 109
6. UltraDev's Graphic and Multimedia Capabilities 137

Part III Developing a Data-Driven Web Site

7. Connecting Your Web Site to a Database 165
8. Creating Visitor Accounts Through Username Validation 193
9. Building Search Capabilities 227
10. Adding Dynamic Images and Text to Search Results 255

Part IV Extending Your Administrative Capabilities

11. Developing a Database Administration Site 279
12. Engaging in eCommerce 313
13. Adding eLearning to Your Site 359
14. Extending UltraDev 389

Appendix A About the Web Site 403

Appendix B Glossary 407

Index 421

Table of Contents

Part I Preparing to Go "Dynamic"

1 Introducing Dreamweaver UltraDev 4   5

Web Development Prior to UltraDev 6
The History of UltraDev 8
    It All Began with Dreamweaver 8
    Drumbeat 2000 Became a Member of the Macromedia
    Family 9
    And the Two Became One 10
    UltraDev 4 Was Born 11
Comparing Dreamweaver and Dreamweaver UltraDev 12
UltraDev's True Talents Revealed! 13
New Features in UltraDev 4 15
    Multiple Views 15
    Syntax Coloring 16
    Remote Database Connectivity 16
    Multimedia Management 17
    Additional Server Behaviors 17
Taking a Look at UltraDev 4 19
    The Document Design Window 20
    UltraDev's Tool Palettes and Toolbars 21
        The Property Inspector 21
        The Objects Panel 21
        The Launcher Toolbar 22
Summary 23

2 Setting Up Your UltraDev Workstation as a Test Server   25

Understanding Web Server Processes 26
Choosing Your Web Server Software 28
    Personal Web Server 28
    Internet Information Server (IIS) 29
    Apache Server 31
Choosing Your Web Server Extension Environment 32
    Active Server Pages (ASP) 33
        JavaScript 33
        JavaScript for a Password Validation Form 34
        VBScript 36
        VBScript for a Password Validation Form 36

Contents   v

Java Server Pages (JSP)	37
Java for a Password Validation Form	38
ColdFusion	40
CFML for a Password Validation Form	40
Configuring Your Machine to Serve Dynamic Web Pages	41
Setting Up Your Windows 9x Workstation	42
Setting Up Your Windows NT4 Workstation to Host Dynamic Pages	43
Setting Up Your Windows 2000 Professional Workstation or Windows 2000 Server to Host Dynamic Pages	46
Setting Up Your Mac Workstation	48
Summary	51

3 Developing Databases for the Web   53

Database Fundamentals	54
The Different Database Models	54
Flat Files	55
Hierarchical Databases	56
Network Databases	58
Relational Databases	59
Choosing a Platform and Database Management System	59
Microsoft Access	60
Microsoft SQL Server	61
MySQL	62
IBM DB2	63
Oracle	63
Building a Database for the Web	64
Building Your Tables	65
Establishing Relationships and Verifying Referential Integrity	68
Connecting Your Database to the Web	70
Communicating with Your Database	73
Understanding How UltraDev Speeds the Process	73
Summary	74

Part II Building a Solid Foundation

4 Building an UltraDev Site from the Ground Up   79

Planning Your UltraDev Site	80
Developing a Site Map	81

Planning Your Pages and Directories 82
Cataloging Your Site Elements 83
Mapping Your Site Using UltraDev's Site Window 86
Setting Up Your Web Server Connection 89
Network Connections 89
FTP Connections 91
WebDAV Connections 92
Connecting to Visual SourceSafe Databases 94
Using the Site Window to Build Your Site 95
Creating a New Page Using the Site Window 96
Creating Automatically Linked Pages 97
Drag and Drop 99
Synchronizing Files 100
Verifying Your Links and Identifying Orphaned Pages 102
Editing Pages in a Workgroup Environment 104
Check In/Check Out 104
Using Design Notes 105
Summary 107

5 The Dreamweaver in Dreamweaver UltraDev 4   109

Choosing Your Page Properties 111
Page Title 111
Background Colors and Images 112
Link Colors 115
Head Tags 115
    Meta Tags 116
    Keywords 117
    Description 118
    Additional Head Tags 119
Designing a Page Layout 120
Choosing a Page Layout View 120
Creating the Main Table 120
Adding a Header Table 122
Adding a Main Data Table 125
Adding a Table for Navigation Links 126
Inserting and Linking Graphics 127
Building a Template File 131
Selecting Editable Regions 132
Creating New Pages from Templates 132
Applying a Template to an Existing Page 132
Disconnecting Pages from Templates 135
Summary 135

6 UltraDev's Graphic and Multimedia Capabilities   137

Introducing the Assets Panel 138
    Gathering Assets for Your Site 139
    Building Your List of Favorite Assets 141
    Adding Assets to Your Pages 143
Creating Dynamic Buttons 144
    Rollover Buttons 144
    Adding Flash Rollover Buttons 148
Adding Movies to Your Pages 153
    Flash Movies 153
    Shockwave Movies 157
    Adding Video to Your Pages 158
Adding Sounds to Your Pages 158
    WAV Files 158
    MIDI Files 159
    MP3 Files 159
Summary 160

Part III Developing a Data-Driven Web Site

7 Connecting Your Web Site to a Database   165

Making Sure Everything Is in Order 166
Setting Up a Database Connection and Recordset 167
Adding Dynamic Data to Your Page 173
Linking to a Detail Page 178
Using Existing Pages and Recordsets to Create Similar Pages 185
    Creating the New Titles Page 185
    Creating the New Titles Detail Page 188
    Creating the Spotlight Items Page and Detail Page 189
Summary 190

8 Creating Visitor Accounts Through Username Validation   193

Enabling Visitors to Create User Accounts 194
    Adding Dynamic Links for Creating an Account,
    Logging In, and Logging Out 195
    Creating a New User Signup Form 201
        Starting with the Template 201
        Adding the Input Form 204
        Verifying That Required Fields Are Filled 208
        Submitting the Data to the Database 209

Avoiding Duplicate Usernames 211
Adding a Confirmation Page 212
Allowing Returning Visitors to Log In and Out 214
Protecting Pages from Unauthenticated Visitors 219
Testing Your New Pages 220
Summary 224

9 Building Search Capabilities 227

Building a Single Parameter Search 228
Adding Links that Conduct the Search 228
Adding the Results Page 230
Creating a Restricted Simple Search Page 235
Creating Links to the Password Lookup Page 236
Adding the Password Lookup Page 237
Validating the User's Credentials 240
Testing the Password Lookup System 243
Adding Advanced Search Capabilities 246
Building the Advanced Search Page 246
Building the Results Page 248
Testing the Advanced Search Page 250
Summary 252

10 Adding Dynamic Images and Text to Search Results 255

Adding Rotating Images and Text 256
Using Time-Dependent Images and Text 263
Using Dynamic Links to Navigate Search Results 267
Building a Record Counter 272
Summary 274

Part IV Extending Your Administrative Capabilities

11 Developing a Database Administration Site 279

Building the Foundation for the Administration Site 280
Beginning with the Login Page 281
Creating a Template for Future Commonly Formatted Pages ..286
Adding a Menu Page to Help Users Navigate the Site 289
Giving Users a Way to Log Out 290
Adding Search Capabilities to the Administration Site 291
Creating a Product Search Page 291
Adding a Results Page to the Administration Site 293

Contents   IX

Adding, Editing, and Deleting Records 297
   Building a New Product Entry Page 297
   Editing Existing Products 299
   Removing Products from the Database 302
   Confirming Additions, Edits, and Deletions 306
Testing the Administration Site 307
Summary 311

12 Engaging in eCommerce   313

Building a Single-Transaction eCommerce Site 314
   Setting Up the Database 315
   Providing a Link to Purchase an Item 316
   Allowing Customers to Confirm Their Shipping
   Information 317
   Confirming the Order Information 320
   Accepting Payment Information 324
   Confirming the Entire Order 329
   Testing the Simple eCommerce Functionality 333
Extending the Model to Include a Shopping Cart 337
   Downloading and Installing the UltraDev Shopping
   Cart 1.2 337
   Defining the UltraDev Shopping Cart 339
   Creating a Link to the Cart 341
   The Shopping Cart Page 344
   Checking Out 348
   Alerting Visitors to an Empty Cart 352
   Testing the Shopping Cart 352
Summary 356

13 Adding eLearning to Your Site   359

Why Use eLearning? 360
Introducing the CourseBuilder Extension for UltraDev 4 361
   Downloading CourseBuilder 361
   Taking a Tour of CourseBuilder 363
Adding a Simple Quiz to Your Site 365
   Building a Quiz Site 366
   Adding a Question to the Quiz 366
   Adding Subsequent Questions 371
   Testing the Quiz 374

Expanding a Simple Quiz to Use Database-Connectivity
 to Track Results 376
   Adding the Learning Site Command Extension 376
   Setting Up Your Learning Site 378
   Modifying the Quiz Questions to Submit a Score to
   the Database 382
   Granting Access and Testing the Quiz 383
   Analyzing Quiz Results 386
 Summary 387

14 Extending UltraDev 389

 Introducing UltraDev Extensions 390
   What Are UltraDev Extensions? 391
   Where Do I Get Them? 391
   How Do I Install Them? 393
   Extension Pros and Cons 393
 Creating New Server Behaviors 395
 Modifying Existing Server Behaviors 398
 Packaging a Newly Created Extension 398
 Summary 399

A About the Web Site 403

 Source Files 404
 Database Files 404
 Third-Party Programs 404
 Feedback 405

B Glossary 407

Index 421

About the Authors

Sean R. Nicholson is the Network Administrator and Web Developer for the Career Services Center at the University of Missouri, Kansas City. Sean has a Juris Doctor from UMKC, but opted to follow a career path in technology rather than law. Sean has been working with computers since the day a shiny new Apple II computer showed up at his house when he was twelve (eighteen years ago). Sean began building Web pages using Notepad and has been developing sites in Dreamweaver after version 1.0 was released. In addition, he has used Drumbeat and UltraDev extensively in both Web-based and Intranet-based projects. Sean's technical publications include *Discover Excel 97* (IDG Books) and *Teach Yourself Outlook 98 in 24 Hours* (Sams) and he has written several legal articles ranging on topics from Canadian water rights to the protection of historic artifacts lost at sea. When he's not glued to a computer, Sean spends time with his family and friends, devoting most of his time to his wife and his two-year-old daughter.

Sean is currently using UltraDev to further develop UMKC's Virtual Career Fair and is building the first interactive Virtual Career Center using Macromedia UltraDev, Flash, and Fireworks. Feel free to contact Sean at seannicholson@kc.rr.com.

John R. Nicholson is a professor of Information Technology at Johnson County Community College in Overland Park, Kansas. He has worked with computers for over 20 years and currently teaches desktop publishing, Web site development, and computer networking with Windows NT and Windows 2000.

John is the father of four children and is closing in on an even half-dozen grandchildren. His best-selling books include *Excel 95 Secrets* (IDG Books), *Discover Excel 97* (IDG Books), and *Teach Yourself Outlook 98 in 24 Hours* (Sams). (Duds are not listed!) He was technical editor for several Microsoft Office User Specialist (MOUS) certification books, and has just completed chapters on Routing and Remote Access Services (RRAS) and Internet Protocol Security (IPSec) for *Windows 2000 MCSE Network Design Exam Prep* book (Coriolis).

John has been designing training materials and writing books for over ten years. He is currently developing materials for *Microsoft Active Directory* and *Designing Windows 2000 Security*. You can reach John at jnichols@jccc.net. He encourages your questions and comments.

About the Technical Editors

David Alcala works for Macromedia Technical Support, where he supports Dream-weaver UltraDev. Although he majored in Economics and Music in college, and worked in finance for five years, his real interest has always been with computers. He has supported UltraDev since its inception and is continually amazed at all of the different things that can be done with the program.

Tom Steeper, who is based in Baltimore, Maryland, is a freelance Web developer, specializing in Intranet solutions for small- to medium-sized companies. He moved to the U.S. in November of 2000 from England. The transition of printed media to the electronic storage of information inside databases prompted Tom to change roles in his work. Tom's first experience with Active Server Pages was using Microsoft FrontPage to view customer databases via a dial-up connection.

Tom is now using Dreamweaver UltraDev, from which he developed a fully featured prospecting system for his employer in England, utilizing the same database as before, but with far greater functionality. Tom is an active member of the UltraDev community, and has extensions available on the Macromedia Exchange and on his Web site at `http://www.webuality.com/t-cubed/`.

Dedication

This book is dedicated to the many members of the Nicholson clan, regardless of their last name. Their love and support over the years have allowed us both to choose (and change) careers according to our whims. Plus, they provide some of the best food possible for family gatherings at Christmas, Thanksgiving, and Easter.

A special dedication to our two babies, Emma (age 2) and Molly (age 20). They keep us on our toes, and make sure our lives are not dull.

Love to you both,

Dads

Acknowledgments

We would like to thank everyone at New Riders for their help on this project, especially Steve Weiss and Theresa Gheen. Steve's enthusiasm and input helped shape our ideas into a great project, and Theresa's friendly support and tireless dedication helped turn that project into a book we can really be proud of. Additional thanks go out to our "safety nets," Development Editor Grant Munroe and Technical Editors Tom Steeper and David Alcala for their tremendous efforts in making this book the best it could possibly be.

We would also like to sincerely thank each and every employee at Macromedia for developing some of the best Web development software on the market. We can't thank you all enough for your dedication to making software that makes our jobs easier.

For our families, a single thank you is not enough, so thank you, thank you, thank you. Without your understanding and support, projects like these simply would not be possible.

Finally, a special thank you to Ron Ramphal, Database Administrator for `www.careerexec.com`. It was Ron who first showed us what a powerful combination a database and a Web browser can be. From that point on, we were convinced.

A Message from New Riders

As the reader of this book, you are our most important critic and commentator. We value your opinion and want to know what we're doing right, what we could do better, in what areas you would like to see us publish, and any other words of wisdom you're willing to pass our way.

As Executive Editor at New Riders, I welcome your comments. You can fax, email, or write me directly to let me know what you did or didn't like about this book—as well as what we can do to make our books better. When you write, please be sure to include this book's title, ISBN, and author, as well as your name and phone or fax number. I will carefully review your comments and share them with the authors and editors who worked on the book.

Please note that I cannot help you with technical problems related to the topic of this book, and that due to the high volume of email I receive, I might not be able to reply to every message. Thanks.

    Email: steve.weiss@newriders.com

    Mail: Steve Weiss
              Executive Editor
              New Riders Publishing
              201 West 103rd Street
              Indianapolis, IN 46290 USA

Visit Our Web Site: www.newriders.com

On our Web site, you'll find information about our other books, the authors we partner with, book updates and file downloads, promotions, discussion boards for online interaction with other users and with technology experts, and a calendar of trade shows and other professional events with which we'll be involved. We hope to see you around.

Email Us from Our Web Site

Go to www.newriders.com and click the Contact link if you

- Have comments or questions about this book.
- Want to report errors that you have found in this book.
- Have a book proposal or are interested in writing for New Riders.
- Would like us to send you one of our author kits.

- Are an expert in a computer topic or technology and are interested in being a reviewer or technical editor.
- Want to find a distributor for our titles in your area.
- Are an educator/instructor who wants to preview New Riders books for classroom use. In the body/comments area, include your name, school, department, address, phone number, office days/hours, text currently in use, and enrollment in your department, along with your request for either desk/examination copies or additional information.

Call Us or Fax Us

You can reach us toll-free at (800) 571-5840 + 0 (ask for New Riders). If outside the U.S., please call 1-317-581-3500 and ask for New Riders. If you prefer, you can fax us at 1-317-581-4663, Attention: New Riders.

> **Note**
>
> **Technical Support for This Book** Although we encourage entry-level users to get as much as they can out of our books, keep in mind that our books are written assuming a non-beginner level of user knowledge of the technology. This assumption is reflected in the brevity and shorthand nature of some of the tutorials.
>
> New Riders will continually work to create clearly written, thoroughly tested and reviewed technology books of the highest educational caliber and creative design. We value our customers more than anything—that's why we're in this business—but we cannot guarantee to each of the thousands of you who buy and use our books that we will be able to work individually with you through tutorials or content with which you may have questions. We urge readers who need help in working through exercises or other material in our books—and who need this assistance immediately—to use as many of the resources that our technology and technical communities can provide, especially the many online user groups and list servers available.

Introduction

They've done it again! With the release of Dreamweaver UltraDev 4, Macromedia continues to set the standard in Web development software. By combining Dreamweaver's popular HTML authoring environment with the ability to rapidly develop dynamic, data-driven

Web sites on a variety of platforms, UltaDev is the most versatile Web-authoring tool on the market today.

The ability to generate dynamic pages, however, requires an understanding of not only Web development, but database design, database connectivity, and Web server technology. *Inside Dreamweaver UltraDev 4* not only brings you a complete resource for learning the database-connectivity process but also helps you understand the underlying technology at work.

Getting the Most from *Inside Dreamweaver UltraDev 4*

As a Web development professional, your time is a valuable commodity. The more time you spend learning new languages and applications, the less time you get to spend putting those technologies to work in your Web pages. As a result, *Inside Dreamweaver UltraDev 4* was designed to provide you with an overview of the applicable technology while showing you how to implement UltraDev's features into your Web site. To accomplish this, the background chapters in Part I familiarize you with the underlying technologies used to power database-driven Web sites, while the exercise-oriented chapters in Parts II, III, and IV show you how to design and manage a database-driven Web site.

Get Familiar with the Dreamweaver Features

UltraDev is based on the Dreamweaver environment and all of the tools available in Dreamweaver 4 are also available in UltraDev 4. If you are not familiar with Dreamweaver and its capabilities, you might want to consider reading up on the process of building static Web pages using Dreamweaver before you focus on the dynamic capabilities of UltraDev.

Use the UltraDev 4 Software with This Book

UltraDev 4 is significantly different from the previous version, UltraDev 1. Although most of the general principles of dynamic Web design remain the same between versions, many of the exercises in this book rely on the advanced features offered in version 4. Because of this, I highly recommend that you purchase or upgrade to version 4 before starting the exercises.

Read the UltraDev 4 Manuals

The manuals that accompany UltraDev 4 provide an overview of UltraDev and some basic tutorials on setting up database-driven pages. In addition, the online lessons built into UltraDev provide a way for you to familiarize yourself with UltraDev's capabilities.

Start at the Beginning of the Book

The first three chapters of *Inside Dreamweaver UltraDev 4* provide an overview of UltraDev, an understanding of how a Web server should be configured to serve dynamic pages, and the fundamentals of database design. An understanding of each of these topics will significantly speed your understanding and application of UltraDev's design tools.

Although you might be tempted to jump right in and start with the exercises, making sure that you are familiar with the technology and that your workstation is configured properly can save you future headaches.

If you really want to skip to a specific chapter in the book, be aware that the book's Web site (www.insideultradev.com) contains the files you will need to copy to your Web server's root directory. For instance, if you want to skip to Chapter 6, "UltraDev's Graphic and Multimedia Capabilities," just browse to the Chapter06 subdirectory on the Web site (www.insideultradev.com/book/chapter6) and copy the insideud4 folder to the root folder of your Web server. The insideud4 folder contains all the files that would have been created had you walked through the exercises in the previous chapters.

Experiment with Each Feature

UltraDev's design capabilities are limited only by your own imagination. While each chapter focuses on a feature and shows you one way to implement it, you may find hundreds of additional uses for the same feature. The best way to learn what UltraDev can and can't do is to experiment.

Use Other UltraDev Resources

As UltraDev's popularity grows, so do the number of resources that are available for helping you develop pages with UltraDev. For instance, Macromedia hosts several online forums that can help you as you develop your UltraDev skills.

In addition, as you develop dynamic Web pages, you will undoubtedly encounter difficulties with third-party applications such as Microsoft's Active Server Pages, Sun's Java Server Pages, and Allaire's (Macromedia) ColdFusion. Take advantage of the extensive online libraries that each of these companies offer for support.

How This Book Is Organized

Inside Dreamweaver UltraDev 4 is divided into four sections:

Part I, "Preparing to Go 'Dynamic,'" helps you understand the history and underlying technologies available to power your dynamic Web pages. Topics such as the history of UltraDev, understanding the process of serving dynamic Web pages, and the fundamentals of database design for the Web are covered.

Part II, "Building a Solid Foundation," focuses on UltraDev's ability to build and manage static and dynamic Web pages using both a page layout format and a code editor. Topics include UltraDev's site management tools, page layout tools, and multimedia capabilities.

Part III, "Developing a Database-Driven Web Site," shows you how to connect your Web pages to a database and how to provide your visitors with dynamically generated pages populated with information from your database.

Part IV, "Extending Your Administrative Capabilities," focuses on building pages that allow you to administer your database via a Web browser. In addition this section demonstrates how UltraDev sites can be extended with the use of eCommerce and eLearning tools.

System Considerations

Compared to its predecessor, Drumbeat 2000, UltraDev is a speed demon. However, you should make sure that your development machine meets the minimum standards required by UltraDev. If you will be testing your Web pages on your local workstation, I highly recommend that you increase your machine's memory beyond the minimum requirements to accommodate the additional Web server software.

> **Note**
>
> **Mac Users** If you are using the Mac version of UltraDev 4, you should be aware that, at this time, you cannot develop and serve database-driven Web pages using Active Server Pages or Java Server Pages using only your Mac. Because of the limited availability of ODBC and JDBC drivers for FileMaker Pro (the most popular Mac database), you will need to save your database and database-driven pages on a Windows or UNIX machine before you can fully develop and test them.

Use Other UltraDev Resources

In addition, support for dual monitors provides an added advantage to users of Windows 98 Second Edition, Windows ME, and Windows 2000. Users of these operating systems can add an additional video card to their systems and extend their desktops to a second monitor. The advantage of this comes from the fact that you can keep all of UltraDev's panels open and slide them onto the second monitor, leaving your page layout environment free of palettes.

Server Considerations

Throughout the book, you will most likely be using your workstation as a Web server. However, you will ultimately want to move your new dynamic site to a true Web server. Keep in mind that many Web hosts do not support database-driven Web sites, or do so at an extra charge. If you are using your organization's Web server to host your pages, you should check with your Web administrator to ensure that the server is properly configured for the platform for which you will be developing your pages.

Words to Work By

Enjoy yourself! Web design can often be a demanding, frustrating process but most of the time it is a lot of fun. UltraDev minimizes many of the potential frustrations by writing most of the code for you. Enjoy the process and be proud of your creations. Keep copies of all Web applications you create to act as your resume or portfolio.

Part I

Preparing to Go "Dynamic"

1	Introducing Dreamweaver UltraDev 4	5
2	Setting Up Your UltraDev Workstation as a Test Server	25
3	Developing Databases for the Web	53

Chapter 1

Introducing Dreamweaver UltraDev 4

Macromedia Dreamweaver UltraDev is setting the standard for Web site development software by offering Web developers a true What You See Is What You Get (WYSWYG) authoring environment combined with the power of a code generator that can provide your Web site with database connectivity, dynamic elements, and a host of additional features. Built using the Dreamweaver platform, UltraDev gives you the tools you need to truly bring your Web site to life.

> **WYSIWYG Editors**
>
> In case you haven't ever heard the term WYSIWYG (pronounced "wiz-ee-wig") before, a WYSIWYG editor is one that allows the developer to see exactly what the pages will look like while they are being developed. WYSIWYG editors are a great step up from traditional code editors that require you to build the pages using markup tags and then view them in a browser before you can see the results.
>
> When early WYSIWYG editors were released in the mid '90s, many hardcore Web programmers shunned them because of their inability to produce consistently cross-browser compatible pages. With the advancements made in WYSIWYG technology, however, many of these code-warriors have turned to applications such as Dreamweaver and UltraDev as their primary development environment.
>
> WYSIWYG editors have not completely replaced code editors, however. Times will certainly arise when you will need to view your code and fine tune it with adjustments. To accommodate those needs, UltraDev 4 has an integrated code editor that allows you to either view the code in full screen mode or split your screen between code and layout. If you find a need to use a third-party code editor, keep in mind that Macromedia also ships a copy of HomeSite 4.5 and BBEdit 6.0 with UltraDev 4.

Before exploring the features and capabilities of UltraDev, it's a good idea to look at how UltraDev was developed and what it can offer to you.

This chapter focuses on the following:

- The history of UltraDev
- A comparison of Dreamweaver and UltraDev
- UltraDev's capabilities
- New features in UltraDev 4
- Familiarizing yourself with the UltraDev environment

Web Development Prior to UltraDev

In the early '90s (you know, the "olden days"), Web design was a much simpler animal than it is today. Back then, the only tools you really needed to develop a Web site were a list of Hypertext Markup Language (HTML) tags, a graphics editor, and a simple text editor such as Notepad. Because of slow download speeds, browser limitations, and restrictions of HTML syntax, Web sites were basic and relatively simple in design.

Due to the limited capabilities of HTML, Web developers who desired features beyond those provided by HTML relied upon applications programmed for the Common Gateway Interface (CGI). CGI provided a standard by which any Web server could process data received from a Web page. Web servers using CGI applications would receive input from the browser (usually from a form) and pass that information to an application stored on the server that would then process the information and perform the appropriate tasks. CGI applications have been used to perform functions such as retrieving data from databases, sending the contents of a form via email, and generating user-oriented Web pages.

The difficulty with CGI arose from the fact that CGI applications required substantial Web server resources. Because the CGI applications are only capable of handling one request at a time, sites with a lot of traffic tend to experience a slowdown during heavy use of the CGI-driven portions of the site.

> **Note**
> **CGI's Utility** Though it may sound like CGI-driven Web sites are a thing of the past, in reality there are still a huge number of sites that continue using CGI to perform many functions. In addition, CGI technology has evolved into the FastCGI standard that is capable of handling multiple CGI requests at a time. The only problem is that you still have to know a programming language such as PERL, C, or C++ to add CGI capabilities to your site.

The late '90s brought about a revolution in Web technology that gave developers new tools and enhanced features to work with. Enhanced Web browsers, WYSIWYG HTML editors, embedded server-side and client-side scripting languages, and animation software all provided Web developers with the ability to build interactive, database-driven Web sites that provided access to information based on the visitor's needs. Advances in modem technology have also increased download speeds, allowing Web sites to provide visitors with more information without forcing them to wait longer. The development of new server environments such as Microsoft's Active Server Pages (ASP), Sun Microsystems' Java Server Pages (JSP), and Allaire's ColdFusion gave developers the ability to create pages that offered the same features as CGI without the extra server load.

Along with these tools, however, came a seemingly endless learning process accompanied by cryptic documentation manuals, tedious online tutorials, and a never-ending list of terms such as SQL, ASP, JSP, CFML, Flash, ODBC, JDBC, VBScript, and JavaScript. As a result, Web developers found themselves responsible for understanding more than just a list of HTML tags and basic graphic design. In today's market, a good Web developer also understands the basics of database design and maintenance, programming fundamentals, Web application server software, extension environments (such as ColdFusion, ASP, and JSP), and basic Web server maintenance.

Having realized that Web developers were now responsible for managing multiple aspects of a data-driven Web site, Macromedia identified the need for a single application to manage static HTML, graphics, databases, and the various flavors of scripting languages. In addition, they understood that this tool needed to work on a variety of server platforms and be able communicate with almost every type of database in use today. Enter UltraDev.

> **Note**
> **UltraDev's Name** Technically, UltraDev's full name is Macromedia Dreamweaver UltraDev 4. To save time (and to keep me from having to type that over and over) we'll just refer to it throughout the book as "UltraDev".

The History of UltraDev

UltraDev 4 is a result of the combination of features found in two products from Macromedia's line of Web development software: Dreamweaver and Drumbeat 2000. Whereas Dreamweaver provided the foundation for UltraDev's HTML authoring capabilities, Drumbeat gave UltraDev the capability to easily connect with databases and generate dynamic Web pages on a variety of platforms.

It All Began with Dreamweaver

In 1997, Macromedia released Dreamweaver 1.0. It was one of the most powerful WYSIWYG HTML authoring tools. Dreamweaver combined the power of cross-browser HTML authoring with the capabilities of creating dynamic behaviors using scripting languages like JavaScript.

> **Note**
> **You'll Love These Behaviors** Dreamweaver was one of the first HTML editors to successfully incorporate behaviors into the WYSIWYG environment. A *behavior* is simply a piece of code that is automatically created and inserted into your Web page based on the chosen menu command. For instance, if you wanted a pop-up message on your page you could just insert the behavior, tell Dreamweaver what you want the pop-up to say, and Dreamweaver would generate the code and insert it for you.

Web developers quickly embraced Dreamweaver for several reasons. (See Figure 1.1.) Unlike some of its competitors, Dreamweaver left native HTML untouched, giving developers the ability to use either Dreamweaver's page layout view to graphically build Web sites or the Code inspector to write raw HTML code. In addition, Dreamweaver's template and Dynamic HTML-related features provided a way to quickly create uniform Web pages that were a step above the traditional static Web site.

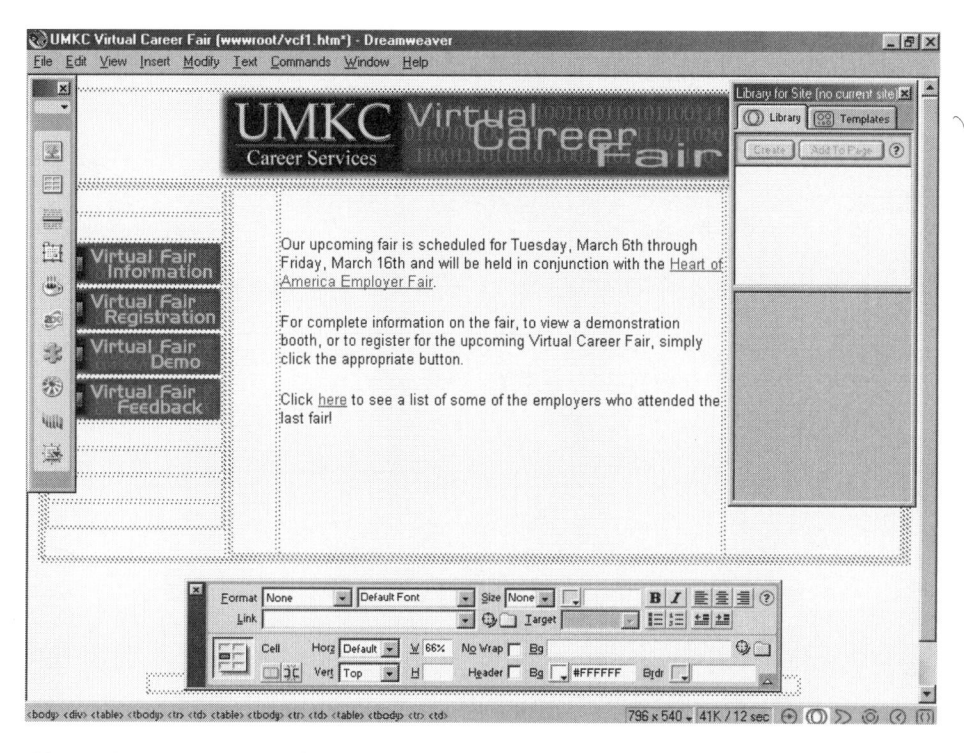

Figure 1.1 Dreamweaver's easy-to-use WYSIWYG environment has been adopted by many Web developers.

Although Dreamweaver has quickly gained popularity among developers for its powerful HTML and JavaScript authoring features, it lacked the capabilities required to create database-driven Web sites and to build Web sites that require the security and customization necessary to conduct eCommerce. As a result, Macromedia recognized a need to provide developers with an HTML editing environment that could also build database-driven Web sites.

Drumbeat 2000 Became a Member of the Macromedia Family

To provide developers with a database connectivity tool, Macromedia announced in 1999 the purchase of the Drumbeat line of products, shown in Figure 1.2, from Elemental Software. Drumbeat 2000 was then offered by Macromedia in ASP, JSP, and eCommerce editions. This application provided Web developers with the ability to build customized online stores complete with database-driven inventory. In addition, Drumbeat offered developers the ability to customize content based on the shoppers' needs and previous purchases.

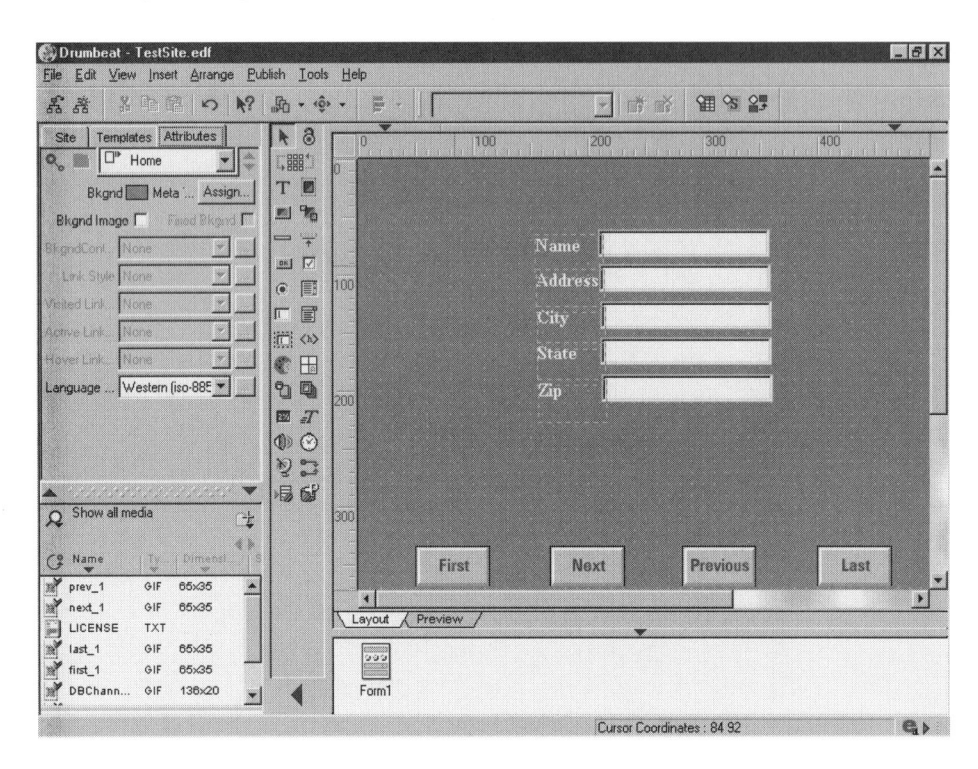

Figure 1.2   Drumbeat 2000 offered database connectivity and eCommerce solutions.

Drumbeat, however, was a much more difficult application to learn and required substantial system resources to build database-driven Web sites. As a result, Macromedia developed its own application merging the easy-to-use interface of Dreamweaver with the database-connectivity features found in Drumbeat 2000. The result was Dreamweaver UltraDev 1, released in July 2000.

And the Two Became One

By merging Dreamweaver's Web authoring and page layout tools with the database-connectivity features of DrumBeat, Macromedia created UltraDev 1, one of the most powerful Web development applications on the market. By completely integrating the Web development and database-connectivity features, developers could build static HTML pages, add JavaScript behaviors, and connect to databases using the Dreamweaver

UltraDev interface, shown in Figure 1.3. In addition, UltraDev provided support for multiple server platforms, including Microsoft's ASP, Sun Microsystems' JSP, and Allaire's ColdFusion, and allowed ASP developers to choose between JavaScript and VBScript as their scripting language of choice.

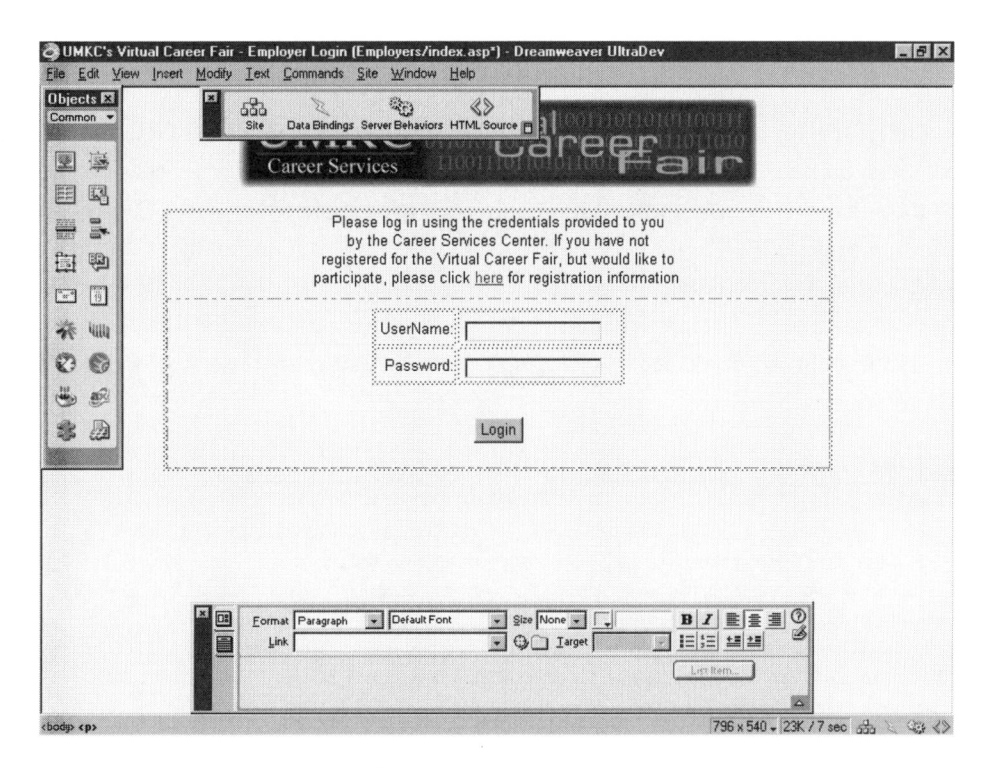

Figure 1.3 UltraDev 1 provided developers with the ability to easily create HTML code, add dynamic behaviors, and connect their Web sites to databases.

One of UltraDev 1's faults was that the product was incomplete in several ways. Certain eCommerce capabilities and security features were missing and many of the Web page behaviors found in Drumbeat were incomplete in UltraDev 1.

UltraDev 4 Was Born

With the release of UltraDev 4 in December, 2000, Macromedia filled in many of the gaps found in version 1 and developed one of the most powerful HTML authoring environments on the market. Not only does UltraDev 4 harness the powerful HTML authoring environment of Dreamweaver 4, but it includes the ability to add eCommerce and eLearning to any Web site and to build secure, database-driven sites quickly and easily.

> **Note**
>
> **What Happened to UltraDev 2 and 3?** No, I didn't skip over UltraDev 2 and 3. To bring UltraDev up to the same revision as Dreamweaver (which provides the foundation for UltraDev), Macromedia opted to skip 2 and 3 and proceed directly to 4, the current Dreamweaver version.

Comparing Dreamweaver and Dreamweaver UltraDev

Although built on the Dreamweaver platform, UltraDev offers Web developers a new set of tools that can be used to build more advanced Web applications and Web sites. In addition to being able to develop HTML in the Dreamweaver environment, UltraDev enables you to easily connect to just about any database format, view the data stored in your database, and develop dynamic pages specifically for each visitor. UltraDev also offers the ability to implement the enhanced security features necessary to operate an eCommerce Web site.

> **Note**
>
> **Do You Need Dreamweaver and UltraDev?** When UltraDev was first released, many were confused as to whether it was an add-on that you needed to purchase in addition to Dreamweaver, or a stand-alone product that simply built on to Dreamweaver's abilities. Be aware that UltraDev is a complete integration of the Dreamweaver WYSIWYG interface and the database-connectivity tools. In other words, you will be able to create both static and dynamic pages using just UltraDev 4. If you plan to purchase UltraDev 4, you do not need to first purchase Dreamweaver 4. Just think of UltraDev as Dreamweaver 4 on steroids.

Table 1.1 shows a breakdown of some of the features offered in UltraDev 4 in comparison with those available in Dreamweaver 4.

Table 1.1   A Comparison of Dreamweaver 4 and UltraDev 4 Features

Feature	Dreamweaver 4	UltraDev 4
Designs static HTML pages using either the page layout view or the source HTML	X	X
Adds JavaScript behaviors to your pages and directly edits JavaScript	X	X
Easily creates complex table layouts	X	X
Manages your Web site, verifies links, and identifies orphaned pages	X	X
Adds multimedia content to your Web pages, including Macromedia Flash objects	X	X
Adds eLearning modules to your pages via the CourseBuilder extension	X	X

Feature	Dreamweaver 4	UltraDev 4
Connects your Web site to a variety of database platforms	-	X
Creates ASP, JSP, and CFML (ColdFusion) pages	-	X
Adds eCommerce to your Web site using the Shopping Cart extension	-	X

> **Note**
>
> **Already Purchased Dreamweaver?** If you have already purchased any version of Dreamweaver, but need the database-connectivity features offered in UltraDev 4, you can upgrade at a reduced price by visiting Macromedia's Web site (www.macromedia.com).

The best way to judge whether you need Dreamweaver or UltraDev is to determine whether you want to connect your Web pages to information stored in a database. If you have no need for the database, eLearning, or eCommerce features, then Dreamweaver is most likely your best choice. If, however, you plan to store and retrieve information from a database to be displayed in your pages or want to operate an eLearning or eCommerce Web site, then UltraDev would be a better selection.

UltraDev's True Talents Revealed!

The true value that UltraDev offers doesn't necessarily come from the fact that it's a great piece of Web development software. Instead, the biggest benefit that UltraDev offers is the ability to save you and your organization time and money. For instance, less time writing code means quicker production of your Web pages. The ability to create dynamically generated Web pages means more options to market your information on the Web without having to build a Web page for each and every product or service that you have to offer. And, most importantly, the combination of UltraDev's HTML authoring tools, database connectivity features, and built-in behaviors means that full-service Web sites can be built by one individual rather than the culmination of efforts from a Web developer, a programmer, and a database administrator.

As an example, imagine this conversation between you and your boss (actually, many of you have probably already lived it or something close to it):

Your Boss: "I'm tired of our competition out-selling us because their products are available on the Internet. I want you to figure out a way for us to extend our Web site to allow our customers to order our product online. In addition, I want each customer to be able to check on his order at any given time to see if it has been shipped."

Your Answer: "Right away, boss!"

As you ponder the assignment you have just been handed, you think about all the time and skills that will be required. Your company has a Web site, but its content is static and aimed more at corporate information than product marketing. You know that all of your product information, such as a product description, pricing information, and number in stock, is stored in a database. In addition, when customers call to order your product, their personal information, payment methods, and shipping details are added to another database.

The only problem is that you don't have a clue as to how to make those databases accessible via the Web and you're not quite sure how to allow each customer to view the information regarding his own account. Fortunately, you have recently heard about UltraDev's capabilities to connect your Web pages to a database and decide to see just how easy UltraDev can make this project.

It is in these situations that UltraDev does its best work. Using UltraDev's HTML authoring environment, you can build the templates for your new eCommerce site using HTML, graphics, and JavaScript behaviors. Next, you can set up connections between UltraDev and your existing databases. Once connected, you can have UltraDev build Structured Query Language (SQL) queries that will draw the information from your database and display it in your Web pages. You can also take advantage of UltraDev's shopping cart add-on, which allows you to take orders via your Web site and update both your product database and your customer database.

Finally, you can assign a tracking number and password to each order as it is processed to permit customers to return and check their order status. Employing UltraDev's user validation tools, you can ensure that anyone checking his shipping status has the appropriate tracking number and password, and you can restrict the pages he is allowed to view (such as only those for his specific order) based on each individual tracking number.

Just think, not only does UltraDev give you the ability to create your pages in an easy-to-use graphical environment, but UltraDev can also write all HTML, JavaScript, VBScript, Java, or ColdFusion Markup Language (CFML) code for you. Additionally, you have the option of publishing these pages on a Windows, UNIX, or Linux platform using a variety of dynamic environments such as ASP, JSP, or ColdFusion.

In fact, since UltraDev saved you so much time, you found you had time to create a satisfaction survey using UltraDev's CourseBuilder add-on as a way to track your customers' impressions of your new, database-driven Web site.

What could be easier? And better yet, what could make you look better in the eyes of your boss?

> **Tip**
>
> **UltraDev is More Than Just Web Authoring Software** It's important that you understand that UltraDev is more than just a piece of software that can help you develop Web pages. Instead, UltraDev is a workplace tool that can help you and your company in the following ways:
>
> - Avoid having to hire outside consultants to design and maintain your corporate Web site or eCommerce site.
> - Decrease the need for Web developers, database administrators, and programmers to build and maintain your database-driven pages.
> - Avoid the need for multiple software titles to build pages that will function on a variety of platforms.
> - Allow you to build pages based on your skills. If you know JavaScript or VBScript, you can use ASP. If, however, you are more familiar with Java, UltraDev will build pages using that language.
>
> Because UltraDev is so flexible and does a lot of the coding for you, the result is that your business saves time, money, and resources.

New Features in UltraDev 4

If you used UltraDev in its original version and are upgrading to UltraDev 4, you should be quite pleased with the new features that have been added. New ways of building pages, managing your site, and connecting to databases can help you speed your design process and reduce the amount of code you have to write.

Multiple Views

The most obvious change in UltraDev 4 is the ability to easily switch between the Design, Code and Design, and Code views. In the previous version of UltraDev, the raw code could be viewed by opening a panel, but the panel obstructed your view of the page layout, making it difficult to see the visual changes to the site. As shown in Figure 1.4, UltraDev now allows you to use the Split view to immediately see the effects that a change in code has on the layout of the page.

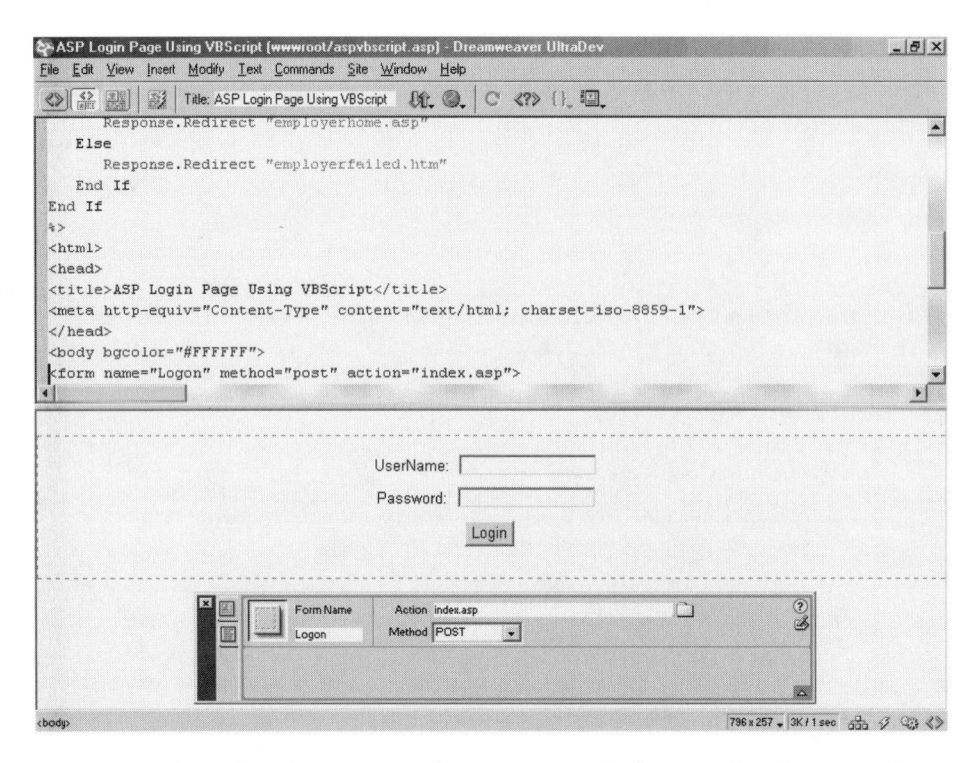

Figure 1.4 The Code and Design view allows you to view both your code and your page layout at the same time.

Syntax Coloring

In addition to making it easier to view the raw code, UltraDev 4 has incorporated distinct syntax coloring into the Code view and the Code and Design view to help you easily distinguish between your text, hyperlinks, embedded scripting code, and invisible elements such as comments. A major benefit to syntax coloring comes from the fact that it can help you identify invalid code containing problems such as open or incorrect HTML, ASP, JSP, or CMFL tags.

Remote Database Connectivity

When building a site on a test server using UltraDev 1, it was necessary to have a copy of the database located on the test server and to have an Open Database Connectivity (ODBC) driver or Java Database Connectivity (JDBC) driver configured on the machine. By choosing to use the DSN on the application server, as shown in Figure 1.5, you can take advantage of UltraDev's remote database connectivity (RDBC) and connect your UltraDev 4 pages directly to the database stored on your application or production server. This means that you don't have to worry about setting up a data source on your local workstation. This minimizes the likelihood of improperly configured servers or experiencing ODBC or JDBC errors when accessing your dynamic Web pages.

> **Note**
> **Good News for Mac Users** Mac users will most likely benefit the most from the remote database connectivity offered in UltraDev 4. With RDBC, Mac users can work directly with a database hosted on a Windows or UNIX machine and forget about searching for and installing third-party ODBC or JDBC drivers that may not function correctly.

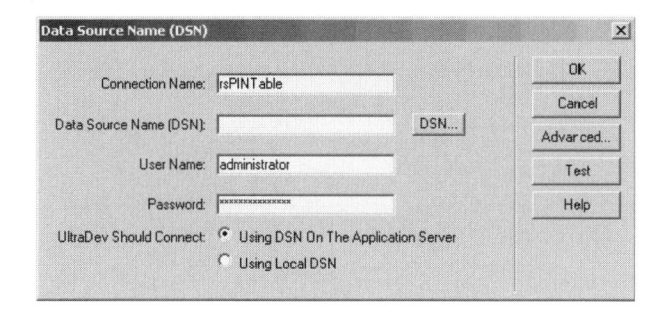

Figure 1.5 You can now choose to use a DSN located on your application or database server using UltraDev's Remote Database Connectivity feature.

Multimedia Management

Expanding upon the concept of libraries used in Macromedia Flash and UltraDev 1, UltraDev 4 now has the ability to access commonly used graphics, sounds, animations, and movie files through the Assets panel. Adding an element stored in the library to your Web site is now as simple as dragging and dropping the element to the desired location.

Shown in Figure 1.6, Macromedia has added the ability to create Flash buttons to your site using UltraDev 4. These vector graphics load quickly and allow you to change scale without reducing the quality of the image.

Additional Server Behaviors

Macromedia has supplemented the server behaviors found in UltraDev 1 with powerful behaviors such as user authentication and the ability to restrict access to pages for those users that have not been properly authenticated. All of the behaviors are available for a number of server models including ASP using VBScript or JavaScript, JSP, or ColdFusion.

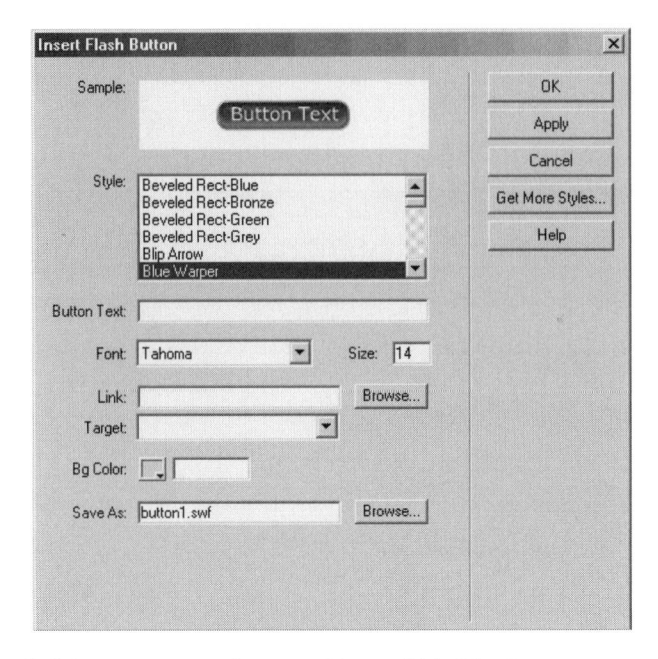

Figure 1.6 Flash buttons can now be created from within UltraDev 4.

The great thing about these server behaviors is the fact that you can easily attach them using the Server Behaviors panel, shown in Figure 1.7.

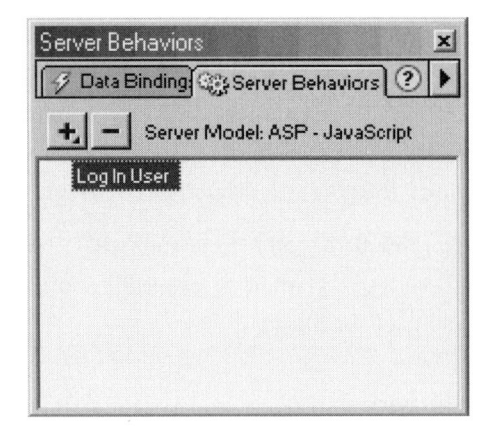

Figure 1.7 Server behaviors can be added to your page via the Server Behaviors panel.

Taking a Look at UltraDev 4

Before you begin developing pages with UltraDev, it's a good idea to familiarize yourself with some of the commonly used tools present in the UltraDev environment. If you have never used Dreamweaver before, you might be a little overwhelmed upon first starting the program. As shown in Figure 1.8, UltraDev offers several toolbars and palettes that are all activated when UltraDev is first opened. During your development process, however, it's likely that you'll hide many of these palettes and keep only those that you use most often.

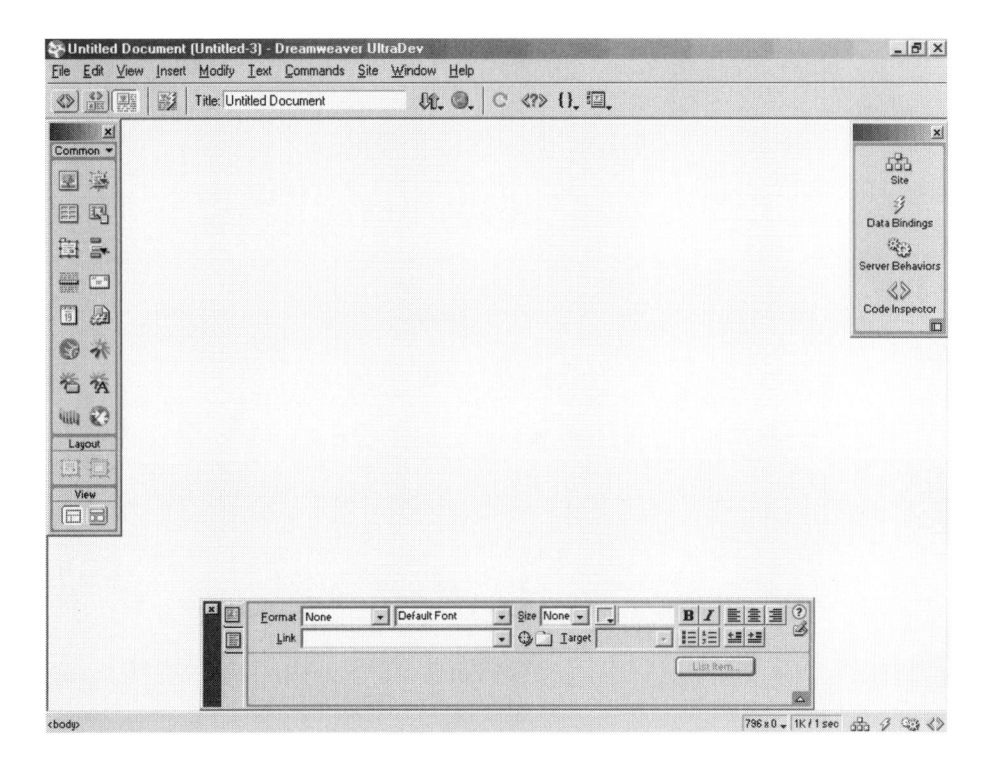

Figure 1.8 By default, UltraDev starts with several palettes on the desktop.

> **Tip**
>
> **Panels, Palettes, and Inspectors! Oh My!** Don't worry if you don't understand the functionality of some of the panels that are introduced. As you use their features throughout the later chapters, you'll be shown the capabilities of each panel and how they can be used to speed up the development process.

The Document Design Window

Think of the Document Design window, shown in Figure 1.9, as the canvas where you will be creating your Web masterpiece. In this window, you are able to see the elements you have added to your pages, manipulate their size and location, and access every feature available in UltraDev through the dropdown menus.

Figure 1.9 The Document Design window is where you will construct your Web pages.

In addition to being able to view the page layout of your Web pages, you can also customize the Document Design window to display your code in either a split-screen or full-screen mode. By using the different Code views, you can tweak any HTML or scripting code generated by UltraDev or you can add your own custom code.

The status bar of the Document Design window, shown in Figure 1.10, also provides you with some valuable information about the page you are developing. For instance, using the Window Size tool, you can adjust the size of the window to match that of different screen resolutions. This enables you to test your pages to ensure that they work in a variety of display environments. Next to the Window Size tool, UltraDev displays the size of your file and the amount of time it takes to load the page at the connection speed set in your UltraDev preferences.

Figure 1.10   The status bar provides important information about your page.

UltraDev's Tool Palettes and Toolbars

To supplement the Document Design window, UltraDev employs a series of palettes that allow you to control each aspect of your HTML elements, manage your multimedia files, and even drag and drop commonly used items right into your page from a variety of libraries.

The Property Inspector

One of the most valuable tools you will use while developing pages with UltraDev is the Property inspector. Shown in Figure 1.11, this tool displays information about each element included in your page. Depending on whether you have a graphic, table, script, sound, text, or any other type of object selected, the Property inspector will allow you to adjust the individual settings for that particular instance of the object.

Figure 1.11   The Property inspector allows you to control different objects within your Web page.

The Properties Palette is also where you will control all the formatting for the text included in your page. You can control your text size and font, select your paragraph alignment, choose color and text properties, and even create hyperlinks.

The Objects Panel

The Objects panel, shown in Figure 1.12, is one of the most powerful tools available in UltraDev; however, it takes a little getting used to in order to understand all of the features it has to offer. By clicking on the dropdown at the top of the palette, you can select from a list of object categories. Each category displays the available objects that can be easily added to your pages.

Beginning at the top of the category list, here are descriptions of the various objects you can expect to find on each of the various palettes:

- **Characters.** Common symbols such as copyright, trademark, and a variety of international monetary symbols.
- **Common.** Objects customarily added to Web pages including images, rollover buttons, tables, and email links. This palette also provides access to objects created in Macromedia Flash and Fireworks.
- **Forms.** Form elements including text boxes, buttons, lists, and radio buttons.
- **Frames.** A variety of options for sites using frames.
- **Head.** Control the information stored in the head section of your pages including Meta tags, keywords, and descriptions.
- **Invisibles.** Elements that are not visible to visitors of your page including anchors, scripts, and comments.
- **Live.** Live-data elements that allow your visitors to navigate pages including data inserted from a database.
- **Special.** Items including Java Applets, browser plug-ins, and ActiveX Control elements.

Figure 1.12 The Objects panel gives you the ability to easily add elements into your pages.

The Launcher Toolbar

Shown in Figure 1.13, the Launcher toolbar allows you to access some of the management tools included in UltraDev.

Figure 1.13 The Launcher toolbar provides shortcuts to some of UltraDev's management tools.

Features such as the Site window, the Data Bindings/Server Behaviors panel, and the Code inspector can all be initiated with the click of a button. This toolbar is also available in the lower-right corner of the Document Design window.

Summary

This chapter has given you a brief look at the history of UltraDev, the features and functionality of UltraDev 4, and some of the modules found in the UltraDev environment. As you move on to Chapter 2, "Setting Up Your UltraDev Workstation as a Test Server," you'll take a look at some of the platforms that UltraDev is capable of supporting and how to set your workstation up as a Web server so that you can begin building and testing your Web pages.

Chapter 2

Setting Up Your UltraDev Workstation as a Test Server

By now you are probably chomping at the bit to get to the development sections of the book and check out the hands-on exercises. However, taking full advantage of

UltraDev's capabilities requires either a server or a workstation capable of serving Web pages, communicating with a database, and building and serving dynamic Web pages. UltraDev was designed to develop Web pages for a variety of server platforms; you must choose a Web server application (such as Personal Web Server or Apache Web Server), an extension environment (Active Server Pages, Java Server Pages, or ColdFusion), and possibly even a scripting language (such as JavaScript or VBScript).

Once you choose a Web server application and an extension environment, and have your UltraDev workstation or server properly configured, UltraDev can write the necessary code to suit your server environment and insert it into your HTML pages. Imagine being able to build dynamic Web pages without ever having to write a line of code.

This chapter helps you accomplish the following:

- Understand the Web server processes
- Choose your Web server application
- Choose a Web server extension environment
- Configure your workstation to serve dynamic Web pages
- Configure UltraDev 4 for your selected server extension environment

Understanding Web Server Processes

Although you might already be familiar with the process of requesting and serving static Web pages written in HyperText Markup Language (HTML), the process of serving a dynamically generated page is a bit more complex. This chapter starts with a quick overview of the steps taken to generate both static and dynamic Web pages, which can help you in planning the initial setup of your workstation, your Web server, and your Web site.

As shown in Figure 2.1, when a Web browser requests a static HTML Web page, the Web server software simply locates the HTML code for the Web page and then transmits it

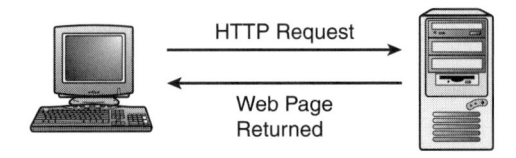

Figure 2.1 The process of serving a static HTML Web page.

to the browser where it is displayed. The code may be stored on the local hard drive, a network server, or on the Internet.

The process of displaying a dynamically generated Web page, as shown in Figure 2.2, incorporates several additional steps on the part of the server. As with a static HTML page, the request is initiated by the workstation browser. Dynamic Web pages, however, have additional programming code embedded in the page. Typically, these are programming languages such as Netscape's JavaScript, Microsoft's VBScript, Allaire's ColdFusion Markup Language (CFML), or Sun Microsystem's Java.

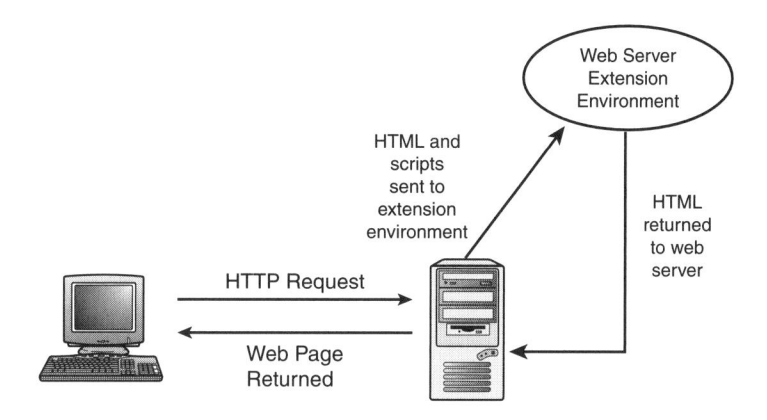

Figure 2.2 The process of serving a dynamically generated Web page.

> **Note**
>
> **A Change of Name for Allaire** When we began writing this book, Macromedia and Allaire were separate companies. During the course of writing this chapter, however, Macromedia and Allaire merged as a single company that retained the Macromedia name. Even though the ColdFusion product line will be offered by Macromedia in the future, we still refer to it as technology developed by Allaire.

Because most Web server applications are designed to handle pages composed of HTML, the Web server software usually does not know how to interpret the additional code. To process a dynamic Web page, the server must be equipped with either a server extension environment such as Active Server Pages (ASP) or Java Server Pages (JSP), or a secondary application server such as Allaire's ColdFusion Server. If the server is properly configured, the code for the Web page is sent to the extension environment, which processes both the HTML and the additional code and sends it back to the Web server that serves it back to the browser.

> **Note**
>
> **UltraDev Offers a Wide Variety of Options** UltraDev is able to build dynamic pages that communicate with a variety of server extension programs and Web application servers including ASP, JSP, and pages designed using the CFML.

Choosing Your Web Server Software

If you work for a medium or large organization, it's likely that the choice of a Web server platform is not up to you because your company may already be running one or more servers on a specific platform. If, however, you are in charge of setting up your Web server from scratch or your department will be running your dynamic Web pages from a departmental server (such as for a departmental intranet), you must decide which Web server software best suits your needs based on the application's platform, stability, and price. The following sections highlight the features of the major Web servers in use today.

Personal Web Server

Personal Web Server, shown in Figure 2.3, is a handy little application that can turn any computer running Windows into a low-volume Web server. Although Personal Web Server is not ideal for a full-blown corporate Web site, it does a relatively good job hosting small Web sites and is an ideal environment for testing Web sites using Active Server Pages. In addition, Personal Web Server is quick to set up, easy to use, and free from Microsoft. This makes Personal Web Server an excellent solution for UltraDev developers who wish to test their ASP pages on their Windows 9x or ME workstation before publishing them to their NT or 2000 server.

There is one potential limitation with respect to Personal Web Server that you should be aware of. Web sites hosted using Personal Web Server are only allowed to have a maximum of 10 users connected at any time. However, this shouldn't be a problem if you are only using the software as a test server or are building a departmental or workgroup Web site. Those wanting to host larger sites might consider moving their server machine to Windows NT 4.0 or Windows 2000 and taking advantage of Internet Information Server (or Services if you are using version 5.0 or later) instead. Any version of Internet Information Server (or Services) is abbreviated as IIS.

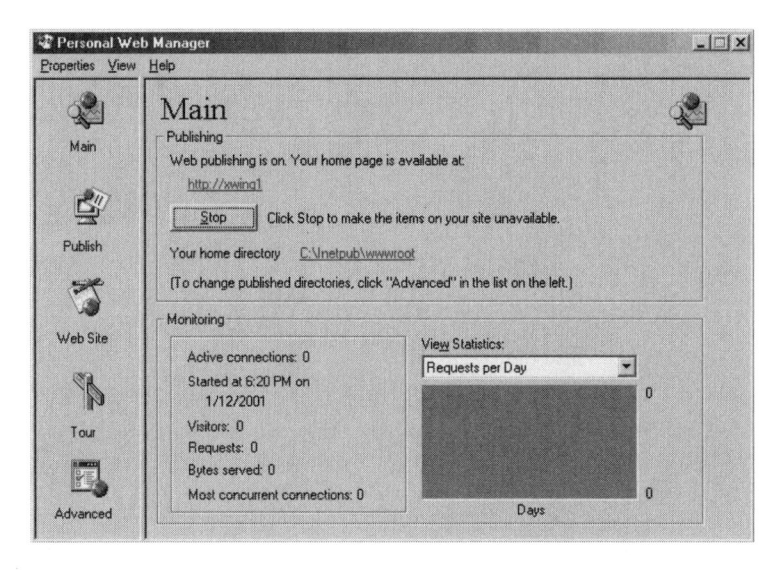

Figure 2.3 Personal Web Server is a free Web server application for Windows users.

> **Note**
>
> **Obtaining Personal Web Server** You can obtain a copy of Personal Web Server from the Add-Ons folder on the Windows 98 CD-ROM or by downloading the NT 4.0 Option Pack from the Microsoft Web site, which includes a version of Personal Web Server for Windows 9x:
>
> http://www.microsoft.com/msdownload/ntoptionpack/askwiz.asp
>
> However, both Microsoft and Macromedia have found that users who install Personal Web Server from the Windows 98 CD-ROM have fewer problems than those who obtain the software from other sources.
>
> You should also be aware that Microsoft does not support Personal Web Server for Windows ME, nor does it recommend that you install it on a Windows ME machine. For more information about Personal Web Server and ME, take a look at the article found at http://support.microsoft.com/support/kb/articles/Q266/4/56.ASP.

Internet Information Server (IIS)

Shown in Figure 2.4, IIS is Microsoft's professional Web server application and is available to users running Windows NT Server, Windows 2000 Professional, and Windows 2000 Server. IIS offers a robust environment capable of easily handling high traffic sites.

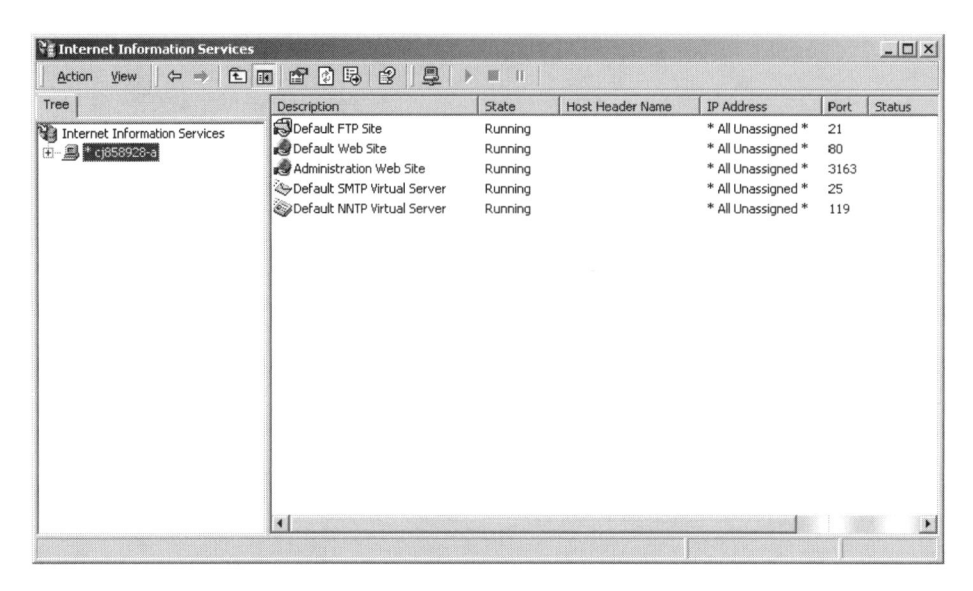

Figure 2.4 IIS is Microsoft's professional Web server application.

IIS also offers administrators a wide variety of management features. These include the ability to password-protect file and folder access, protect information using Secure Sockets Layer (SSL) encryption, and manage the Web server via an available Web interface application. Because IIS comes free with the NT Option Pack, it is generally the Web server of choice for companies running their Web server on the Windows NT or 2000 platform.

> **Note**
>
> **Things to Consider When Using Personal Web Server** If you are using Personal Web Server as your choice of Web server software, you need to be aware of some potential limitations when selecting your extension environment. While ASP functions fully under Personal Web Server, the ColdFusion Server and Studio do not function properly under the version of Personal Web Server shipped with Windows 98. For more information on the workaround for these products, check Allaire's Web site:
>
> http://www.allaire.com/Handlers/index.cfm?ID=13084&Method=Full
>
> In addition, if you plan to use JSP as your extension environment, be aware that some extensions (discussed in later sections) such as Apache Software Foundation's Tomcat are written specifically for IIS, rather than for Personal Web Server. Others, such as Allaire's JRun, are fully functional under Personal Web Server.

> **Tip**
>
> **Different Names, Similar Product** Don't get confused if you see IIS referred to as both Internet Information Server and Internet Information Services. For NT 4.0 users, IIS 4.0 is commonly referred to as Internet Information Server, while Windows 2000 users will see IIS 5.0 is called the Internet Information Services.

Apache Server

For those running servers on platforms other than Windows, Apache Software Foundation's Apache Server is one of the fastest Web server applications on the market. Used by the vast majority of Web servers on the Internet, Apache is an open source application (which means the software is free as long as it is used according to the licensing guidelines) developed to run on any server regardless of platform.

> **Note**
>
> **A New GUI for Apache** Most UNIX developers run the Apache services from the command line, but taking a screen capture of the command line doesn't paint a very pretty picture of Apache. Figure 2.5 shows a new Graphical User Interface (GUI) for Apache, called Comanche. The Comanche interface is currently being developed by the Apache Software Foundation and more information about it can be found at `http://www.comanche.org`.

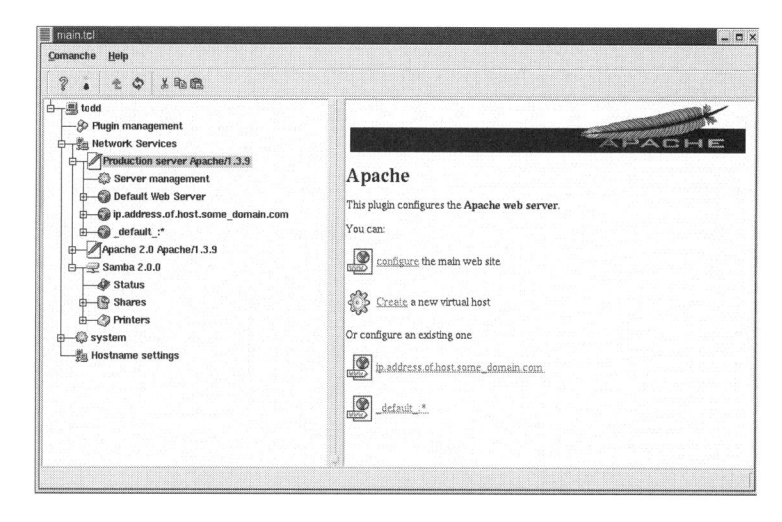

Figure 2.5 The Comanche Graphical User Interface for Apache.

Apache is also capable of serving ASP, JSP, and ColdFusion pages, with the help of additional Web server extension applications. Allaire has created several versions of the

ColdFusion Server designed specifically for UNIX and Linux. Sun Microsystems and Apache Software Foundation have developed the Tomcat JSP add-on for JSP.

Be aware, however, that running ASP on a machine running UNIX, Linux, or a Mac operating system is a bit more tricky. Because ASP is a technology developed for the Windows platform, you will need a piece of software called Sun Chili!Soft ASP if you want to bring ASP to the UNIX or Linux environments. Although UNIX and Linux are free of charge, Chili!Soft must be purchased from Chili!Soft, a subsidiary of Sun Microsystems.

> **Tip**
> **Chili!Soft** You can check out the Chili!Soft Web site at http://www.chilisoft.com.

Just about the only drawback to running Apache is the fact that there is no commercial technical support. If your Web services stop responding at 3 a.m., there is no 1-800 tech support number to call. Apache does, however, have one of the strongest peer-support systems on the Internet. If you have a browser, an Internet connection, and a search engine, you can pick and choose from the thousands of Web sites focused on answering Apache-related questions.

Choosing Your Web Server Extension Environment

Another decision that needs to be made prior to building your dynamic Web site is the extension environment that your Web site will operate in. In other words, will you use ASP, JSP, or CFML to build your dynamic pages? Once again, if you are in a corporate environment, this decision may have already been made for you. Even if it has, however, it's a good idea to understand how each of the technologies work and the pros and cons of each platform. To help you understand the various extension environments that are available, the next few sections focus on the benefits and drawbacks of the extension environments. Even if your organization has already chosen an extension environment for your site, you might want to take a look at the other available options so you know what other technologies are available for future projects.

> **Note**
> **A Focus on ASP** Because ASP is currently the most popular of the three extension environments, the exercises in this book are focused mainly on developing for ASP. We will, however, point out differences that may occur in the ColdFusion and JSP environments when they arise.

Active Server Pages (ASP)

ASP is a server-side scripting environment (meaning that the bulk of the work processing the script is done by the server rather by the browser) that allows you to embed JavaScript or VBScript code into your HTML documents. That code can then be processed by the server to accomplish a wide variety of tasks. ASP pages can communicate with databases, customize each visitor's Web site experience through the use of cookies, and even password-protect your entire site so that each visitor has to log on and be properly authenticated before gaining access.

> **Note**
>
> **Avoiding ASP Confusion** ASP stands for Active Server Pages and those pages with an .asp extension are commonly referred to as "ASP pages." Although writing "ASP pages" (which technically stands for "Active Server Pages pages") may seem redundant and repetitive, it makes reading the sentence easier, so it is the convention used throughout this book.

Because ASP pages rely on JavaScript or VBScript to implement the server-side behaviors, these pages are relatively easy to build and maintain. Just create your traditional HTML page, add the server-side behaviors in the scripting language of your choice, rename the file to have an .asp extension, and you have yourself an ASP page. Or better yet, design your traditional HTML page, let UltraDev write the scripting code for you, save your page with an .asp extension, and you can create ASP pages faster than ever.

> **Caution**
>
> **ASP Is Free for Some, Costly for Others** Although the ASP environment is free for those who are running machines on the Windows platform, those running UNIX or Linux machines may find themselves forking over a pretty penny for third-party software just to be able to run ASP. Companies like Chili!Soft have developed application servers that port ASP technology to non-Windows environments. Their software, however, can cost thousands of dollars per server to gain ASP capabilities.

Building and maintaining ASP pages usually does require some understanding of a scripting language. Situations always arise when you need to tweak a script or write a custom script that may not match one of UltraDev's built-in behaviors. It's during these times when understanding a little about the scripting language and how to read its syntax will save you time and frustration.

JavaScript

Developed by Netscape to enhance HTML capabilities, JavaScript is an interpreted scripting language that does not need to be compiled to run. The syntax of JavaScript is similar to other object-oriented languages such as Java and C++, making it an easy environment for those with programming experience to develop in. Its simplicity, however, also lends itself to Web developers with little or no programming experience.

> **Tip**
>
> **UltraDev Builds the Code for You** Throughout this chapter, we show you examples of code generated by UltraDev in the languages and environments UltraDev is capable of working with. Don't worry about understanding exactly what is going on in the code; the examples are there to demonstrate UltraDev's ability to save you time by generating code on a variety of platforms.
>
> We also include the full code of each page generated throughout the book on the book's Web site. If you're interested in looking at the code more closely or even copying pieces of the code into your own Web site, check out www.insideultradev.com.

JavaScript for a Password Validation Form

This JavaScript function would be added to a traditional HTML password validation form to ensure that the username and password were present in the database and were correct. We provide this code so you can compare it to the code generated by VBScript, CFML, and Java.

```
<%@LANGUAGE="JAVASCRIPT"%>
<!—#include file="../Connections/connLogon.asp" —>
<%var rsLogin__strUserID = "xyz";
if(String(Request.Form("UserID")) != "undefined") {
  rsLogin__strUserID = String(Request.Form("UserID"));}%>
<%var rsLogin__strPIN = "123";
if(String(Request.Form("PIN")) != "undefined") {
  rsLogin__strPIN = String(Request.Form("PIN"));}%>
<%var rsLogin = Server.CreateObject("ADODB.Recordset");
rsLogin.ActiveConnection = MM_connLogon_STRING;
rsLogin.Source = "SELECT *  FROM PIN_Table  WHERE UserID=""+
rsLogin__strUserID.replace(/'/g, "''") + "" AND PIN=""+
rsLogin__strPIN.replace(/'/g, "''") + """;
rsLogin.CursorType = 0;
rsLogin.CursorLocation = 2;
rsLogin.LockType = 3;
rsLogin.Open();
var rsLogin_numRows = 0;%>
<%// *** Validate request to log in to this site.
var MM_LoginAction = Request.ServerVariables("URL");
if (Request.QueryString!="") MM_LoginAction += "?" +
Request.QueryString;
var MM_valUsername=String(Request.Form("UserID"));
if (MM_valUsername != "undefined") {
  var MM_fldUserAuthorization="";
  var MM_redirectLoginSuccess="employerhome.asp";
  var MM_redirectLoginFailed="employerfailed.htm";
  var MM_flag="ADODB.Recordset";
```

```
var MM_rsUser = Server.CreateObject(MM_flag);
MM_rsUser.ActiveConnection = MM_connLogon_STRING;
MM_rsUser.Source = "SELECT UserID, PIN";
if (MM_fldUserAuthorization != "") MM_rsUser.Source += ","
+ MM_fldUserAuthorization;
MM_rsUser.Source += " FROM PIN_Table WHERE UserID='" +
MM_valUsername + "' AND PIN='"
+String(Request.Form("PIN")) + "'";
MM_rsUser.CursorType = 0;
MM_rsUser.CursorLocation = 2;
MM_rsUser.LockType = 3;
MM_rsUser.Open();
if (!MM_rsUser.EOF || !MM_rsUser.BOF) {
  // username and password match - this is a valid user
  Session("MM_Username") = MM_valUsername;
  if (MM_fldUserAuthorization != "") {
    Session("MM_UserAuthorization") =
String(MM_rsUser.Fields.Item(MM_fldUserAuthorization).Value;
  } else {
    Session("MM_UserAuthorization") = "";
  }
  if (String(Request.QueryString("accessdenied")) !=
  "undefined" && false) {
    MM_redirectLoginSuccess =
    Request.QueryString("accessdenied");}
  MM_rsUser.Close();
  Response.Redirect(MM_redirectLoginSuccess);
}
MM_rsUser.Close();
Response.Redirect(MM_redirectLoginFailed);}%>
```

In fact, many Web developers using WYSIWYG editors, such as Macromedia's Dreamweaver, often insert JavaScript commands without actually knowing it. Common Web site behaviors such as rollover buttons, pop-up windows, and status bar messages usually come from simple JavaScript functions that your editor adds for you.

> **Tip**
>
> **Client-Side Behaviors Versus Server-Side Scripting** UltraDev has a variety of JavaScript Behaviors available for developers to include in their Web creations without ever writing a single line of code, including the rollovers, pop-ups, and messages mentioned earlier. The code that UltraDev adds to your pages, however, is processed by the Web browser on the visitor's machine and may slow down the load times for your pages. This type of scripting is commonly referred to as client-side scripting.
>
> Server-side scripts, on the other hand, are processed by the Web server itself and require no processing on the client-side. Examples of server-side scripts include those that extract data from a database or restrict access to certain pages based on authentication.

Currently, JavaScript is the ideal language for developers who are developing ASP pages but don't currently know a scripting language. Because the last few releases of both

Netscape Navigator and Internet Explorer interpret JavaScript syntax relatively well, you can learn one language that allows you to write both server-side scripts and client-side scripts.

> **Caution**
> **JavaScript Versus Jscript** Don't confuse JavaScript and JScript. JScript is Microsoft's version of JavaScript and depends on a completely different Document Object Model (DOM) from JavaScript. While Microsoft's JScript is supposed to be compatible with Netscape Navigator, it just doesn't seem to work out that way. I have always had better experiences developing in JavaScript because scripts that function in Navigator usually function in Internet Explorer as well.

The only downside to using JavaScript in your pages comes when you add client-side JavaScript Behaviors to your pages because they only run in Internet Explorer 4.0 or greater and Netscape 4.0 or greater. When it comes to JavaScript for your server behaviors, however, you should have no problems because the JavaScript code is processed on the server side and passed back to the browser as HTML.

VBScript

Developed by Microsoft, VBScript offers a relatively easy scripting language to learn and use. In fact, anyone with familiarity of Microsoft's Visual Basic language will feel quite comfortable jumping in with VBScript. Non-programmers can find a wide variety of tutorials and books that will teach you the syntax and control structures and get you programming with VBScript in no time.

> **Tip**
> **Learn More About VBScript** A good place to learn more about VBScript and Microsoft's endeavors to create a VBScript interpreter plug-in for Netscape is Microsoft's scripting Web page at http://msdn.microsoft.com/scripting/.

The following is the function for the same password validation form used in the previous JavaScript section. The only difference is that the code uses VBScript rather than JavaScript.

VBScript for a Password Validation Form

This VBScript function would be added to a traditional HTML password validation form to ensure that the username and password were present in the database and were correct.

```
<% @LANGUAGE="VBSCRIPT" %>
<!—#include file="../Connections/connLogon.asp" —>
<% Dim rsLogin__strUserID
```

```
rsLogin__strUserID = "xyz"
if(Request.Form("UserID") <> "") then
rsLogin__strUserID = Request.Form("UserID")
Dim rsLogin__strPIN
rsLogin__strPIN = "123"
if(Request.Form("PIN") <> "") then
rsLogin__strPIN = Request.Form("PIN")%>
<% set rsLogin = Server.CreateObject("ADODB.Recordset")
rsLogin.ActiveConnection = "dsn=connVcfemployers;"
rsLogin.Source = "SELECT * FROM PIN_Table WHERE UserID='"
+ Replace(rsLogin__strUserID, "'", "''") + "' AND PIN='" +
Replace(rsLogin__strPIN, "'", "''") + "'"
rsLogin.CursorType = 0
rsLogin.CursorLocation = 2
rsLogin.LockType = 3
rsLogin.Open
rsLogin_numRows = 0 %>
<% If rsLogin__strUserID <> "xyz" then
   IF Not rsLogin.EOF Then
      Session("svUserID") =
      (rsLogin.Fields.Item("UserID").Value)
        Response.Redirect "employerhome.asp"
   Else
        Response.Redirect "employerfailed.htm"
   End If
End If %>
```

The biggest downside to using VBScript is the fact that Netscape Navigator does not fully support the language in its browser. Therefore, programming client-side elements in your ASP site in VBScript could leave some visitors with those nasty browser errors. Again, keep in mind that the VBScript added to your pages to run server-side commands won't be affected because they are processed on the server and then sent to browser as HTML.

Java Server Pages (JSP)

The JSP environment is unique from ASP or ColdFusion in that its technology is based on Java—a compiled, object-oriented programming language. This extends the capabilities of what you can do with JSP pages to just about anything you can do with the Java language.

Instead of embedding a script in the HTML page or using additional extension tags, as ASP and ColdFusion pages do, JSP includes a small program referred to as a *servlet*. These servlets run on the server and modify the HTML of the page before they are sent back to the browser. Servlets can perform tasks such as inserting data from a database, controlling the behaviors of HTML elements, and even rewriting the HTML code completely.

Java for a Password Validation Form

Once again, this servlet performs a similar function to the previously shown scripts.

```
<%@page contentType="text/html; charset=iso-8859-1" language="java"
import="java.sql.*"%>
<%@ include file="Connections/connPINTable.jsp" %>
<%
String Recordset1__MMColParam = "1";
if (request.getParameter("UserID") !=null) {Recordset1__MMColParam =
(String)request.getParameter("UserID");}
%>
<%
Driver DriverRecordset1 = (Driver)Class.forName(MM_connPINTable_DRI-
VER).newInstance();
Connection ConnRecordset1 =
DriverManager.getConnection(MM_connPINTable_STRING,MM_connPINTable_USER-
NAME,MM_connPINTable_PASSWORD);
PreparedStatement StatementRecordset1 =
ConnRecordset1.prepareStatement("SELECT UserID, PIN FROM PIN_Table WHERE
UserID = '" + Recordset1__MMColParam + "'");
ResultSet Recordset1 = StatementRecordset1.executeQuery();
boolean Recordset1_isEmpty = !Recordset1.next();
boolean Recordset1_hasData = !Recordset1_isEmpty;
Object Recordset1_data;
int Recordset1_numRows = 0;
%>
<%
// *** Validate request to log in to this site.
String MM_LoginAction = request.getRequestURI();
if (request.getQueryString() != null &&
request.getQueryString().length() > 0) MM_LoginAction += "?" +
request.getQueryString();
String MM_valUsername=request.getParameter("UserID");
if (MM_valUsername != null) {
  String MM_fldUserAuthorization="";
  String MM_redirectLoginSuccess="success.jsp";
  String MM_redirectLoginFailed="failure.jsp";
  String MM_redirectLogin=MM_redirectLoginFailed;
  Driver MM_driverUser =
(Driver)Class.forName(MM_connPINTable_DRIVER).newInstance();
  Connection MM_connUser =
DriverManager.getConnection(MM_connPINTable_STRING,MM_connPINTable_USER-
NAME,MM_connPINTable_PASSWORD);
    String MM_pSQL = "SELECT UserID, PIN";
    if (!MM_fldUserAuthorization.equals("")) MM_pSQL += "," +
MM_fldUserAuthorization;
    MM_pSQL += " FROM PIN_Table WHERE UserID='" + MM_valUsername + "' AND
PIN='" + request.getParameter("PIN") + "'";
    PreparedStatement MM_statementUser =
MM_connUser.prepareStatement(MM_pSQL);
    ResultSet MM_rsUser = MM_statementUser.executeQuery();
    boolean MM_rsUser_isNotEmpty = MM_rsUser.next();
    if (MM_rsUser_isNotEmpty) {
```

```
    // username and password match - this is a valid user
    session.putValue("MM_Username", MM_valUsername);
    if (!MM_fldUserAuthorization.equals("")) {
      session.putValue("MM_UserAuthorization",
MM_rsUser.getString(MM_fldUserAuthorization).trim());
    } else {
      session.putValue("MM_UserAuthorization", "");
    }
    if ((request.getParameter("accessdenied") != null) && false) {
      MM_redirectLoginSuccess = request.getParameter("accessdenied");
    }
    MM_redirectLogin=MM_redirectLoginSuccess;
  }
  MM_rsUser.close();
  MM_connUser.close();
  response.sendRedirect(response.encodeRedirectURL(MM_redirectLogin));
}
%>
```

One of the biggest benefits to running JSP is the fact that some vendors, such as the Apache Software Foundation and Sun Microsystems, are working to develop open-source JSP servers that operate on any platform and are free to use. Currently, the Jakarta Project (a subproject of Apache) is offering Tomcat for UNIX, Linux, and Win32 platforms on their Web site at http://jakarta.apache.org. However, support for Tomcat is often difficult to obtain and comes only in the form of peer support.

If you are interested in running JSP, but want the security of commercial support, consider IBM's WebSphere application server (a demonstration copy is included with UltraDev 4) or Allaire's JRun Server. Both are commercial JSP application servers that run on the Windows, UNIX, and Linux platforms.

> **Note**
>
> **J2EE—The New Breed of JSP** There is a new era of JSP currently being implemented called Java 2 Enterprise Edition (J2EE) server solutions. Most major JSP projects rely upon the enhanced capabilities of J2EE servers to reuse code and handle increased traffic. However, using J2EE is much more costly than implementing a traditional JSP server. For more information about J2EE, check out the information provided by Sun Microsystems at http://www.j2ee.com.

There are two drawbacks to using JSP as your Web server extension environment. First, if you use an open-source JSP server such as Tomcat you're going to have to do quite a bit of work to find support when things go wrong. On the other hand, if you choose to use a product that offers commercial support, you're going to have to pay for your JSP server. The second drawback is the fact that JSP relies on Java, which is a full-blown object-oriented programming language. If you aren't already familiar with Java and you don't want to spend quite a bit of time learning a programming language, you are probably better off sticking to ASP or ColdFusion.

ColdFusion

Allaire has developed an extension environment of its own with the creation of the ColdFusion Server application and CFML. CFML is unique in the fact that rather than embedding additional code within the HTML, it simply extends HTML by giving you additional tags that the ColdFusion Server is able to interpret and convert to HTML. This means that developers who are familiar with HTML tags only need to learn the additional CFML tags before they can begin creating ColdFusion pages.

CFML for a Password Validation Form

Once again, this CFML performs a similar function to the scripts shown previously.

```
<cfinclude template="Connections/connPasswordDB.cfm">
<cfif IsDefined("FORM." & "UserID")>
<cfscript>
    MM_valUsername=Evaluate("FORM." & "UserID");
    MM_fldUserAuthorization="";
    MM_redirectLoginSuccess="success.cfm";
    MM_redirectLoginFailed="failure.cfm";
    MM_dataSource=MM_connPasswordDB_DSN;
    MM_queryFieldList = "UserID,PIN";
    if (MM_fldUserAuthorization IS NOT "")
MM_queryFieldList=MM_queryFieldList & "," & MM_fldUserAuthorization;
</cfscript>
<cfquery datasource=#MM_dataSource# name="MM_rsUser"
username=#MM_connPasswordDB_USERNAME# password=#MM_connPasswordDB_PASS-
WORD#>
SELECT #MM_queryFieldList# FROM PIN_Table WHERE
UserID='#MM_valUsername#' AND
PIN='#Evaluate("FORM." & "PIN")#'
</cfquery>
<cfif MM_rsUser.RecordCount GREATER THAN 0>
<cfscript>
        // username and password match - this is a valid user
        Session.MM_Username = MM_valUsername;
        if (MM_fldUserAuthorization IS NOT "") {
           Session.MM_UserAuthorization =
MM_rsUser[MM_fldUserAuthorization][1];
        } else {
           Session.MM_UserAuthorization = "";
        }
        if (IsDefined("accessdenied") AND false) {
           MM_redirectLoginSuccess = Evaluate("accessdenied");
        }
```

```
</cfscript>
<cflocation url="#MM_redirectLoginSuccess#" addtoken="no">
</cfif>
<cflocation url="#MM_redirectLoginFailed#" addtoken="no">
<cfelse>
<cfscript>
    MM_LoginAction = CGI.SCRIPT_NAME;
    if (CGI.QUERY_STRING NEQ "") MM_LoginAction = MM_LoginAction & "?"
& CGI.QUERY_STRING;
</cfscript>
</cfif>
```

The fact that CFML is one of the easiest extension languages to learn makes it an attractive environment for developers who are not necessarily programmers. In addition, CFML is capable of supporting objects created in both C++ and Java, making it an extremely robust language.

The drawbacks to using ColdFusion are few and far between. ColdFusion has an excellent support structure in the form of both corporate technical support and from the numerous peer-support groups. Its most significant downfall is the fact that the ColdFusion Server will cost you, while ASP and JSP both offer free extension programs for specific platforms. The cost, however, is often justified by the excellent technical support available and the powerful development environment provided in the ColdFusion Studio.

> **Note**
>
> **Using ColdFusion with UltraDev** UltraDev ships with a single-license demonstration version of ColdFusion server. This application allows you to build and test CFML pages on your local machine to determine if ColdFusion is an environment that suits your needs. If you choose to develop in the ColdFusion environment, you must either purchase one of the commercial versions of ColdFusion server to run in conjunction with your Web server software or find a Web host that hosts ColdFusion pages.

Configuring Your Machine to Serve Dynamic Web Pages

Configuring your local workstation to act as a test server for your dynamic pages can be advantageous in several aspects. For instance, a test server allows you to develop and change your Web site without any effect on your production server. The fact that database-driven pages rely on additional factors such as database integrity and proper database connections makes it even more logical to test your pages thoroughly on a test server before migrating your pages to your Web server. In addition, by using your workstation as your test server, you don't have the cost and maintenance associated with a second server. Finally, for those Web developers whose sites are hosted remotely, it can save you the time of having to transfer your files to your server every time you want to test them.

> **Tip**
>
> **Avoid Editing "Live" Pages** It is always a good idea to have a test server on which you can edit your Web pages and work out any kinks before making them "live." Editing pages directly from your production server is unwise because it places your data at risk of corruption. If you already have a test server in place and configured to serve dynamic pages, you may want to skip the following exercises.

Setting Up Your Windows 9x Workstation

Serving dynamic Web pages from a Windows 9x machine requires the installation of Microsoft's Personal Web Server. This exercise walks you through the installation and configuration process for serving up ASP pages.

> **Caution**
>
> **FrontPage Personal Web Server is Not Personal Web Server** Be careful not to confuse Personal Web Server with the FrontPage Personal Web Server. If you have designed Web pages using Microsoft's FrontPage, you have probably installed the FrontPage Personal Web Server on your machine for testing those pages. This is not the same product as Microsoft's Personal Web Server and will not help you in testing your database-driven pages because it does not support ASP. If you have previously installed FrontPage on your machine, it would be best if you uninstall the FrontPage Personal Web Server and install the version of Personal Web Server available on the Windows 98 CD or from the Microsoft Web site. Don't worry: You can still test any pages created in FrontPage using Personal Web Server.

Exercise 2.1 Setting Up Personal Web Server on a Windows 9x Machine

1. Run the setup.exe program for Personal Web Server that you have either downloaded from Microsoft or have located on your Windows 98 CD in the Add-Ons folder. The installation welcome screen is displayed.
2. Click the Next button and choose a typical installation as your choice of installation preference.
3. Figure 2.6 shows the dialog box that allows you to choose the publication folder that will act as the root folder for your Web pages. Unless you would like the root on another drive, leave the default folder and click the Next button.
4. Once Personal Web Server finishes copying the necessary files, click the Finish button and then choose to restart your computer.

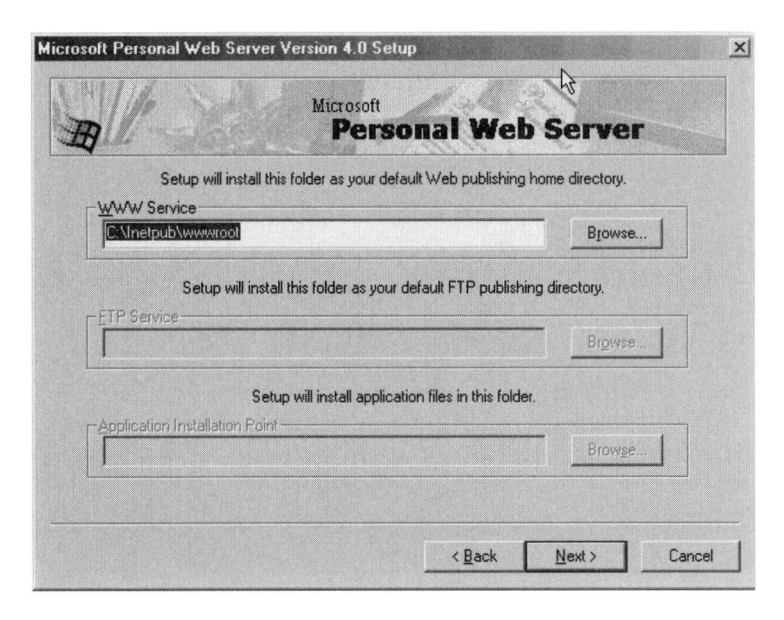

Figure 2.6 Choose the folder that you would like to act as the root for your Web pages.

After your computer is restarted, Personal Web Server should be running and an icon should be active in your system tray. At this point you are ready to develop, publish, and test ASP pages on your local machine. You can access information about your Personal Web Server site by right-clicking on the icon and choosing Properties.

> **Tip**
> **Testing Your Personal Web Server Installation** If you want to test your Personal Web Server installation to ensure that your machine is currently capable of serving ASP pages, just click the Start button and select Programs. Find the Personal Web Server folder. If your machine is serving ASP pages properly, you will see the complete Personal Web Server Documentation page. If Personal Web Server is not fully installed or is not configured correctly, the page will only partially load.

Setting Up Your Windows NT4 Workstation to Host Dynamic Pages

If you are using Windows NT Workstation, you have the advantage of using a scaled-down version of IIS 4.0 called Peer Web Services, rather than Personal Web Server. This version of IIS offers all the features and control over your Web site, but limits the number of concurrent connections in the same way that Personal Web Server is limited.

44   Part I   Preparing to Go "Dynamic"

> **Note**
>
> **Personal Web Server on an NT4 Workstation** If, for some reason, you do not want to use Peer Web Services on your NT4 Workstation, Personal Web Server can be used instead. Just follow the installation steps for the Windows 9x machine in the previous section.

Exercise 2.2 Setting Up Peer Web Services on a Windows NT Workstation

> **Tip**
>
> **Checking Whether Peer Web Services is Already Installed** Peer Web Services may have been installed on your machine during the NT4 Workstation installation. To see whether the service is already installed, right-click on the Network Neighborhood icon on your desktop and choose Properties from the drop-down menu. From the Network Control Panel, click the Services tab. If Personal Web Services is already installed it will be listed.

1. To install the Personal Web Services, right-click the Network Neighborhood icon on your desktop and choose Properties from the drop-down menu.
2. In the Network Control Panel, select the Services tab and click the Add button.
3. From the list of available services, select the Microsoft Peer Web Server, as shown in Figure 2.7, and click OK. If prompted, fill in the location of your Windows NT Workstation setup CD.

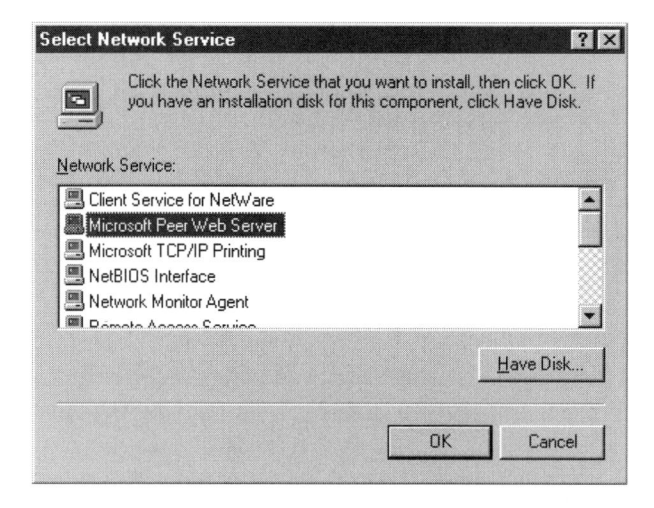

Figure 2.7   Add the Peer Web Server from the list of available services.

4. From the Microsoft Peer Web Services dialog box, click OK.
5. In the Peer Web Services Options dialog box, shown in Figure 2.8, make sure that all the options are selected for installation and click OK.

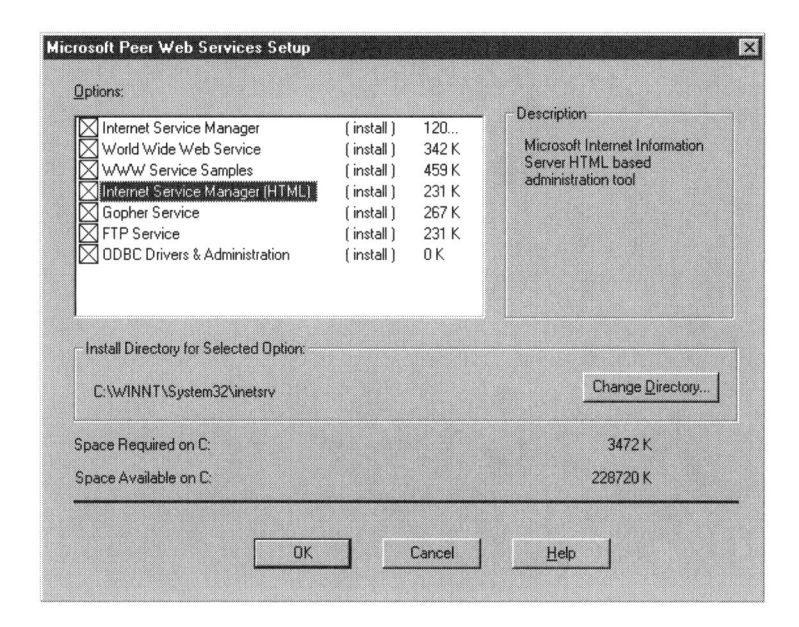

Chapter 2 Setting Up Your UltraDev Workstation as a Test Server 45

Figure 2.8 Add all options in the Peer Services Options dialog box.

6. The Publishing Directory dialog box that appears allows you to choose the location where your Web pages will be located. If you do not wish to change the location, leave the defaults and click OK.

7. After the Peer Web Services installation is finished copying the necessary files, click OK to close the Network Control Panel and begin the ODBC installation. The ODBC installation process begins automatically after you close the Network Control Panel.

8. As shown in Figure 2.9, the Install Drivers dialog box allows you to add ODBC drivers for connecting your ASP pages to databases. In the Install Drivers box, select the SQL Server drivers for installation and click OK.

9. After the SQL Server drivers are installed, click OK in the dialog box that confirms that the Peer Web Services were installed correctly.

Once the Peer Web Services are installed, you can access the services by choosing Start/Programs/Microsoft Peer Web Services/Internet Service Manager. The Peer Web Services Control Panel, shown in Figure 2.10, is similar to the IIS 4.0 Management Console found in Windows NT Server.

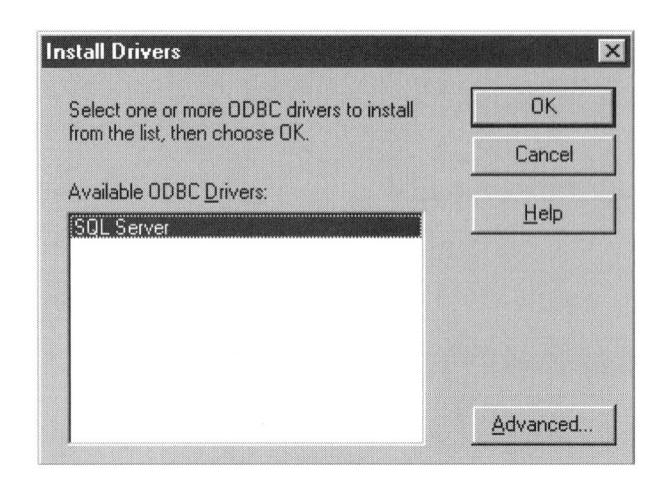

Figure 2.9 The Install Drivers dialog box allows you to add ODBC drivers.

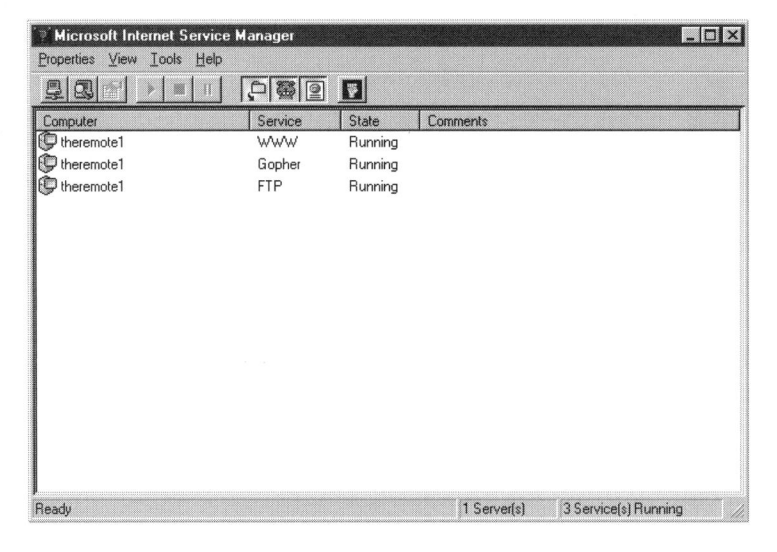

Figure 2.10 The Peer Web Services Control Panel allows you to start and stop your Web services.

Setting Up Your Windows 2000 Professional Workstation or Windows 2000 Server to Host Dynamic Pages

Configuring Internet Information Services on your Windows 2000 Professional workstation is a simple matter. The following exercise takes you through each of the steps.

Exercise 2.3 Setting Up IIS 5 on a Windows 2000 Professional Workstation

1. From the Start menu, click Settings/Control Panel, and then double-click Add/Remove Programs.
2. On the left side of the dialog box, select Add/Remove Windows Components. The Windows Components Wizard, shown in Figure 2.11, is displayed. Select the Internet Information Services (IIS) component and click the Next button.

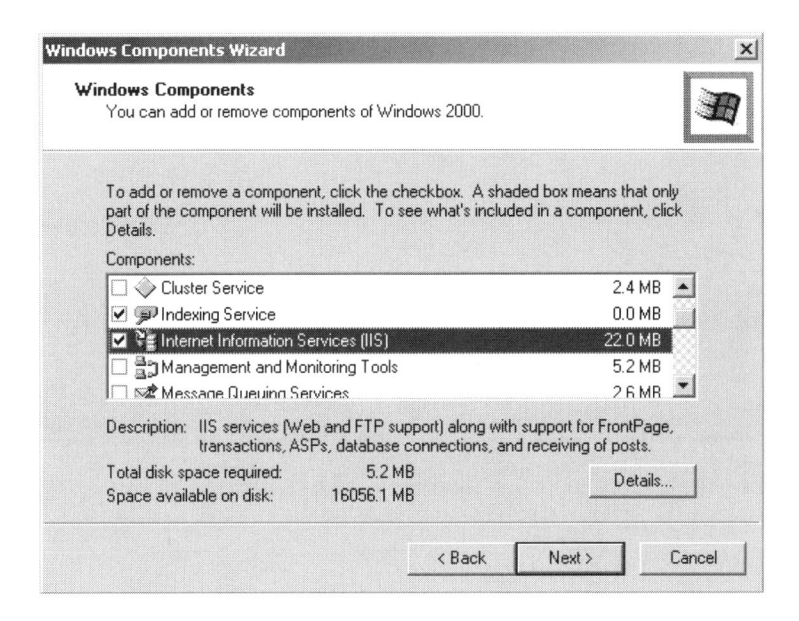

Figure 2.11 The Windows Components Wizard allows you to quickly add IIS to your Windows 2000 Professional workstation.

The next screen begins the loading of IIS. You must either have the Windows 2000 Professional CD-ROM in the drive, or browse to the location of the I386 folder on your hard drive.

3. It may take several minutes to install IIS on your computer. When finished, click Finish to close the dialog box.
4. To start or stop ISS, choose Start/Programs/Administrative Tools/Internet Information Services. The IIS dialog box, shown in Figure 2.12, is displayed.

   To view the various services, click the plus sign next to the name of your computer. Available services are shown in Figure 2.13.
5. Close the dialog box.

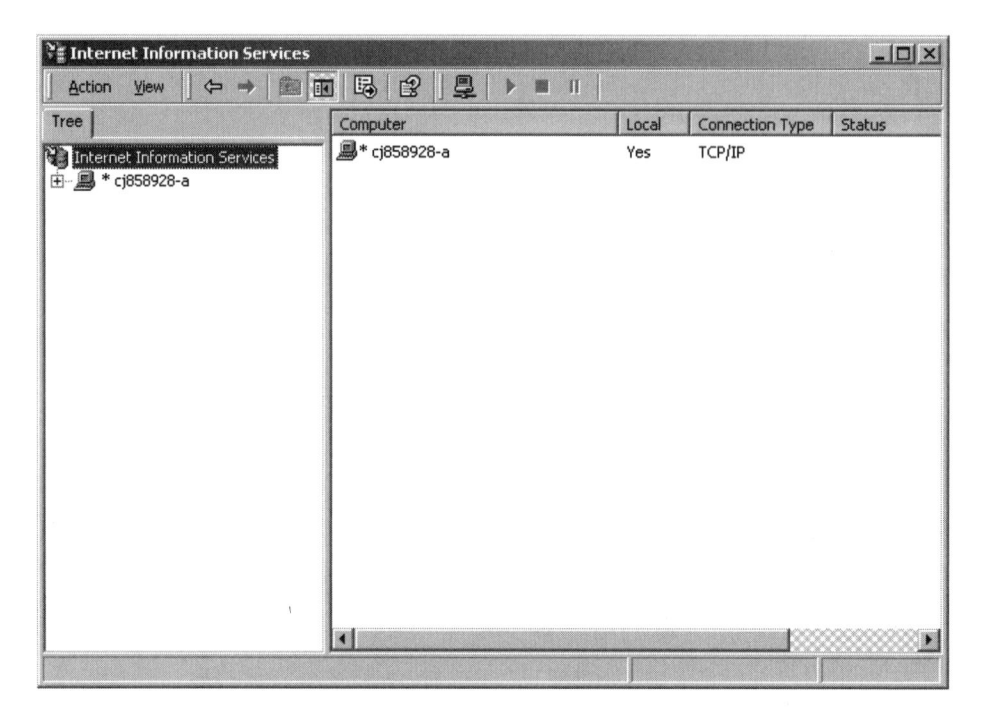

Figure 2.12 The Internet Information Services dialog box allows you to start and stop the Internet services.

Setting Up Your Mac Workstation

With all this talk about Windows machines, it wouldn't be proper not to give you Mac fans the chance to use your machines as a test server as well. Unfortunately, your abilities to serve database-driven pages directly from your machine are severely limited due to the lack of ODBC and JDBC drivers for Mac databases. Because of this, any database-driven pages you create will have to be tested on a Windows or UNIX server.

Although you can't serve dynamic pages, you can set your Mac up as a Web server if you have Mac OS8 or greater by taking advantage of the Personal Web Sharing services that are featured with the OS. If, however, you don't want to use the Personal Web Sharing service or don't have OS8, you can use the version of Microsoft's Personal Web Server created for the Mac.

> **Tip**
> **Personal Web Server for the Mac** You can download the Mac version of Personal Web Server from the Microsoft Web site:
> http://support.microsoft.com/support/kb/articles/Q164/5/71.asp

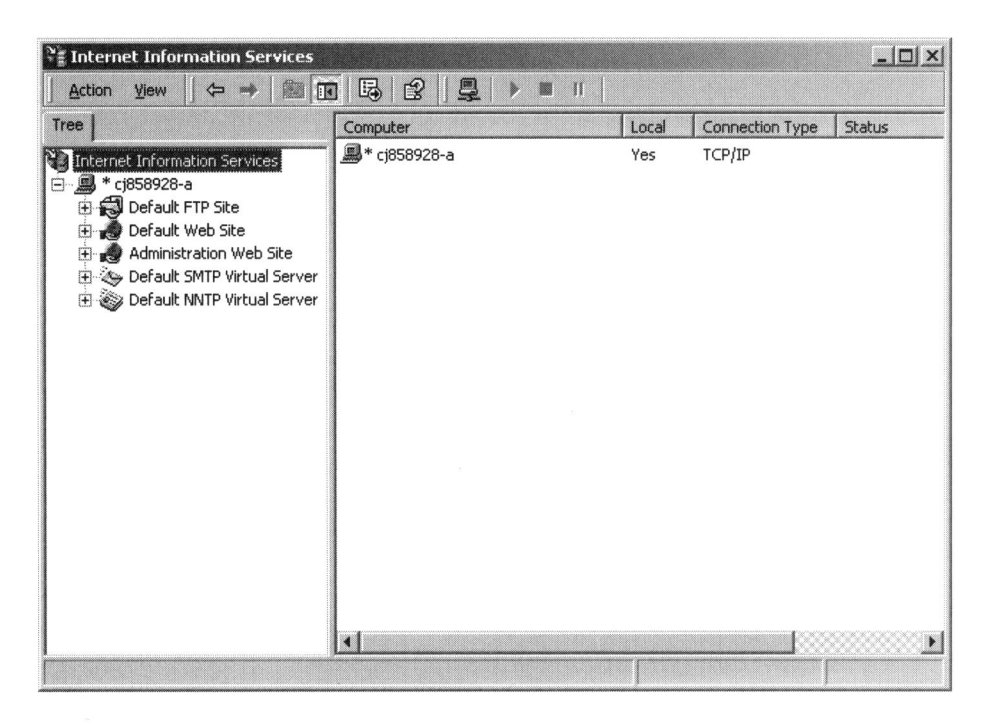

Chapter 2 Setting Up Your UltraDev Workstation as a Test Server   49

Figure 2.13 The IIS services are displayed.

Exercise 2.4 Setting Up Personal Web Server on a Mac Workstation

1. Download the Microsoft Personal Web Server for Mac from the Web address listed in the preceding Tip.
2. Run the Setup program for Personal Web Server and accept the license agreement.
3. In the Personal Web Server Installer, make sure the Easy Install option, shown in Figure 2.14, is selected and click Install.

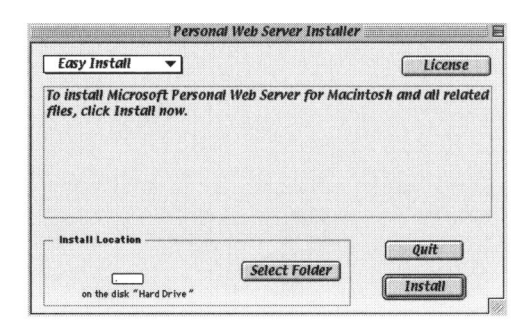

Figure 2.14 Installing the Personal Web Server using the Easy Install option.

4. When the Personal Web Server is finished installing, open the program by clicking the Personal Web Server executable.
5. From the Personal Web Server Control Panel, click the Set Folder button to select the location of your Web site files as shown in Figure 2.15. The default location is the My Personal Web site folder.

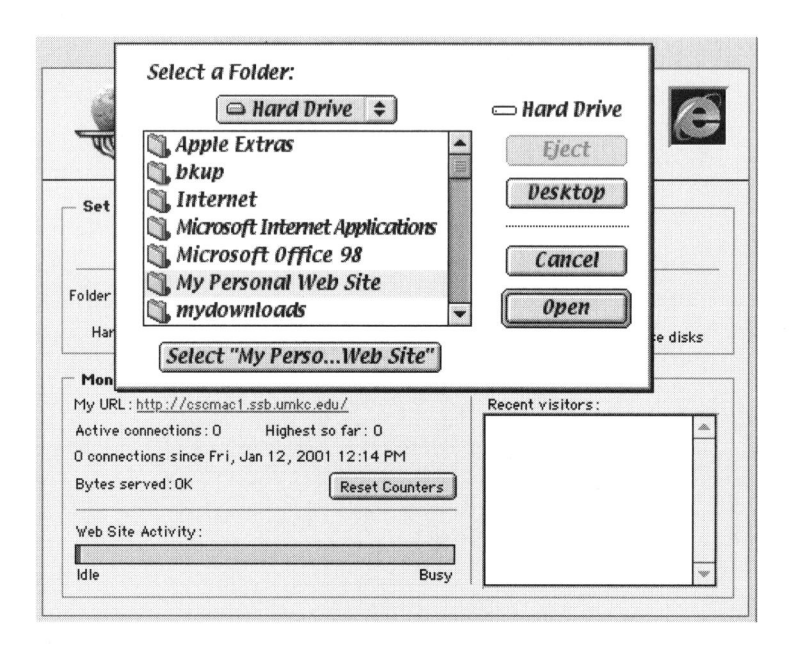

Figure 2.15 The Personal Web Server Control Panel lets you choose the folder that is shared on the Web.

6. Click the Start button to start the Web services. As shown in Figure 2.16, the button changes to Stop and the URL to your Web site is displayed in the Monitor Web Site panel.
7. Test your site by clicking the link to your Web site in the Monitor Web Site panel. If the default.asp page displays, you are ready to begin developing ASP pages on your Mac.

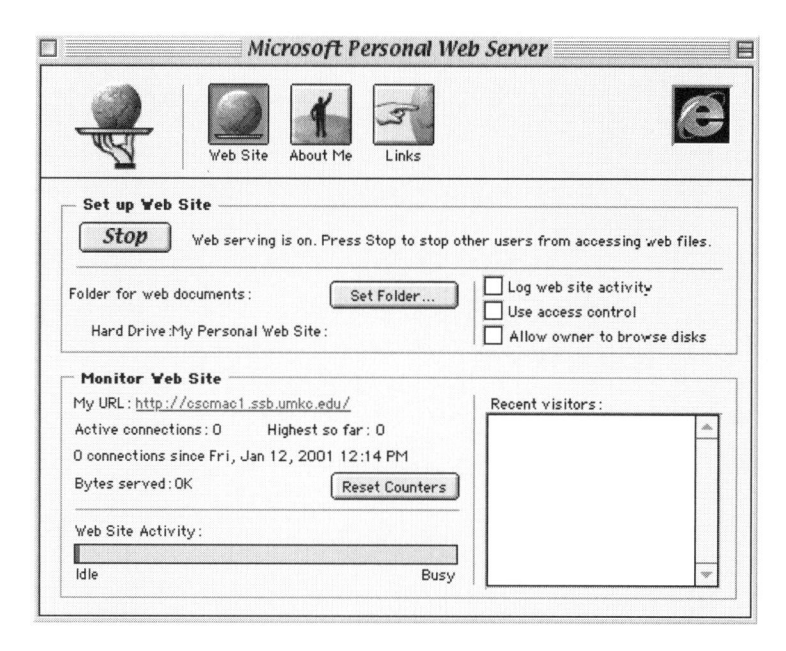

Figure 2.16 When the Web services are started, the URL to your site is displayed.

Summary

This chapter introduced you to a wide variety of Web server applications, Web server extension environments, and scripting languages. In addition, you should now have a workstation that is suitable for serving Active Server Pages so you can take advantage of the hands-on exercises in the later sections of the book. However, before you begin on the development side, Chapter 3, "Developing Databases for the Web," reviews the concepts of databases and how they are connected to Web pages.

Chapter 3

Developing Databases for the Web

Over the last decade, databases have played an integral role in the growth of the Internet. Sites that integrate databases in their design through the use of dynamically built pages are often able to provide visitors with more information while using fewer developmental resources than those sites using static pages. To fully capitalize on the advantages offered by databases, it is important that you understand the fundamentals of database design and the tools used to build and manage databases.

This chapter looks at the following:

- The various database models
- The advantages that databases offer Web developers
- Methods of designing a database for the Web
- Some available database platforms and Database Management Systems
- Constructing a database and preparing it for connection to the Web

Database Fundamentals

As a professional in the arena of Web development, you may not have ever had to work with databases other than the occasional departmental-sized database created using an application like Microsoft Access. However, understanding how to design a database and connect it to the Web requires an understanding of the various types of databases, the database platforms that are available, and the technology used to allow HTML pages to access the information stored within a database.

> **Tip**
> **Getting to Know Your DBA** If your company has a Database Administrator (DBA), now would probably be a good time to find out who he or she is and introduce yourself. If your company already has a database established that you will be using to drive your dynamic pages, the DBA can be an invaluable resource when you encounter difficulties or have questions.

One of the great things about UltraDev's database-connectivity tools is the fact that you don't have to be an expert at developing and using databases to build your dynamic pages. However, because you will need to understand the basic structure of your database and the terminology used by UltraDev to access your data, a quick review of the different types of databases and the basic elements used to construct a database are worth a look.

The Different Database Models

Raw, unorganized data is usually meaningless to most of us. Imagine trying to look up a telephone number if the phone book were not organized in alphabetical order listing the name and the phone number. To facilitate the organization of data, several database models have been developed, each using a different method of organizing data and, as a result, having its own set of pros and cons.

Flat Files

Although technically not one of the major database models, flat files deserve to be mentioned because they are commonly used on the Web in conjunction with CGI scripts to perform small-scale tasks including password authentication, site-wide search engines, and newsletter subscriptions. Essentially, a flat file is nothing more than a collection of data organized using minimal structure. For example, the flat file as seen in Figure 3.1 could represent the mailing information of those visitors to your site who requested more information about your products.

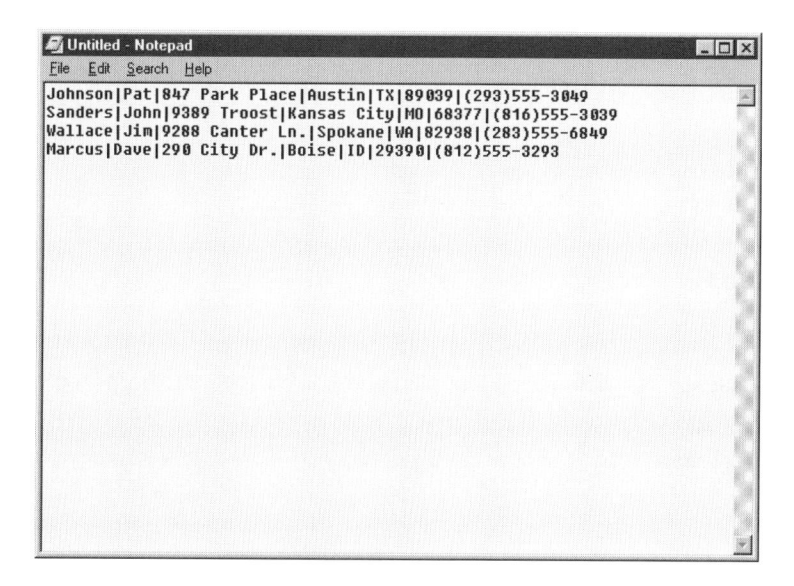

```
Untitled - Notepad
File  Edit  Search  Help
Johnson|Pat|847 Park Place|Austin|TX|89039|(293)555-3049
Sanders|John|9389 Troost|Kansas City|MO|68377|(816)555-3039
Wallace|Jim|9288 Canter Ln.|Spokane|WA|82938|(283)555-6849
Marcus|Dave|290 City Dr.|Boise|ID|29390|(812)555-3293
```

Figure 3.1   A flat file database representing visitor data.

> **Note**
> **Limitations on Graphical Flat File Databases**   Graphical flat file databases, such as those found in Microsoft Excel and Works, can access only one table of data at a time. Relational databases can access multiple database tables simultaneously.

Because a flat file contains only data and does not store any information about the file structure itself, each individual piece of information has to be stored sequentially, using either a fixed number of characters or a unique character to identify where that piece of data ends. This format is extremely easy to set up using a simple text editor and can be updated just by adding new information at the end of the file.

While simplicity is the most obvious reason to use a flat file, the problems that arise with this format often outweigh any benefits. For example, flat file databases cannot be linked with other flat file databases. This means that the same piece of information (such as a customer's address) might be stored in multiple locations, taking up additional storage space. In addition, if that information changes, each flat file database must be updated individually or the risk of storing incorrect information in one of your files arises. Duplicating input of information increases the chance of data entry errors.

As you can see, using flat files for anything more than a simple task can quickly turn into an administrative nightmare. Today's businesses nearly always use some form of relational database.

> **Note**
> **When Are Flat Files Useful?** There are times when flat files are useful. If you have a small set of static information that is unlikely to need frequent updating, such as a list of videos you own, a flat file may serve your purposes.

Hierarchical Databases

To avoid the administrative difficulties of updating multiple flat file databases, the hierarchical database model was developed. Hierarchical databases use a "tree" structure based on a single table specified as the root. As shown in Figure 3.2, links between tables can be established using a parent-child relationship. Under this structure, each child table can only have one parent table, although a parent table may have more than one child.

The biggest advantage to a hierarchical database is the structure provided for your data. To access data stored in a hierarchical database, you simply start at the root and make decisions as to which data path you want to follow. Each step provides you with more and more detailed information stored in the database.

One good example of a hierarchical database is the file structure used by your computer. For example, suppose you want to find the C:\windows\media\tada.wav file on your Windows machine. You could open Windows Explorer, shown in Figure 3.3, and click the icon for the C: drive to display the root directory. Next you click the Windows folder and then the Media folder underneath that. Within the Media folder, you would see the tada.wav file that you are looking for. By following this structure, you navigate the hierarchy of your Windows directory system.

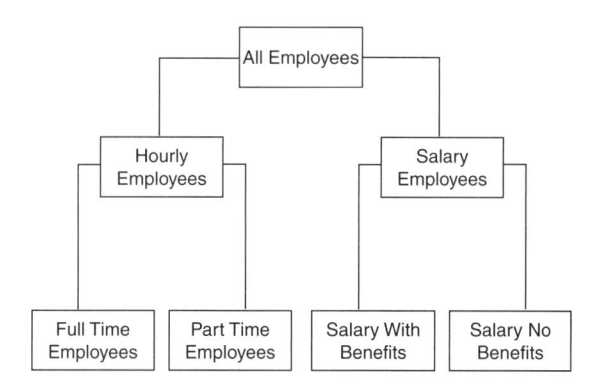

Figure 3.2 The tree structure of a hierarchical database.

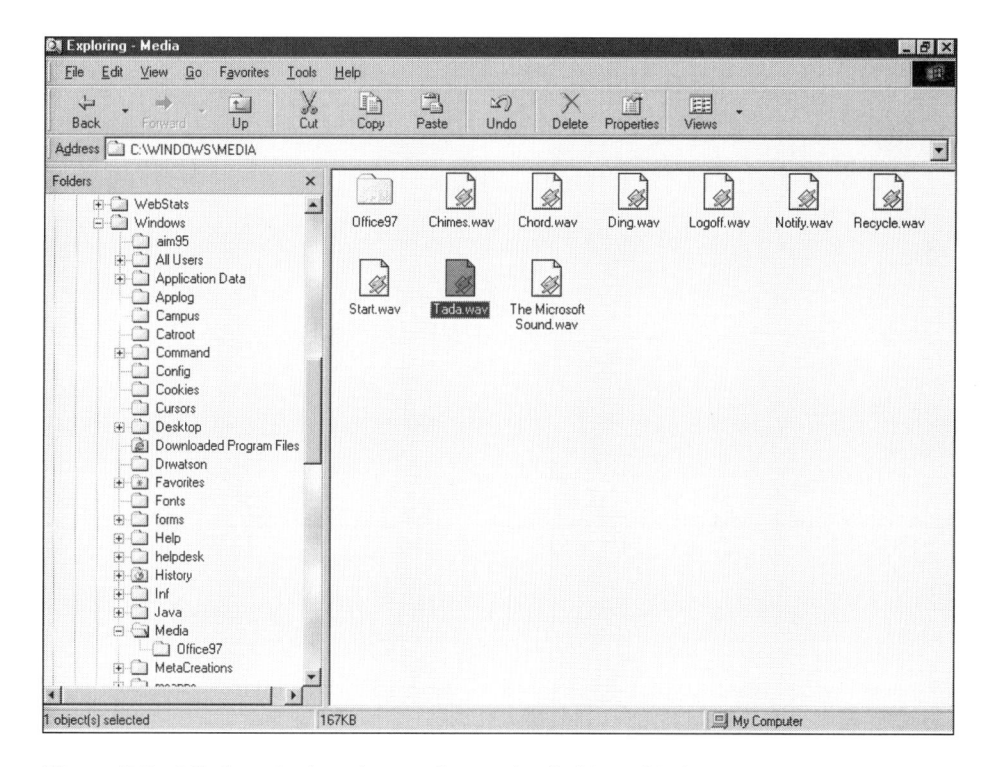

Figure 3.3 Windows Explorer is a good example of a hierarchical structure.

While hierarchical databases do provide a basic structure for your data, there are still problems that can arise. For example, hierarchical databases may still require redundant data to be stored throughout the system due primarily to the fact that child tables cannot be linked to more than one parent table.

> **Note**
> **Table Relationships** Because parent tables can be linked to numerous child tables, they are said to have a "one to many" relationship. Later models developed the ability to create "many to many" relationships by allowing child tables to have more than one parent.

Network Databases

To resolve the data redundancy problems found in flat files and hierarchical databases, the Network Database model, shown in Figure 3.4, was developed.

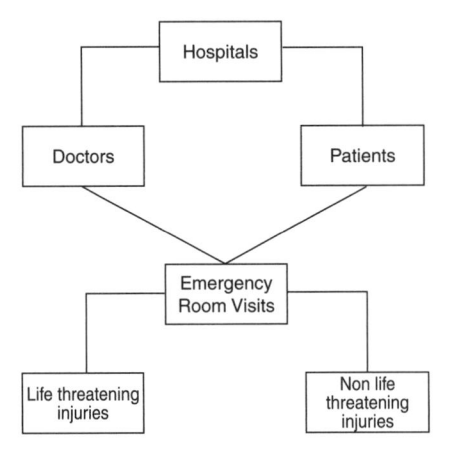

Figure 3.4 The Network Database model.

While very similar in structure to hierarchical databases, child tables in network databases are capable of having more than one parent. With this capability, network databases were the first to accomplish many to many relationships, effectively ending the need for any redundant data.

The problem with network databases is that developing and maintaining the structural integrity of the model was very difficult. With the addition of each new table, its relationship with each potential parent table had to be analyzed and the effect on the other child tables considered. As a result, network databases are usually not considered as a realistic model for most databases.

Relational Databases

The most effective solution to the problems found in the other database models comes in the form of the Relational Database model. A relational database is comprised of tables that are uniquely named. Each table is then made up of records (commonly referred to as rows) and fields (also called columns). Rather than using the structure of the database as the previous models did, relational databases use the value of the data stored in the tables themselves to determine what data is retrieved.

For instance, suppose your relational database has a table called All_Employees, similar to the one shown in Table 3.1, that stores the names, phone numbers, and departmental information for each employee in your company.

Table 3.1 An Example of a Table in a Relational Database

Last Name	First Name	Phone	Department	Title
Holman	Doug	(555)213-4956	Accounting	Auditor
Hughes	Mark	(555)213-9485	Human Resources	Consultant
Haines	Sally	(555)213-3948	Information Technology	Coordinator
Davis	Anna	(555)213-4995	Human Resources	Director

Because the Relational Database model relies only on the value of the data itself, you could find all the employees in your Human Resources department by searching the Department field in the table for values that equal "Human Resources." You could further refine that query by searching for values in the Department field that equal "Human Resources" that also have "Director" in the Title field.

The fact that the structure of the database itself is relatively unimportant makes relational databases very easy to develop and manage. As a result, relational databases have become the postpopular database system in use today. In fact, most Database Management Systems on the market today are based on the Relational Database model.

Choosing a Platform and Database Management System

If your company already has a database that you want to connect to your Web site, you probably don't need to worry about what platform your database will be built on. If, however, you are in charge of organizing and developing a database for your site, the choice of platform can be a big decision. In addition to the selection of database platform, you will also need to select a Database Management System (DBMS) that allows you to build and update your database.

The factors that you should consider in choosing a platform and DBMS include the amount of data being stored, the number of users that will be connecting to your database, and your budget. There is a wide variety of tools on the market that offer everything from inexpensive, personal databases to extremely robust, corporate-oriented tools that cost a small fortune.

Microsoft Access

When most of us think about databases, Access often comes to mind. Included with the Microsoft Office Professional suite, Access is a tool that can be found on most corporate workstations as well as many home computers. Shown in Figure 3.5, the widespread availability of Access makes it an ideal environment for developing databases that can then be upgraded to SQL, MySQL, and Oracle platforms.

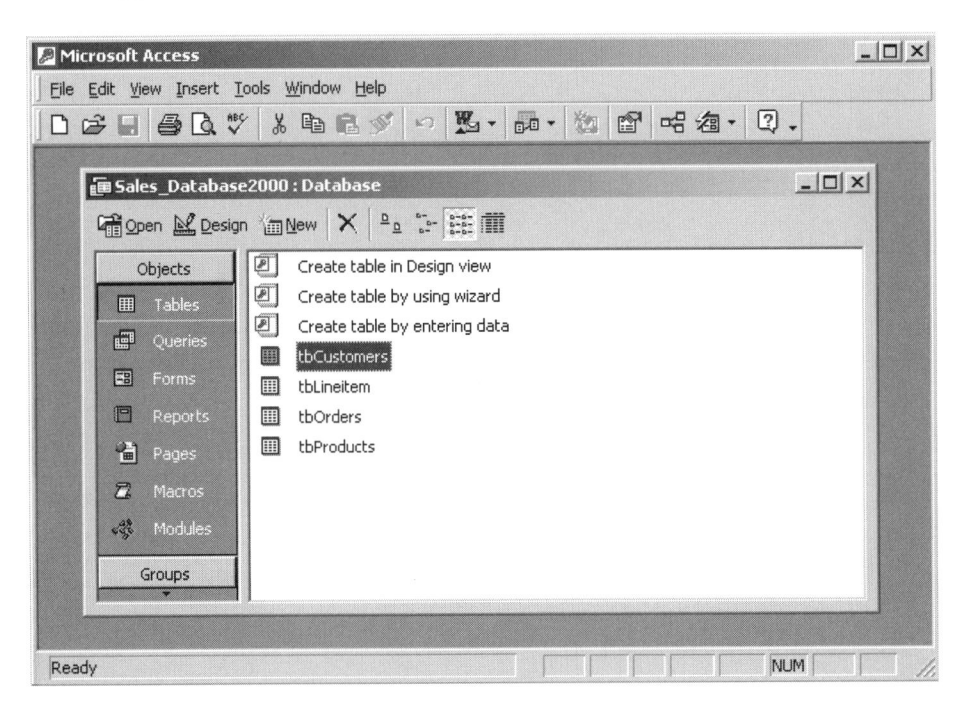

Figure 3.5 Microsoft Access can be found on most corporate workstations.

> **Note**
>
> **Support for Microsoft Access** Although you used to get unlimited support from Microsoft when using Access, Microsoft has decided that Access is a development tool, rather than a user's tool. Because of this distinction, you get two no-charge calls. After that, you must pay a fee for each call you make.

The viability of Access on the Web, however, is limited to relatively small databases because its file size is limited to 1GB for Access 97 and 2GB for Access 2000. In addition, Access is limited to 255 concurrent users at a time. Because of this, forget building the next Amazon.com using Access.

> **Note**
> **Access 2000 Still Has Its Limitations** Although Access 2000 has increased the file size limit to 2GB, the 255 concurrent user limit is still in place.

If your goal is to develop a departmental Web site using a small database that can be easily managed, Access is probably the ideal candidate for the PC. If, however, you are building the next Amazon.com or eBay, you should skip Access and select a more robust database with fewer limitations.

> **Tip**
> **Using Databases with the Exercises** In the exercises throughout this book, you will be using Access databases simply because most PC users will have access to Access (sorry, I just couldn't help myself). If you are not a PC user, the sample databases are also available in MySQL format for UNIX and Linux users or Windows users who prefer JDBC. These files can be found on the book's Web site.

Microsoft SQL Server

Commonly viewed as the big brother to Microsoft Access, SQL Server provides a robust, enterprise-level DBMS capable of powering some of the largest sites on the Web. A sample SQL Server screen is shown in Figure 3.6.

> **Tip**
> **SQL in Action** Want to see SQL Server in action on the Web? Check out Dell.com or Monster.com. Both use SQL Server databases to power their Web sites.

There are a couple of drawbacks to choosing SQL Server as your DBMS. First, SQL Server runs only on the Windows platform, so UNIX and Linux users are out of luck. Second, if you are going to connect your SQL Server version 6.0 or 7.0 databases to the Web, you are required by Microsoft to purchase the SQL Internet Connector, which gives you an open license for Internet visitors. If, however, you are using SQL Server 2000, you must purchase one license of SQL Server per processor in the machine that is running the database. This means that as your Web site grows to require more server power, you'll continue to pay Microsoft for additional licenses.

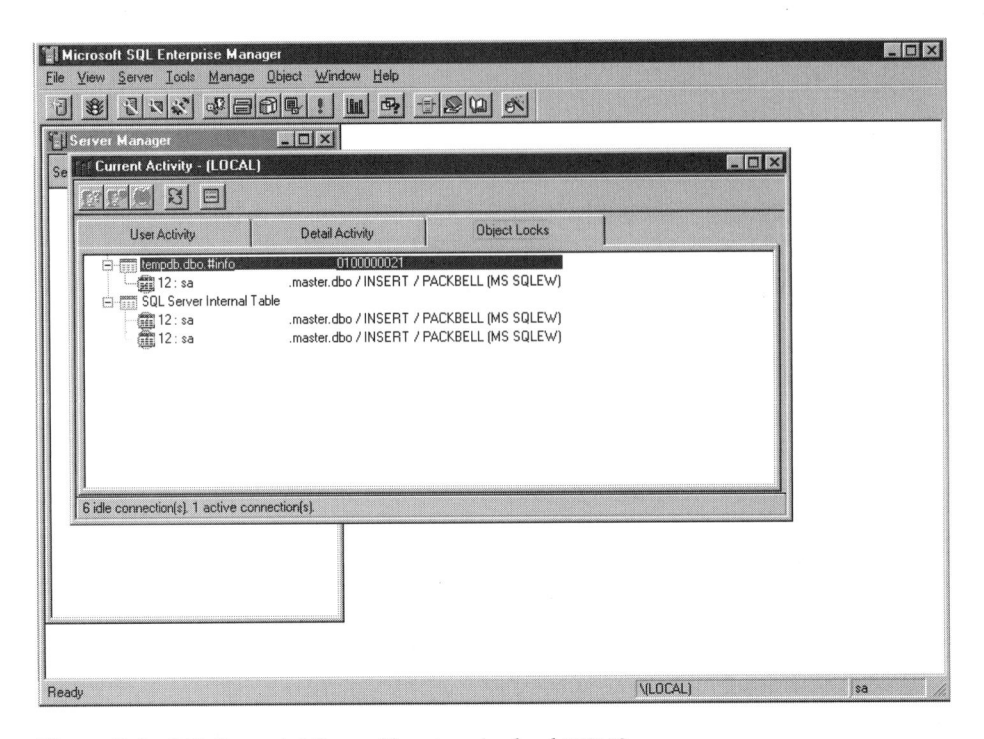

Figure 3.6 SQL Server is Microsoft's enterprise-level DBMS.

MySQL

MySQL is rapidly becoming one of the most popular databases on the Web for small to medium-sized Web sites. Because this DBMS runs on UNIX, Linux, Windows, and just about any other operating system, it is extremely versatile and transports easily between machines. This means that you can develop your database tables on a Windows machine and easily migrate your MySQL database to your UNIX Web server.

The biggest benefit to using MySQL, shown in Figure 3.7, is the fact that it is Open Source software. This means that it is free for most uses. The fact that it is Open Source, however, also means that support is not as readily available as it might be for applications such as Access or SQL Server.

> **Note**
> **MySQL Additional Information** If you would like more information as to free uses of MySQL, check out their Web page at http://www.mysql.com/information. You can also learn about General Public Licensing of Open Source applications at http://www.gnu.org/copyleft/gpl.html.

Figure 3.7 MySQL is an Open Source DBMS whose popularity is rapidly growing.

IBM DB2

IBM's client-server database, shown in Figure 3.8, balances powerful performance with a cost that won't send your accountant reeling. Although originally developed as a mainframe DBMS, DB2 has made the transition to a PC version. One of the most powerful features within DB2 is the integrated Java support, making it an ideal candidate for those developers who choose Java Server Pages (JSP) as their dynamic Web page environment.

Although DB2 is not as expensive as Oracle, its cost still exceeds that of SQL Server. In addition, if you are looking for a DBA to manage your DB2 databases, you might find that the number of professionals skilled in DB2 is limited, while those trained in Oracle or SQL Server are more numerous. This could have the end effect of a higher cost of operating on the DB2 platform.

Oracle

Generally regarded as the most powerful database on the Web today, Oracle also provides some of the most robust security measures of any DBMS on the market. Oracle runs on most UNIX flavors and on the Windows platform and places no limits on the size of databases it can manage. Oracle offers a wide range of DBMS choices, ranging from its Personal Edition to its Enterprise Edition, all of which provide an excellent balance between speed and security.

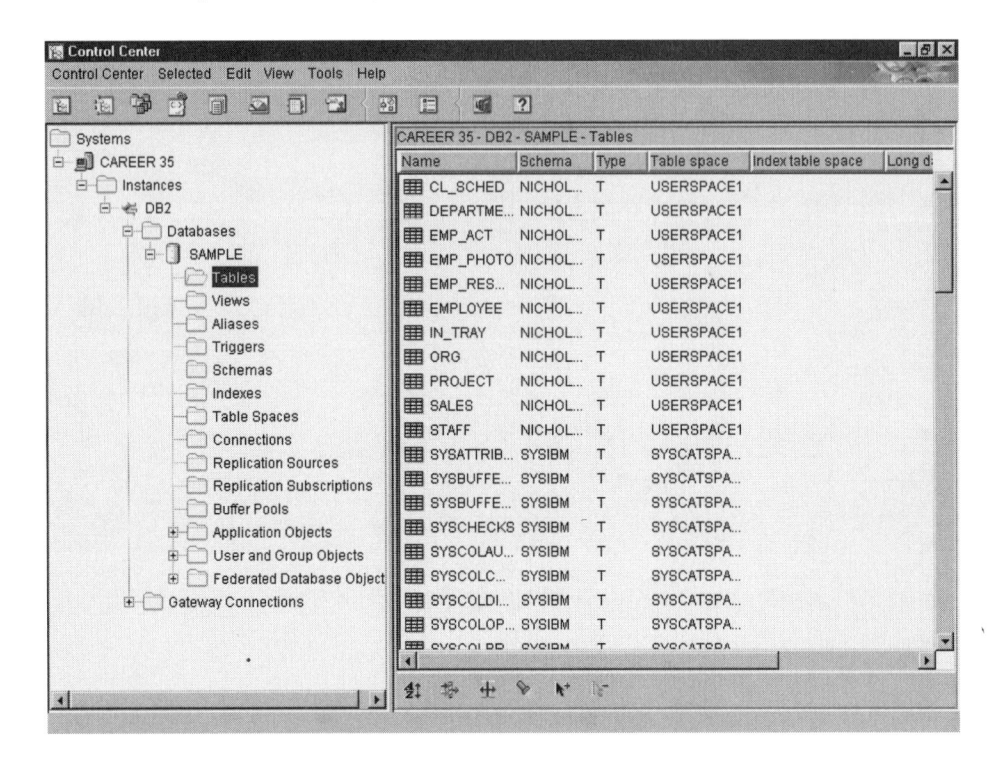

Figure 3.8 IBM's DB2 offers many features including integrated Java support.

The biggest drawback to choosing Oracle as your DBMS of choice is cost and training. Traditionally, Oracle's Enterprise Edition has cost nearly double that of the SQL Server Enterprise Edition, and Oracle databases require very advanced training to operate and maintain. However, the stability, support, and data protection offered by Oracle often make up for the extra money spent.

Building a Database for the Web

What does it take to design a database that will be accessible via the Web? In most cases the process is the same as building a personal database or a departmental database. Through the use of tables, relationships, and queries, you can build a database that UltraDev can connect to your Web pages.

> **Note**
>
> **Database Examples** In the remainder of the chapter, you'll be looking at the sample tables that will be used throughout the rest of the book. Familiarizing yourself with these tables now will save you time in the later chapters when you are connecting your database to your Web pages.
>
> The sample databases have been created in several formats in order to accommodate the various DBMS options available. For PC users, the sample database is available in Access 97, Access 2000, and MySQL formats.

Building Your Tables

Tables are the heart and soul of every database, and the functionality of the database is only as good as the structure of its tables. Therefore, it's important that you carefully consider the structure of your tables prior to building your database-driven pages. Nothing is more frustrating than getting halfway through your Web site design process and realizing that you need to revamp your database to accommodate something you forgot.

As stated earlier, every relational database is comprised of tables that are made up of fields (columns) and records (rows). Take a couple of minutes and look at the sample database included on the book's Web site (www.insideultradev.com). This database will serve as the foundation for all the exercises in the following chapters, so it's a good idea to familiarize yourself with its layout.

> **Caution**
>
> **Database Design Skills** Not all Web developers are familiar with database design. If terms like primary key, table relationships, or referential integrity don't ring a bell, then you might want to brush up on your database skills.

Exercise 3.1 Familiarizing Yourself with the Sample Database

1. Using Windows Explorer, browse to your Web site's root directory and create a subfolder called **insideud4**. Within the insideud4 folder, create another subfolder and name it **database**.

2. Copy the database named Sales_Database from the SampleDatabase folder on the book's Web site to the new database folder. If you are using Personal Web Server, the path to your database should now be `C:\InetPub\wwwroot\insideud4\database\Sales_Database.mdb`.

3. Open the Sales_Database.mdb file using Microsoft Access.

> **Tip**
>
> **Database Filenames** If you are using Microsoft Access 97, open Sales_Database.mdb or open the Sales_Database2K.mdb if you are using Access 2000. If you opt to use MySQL, the filename is simply Sales_Database. Throughout the following exercises, however, Microsoft Access will be used to demonstrate the structure of the tables.

4. Sales_database.mdb has been constructed using four different tables. Open the tbCustomers table. As shown in Figure 3.9, the tbCustomers table is comprised of information that you might collect from someone ordering one of your products.

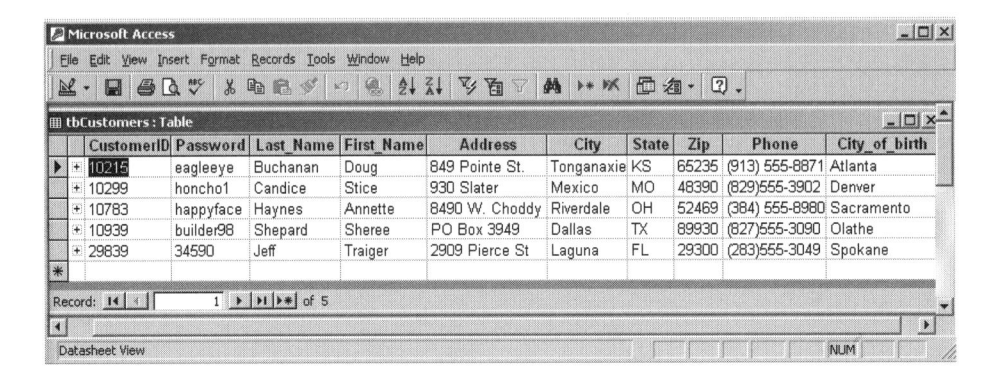

CustomerID	Password	Last_Name	First_Name	Address	City	State	Zip	Phone	City_of_birth
10215	eagleeye	Buchanan	Doug	849 Pointe St.	Tonganaxie	KS	65235	(913) 555-8871	Atlanta
10299	honcho1	Candice	Stice	930 Slater	Mexico	MO	48390	(829)555-3902	Denver
10783	happyface	Haynes	Annette	8490 W. Choddy	Riverdale	OH	52469	(384) 555-8980	Sacramento
10939	builder98	Shepard	Sheree	PO Box 3949	Dallas	TX	89930	(827)555-3090	Olathe
29839	34590	Jeff	Traiger	2909 Pierce St	Laguna	FL	29300	(283)555-3049	Spokane

Figure 3.9 The tbCustomers table stores information about your customers.

The descriptions of each of the fields that are included in the tbCustomers table are as follows:

- **CustomerID.** This field is the primary key for this table, providing each customer with a unique identifier. This avoids any potential problems that could occur with two different customers named Jane Smith. In addition, CustomerID is linked to the CustomerID field in the tbOrders table.
- **Password.** This field stores the password specified by users when they first register with the Web site. This password is used to validate the user's access to the eCommerce section of the Web site.
- **Last_Name.** This field stores the customer's last name.
- **First_Name.** This field stores the customer's first name.
- **Address.** This field stores the customer's address.
- **City.** This field stores the customer's city.
- **State.** This field stores the customer's state.

- **Zip.** This field stores the customer's ZIP code.
- **Phone.** This field stores the customer's telephone number.
- **City_of_Birth.** This field stores the customer's city of birth. Later you will learn how a field such as this one can be combined with the customer's ZIP code or telephone number to provide customers with a method to retrieve a lost password.

5. Close the tbCustomers table and open the tbLineitem table. This table is used to store the number of orders for each of the individual items. The benefit of this table is to give us direct access to the number of times a specific product has been ordered at any given time. The fields used in this table are as follows:
   - **Order_No.** This field is one of the two primary keys for this table and provides each order with a unique order number. This field is also linked to the Order# field in the tbOrders table.
   - **Product_No.** This field stores the product number and is linked to the tbProducts table.
   - **Qty.** This field displays the quantity of that product that has been ordered.

6. Close the tbLineitem table and open the tbOrders table. This table stores information about each order that is placed. The fields in the tbOrders table are as follows:
   - **Order_No.** This field is the primary key for this table and provides each order with a unique order number. This field is also linked to the Order# field in the tbLineitem table.
   - **CustomerID.** This field stores unique customer ID numbers and is linked to the tbCustomers table.

> **Tip**
>
> **Choosing Your Primary Key** CustomerID stores the customer number that is the primary key in the tbCustomers table. It can't be a primary key in this table because customers might place more than one order. The second order would mean a duplicate CustomerID, and an error would occur. When choosing your primary key, it's important that you consider whether duplicates are possible and when they could possibly occur. Because a primary key should be unique to the record, you should do everything possible to ensure that no duplicates can occur.

- **Order_Date.** This field displays the date the order was placed.
- **Ship_Meth.** This field stores the method of shipping chosen by the customer.
- **Payment.** This field displays the payment method selected by the customer.

- **CC_Type.** This field displays the credit card type that was selected by the customer.
- **CC_Number.** This field stores the credit card number that was entered by the customer.
- **CC_Exp.** This field displays the expiration date of the credit card that was entered by the customer.

7. Close the tbOrders table and open the tbProducts table. This table stores the relevant information about each product offered on the Web site. The fields stored are as follows:
   - **Product_No.** This field is the primary key for this table and provides each order with a unique order number. This field is also linked to the Product# field in the tbLineitem table.
   - **Title.** This field stores the name of the artist who performed the show.
   - **Entry_Date.** This field tracks the date the record was added to the database.
   - **Description.** This field provides a more detailed description of the product.
   - **Episode_Title.** This field displays the title of the individual episode.
   - **Air_Date.** This field stores the date the episode was originally aired.
   - **Genre.** This field stores the genre category (such as Action, Family, and so on) that pertains to the product.
   - **Photo_URL.** This field displays the URL to a photo that will accompany the product information on the Web page.
   - **Spotlight.** This field is a yes/no field that designates an item as a Spotlight item.
   - **Price.** This field displays the price of the product.
8. Close the tbProducts table.

Establishing Relationships and Verifying Referential Integrity

The next step in developing your relational database is to create relationships between your tables. Relationships ensure that redundant data is kept to a minimum by allowing you to store in a field a pointer to the data in another table, rather than entering the data in both tables.

In addition, it is important to verify that the referential integrity of the relationships is enabled. This ensures that when data is changed in a field in a parent table, the data in the child table will be updated as well.

> **Caution**
> **Referential Integrity** Without defining the referential integrity of your relational database, you risk storing inconsistent data in your different tables.

Exercise 3.2 Establishing Relationships and Verifying Referential Integrity

1. With the Sales_Database open, chose Tools/Relationships from the drop-down menu. As shown in Figure 3.10, each table is linked to another through one or more fields.

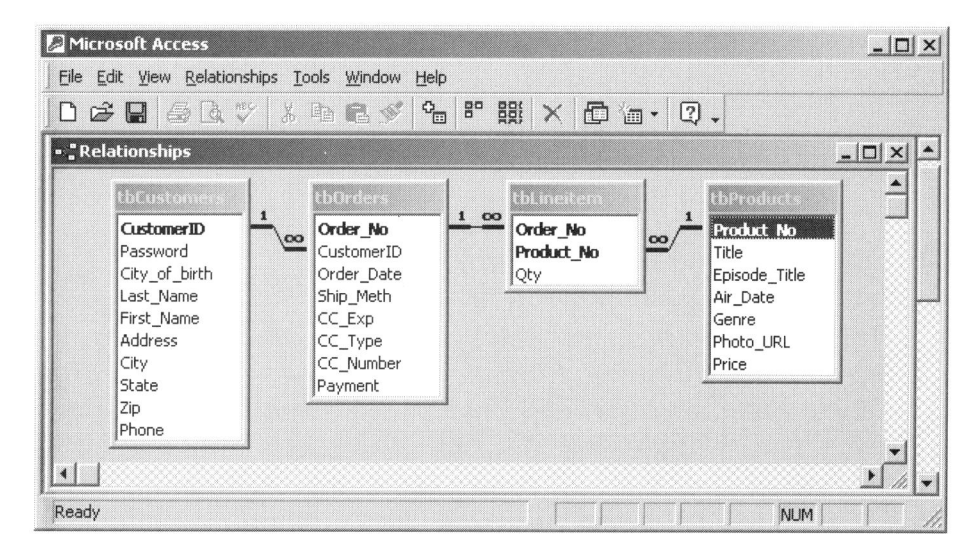

Figure 3.10 Each table is linked through a relationship between fields common to both tables.

2. Right-click on the link between CustomerID in the tbCustomers table and CustomerID in the tbOrders table and choose Edit Relationship.
3. In the Relationships dialog box, shown in Figure 3.11, ensure that Enforce Referential Integrity and Cascade Update Related Fields are checked. Checking these boxes will ensure that any changes you make to this field in the parent table will be updated in the child table. Click OK to close the Relationships dialog box.
4. Repeat Step 3 to check each of the three relationships between the four tables.
5. Close the Relationships dialog box window.
6. Close the database.

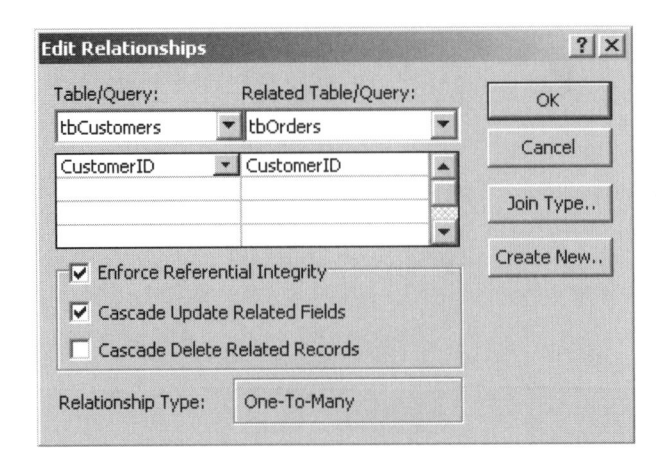

Figure 3.11 The Relationships dialog box allows you to enable referential integrity.

Connecting Your Database to the Web

After you have built your database and have it located on your Web server, the next step in building your database-driven site is to create an avenue of communication between your Web server and the database. Although this can be accomplished using drivers designed specifically for your database, it is much easier to use the Open Database Connectivity Driver (ODBC) or the Java Database Connectivity Driver (JDBC) to accomplish the task.

ODBC and JDBC are standards that have been developed for communicating with modern databases. Most of today's databases, including Access, SQL Server, and DB2, are capable of using the ODBC driver. Other databases are capable of using the JDBC driver. For instance, MySQL can use either the standard JDBC driver or connect through the ODBC driver using an additional program called MyODBC.

> **Tip**
>
> **How Many Drivers Do You Need?** An ODBC or JDBC driver must be set up for each database that you want to connect to the Web.
>
> UltraDev also requires that you have the most recent ODBC drivers available in order to function properly. When you first installed UltraDev, you should have received a warning that UltraDev requires the Microsoft Data Access Components (MDAC) 2.5. If you have not already installed MDAC 2.5, it is recommended that you take a moment and download them from http://www.microsoft.com/data/download_250rtm.htm and install them on your machine.

Chapter 3 Developing Databases for the Web 71

Exercise 3.3 Establishing an ODBC Data Source for Your Database

1. Setting up an ODBC data source on your workstation differs among operating systems. If the machine that you set up as your Web server in Chapter 2, "Setting Up Your UltraDev Workstation as a Test Server," is a Windows 9x machine, click Start/Settings/Control Panel. In the Control Panel, select ODBC Data Sources (32bit).

   If you are using Windows NT, select Start/Settings/Control Panel and select the Data Sources (ODBC) icon.

   If, however, your machine is using Windows 2000, you should select Start/Settings/Control Panel and choose the Administrative Tools icon. Within the Administrative Tools window, choose the Data Sources (ODBC) icon.

2. Choose the System DSN tab from the ODBC Data Source Administrator dialog box, shown in Figure 3.12, and click the Add button.

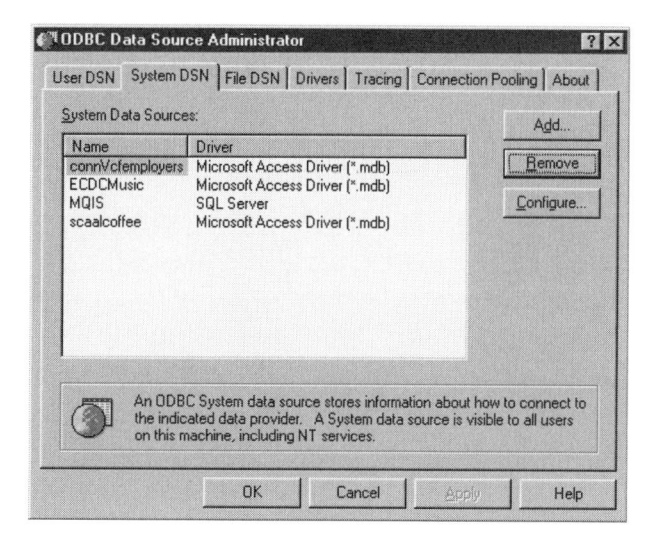

Figure 3.12 The System DSN tab allows you to create a data source that can be shared on the Internet.

> **Caution**
> **Using a System DSN** To make a database available to your Web page visitors, you must create the ODBC source under the System DSN tab.

3. Select the Microsoft Access driver and click Finish.
4. In the ODBC Microsoft Access Setup dialog box, shown in Figure 3.13, type **dsSales_Database** in the Data Source Name field.
5. In the Database panel of the ODBC Microsoft Access Setup dialog box, click the Select button.

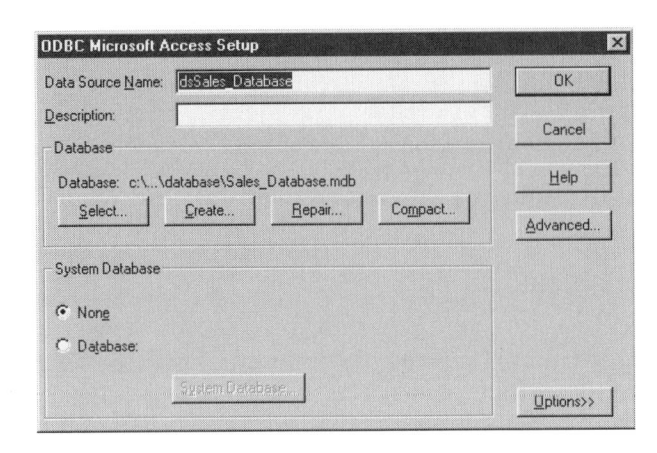

Figure 3.13 The ODBC Microsoft Access Setup dialog box allows you to create a data source using your Access database.

6. Navigate to the C:\InetPub\wwwroot\insideud4\database\Sales_Database.mdb file and click OK.
7. Click the Options button located in the lower-right corner of the ODBC Microsoft Access Setup dialog box. In the Page Timeout field, type **5000**.
8. Click OK to close the ODBC Microsoft Access Setup dialog box.
9. As shown in Figure 3.14, the ODBC Data Source Administrator dialog box now shows a data source for dsSales_Database.

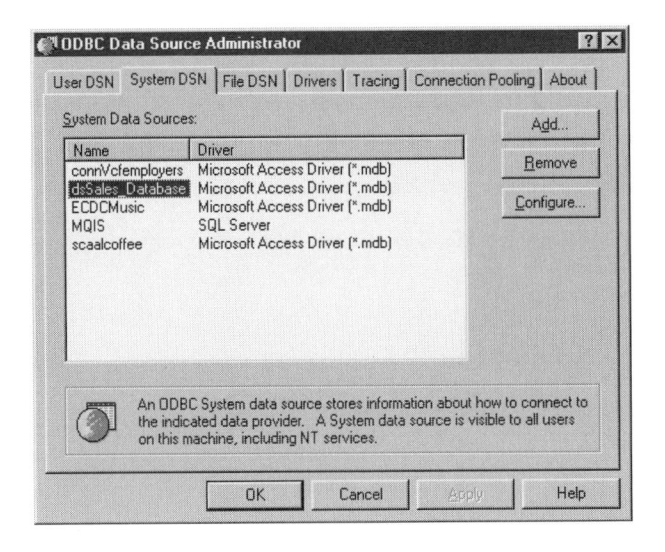

Figure 3.14 A data source has been created for your database.

Communicating with Your Database

The final element of adding a database to your Web pages that you should understand is the language used to manipulate the data stored in your database. When you set up your ODBC data source, you gave your machine the ability to use a set of command strings to communicate with your database. The set of these strings is called the Structured Query Language (SQL).

> **Note**
> **Pronouncing SQL**   The debate rages on as to the correct pronunciation of SQL. Hardcore programmers like to pronounce it by saying the letters ES-Que-EL, while the rest of the world refers to it as Sequel. No matter how you choose to pronounce it, be prepared to be corrected by those who pronounce it differently.

Using SQL commands, you can extract data from your tables, perform comparisons between terms you (or your visitors) provide and the values in your database, and even add and remove data. Keep in mind that SQL commands vary slightly depending on the DBMS that you choose. While the principle functionality remains the same, you should familiarize yourself with the "flavor" of SQL that your database uses.

The biggest advantage that SQL has to offer Web developers is a single language that can be used to communicate with just about any database on the market. If the database is capable of connecting to an ODBC or JDBC driver, SQL can be used to communicate with it. This means as a Web developer you only need to know the basics of SQL and you can add a number of different database platforms to your Web site.

Understanding How UltraDev Speeds the Process

By this time you may be wondering what all this has to do with UltraDev. To fully understand the power of UltraDev as a Web development tool, you need to realize that once a data source has been established for your database, the process of adding dynamic data to your Web pages can be done automatically through the use of UltraDev's database connection tools.

In addition, you can quickly develop pages that allow you to add, edit, and delete data directly to or from your database. The biggest bonus, however, is the fact that all thanks to UltraDev, you can do this without having to write a single line of code.

Summary

This chapter introduced you to the basics of databases and their structure. In addition, you set up an ODBC data source for your database and learned how UltraDev uses SQL to add database connectivity to your Web pages.

In the next chapter, you begin building a database-driven Web site from the ground up. Hold on to your hats, ladies and gentlemen! We're about to take your Web development skills to the next level!

Part II

Building a Solid Foundation

4	Building an UltraDev Site from the Ground Up	79
5	The Dreamweaver in Dreamweaver UltraDev 4	109
6	UltraDev's Graphic and Multimedia Capabilities	137

Chapter 4

Building an UltraDev Site from the Ground Up

Creating and maintaining any Web site requires more than just a knowledge of HTML and access to a Web server. In fact, diligent Web developers often spend a considerable amount of time just thinking about what their site will look like and then even more time developing additional pages, updating existing data, and checking their pages for broken links. UltraDev makes processes such as these simple through the use of the Site window and its many features.

This chapter looks at the following:

- Planning your UltraDev site
- Creating a Web server connection
- Adding pages using the site window
- Verifying your Web site links
- Using UltraDev in a workgroup environment

Planning Your UltraDev Site

When I was a kid, I used to love to build model cars. In particular, I took pride in the fact that I was able to convert a bunch of steel gray plastic parts into a fire-engine red sports car or a lean, mean, battle-ready jet fighter. One of the first models I ever worked on was a 1957 Chevy Bel Air, and I remember standing in the store and looking at the picture on the box knowing that one day soon I would have a replica of this hot rod sitting on my shelf.

Unfortunately, I also remember taking the model home, dragging out all the pieces and slapping together the plastic parts as quickly as possible so I could paint it and show all my friends how cool it was. By the end of the process, I had lost a couple of parts, glue was everywhere, and my model looked more like a '57 Chevy rusting behind a barn somewhere instead of the showroom beauty that I had hoped for.

However, I quickly learned that there was more to model building than just gluing and painting. In fact, I discovered that the planning process and the procedures followed during the construction were just as important to the building of the model as the wheels or the doors. For instance, I discovered that I could avoid losing parts if I left them in the box until I needed them and that my paint jobs improved significantly if I let the glue dry first.

While reminiscing about my model-building days might be a lot of fun for me, you might be wondering what on Earth this has to do with building Web sites using UltraDev. Essentially, a dynamic Web site is nothing more than a model built using raw code, hyperlinks, and databases instead of plastic parts, glue, and paint. In addition, the planning phase of building a Web site and the procedures followed throughout the process always have a direct influence on the quality of the end-result.

Developing a Site Map

One of the most useful tools you can use in the development of any Web site is a site map. A *site map* is a diagram that visually represents the pages that comprise your site and the relationships between those pages. Depending on the size and complexity of your Web site, you may be able to draw a diagram similar to the one in Figure 4.1 using pen and paper, or you may need diagramming software such as Microsoft Visio or netViz Professional.

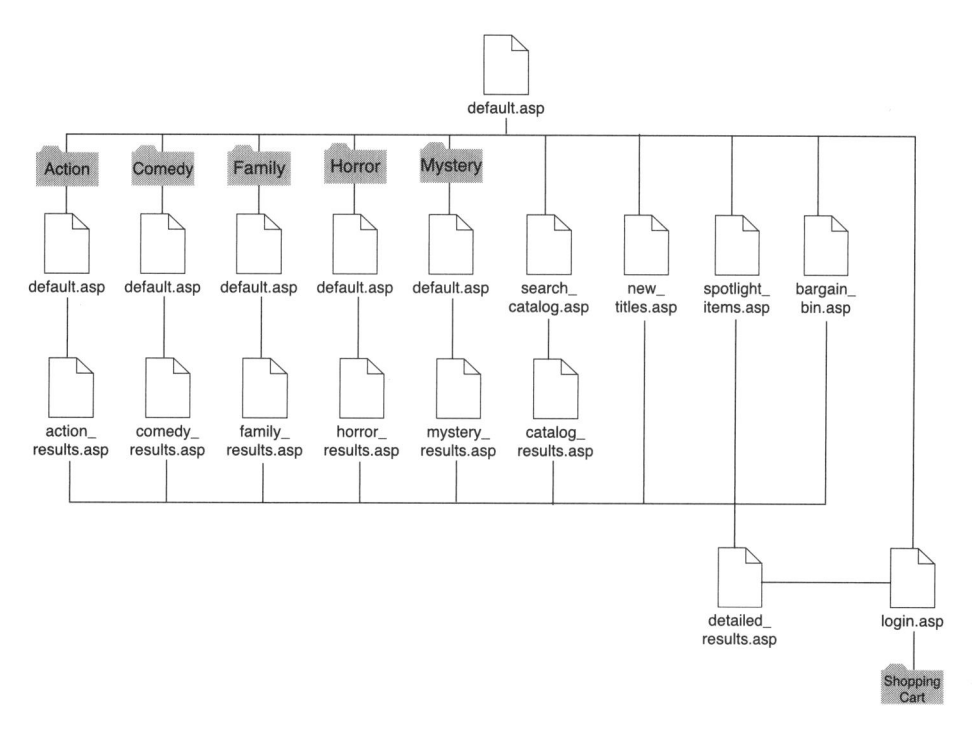

Figure 4.1 A site map can speed the development process by giving your site direction.

Also, keep in mind that a site map is always a work in progress. As your plans for your site change, so will the look and feel of your site map. Don't be afraid to mark it up or make additions or deletions to it. I always keep a photocopy handy of any site map that I make so I can draw all over it as ideas come to mind.

> **Tip**
>
> **UltraDev's Site Mapping Tool**   UltraDev comes with some pretty cool site mapping tools that can definitely help you identify and resolve problems in your site. However, while these tools are handy for checking the relationships between your pages, they won't help you plan your site before you build it. Writing out a site map prior to the building phase will help you conceptualize the structure your site requires, something that UltraDev's site map can't do because it only works after the site is built.

> **Tip**
>
> **Building a Better Site Through Documentation**   Documenting your site, its pages, and its links is critical to the success of your site. A site that is difficult to navigate and contains broken links to other pages or sites quickly discourages the average user.

Planning Your Pages and Directories

When building your site map, you should consider the file structure that your site will be using. It's likely that your site can be categorized into specific areas of functionality, and these areas can usually be represented by individual directories. In addition, you should take into account any special directories that might be needed to store databases, images, or other multimedia elements.

By diagramming the pages, directories, and databases you intend to use throughout your site, you give yourself a roadmap to guide your creative efforts. In addition, a site map gives you a quick reference to the relationships between documents and site elements and a way to visualize the structure of your Web site.

> **Caution**
>
> **A Good Naming Convention Goes a Long Way**   When planning your pages, it is a good idea to develop a naming convention that is easily identifiable to others who may need to work with the files. Giving your files cryptic names serves no purpose other than to confuse yourself and others when it comes time to find a file. Also, it's a good idea to avoid using spaces or symbols in your file names because different browsers and Web servers interpret these characters differently.
>
> Finally, although NT servers are not case sensitive when it comes to filenames, UNIX and Linux servers treat uppercase filenames differently than lowercase filenames. Therefore help.htm and Help.htm are two entirely different files.

> **Tip**
>
> **Stick to Lower Case**   For consistency, use file names that are all lower case. That way, you don't need to worry about the case of the file name when other users try to reach it.

Cataloging Your Site Elements

In addition to laying out the relationships between pages, it's usually a good idea to get a clear idea of what elements will be required to construct each page. Examples might include images, sounds, scripts, forms, database connections, or a host of other options. By defining what elements each page relies upon, you document the files you need to gather before the building process begins.

> **Tip**
>
> **Gather What You Can**   Sometimes it is impossible to have every graphic, sound, or database in front of you when you start the design process. Other times, you may find that you need an element that you had not originally anticipated. Luckily, UltraDev allows you to put a placeholder where an element should be and replace it at a later date using the search and replace tools discussed later in this chapter.

Although not absolutely necessary, you might also consider creating an additional extended site map that includes a description of each element that your pages require. An extended site map helps you quickly identify which elements are needed to build a page and can be used to keep track of the elements you may need to create or collect from other departments.

Static Pages

Although you are building a dynamic Web site, it is likely that you may still have a need for static Web pages. Keep in mind that static pages have the advantage of being easy to update without the worry of altering any of your site's database connections.

> **Tip**
>
> **Choosing Your File Name Extensions**   When developing your site, you may be tempted to use the same extension for both your dynamic pages (.asp, .jsp, or .cfm) and your static pages to provide uniformity throughout your site. I have found that maintaining the .htm or .html extension for static pages has the benefit of making them easy to identify and lets me know whether a page should be performing a dynamic function without ever having to open it. Also, because an HTML document requires no additional processing on the server side, this results in a reduced server load and your HTML page may load faster than a similar ASP page. Your visitors will appreciate this.

Dynamic Pages

Depending on the size and purpose of your site, it is possible that you may be using more than one database throughout your site. By cataloging your dynamic pages, you can specify which database connections each page relies on and the tables each connection needs to make the data available via the Web.

> **Caution**
>
> **Identifying Dynamic Pages** When laying out your site map and determining which folders will store dynamic pages, it is a good idea to mark those folders with dynamic identifiers. Because dynamic pages require different permissions from those of static pages, you can run into trouble quickly if you forget to adjust the folder permissions accordingly. Labeling the folders can help remind you to adjust the permissions when you begin building your site.

If you do choose to reserve the .asp, .jsp, or .cfm extensions for your dynamic pages, you should have no difficulty distinguishing your dynamic pages from your static pages. If, however, you choose to maintain the same extension for all pages in your site, you might consider adding a distinguishing mark to both your static and dynamic pages when creating your site map. As shown in Figure 4.2, I use the lightning bolt icon that UltraDev uses to show that a page relies on a database connection.

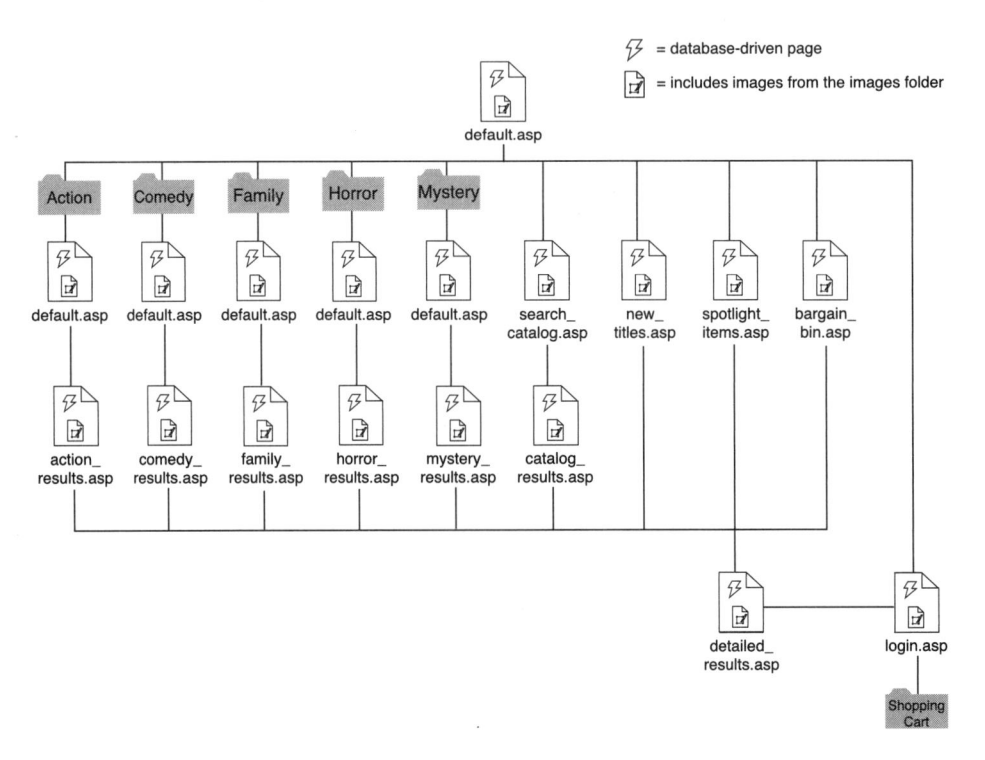

Figure 4.2 Distinguishing your dynamic pages helps you easily identify those that rely on database connections.

> **Tip**
>
> **Finding the Lightning Bolt** Just in case you want to use the lightning bolt icon for your site map, it can be found in the Macromedia\Dreamweaver UltraDev 4\Configuration\DataSources\ASP folder on your local hard drive. The file name is DSL_D.gif.

Databases

The driving force behind your dynamic Web site is obviously your database, and before building your site, you should have already given careful consideration to the database design. Complex dynamic pages can get very tricky when you are building pages that draw from more than one table or even multiple databases. As shown in Figure 4.3, a comprehensive site map should include references to the databases and tables being used.

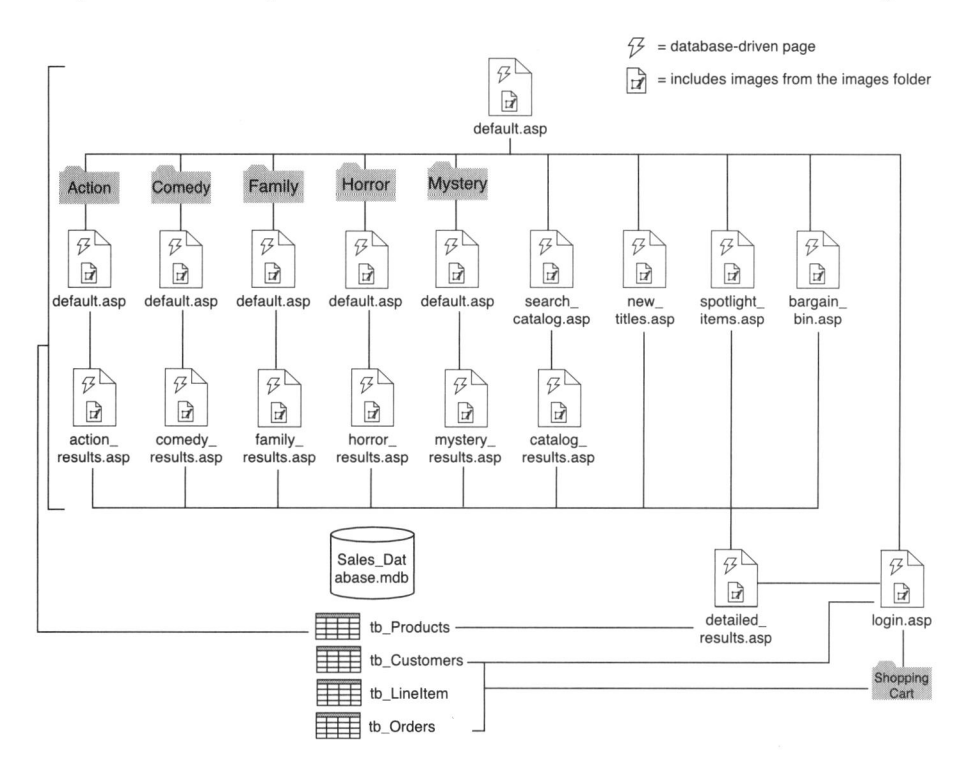

Figure 4.3 Your site map should also include database connections.

Images, Sounds, and Multimedia

If content is king on the Internet, the look and feel of your Web site is certainly queen. Adding attractive graphics to your site not only enhances its physical presence, but also helps your visitors navigate your site.

Unless you are building a site for a corporate Intranet where you know the processor capabilities and browser that your visitors will be using, remember that multimedia elements function differently when accessed from different browsers. In addition, packing your page with tons of graphics might look nice to someone with a T1 LAN connection, but may frustrate a visitor with a 28.8 connection enough to force them to leave.

> **Tip**
>
> **Avoiding Bandwidth Thieves** Placing your images in a separate folder can help you detect bandwidth thieves. These people build Web pages that link directly to the images stored on your Web site rather than storing the images on their own servers. Theft of bandwidth can substantially slow the performance of your Web site because your server will be serving images for multiple sites.
>
> By placing all your images in a separate folder, you can quickly scan your server's log files and assure that the images are only being requested by pages on your site. If other Web sites are consistently requesting your images, you can investigate and determine whether they are, indeed, stealing your bandwidth.

Mapping Your Site Using UltraDev's Site Window

One of the most overlooked tools that UltraDev has to offer is its ability to maintain a basic site map for you. Once you have defined the parameters for your site, you can use the UltraDev site map to ensure that the relationships between your pages match the proposed relationships that you developed in your original site map. Think of it as an easy way to check your work as you go.

Before you can take advantage of UltraDev's Site Management tools, you have to define the parameters of your site. Defining a site is an easy process and you can define as many different sites as you wish.

Exercise 4.1 Defining Your UltraDev Site

1. In the root directory of your Web server folder, create a new folder and name it **InsideUD4**. Throughout the rest of the chapters, you will use this folder to build a database-driven Web site. If you do not have Personal Web Server or IIS installed on your workstation, or your site is hosted remotely, create a new folder on your local hard drive with the path C:\UD4Sites\InsideUD4.

> **Tip**
>
> **Finding Your Root Folder** Remember, if you are using Personal Web Server, Internet Information Server 4, or the Internet Information Services 5 on your local machine, the default path to your Web server root is C:\Inetpub\wwwroot\. Other Web server software, such as Apache, may use /usr/local or /usr/local/htdocs as the Web server root.

2. Open UltraDev 4 and choose Site/Define Sites from the drop-down menu. In the Define Sites dialog box, click the New button. As shown in Figure 4.4, UltraDev opens the Site Definition dialog box for your new site.

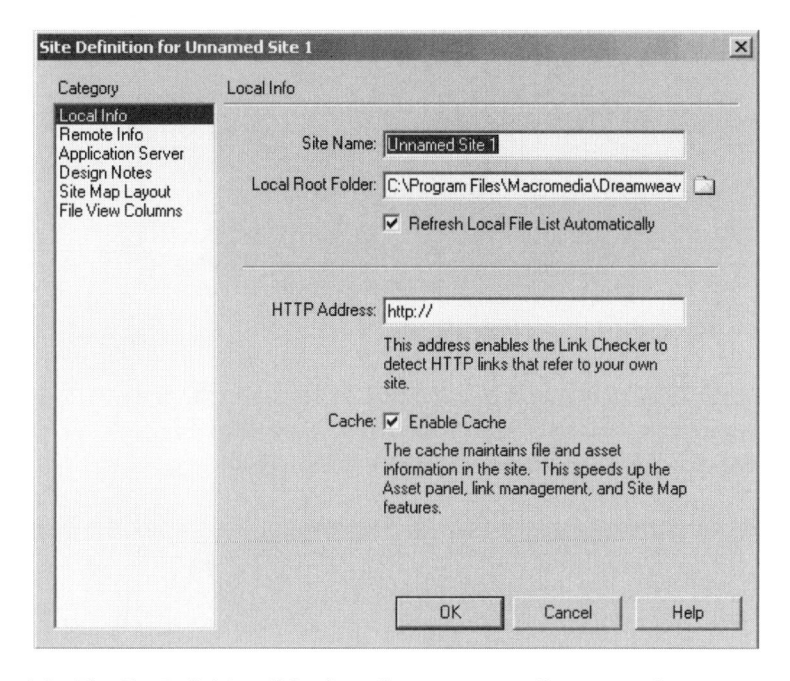

Figure 4.4 The Site Definition dialog box allows you to configure your site.

3. With the Local Info category selected in the Category column on the left side of the dialog box, type **InsideUD4** for the Site Name and choose the path to the InsideUD4 folder that you created in Step 1.

4. Leave the box checked next to Refresh Local File List Automatically. If you have a Fully Qualified Domain Name (FQDN), you can enter it in the HTTP Address box. Entering your domain name gives UltraDev the ability to check links within your site that use that domain name.

5. To maximize the performance of UltraDev's Site window, leave the box checked next to Cache.

6. Click OK to close the Site Definition dialog box. UltraDev indicates that an initial cache for the site will be created. Click OK to close the pop-up box. As shown in Figure 4.5, you should now see your site listed in UltraDev's Define Sites box.

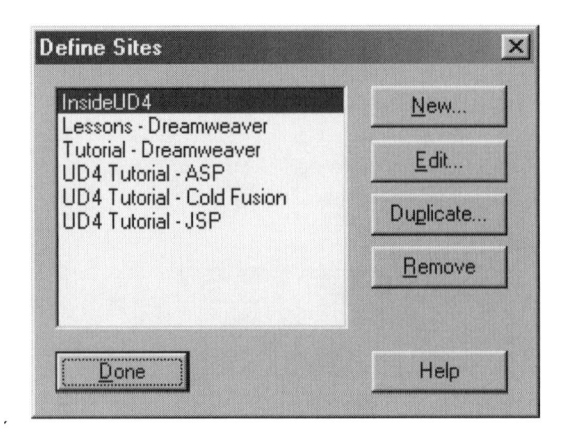

Figure 4.5 Your new site has been successfully created.

7. Click the Done button and UltraDev will bring you to the Site window. As shown in Figure 4.6, you should now have a blank site with the Local Folder (in the right pane) pointing to your new Web site root.

Figure 4.6 The Site window now displays the root folder for your site.

8. For now, leave the Site window open.

> **Note**
> **Mapping Existing Sites** If you already have an existing site and are adding dynamic capabilities, you can configure UltraDev to map those files as well. Simply set up your new UltraDev site using your existing site's root folder and UltraDev will do the rest.

Setting Up Your Web Server Connection

If you are developing a Web site for an organization that maintains its own Web server, you may have a network connection to your Web server through a mapped network drive. If this is the case, maintaining your pages is as simple as developing them on your test machine and then dragging and dropping them to your Web server using UltraDev's Site window.

If, however, your organization doesn't have its own server, it's likely that you'll be maintaining your site using File Transfer Protocol (FTP). In the past, FTP has been an awkward method of transferring files because you had to develop your pages in one application and then transfer them using an FTP Client. With FTP, certain files such as HTML documents and scripts had been transferred using ASCII mode, while graphics needed to be transferred in Binary mode to avoid corruption.

Luckily, those days of third-party FTP clients have come to an end. By using UltraDev's Site window, you can synchronize the files you have edited on your local machine with those stored on your Web server with the click of a button.

Network Connections

Configuring your site to access your files through a network share is very easy. Before you do, however, you need to decide whether you will be accessing your Web server and editing your files directly from the Web server, or if you will be maintaining a copy of your Web site on your local machine and synchronizing the files when changes are made.

The benefit of editing the pages stored directly on the Web server is that you don't have to worry about maintaining two separate copies of your Web site—one on the server and one on your workstation. The downside, however, comes from the fact that once you save the file you are editing, it is live on your Web site. Doing this is very perilous as you risk publishing files that may not be ready for production. Because of this, I highly recommend that you opt to edit the files on your local machine and then synchronize when you are sure they are ready.

Exercise 4.2 Configuring Your Site to Use a Network Connection

1. In the Site window, choose Site/Define Sites from the drop-down menu. InsideUD4 should already be displayed. Click Edit.

> **Tip**
>
> **Accessing Site Properties** If you already have the Site window open to the InsideUD4 site, you can easily access the properties for the site by choosing Define Sites from the Site drop-down menu on the toolbar.

2. As shown in Figure 4.7, select Remote Info from the Category list and choose Local/Network from the Access drop-down menu.

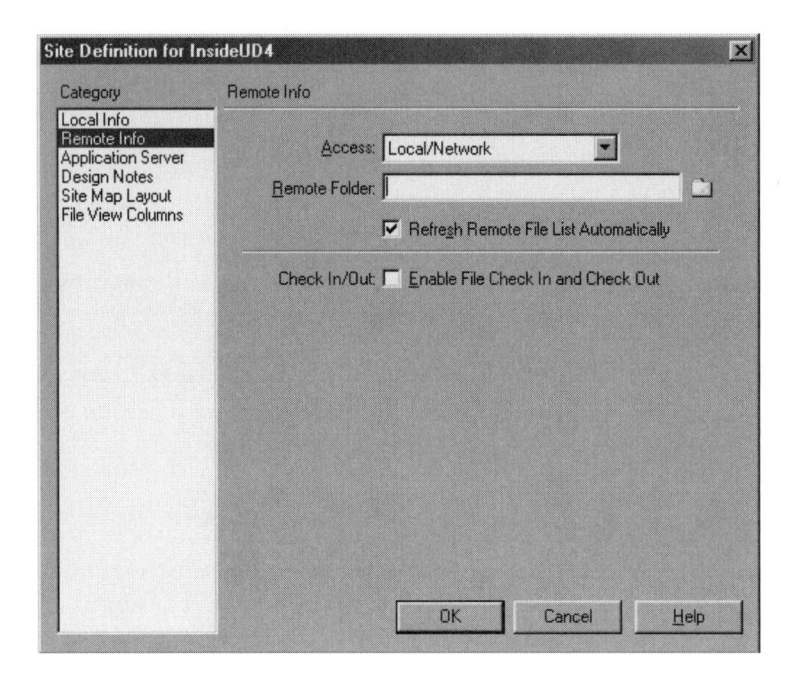

Figure 4.7 Selecting Local/Network establishes a connection to your network Web server.

> **Note**
>
> **Editing Live Pages** If you decide you really want to edit your pages directly on your Web server, set the Access dropdown to None.

3. To browse to the Remote Folder on your Web server where your Web site files are stored, click the folder icon. The Select box should contain the InsideUD4 folder. Click Select.
4. Leave the box checked next to Refresh Remote File List Automatically.

5. Click the OK button to return to the Define Sites dialog box.
6. Click Done.

FTP Connections

Configuring UltraDev to access your Web server through FTP is just as easy as configuring any third-party FTP client. Once configured, however, you can synchronize your files with a single click.

Exercise 4.3 Configuring Your Site to Use an FTP Connection

1. Open UltraDev 4 and choose Site/Define Sites from the drop-down menu. Select the InsideUD4 site you created earlier and click Edit.
2. As shown in Figure 4.8, select Remote Info from the Category list and choose FTP from the Access dropdown.

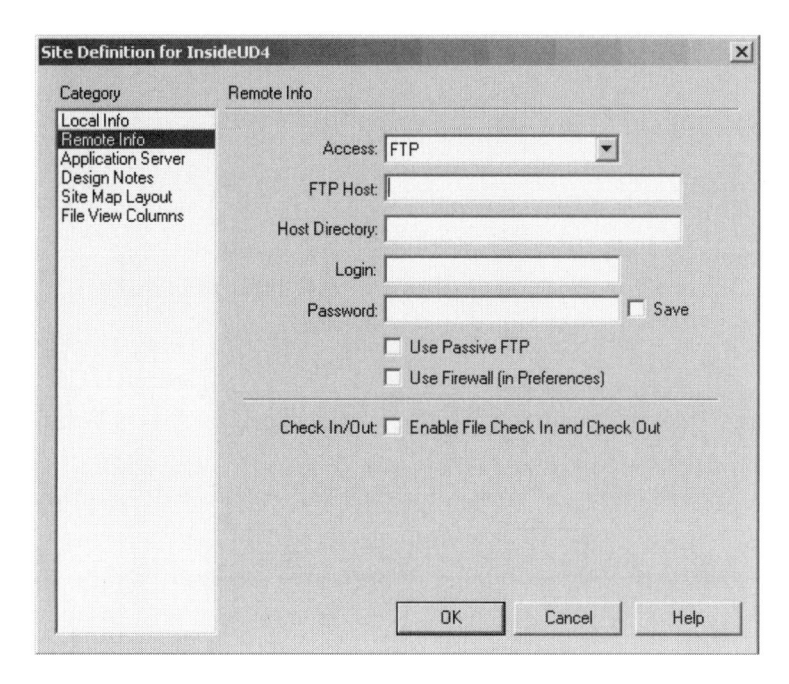

Figure 4.8 Selecting FTP Access configures UltraDev to transfer files to your Web server using the built-in FTP Client.

3. Fill in the FTP Host and Host Directory information provided to you by your Web host or Webmaster.

4. Enter your Login and Password. If you check the Save box, UltraDev will remember your password and you will not be required to enter it each time you want to work on your UltraDev site or synchronize your files.

5. Depending on whether your network is behind a firewall, you may have to provide additional information or use Passive FTP (a more secure method than traditional FTP) to access external FTP sites.

   If you aren't sure whether you are behind a firewall or need to use Passive FTP, leave these boxes unchecked and then try to connect to your FTP server by choosing Site/Connect from the drop-down menu in the Site window. If you are unable to connect, try checking the Use Passive FTP box and try connecting again. If you are still unable to connect, contact your Network Administrator to determine the firewall information that UltraDev requires.

   If you do have to configure UltraDev to navigate your company's firewall, you need to adjust the UltraDev preferences by choosing Edit/Preferences and selecting the Site Category.

6. Click the OK button to return to the Define Sites dialog box.

7. Click Done.

WebDAV Connections

If you have been following the buzz that surrounds the World Wide Web Consortium, you are probably familiar with the term WebDAV as an up and coming extension to the Hypertext Transfer Protocol (HTTP). If you're not familiar with WebDAV, it stands for World Wide Web Distributed Authoring and Versioning and it offers an attractive alternative to traditional FTP.

In its current implementation, the HTTP protocol allows you to read Web pages from servers that are capable of accepting HTTP requests. The WebDAV protocol, however, extends HTTP and gives your browser the ability to read *and* write files, which means that you can author your Web pages using UltraDev and transfer them to your Web server using the HTTP protocol rather than the FTP protocol. Because you use the HTTP protocol, you can take advantage of features such as strong authentication and encryption that FTP does not currently support.

To take advantage of WebDAV, however, your Web server must be capable of interpreting the WebDAV protocol and be configured as a WebDAV server. Currently, both Apache Web Server and Microsoft's Internet Information Services 5.0 support WebDAV connections.

Exercise 4.4 Configuring Your Site to Connect to a WebDAV Server

1. Open UltraDev 4 and choose Site/Define Sites from the drop-down menu. Select the InsideUD4 you created earlier and click Edit.

2. As shown in Figure 4.9, select Remote Info from the Category list and choose WebDAV from the Access dropdown.

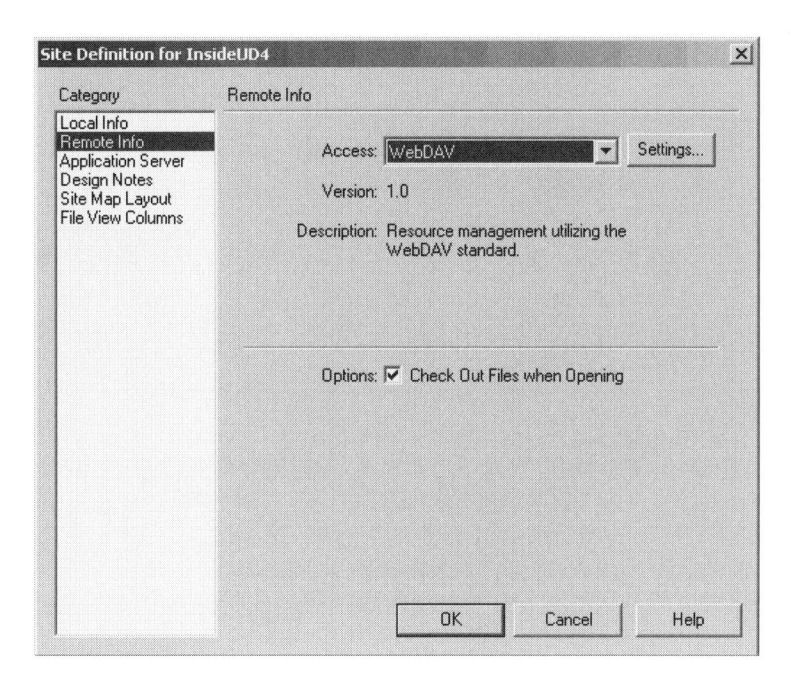

Figure 4.9 UltraDev includes support for WebDAV servers.

3. Click the Settings button and in the WebDAV Connection dialog box, shown in Figure 4.10, fill in the HTTP address of your server.

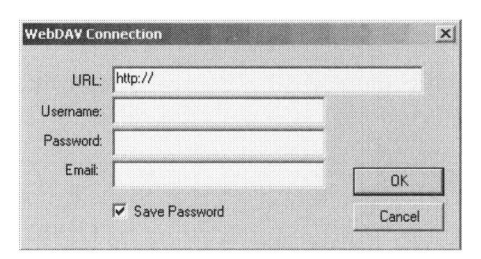

Figure 4.10 Filling in the appropriate information allows UltraDev to transfer files via WebDAV.

4. Enter your Username, Password, and email address in the appropriate boxes. If you check the Save Password box, UltraDev will remember your password and you will not be required to enter it each time you synchronize your files. Click OK.
5. Click the OK button to return to the Define Sites box.
6. Click Done.

Connecting to Visual SourceSafe Databases

If you have ever accidentally overwritten a file or deleted something you shouldn't have, you can appreciate the features offered by Microsoft's Visual SourceSafe (VSS). What VSS does is keep track of every version of your files, whether they are documents, Web pages, or applications, throughout the development process. If you make a mistake or simply want to revert your file back to a previous version, you simply tell VSS which version you want to revert to and VSS rebuilds the file.

> **Caution**
>
> **Visual SourceSafe Requirements** While Visual SourceSafe is a great tool for protecting changes to your database, UltraDev 4 requires that Windows users have the Visual SourceSafe client 6.0 installed and Mac users need the MetroWerks SourceSafe version 1.1.0.
>
> If you are not sure what version of the VSS client your are running, download and install the SourceSafe Updater from the Macromedia download site at http://www.macromedia.com/support/dreamweaver/downloads.html

Exercise 4.5 Configuring Your Site to Connect to a Visual SourceSafe Database

1. Open UltraDev 4 and choose Site/Define Sites from the drop-down menu. Select the InsideUD4 you created earlier and click Edit.
2. As shown in Figure 4.11, select Remote Info from the Category list and choose SourceSafe Database from the Access dropdown.
3. Click the Settings button to open the Open SourceSafe dialog box shown in Figure 4.12.
4. In the Database Path field, enter the location of your VSS database or browse to it using the Browse button.
5. Select the project name that you wish to access and enter your Username and Password. If you would like to avoid entering your password every time you access the VSS database, make sure there is a check in the Save checkbox.
6. Click OK to close the Open SourceSafe Database dialog box.
7. Click OK to close the Site Definitions dialog box.
8. Click the Done button in the Define Sites dialog box.

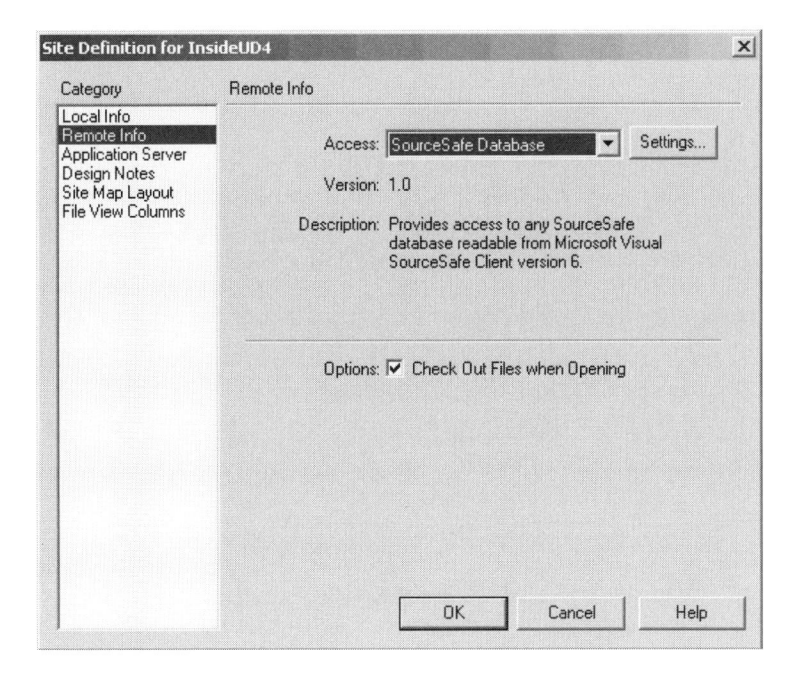

Figure 4.11 You can access your Visual SourceSafe database using UltraDev 4.

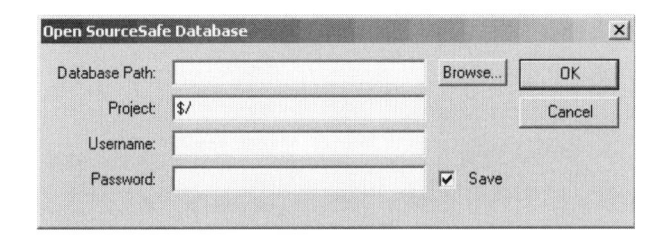

Figure 4.12 The Open SourceSafe Database dialog box lets you specify the settings for your VSS database.

Using the Site Window to Build Your Site

After you have established a connection to your local hard drive or Web server, you are ready to start building and managing your pages. As with other WYSIWYG editors, you could start by creating a new page, adding links to other pages, and then save it using the appropriate file name.

On the other hand, you could simplify the process by using UltraDev's Site window and build the page, links, and all, in a matter of seconds. In addition, using the Site window you can update existing pages and even synchronize your files to ensure that the files stored on your server are current.

Creating a New Page Using the Site Window

If you are building your site from scratch, you can use UltraDev's Site window to configure your site for dynamic pages and to specify your site's home page.

Exercise 4.6 Specifying a Home Page and Configuring Your Site to Build Dynamic Pages

1. In UltraDev's Site window, click Site/Define Sites.
2. The InsideUD4 you created earlier should still be highlighted. Click Edit.
3. With Remote Info selected in the Category list, select Local/Network in the Access field.
4. In the Remote Folder field, browse to the InsideUD4 folder you created earlier.
5. In the Check Out Name field, type your name.
6. As shown in Figure 4.13, select Site Map Layout from the Category list and type **default.asp** in the Home Page dialog box. Do *not* click OK.

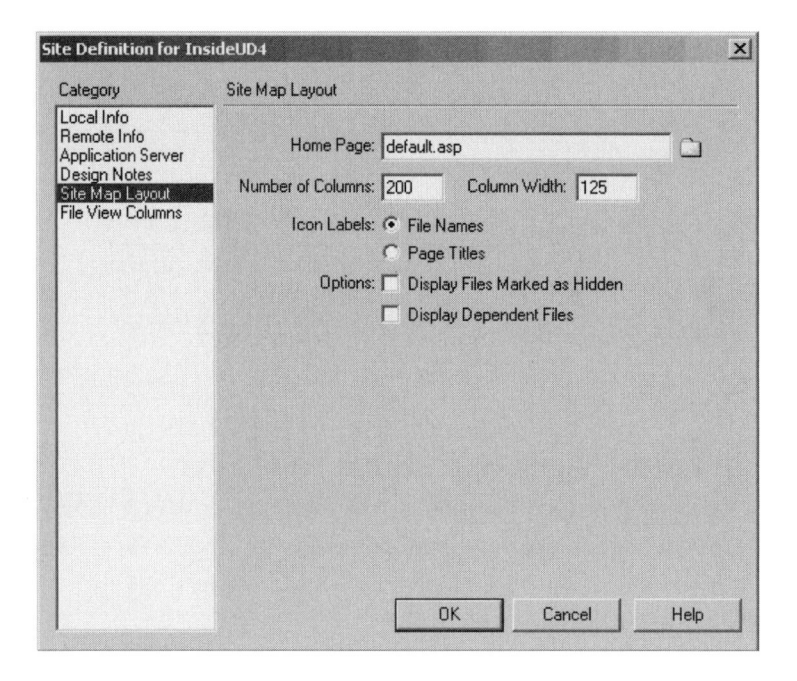

Figure 4.13 You can create your home page using the Site window.

Chapter 4 Building an UltraDev Site from the Ground Up

7. Select Application Server from the Category listing. Respond OK to the popup that asks whether you want UltraDev 4 to create default.asp.
8. As shown in Figure 4.14, select ASP 2.0 from the Server Model dropdown and VBScript as the Scripting Language and .asp as the Page Extension. Click OK.

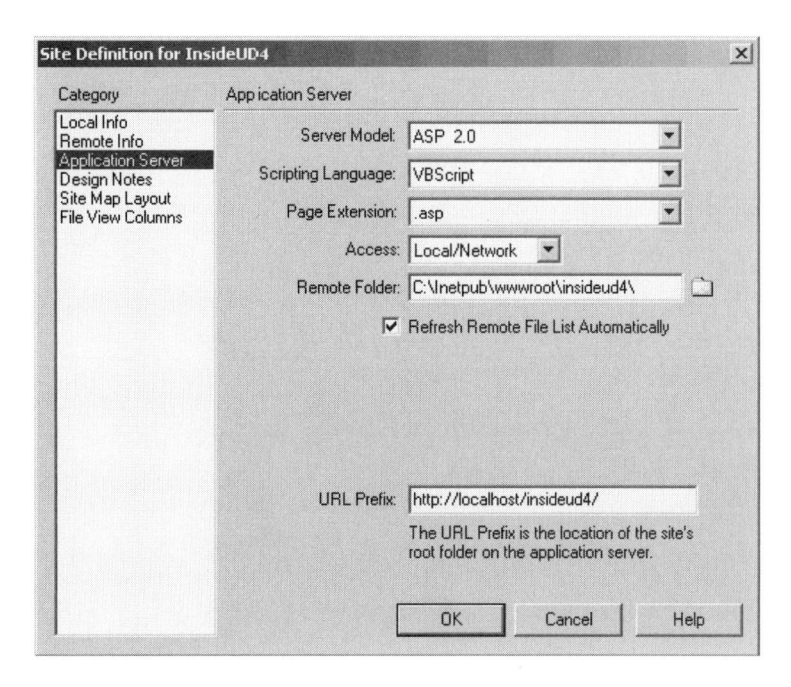

Figure 4.14 Select the dynamic environment you will be developing in.

9. Click Done from the Define Sites dialog box.
10. As you can see in Figure 4.15, the Site window has now added default.asp to your site.

Creating Automatically Linked Pages

One of the quickest ways to add pages to your site is to let UltraDev add them for you. If you developed your site map and want to build a site based on your design, the easiest way to accomplish that is by using UltraDev's site map features.

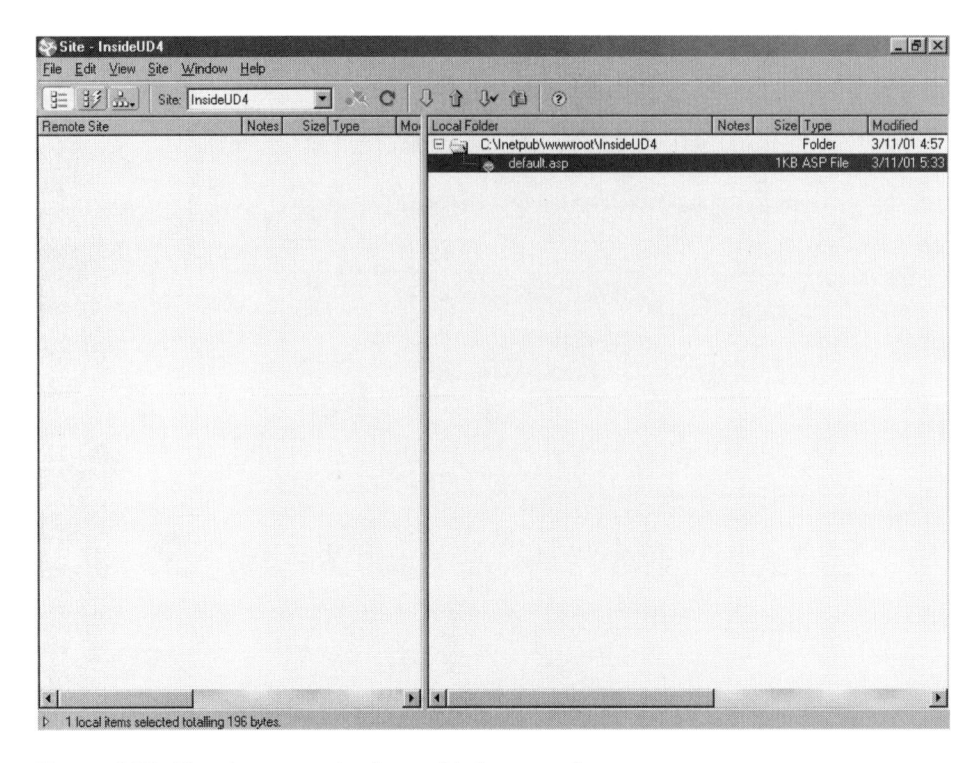

Figure 4.15 Your home page has been added to your site.

Exercise 4.7 Adding Automatically Linked Pages to Your Site

1. Open the Site window for the InsideUD4 you created earlier and click the Site Map button, which is located third from the left on the toolbar. Choose Map Only. As shown in Figure 4.16, the Site window displays the default.asp page that you created earlier.
2. Right-click on the default.asp page and choose Link to New File.
3. In the Link to New File box, shown in Figure 4.17, type **bargain_bin.asp** for the File Name. Type **Bargain Bin** in the Title box and in the Text of Link box.
4. Click OK. Figure 4.18 shows the newly created linked file in your site map.

Figure 4.16 The Site Map view shows the default.htm page as the only page in the site.

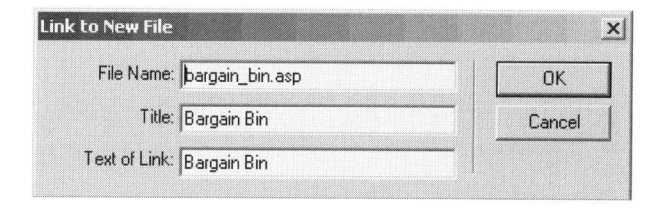

Figure 4.17 Enter the File Name, Title, and Text of Link to be included in your page.

Drag and Drop

After you have created your site and established a connection to your Web server through a network connection, FTP, or WebDAV, the easiest way to transfer files from your workstation to your Web server is to drag and drop them in the Site window. The benefit of using the Site window comes from the fact that before transferring the file, it will analyze all the dependent files (such as graphics or other linked files) and then ask if you would like to transfer them as well. This saves you the hassle of having to transfer each file manually as you would have to do with a traditional FTP or network connection.

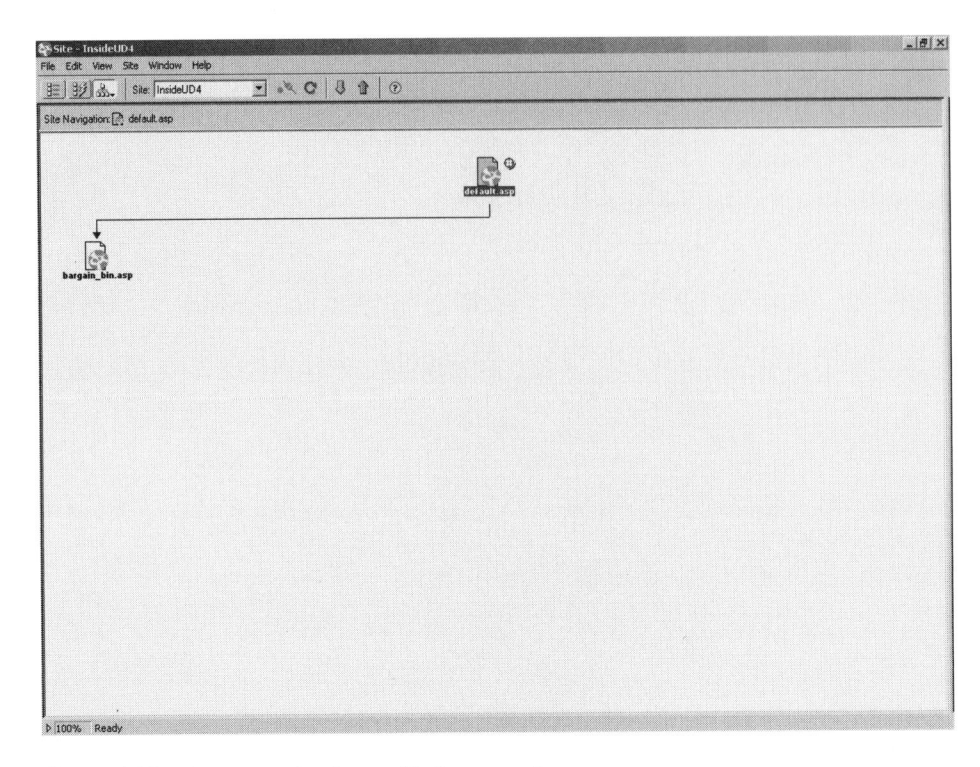

Figure 4.18 A new page has been added to your site map.

> **Note**
>
> **Dragging Files to the Remote Site** To move a file to the root directory, simply drag the file from the Local Host pane to your root folder in the Remote Site pane. If, however, you want the file to be located in a subdirectory, be sure to drop that file directly onto the name of that folder.

Synchronizing Files

After you have developed pages on your workstation and are ready to transfer them to your Web server, you can synchronize both sites to ensure that the Web server accurately reflects the changes you have made to the site. Synchronizing your files has the added benefit of allowing you to roll back your workstation to reflect the files on the Web server if something goes wrong while you are building or updating your pages.

Chapter 4 Building an UltraDev Site from the Ground Up   101

> **Caution**
>
> **Use Caution When Synchronizing** Be very careful when using the synchronize feature. If the files stored on your workstation are not functioning correctly and you tell UltraDev to put the newer files on the remote, you will overwrite your functional pages with the non-functional pages from your workstation.
>
> Remember that UltraDev cannot read your mind. It only does what it is told. If you tell it to overwrite the good files with the bad files, it will comply.

Exercise 4.8 Synchronizing Your Site's Files

After you have established a connection to your Web server, you can synchronize your files by following these steps:

1. Open the Site window for the InsideUD4 you created earlier and click the Site Files button, which is the first from the left on the toolbar.
2. As shown in Figure 4.19, the Site window displays the files stored on the Remote Site in the left pane and those in the Local Folder in the right.

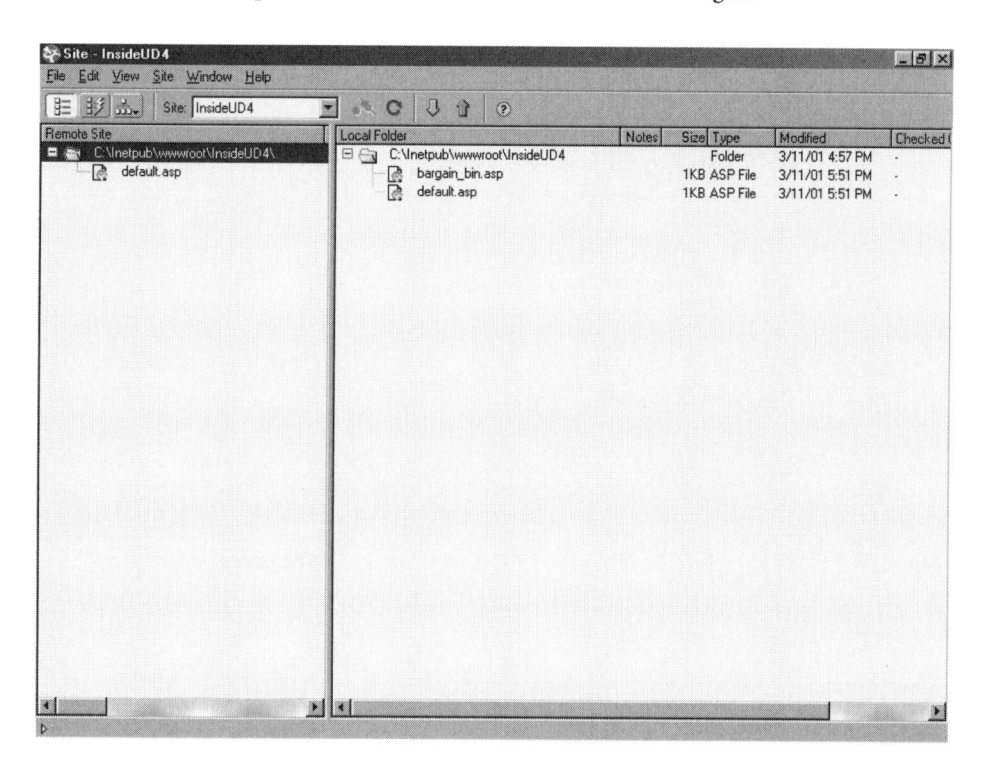

Figure 4.19 Once a connection is made, you can view the files on both your server and your workstation.

3. Select Site/Synchronize from the menu bar.

4. As shown in Figure 4.20, you can select from a variety of synchronization options. Choose to synchronize the entire InsideUD4 site and select the Put newer files to remote option. Click the Preview button. Because your local and remote folders are the same, UltraDev indicates that no synchronization is necessary.

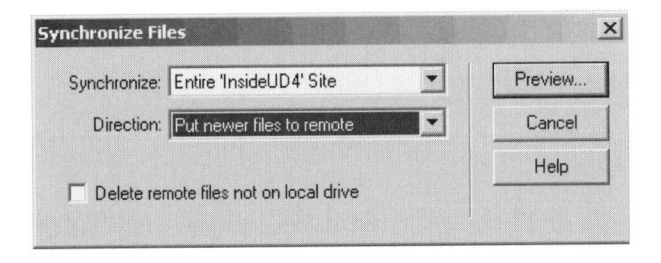

Figure 4.20 Choose from a variety of synchronization options.

5. Choose from the variety of synchronization options. If, however, your remote folder were located on another machine, Figure 4.21 shows the dialog box that indicates the files that would be scheduled to be synchronized.

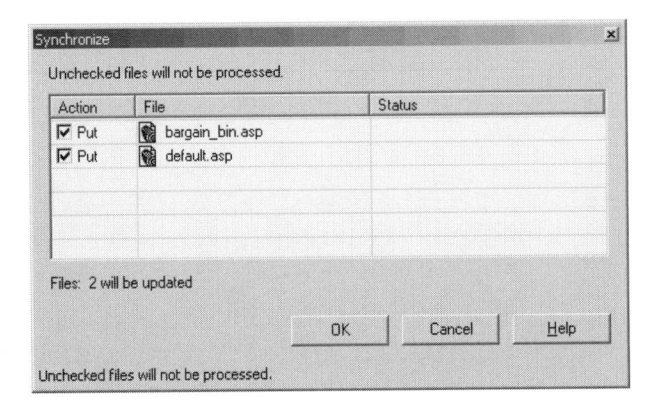

Figure 4.21 The synchronization preview displays the tasks scheduled for completion.

Verifying Your Links and Identifying Orphaned Pages

Have you ever been showing off your Web site to a friend or colleague only to stumble across a broken link? If you're like I used to be, I would get all embarrassed and spend the next couple of hours just clicking on links to make sure they all worked. Fortunately, those days are a thing of the past. By taking advantage of the site management features UltraDev has to offer, you can check all your links automatically in a matter of seconds.

In addition, you can quickly determine what files are located on your server or local folder that have been *orphaned*—meaning that no other page is linked to them.

Exercise 4.9 Identifying Broken Links and Orphaned Pages

1. Open the Site window for the InsideUD4 you created earlier. From the Site menu, choose Check Links Sitewide. UltraDev provides a report similar to the one in Figure 4.22.

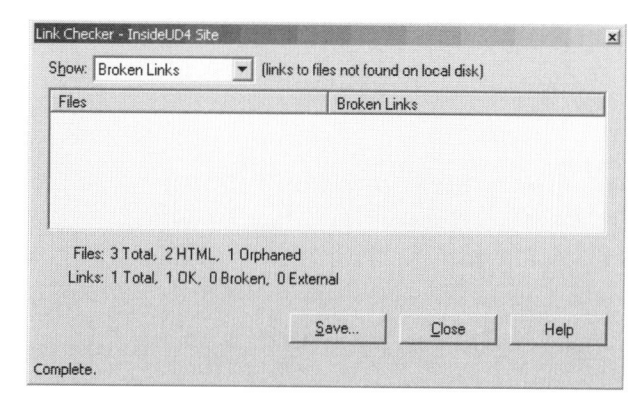

Figure 4.22 UltraDev can check your links and orphaned files for you.

2. To see the files that have been orphaned, choose Orphaned Files from the Show drop-down menu.
3. If you would like to see a list of links that are not part of your site, but are linked to your site, select External Links from the Show dropdown.
4. Close the Link Checker dialog box.

> **Tip**
>
> **Changing Links Throughout a Site** Have you ever built multiple pages using the same page design, only to discover later that one of the links was incorrect? This is no longer a worry either. If you discover that one of your links is incorrect for several of your pages, just choose the Change Link Sitewide from the Site menu and specify how the improper link should be replaced.

Editing Pages in a Workgroup Environment

Editing a Web site in a workgroup can have advantages and disadvantages. By providing each member of the workgroup with access to the page, several people can edit and update their specific areas of the site without having to ask for access to the files. The disadvantage to this, however, arises when two or more people work on the same document at the same time. Inevitably, someone's work is going to be overwritten and their time wasted.

To resolve these potential problems, UltraDev includes a couple of handy tools that not only reduce the possibility of lost data, but allow group members to flag the status of a page and attach notes to a document that are visible to team members, but invisible to visitors.

Check In/Check Out

Borrowing from the time-tested format of every public library, UltraDev includes a system that enables each member of a workgroup to "check out" a file, essentially blocking others from being able to access the file at the same time. Any other group member who tries to access the file is informed that the file is checked out and they are given the name of the person working on the file and the time and date they checked it out.

Once the changes are made, that person can "check in" the file, enabling others to make changes or check the file out. By allowing groups to restrict the number of people editing a page at the same time, this system reduces the chance that someone could overwrite your hard work.

Exercise 4.10 Enabling Check In/Check Out

1. To enable the check in/check out system, open the Site window for the InsideUD4 you created earlier. Make sure the Site drop-down box (not the Site menu) displays the site name. Double-click the InsideUD4 name to display the Site Definition dialog box.
2. As shown in Figure 4.23, select the Remote Info Category and check the Enable File Check In and Check Out box.
3. To ensure that files are locked when opened, make sure there is a checkmark in the box marked Check Out Files When Opening.
4. Provide your name and email address in the appropriate boxes. Other members of the workgroup will be able to see this information when they attempt to open a file that you have checked out.
5. Click OK to close the Site Definition dialog box.

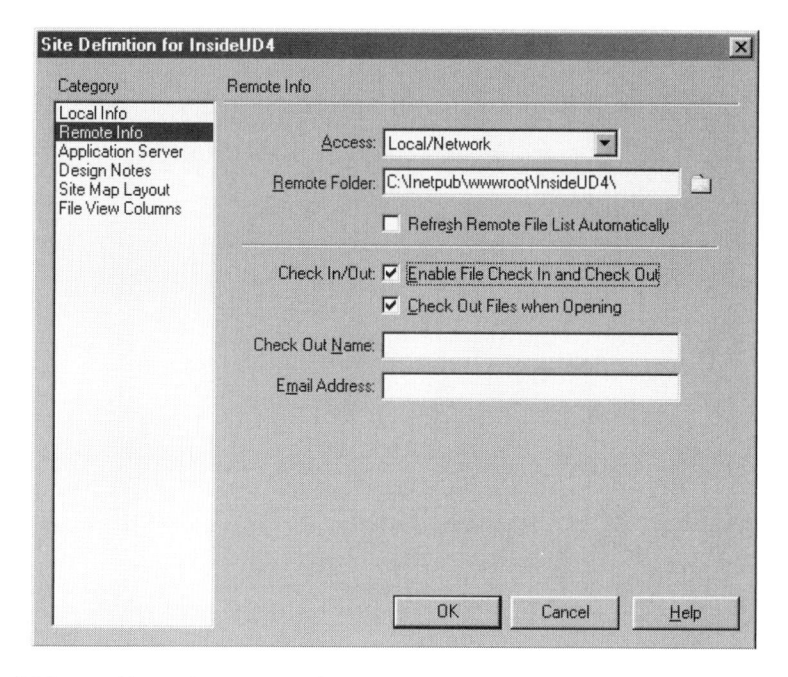

Figure 4.23 Enabling File Check In and Check Out.

Using Design Notes

One additional tool that UltraDev offers to workgroups is the Design Notes feature. When a user makes updates to a page, he has the option of adding a design note to indicate what changes were made and when. These notes are then stored in the notes folder located in the root directory of the site. Other members of the group are then able to see when changes were made, what development stage the pages is in, when it was last updated, and by whom.

This feature is not just for workgroups, either. Anyone who wants to log the changes made to pages or to remind themselves of the status of a page can see the value that UltraDev's design notes offer.

Exercise 4.11 Attaching Design Notes to a Page

1. Open the Site window for the InsideUD4 you created earlier.
2. In the Local Folder pane (on the right side of the screen) right-click on the default.asp file and select Design Notes.
3. Using the Basic Info tab, shown in Figure 4.24, set the status of this file as Draft and type your initials and the date in the Notes field.

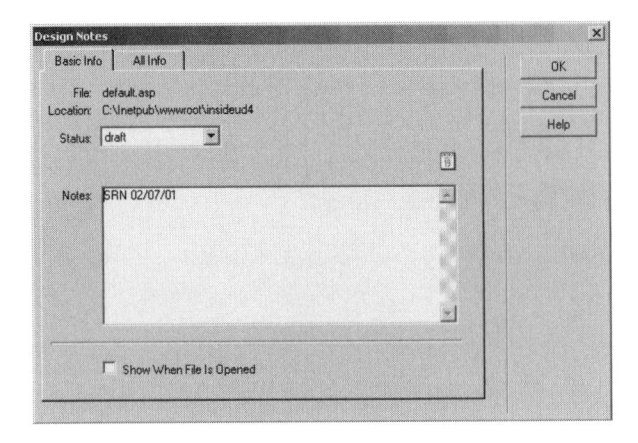

Figure 4.24 Design notes track information about page updates.

4. If you are familiar with the Extensible Markup Language (XML), you can click the All Info tab and add or remove information through the use of the plus and minus buttons.

5. Click OK to apply the design note to the page. As you can see in Figure 4.25, a callout icon has been placed in the notes column of the Local Folder next to the default.asp file. This indicates that a design note has successfully been attached to the file. To read the note, simply double-click the icon.

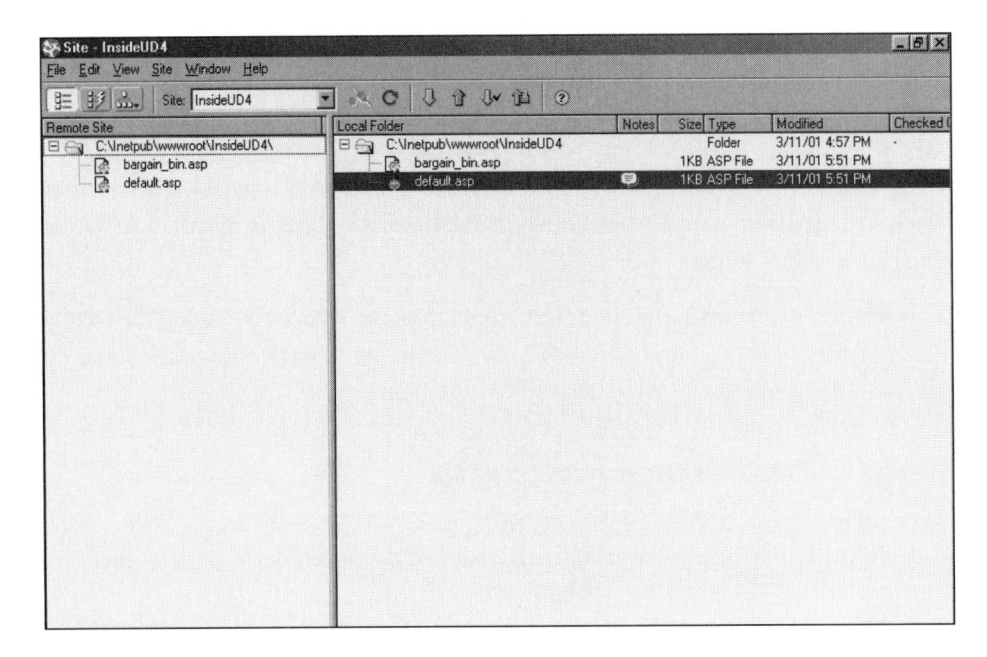

Figure 4.25 A design note has been attached to the file.

Summary

This chapter introduced you to many of the site management features that UltraDev offers. Getting in the habit of using the Site window can not only save you time by helping you automate processes like checking for broken links, but help you avoid difficulties with lost or overwritten data through the use of the check in/check out process.

In the next chapter, you take a look at the Dreamweaver design tools used to build the framework of a dynamic Web site. An introduction to these tools is particularly important for developers who are not familiar with Dreamweaver, its libraries, or its tool palettes. Those who are familiar with previous versions of Dreamweaver will also benefit from an introduction to additional features offered in UltraDev 4.

Chapter 5

The Dreamweaver in Dreamweaver UltraDev 4

Have you ever had a friend or family member who spent every spare minute of his time rebuilding the engine of his muscle car, yet seemed to overlook the fact that the only thing holding the chassis together was rust and dirt? I have a couple of friends like this, and I am always giving them grief about the fact that they focus all their efforts (and a considerable amount of money) on the car's power plant, yet they remain blind to the fact that the structure of their car is just short of a death-trap.

The reason I bring this up is because building a dynamic Web site is a lot like building a car from scratch. Although a robust database and powerful scripting languages are as important as the power plant and transmission for your site, a well-designed page layout and attractive graphics are just as important because they serve as the chassis. After all, before your visitors ever give your database a run for its money, they will have already evaluated your site based on the visual appeal and functionality that you have designed using HTML elements. First impressions count!

Behind UltraDev's database-connectivity, eCommerce, and eLearning features is Dreamweaver 4, one of the most powerful HTML authoring applications available. Using the authoring tools, you can ensure that the static infrastructure of your Web pages is just as sound as the database that drives them.

This chapter focuses on using the HTML design tools found in UltraDev 4 to build the foundation for your dynamic Web site. Each exercise introduces you to tools used to create an individual element of a Web page.

These topics include the following:

- Choosing your page properties
- Designing your page layout
- Building and manipulating tables
- Adding and linking graphics
- Constructing template files

> **Note**
>
> **Just the Dreamweaver Basics** Keep in mind that the purpose of this chapter is to familiarize you with the features commonly used to build the static portions of a Web page. If you are already comfortable with Dreamweaver 4, you should be able to walk through these exercises with little difficulty. If, however, you find yourself confused about some of the HTML authoring tools that UltraDev 4 has to offer, I highly recommend that you check out the Using Dreamweaver 4 manual that comes with the UltraDev 4 software and walk through the Dreamweaver tutorial found on the UltraDev 4 Help menu.

Choosing Your Page Properties

The first step in building an attractive chassis for your Web page is to configure the properties that each page will rely upon. Settings such as the background and link colors are important because they directly affect the way your visitors view your site. Other data, such as the page description and keywords are equally important because they may influence the way that your pages are indexed and displayed in many search engines.

Page Title

If you've been building Web pages for a while, you might think it's a little silly that I'm writing a section on adding a page title to a Web page. Unfortunately, the importance of a good page title is sometimes overlooked, which could result in confusion on the part of the visitor and poor rankings in the search engines.

Think about it for a second. Suppose you have just released your newest Web creation selling handcrafted furniture. Although you're marketing your site through traditional avenues such as media advertising and word-of-mouth, you are hoping to attract significant traffic from the major search engines. However, even if your site description and keywords earn you a top ranking in the search engines, potential customers may not visit your site if the title is not attractive, because it is the title that is displayed as the link to your page. And it's not just personal Web sites that are forgetting the title. Running a search on AltaVista using the terms "Untitled Document" turns up everything from small businesses to major software companies.

The point in all this is not to forget the little details when developing your pages. Sure, it's important to make sure that you have an attractive design and a well-designed database, but what good does it do for your business if you have no traffic?

> **Tip**
>
> **Seeing the "Big" Picture** The first time you open UltraDev 4, the Page view may not be maximized to fit your entire screen. If you want UltraDev maximized every time you open it, just maximize the screen and the close the program. UltraDev then "remembers" to open maximized next time.
>
> Another issue arises if you are using the Microsoft Office toolbar and it is set to always be on top. It may cover the minimize and maximize buttons. You can either close the Office Toolbar or right-click anywhere in the UltraDev Page Title bar and choose a window resize option.

Exercise 5.1 Adding a Page Title

1. Open UltraDev 4. If the Objects panel (generally the vertical toolbar on the left side of the screen) is turned on, turn it off by clicking its close button. If the Data Bindings/Server Behaviors panel (usually in the upper-right area of the screen) is open, close it, too.

> **Tip**
>
> **About Closing and Opening**   Don't worry about opening and closing panels, inspectors, or toolbars. You can easily open them again by dropping down the Window menu and selecting the object to toggle it on and off.

2. Choose Site/Open Site/InsideUD4 from the drop-down menu.
3. In the local folder pane (the right pane) of the Site window, double-click the default.asp file created in Chapter 4, "Building an UltraDev Site from the Gound Up." UltraDev opens default.asp for editing.

> **Note**
>
> **Viewing the Site Files**   If you have only a single pane in your Site view (the screen isn't split into a left and right half), you are most likely viewing the site in the Site Map layout. To view the site files, click the left-most button (Site Files) on the toolbar near the top of the screen.

4. You should see the link to Bargain Bin created in the previous chapter. Select it, and press the Delete key on your keyboard to delete the text and the link.
5. In UltraDev 4, Macromedia has made it extremely easy to change the page title of each page by placing a Title field in the toolbar. In that field, highlight the current name (Untitled Document), type **Nostalgic Radio Favorites**, and press Enter. As shown in Figure 5.1, the title of your page is now updated.

> **Tip**
>
> **Renaming Revisited**   If you upgraded from UltraDev 1 or from any previous version of Dreamweaver, you can still modify the page title by selecting Modify/Page Properties or by right-clicking on any blank space in your page and selecting Page Properties from the context menu.

6. Save the default.asp page.

Background Colors and Images

One of the most prominent ways to customize the way your visitors view your Web pages is to provide a custom background color or background image. You should, however, exercise caution when choosing either of these options. Choosing bright or flashy colors can be annoying and discourage would-be customers. Dark colors, on the other hand, can interfere with the way text is displayed and make your content difficult to read. Whatever color you choose, you should ensure that it falls within the 216 colors that comprise the Web-safe palette offered by UltraDev whenever you choose colors.

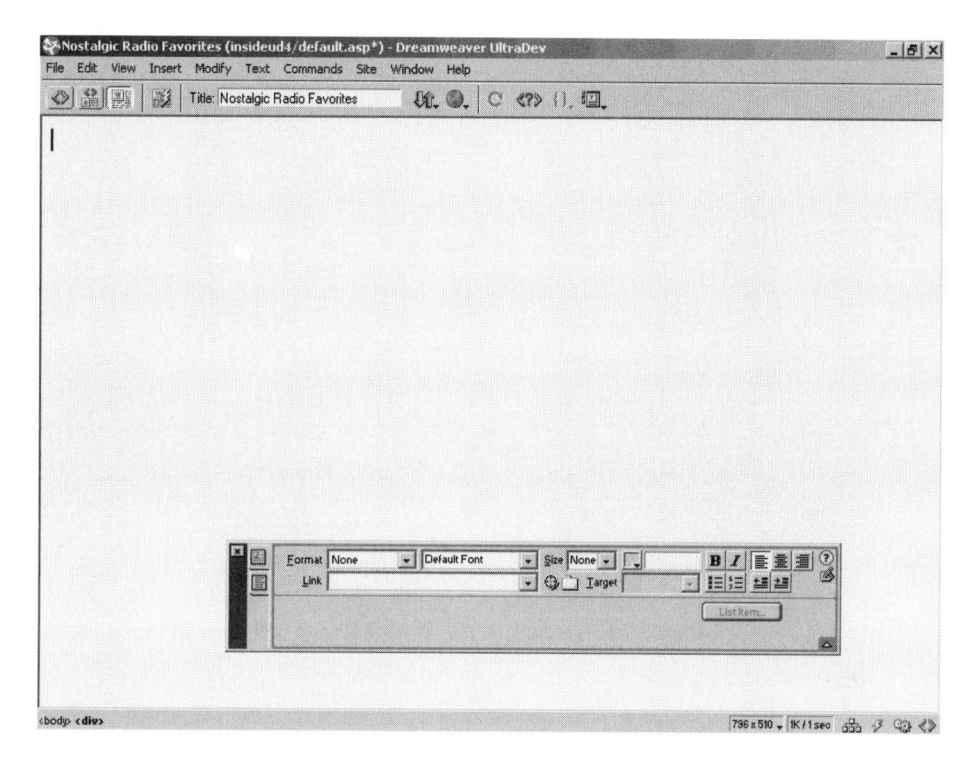

Figure 5.1 Add a title to your site by typing it into the Title field.

Similar cautions should be stated regarding background images. With a variety of display resolutions, color settings, and modem speeds out there, you should be sure that your background doesn't interfere with your text at various resolutions and doesn't create a significant increase in the amount of time it takes dial-up visitors to view your page.

At this point, you don't need to change the background because you are using a white background in the exercises. If you need to add or change the background color or image for your own pages, follow these steps:

1. Select Modify/Page Properties. As shown in Figure 5.2, UltraDev 4 opens the Page Properties dialog box.

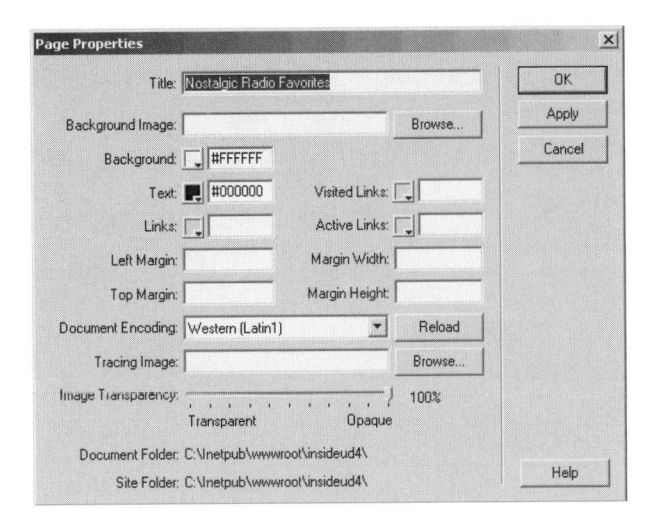

Figure 5.2 The Page Properties dialog box allows you to customize many visual elements on your page.

2. To select a background image, enter the path to the file or click the Browse button to navigate to the file.

3. To choose a background color, you can enter a hexadecimal value that corresponds to the appropriate Red, Green, and Blue (RGB) values. If you don't know the value for your color, you can click the color box and select from one of the 216 colors from the Web-safe palette shown in Figure 5.3.

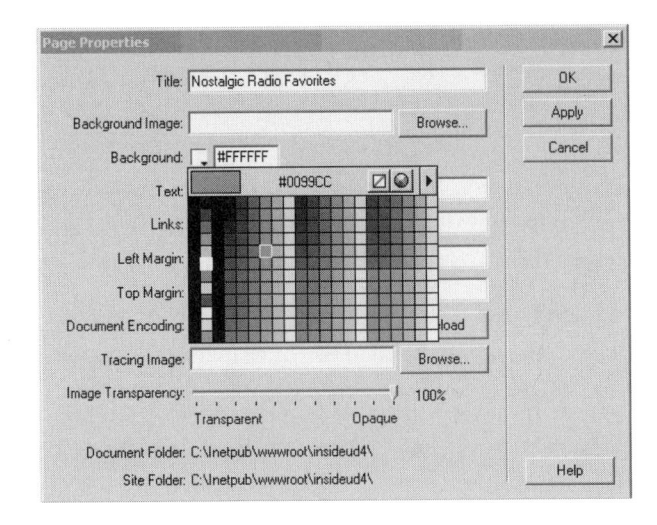

Figure 5.3 UltraDev's Web-safe palette lets you choose from colors that browsers can safely display.

4. You can also select a color outside the Web-safe palette by clicking the color wheel in the upper-right corner of the Web-safe palette.

5. After you have selected the background color or image of your choice, click the OK button.

Link Colors

Another way to customize the color scheme that your pages use is to choose colors for the various hyperlinks that you may include. UltraDev 4 allows you to specify values for links, active links, and visited links. Once colors are chosen, links that have not been clicked before will automatically inherit the Links value, those that are in the process of being clicked will inherit the Active Link value, and those that have been clicked before will inherit the Visited Links value. Link colors are specified in the Page Properties box in the same manner that background colors are chosen.

> **Caution**
>
> **Watch Those Link Colors!** When selecting link colors, you should also remember to stick with the 216 Web-safe colors. In addition, you should keep in mind that visitors to your Web site can adjust their browsers to override the colors you specify, so make sure your site's color scheme works with all link colors.

Head Tags

When someone makes a request for one of your Web pages, your Web server sends the header information for that page. The information stored in the header provides information on how to display the page, authoring details, and quite a bit of information that is used by search engines.

As you can probably tell from my little rant on page titles, I am a big believer in doing everything possible to make Web sites successful in the search engines. So bear with me through one more section while I talk about the importance of the information that is placed in the head section of your pages.

Unfortunately, pages that use dynamic Web pages are already at a distinct disadvantage when it comes to search engines. If you are not familiar with the way search engines work, you should be aware that when you submit your page to be included in a search engine's directory, a small program known as a spider visits your Web site and its pages and extracts information such as the page titles, header information, and a small portion of the text from each page that is linked. It is that information that determines where you are ranked and whether or not your site will be indexed.

Spiders, however, are not capable of pressing the "submit" button on your pages, so they aren't capable of running any of the database queries that build the dynamic pages that your human visitor might see. Therefore, it is entirely possible that large pieces of information—such as your product catalog, employee database, or other information stored in a database would have no bearing on your search engine placement.

> **Note**
>
> **Increasing Spider I.Q.** As search engine technology advances, spiders are getting "smarter." There is a new search engine that is in beta testing that claims to be able to spider your database as well as your Web pages. If you're interested in checking it out, take a look at http://beta.profusion.com/.

The fact that you are using dynamic pages doesn't completely exclude you from being listed in the search engines. Any page that is not built dynamically can still be included in the search engines. In fact, if you place relevant information in the head section of your pages, you should still be able to attract significant traffic from the search engines.

Meta Tags

Think of Meta tags as tidbits of information that tell the browser how to behave when it is displaying your pages. Certain tags, such as the window-target tag, can ensure that no one places your pages in a frame. Other tags like the set-cookie tag and the robots tag can grant or restrict access to areas of your site to both users and search engine spiders.

You should also be aware that there are two types of Meta tags: the HTTP-EQUIV and those with a Name attribute. HTTP-EQUIV tags are processed by the browser just as though they were head tags. This means that they can control the way the browser behaves while displaying your pages. For instance, many site creators have used these tags to create entrance and exit effects that make the page look as though it is sliding on or off the page.

Meta tags that use the Name attribute are a little different. Rather than just using the HTTP-EQUIV tag, they assign a value to the tag in the form of a name. Because they are named, they have no effect on how the browser displays your page, but instead provide additional information about your page content. Some common tags using the Name attribute include the following:

- `<META Name="author" CONTENT="Your Name">`
- `<META Name="copyright" CONTENT="Copyright 2001 by Your Name. All rights reserved.">`

Exercise 5.2 Adding a Copyright Meta Tag to Your Page

1. In the default.asp page, select Insert/Head Tags/Meta from the UltraDev 4 menu bar. UltraDev prompts you to enter the tag's Attribute, Value, and Content.
2. In the Insert Meta dialog box, shown in Figure 5.4, select the Name Attribute.

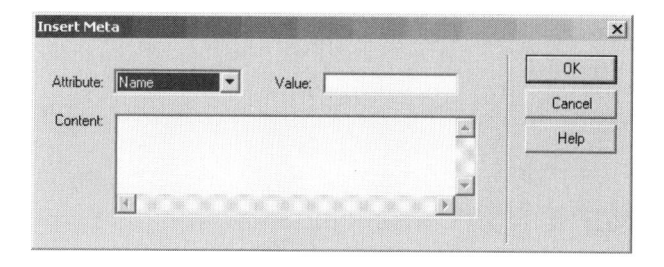

Figure 5.4 The Insert Meta dialog box helps you quickly create custom tags for your pages.

3. In the Value field, type **copyright**.
4. In the Content field, type **Copyright 2001 by (Your Name). All Rights Reserved**.
5. Click OK. Although you can't see it in the Design view, UltraDev places the appropriate tag in the head section of your page's code.
6. Click the Show Code View button on the toolbar where you can see that the copyright Meta tag has been added to the code.
7. Switch back to the Design view by clicking the Show Design View button on the toolbar.
8. Save your default.asp page.

Keywords

In your efforts to promote your pages in the search engines, keywords will probably have the most effect on whether you are listed. Some search engines, such as AltaVista, scan your pages for the Keywords Meta tag and compare those keywords to the actual content in your page. If they match, then your page is usually included in the index. If, however, you tried to get cute and add *sex* (still the most popular search term according to searchterms.com) as a keyword for your furniture store, many of the search engines would deny you a listing for "spamming" their index.

There are a couple of other things you should know about keywords. First, each page should have its own set of unique keywords. Don't add a generic set of keywords to a page template, use those keywords for every page, and then expect to be successful in the search engines. It won't happen. Second, to customize each page, you should analyze the page content and determine ten to twelve words that visitors to a search engine might use to find your pages. Try your best to get into the mind of one of your customers or, if the opportunity arises, ask some of your customers what search terms they might use to find information about your business.

Exercise 5.3 Adding Keywords to Your Page

1. In the default.asp page, select Insert/Head Tags/Keywords from the UltraDev 4 menu bar.
2. As shown in Figure 5.5, UltraDev allows you to enter your keywords separated by commas.

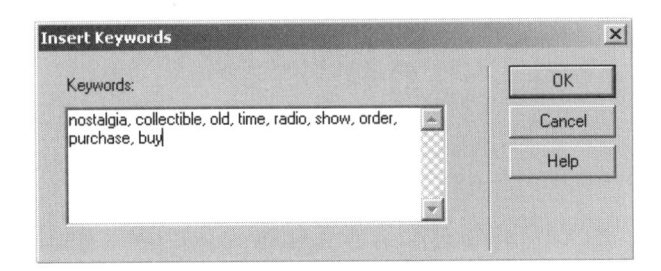

Figure 5.5 Customize your site by adding page-specific keywords.

3. Type **nostalgia, collectible, old, time, radio, show, order, purchase, buy**. When you have entered your keywords for the page, click OK.
4. Again, switch to the Code view to see the additions that UltraDev has made to your code.
5. Switch back to the Design view and save the default.asp.

> **Caution**
> **Beware of Trademarked Keywords** Be very careful which keywords you apply to your Web pages. There have been instances where trademarked keywords have been used without the permission of the owner (the most notable being Playboy) and the owner of the trademark has sued for, and won, millions of dollars.

Description

The final piece of information that can have an effect on your ability to attract visitors from the search engines is the Description tag. Most search engines display a synopsis of the site underneath the link that gives an idea of what the page is about, and many search engines draw this information from the Description tag. Again, try to conceptualize what the person searching for your site would want to see in the page description. As with the Keywords tag, the Description tag should be unique from page to page.

Exercise 5.4 Adding a Description to Your Page

1. In the default.asp page, select Insert/Head Tags/Description from the UltraDev 4 menu bar.
2. As shown in Figure 5.6, UltraDev allows you to enter a description for your page. Keep your description short and concise.

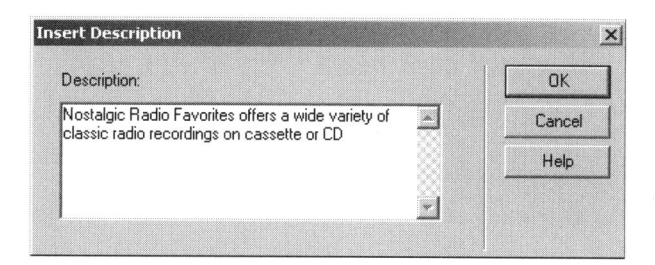

Figure 5.6 Enter a description for your page.

3. Type **Nostalgic Radio Favorites offers a wide variety of classic radio recordings on cassette or CD**. When you have entered your description for the page, click OK.
4. Once again, switch to the Code view to see the Meta tag that UltraDev added to your code.
5. Switch back to the Design view and save the default.asp page.

Additional Head Tags

There are three additional tags, shown in Table 5.1, that UltraDev 4 can insert into each of your pages. Although not useful on a regular basis, each provides a function that is useful from time to time.

Table 5.1 Additional Meta Tags

Head Tag	Function
Refresh tag	This tag instructs the browser to refresh after a certain period of time and can redirect the visitor to another site after the time.
	The Refresh tag has been abused and is discouraged by the search engines, but can be beneficial if you have a page with dynamic elements that should be refreshed periodically (such as a featured item).
Base tag	This tag specifies the location of a base document for all document-relative links within the page.
Link tag	The Link tag sets up a relationship with another document in plain terms. For instance, if you set the word contents to equal toc.htm, you could create a link to your table of contents page by simply using the word contents rather than the page name toc.htm.

Designing a Page Layout

After you have configured your page settings, you are ready to begin building your pages. At this point, you should already have an idea of what your pages are going to look like and the relationships that will exist between pages. In the exercises that follow, you will be building a page that you will use as a template throughout the remainder of the book. Although this chapter focuses on the static elements within the page, the template will evolve throughout the rest of the chapters to include dynamic elements, content drawn from a database, and both eCommerce and eLearning elements.

Choosing a Page Layout View

If you have created Web pages before, you are probably familiar with the use of tables to align the various objects throughout your individual pages. Unlike many desktop publishing applications, such as Adobe PageMaker or Microsoft Publisher, WYSIWYG editors do not allow you to insert images and text blocks and drag them to wherever you want them located. Instead, you build the layout of your page by creating tables and then placing tables within those tables (referred to as "nesting"). If you haven't used tables to control page layout before, bear with me for a minute as the exercises will demonstrate exactly what I'm referring to.

In an effort to make the Web page development process more like desktop publishing, UltraDev 4 now offers two options for creating tables within your Web pages. The first is the Standard View, which is the default view you see when you start UltraDev 4. This view allows you to see the page as it would be displayed in a browser. The second option is the Layout View, which will be more comfortable for those who are used to desktop publishing applications. This view allows you to create tables and cells by clicking and dragging and to adjust the sizes of each table using rulers and guides for specific measurements.

Creating the Main Table

To begin building the Web page template, use a single table that provides your pages with left and right margins. In addition, the table is set to expand to fill the screen vertically for every resolution.

Exercise 5.5 Inserting the Main Table

1. In the default.asp page, open the Property inspector, if it is not already showing, by choosing Window/Properties from the menu bar (see Figure 5.7).
2. If the Property inspector is not fully expanded to show all properties, click the expander arrow.

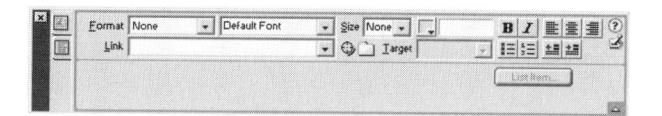

Chapter 5 The Dreamweaver in Dreamweaver UltraDev 4   121

Figure 5.7 UltraDev 4's Property inspector.

> **Note**
>
> **Expanding the Property Inspector** By default, the Property inspector displays only the most commonly accessed properties of an element. You can view all of the properties by clicking the expander arrow in the lower-right corner of the Property inspector. Personally, I keep the properties showing at all times, but whether you choose to is your personal preference.

3. Place your cursor in the Document window and click the Align Center button on the Property inspector. Your cursor should now be aligned in the center of the page.
4. Select Insert/Table from the menu bar. The Insert Table dialog box allows you to specify the dimensions of your table.
5. As shown in Figure 5.8, enter **1** row and **1** column and set the Width to be **90%** with a Border of **1**. Set Cell Padding and Cell Spacing both to **0**. Click OK.

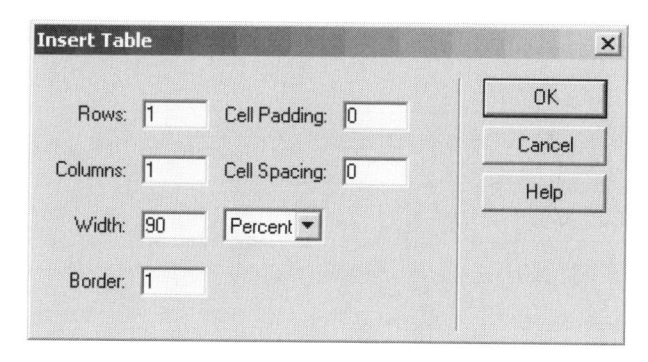

Figure 5.8 Easily create your table by filling in the fields in the Insert Table dialog box.

6. With the table selected, enter **#999966** as the border color in the Property inspector. The border color should turn khaki colored. Border changes are not shown until the table is deselected.

> **Tip**
>
> **Selecting a Table the Easy Way** You can select a table at any time by right-clicking anywhere in the table and selecting Table/Select Table from the context menu. Alternatively, you can also place your cursor anywhere in the table and click the <table> tag in the bottom-left corner of the design window.

7. In the Property inspector, type **tbMainTable** in the Table Name field of the Property inspector. Press Enter.

> **Note**
>
> **Choosing a Naming Convention** This is probably a good time to talk about naming the objects located throughout your Web site. When Web pages only consisted of static HTML, there was not a lot of incentive to name related images and tables. Because they were generally static items, there was little need to reference them and, hence, a lesser need to name them.
>
> Dynamic pages, however, rely heavily upon the naming of objects within your pages. Scripts can perform actions like swapping images, moving layers, or filling in form fields. These actions cannot be done, however, without referencing the object by name. Therefore, it is a good idea to get in the habit of naming every element whether it is static or dynamic.
>
> As a personal preference, I like to add a two-letter code at the front of each element that lets me know at a glance what type of element I am looking for. For example, the name for the table you just entered is tbMainTable. If I were looking at the code alone, I would quickly be able to discern that this is a table.
>
> The naming convention you choose for your sites is usually based on personal preference. However, it is a good idea to develop a style and apply it to all your Web applications.

8. With the table still selected, enter **100** percent in the Height (H) field on the Property inspector. Press Enter. As a result, the table adjusts to fill your screen.

> **Warning**
>
> **Percent, Not Pixels** Make sure you choose percent and don't leave it at the pixels default setting.

9. Drop the insertion point inside the table's single cell and click. Now click the Align Center button on the Property inspector.
10. Finally, adjust the Vertical alignment to be Top on the Property inspector. Leave the Horizontal alignment at default.
11. As shown in Figure 5.9, you should now have a single table bordering your page. Save your file.

Adding a Header Table

The next step in developing your page layout is to add a header table. This table is nested within your main table and will eventually contain the site logo and the navigation tabs for the various areas of the site.

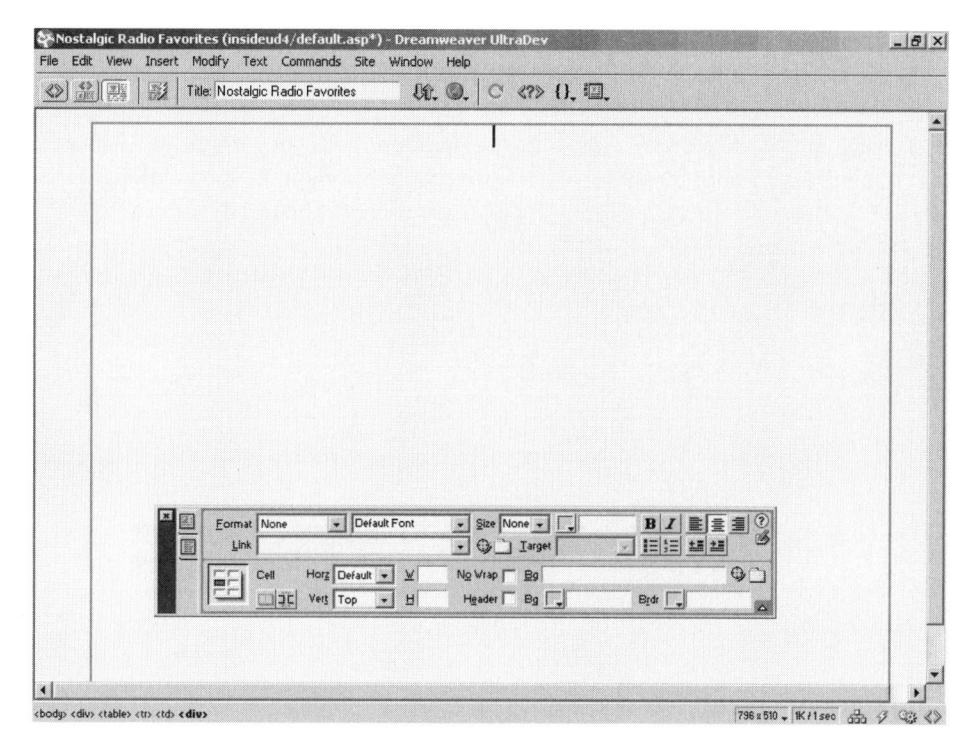

Chapter 5 The Dreamweaver in Dreamweaver UltraDev 4   123

Figure 5.9 The main table now borders the page.

Exercise 5.6 Adding a Header Table to the Page

1. From the menu bar, select Insert/Table. As shown in Figure 5.10, create a table that consists of **2** rows, **3** columns, has a Width of **100%** and no border. In addition, set the Cell Padding and Cell Spacing to **0**. Press Enter. UltraDev 4 inserts a new table with six cells in your main table.

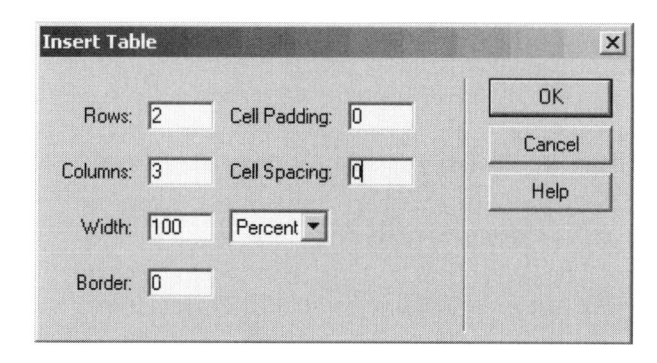

Figure 5.10 Create your header table.

2. Highlight the new table by right-clicking inside the table and choosing Table/Select Table. In the Property inspector, type **tbHeaderTable** in the Table Name field and press Enter.

3. Highlight the top row of cells in the header table by clicking on the top-left cell and dragging your cursor across the two cells to the right. As shown in Figure 5.11, the cells indicate that they are highlighted by the black border that surrounds them.

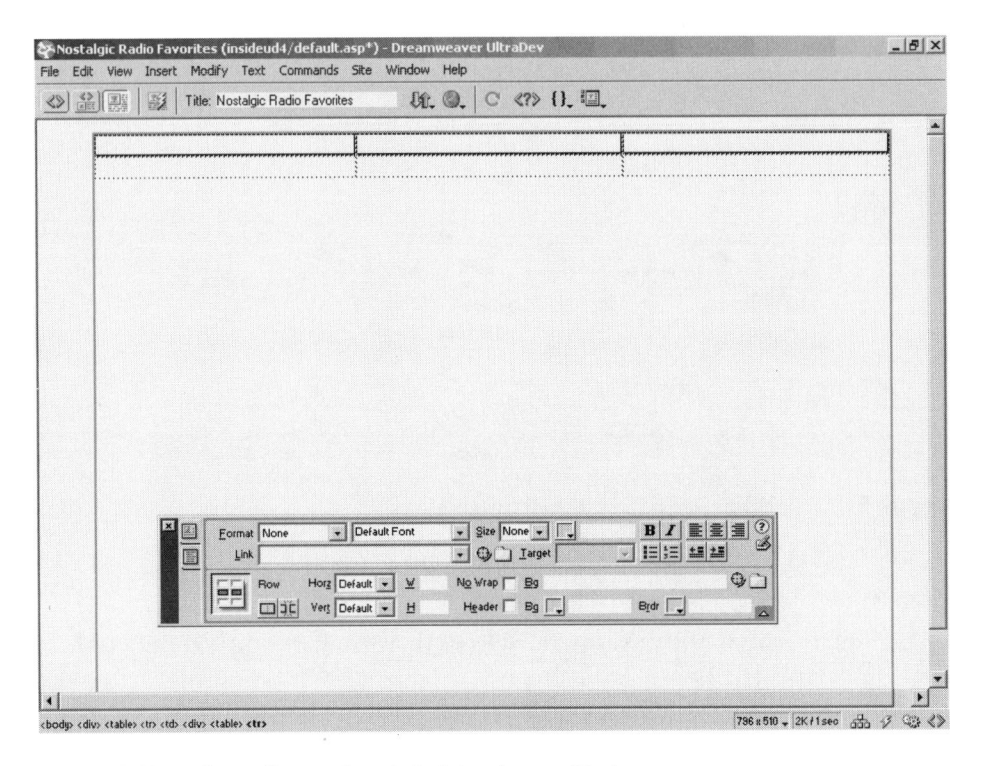

Figure 5.11 When cells are selected, their borders are black.

4. Set the vertical alignment for these cells to Bottom by choosing that option from the Vert field in the Property inspector. Set the width for the fields to **33%** by typing the percentage in the W field of the Property inspector. Don't forget the percent sign or UltraDev will default to pixels. Press Enter.

5. Highlight the bottom row of cells in this table and change the background color for these cells to **#999966** by typing that value in the Bg field of the Property inspector that has a color box next to it. Press Enter. In addition, set the Height of these cells to **10** pixels in the H field of the Property inspector and press Enter.

6. Save your document.

Adding a Main Data Table

The next item to add to the page is the main data table. This table serves as the location for both static information that you will enter and dynamic data that is generated from your database.

Exercise 5.7 Constructing a Main Data Table

1. In the default.asp page, place the insertion point in the main table below the header table.
2. Select Insert/Table from the menu bar and add a table that has **1** row, **2** columns, and occupies **100%** of the Width. In addition, set the Border, Cell Padding, and Cell Spacing to **0**. Click OK. Your page should look like Figure 5.12.

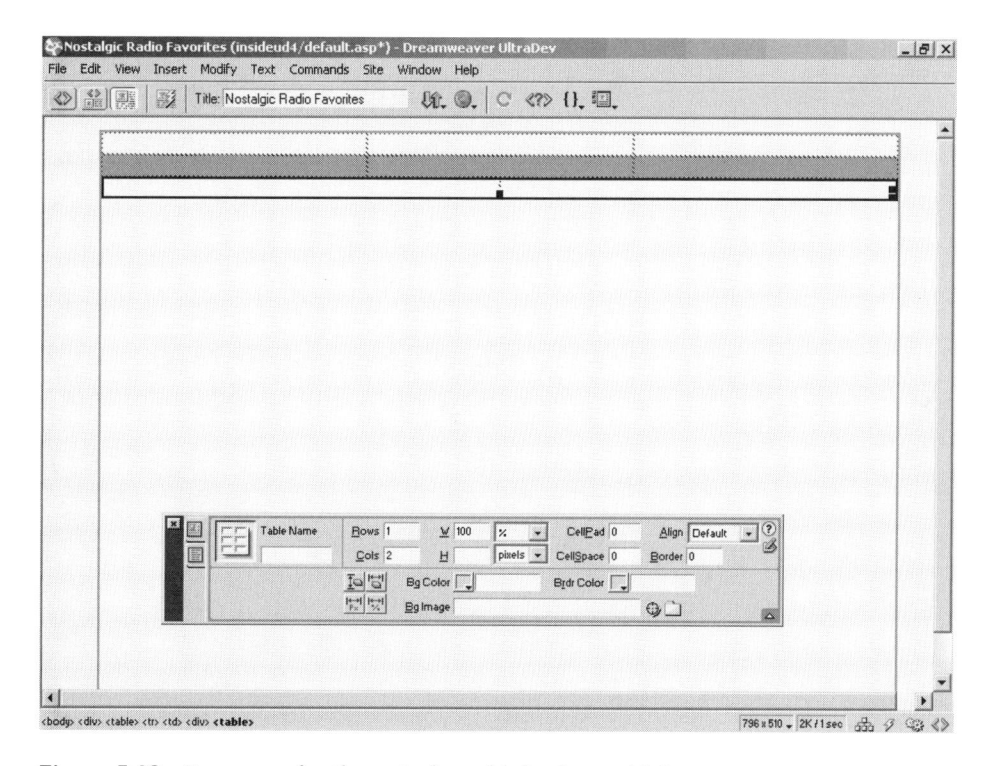

Figure 5.12 Your page after the main data table has been added.

3. Highlight the table by right-clicking inside one of the table cells and choosing Table/Select Table. In the Property inspector, name the table **tbMainData**. Press Enter.
4. Place your cursor in the left cell of the main data table and change the background color for the cell to **#999966** by entering the value in the Bg field of the Property inspector. Press Enter.

5. In addition, enter **10%** for the cell width in the Property inspector. As shown in Figure 5.13, UltraDev 4 automatically adjusts the size of the column.

6. Place your cursor in the right cell of the Main Data table and click the Align Center button on the Property inspector. Set the vertical alignment of the cell to top by choosing Top from the Vert dropdown on the Property inspector.

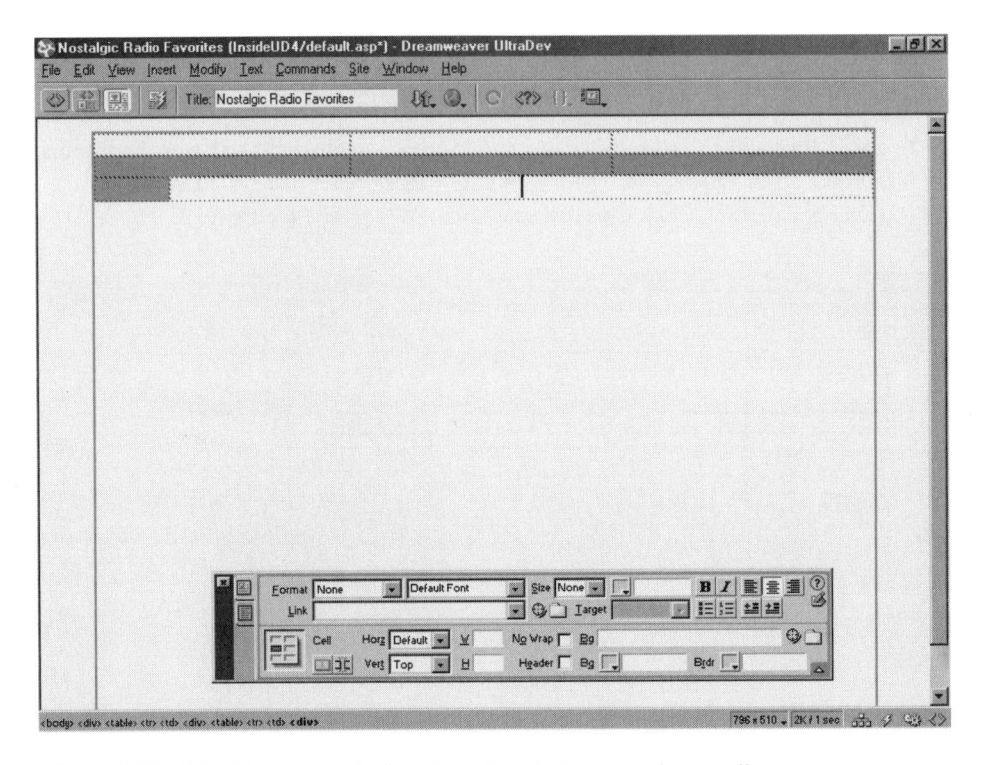

Figure 5.13 UltraDev automatically adjusts the relative sizes of your cells.

7. Save your document.

Adding a Table for Navigation Links

The final step in laying out your table design is to add a table for your navigation links. This table is nested within the Main Data table and provides an easy way to organize the buttons that your visitors will use to navigate some of the site's functions.

Exercise 5.8 Adding a Navigation Links Table

1. In the default.asp page, place the insertion point in the left cell of the main data table. Select Insert/Table from the menu bar and create a table that consists of **6**

rows, **1** column, and occupies **100%** of the Width. In addition, set the Border, Cell Padding, and Cell Spacing to **0**.

2. Select the table by right-clicking in one of the table cells and choosing Table/Select Table.
3. In the Property inspector, name the table **tbNavTable**.
4. Finally, highlight the cells in the table by clicking on the top cell and dragging your mouse over the rest of the cells. Click the Align Center button on the Property inspector. As shown in Figure 5.14, you now have a series of tables that are ready to hold your site's images and data.

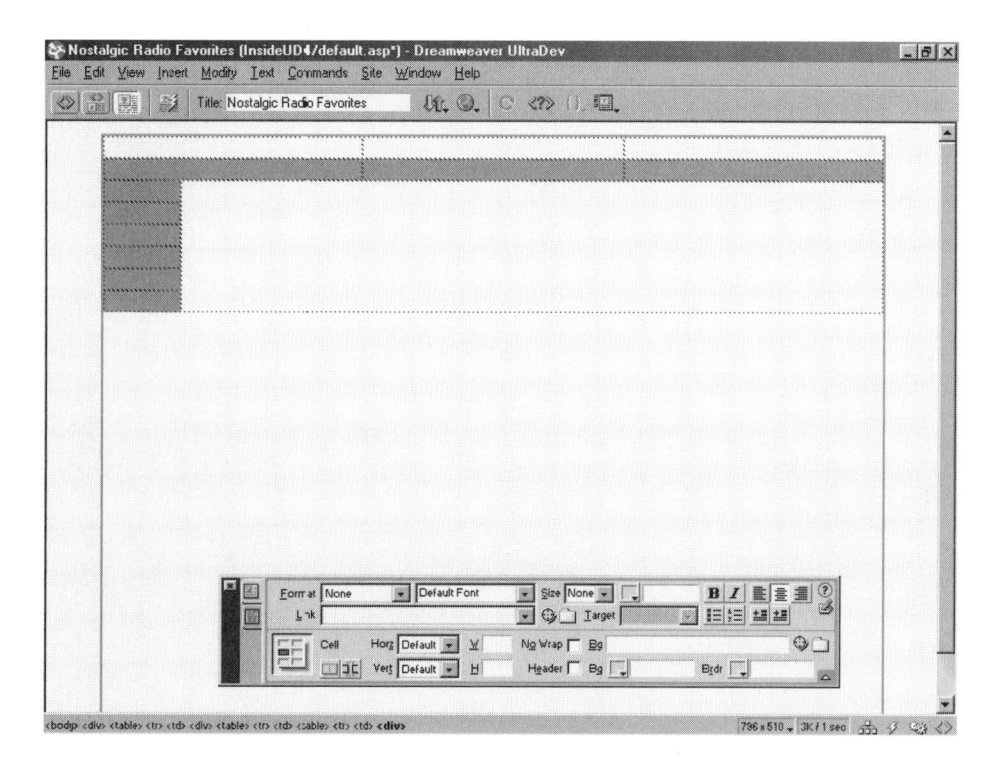

Figure 5.14 Your page with all the necessary tables.

5. Save your document.

Inserting and Linking Graphics

What would a Web page be without graphics? Images and buttons (affectionately referred to as "eye-candy") provide your visitors with visual links to the services that your site offers. Remember, however, that large graphics or those that are not optimized for the Web can slow your pages' load times significantly. As you add images to your site, keep an eye on UltraDev 4's status bar, which will let you know approximately how fast your page will load.

> **Note**
>
> **Give Fireworks a Try** If you haven't already given Macromedia Fireworks a try, I highly recommend it for optimizing your graphics for the Web. Fireworks consistently produces some of the smallest graphic file sizes without sacrificing the quality of your image. You can download a free 30-day trial of Fireworks at http://www.macromedia.com/software/fireworks/.

Exercise 5.9 Adding and Linking Images

1. Before you can add the graphics to your site, you need to copy them to your local site root. Using the book's Web site, locate the images for Chapter 5 in the chapter's subdirectory (www.insideultradev.com/book/chatper5). Copy all the images to the root directory for the InsideUD4 site on your local hard drive. If you are using Personal Web Server, you would place the image folder and its contents in the C:\inetpub\wwwroot\insideud4 folder.

2. In the default.asp page, place the insertion point in the top-left cell of the header table.

3. Select Insert/Image from the menu bar. As shown in Figure 5.15, browse to the nrf_logo.gif image stored in the images subdirectory of your site and click OK. UltraDev 4 adds the site logo to your page.

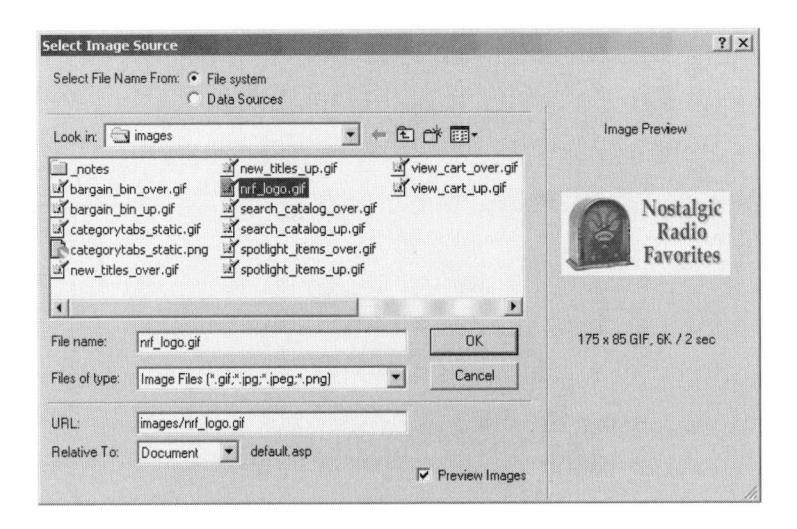

Figure 5.15 Choose the nrf_logo.gif image to add to your page.

4. Highlight the site logo by clicking on it and type **http://localhost/insideud4/** in the Link field of the Property inspector. This makes the image a hyperlink to the root of your site.

> **Caution**
>
> **Adjust Those Links if Necessary** If you are using a different directory or are using a folder on a different machine (such as your Web server), you need to adjust the hyperlinks to meet your needs. In addition, if you are using Web server software other than Personal Web Server or IIS, you should enter your machine's network name or IP address rather than localhost in your URLs throughout each exercise.

5. Place the insertion point in the rightmost cell of the header table and click the Align Right button on the Property inspector.
6. Choose Insert/Image from the menu bar and browse to the image named categorytabs_static.gif. Click OK. As shown in Figure 5.16, UltraDev 4 inserts an image containing tabs for a variety of topics.

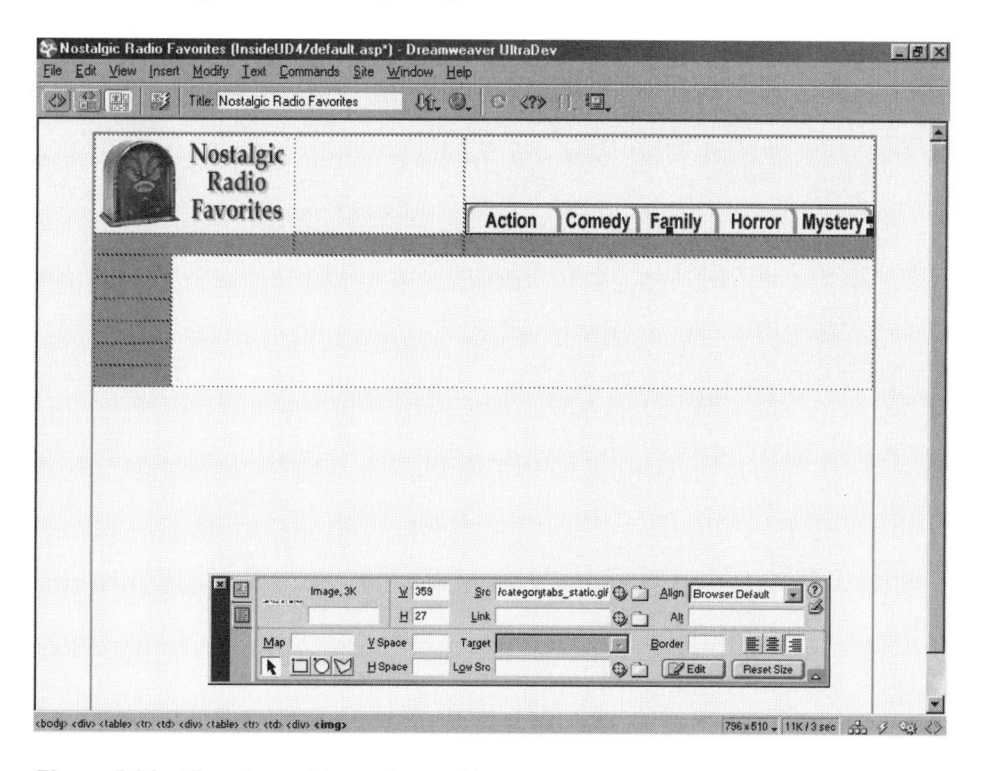

Figure 5.16 The category tabs are inserted into your page.

7. With the categorytabs_static.gif image highlighted, click the Rectangular Hotspot Tool at the bottom-left corner of the Property inspector and create a

130   Part II   Building a Solid Foundation

hotspot by using the tool to draw a rectangle over the word Action. As shown in Figure 5.17, the Property inspector allows you to specify information about the new hotspot.

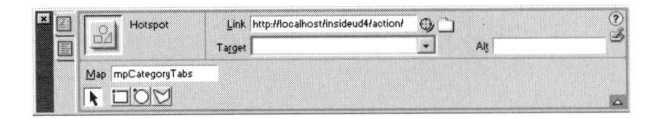

Figure 5.17   Specify the properties for your new hotspot.

8. In the Map box, delete the word Map, type **mpCategoryTabs**, and press Enter. Delete the # character from the Link field and type **http://localhost/insideud4/action/** to link the hotspot to the action folder. Press Enter.

9. Create hotspots for the remaining four tabs by following the same procedures. When completed, your page should look like Figure 5.18.

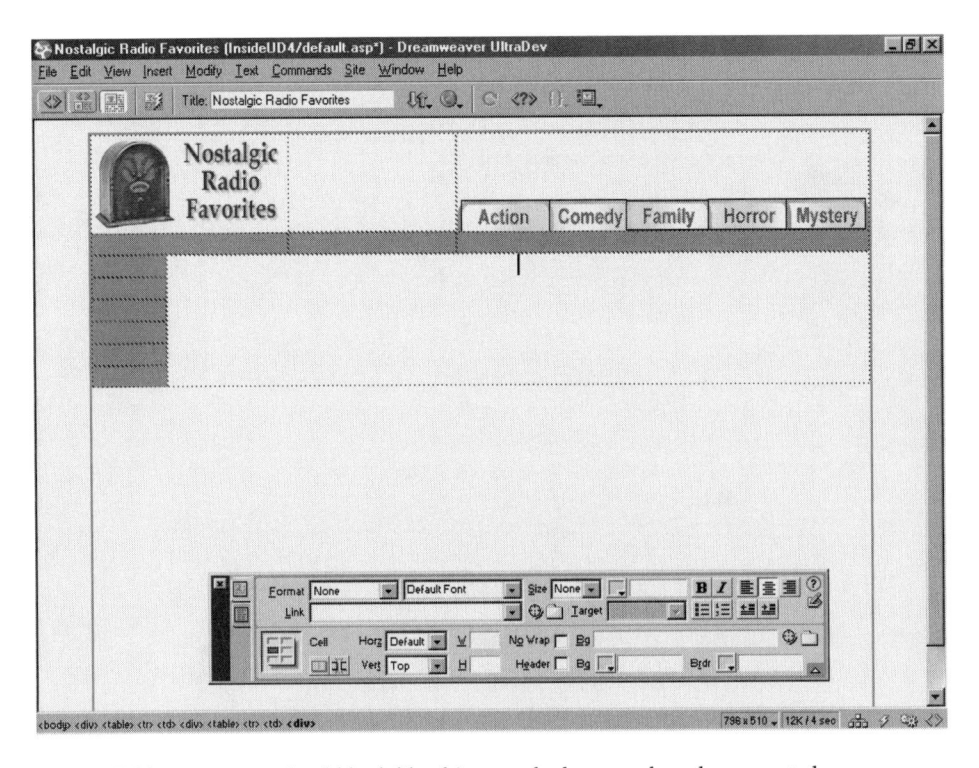

Figure 5.18   Your page should look like this once the hotspots have been created.

10. Save your document.

Building a Template File

One of the most timesaving tools found in UltraDev 4 is its capability to create customized page templates. By creating a template file and building pages based on that template, you can quickly create pages using a common page layout and elements that are present on every page. In addition, after you have created the pages, you can easily update every page that relies on the template by simply making the changes in the template file. Imagine updating hundreds of Web pages in a matter of minutes.

Templates do have their downside, too. Once you commit to a template, making major changes across your site can be a bit tricky. In addition, because the Head section of any page is dependent on a template, it is not editable; you may encounter difficulties applying Cascading Style Sheets (CSS), dynamic data, or behaviors. However, if you are confident in the page layout you have chosen and want to develop pages that share the same layout, a template may be the right choice.

Exercise 5.10 Creating a Template File

1. With the default.asp file open, choose File/Save As Template from the menu bar.
2. As shown in Figure 5.19, UltraDev 4 asks you to choose a site where the template will be applied and to choose a name for the template.

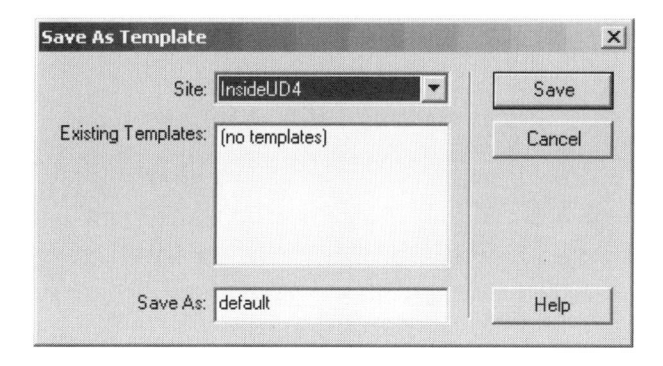

Figure 5.19 Select the site and template name.

3. Highlight the InsideUD4 site in the Site dropdown and type **nrfdefault** in the Save As field. (The beginning of the name is an abbreviation of Nostalgic Radio Favorites.) Click Save. You will notice that the name of your file in the Windows title bar is updated to reflect that you are now working with a template, rather than your original default.asp document.

> **Caution**
>
> **Template Location** When you create a template for your site, UltraDev 4 creates a templates subdirectory where the template files are stored. Do not ever delete or move that template folder or you risk corrupting any page that relies on the page layout store in the template files.

Selecting Editable Regions

After you have created a template file, the next step is to specify which areas of the pages should be customizable from page to page. To do this, we set regions of the page as editable. Once you specify which regions are editable, all other regions in the template are set as noneditable and are locked in all pages depending on the template.

Exercise 5.11 Specifying Editable Regions in the Template

1. In the nrfdefault.dwt file, place the insertion point in the right cell of the main data table.
2. From the menu bar, select Modify/Templates/New Editable Region. In the New Editable Region dialog box, type **erMainData**. Click OK. As shown in Figure 5.20, UltraDev 4 adds a highlighted comment to the cell, showing that it has been set as an editable region.
3. Save the template file. If UltraDev 4 asks you whether you want to automatically update all files that are dependent upon the template, choose Don't Update.

Creating New Pages from Templates

After you have developed your template, creating new pages that inherit the template properties is a snap. You can easily create a new file that is based upon a template by choosing File/New from Template from the UltraDev 4 menu bar. After you select which template you would like applied, UltraDev 4 will automatically generate a new page for you to work with.

Keep in mind, however, that within that new page, the only sections you will be able to customize are the regions designated as editable in the template and the page's title.

Applying a Template to an Existing Page

When you created your template, the default.asp document that you created was not automatically linked to the template. Therefore, the next step in ensuring that the home page is updated whenever the template is updated is to apply the template to the home page.

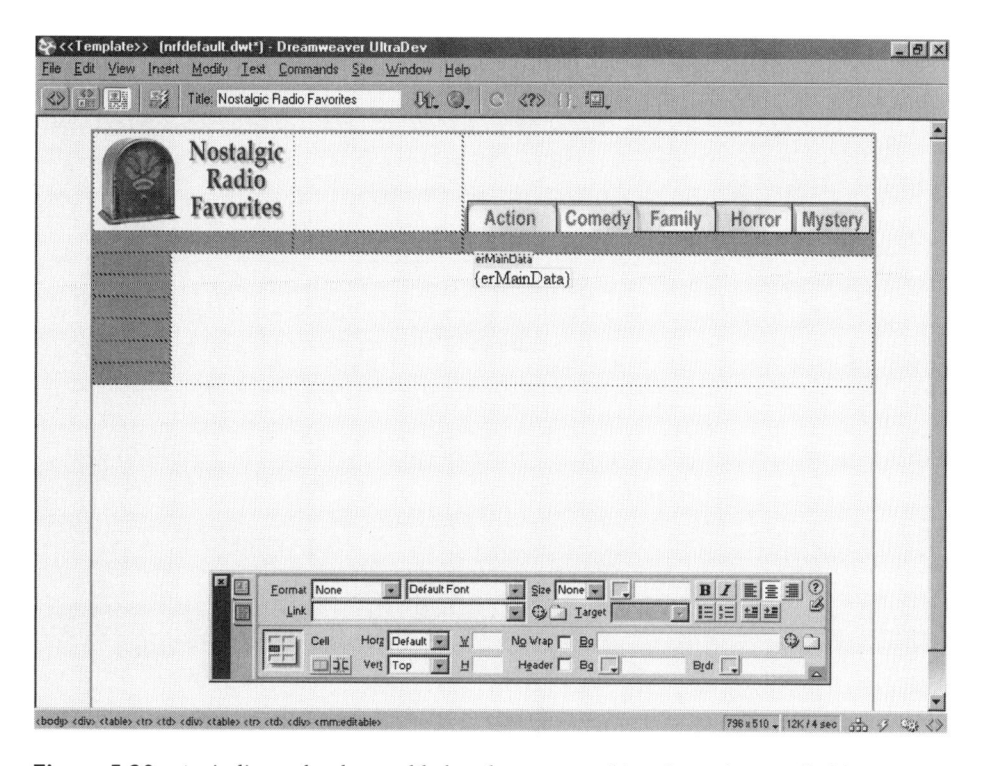

Chapter 5 The Dreamweaver in Dreamweaver UltraDev 4   133

Figure 5.20 An indicator has been added to the page, marking the region as editable.

Exercise 5.12 Applying a Template to a Page

1. Open the default.asp page and select Modify/Templates/Apply Templates to Page from the menu bar.
2. As shown in Figure 5.21, UltraDev 4 asks you to specify which template you would like to apply.

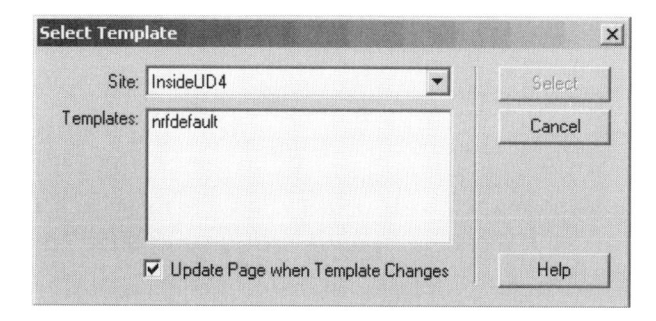

Figure 5.21 Specify the template you would like to apply to the page.

3. Highlight the nrfdefault and make sure there is a check in the Update Page when Template Changes checkbox. Click the Select button.

4. Because your default.asp page already has existing content, UltraDev 4 asks you what to do with it. Since we will be applying the exact same layout to this page, you should select the (none) option and click OK.

> **Note**
>
> **A Page Within a Page** If you were to choose the erMainData option, UltraDev 4 would take all the tables and images that are currently on the page and place them inside the erMainData editable region. Essentially, you would have a duplicate page inside the editable region.

5. As shown in Figure 5.22, you now have an editable region where you can make changes to the default.asp document. If you try to place the insertion point in any of the other tables, you will notice that UltraDev 4 has locked access to them because they were not marked as editable.

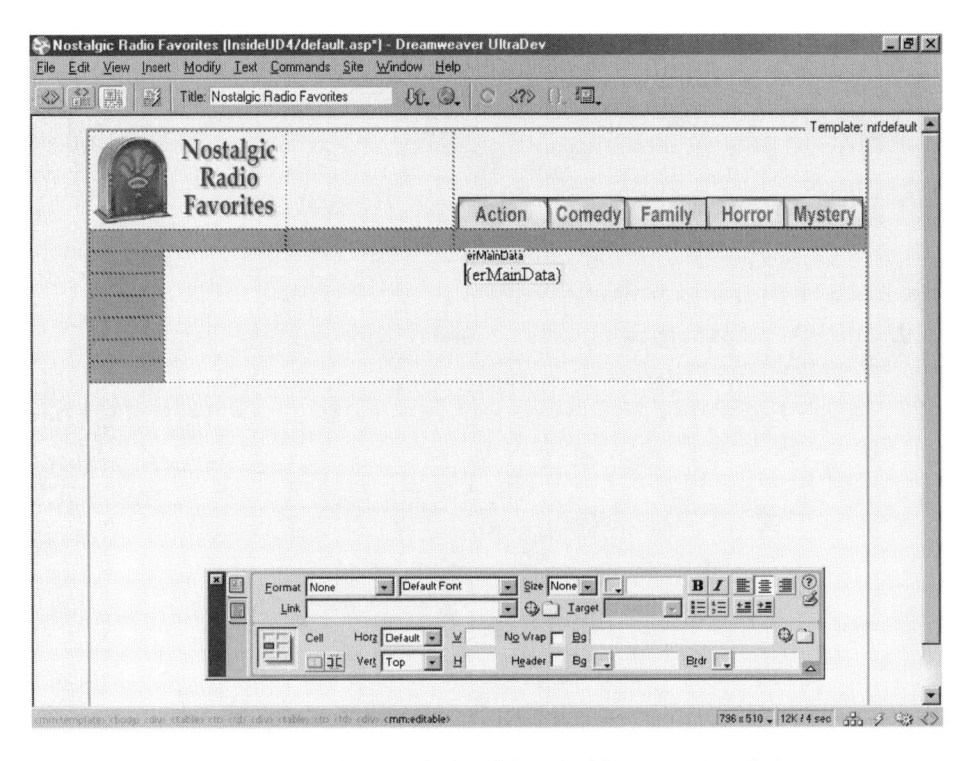

Figure 5.22 The template has been applied and the editable region identified.

6. Save the default.asp document.

Disconnecting Pages from Templates

There may come a time when you no longer want a page to be governed by a template. For instance, you may need to customize an individual page's Meta tags, but the template restricts access to the head section of the document. In this case, you can build the page from the template and then disconnect it to regain access to the head section.

To disconnect a page from a template, simply open the document and select Modify/Templates/Detach from Template.

Summary

This chapter introduced you to many of the HTML authoring tools that UltraDev 4 has adopted from Dreamweaver 4. These tools can help you develop a page layout and insert images in your pages. In addition, you learned how to build and use templates to quickly create pages that have the same characteristics.

In the next chapter, you look at the multimedia management capabilities that UltraDev 4 offers. So turn up those speakers and get ready to add sounds, rollover buttons, and animated layers to your pages.

Chapter 6

UltraDev's Graphic and Multimedia Capabilities

When it comes to building a Web site, one aspect I really enjoy is finding ways to bring the pages to life through graphics and multimedia. While static images and text may offer functionality and speed, they rarely provide the "wow" effect that elements such as rollover buttons, Flash movies, and sounds generate.

I do, however, recognize that too much eye-candy can cause problems. Although I love the look and feel of a well-designed, graphically rich Web site, I have also visited sites that have bombarded me with awful MIDI renditions of pop favorites or took way too long to download graphics or movie files. Therefore, when designing pages, I always try to balance the utility of the dynamic element with its functionality and use the element only when it will benefit the page's design without detracting from the visitor's experience.

Fortunately, UltraDev 4 offers quite a few options when it comes to managing and inserting graphics and multimedia content into your pages. Whether you're building a simple eCommerce site to sell your products or a corporate eLearning site to train your employees, you can take advantage of UltraDev's ability to handle multimedia.

To demonstrate UltraDev's multimedia features, this chapter takes a look at the following:

- UltraDev 4's Assets panel
- Creating dynamic buttons
- Adding movies to your pages
- Adding sounds to your pages

If you have never used Dreamweaver or UltraDev before, you'll be surprised at just how easy it can be to add dynamic graphics and multimedia to your pages. So turn up those speakers and see what UltraDev can do!

Introducing the Assets Panel

I am a naturally unorganized person. In my office, I often find myself the victim of my own filing system, which consists of piles of (somewhat) related papers, books, and disks occupying every square inch of my desk. Unfortunately, this cluttered lifestyle has led me on a few hour-long hunts for an item that turned out to be within arm's reach but was covered by a file folder or underneath a book.

Because of this disorganized lifestyle, I love it when an application comes along and helps me organize my projects. With UltraDev 4's addition of the Assets panel, shown in Figure 6.1, Macromedia has created a way for me to keep track of all the different elements that I use in my pages, including images, sounds, links, movies, scripts, and even colors.

Figure 6.1 The Assets panel organizes the various elements included in your pages.

The best thing about the Assets panel, however, is that with a click of your mouse, UltraDev will do all the work for you by determining the assets present in your site and how they should be categorized, and then allowing you just to drag and drop them right onto your pages.

Gathering Assets for Your Site

Have you ever built a Web site or maybe taken one over from some other developer where a generic naming scheme was used for the graphics? I recently did an update on a site where the original developer generically named the navigation buttons "button1.gif," "button2.gif," and so forth. In the past, updating these pages would have been a tedious process because I would have had to open every graphic to see what they looked like before I could even start.

Fortunately, UltraDev saved me from all this extra labor by adding the graphics to the Assets panel once I specified the site settings in the Site window. Then, instead of having to open each graphic in my graphics editor, I could see what each image looked like just by clicking the filename in the Assets panel.

> **Caution**
>
> **Choose Your Site Carefully** If you are managing multiple sites from the same machine, it's important that you make sure you have the right site open before opening your Assets panel. Because UltraDev builds the list of assets from the folders included in the open site, it's always a good idea to drop down the Site menu, click Open Site, and make sure that the correct site has a check next to it.

Exercise 6.1 Adding Elements to the Assets Panel

1. On the Web site for the book, locate the Chatper 6 subdirectory. From the Chapter6 folder, copy the media folder to the root folder of your local site. If you are using Personal Web Server, the path to your media folder should now be C:\Inetpub\wwwroot\insideud4\media.

2. Open UltraDev 4 and click Site/Open Site/InsideUD4. You should now see the Site window displaying the files and folders contained within the InsideUD4 site.

3. Switch to the Document window where an Untitled Document should be displayed. Select Window/Assets from the menu bar. The Assets panel should now be displayed.

4. If it is not already highlighted, select the Images category by clicking the Images category button on the left side of the Assets panel. As shown in Figure 6.2, UltraDev displays every GIF, JPEG, or PNG file located within the site.

5. Next, choose the Colors category and notice that UltraDev has stored each custom color that you have used throughout the site.

6. Click the button for each of the other categories in the site. You'll notice that with the exception of the template you created in Chapter 5, "The Dreamweaver in Dreamweaver UltraDev 4," the Assets panel is relatively empty. Don't worry: You'll be adding elements soon.

> **Tip**
>
> **Refreshing the Assets Panel** If you add an asset to your site, but it isn't showing up in the Assets panel, you can force UltraDev to refresh the Assets panel by clicking the Refresh Site List button at the bottom of the Assets panel. If your graphic still doesn't show up, try opening the Assets panel menu by clicking the black arrow in the upper-right corner of the panel. From the menu, select Recreate Site List.

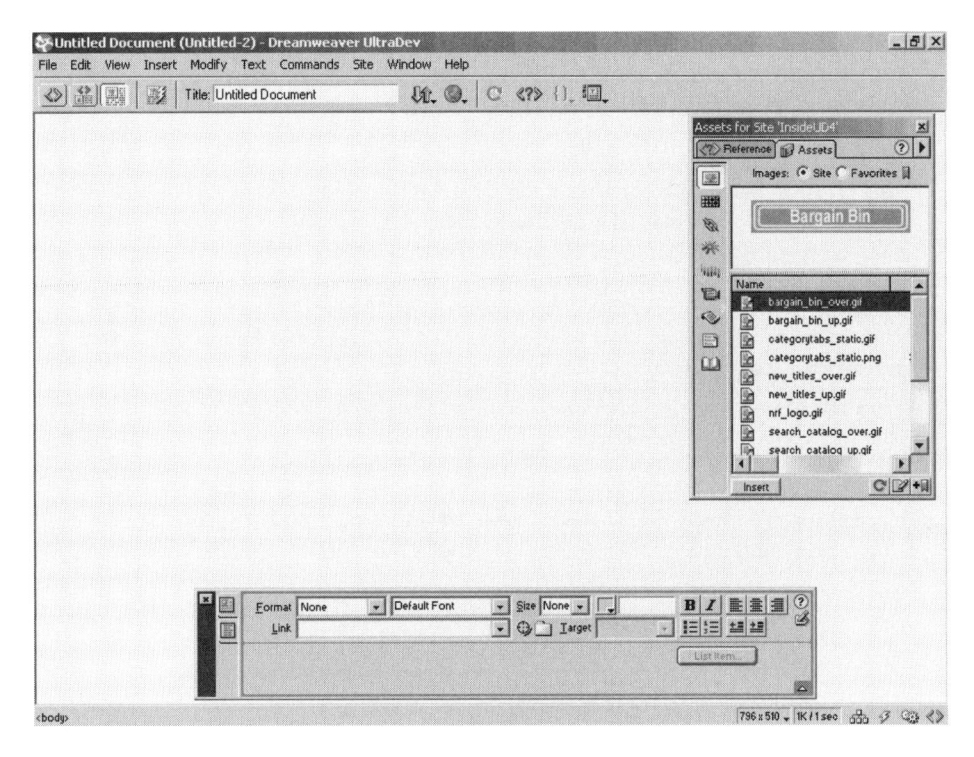

Chapter 6 UltraDev's Graphic and Multimedia Capabilities 141

Figure 6.2 The Assets panel categorizes all the elements located within your site.

Building Your List of Favorite Assets

By default, UltraDev displays the Assets panel using the Site view, which displays every element included in any page located in your site. Right now it may be a convenient way to view your site's assets, but as your site grows, so does the number of elements located in the Assets panel. It's possible that several of those elements may only be used in one page in your site and you don't need to view them while building new pages. To provide a more streamlined view, it's a good idea to set up a Favorites list consisting of those assets that you need to access more frequently.

Exercise 6.2 Setting Up the Favorites List

1. With the Assets panel open, select the Images category by clicking the Images category button.
2. In the list of Images, scroll down until you see categorytabs_static.gif and click it to select it.
3. In the lower-right corner of the Assets panel, click the Add to Favorites button that looks like a ribbon with a plus sign next to it.

Note

Why Is the My Favorites Button Unavailable? Here is a note without a good explanation. If your Favorites button in the lower-right corner of the Assets panel is grayed out, don't be alarmed. This seems to be a bug (or a feature?) on every machine we tried it on. To make it active, add a graphic manually by clicking the right-pointing black arrow in the upper-right area of the screen and choosing Add to Favorites. You'll get an information box that says it has been added. Click OK. Although you now have a graphic in the Favorites area, you still can't add one by clicking in the bottom-right corner of the panel. The answer is simple (although it took me a long time to figure out). Click on the Favorites radio button (next to the Site button near the top of the screen). Delete the graphic. Now your Add to Favorites is colored (rather than grayed out) and ready to be used.

If this still doesn't work, you can always just right-click on the graphic and select Add to Favorites from the pop-up menu.

4. As shown in Figure 6.3, UltraDev displays a message notifying you that the asset has been added to your Favorites list. Click OK.

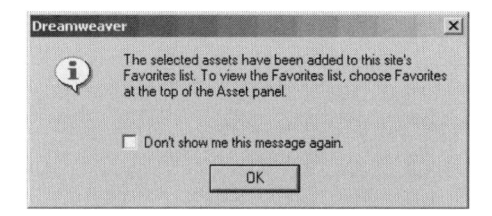

Figure 6.3 UltraDev confirms that the selected assets were added to your Favorites list.

5. In the Assets panel, click the Favorites radio button. As shown in Figure 6.4, the categorytabs_static.gif asset is displayed in your list of Favorites.

Tip

A Categorized Favorites List Just as the Site view of the Assets panel is broken down into categories, so is the Favorites view. If you add an asset to your Favorites list, but don't see it, check to be sure you are viewing the correct category.

6. Removing an asset from your Favorites list is just as easy as adding one. In the Favorites view, highlight the categorytabs_static.gif asset. In the bottom-right corner of the Assets panel, click the Remove from Favorites button, which looks like a ribbon with a minus sign next to it. UltraDev removes the image from your Favorites list.

7. Select the Site radio button to return to the default view of the Assets panel.

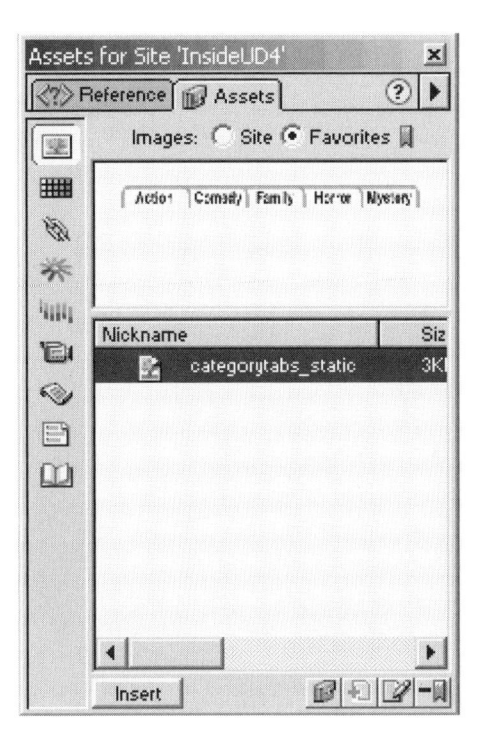

Figure 6.4 Your Favorites list now includes an image.

Adding Assets to Your Pages

Once you have organized your assets, it's easy to add them to your pages. By simply dragging elements such as graphics or movies from the Assets panel and dropping them onto your page, you can easily add images to your site.

Exercise 6.3 Adding a Graphic to Your Page from the Assets Panel

1. Open the nrfdefault.dwt template from the templates folder within the InsideUD4 site. If you have not created the nrfdefault template, refer to Chapter 5 for more information.
2. With the Assets panel open, select the Images category by clicking the Images category button.
3. From the list of Images, drag the bargain_bin_up.gif image into the top cell of tbNavTable table. As shown in Figure 6.5, the Bargain Bin button has now been added to your site.
4. Click on the bargain_bin_up.gif button and press the delete key on your keyboard to remove the button from your page.

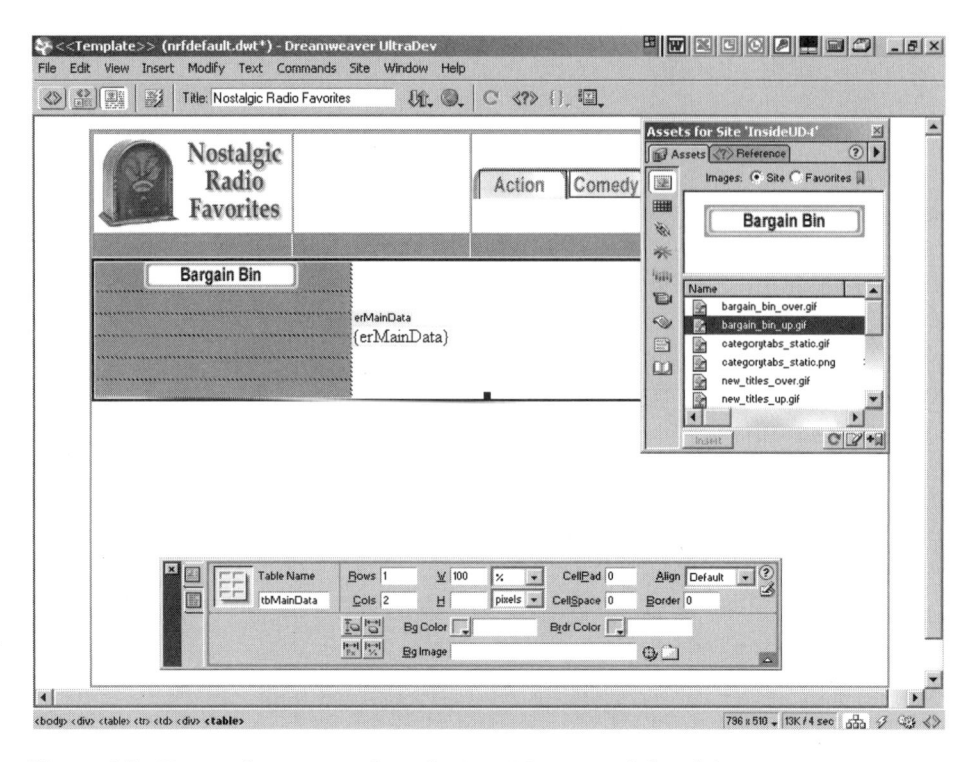

Figure 6.5 You can drag an asset from the Asset Manager and drop it in your page.

Other assets like colors or links can be used to modify the existing attributes of a page element. For instance, colors can be dragged onto highlighted text and links can be dropped onto images to create instant hyperlink buttons.

Creating Dynamic Buttons

Using UltraDev 4, you have the option to easily include JavaScript-driven rollover buttons or Flash buttons. Either style of button is easy to create and add to your pages, but both come with minor limitations that should be considered.

Rollover Buttons

One of the easiest ways to bring your pages to life is to use buttons that change when the visitor moves his mouse cursor over them. These buttons (commonly referred to as *rollover* buttons) can do everything from changing colors, text, or graphics to building submenus for the user to navigate. Because UltraDev is simply building a JavaScript behavior that swaps one image for another, you are limited only by your creativity and your graphics editor.

> **Tip**
>
> **Animated Rollover Buttons** If you are developing for an intranet environment and you know your visitors will have a fast connection, try using animated rollovers for an added effect. Just create two different animated GIF files, using a graphics editor like Fireworks, to represent the up and over states. Once the rollovers are created, the visitor will see one animated GIF when their mouse is not over the graphic and another when the mouse rolls over it.

So far you have seen two different ways to add static images to your pages. In Chapter 5, you used the Insert/Image command and in the previous sections you were shown how to drag and drop images using the Assets panel. After you add these images to your page design, UltraDev automatically creates the necessary HTML code and adds it to your page.

Rollover buttons, however, are slightly more complex than static buttons in the fact that they require HTML and JavaScript. Luckily, UltraDev handles rollover buttons just as easily as it does static buttons. With a few clicks of your mouse, UltraDev can create any code your rollovers need to work. Just tell it where your images are stored and it will do the rest.

Before we start, however, keep in mind that before creating a rollover button, you need to create the images that will serve as your "up" state and another one for your "over" state. Typically, the easiest way to do this is to create the first state in your graphics editor, export it to a file with the name yourfilename_up.gif, and then make changes to the file and export those changes to yourfilename_over.gif.

You should also keep in mind that by default, UltraDev preloads rollover images, so buttons that have a large file size increase your site's load time.

> **Tip**
>
> **Let Fireworks Create Your Buttons** If you aren't already familiar with Macromedia's Fireworks graphics manipulation software, I highly recommend that you check it out. If you choose to develop your rollover buttons using Fireworks, you can have Fireworks generate all the necessary code to make the buttons function properly. You can then simply copy and paste the code into the appropriate section of your page and your rollover button is complete.
>
> Macromedia also has some great Fireworks extensions available on the Macromedia Exchange that help with creating buttons. Just visit the Exchange at `http://www.macromedia.com/exchange` and search for "fireworks."

Exercise 6.4 Creating Rollover Buttons

1. In the nrfdefault.dwt template, place the insertion point in the top cell of the tbNavTable table. From the menu bar, select Insert/Interactive Images/Rollover Image. As shown in Figure 6.6, UltraDev displays the Insert Rollover Image dialog box.

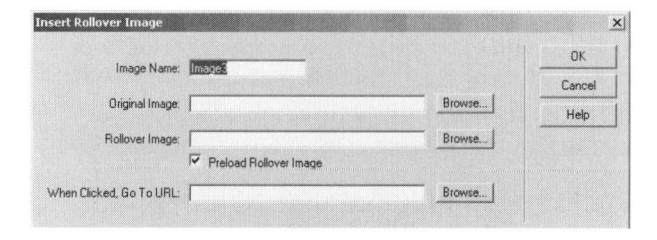

Figure 6.6 The Insert Rollover Image dialog box lets you specify the attributes of your rollover buttons.

2. In the Image Name field, type **rbSearchCatalog**.
3. Click the Browse button next to the Original Image field and select the search_catalog_up.gif image in the images subfolder of your site. Click OK in the Original Image search box.
4. Click the Browse button next to the Rollover Image field and select the search_catalog_over.gif image in the images subfolder of your site. Click OK in the Rollover Image search box.
5. Make sure that the Preload Rollover Image check box has a check in it.
6. In the When Clicked, Go to URL field, type **http://localhost/insideud4/search_catalog.asp**. Your dialog box should look like Figure 6.7.

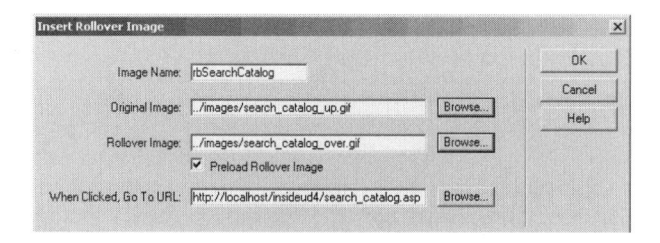

Figure 6.7 When completed, the attributes for your rollover button should look like this.

7. Click OK. You should now see a new button added to your page.
8. To confirm that this button has been set up as a rollover, select the button and choose Window/Behaviors from the menu bar. The Behaviors panel, shown in Figure 6.8, shows two behaviors assigned to this button: a swap image restore and a swap image.

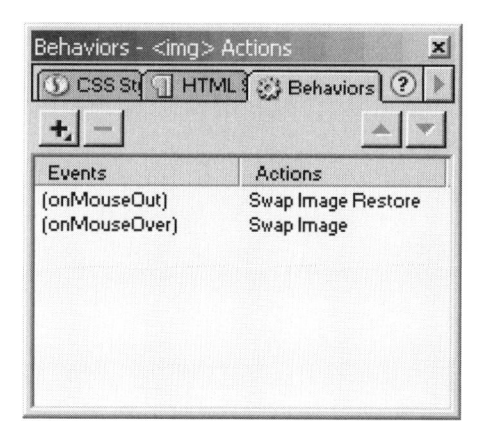

Figure 6.8 The Behaviors panel displays the behaviors associated with the selected rollover button.

> **Note**
>
> **Behavior Order** Don't worry if the Swap Image Restore is listed before the Swap Image in the Behaviors panel. UltraDev may not list the behaviors in the order that they would occur on the Web page, but the script that UltraDev generates to handle the behaviors will make sure they work correctly.

9. Close the Behaviors panel.

> **Note**
>
> **Rollover Button-Naming Convention** When creating the rollover buttons, add the button name with the _up.gif in the Original Image box and the _over.gif for the Rollover Image box.

10. Place the insertion point in the second cell in the tbNavTable table and add the New Titles rollover button following the same steps. Name the New Titles button **rbNewTitles** and link the button to http://localhost/insideud4/new_titles.asp.

11. In the third cell, add the Spotlight Items rollover button. Name this button **rbSpotlightItems** and link the button to http://localhost/insideud4/spotlight_items.asp.

12. In the fourth cell, add the Bargain Bin rollover button and name it **rbBargainBin**. Link the button to http://localhost/insideud4/bargain_bin.asp.

13. Finally, place the insertion point in the fifth cell in the tbNavTable table and build the View Cart rollover. Name this button **rbViewCart** and link the button to http://localhost/insideud4/view_cart.asp.

14. Close the Assets panel. Your page should now look like Figure 6.9.

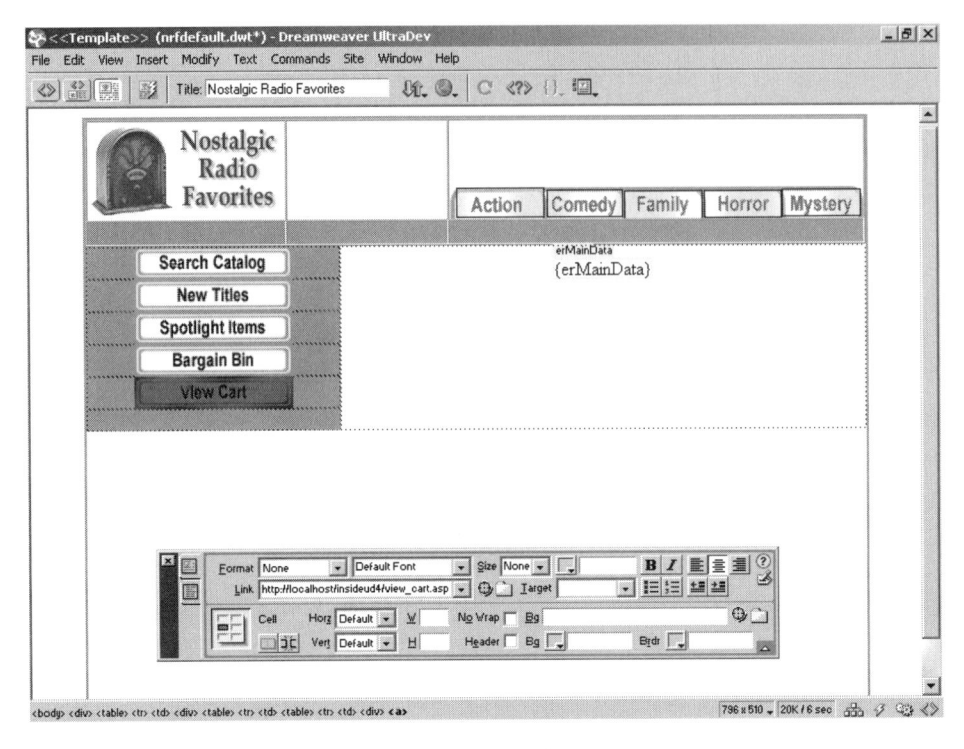

Figure 6.9 The navigation rollovers have been added to your page.

15. Save the template. When UltraDev asks you if you would like to update the pages that rely on the template, choose Update.
16. In the Update Pages box that displays the report of updated pages, click Close.
17. To confirm that your rollovers function properly, open your browser and type **http://localhost/insideud4** in the address bar. Your default.asp page should look like Figure 6.10.
18. Test each button by rolling over it. Note, however, that the links will not work yet because you have not created those pages.

Adding Flash Rollover Buttons

Another way to add dynamic buttons to your site is to use the Flash button templates that are included in UltraDev. These templates allow you to choose from a limited number of pre-created Flash buttons and customize them to fit your needs.

If you are a Flash developer and want to create your own buttons for use in UltraDev, you can create Generator template files and add them to the standard templates included with UltraDev. If you don't develop in Flash, but want some additional buttons to choose from, check out the Macromedia Exchange at `http://www.macromedia.com/exchange/ultradev`.

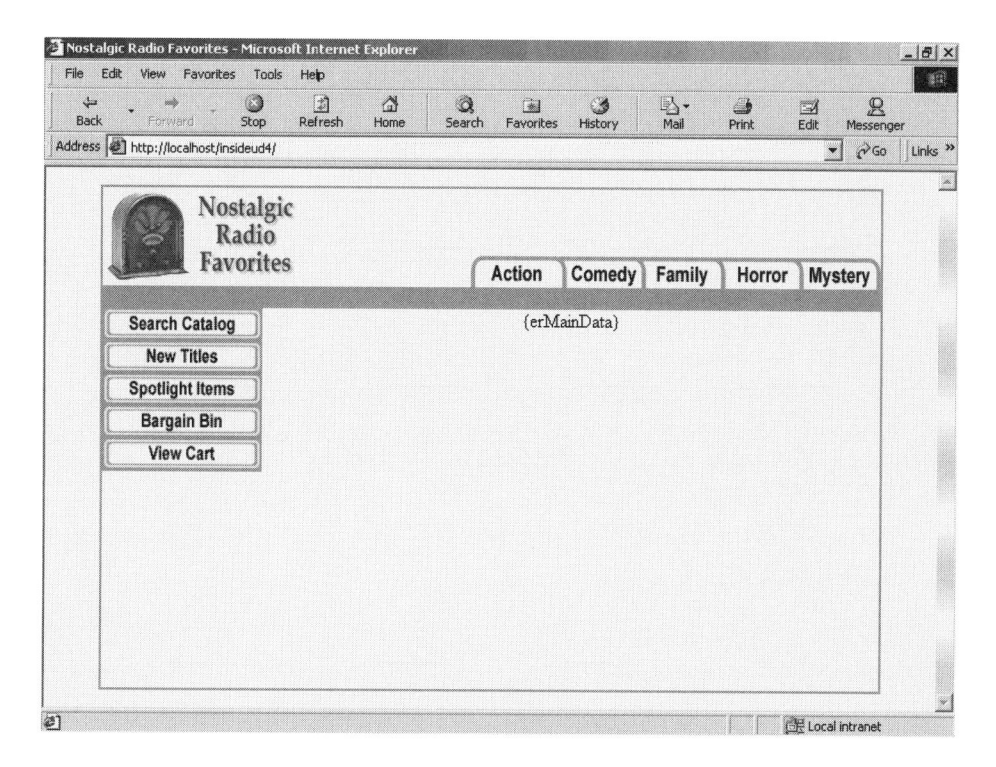

Figure 6.10 Your default.asp page as viewed from a browser.

The biggest disadvantage to using Flash buttons is the fact that other than a link and a target, no additional behaviors can be added to them. This means that Flash buttons cannot control Flash movies, play sounds, or swap images on the page. Because of these limitations, Flash buttons should only be used as links to other pages.

Exercise 6.5 Adding Flash Buttons

1. Before starting this exercise, it's important that you understand that you will be creating the Flash buttons so you can see how they work, but that you will be removing them from the page at the end of the exercise. Because Flash buttons are not suitable for controlling other Flash movies, they don't serve the requirements of later exercises.

2. Open the default.asp page. In the right cell of the tbMainTable table, highlight the text that reads {erMainData} and press the Delete key on your keyboard.

150   Part II   Building a Solid Foundation

This text was placed there by UltraDev when you attached this file to the template to show where the editable region is.

3. Create a table by choosing Insert/Table from the menu bar. The table should have **2** rows and **1** column, and should be **80%** in width. Set the border, cell padding, and cell spacing to **0**. Click OK.

4. With the table selected, set the Align value in the Property inspector to Center. As shown in Figure 6.11, you should now have a new table in your page.

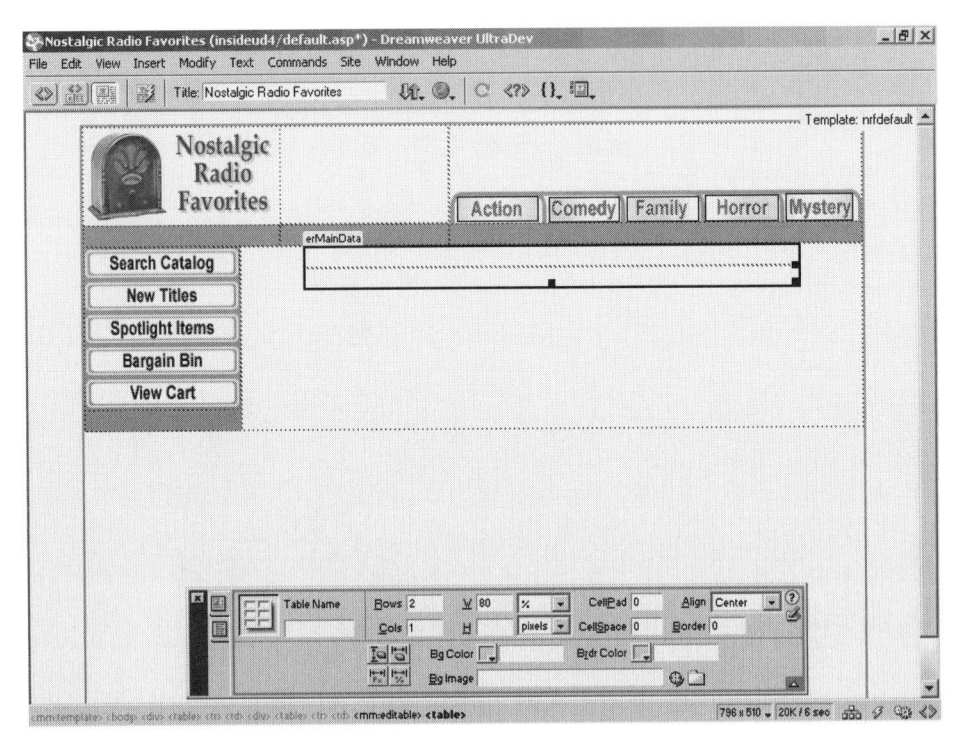

Figure 6.11   Your default.asp page should now have an additional table.

5. Right click in the bottom cell of the new table and select Table/Split Cell from the context menu. In the Split Cell dialog box, choose to split the cell into columns and set the Number of Columns value to **2**, as shown in Figure 6.12. Click OK.

6. Place the insertion point in the bottom-left cell of the new table and click the Align Right button on the Property inspector. Select Insert/Interactive Images/Flash Button from the menu bar. UltraDev opens the Insert Flash Button dialog box, shown in Figure 6.13.

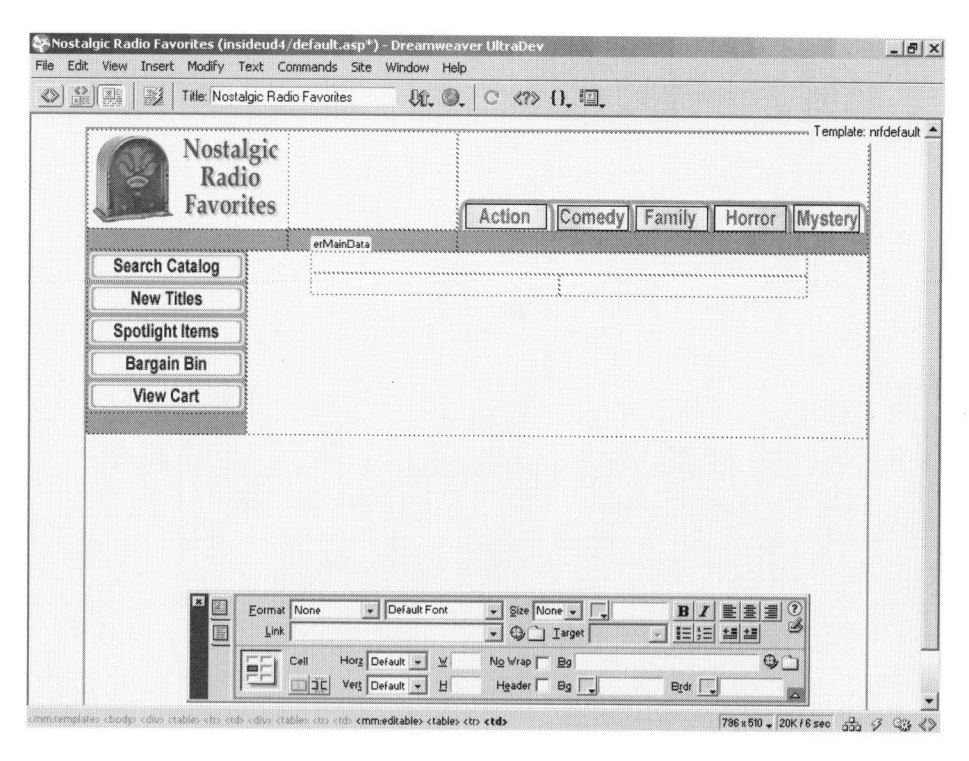

Figure 6.12 Split the cell in half by using the Split Cell dialog box.

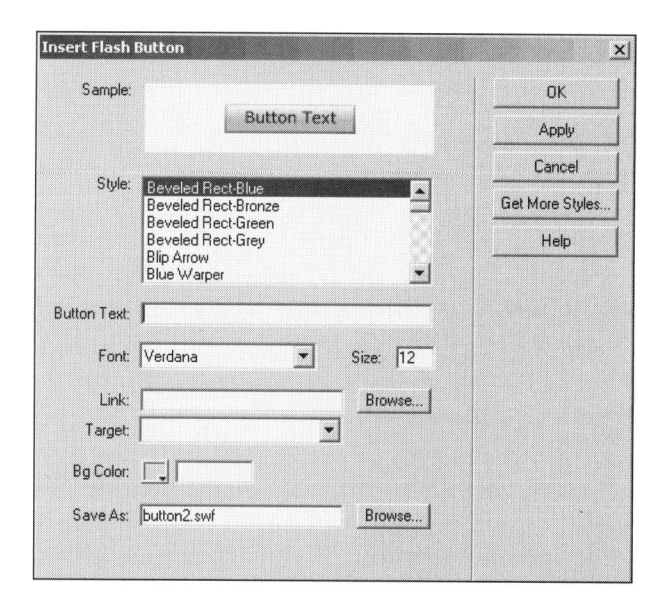

Figure 6.13 The Insert Flash Button dialog box allows you to add Flash buttons to your page.

7. From the Style choices select the Beveled Rect-Bronze button.
8. In the Button Text field, type **Play Intro**.
9. Leave the Font as Verdana 12 and leave the link, target, and Bg Color choices empty.
10. In the Save As field, type **images/play_intro.swf**. The dialog box should look like Figure 6.14. Click OK.

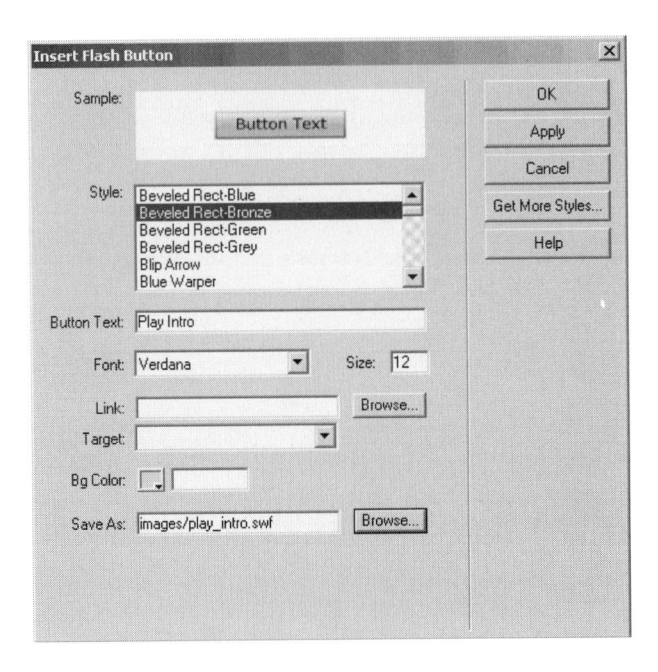

Figure 6.14 The settings for your new Flash button.

11. Place the insertion point in the bottom-right cell of the new table and click the Align Left button on the Property inspector. Create another Flash button. Using the same style and font, create a button that says Stop Intro and save it to **images/stop_intro.swf**. Click OK. With both buttons inserted, your page should look like Figure 6.15.
12. Save your default.asp page and view the page by opening your browser and typing **http://localhost/insideud4/**.
13. Notice that when you move the pointer over a Flash button, it changes colors. When you have finished viewing the Flash buttons, close the browser, return to the default.asp page in UltraDev, and remove the buttons from the page by clicking each button and pressing the Delete key on your keyboard. Because Flash buttons cannot be assigned behaviors, you will not be using them in your pages.
14. Save the page.

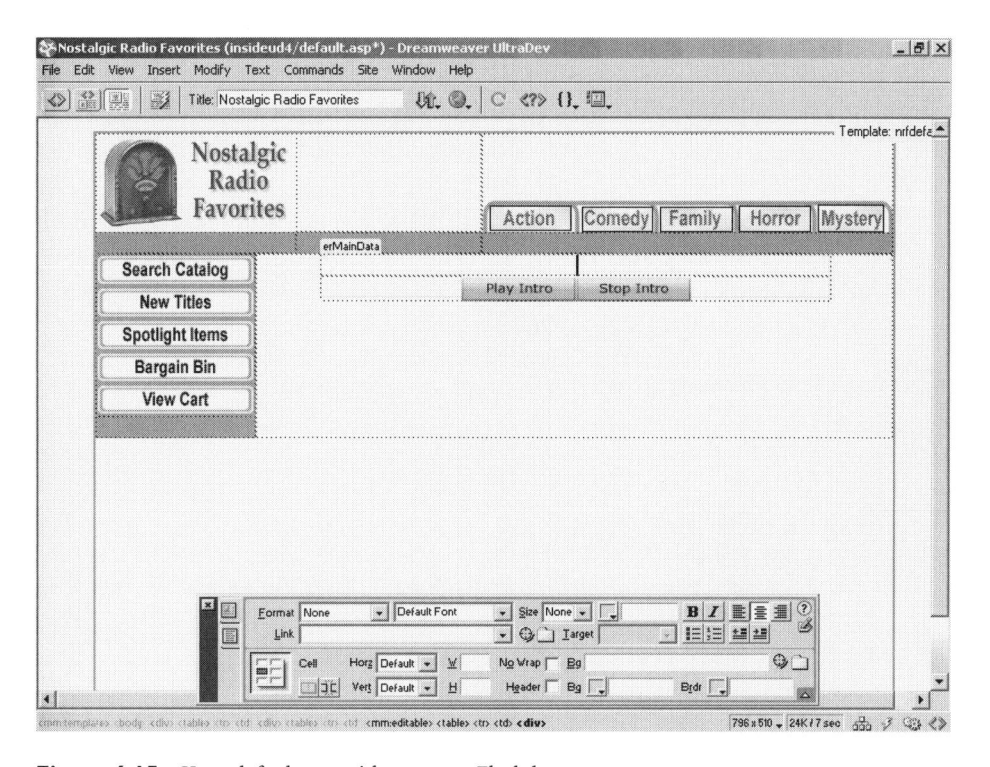

Figure 6.15 Your default.asp with two new Flash buttons.

Adding Movies to Your Pages

As Web sites strive to become more interactive and high-speed Internet connections such as DSL and cable modem technology continue to develop, the inclusion of complex animations and video content becomes more feasible. In fact, with software advances in technologies such as Flash, RealVideo, and QuickTime, sites that rely on visual content have already begun making video footage available.

UltraDev offers developers the opportunity to work with numerous animation and video formats. Inserting and configuring a movie element is just about as easy as adding static graphics to your pages.

Flash Movies

Macromedia's Flash has revolutionized animation on the Internet. By enabling developers to present high-quality sound and animation, Flash can be used to create everything from small animations to entire Web sites.

154 Part II Building a Solid Foundation

Flash has not been without its critics, however. Some developers fear losing visitors due to the fact that Flash movies require an Internet Explorer ActiveX control or a Netscape plug-in in order to be viewed. Others feel that the bandwidth consumed by Flash content could be better used elsewhere.

According to Macromedia, many of these concerns have been addressed since more than 96% of the Internet community now has the Flash Player installed (`http://www.macromedia.com/software/player_census/flashplayer/`) and the latest releases of Flash provide substantial control over the size and quality of the animations.

Regardless of whether you currently use or plan to use Flash, UltraDev provides you with the ability to add Flash content to your pages and customize the way your animations are viewed.

Exercise 6.6 Adding and Controlling a Flash Movie

1. In the default.asp page, place your insertion point in the top cell of the table that you created in the last exercise. Click the Align Center button on the Property inspector.
2. Select Insert/Media/Flash from the menu bar.
3. In the Select File dialog box, browse to the media folder in your site's root, select the radio_shows.swf file, and click OK. As shown in Figure 6.16, UltraDev inserts a placeholder graphic for the Flash animation.
4. Select the Flash animation by clicking it and type **flaRadioShows** in the name field, which is located next to the Flash logo in the Property inspector.
5. Set the Quality option in the Property inspector to Auto Low. This setting allows the animation to download faster, but then improves in quality once fully downloaded.
6. Remove the check from the Loop checkbox.
7. Preview the animation by clicking the Play button on the Property inspector.
8. Remove the check from the AutoPlay checkbox.

> **Tip**
>
> **Preview First** Always remember to preview your animation *before* unchecking the AutoPlay checkbox. Once you uncheck that box, you are no longer able to preview the animation until the box is checked again.

9. Place the insertion point in the bottom-left cell of the table and select Insert/Image from the menu bar. Browse to the images subfolder within your site and select the play_intro.gif image. Click OK.

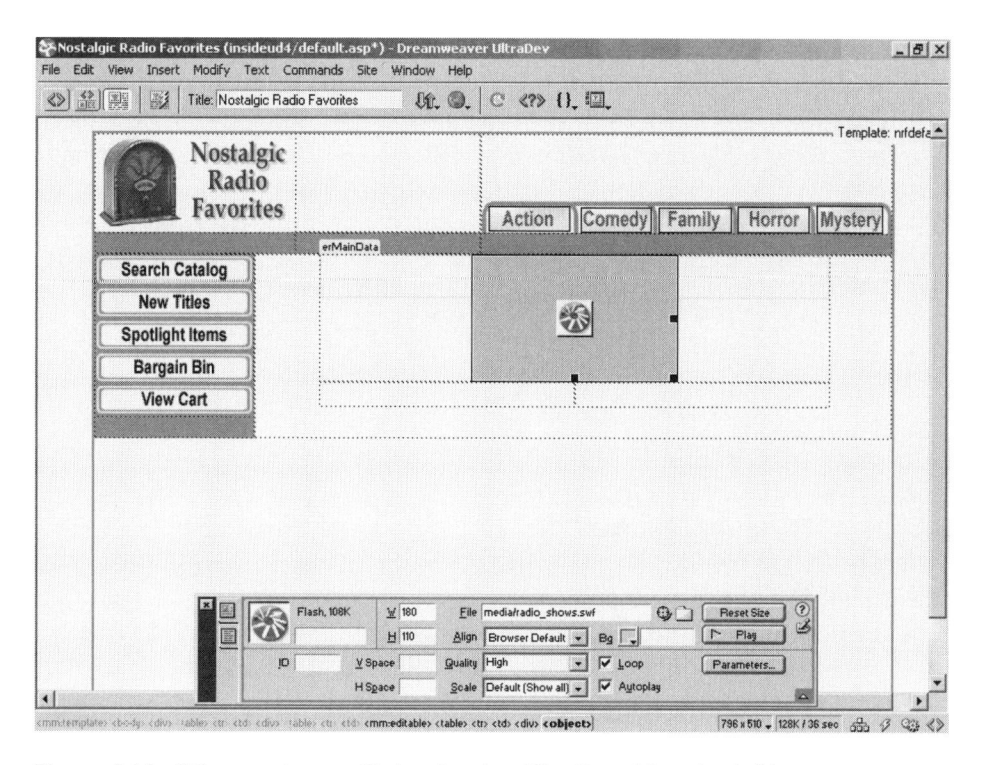

Chapter 6 UltraDev's Graphic and Multimedia Capabilities   155

Figure 6.16 When you insert a Flash animation, UltraDev adds a placeholder to your page.

10. With the Play Intro button selected, type a # in the Link field of the Property inspector. Without the # or a link to another page, the browser will not recognize the button as a link and the visitor's cursor will not change to indicate that the item can be clicked.

> **Tip**
>
> **Using Behaviors Without Assigning a Link** Some UltraDev behaviors require that you assign a link to the object before you can assign the behavior to the object. There are times, however, when you may not want to assign a link, but instead want to use the behavior to perform a function.
>
> For instance, suppose you want to create a button that opens a new window to a page outside your site. You don't want the main window to go to a new page, but you do want to assign the "Open Browser Window" behavior. To trick UltraDev into thinking that a link has already been created, just type the pound sign (#) in the link field of the Property inspector. The pound sign is used in UltraDev as a link to the currently displayed page.
>
> Keep in mind, however, that when the link is clicked not only will the new browser window open, but the currently displayed page will reload.

11. Open the Behaviors panel by selecting Window/Behaviors from the menu bar.
12. With the Play Intro button selected, click the plus sign on the Behaviors panel and select Control Shockwave or Flash. In the Control Shockwave or Flash dialog box, shown in Figure 6.17, select flaRadioShows from the Movie dropdown and click the Play radio button.

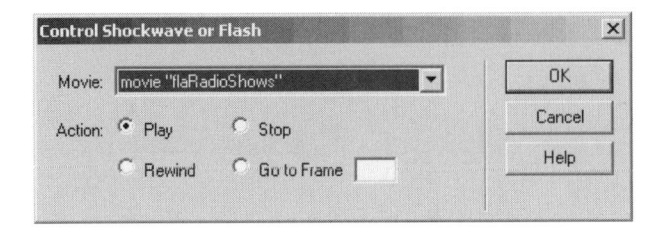

Figure 6.17 The Control Shockwave or Flash dialog box lets you specify what action the button should perform.

13. Click OK.
14. In the Behaviors panel, select the newly assigned behavior and click the down arrow located next to the onMouseDown event. From the Context menu that appears, select Show Events For/4.0 and Later Browsers.
15. Click the down arrow again and select (onClick). Selecting this option requires the user to click the button before the behavior is processed.
16. Place the insertion point in the bottom-right cell of the table and select Insert/Image from the menu bar. Insert the stop_intro.gif button from the images folder within your site. Click OK.
17. With the Stop Intro button selected, type a # in the Link field of the Property inspector and click the plus sign on the Behaviors panel.
18. Add the Control Shockwave or Flash dialog box and select flaRadioShows from the Movie dropdown. Click the Stop button and click OK.
19. With the Stop Intro button selected, click the plus and select Control Shockwave or Flash. In the dialog box, choose Stop and click OK. Click the down arrow next to (onMouseDown) and select (onClick) instead.
20. Save the page.
21. View your page in your browser. As shown in Figure 6.18, the Flash movie and the buttons have been added to your page.
22. Once the page has loaded, click the Play Intro button.
23. To stop the movie at any time, click the Stop Intro button.
24. Close the browser.

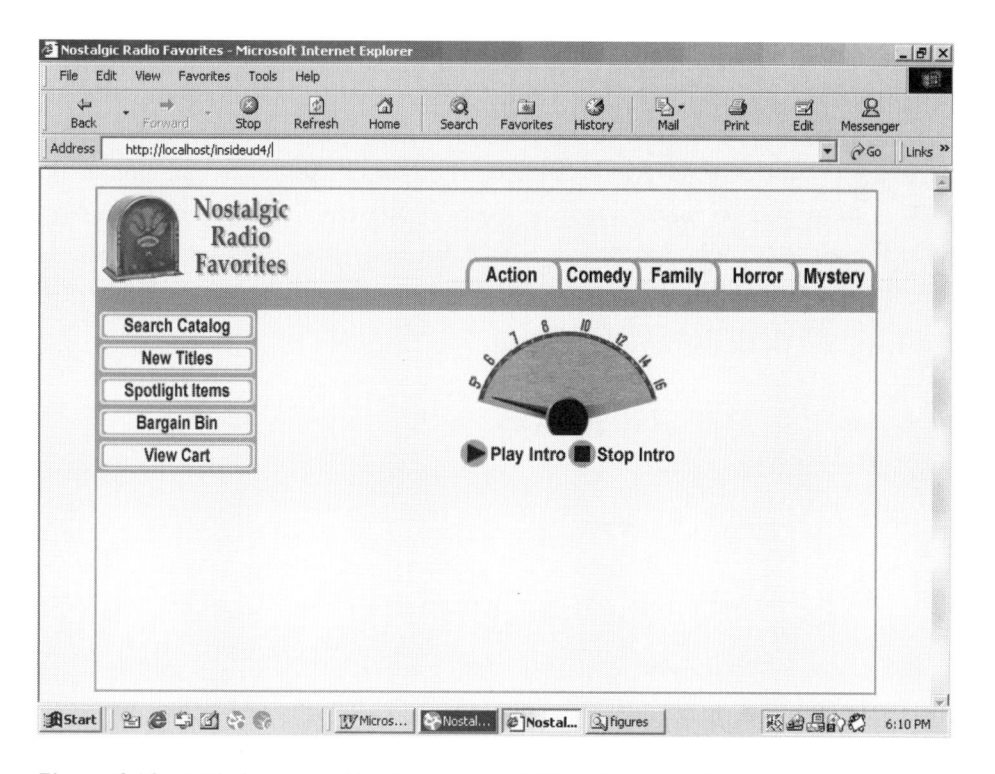

Chapter 6 UltraDev's Graphic and Multimedia Capabilities   157

Figure 6.18 A Flash intro and buttons to control it have been added to your page.

> **Caution**
>
> **Check Those Loop Settings** When you publish your Flash movies, you have the option of specifying whether the movie should replay in a loop. Even if you set your movie so it doesn't loop in Flash, you still need to uncheck the loop checkbox in UltraDev or the movie will play repeatedly.

Shockwave Movies

In addition to supporting Flash movies, UltraDev allows you to insert Shockwave movies as well. Shockwave movies are developed using Macromedia's Director and are capable of combining audio, animation, and video to create interactive Web-based content.

You should be aware, however, that although inserting Shockwave media into your pages is as simple as adding a Flash animation, the Shockwave Player required to view Shockwave presentations is not quite as popular as the Flash Player. This means that some of your visitors may be required to install the Shockwave Player prior to being able to view your pages properly.

Adding Video to Your Pages

UltraDev can also assist you in the addition of video content in a number of different formats. Although you cannot place the video file directly into your page, you can embed the ActiveX Control for the Windows Media Player or the RealPlayer and indicate the URL of the file you would like it to play. To embed an ActiveX Control into your page, place the insertion point where you would like the media embedded and choose Insert/Media/ActiveX. You will need to know the class ID and the URL to the file that you would like to display on your page.

> **Tip**
> **Embedding the Windows Media Player** For complete information on embedding the Windows Media Player into your pages, visit http://msdn.microsoft.com/library/psdk/wm_media/wmplay/mmp_sdk/embeddingwindowsmediaplayer.htm.

Adding Sounds to Your Pages

With UltraDev 4, placing sounds on your pages is just as easy as adding movies or animations. Depending on your needs, UltraDev provides the ability to control the sound using a behavior, embed certain formats in your page that will play in any browser, or link to a file that uses a third-party plug-in such as RealNetworks' RealPlayer.

> **Caution**
> **Are Sounds Appropriate?** When considering the addition of sound to your site, take into account whether it will assist the visitor or merely become annoying. For instance, the site you are building in these exercises focuses on old-time radio shows. At certain points in the visitor's navigation of the site she might want to listen to a sample clip of one of the products. In this case, audio would be appropriate. However, bombarding the visitor with a rendition of the latest top 40 hit rendered in MIDI format would probably be less than professional and may even cause the visitor to leave.

Each of the audio formats supported by UltraDev has its own advantages and disadvantages. If you have determined that your site could benefit from the inclusion of audio, it would be a good idea to familiarize yourself with the various formats and pick the one that best suits your needs.

WAV Files

The WAV format is the standard sound format used on PCs today and audio files in the WAV format can be identified by their .wav extension. WAV files can produce high-quality audio, and because both Internet Explorer and Netscape support the WAV format, they are easily embedded in Web pages.

Probably the biggest benefit of WAV files is the fact that they are so easy to create. Using the microphone or line-in jack on your sound card, any Windows user can create a WAV file using the Windows Sound Recorder in a matter of minutes.

The downside to the WAV format is the file size required to produce them. Because they are uncompressed, they are usually only suitable for short sounds such as sound effects and aren't useful for lengthy audio files.

MIDI Files

MIDI stands for Musical Instrument Digital Interface and is the standard used for recording and playing music that is digitally synthesized on a computer. The advantage of MIDI is that the files produced are very small in size, but the disadvantage is the annoyance factor. Anyone who has ever been to a Web page that plays an embedded MIDI music file knows just how irritating it can be—especially when there are no controls to stop the music.

For any site that does not specifically focus on MIDI music as its topic, I highly recommend avoiding the inclusion of MIDI files in your pages. Sure, they're cute and funny at first, but visitors soon tire of the cuteness factor and they rarely enhance the visitor's experience.

MP3 Files

MPEG-1 Audio Layer-3, also known as MP3, is a compression standard used to reduce raw audio files, such as WAVs, to a significantly smaller file size while maintaining the sound quality of the original recording. Although you can insert MP3 files into your pages using UltraDev, visitors who want to play them will require a third-party application such as the Windows Media Player, WinAmp, or MacAmp to listen to the recordings.

Exercise 6.7 Adding an Audio Behavior to Your Page

1. In the default.asp page, click the Play Intro button.
2. In the Behaviors panel, click the plus symbol and select Play Sound. As shown in Figure 6.19, UltraDev asks you to specify the path to the sound you would like to play.
3. Browse to the media folder in your site, select click.wav, and click OK.
4. In the Play Sound dialog box, click OK. You'll notice that UltraDev now displays the Play Sound behavior in the Behaviors panel.

Figure 6.19 The Play Sound dialog box allows you to specify the sound that you would like to add to your page.

5. Click the Stop Intro button and follow the same steps to add the Play Sound behavior to this button. Use the click.wav file for this button as well.
6. Save the default.asp page.
7. Open your page in your browser by typing **http://localhost/insideud4** in the address bar.
8. Click your mouse on the Play Intro and Stop Intro buttons. Each should play the click.wav sound.

> **Note**
>
> **Playing Sounds with QuickTime Installed** If you are using Netscape Navigator and have the QuickTime plug-in installed, you may have difficulties with embedded sounds. Because QuickTime assumes control over playing all embedded sounds, when you place your cursor over the image, you are then taken to a new page where the sound is played using the QuickTime controls. To resolve this problem, you can uninstall QuickTime and use a different plug-in such as BeatNik. Keep in mind, however, that visitors to your site may experience the same difficulties.

Summary

As the Internet develops, dynamic graphics and multimedia elements in Web pages are becoming increasingly common. Understanding when these elements are appropriate and how to apply them to your pages correctly can enhance your visitors' Web site experience.

Throughout this chapter you looked at several ways UltraDev can be used to animate graphics and add multimedia content to your pages. Deciding when and where to use these features, however, is up to you.

In the next chapter, you begin looking at the basics of connecting your pages to a database and UltraDev's ability to dynamically generate database-driven pages.

Part III

Developing a Data-Driven Web Site

7	Connecting Your Web Site to a Database	165
8	Creating Visitor Accounts Through Username Validation	193
9	Building Search Capabilities	227
10	Adding Dynamic Images and Text to Search Results	255

Chapter 7

Connecting Your Web Site to a Database

Now that you have covered the basic Web authoring features available in UltraDev 4, you're ready to move on to the really fun stuff! UltraDev 4 is all about dynamic data, and this chapter shows you just how easy it is to build pages that display dynamic data based on the criteria used to query the database.

Before you start, though, I have to warn you that this is a very exercise-oriented chapter. I encourage you to sit down and walk through every exercise so that you can see how easy it is not only to add dynamic data to your pages, but to add pages by simply reusing existing pages and making slight modifications.

This chapter focuses on the following:

- Setting up a database connection
- Adding dynamic data to your pages
- Creating and linking to detail pages

If you're ready to build some dynamic pages, fill up that coffee cup, grab a snack, and let's get to it!

Making Sure Everything Is in Order

Before you go further into this chapter, there are a couple of things that you have to make sure are present in your site. If you have completed all the exercises in the previous chapters, each of these elements will be present. If you skimmed over a chapter or two and didn't complete the exercises, it's important that you go back and walk through the exercises so your site is ready to host database-driven pages that are based on your template.

To perform the exercises in this chapter, you need the following:

- A workstation or server configured to host Active Server Pages (Chapter 2, "Setting Up Your UltraDev Workstation as a Test Server").
- A database subfolder within the root folder of your InsideUD4 site. This folder should contain the Sales_Database.mdb database. You should also have an ODBC system data source defined for the Sales_Database.mdb (Chapter 3, "Developing Databases for the Web").
- An InsideUD4 site defined and configured (Chapter 4, "Building an UltraDev Site from the Ground Up").
- An images subfolder within the root folder of the InsideUD4 site (Chapter 5, "The Dreamweaver in Dreamweaver UltraDev 4").
- An nrfdefault.dwt template defined within the InsideUD4 site (Chapter 5).

If one or more of these elements doesn't sound familiar, I suggest you take a moment to look through the relevant chapter exercises to ensure that your site is configured properly. Although UltraDev 4 makes creating dynamic pages relatively easy, an improperly configured site or missing element will slow your development process.

Setting Up a Database Connection and Recordset

The first step in building dynamic pages is to familiarize yourself with the process of communicating with the database and adding placeholders for your dynamic data to your page. When you created the ODBC data source for your database in Chapter 3, you gave your Web server software the ability to talk directly to the database.

Dynamic pages, however, aren't able to talk directly to the ODBC data source without a helper known as a *database connection*. This connection lets UltraDev know the path to your database and the type of database (such as Access, MySQL, or Oracle) you are using.

Exercise 7.1 Creating a Connection to Your Database

1. Open UltraDev 4. If the Site window opens, minimize it.
2. Make sure you are in the InsideUD4 site by choosing Site/Open Site/InsideUD4 from the menu bar.
3. Select File/New From Template from the menu bar. As shown in Figure 7.1, UltraDev opens the Select Template dialog box.

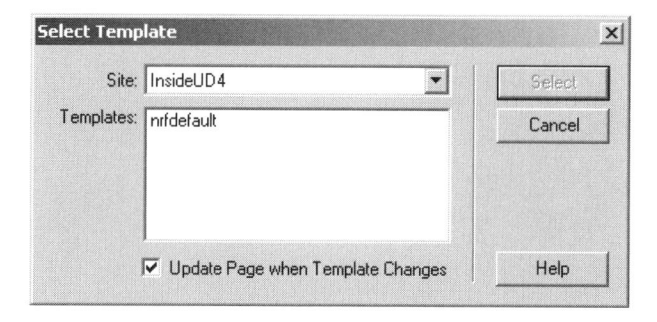

Figure 7.1 The Select Template dialog box allows you to build new pages directly from an existing template.

4. Select the nrfdefault template and make sure the Update Page When Template Changes check box has a check in it. Click Select. UltraDev creates a new page for you based on the template. If the Behaviors panel is still open, close it.

5. In the Title field on the toolbar, type **Bargain Bin** and press the Enter key.
6. Save this page in the InsideUD4 folder as **bargain_bin.asp**. Earlier in Chapter 4, you created a page called bargain_bin.asp. If UltraDev asks you if you want to overwrite that file, click Yes.
7. Open the Data Bindings panel, shown in Figure 7.2, by selecting Window/Data Bindings from the menu bar.

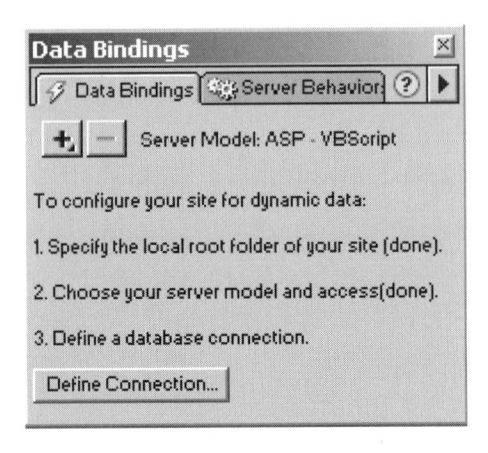

Figure 7.2 The Data Bindings panel specifies the steps you need to take to configure your site to serve dynamic pages.

8. Because you haven't created a database connection, the Data Bindings panel displays the Define Connection button. Click the Define Connection button and UltraDev displays the Connections for Site 'InsideUD4' dialog box shown in Figure 7.3. Because we have no connections defined, the box is empty.

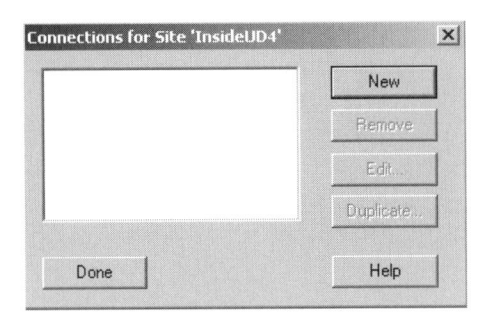

Figure 7.3 There are currently no connections defined in our site.

9. Click the New button and select Data Source Name (DSN) from the menu. As shown in Figure 7.4, UltraDev displays the DSN dialog box.

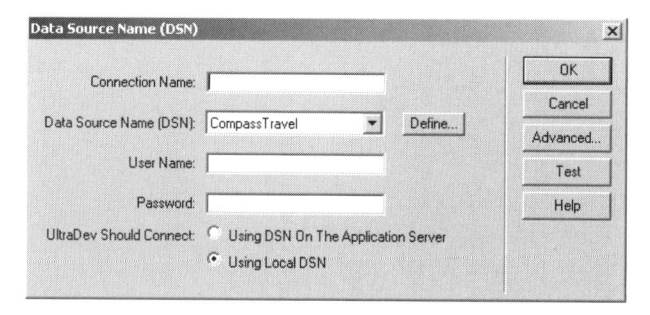

Figure 7.4 The Data Source Name (DSN) dialog box lets you establish a connection to your database.

> **Note**
>
> **Other Options for Creating a Connection** A DSN connection is only one of four different types of connections that you can build in UltraDev. UltraDev also allows you to create your own custom connection string, which allows you to connect to your database without having to define an ODBC data source on your workstation. The only downside to the custom connection strings is the fact that they are a little more cumbersome to work with because you must understand the syntax of the strings.
>
> If you are using ColdFusion, UltraDev allows you to create a connection using a process similar to the ASP DSN connection. In fact, the only difference between the two that your DSN is a ColdFusion DSN rather than an ODBC DSN.
>
> Finally, if you are using the JSP server model, you may have a little more work on your hands depending on what type of database you are using. UltraDev is able to build a connection to several popular databases or allow you to create a custom JDBC connection if your database driver is not listed in UltraDev's available connections. The custom string, however, requires that you know the name of the driver you will be using and the URL to the database location.

10. In the Data Source Name (DSN) dialog box, type **connSales_Database** in the Connection Name field.
11. In the Data Source Name (DSN) dropdown, select dsSales_Database.
12. Leave the User Name and Password fields blank and make sure the Using Local DSN radio button is selected.
13. Click the Test button. If UltraDev is able to communicate with the DSN, the confirmation shown in Figure 7.5 is displayed.
14. Click OK to close the confirmation popup.
15. Click OK to complete the setup of your database connection. As shown in Figure 7.6, you now have a connSales_Database connection established for your site.
16. Click Done to return to the Design view.

Figure 7.5 A successful connection to the DSN was made.

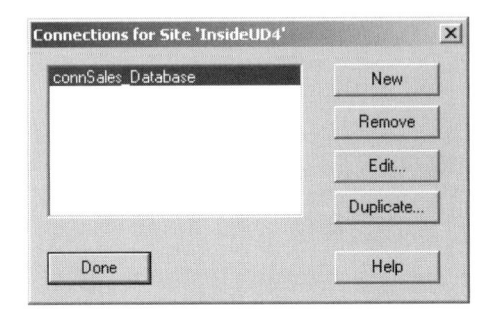

Figure 7.6 A database connection has been added to your site.

As if an ODBC data source and a database connection weren't enough, there is one more step you have to take before you are ready to build your dynamic pages. Because your pages are not able to communicate directly with the information in the database, each dynamic page has to query the database and then create a *recordset*, which represents all the data returned from the query. Once the recordset is created, you can then manipulate the items in that recordset or add them to your page to be displayed. When your pages are viewed by visitors, each page queries the database, builds the recordset, and performs any manipulation and formatting that you have assigned.

Exercise 7.2 Adding a Recordset to Your Page

1. In the bargain_bin.asp page, click the plus sign on the Data Bindings tab of the Data Bindings panel. From the menu, select Recordset (Query). As shown in Figure 7.7, the Recordset dialog box is displayed.
2. In the Name field, type **rsResults_Page** and select connSales_Database from the Connection dropdown.
3. Since our Bargain Bin will display information about the products offered on our site, select the tbProducts from the Table dropdown.

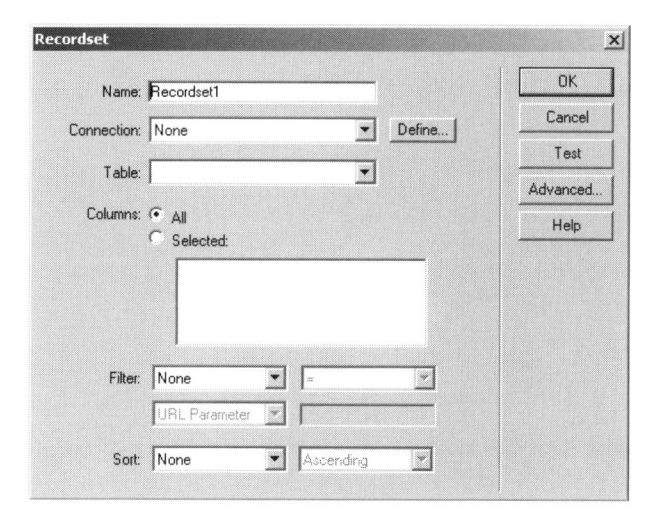

Figure 7.7 The Recordset dialog box helps you define your recordset.

4. The information that we will be showing our visitors in the Bargain Bin includes the title of the radio show, the episode title, the genre, and (of course) the price. From the Columns radio buttons, click Selected and choose Product_No, Title, Episode_Title, Genre, and Price as our selected columns.

> **Tip**
>
> **Making Multiple Selections** As with many applications, UltraDev allows you to select multiple items from the Selection menu by clicking on an item and pressing the Ctrl key on your keyboard while clicking on additional items. To select a range of items, click the topmost item, hold the Shift key, and then click the bottommost item you want selected and everything in between will be selected.

5. Because this is our Bargain Bin page, we only want items that have a price of less than $6.00. Select Price from the Filter dropdown and choose the < (less than) symbol from the operators dropdown. Select Entered Value in the third drop-down and type **6.00** in the final field.
6. Sort the data by selecting Title from the Sort drop-down menu and selecting the Ascending parameter. When finished, your Recordset dialog box should look like Figure 7.8.
7. Click the Test button to see the results of the query. As shown in Figure 7.9, two records should be returned and they should both have a price of less than $6.00. In addition, the records are sorted alphabetically by title in ascending order.

172   Part III   Developing a Data-Driven Web Site

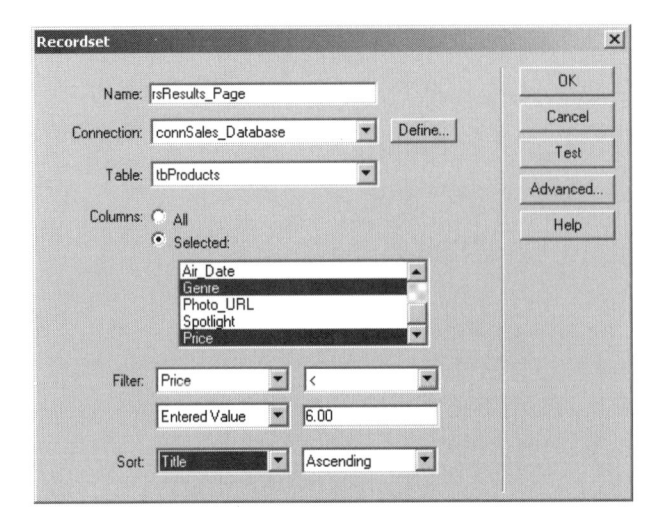

Figure 7.8   Your Recordset dialog box should look like this.

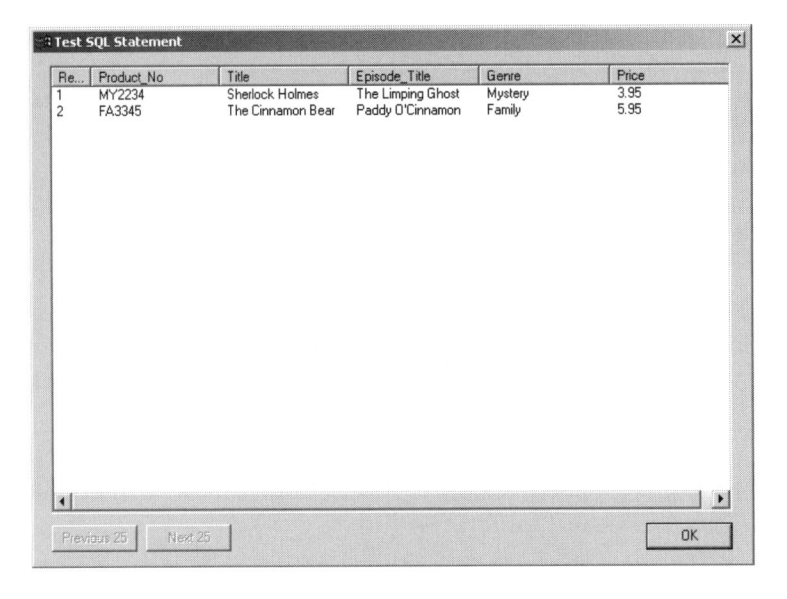

Figure 7.9   The results of your test SQL statement.

8. Click OK to close the Test SQL Statement dialog box.
9. Click OK to complete the creation of the recordset. Figure 7.10 shows the new recordset displayed in the Data Bindings panel.
10. Save the page.

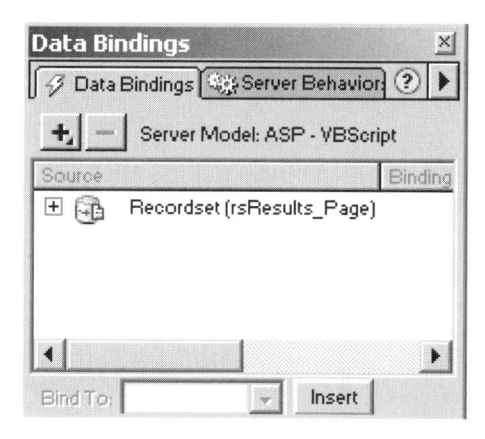

Chapter 7　Connecting Your Web Site to a Database　　173

Figure 7.10　The Data Bindings panel shows the Recordset for rsResults_Page.

Adding Dynamic Data to Your Page

Now that you have created the various avenues of communication between your page and your database, you'll be amazed how easy UltraDev 4 makes it to add dynamic data to your pages. In many cases you can just drag and drop directly from the Data Bindings panel and you're ready to go.

> **Note**
>
> **A Quick Note About Formatting**　Tables and formatting contribute much to the display of dynamic data. One of the things I really like about UltraDev is that you can format your table and the placeholders for your dynamic data, and when the data is inserted, it will automatically adopt the font, style, alignment, and any other formatting you have applied.

Exercise 7.3　Adding Dynamic Data to the Page

1. In the bargain_bin.asp page, place your insertion point in the editable region marked erMainData and delete the {erMainData} text.
2. Insert the image bargain_bin_logo.gif from the images folder. Press the right arrow key to deselect the graphic.
3. Press the Enter key for a new line.
4. Insert a table into your editable region by selecting Insert/Table from the menu bar. Your table should have **2** rows, **5** columns, occupy **90%** of the width, and have a border of **1**. Set the cell padding and cell spacing to **0**. Click OK.

5. In the top-left cell, type **Product Number**. Type **Show Title** in the next cell to the right. In the next cell, type **Episode Title**. In the fourth cell, type **Genre** and in the top-right cell type **Price**.

6. Select the top five cells in the new table by clicking in the top-left cell and dragging your cursor to the top-right cell. Click the Align Center button on the Property inspector.

7. Set the background color for these cells to **#006699** by typing this value in the Bg field of the Property inspector that has a color picker.

8. Select Arial, Helvetica, sans serif in the default font dropdown of the Property inspector. Set the font size to **3** and the text color to white (**#FFFFFF**). Click the Bold formatting button. Your page should look like Figure 7.11.

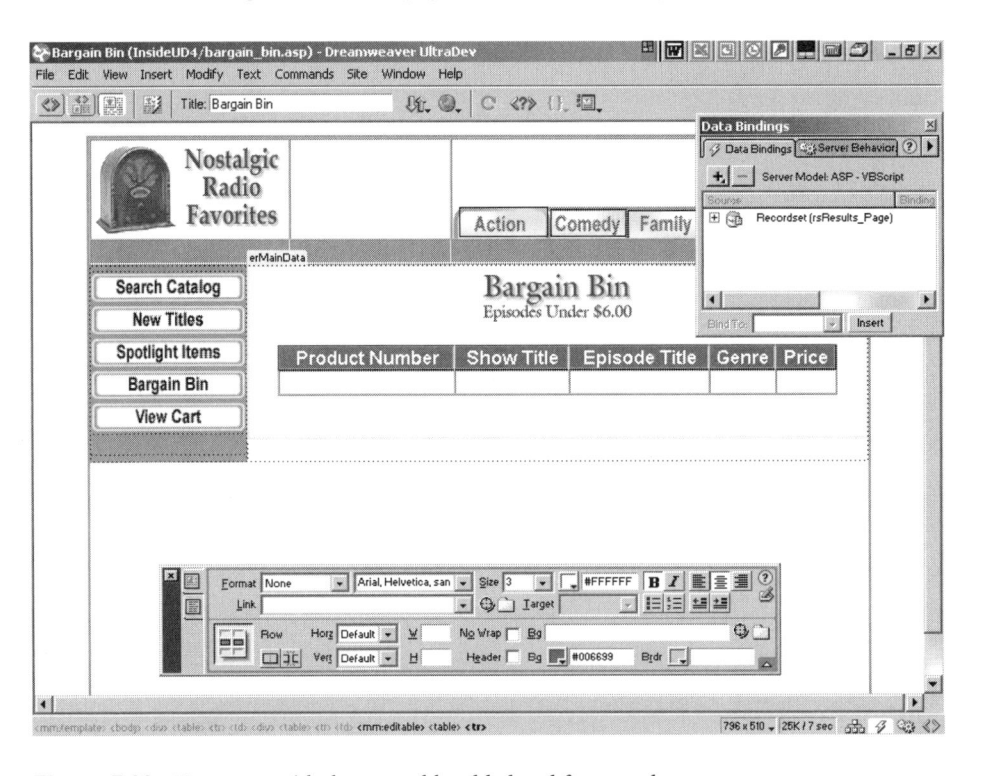

Figure 7.11 Your page with the new table added and formatted.

9. In the Data Bindings panel, make sure the Data Bindings tab is active. Click the plus sign next to the rsResults_Page recordset to expand the elements.

10. Click on the Product_No data binding and drag it into the bottom-left cell of the new table.

11. Drag the Title data binding to the next cell to the right.

Chapter 7 Connecting Your Web Site to a Database 175

> **Note**
>
> **A Case of Language** Macromedia refers to the major components in the Data Bindings panel (such as recordsets) as data bindings. The items that fall beneath each of these components are then referred to as Column names. To avoid confusion when placing these elements into tables, I simply refer to all of the items in the Data Bindings panel as data bindings.

12. Drag the Episode_Title, Genre, and Price data bindings to their appropriate cells.
13. Select the bottom five cells by placing your cursor on the left edge of the bottom-left cell and dragging across all five cells.
14. Set the font for these cells to Arial, Helvetica, sans serif with a size of **2**. Leave the color and formatting at their default settings.
15. Click the Align Center button. Your page should look like Figure 7.12.

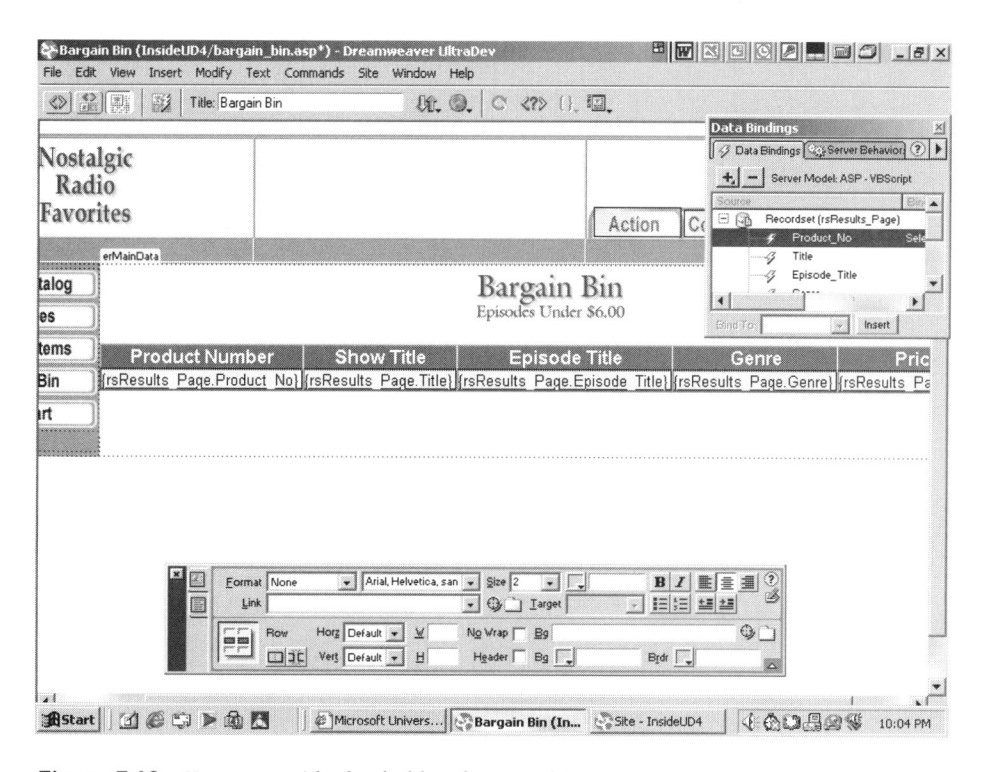

Figure 7.12 Your page with placeholders for your data.

16. Click the Show Live Data View button on your toolbar. As shown in Figure 7.13, UltraDev inserts the first row of data in the cells.
17. Switch back to the Page Design view.

176 Part III Developing a Data-Driven Web Site

> **Note**
> **Permission Denied** If you get an error message stating that Microsoft Jet Database Engine cannot open the file, it is likely that the permissions for the InsideUD4 folder are not set correctly. You can check the permissions by right-clicking on the folder from within Windows Explorer and selecting Properties from the context menu.

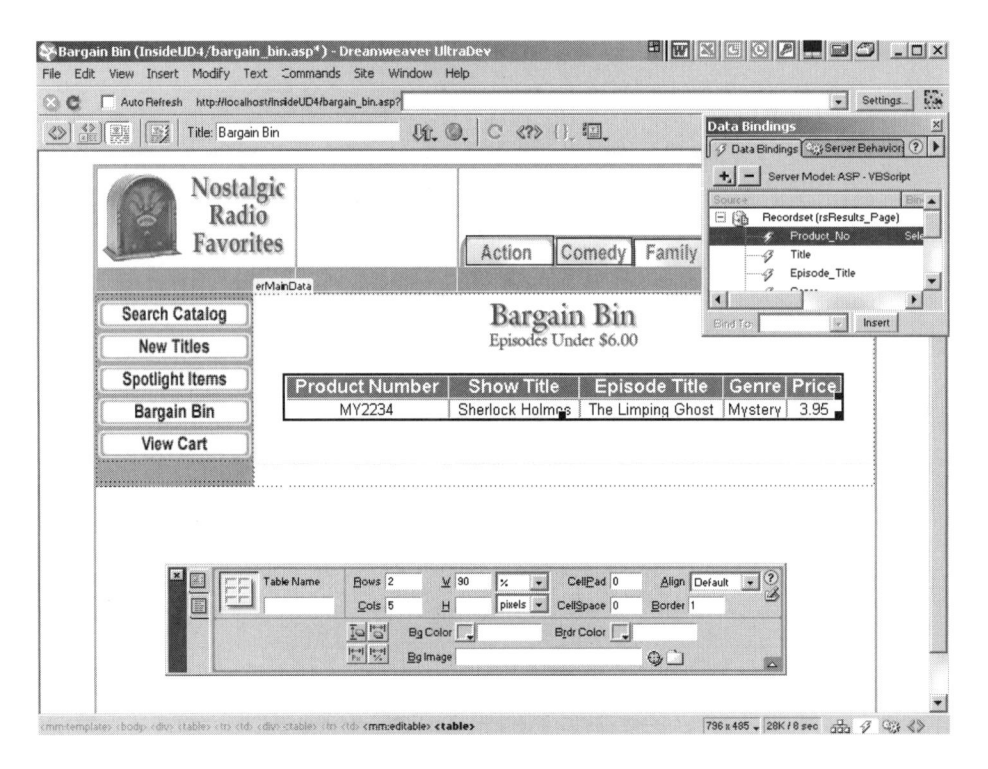

Figure 7.13 The Live Data view displays a sample of your data.

18. Because you would like to see all the records that match your query and not just the first one, you have to apply a server behavior that tells the page to keep displaying records until there aren't any more.

    To do this, highlight the bottom five cells where the data placeholders are located and click the Server Behaviors tab on the Data Bindings panel.

19. Click the plus button and select Repeat Region. The Repeat Region dialog box, shown in Figure 7.14, lets you control the repeat parameters.

20. In the Repeat Region dialog box, make sure the rsResults_Page recordset is highlighted. Select the radio button to show All Records and click OK.

21. Save your page.

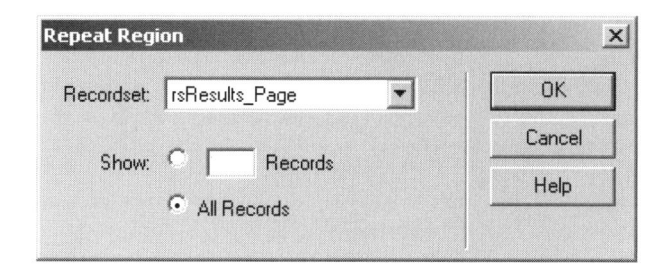

Chapter 7 Connecting Your Web Site to a Database 177

Figure 7.14 The Repeat Region dialog box lets you control how often the behavior is repeated.

22. View the Bargain Bin in your browser by typing the URL **http://localhost/insideud4/bargain_bin.asp** in the address line. Your page should look like Figure 7.15.

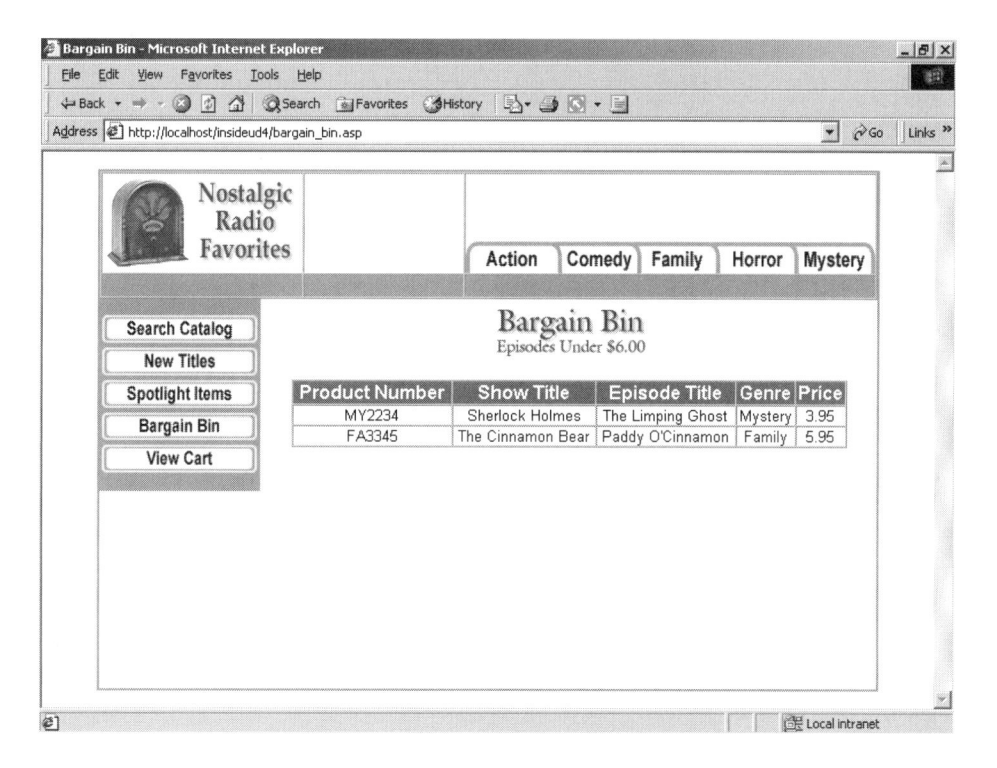

Figure 7.15 The Bargain Bin with dynamic data.

23. Close your browser.

> **Tip**
>
> **Previewing Your Pages in Your Browser** UltraDev has a nice built-in feature that allows you to preview your pages in your browser by simply clicking the F12 key. If you are using multiple browsers on your machine, you can specify which browser should be your default browser by selecting File/Preview in Browser/Edit Browser List.

Linking to a Detail Page

Now that your visitors can view some of the records stored in your database, it's likely that they might want to get additional information about a specific product. To provide that information, you can create a detail page that displays additional information about the product. To successfully add a detail page to your site, however, UltraDev must first know what record the detail page should display, which page it should display the information in, and then in what format it should display it.

Luckily, UltraDev makes this process very simple through the implementation of the Go to Detail Page server behavior.

Exercise 7.4 Creating a Link to a Details Page

1. In the bargain_bin.asp page, highlight the dynamic data placeholder called {rsResults_Page.Episode_Title} by clicking it.
2. On the Server Behaviors palette, click the plus symbol and select Go to Detail Page. As shown in Figure 7.16, the Go to Detail Page dialog box allows you to choose the location of your detail page. Notice that the Link field has already been filled with the data placeholder that you selected.

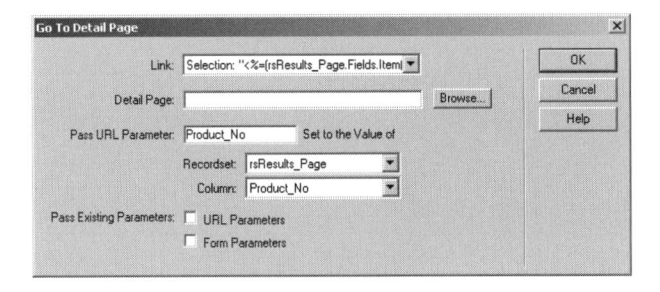

Figure 7.16 The Go to Detail Page dialog box allows you to select a destination link.

3. In the Detail Page field, type **bargain_bin_details.asp**.
4. In the Pass URL Parameter field, make sure Product_No is displayed. This is the unique piece of information that lets the detail page know which record to

display. In your case, each product has a unique product number, so this is the easiest way to distinguish between records.

> **Tip**
>
> **Letting UltraDev Create the Link** If you haven't already identified the text that you would like to use as the link to the detail page, UltraDev can create one for you. For instance, suppose that instead of using a dynamic field as the link, you choose to create a new field with a link that reads "Additional Info." To accomplish this, you would add the Go to Detail Page behavior to the page (with nothing selected) and then select the Create New Link: Detail option in the Link field. UltraDev would then insert the word "Detail" into your page that links to the detail page. In the Design view, you could then highlight the link and change it to say Additional Info.

5. In the Recordset field, make sure rsResults_Page is selected and Product_No is displayed in the Column field.
6. Make sure that the two check boxes remain unchecked. These boxes allow you to retain any URL or Form parameters that might have been passed to the bargain_bin.asp page. These are not appropriate here and checking them could result in errors when visitors view your pages.
7. Click OK to apply the behavior.
8. Place your insertion point anywhere in the page that is not inside a table, and notice that the placeholder for Episode Title, shown in Figure 7.17, is now a hyperlink.
9. Click the Live Data View button on the toolbar and notice that the episode titles are also hyperlinks. Keep in mind, however, that these links currently won't work because you haven't created the detail page yet.
10. Turn off the Live Data view.
11. Save the page.

After you have a link to your detail page, you need to create the page itself. Because a detail page is nothing more than a dynamic page similar to the one you just created, it should be a snap to create.

Exercise 7.5 Building a Detail Page

1. From the menu bar, select File/New From Template.
2. In the Site Template dialog box, choose the nrfdefault template and click Select.
3. Change the title of the new page to **Bargain Bin Details** and save the new page as **bargain_bin_details.asp**.
4. In the new page that is created, place your insertion point in the main data editable region and remove the {erMainData} text.

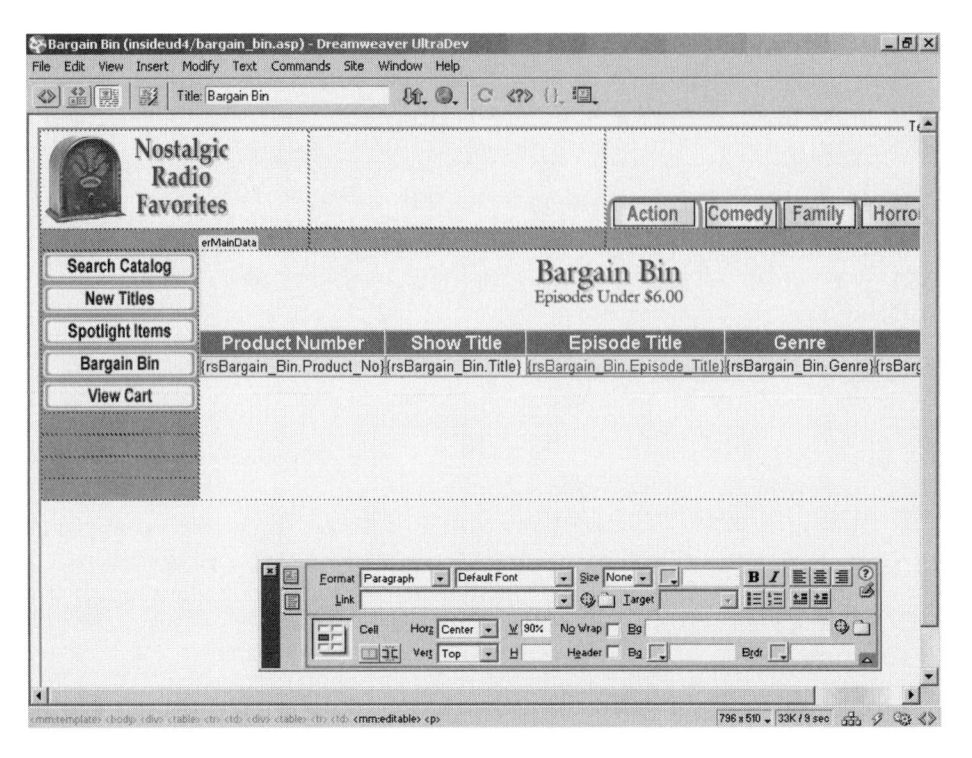

Figure 7.17 A link to your detail page has been created.

5. Insert the bargain_bin_logo.gif image from the images subfolder of your site. Press the right arrow key on your keyboard to move to the right of the image and press the Enter key to move to a new line.

6. On the new line, insert a new table. The table should have **1** row and **1** column, and have a width of **90%**. Set the border, cell padding, and cell spacing to **0**. Click OK.

7. Drop the insertion point inside the new table and click the Align Center button on the Property inspector.

8. Click the Data Bindings tab in the Server Behaviors panel. Click the plus sign and choose Recordset (Query).

9. In the Recordset dialog box, create a recordset that is connected to the connSales_Database and name it **rsResults_Page_Details**.

10. In the Table field, select tbProducts and select the All radio button to retrieve all of the records in the table.

11. Because this is a detail page and you want to display only the record that is being requested, you need to apply a filter. In the Filter fields, set the first field to Product_No. The second field should be set to =, and the third and fourth fields should be URL Parameter and Product_No. This looks for the specific record that has the product number which matches the one that was passed in the URL when the link was clicked.

> **Note**
>
> **Another Way to Display a Detail Page** Another way to display a detail page is to use the Move to Specific Record server behavior. When applying this behavior, however, you might consider the size of your recordset. If you are working with a relatively small recordset, the behavior works well. If, however, you are using a recordset that contains a large number of records, the Move to Specific Record server behavior runs more slowly than creating a smaller recordset and using a filter.

12. Click the test button. Because this test query relies on information that will be passed via the URL when a link is clicked, you must provide a piece of test data. As shown in Figure 7.18, type **AC8989** and click OK. The test query should return the record with the product number AC8989.

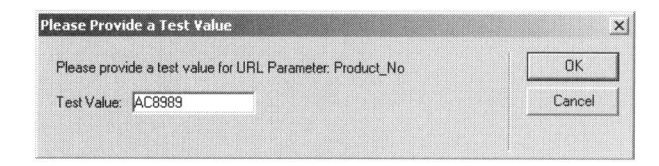

Figure 7.18 Testing a query that relies on a URL parameter requires a test value.

13. Click OK to close the Test SQL Statement results box.
14. Click OK to close the Recordset dialog box.
15. In the Data Bindings panel, click the plus sign next to rsResults_Page_Details to display the available data bindings.
16. Click and drag the Title data binding from the Data Bindings panel to your new table. Press the right arrow key on your keyboard to move your insertion point to the right of the Title placeholder.
17. Press the hyphen (-) key on your keyboard and drag the Episode Title into the table to the right of the dash. Your page should look like Figure 7.19.
18. Press the Tab key on your keyboard to create a new row.
19. Right-click in the new row and choose Table/Split Cell. Choose to split the cell into two columns and click OK.
20. With the insertion point in the left cell, choose Insert/Image. In the Insert Image dialog box, choose the Data Sources radio button from the Select Filename From option.

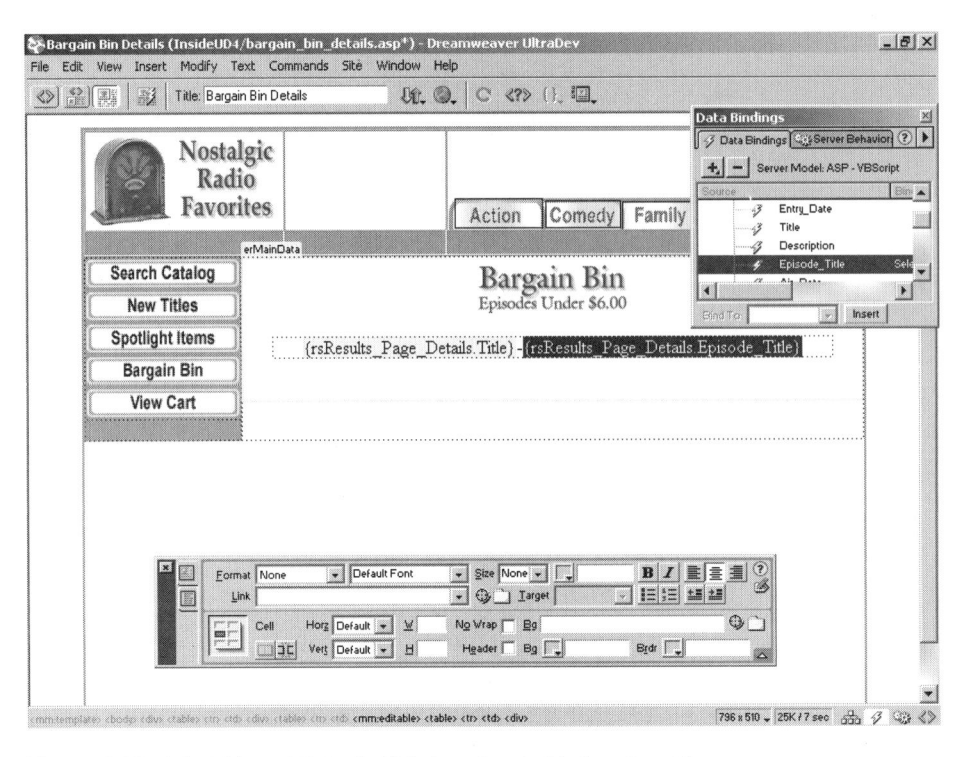

Figure 7.19 The Title and Episode Title have been added to the table.

21. In the Data Sources view of the Select Image Source dialog box, click the plus sign next to the rsResults_Page_Details recordset to expand the options. As shown in Figure 7.20, you now have access to all the data bindings in the recordset.
22. Select the Photo_URL data binding and click OK. As shown in Figure 7.21, UltraDev has now inserted a placeholder for the image.
23. Press the Tab key twice to create a new row.
24. In the left cell in the bottom row, type **Product Number:**.
25. Drag and drop the Product_No data binding into the bottom-right cell of the table.

    It's possible that UltraDev may have shrunk the right column when you inserted data into the left column. To make your right column visible again, place the insertion point in any cells in the left column and set the width of that cell to **50%** in the Property inspector. You will then be able to see both columns again.

26. Press Tab to create a new row. In the left cell, type **Air Date:**. Drag and drop the Air_Date data binding to the right cell.
27. Press Tab to create a new row. In the left cell, type **Price:**. Drag and drop the Price data binding to the right cell.

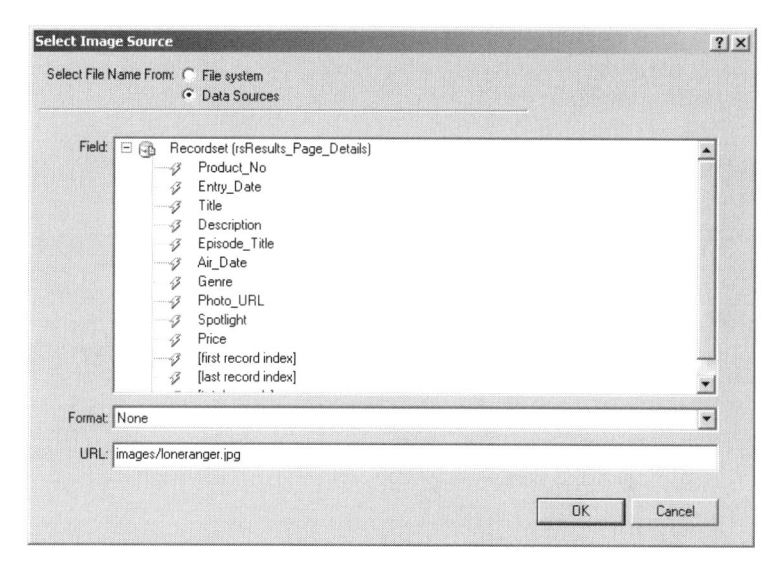

Chapter 7 Connecting Your Web Site to a Database 183

Figure 7.20 The Data Sources view of the Select Image Source dialog box allows you to insert dynamic images.

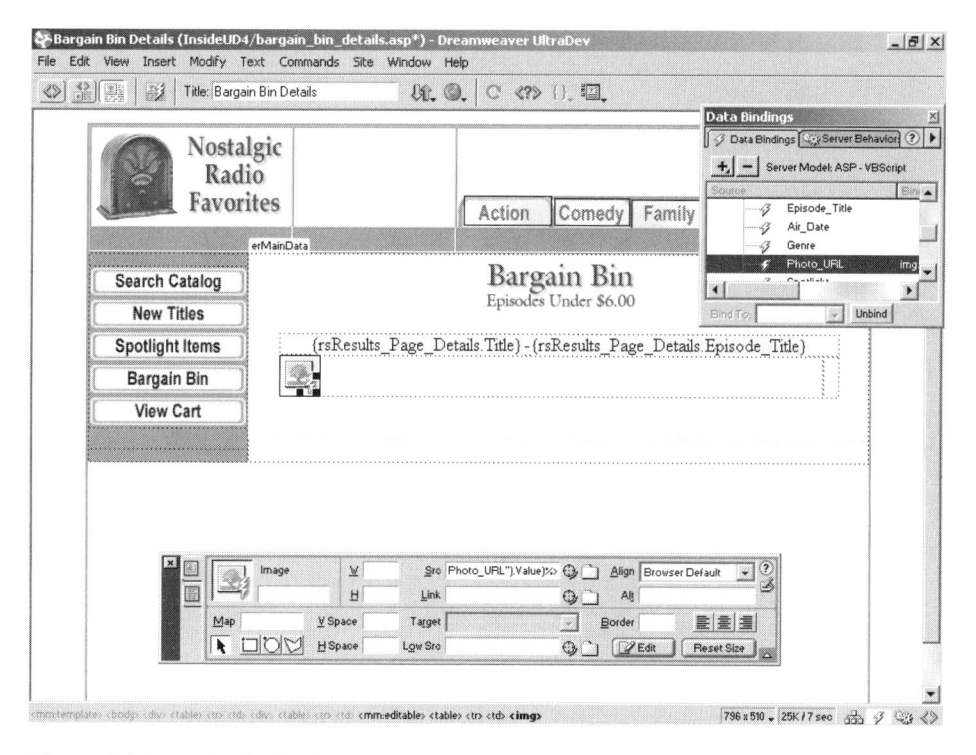

Figure 7.21 A placeholder has been inserted for your dynamic image.

28. Press Tab to create a new row. In the left cell, type **Description:**. Drag and drop the Description data binding to the right cell. Your page should now look like Figure 7.22.

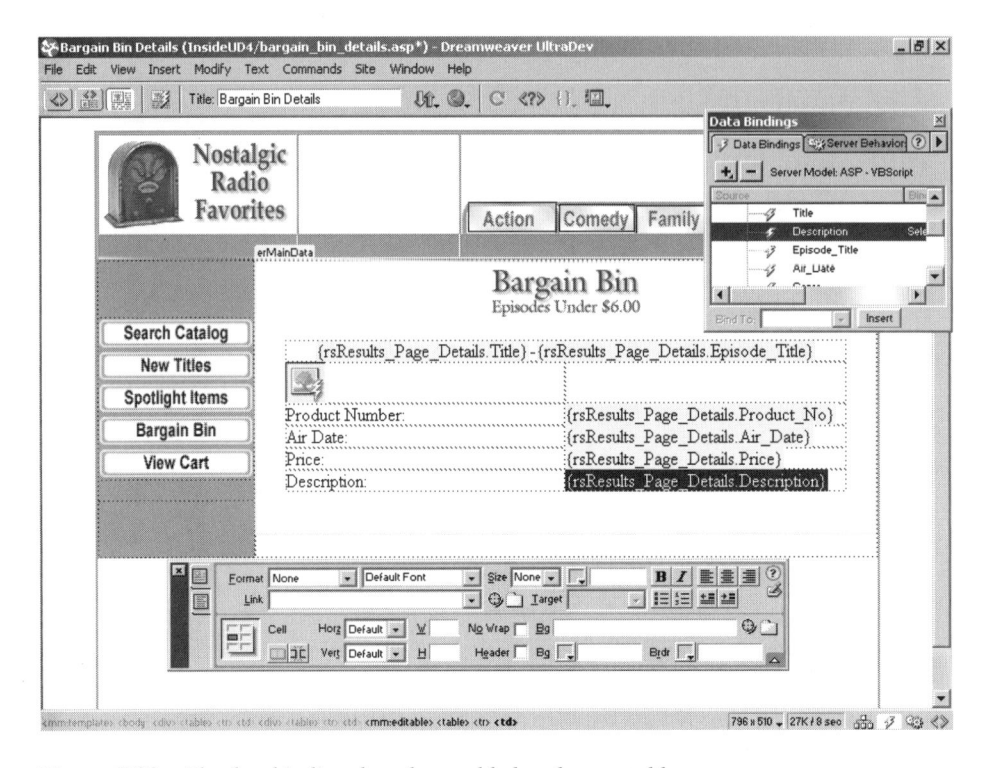

Figure 7.22 The data bindings have been added to the new table.

29. Select all of the cells in the table by clicking in the bottom-right cell and dragging your cursor to the top-left cell.

> **Tip**
> **Be Careful When Selecting Cells** When you are selecting cells by dragging, make sure you don't accidentally click on the data that is stored in the cell. If you do, your data will move wherever you drag your cursor.

30. In the Property inspector, set the Font to Arial, Helvetica, sans serif and the size to **3**. Set the vertical alignment of the cells to Top in the Vert field.

31. Save your page.

32. Open your Web browser and type **http://localhost/insideud4**. This will take you to the home page for your site.

33. Click the Bargain Bin button. The Bargain Bin should display items that have a price of less than $6.00.
34. Click the link to "The Limping Ghost" and you should see the detail page shown in Figure 7.23.

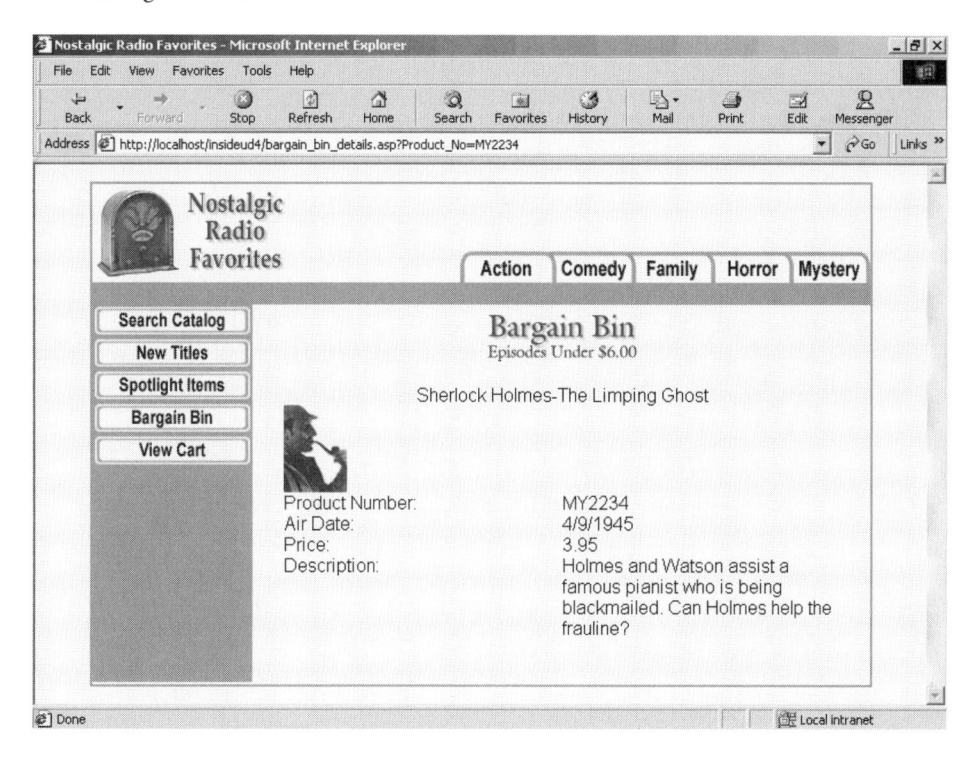

Figure 7.23 Your detail page is complete!

Using Existing Pages and Recordsets to Create Similar Pages

Although building database-driven results is relatively easy using UltraDev, there are quite a few steps involved. To speed up the development process, you can often reuse pages and simply make minor adjustments to bring a whole new page to life. Doing this not only saves time, but it reduces the number of potential mistakes you could make when creating pages from scratch.

Creating the New Titles Page

Now that you have the Bargain Bin set up and the Bargain Bin detail page properly displays the additional information for each product, you can use these two pages as the starting point to create several of the other pages in your site.

For instance, suppose your returning visitors want an easy way to see items that have recently been added to your database. To accomplish this, you can create a New Titles page that dynamically displays the five most recent records that were entered into the database. To accomplish this, use a field in the database that keeps track of the date the record was created and then display only the most recent five in descending order.

Exercise 7.6 Creating the New Titles Page

1. Open the bargain_bin.asp page. Select File/Save As from the menu bar.
2. In the Save As dialog box, change the filename to **new_titles.asp** and click the Save button.

> **Note**
> **Using Save As with Files Attached to Templates** When you use the Save As command to create a new document, the new page is still attached to the same template as the original document.

3. In the Title field of the new page, type **New Titles** and press the Enter key.
4. Highlight the Bargain Bin image by clicking on it. In the Property inspector, change the Src field to **images/new_titles_logo.gif**.
5. In the Data Bindings panel, double-click the rsResults_Page recordset.
6. In the Columns field, add Entry_Date to the recordset by pressing the Ctrl key on your keyboard and clicking Entry_Date.
7. Since the purpose of your New Titles page is to display the most recent five records, you have to adjust the way your results are filtered and sorted. Set the Filter field to None.
8. In the Sort fields, select Entry_Date in the first field and Descending in the second field.
9. Click the Test button. As shown in Figure 7.24, UltraDev returns the results of your test query. Notice that all the records are displayed with the most recent entries at the top.
10. Click OK to close the Test SQL Statement dialog box. Click OK to close the Recordset dialog box.
11. In the Server Behaviors panel, double-click the Repeat Region behavior assigned to your page.
12. As shown in Figure 7.25, change the server behavior to show only the first five records. Click OK to update the server behavior.

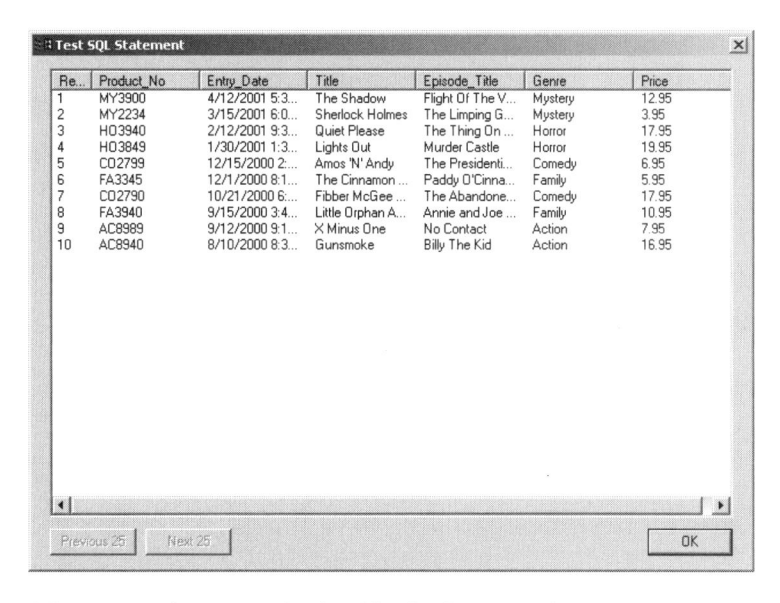

Chapter 7 Connecting Your Web Site to a Database 187

Figure 7.24 Your results are now displayed by the date entered.

> **Caution**
>
> **Save As and Recordset Naming Conventions** When you are creating your recordsets, you might be tempted to give them unique names that match the page where they are located. If you do so, you may run into problems when creating new pages using the Save As method because the new page inherits all the recordsets and their properties from the first page.
>
> For instance, if you had named the recordset for your Bargain Bin page rsBargain_Bin, then the New Titles page that was created by using Save As would also have an rsBargain_Bin recordset. This isn't really a big problem unless you try to update the name of the recordset in the New Titles page.
>
> If you updated the name of the recordset to rsNew_Titles, you would also have to go through each of your server behaviors and update the name of the recordset that they are dependant upon. This could be a time-consuming process if you have a lot of server behaviors assigned.
>
> If you are planning to use the Save As method to create new pages, be sure to use relatively generic recordset names so that they apply to all your pages.

13. The final step is to designate the new location of your detail page. In the Server Behaviors panel, double-click the Go to Detail Page data binding. In the Go to Detail Page dialog box, type **new_titles_details.asp** in the Detail Page field.
14. Click OK to update the change.
15. Save your page.

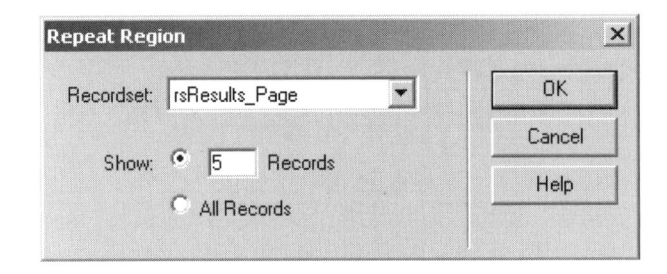

Figure 7.25 Change the Repeat Region behavior to display only five records.

> **Note**
>
> **Another Way to Show the Top Five Records** If you are using a recordset that contains a small number of records, the easiest way to show the top five records is to create the recordset and then limit the number of records that appear. If, however, you have a recordset that contains thousands of records, it would be inefficient to build the entire recordset and then only display the top five records.
>
> If you are working with a large recordset, you might consider using an advanced SQL query in your recordset and using the SELECT TOP5 SQL statement.

Creating the New Titles Detail Page

After you have created your New Titles page, you also need to create a detail page that is customized for the new titles. Because we already created a detail page for the Bargain Bin, we can simply reuse that page and make some slight alterations.

Exercise 7.7 Creating the New Titles Detail Page

1. Open the bargain_bin_details.asp page. Select File/Save As from the menu bar.
2. In the Save As dialog box, change the filename to **new_titles_details.asp** and click the Save button.
3. In the Title field of the new page, type **New Titles Details** and press the Enter key.
4. Highlight the Bargain Bin image by clicking on it. In the Property inspector, change the Src field to **images/new_titles_logo.gif**. Press Enter.
5. Save your page.
6. Minimize UltraDev.
7. View your New Titles and New Titles Results pages in your browser by typing **http://localhost/insideud4/new_titles.asp** in the address bar. As shown in Figure 7.26, you now see only the five most recent entries into the database.

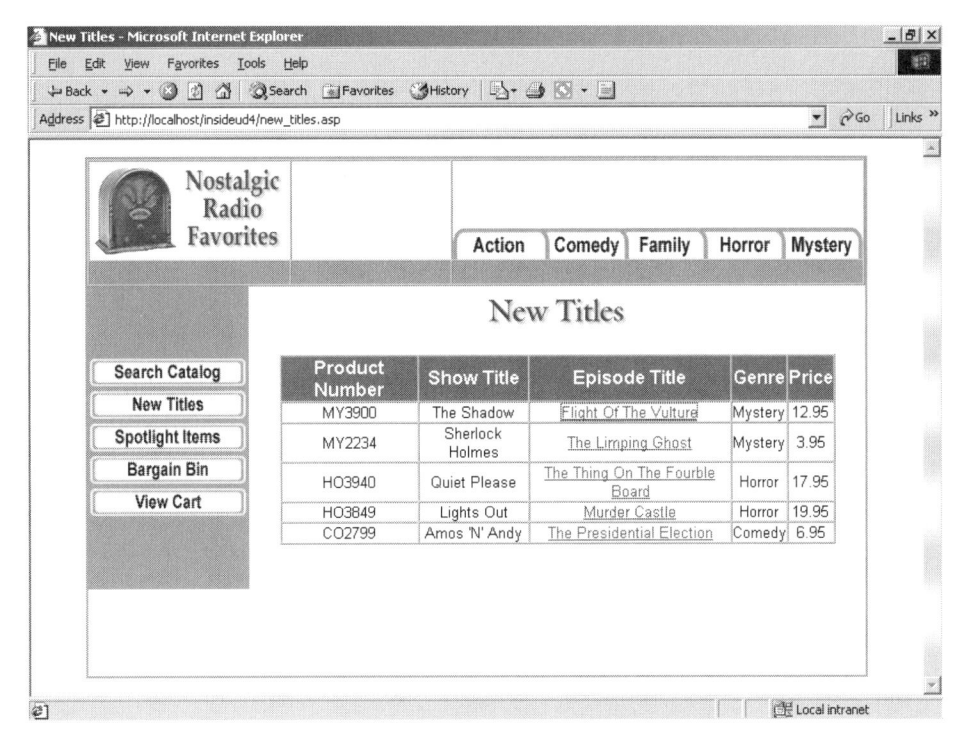

Figure 7.26 Your page now displays the five most recent entries into the database.

8. Click the Flight of the Vulture link. Your detail page now displays the details with the New Titles logo at the top.
9. Close your browser.

Creating the Spotlight Items Page and Detail Page

The final step in this chapter is to create a page that displays all of the "spotlight items" that you have designated in the database. These products may be overstocks that are on sale, or may be rare recordings that you are just now able to offer to the public.

Regardless of why you choose to designate an item as a spotlight item, you can easily build a results page and a detail page that displays those records designated in the database by using the same methods you used in developing your New Titles pages.

I am going to leave the creation of these two pages up to you, although the following bulleted lists serve as a guide for what changes you should make in both the new pages.

For the spotlight_items.asp page, try the following:

- Create the page by opening the bargain_bin.asp page and doing a Save As **spotlight_items.asp**.
- Change the page title to **Spotlight Items**.
- Change the page logo to the spotlight_items_logo.gif.
- Change the recordset to filter the pages where the Spotlight field is equal to the Entered Value of Yes.
- Change the Detail Page location in the Go to Detail Page server behavior to spotlight_items_details.asp.

For the spotlight_items_details.asp page, try the following:

- Create the page by opening the bargain_bin_details.asp page and doing a Save As **spotlight_items_details.asp**.
- Change the name of the page.
- Change the logo for the page.
- Minimize UltraDev and check the pages in your browser.

Summary

This chapter has shown you how easy it is to build database-driven pages using UltraDev. In addition, you have learned how to insert dynamic images, link to results pages, and create detail pages that provide visitors with additional information.

The next chapter focuses on the security features that can be added to your pages and demonstrates how to allow visitors to create user accounts. In addition, you will learn how to restrict access to pages based on whether the visitor has logged on to your site using a valid username and password.

Chapter 8

Creating Visitor Accounts Through Username Validation

Over the last few years, there has been a substantial increase in the number of sites that are allowing visitors to create and maintain their own user accounts. Most of these sites allow their visitors to browse through the "public" sections of their site, but require the creation of an individual account when it comes time to order products, contribute content, or view pages that the organization just doesn't want available to the general public. In most cases, the visitor is asked to provide the appropriate demographic information, select a username, and then choose a password. This information is stored in a database, and registered users can return to the site at any time, log in to their accounts, and surf the site in its entirety.

Registering visitors has the added benefit of providing organizations with the ability to gain a more detailed understanding of who is visiting the site and to develop custom content that focuses on the individual visitor. For instance, some sites currently track the search terms that are used to locate products. This information is then used to customize the site's content to meet the perceived needs of the visitor during the next visit. Whether it be for purchasing products, searching for a job, or maybe just playing a few games online, many sites are customizing content for their visitors based upon their activities while logged in to an individual account.

From a Web developer's point of view, adding this functionality to a site has the added benefit of providing you with the ability to collect valuable information about your visitors. Whether it be a shipping address so you can quickly deliver products or an email address so you can notify customers of upcoming promotions, the more you know about your visitors, the more likely you can develop content that suits their needs. For instance, if you track the expressions entered into a product search box, you might be able to better understand what items your customer wanted to see and be able to add products that you might not have previously offered.

To assist you in adding individual accounts to your site, UltraDev has several built-in server behaviors that speed up the development process. In particular, this chapter focuses on three things:

- Enabling visitors to create individual accounts
- Protecting pages from unauthenticated visitors
- Testing your new pages

Enabling Visitors to Create User Accounts

The first step in allowing users to access password-protected areas of your site is to develop a process that allows each user to create an account. The most common way to do this with UltraDev is to create a signup page including a form that allows each user to enter the necessary information and choose a username and password. When the form is submitted, the contents are placed into a database where they can be referenced for validation when the visitor returns and attempts to log in again.

The site must also include several additional elements that help returning visitors access their accounts and the secured sections of the site. First, the site needs links that allow the user to log in and log out. Ideally, the site should be able to detect whether an individual has logged in or not and should then only display the Login link to visitors who haven't yet signed in. Likewise, authenticated users should only see the Logout link.

The last element a site needs for minimal functionality is a login page for returning visitors. This page usually includes a form that accepts a username and password and submits the information to the Web server. The user's credentials are then checked against the values stored in the database and the user is validated or denied access based on whether or not the values match.

Luckily, UltraDev makes the process of adding user accounts relatively easy. From the menu bar you can quickly add forms, text fields, and buttons to your pages. In addition, built-in server behaviors help you add new users to your database and validate credentials supplied by returning visitors.

Adding Dynamic Links for Creating an Account, Logging In, and Logging Out

The first step to adding user accounts and allowing returning visitors to log in and log out is to provide appropriate links. As I mentioned before, the goal is to create dynamic links that are only visible at the appropriate time. To accomplish this, we can use UltraDev's Show Region behavior to display only the Login and Create New Account links when the user has not already logged in. Likewise, the same behavior can be used to display the Logout link only when the user has successfully logged in.

Exercise 8.1 Adding Dynamic Links

1. Open UltraDev. Open the nrfdefault.dwt page located in the Templates folder of the InsideUD4 site.
2. Open the Server Behaviors panel by selecting Window/Server Behaviors from the menu bar.
3. Click the plus sign on the Server Behaviors panel and select Recordset (Query) from the drop-down menu.

4. In the Recordset dialog box, type **rsLogin** in the Name field. Select the connSales_Database connection from the Connection dropdown. If you do not see the connSales_Database connection, please refer to Exercise 7.1.

5. Click the Advanced button. The Advanced view of the Recordset dialog box, shown in Figure 8.1, provides you with the ability to create your own custom SQL queries. Notice that UltraDev has already begun a SQL query for us indicating that the query should select everything (indicated by the asterisk following SELECT in the SQL panel) from the tbCustomers table.

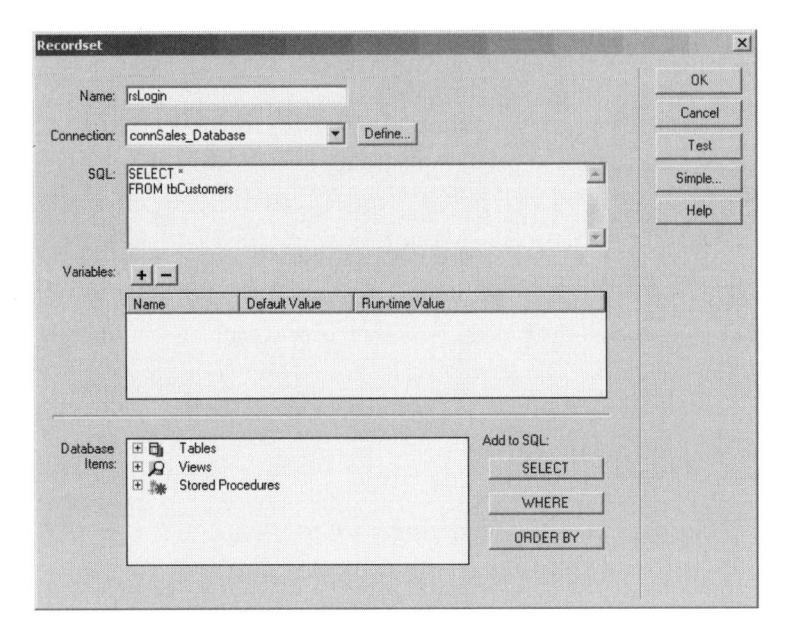

Figure 8.1 The advanced view of the Recordset dialog box allows you to define custom SQL queries.

6. Place the insertion point in the SQL panel after the word tbCustomers.

7. In the Database Items panel, click the plus symbol next to Tables. Click the plus symbol next to tbCustomers. You should now see all the columns (fields) available in your database.

8. Highlight the CustomerID column and click the WHERE button. Notice that UltraDev automatically adds a qualifier to your SQL query.

9. Highlight the Password column and click the WHERE button.

10. Fill in the rest of the SQL query as shown in Figure 8.2. To add the variables, simply click the plus sign and type the variable entries.

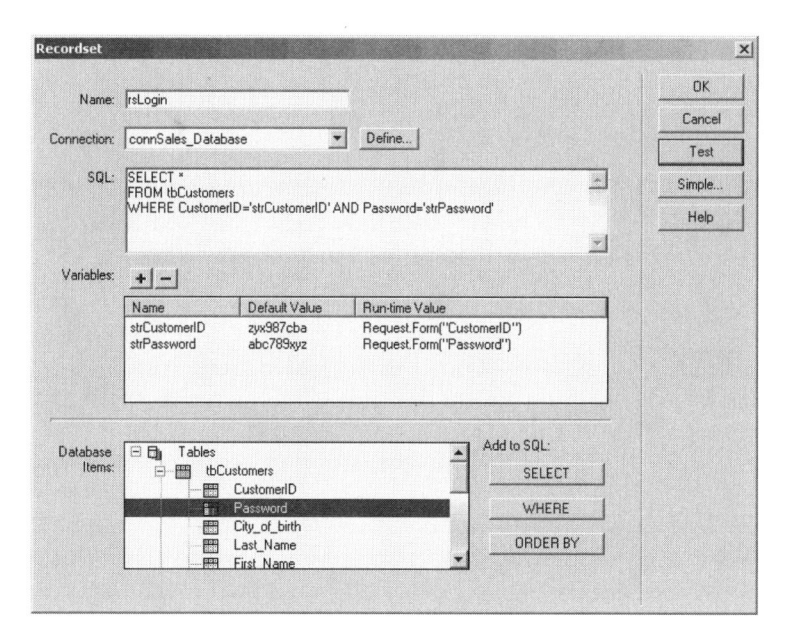

Chapter 8 Creating Visitor Accounts Through Username Validation 197

Figure 8.2 Your SQL query and variables should look like this.

11. Click the Test button. This query simply takes whatever values are stored in the CustomerID and Password text fields of a form and compares them to the CustomerID and Password fields in the database. Because there are no entries in the database that match the default customer ID or password, the test query should return no data.

> **Caution**
>
> **Selecting Default Values for Your SQL Queries** Whenever you create a custom SQL Query in UltraDev, you have the ability to test the query with default values to ensure that the query behaves properly. However, if you choose default values that are common, you could create a potential security problem within your site.
>
> For instance, suppose you enter a default value of abc for the CustomerID and 123 for the Password. If a visitor comes along and creates a user account that uses abc and 123 for his username and password, everyone will now be able to access your account without supplying a username and password because of the default values that exist in the database.
>
> Therefore, when selecting default values, be sure to enter values that are exotic and that no visitor is likely to choose. When you are done testing your pages, you can either leave the exotic default values or change the default values to input information from a session variable.

12. Click OK to close the Test SQL Statement dialog box and click OK in the Recordset dialog box. UltraDev now displays the rsLogin recordset in the Server Behaviors panel.

13. Switch to the Code view by clicking the Show Code View button.
14. Scroll to the top of the code and find the line that reads

    ```
    rsLogin__strCustomerID = "Session("MM_Username")"
    ```

    Remove the outer quotes from around the session information and change this line to read as follows:

    ```
    rsLogin__strCustomerID = Session("MM_Username")
    ```

15. A few lines down, find the line that reads

    ```
    rsLogin__strPassword = "Session("MM_Password")"
    ```

    Remove the quotes from around this session information as well. The line should now read

    ```
    rsLogin__strPassword = Session("MM_Password")
    ```

    The default variables that were initially entered in the rsLogin recordset tell the recordset to check whether the user has previously logged in and created a session variable. If he has logged in, the rsLogin recordset contains the appropriate record from the tbCustomers table.

    The only problem with this arises from the fact that UltraDev places quotes around the session code, which results in an empty recordset. To resolve the issue, you can simply remove the quotes in the Code view.

    Keep in mind, however, that if you open the recordset on any particular page, UltraDev will "fix" the problem. To undo UltraDev's fix, just view the code again and retype the session information.

16. Switch back to the Design view. Notice that the rsLogin recordset now has an exclamation point next to it because you removed the quotation marks from the session variable information. Don't worry about this; the recordset still functions properly.

> **Note**
>
> **Adding Recordsets and Server Behaviors to a Template** When you add a recordset or server behavior to a template, all pages that are built from the template will also inherit the recordset and server behavior that are associated with the template at the time. Adding these elements to your templates is a quick and easy way to add a dynamic behavior to all the pages in your site.
>
> Keep in mind, however, that there are times when you won't want to apply a server behavior to all your pages. For instance, suppose you want to limit access to a certain area of your site to users who have entered a valid username and password. Applying these limitations to a template could result in protecting pages that you wanted to remain available to all visitors. In this case, you might consider creating a second template for use with those pages that should be password protected.

Chapter 8 Creating Visitor Accounts Through Username Validation 199

17. Place the insertion point in the empty cell below the View Cart button on the left side of the template. In the cell, type **Create Account**.
18. Highlight the Create Account text and type **http://localhost/insideud4/newuser.asp** in the Link field of the Property inspector. Press Enter.
19. With the Create Account text highlighted, click the plus sign on the Server Behaviors panel and select Show Region/Show Region If Recordset Is Empty. From the dialog box shown in Figure 8.3, select the rsLogin recordset and click OK. This behavior has the effect of only showing the Create Account link if the user has not logged on using a valid username and password.

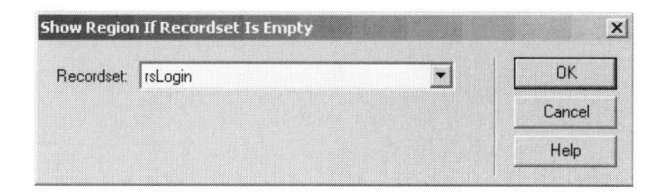

Figure 8.3 Select the rsLogin recordset.

20. Place the insertion point after the Create Account text and press the Tab key on your keyboard to create a new cell. With the insertion point in the new cell, click the Align Center button on the Property inspector.
21. Type **Login** in the cell.
22. Highlight the Login text and type **http://localhost/insideud4/login.asp** in the Link field of the Property inspector. Press Enter.
23. With the Login text highlighted, click the plus sign on the Server Behaviors panel and select Show Region/Show Region If Recordset Is Empty. From the dialog box, select the rsLogin recordset and click OK. Again, this behavior has the effect of showing the Login link only if the user has not entered a valid username and password.
24. Place the insertion point after the Login text and press the Tab key on your keyboard to create a new cell. With the insertion point in the new cell, press the Align Center button on the Property inspector.
25. Type **Logout** in the cell.
26. Highlight the Logout text and type **http://localhost/insideud4/logout.asp** in the Link field of the Property inspector. Press Enter.
27. With the Logout text highlighted, click the plus sign on the Server Behaviors panel and choose Show Region/Show Region If Recordset Is Not Empty.

200   Part III   Developing a Data-Driven Web Site

28. From the dialog box, select the rsLogin recordset and click OK. This behavior displays the Logout text only after a user has entered a valid username and password. As shown in Figure 8.4, you should now have login and logout links that have server behaviors.

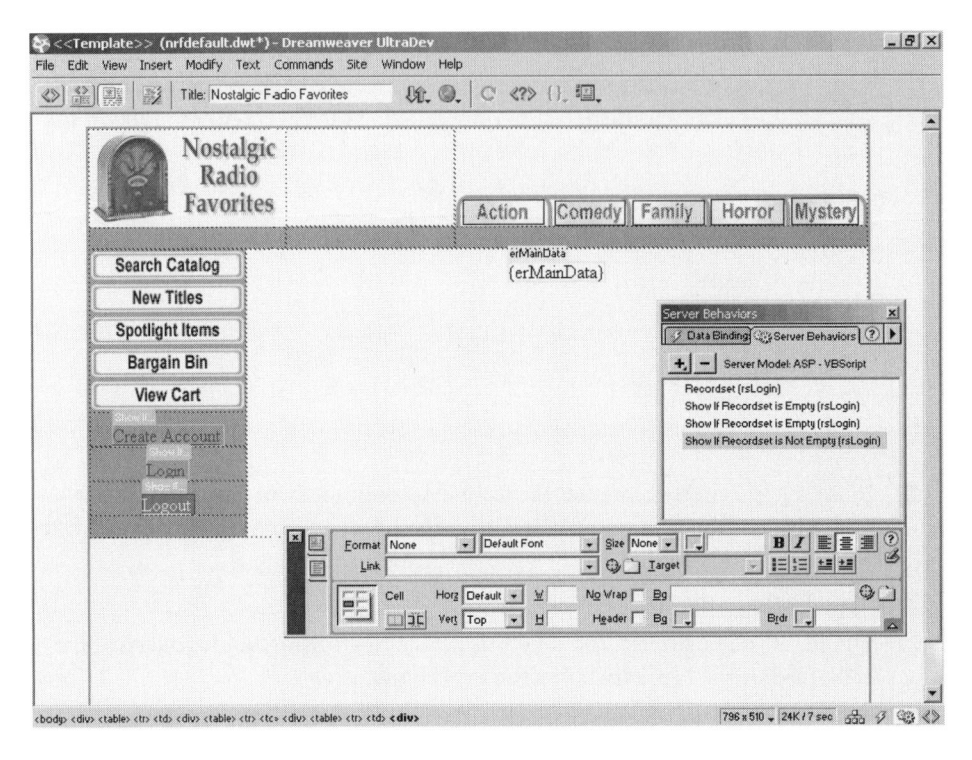

Figure 8.4   Your template with login and logout links.

29. Save your template. When asked whether dependent pages should be updated, respond Yes.
30. Close the Update Pages dialog box and close the nrfdefault.dwt template.
31. Do not close UltraDev.

> **Note**
>
> **Testing the Additions to Your Pages**   With the links added to your pages, you have taken the first step toward allowing users to create their own user accounts. At this point, however, the links are pointing to pages that don't exist so don't worry about testing the new additions to your page just yet. When you get to the end of the chapter, you'll have the opportunity to see everything in action and test the site's added functionality.

Creating a New User Signup Form

A couple of years ago, the university where I work began developing a Web-based employment database. When we considered what information we needed to collect from our job seekers, we came up with an extensive list of items ranging from their personal information (such as name and address) and demographic information (such as gender, race, and age) to their employment history (such as degrees earned and relevant experience). Although a lot of the data seemed irrelevant to the job search process, we decided to collect as much information as possible and then filter the information that was visible to employers to include only data that was relevant to a job search.

A few months after implementing the database, however, we discovered that a lot of the information that was unrelated to the individual's job search was helpful to us in understanding who our job seekers were and what types of employment opportunities were being sought. With this information in mind, we were able to market our database to employers who were more likely to offer positions that met the needs of our job seekers.

The point here is that one of the biggest difficulties in developing a new user signup form is to determine what information you should collect from your visitors. Not only is it imperative that you think about information that is absolutely necessary, but you must also break out your crystal ball and predict what information could conceivably be needed in the future.

> **Caution**
>
> **Balancing What You Want with What You Need** When developing a new user form, you should always keep in mind that no one likes to fill out a form that requests too much information and takes too long to complete. If the form takes each visitor more than a couple of minutes to fill out, you might reconsider some of the data you are requiring. The last thing you want to do is drive visitors away from your site because they don't want to take the time to create an account.

Starting with the Template

As with the other pages in your site, you can develop your new user account page from scratch or save time by using a previously created template. Pages that include simple forms that interact with your database should cause no problems when built from a template. Keep in mind, however, that using a template restricts access to the Head section of your code. Because of this, any forms that use JavaScript behaviors (such as checking for required fields) will have to be disconnected from the template before the behaviors can be applied.

202   Part III   Developing a Data-Driven Web Site

> **Note**
>
> **Learning More About Templates**   If you are interested in learning more about the potential limitations of templates, check out this TechNote on the Dreamweaver Support Pages:
>
> http://www.macromedia.com/support/dreamweaver/ts/documents/behavior_templates.htm

Exercise 8.2 Creating a New User Account Page

1. Open UltraDev, if it isn't already open, and select File/New from Template from the menu bar.
2. From the Select Template dialog box, choose the InsideUD4 site and select nrfdefault from the available templates. Click Select. As shown in Figure 8.5, UltraDev creates a new page based on the previously developed template.

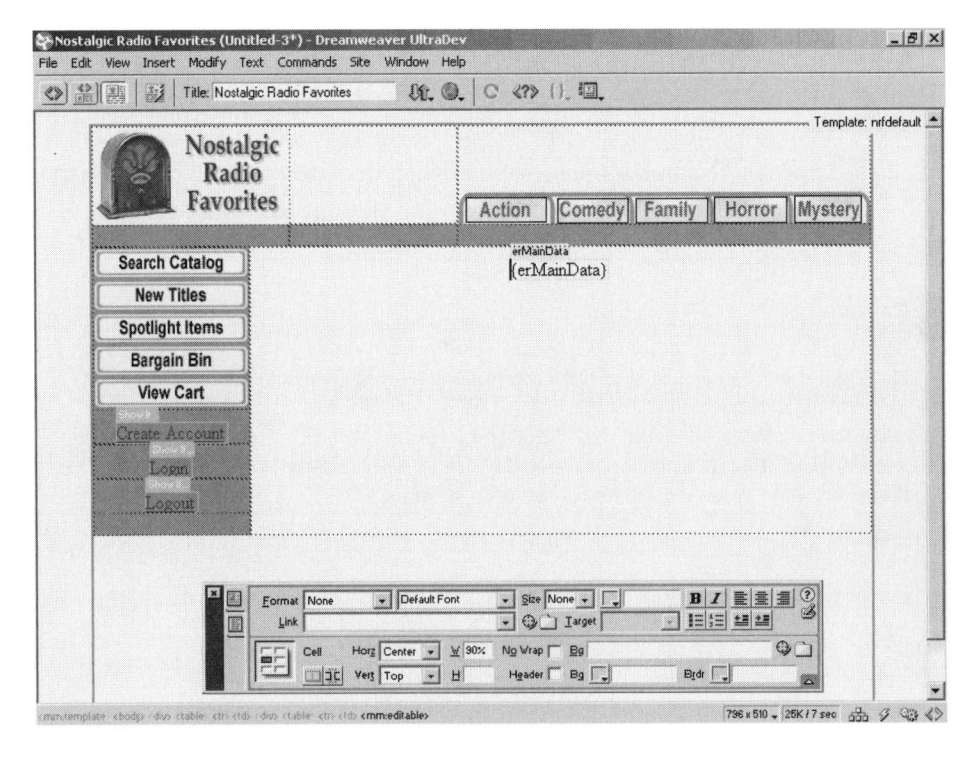

Figure 8.5   A new page has been created from the template.

3. In the erMainData editable region, highlight the {erMainData} text and delete it. In the editable region, type **Create New User Account**.

Chapter 8 Creating Visitor Accounts Through Username Validation   203

4. Highlight the text and select Heading 1 from the Format dropdown on the Property inspector. In addition, select Arial, Helvetica, sans serif as the font style and **3** for the font size. Click the Bold button.

5. Place the insertion point at the end of the line and press Enter. From the menu bar, select Modify/Templates/Detach from Template. As shown in Figure 8.6, the editable regions are removed from the page.

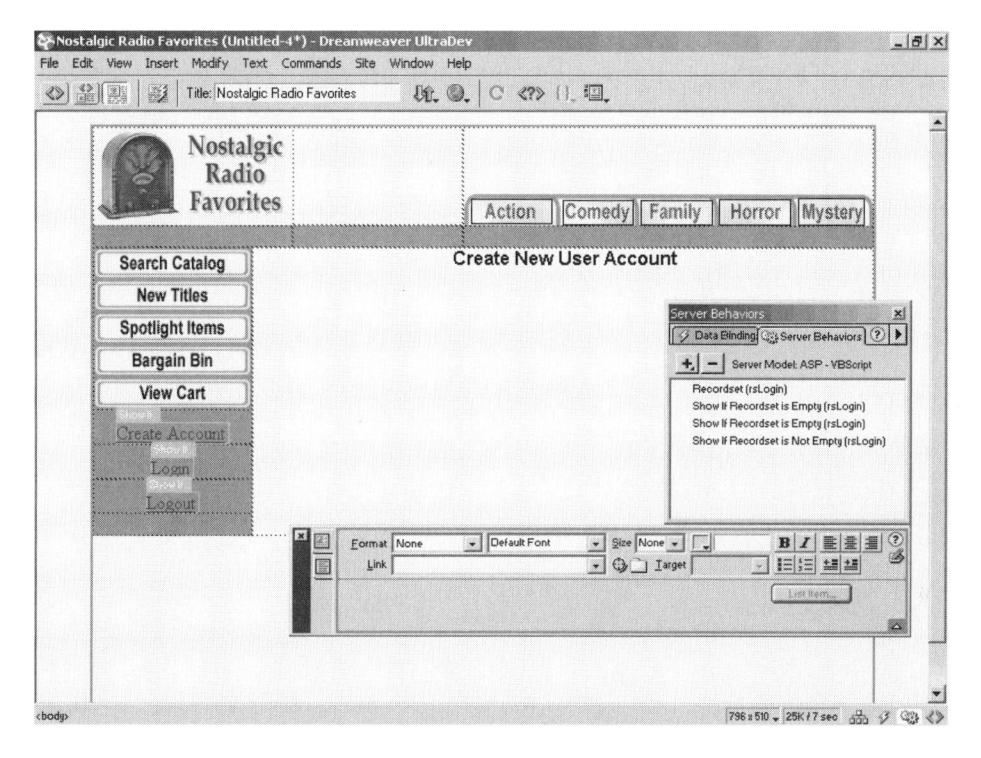

Figure 8.6 The page has been detached from the template.

6. Save your page in the root directory of your InsideUD4 site. The filename should be newuser.asp.

> **Tip**
>
> **Tracking Pages that Don't Rely on Templates**   Creating a page from a template is a quick way to maintain uniformity across your site. Keep in mind, however, that any pages you detach from the template won't be updated when you change the template. For this reason, it's a good idea to make a note on your site map when you detach a page. This serves as a reminder to manually make the updates to the detached pages whenever you update your templates.

Adding the Input Form

The next step to creating your new user account page is to add a signup form that includes the appropriate text labels, text fields, and buttons. Whereas a typical new user account might ask a user to enter personal information, demographic information, and account information (such as username and password), a new user account form can ask for as little or as much information as your organization needs. The only requirement is that your database have a table with a single field established where the data entered into the form can be stored. Once you have created the appropriate fields in your database, you can use UltraDev menus to develop your signup form with a few clicks of your mouse.

Exercise 8.3 Adding an Input Form to the New User Account Page

1. In the newuser.asp page, place the insertion point on the line below your Header text.
2. From the menu bar, select Insert/Form. As shown in Figure 8.7, UltraDev places a blank form in the editable region indicated by a red, dashed border.

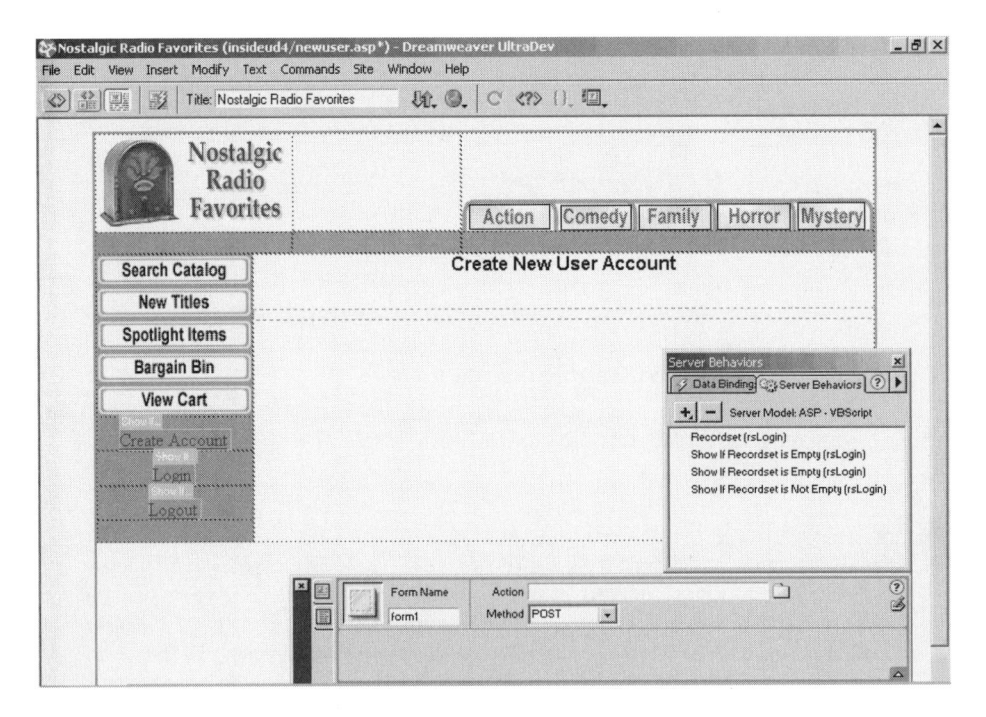

Figure 8.7 A form has been added to the page.

Chapter 8 Creating Visitor Accounts Through Username Validation 205

3. In the Property inspector, type **fmNewuser** into the Form Name field. If you do not see the Form Name field, the form is not selected. To select the form, click anywhere on the form's red border.

4. With the form selected, choose Insert/Table from the menu bar. Add a table with **11** rows, **2** columns, and a width of **100%**. Set the border at **0**. Set the cell padding and cell spacing to **1**. Click OK.

5. Highlight all the cells by clicking in the top-left cell and dragging your cursor to the bottom-right cell. Click the Align Right button on the Property inspector. Set the cell width to **50%** by typing the value in the W field of the Property inspector.

6. Place the insertion point in the top-left cell and type **Choose Username:**. Select Insert/Form Objects/Text Field from the menu bar. As shown in Figure 8.8, UltraDev adds a text field to your form.

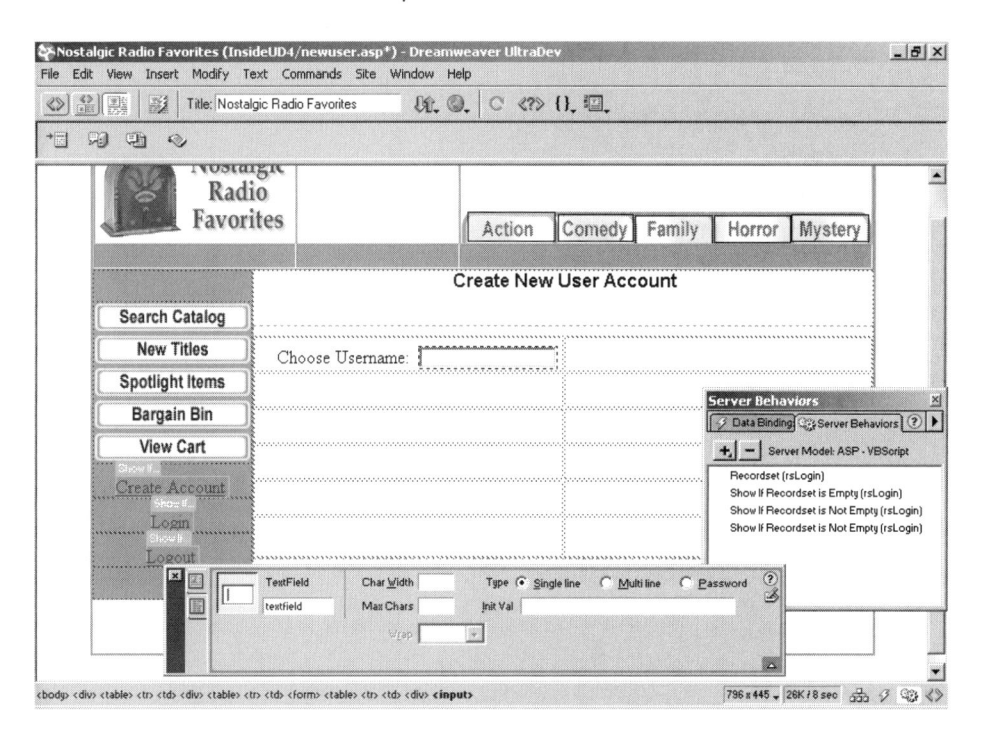

Figure 8.8 The text field has been added.

7. With the text field selected, type **tfUsername** in the TextField field of the Property inspector. Press Enter.

8. Place the insertion point in the top-right cell and type **Choose Password:**. Select Insert/Form Objects/Text Field from the menu bar. Name this text field **tfPassword**.

9. With the tfPassword text field selected, choose the text field type Password from the Property inspector. Selecting the Password type will cause the browser to display an asterisk each time a character is typed rather than the actual character.

> **Tip**
>
> **Verifying Passwords** Although you aren't going to do it in this exercise, you may want to add a Re-enter Password field where the user is required to enter his new password a second time. You can then compare the first password field and the second to ensure that they are identical. Doing this verifies that the user entered what he intended and saves him from the hassle of having to retrieve his password due to a mistyped character.
>
> If you want to add a little script to your page that verifies that the entered passwords match, just create two password fields and name them tfPassword and tfPassword2. Switch to the Code view. Add the following code to the Head section of your page:
>
> ```
> <SCRIPT LANGUAGE = "JavaScript">
>
> function verifyPassword(){
> paswd1 = document.fmNewuser.tfPassword.value;
> paswd2 = document.fmNewuser.tfPassword2.value;
>
> if (paswd1 != paswd2){
> alert("Passwords do not match!");
> document.fmNewuser.tfPassword.focus();
> document.fmNewuser.tfPassword2.select();
> }
> else{
> alert("Your password has been accepted");
> }
> }
> </SCRIPT>
> ```
>
> In addition, you will need to highlight the form and switch to the Code view. Find the line of code that reads
>
> ```
> <form name="fmNewUser" method="post" action="">
> ```
>
> Edit the line to read as follows:
>
> ```
> <form name="fmNewUser" onSubmit="verifyPassword()" method="post"
> ↪action="">
> ```
>
> When the form is submitted, the script is called and checks the contents of the two password fields and then displays an alert as to whether or not the passwords match. Keep in mind that this function relies on the proper naming of your form and password text fields. If your form is not named fmNewuser or your field names are not tfPassword and tfPassword2, the function will fail.

10. Continue filling in the cells using the information shown in Table 8.1. Remember to name each text field and set all text field types to single line.

Table 8.1 Label and Text Field Criteria

Text Field Label	Text Field Name
First Name:	tfFirstname
Last Name:	tfLastname
Street Address:	tfAddress
City:	tfCity
State:	tfState
Zip:	tfZip
Phone Number:	tfPhone
City of Birth:	tfCityofbirth

11. Place the insertion point in the bottom-left cell and choose Insert/Form Objects/Button. In the Property inspector, name the button btSubmit. Leave the label as Submit and the Action as Submit form.

12. Place the insertion point in the bottom-right cell and click the Align Left button on the Property inspector. Choose Insert/Form Objects/Button from the menu bar. Rename the second button btReset and change the label to Reset. Change the button Type to Reset form. Your page should now look like Figure 8.9.

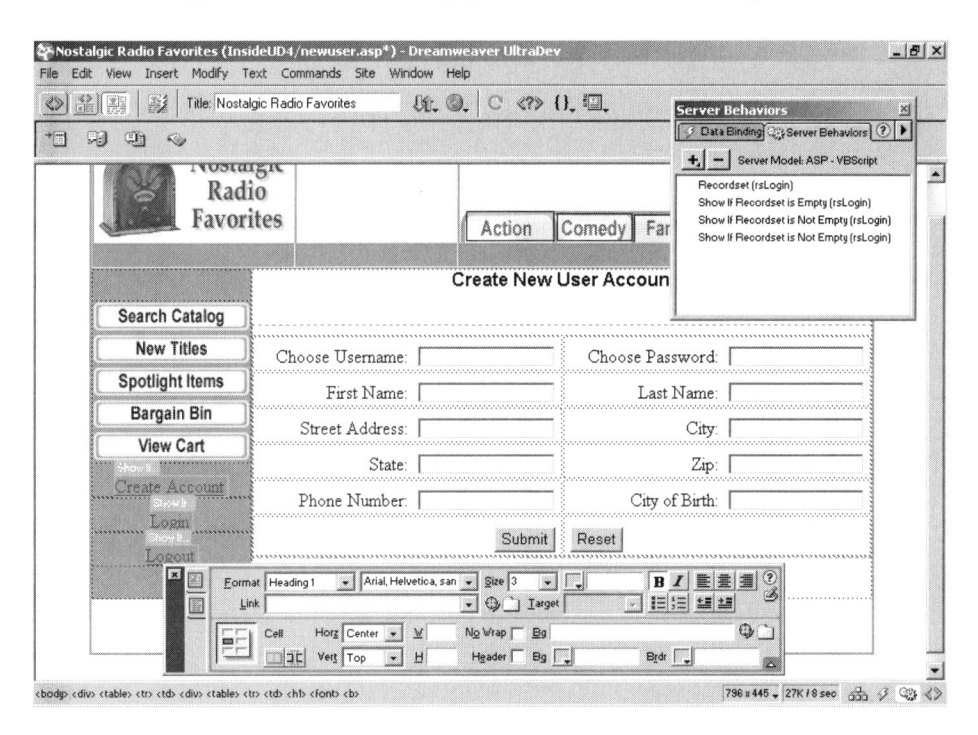

Figure 8.9 The form, table, and form elements have been added.

13. Save your page.

> **Note**
>
> **How Secure Is That Form?** Web site security should always be on the mind of every Web developer. When your users transmit their personal data to your database, they are relying on you to provide them with as much privacy as is appropriate. Unfortunately, some Web developers fail to realize that information submitted via a standard form is available to prying eyes because no encryption is used when the data is transmitted.
>
> Therefore, when the need arises to transfer confidential information such as credit card information or social security numbers, or other highly personal information, Web developers should consider the use of a Secure Sockets Layer (SSL) connection. SSL is a protocol developed by Netscape that provides a secure connection between the visitor's Web browser and the Web server by encrypting any information transmitted between the two.
>
> If you will be collecting information beyond traditional "directory" information (such as name, address, and phone number), you might consider looking into adding SSL functionality to your site. For more information on SSL, check out
>
> `http://home.netscape.com/security/techbriefs/ssl.html`

Verifying That Required Fields Are Filled

When you are considering what data you would like to collect from your visitors, you might also want to decide what information should be required to create a new user account. For instance, if you are shipping a product to the user, his street address, city, state, and zip would obviously be necessary. In other instances, you may need his phone number, credit card number, or some other information. In any case, it's likely that information such as the new username and password will always be required.

To verify that the visitor has entered data into a specific field, you can use the UltraDev form validation behavior. With this behavior, JavaScript is used to verify whether or not a value has been entered into a text field and whether the entered data is a number, an email address, or falls within a range of numbers. Because the validation process takes place on the client side, prior to submitting the data to the database, the visitor will be notified if a required field has been left empty. The information can be changed and resubmitted.

> **Tip**
>
> **Advanced Form Validation** If you want a more advanced form validation option, check out the JavaScript Integration Kit extension found on the Dreamweaver Exchange. Although this extension says it is for Flash 5, installing it in UltraDev gives you added password validation options.

Exercise 8.4 Verifying Form Fields

1. In the newuser.asp page, select the fmNewuser form by clicking on the red border. Open the Behaviors panel by choosing Window/Behaviors from the menu bar.
2. Click the plus sign on the Behaviors panel and choose Validate Form.
3. From the Validate Form dialog box, shown in Figure 8.10, highlight each entry in the list one at a time and click the Required checkbox. This results in requiring the visitor to fill in every text box before the form can be submitted.

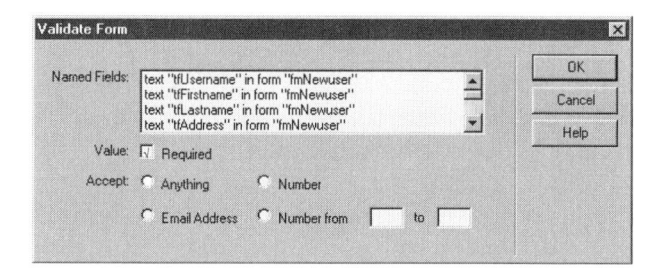

Figure 8.10 The Validate Form dialog box ensures that required fields are filled.

4. Click OK to close the Validate Form dialog box.
5. Close the Behaviors panel.

> **Note**
>
> **Using JavaScript for Form Validation** Although UltraDev makes it very easy to validate a form using the built-in behavior, there is a downside. Since the form validation behavior uses JavaScript, it can be disabled on the browser side. Those who have disabled JavaScript in the browser may be able to slip in entries that are not complete. Your alternative is to employ server-side scripting, such as a CGI Script. This, however, places a larger load on the Web server and may slow down your site's performance.
>
> My suggestion is to give the JavaScript behavior a try. If you find numerous incomplete forms, consider switching to a CGI form.

Submitting the Data to the Database

After the visitor fills in the form and clicks the Submit button, you want the data to be placed into the appropriate database fields. To accomplish this, UltraDev provides the Insert Record server behavior that does all the work for you. All you have to do is tell UltraDev which database it should connect to and then specify which form field should be linked to which database field and UltraDev does the rest.

Exercise 8.5 Linking Form Fields to the Appropriate Database Fields

1. If it is not already visible, open the Server Behaviors panel.
2. Click the plus sign on the Server Behaviors panel and choose Insert Record from the drop-down menu.
3. In the Insert Record dialog box, shown in Figure 8.11, select the connSales_Database connection.

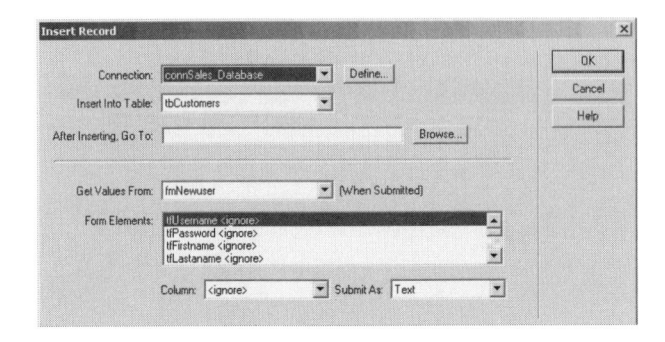

Figure 8.11 The Insert Record dialog box helps you add your form's contents to the database.

4. From the Insert Into Table dropdown, choose the tbCustomers table.
5. In the After Inserting/Go To field, type **newuser_confirmation.asp**.
6. Select the fmNewuser form from the Get Values From drop-down menu.
7. In the Form Elements panel, highlight the tfUsername element. In the Column field, choose the CustomerID column. As shown in Figure 8.12, the Element now shows that the information stored in tfUsername will be inserted into the CustomerID column.

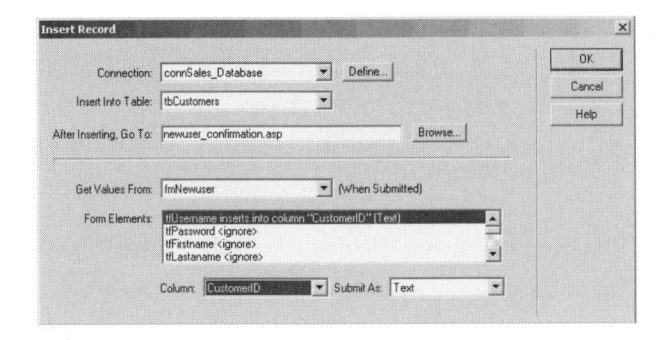

Figure 8.12 The tfUsername field is now linked to the CustomerID column of the database.

8. Using the values in Table 8.2, assign the appropriate form element to the column. Each value should be submitted as text to the database.

Table 8.2 Form Elements and Their Corresponding Columns

Form Element	Database Column
TfPassword	Password
tfFirstname	First_Name
tfLastname	Last_Name
tfAddress	Address
tfCity	City
tfState	State
tfZip	Zip
tfPhone	Phone
tfCityofbirth	City_of_birth

> **Caution**
>
> **Duplicate Insert Entries** Be very careful when assigning your form elements to their corresponding columns. If you assign multiple form elements to update the same column, the insert action will fail and you will receive a nasty error message notifying you that updating a single column from multiple form elements is not allowed.

9. Click OK to close the Insert Record dialog box.
10. Save your page.

Avoiding Duplicate Usernames

Now that your have your form tied to your database fields, you need to make sure that the username the visitor has chosen is unique. To do this, use the UltraDev Check New Username server behavior. When the behavior is applied to a form field, UltraDev adds a function to your page that searches the specified username field for an entry that matches the one entered into the form. If the username already exists, the visitor is redirected to a new page where they are notified of the problem.

Exercise 8.6 Checking for Duplicate Names

1. In the Server Behaviors panel, click the plus sign and choose User Authentication/Check New Username from the drop-down menu.
2. In the Check New Username dialog box, shown in Figure 8.13, select tfUsername from the Username Field dropdown.
3. In the If Already Exists, Go To field, type **username_taken.asp**. Click OK.
4. Save your newuser.asp page.
5. From the menu bar, select File/New From Template. In the Select Template dialog box, choose the InsideUD4 site and the nrfdefault template. Click Select.

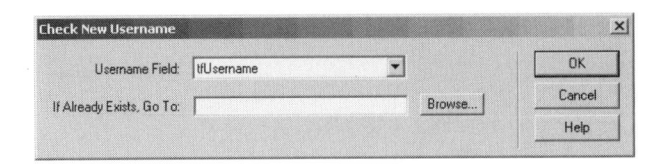

Figure 8.13 The Check New Username dialog box allows you to avoid duplicate usernames.

6. With the new page displayed, select Modify/Templates/Detach From Template. You are detaching this page from the template because you are going to use a JavaScript behavior that needs to be placed in the Head section of the document.

7. Highlight the {erMainData} text and delete it.

8. With the insertion point placed where the erMainData text was, choose Insert/Table from the menu bar. Add a table that has **2** rows, **1** column, and a width of **80%**. Set the border, cell spacing, and cell padding to **0**. Click OK.

9. Highlight both cells by clicking in the top cell and dragging your cursor to the bottom cell. Click the Align Center button on the Property inspector.

10. In the top cell, type the following text block:

    We're sorry, but the username you have selected has already been taken. Please click the Back button on your browser's button bar or click the link below to return to the form and choose a different username.

11. In the bottom cell, type **Return to the form**. Higlight this text and type a pound sign (#) in the Link field of the Property inspector. This converts the text to a link that has no destination. Press Enter. Your page should now look like Figure 8.14.

12. To create a link that performs the same function as the browser's Back button, we call a simple JavaScript function. Open the Behaviors panel by choosing Window/Behaviors.

13. With the text still highlighted, click the plus sign on the Behaviors panel and choose Call JavaScript.

14. In the Call JavaScript dialog box, shown in Figure 8.15, type **history.back();**. Click the OK button.

15. Save the page as **username_taken.asp**.

Adding a Confirmation Page

The final step in developing the new user registration process is to create a confirmation page that lets the new user know that his account was created successfully. A well-designed confirmation page not only informs the user that no errors occurred in the process, but also provides the user with his first opportunity to log in.

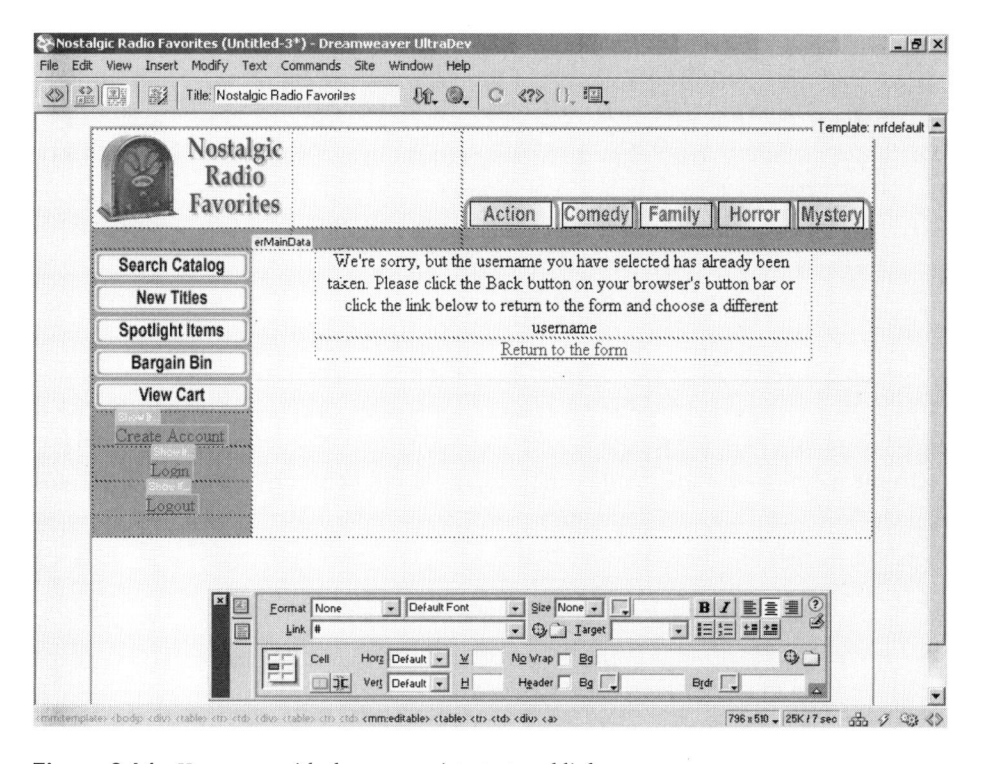

Chapter 8 Creating Visitor Accounts Through Username Validation 213

Figure 8.14 Your page with the appropriate text and link.

Figure 8.15 The Call JavaScript dialog box allows you to add custom scripts to your pages.

Exercise 8.7 Creating a Confirmation Page

1. From the menu bar, select File/New From Template. In the Select Template dialog box, choose the InsideUD4 site and the nrfdefault template. Click Select.
2. Highlight the {erMainData} text and delete it.
3. With the insertion point placed where the erMainData text was, choose Insert/Table from the menu bar. Add a table that has **2** rows, **1** column, and a width of **80%**. Set the border, cell spacing, and cell padding to **0**. Click OK.
4. Highlight both cells by clicking in the top cell and dragging your cursor to the bottom cell. Click the Align Center button on the Property inspector.

5. In the top cell, type the following text block:

   Congratulations! Your account has been created successfully and your information has been added to our database.

6. Place the insertion point in the bottom cell and type **To log in for the first time, click here.**

7. Highlight the words "click here." In the Link field of the Property inspector, type **login.asp**. Press Enter.

8. Save the page as **newuser_confirmation.asp**.

Allowing Returning Visitors to Log In and Out

Now that visitors have the opportunity to create their own user accounts, it's time to give them the means to use them. Although a login form may seem like just a simple form that checks to see if the username and password match the values stored in the database, there is actually a lot more to it than that.

When a visitor logs in to your site, he should then be able to view all of the pages that were previously restricted to the general public. This means that you somehow have to let all the pages in the site know that this user has successfully entered his username and password and has been admitted to the site.

To accomplish this, insert a small piece of code into your login page that stores a small text file, also known as a *cookie*, on the visitor's hard drive. This cookie is updated as the user actively navigates the site. By default, the session expires once the visitor leaves the site, closes his Web browser, or is idle for 20 minutes.

The only downside to using cookies to maintain a session is the fact that visitors can set their browsers to stop cookies from being placed on their computer. If your site relies upon cookies to maintain a session, a visitor who has cookies disabled won't be able to effectively navigate your site.

Exercise 8.8 Creating a Login Form

1. Create a new page from the nrfdefault template. Close any other open pages. Close the Behaviors panel.

2. Highlight the {erMainData} text and type the following text:

   Welcome Back! Please use the following form to log in to our site.

3. Press Enter.

4. From the menu bar, select Insert/Form. Name the Form **fmLogin**.

> **Tip**
>
> **Allowing Access to Your Pages by Passing Variables** Another way to give visitors access to your pages after they are authenticated is to pass a variable from page to page. Each page would then check whether that variable exists in the database and allow access to the page when appropriate. A variable is passed from one page to another by appending the variable to the URL for the page.
>
> For instance, suppose you clicked on a link to http://localhost/insideud4/newpage.asp and you are an authenticated user. The original page could pass your username to the next page by changing the link to http://localhost/insideud4/newpage.asp?username=yourusername. The newpage.asp document would then understand that you are allowed access to the page and would enable you to view its content.
>
> This method, however, has its drawbacks. While it may be useful for passing small variables from page to page, it quickly becomes cumbersome when passing a large number of variables from page to page. For instance, suppose you wanted to give your visitors the ability to maintain a shopping cart that lasted throughout their sessions. As they moved through the site adding items to their carts, the list of variables being passed from page to page could become huge. The more effective approach would be to create a session using a cookie, and to store the shopping cart information in the cookie. Because some servers place a limit on the maximum number of characters that can be placed in a URL, this effectively restricts the viability of this method for passing large amounts of data.
>
> Another disadvantage of passing URL parameters is that they could pass sensitive information such as passwords or credit card information in a visible manner. In cases where you are passing sensitive information, you are much better off using session variables or cookies. This way, the sensitive information is stored on the user's computer in a much more secure manner.

5. With the form selected, select Insert/Table from the menu bar. Create a table that has **3** rows, **2** columns, and a width of **50%**. Set the border, cell padding and cell spacing to **1**. Click OK.

6. Select the cells in the left column by moving your cursor to the top of the left column. When your cursor becomes a downward-pointing arrow, click the mouse button.

7. On the Property inspector, click the Align Right button.

8. Select the cells in the right column and click the Align Left button on the Property inspector.

9. In the top-left cell, type **Username:**. In the middle-left cell, type **Password:**.

10. Place the insertion point in the top-right cell and select Insert/Form Objects/Text Field from the menu bar. Name the new text field **tfCustomerID**.

11. In the middle-right cell, add an additional text field and name it **tfPassword**. In the Property inspector, set the text field type to Password.

12. In the bottom-left cell, add a submit button by choosing Insert/Form Objects/Button. Name the button **btSubmit**. Press Enter.

216 Part III Developing a Data-Driven Web Site

13. Add a Reset Form button to the bottom-right cell. Name the button **btReset**. Your page should now look like Figure 8.16. Press Enter.

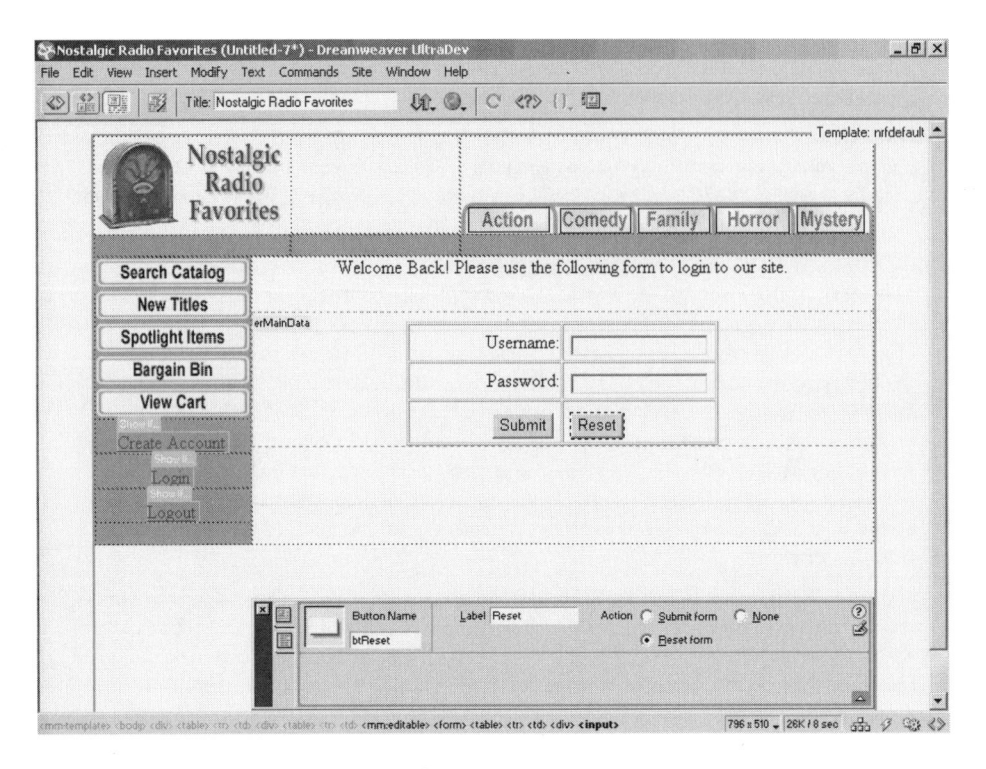

Figure 8.16 Your page with the login form.

14. Highlight the form by clicking on the red border. In the Property inspector, type **validation.asp** in the Action field. Press Enter.
15. Place the insertion point below the bottom border of the form and type **Click here to create an account**. Select the text and type **newuser.asp** in the Link field of the Property inspector. Press Enter.
16. Save the page as **login.asp**.

Once the form is successfully submitted and the username/password combination is validated or denied, the visitor is automatically redirected to a page that lets him know whether he was successfully logged on. This page also has the added functionality of creating the user's session and storing his session information on his local hard drive if he is successfully logged on.

> **Note**
>
> **UltraDev's Log In User Server Behavior** It's probably worth mentioning that UltraDev does include a Log In User server behavior that is easy to apply to a form. This behavior checks whether the username and password match those stored in the database and then redirects the visitor based on whether he was authenticated.
>
> The behavior, however, has two major drawbacks. First, it does not allow Web developers to pass request variables in any way. This means that the behavior is really only good for protecting one page at a time. Second, UltraDev has identified a bug in the behavior that can compromise the security of your site. For more information on these problems, check out the following articles:
>
> Passing form data from a login page to successive pages is unsuccessful
>
> http://www.macromedia.com/support/ultradev/ts/documents/loginformdata.htm
>
> and
>
> Log in user server behavior security issue
>
> http://www.macromedia.com/support/ultradev/ts/documents/login_sb_security.htm

Exercise 8.9 Adding a Validation Page

1. From the nrfdefault template, create a new page. Close the Login.asp page.
2. Delete the {erMainData} text and insert a table that consists of **2** rows, **1** column, and a width of **80%**. Set the border, cell padding, and cell spacing at **0**. Click OK.
3. Highlight both cells and click the Align Center button on the Property inspector.
4. In the top cell of the table, type the following text block:

    You were successfully logged in. Please click here to continue viewing our site as an authenticated user.

5. Highlight the "click here" text and type **default.asp** in the Link field of the Property inspector. Press Enter.
6. In the bottom cell, type the following text:

    We're sorry, but we were unable to validate your username and password. Please click the Back button on your browser's button bar to return to the login form.

7. Just as you did earlier with your dynamic login and logout links, the goal here is to display only the text that is appropriate depending on whether the login information submitted in the form was correct. Highlight the text in the top cell and click the plus sign on the Server Behaviors panel. From the menu, select Show Region/Show Region If Recordset Is Not Empty.

8. From the following dialog box, select the rsLogin recordset. Click OK.
9. Highlight the text in the bottom cell and click the plus sign on the Server Behaviors panel. From the menu, select Show Region/Show Region If Recordset Is Empty.
10. From the following dialog box, select the rsLogin recordset and click OK.
11. Highlight the text in the top cell and switch to the Source Code view by clicking the Show Code View button on the button bar. This code, shown in Figure 8.17, displays the text only if the user has been properly authenticated.

```
149    <% If Not rsLogin.EOF Or Not rsLogin.BOF Then %>
150    You were successfully logged in. Please <a href="default.asp">click
151    here</a> to continue viewing our site as an authenticated
152    user.
153    <% End If ' end Not rsLogin.EOF Or NOT rsLogin.BOF %>
```

Figure 8.17 The code in your page that displays the successful login message if the user is properly authenticated.

12. After the first line of this code, add the following lines:

    ```
    <%session("MM_Username")=rsLogin.Fields.Item("tfCustomerID").Value%>
    <%session("MM_Password")=rsLogin.Fields.Item("Password").Value%>
    ```

    Press Enter. Your code block should now look like Figure 8.18.

```
<% If Not rsLogin.EOF Or Not rsLogin.BOF Then %>
<%session("MM_Username")=Request.Form("tfUsername")%>
You were successfully logged in. Please <a href="default.asp">click
here</a> to continue viewing our site as an authenticated
user.
<% End If ' end Not rsLogin.EOF Or NOT rsLogin.BOF %>
```

Figure 8.18 After adding the code to create a session, your code should look like this.

Because this session will be used in conjunction with one of UltraDev's built-in server behaviors to restrict access to certain pages, it is important that you give the session the MM_Username name. Selecting a different name would result in the server behavior failing to restrict access.

13. Switch back to the Show Design View and notice that UltraDev has added a yellow ASP marker to your page. Save the page as **validation.asp**.

The final step in the login process is to provide visitors with the ability to log out. Although their sessions will close after an extended length of inactivity or whenever they close their browser windows, it's always a good idea to give your visitors the ability to manually close their sessions. This specifically protects visitors who may be surfing your site from public computers at a library or a student computer lab.

Since you added the logout link earlier, the only thing left to do is to add the logout page. This page simply thanks the visitor for logging out and uses one of UltraDev's server behaviors to close the user's session.

Exercise 8.10 Creating a Logout Page

1. Using the nrfdefault template, create a new page. Close the Validation.asp page.
2. In the new page, replace the {erMainData} text with the following text block:

   Your session has ended. Thanks for visiting our site. Feel free to log back in by clicking the Login link.
3. On the Server Behaviors panel, click the plus symbol and choose User Authentication/Log Out User from the menu.
4. In the Log Out User dialog box, shown in Figure 8.19, select Log Out When: Page Loads. Leave the When Done, Go To field blank and click OK.

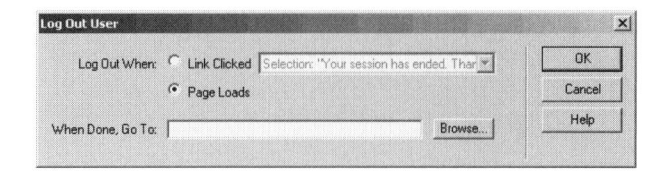

Figure 8.19 The Log Out User dialog box lets you dictate when the user is logged out.

5. Save the page as **logout.asp**.

Protecting Pages from Unauthenticated Visitors

The final piece of adding user authentication to your site is to protect those pages that should not be available to unauthenticated visitors. Since you created a session using the visitor's username as the session variable that is passed from page to page, you can add one of UltraDev's server behaviors to the protected pages that verifies that the user has entered a valid username and password prior to requesting the protected page.

Exercise 8.11 Restricting Access to a Page

1. Using the nrfdefault template, create a new page. Close the Logout.asp page.
2. Remove the {erMainData} text and replace it with the following text block:

   Welcome to your shopping cart. Because you were properly authenticated, you are able to see this page.

3. On the Server Behaviors panel, click the plus sign and select User Authentication/Restrict Access To Page.
4. In the Restrict Access To Page dialog box, shown in Figure 8.20, choose to restrict the page based on Username and Password. In the If Access Denied, Go To field, type **http://localhost/insideud4/login.asp**.

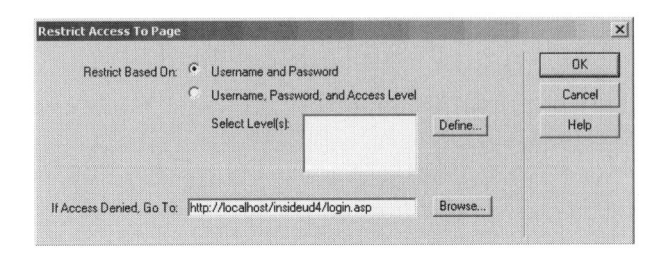

Figure 8.20 The Restrict Access To Page dialog box keeps unauthenticated visitors from viewing content.

5. Click OK. Save the page in the root of your site as **view_cart.asp**.

Testing Your New Pages

Are you ready to view the fruits of your labor? Now that you have added all the required recordsets, forms, and behaviors to your pages, you are ready to test them. Although this section takes a brief look at the results of the chapter exercises, I highly recommend that you take some time to play around with the new pages you've developed. Understanding what your visitors will see when they attempt to log on can help you streamline your pages and make them as user-friendly as possible.

Exercise 8.12 Testing the User Account Pages

1. Close all of your pages and close UltraDev.
2. Open your Web browser and enter **http://localhost/insideud4/default.asp** in the address field.
3. As shown in Figure 8.21, you should now see your home page with the Create Account and Login links showing. Because you have not logged in, the Logout link is hidden.
4. Click the View Cart button. Because you are not an authenticated user, you are automatically redirected to the login.asp page.
5. Click the Create Account link on the left side of your page. The Create New User Account page now allows you to enter your information and create a user account.

Chapter 8 Creating Visitor Accounts Through Username Validation   221

> **Note**
>
> **Taking Care of Orphaned Pages** As I mentioned earlier, when it comes to updating pages built using templates, UltraDev doesn't do a very good job of transferring recordsets to older pages. Because of this, it's probably a good idea to do a little cleanup before you test your pages.
>
> Prior to this chapter, you have built six pages that rely on your nrfdefault template:
>
> - new_titles.asp
> - new_titles_details.asp
> - spotlight_items.asp
> - spotlight_items_details.asp
> - bargain_bin.asp
> - bargain_bin_details.asp
>
> When you try to access each of these pages in your browser, you may receive an error. If you do, open your nrfdefault.dwt page and open the Server Behaviors panel. Right-click on the rsLogin recordset and choose Copy from the pop-up menu.
>
> Next, open each of the six pages, right-click in the Server Behaviors panel and click Paste. Save each page and the problem should now be resolved.

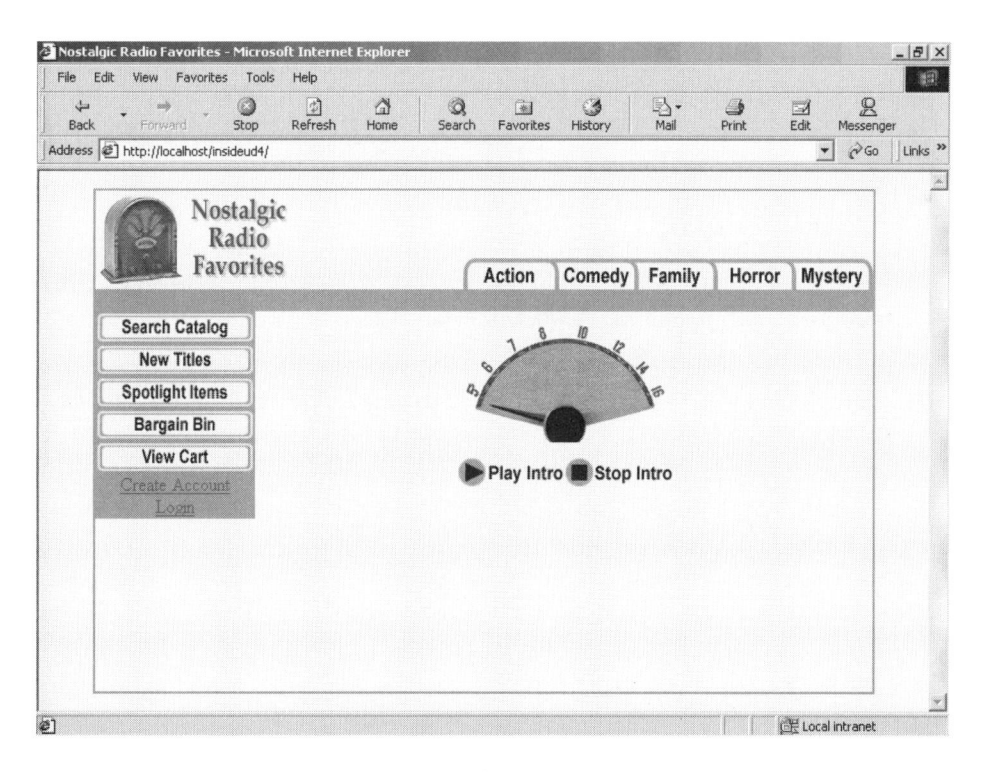

Figure 8.21 Your home page with dynamic links in place.

6. In the Choose Username field, type **testuser**.
7. Click the Submit button. Because all the required fields have not been completed, a pop-up message, shown in Figure 8.22, lets you know that you need to finish filling out the form.

Figure 8.22 An alert informing you that the required fields have not been filled in.

8. Click OK to close the pop-up box.
9. In the Choose Password field, type **testuser**. Because the field was designated as a password field, the actual text is replaced by asterisks.
10. Fill in the rest of the form as shown in Figure 8.23.
11. Click the Submit button. Having submitted a form that did not contain a username already in the database and with every field filled, you should now see the new user confirmation page shown in Figure 8.24.
12. Click the text that reads "click here" to login using the account you just created.
13. In the login form, type **testuser** for the username and **testuser** for the password. Click the Submit button. You should now see the validation.asp page letting you know that you successfully logged in.
14. Click the Logout button that is now visible on the left side of the page. As shown in Figure 8.25, UltraDev ends your session.

Figure 8.23 Complete the new user account form using this information.

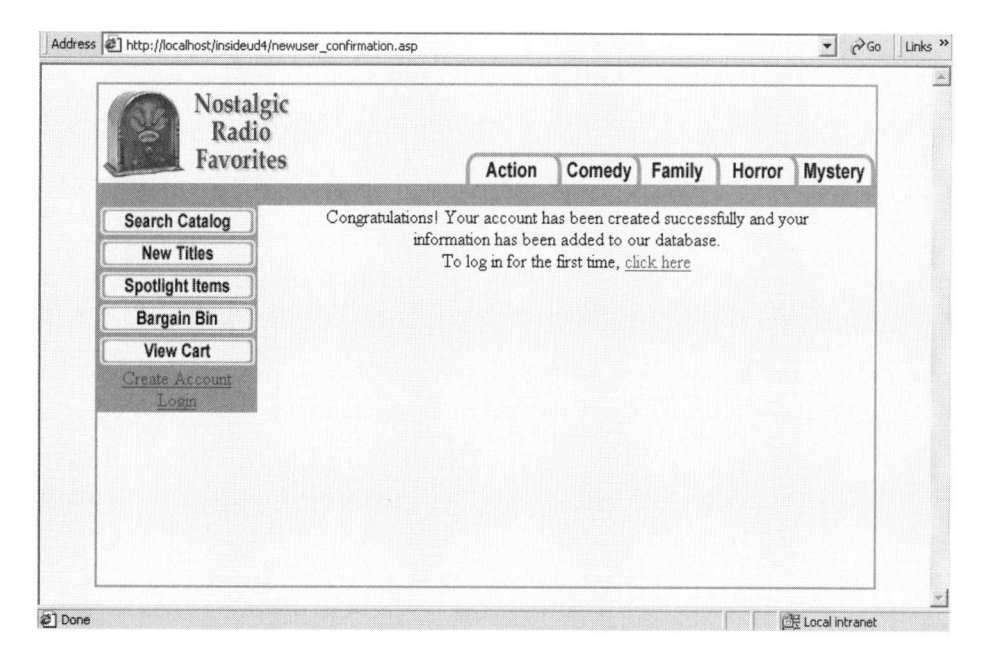

Figure 8.24 Congratulations! You've added a new user to the database.

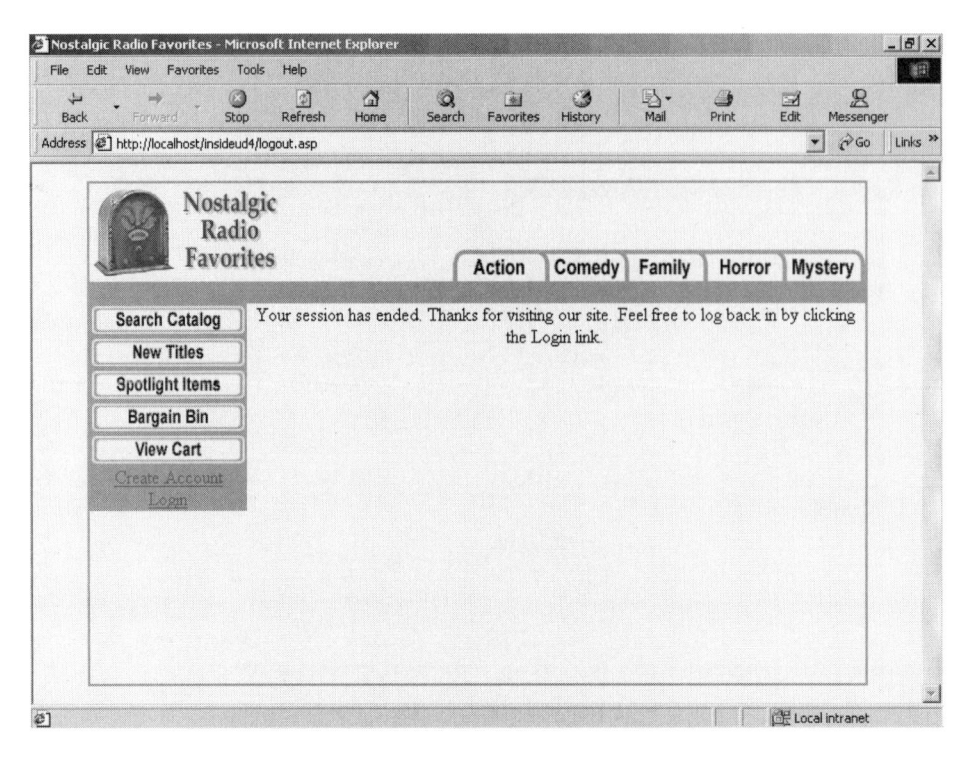

Figure 8.25 The logout page confirms that your session has ended.

Summary

This chapter demonstrated how to add pages to your site that allow visitors to create their own user accounts. In addition, it discussed adding dynamic links to your site, developing session variables, and protecting pages from unauthorized visitors.

The next chapter takes a look at adding search capabilities to your site and shows you how to allow your visitors to search your site using input forms.

Chapter 9

Building Search Capabilities

You've done it! You just finished putting the final touches on the new line of products that will change the world as we know it. Or maybe you just want to increase your sales by 200% by making your products available on the Web. All that stands between you and total success is a way to let your customers see and order your products.

So what's next? You could create a single Web page that lists every product you offer, complete with description and photo, but that would take hours to load. How about building a page for each product and then creating and maintaining a page that links to each of the product pages? Yeah, right! Like you have that much spare time.

The solution is to take advantage of UltraDev's database-connectivity features: Put all your products and their pertinent information into a single, easy-to-maintain database and create a page that allows your visitors to search the database using the keywords criteria that they choose. Sound difficult? Not with UltraDev!

To show you just how easy it is to build a variety of search applications using UltraDev, this chapter focuses on the following:

- Building a single parameter search
- Building a restricted simple search
- Adding advanced search capabilities

Whether it's searching your product catalog or helping a visitor recall their password, UltraDev's server behaviors will have the search section of your Web site up and running in no time.

Building a Single Parameter Search

The most basic search that a visitor may want to conduct is a single parameter search. Single parameter searches query a database using a single piece of data and return only the fields that contain a match. Often, the search criteria are built into a link and when the visitor clicks the link, the server simply collects the data from the link and then returns any matching results.

Adding Links that Conduct the Search

Using the Nostalgic Radio Favorites site as an example, suppose visitors might want the ability to quickly view all titles that fall under a specific genre, such as comedy or action. To provide them with this, you can simply create a link with a search term included in it that sends the visitor directly to a results page. This page then takes the search term from the URL or the page and returns all records that have a genre equal to the search term.

Constructing these links in UltraDev is not much different than creating a traditional link. All you have to do is append the proper search criteria to the end of the regular link and then make sure that the target page understands how to interpret the search term that is being passed.

Exercise 9.1 Creating Links that Run Single Parameter Searches

1. Open the nrfdefault.dwt template located in the Templates folder of the InsideUD4 site.
2. Select the hotspot located over the Action tab at the top the page. As shown in Figure 9.1, hotspots are, by default, indicated by a light blue highlight covering the hotspot region. If you do not have a hotspot located over the Action tab, refer to Chapter 5, "The Dreamweaver in Dreamweaver UltraDev," for information on creating hotspots.

Figure 9.1 The hotspots located in the nrfdefault.dwt template.

3. In the Link field of the Property inspector, change the link to **http://localhost/insideud4/genreresults.asp?genre=action**.

   By adding ?genre=action, you are automatically passing the appropriate variable (genre) and value (action) for the genreresults.asp page to interpret. Once the variable is passed, the results page builds the recordset based on the value of the variable.

4. Using Table 9.1, change the Comedy, Family, Horror, and Mystery hotspots to link to the genreresults.asp page using the appropriate variables and values.

Table 9.1 Hotspot links for the single parameter search

Hotspot	Link
Comedy	`http://localhost/insideud4/genreresults.asp?genre=comedy`
Family	`http://localhost/insideud4/genreresults.asp?genre=family`
Horror	`http://localhost/insideud4/genreresults.asp?genre=horror`
Mystery	`http://localhost/insideud4/genreresults.asp?genre=mystery`

5. Save the template.

6. When asked whether dependent pages should be updated, click Yes.
7. Once the pages are updated, close the Update Pages dialog box.

> **Note**
>
> **Don't Forget: Some Pages Aren't Updated by the Template** Remember that we have created several pages that were detached from the template because they needed special JavaScript behaviors that were not accessible when attached to a template. These pages can be easily updated by switching to the Site window and doing a sitewide search and replace.
>
> To do this, just select Edit/Find and Replace from the Site window and have UltraDev replace all instances of `http://localhost/insideud4/action/` with `http://localhost/insideud4/genreresults.asp?genre=action`. You can then replace the Comedy, Family, Horror, and Mystery links the same way.
>
> Be careful, however, when doing a sitewide search and replace. You are able to replace these links because an action folder has not been created and (other than the hotspots) there are no links to pages within the action folder. If we had created pages and links, a sitewide search and replace might not be the best approach since it might replace links that we had not intended to change.
>
> Think of this like a word processing replacement. If you choose to replace all instances of "the" with "hello", you will find words like "hellore", "helloir", and "helloater". (These are the changes to "there", "their", and "theater".) In other words, doing a full site replacement will replace instances of the string, even if the string of text is inside a longer string of text.

Adding the Results Page

Once the links have been created, you need to create the page that displays the results of the single parameter query. The best way to do this is to create a single results page that then "reads" the parameter that is passed through the URL and builds a results table accordingly. This can be done relatively easily using several of the server behaviors discussed in Chapter 7 "Connecting Your Web Site to a Database."

> **Note**
>
> **A Different Approach to Single Parameter Searches** Another way to provide visitors with the results of a specific genre would be to create a file named action.asp that would then have its own recordset that extracts only records that have an action genre specified. This, however, would require you to create five different pages and five different recordsets for the Nostalgic Radio Favorites site. As you can see, using a single parameter search has its advantages because it not only saves time, but also hard drive space.

Chapter 9 Building Search Capabilities 231

Exercise 9.2 Creating a Dynamic Results Page

1. On the menu bar, select File/New Page from Template and create a page based on the nrfdefault template. Close the nrfdefault.dwt page.
2. Delete the {erMainData} text and type **Genre Results**.
3. Highlight the text and select Heading 1 from the Format dropdown on the Property inspector. Set the font to Arial, Helvetica, sans serif and the size to **3**. Click the Bold button.
4. Press the right arrow key to move to the end of the line and press the Enter key to move to a new line.
5. From the menu bar, select Insert/Table. Create a table that has **2** rows, **5** columns and has a width of **90%**. Set the border, cell padding, and cell spacing to **1**.
6. Highlight the cells in the new table by clicking in the top-left cell and dragging your cursor to the bottom-right cell. Click the Align Center button on the Property inspector.
7. In the top-left cell, type **Product Number**. Press the Tab key to move to the next cell.
8. Type **Show Title** in the second cell and press the Tab key.
9. Type **Episode Title** in the third cell and press the Tab key.
10. Type **Genre** in the fourth cell and press the Tab key.
11. Type **Price** in the top-right cell.
12. Select the cells in the top row by clicking in the top-left cell and dragging your cursor to the top-right cell. In the Bg field of the Property inspector that has a color picker next to it, type **#006699** and press Enter.
13. With the top cells still selected, set the Size field on the Property inspector to **3** and type **#FFFFFF** in the field between the Size dropdown and the Bold button. Press Enter to set the text color to white.
14. If necessary, open the Server Behaviors panel by selecting Window/Server Behaviors from the menu bar.
15. On the Server Behaviors panel, click the plus sign and select Recordset (Query) from the popup menu. UltraDev opens the Recordset dialog box, shown in Figure 9.2.

    If you see the Advanced Recordset dialog box instead, click the Simple button.
16. Name the recordset **rsSearch** and select the connSales_Database connection and the tbProducts table.
17. On the Columns panel, click the Selected radio button and click Product_No. Press and hold the Ctrl key and click Title, Episode_Title, Genre, and Price.
18. From the Filter dropdowns, select Genre, =, URL Parameter, and then type **Genre** in the fourth box. Your recordset should now look like Figure 9.3.

232 Part III Developing a Data-Driven Web Site

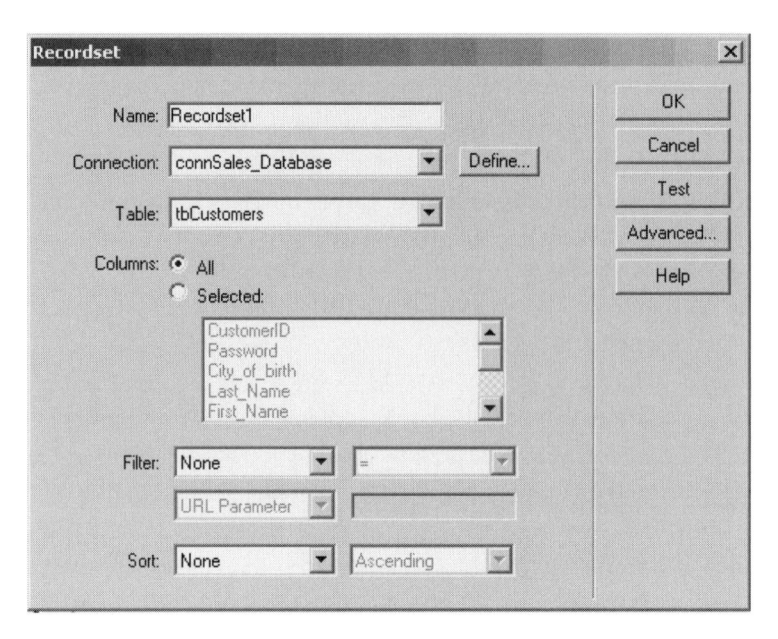

Figure 9.2 The Simple Recordset dialog box.

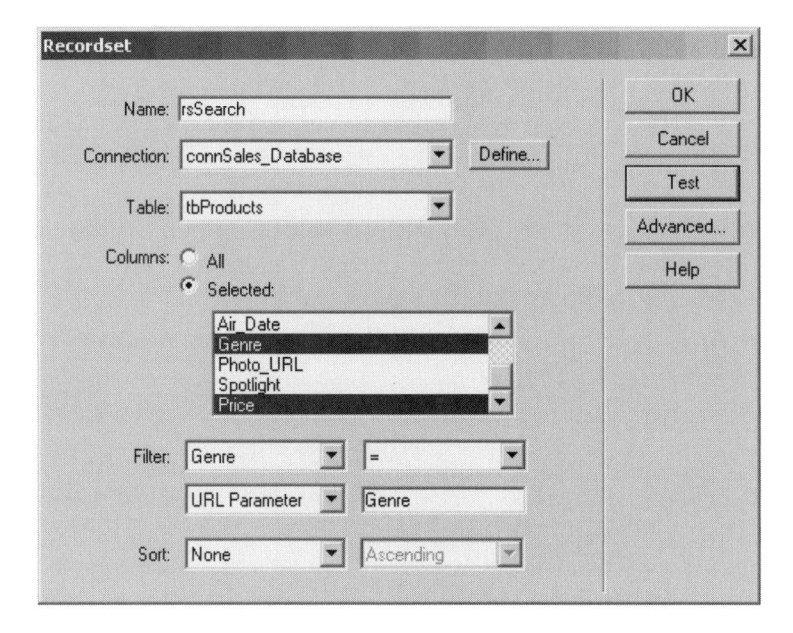

Figure 9.3 The new rsSearch recordset.

19. Click the Test button. Because this recordset relies on a value being passed in the URL, the Please Provide a Test Value dialog box, shown in Figure 9.4, asks for a test value.

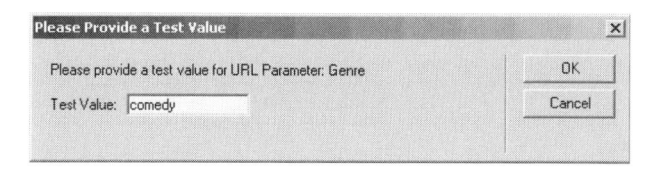

Figure 9.4 Testing the recordset requires a test value.

20. Type **comedy** in the Test Value field and click OK. UltraDev returns the test results shown in Figure 9.5 of all records with a genre value of "comedy."

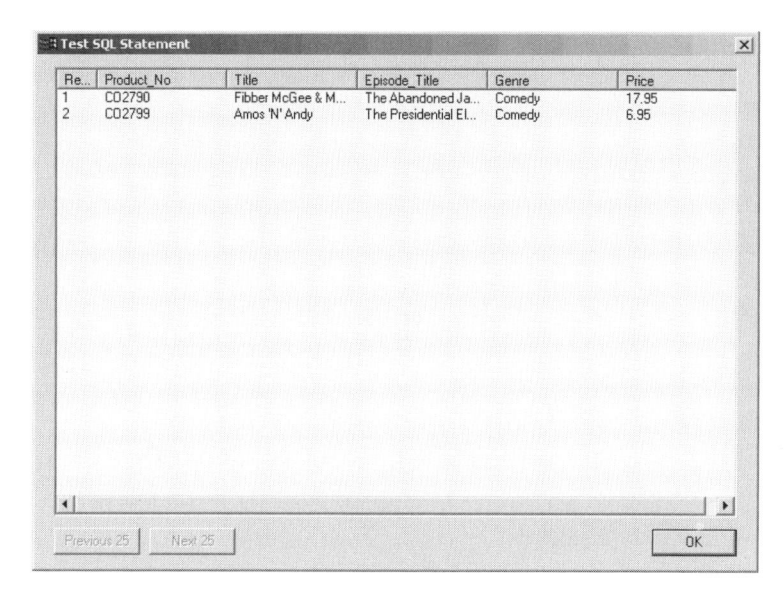

Figure 9.5 The test results using the "comedy" value.

21. Click OK to close the Test SQL Statement dialog box and click OK to close the Recordset dialog box.
22. Click the Data Bindings tab on the Server Behaviors panel and click the plus sign next to the rsSearch recordset.
23. Click Product_No data source and drag it to the bottom cell in the Product Number column of the table in your page.
24. Drag the Title data source to the bottom cell in the Show Title column and drag the Episode_Title, Genre, and Price sources to their appropriate cells. As shown in Figure 9.6, UltraDev inserts placeholders into the fields.
25. Select the bottom row of the table by placing the insertion point inside the page and clicking the <tr> symbol on the status bar. You can also highlight the row by placing your cursor on the left border of the row. When the cursor changes to a black arrow, click to highlight the entire row.

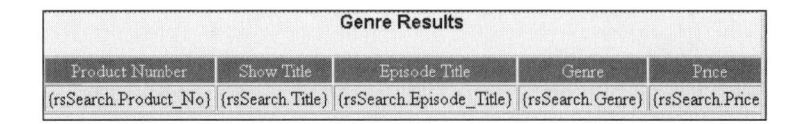

Genre Results				
Product Number	Show Title	Episode Title	Genre	Price
{rsSearch.Product_No}	{rsSearch.Title}	{rsSearch.Episode_Title}	{rsSearch.Genre}	{rsSearch.Price}

Figure 9.6 Placeholders have been inserted into the table.

> **Note**
>
> **Using the Status Bar to Select Nested Tables** Nested tables (tables that are inserted into another table) are a common occurrence in complex Web pages. Unfortunately, when you nest tables, your code can become very confusing. UltraDev has made it easy to select nested tables by adding the tags that define the page's table structure to the left side of the status bar. When you click on any of the table tags, UltraDev will select the appropriate table or table element.
>
> Keep in mind that the table structure of the page moves from left to right with the outermost table tags on the far left and the innermost table tags on the far right. Also, if some of your table tags are grayed out, it is most likely due to the fact that your page relies on tables that are part of a template.

26. Click the Server Behaviors tab on the Data Bindings panel and click the plus sign. Select Repeat Region from the popup menu.
27. In the Repeat Region dialog box, select the rsSearch recordset and click the All Records radio button. Click OK.
28. Save the page as **genreresults.asp** in the root folder of the InsideUD4 site.
29. Minimize UltraDev and open a browser window. In the address bar, type **http://localhost/insideud4**.
30. Click the Comedy button from the category tabs in the top-right section of the page. As shown in Figure 9.7, all records within the Comedy genre are now displayed.

    Take note of the URL that was passed when the link to the page was clicked. Notice that when the link was clicked, the variable and value were passed to the results page to be used in the query.

The last step to finishing off the single parameter search would be to add the proper server behaviors that automatically turn the values in one of the columns into links that take the visitor to a details page. Since you already covered this process in Chapter 7, I'll leave it up to you to finish up the process.

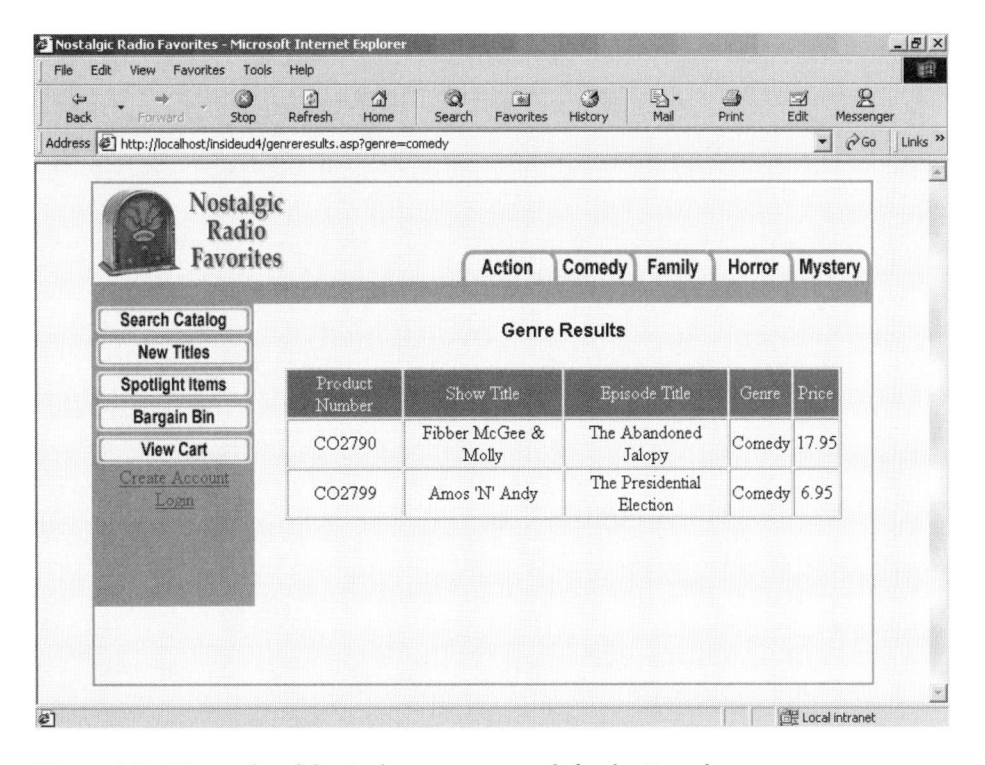

Figure 9.7 The results of the single parameter search for the Comedy genre.

Creating a Restricted Simple Search Page

With privacy issues becoming a growing concern on the Internet, the number of passwords users have to remember is growing beyond belief! From online banking codes to Internet service provider logons to ordering profiles on a hundred different Web sites, Web surfers are constantly being instructed to provide a password. And what happens when they just can't recall that password they created six months ago? Hopefully, the Web developer for the site considered this and developed a method for looking up the password.

These password lookups usually require the entering of the visitor's username and a unique piece of data that the visitor provided when initially creating their account, usually their mother's maiden name, city of birth, or some other identifying criteria.

Because a password lookup usually only requires a couple of search terms, it can still be considered a simple search. In order to be effective and provide the required security, however, certain restrictions have to be placed on the form being submitted. First, all the fields must be completed before the form can be submitted. Second, each piece of data submitted via the form must match the information stored in the Web site's database. Because this search requires only two search terms and the restrictions are placed on the search page and its form, we refer to the search as a restricted simple search.

Building this type of search with UltraDev, however, doesn't take any extra effort. Using UltraDev's form verification behavior, you can specify which fields are required to be filled before the visitor can submit the form. Combined with UltraDev's server behaviors, you can query your database to see if the form contents match the information provided by the visitor when he created his profile. If the information matches, the site can automatically display his password. If the information is incorrect, however, the visitor is notified and asked to try again.

> **Caution**
>
> **Displaying Passwords and SSL** Sending a password to a page that is displayed on the screen is not the most secure method to provide a visitor with their password. However, it is very easy to configure and provides the visitor with instant access to their information. If you want to offer your visitors the convenience of displaying their passwords, I highly recommend that you use a Secure Sockets Layer (SSL) to ensure that the data is protected from prying eyes.
>
> To accomplish this, you need to obtain a Web site security certificate from a company like VeriSign (www.verisign.com). Once you have obtained your certificate, you can then enable SSL security in your Web server software.

Creating Links to the Password Lookup Page

The first step to creating a password lookup system is to give the visitor somewhere to click in order to access the system. Using the Show Region behavior you used to create your dynamic login and logout links, you can add a lost password link that is visible to visitors who haven't logged on yet.

Exercise 9.3 Adding Lost Password Links

1. Open UltraDev. Open the login.asp page that was created in Chapter 8 "Creating Visitor Accounts Through Username Validation."
2. Place the insertion point at the end of the line that reads "Click here to create a new account." Press Enter to move to a new line.
3. On the new line, type **Click here if you forgot your password**.

Chapter 9 Building Search Capabilities 237

4. Highlight the text and type **http://localhost/insideud4/passwordlookup.asp** in the Link field of the property inspector. Press Enter. As shown in Figure 9.8, your page should now include a link to the password lookup page.

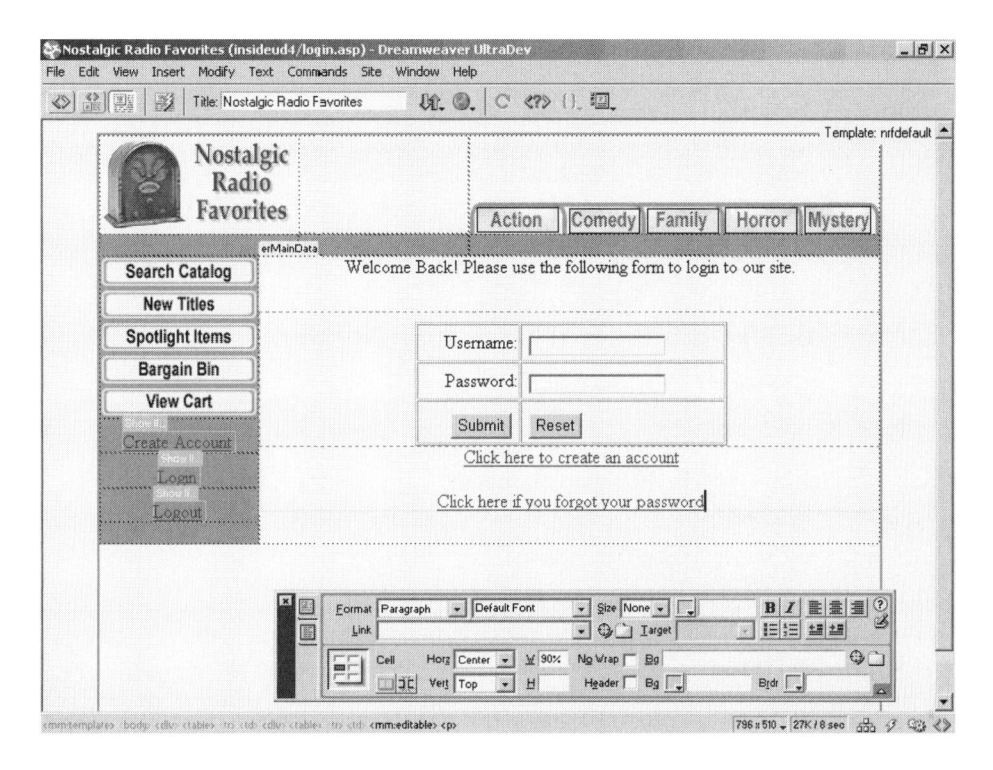

Figure 9.8 The login page with a new password lookup link.

5. Save the file.

Adding the Password Lookup Page

Now that links have been created to help the user get to the password lookup page, you need to create a page that contains a form. To verify that the user is who he claims, the form will ask him to provide his username and city of birth.

Exercise 9.4 Building the Password Lookup Form

1. From the menu bar, select File/New from Template and create a page based on the nrfdefault template in the InsideUD4 site. Close the login.asp page.
2. On the new page, highlight the {erMainData} text and delete it. Type **Password Lookup** and press the Enter key.

3. From the menu bar, select Insert/Form. In the Property inspector, name the form **fmLookup** and type **lookupresults.asp** in the Action field. Press Enter.
4. Click the insertion point inside the form and select Insert/Table. Create a table that has **3** rows, **2** columns, and a width of **60%**. Set the border, cell padding, and cell spacing to **1**.

> **Tip**
>
> **Getting the Insertion Point Inside an Empty Form** When working with forms in UltraDev, sometimes it's really difficult to get the insertion point inside the form. In fact, when the insertion point is inside an empty form, it looks more like the I-bar is half-in and half-out of the form. The way to be sure that the insertion point is inside the form is to make sure that the top of the I-bar is lined up with the top, red border of the form before clicking.

5. Highlight the cells in the left column of the table and click the Align Right button on the Property inspector. Set the column width at **50%** by typing the value and the percent sign in the W field of the Property inspector.
6. Highlight the cells in the right column and click the Align Left button on the Property inspector.
7. In the top-left cell, type **Username:**.
8. In the middle-left cell, type **City of Birth:**.
9. In the top-right cell, insert a text field by choosing Insert/Form Objects/Text Field from the menu bar. Name the text field **tfUsername** in the Property inspector.
10. In the middle-right cell, insert another text field and name it **tfCityofbirth**.
11. Place the insertion point in the bottom-left cell and choose Insert/Form Objects/Button from the menu bar. Name the button **btSubmit**.
12. In the bottom-right cell insert another button and name the button **btReset**. In the Label field on the Property inspector, type **Reset** and select the Reset Form action. Your page should now look like Figure 9.9.
13. Open the Behaviors panel by selecting Window/Behaviors from the menu bar.
14. Select the Submit button in the form and click the plus button on the Behaviors panel (make sure you don't choose the Server Behaviors panel!). Choose Validate Form from the pop-up menu.
15. In the Validate Form dialog box, shown in Figure 9.10, highlight the first named field and check the Value Required check box.
16. Select the second named field and check the Value Required check box.
17. Click OK to close the Validate Form dialog box. Close the Behaviors panel.
18. Save the page as **passwordlookup.asp** in the root folder of the InsideUD4 site.

Chapter 9 Building Search Capabilities   239

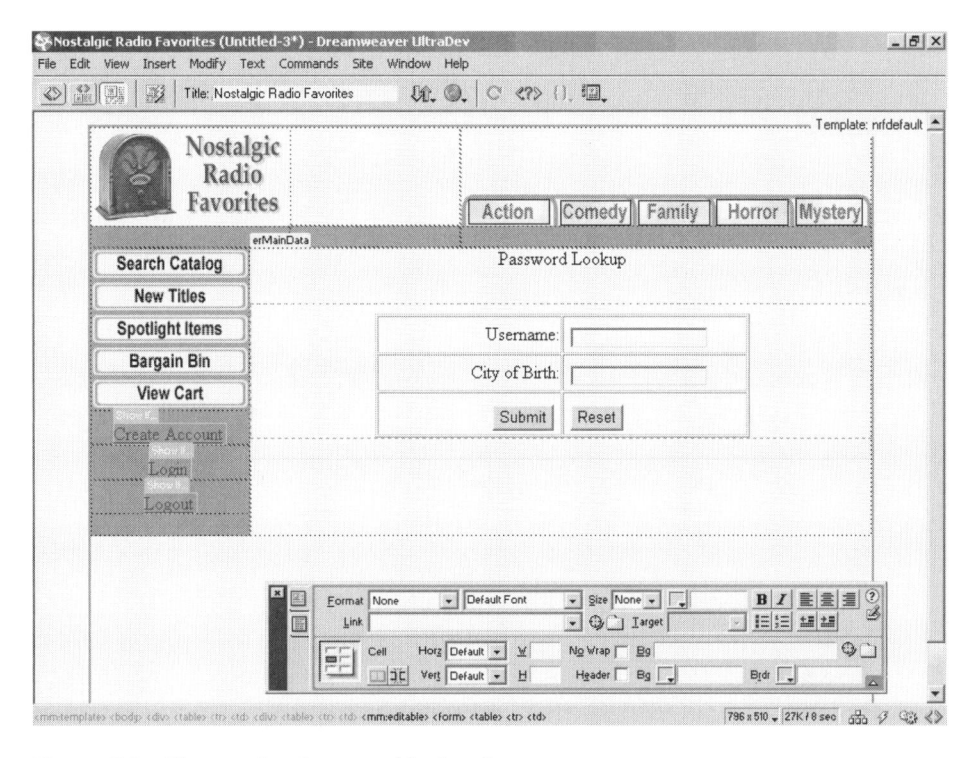

Figure 9.9 The completed password lookup form.

> **Caution**
>
> **Tying the Validate Form Behavior to an Object** When you add the Validate Form behavior to a page, be sure that you first highlight the item that will initiate the behavior such as a button or image. If you don't have an object selected in the page, UltraDev will associate the onLoad event with the behavior, and every time your page is loaded, the browser will check to see if the fields are empty. Since the fields are empty by default, your visitors will receive an error alerting them to the fact that the form fields are empty when they first load the page.

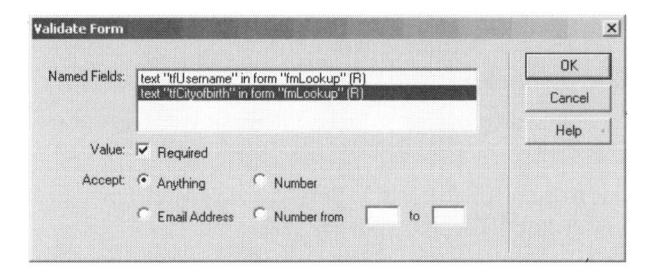

Figure 9.10 The Validate Form dialog box.

Validating the User's Credentials

The final step in creating the password lookup system is to build the page that validates the form data and then displays the password if appropriate. The page should also be able to inform the visitor if his credentials are incorrect.

Using UltraDev's Show Region behavior again, this can be accomplished by using one page that displays the appropriate information depending on whether the information submitted in the form matches the data stored in the database.

Exercise 9.5 Building the Password Lookup Results Page

1. Create a new page from the nrfdefault template. Close the passwordlookup.asp page.
2. Highlight the {erMainData} text and delete it.
3. In the editable region, insert a new table with **2** rows, **1** column, and a width of **80%**. Set the border, cell padding, and cell spacing to **0**. Click OK.
4. In the top row of the table, type the following text block:

    We're sorry, but the username/city of birth combination you provided was not correct. Please click the back button on your browser's button bar to return to the form.

5. Place the insertion in the bottom row of the table and type the following text block:

    Thank you . We were able to validate your username/city of birth combination. Your password is .

    Note that you should insert an extra space before the first and the last periods. This leaves room to insert the visitor's data.

6. If necessary, open the Server Behaviors panel.
7. Click the plus sign on the Server Behaviors panel and click Recordset (Query) from the pop-up menu. In the Recordset dialog box, click the Advanced button.
8. Complete the Recordset as shown in Figure 9.11. This recordset checks to see if the form elements submitted match any records in the database.
9. Click OK to close the Recordset dialog box.
10. Highlight the text in the top row and click the plus sign on the Server Behaviors panel. Select Show Region/Show Region If Recordset Is Empty from the pop-up menu.
11. In the Show Region If Recordset Is Empty dialog box, shown in Figure 9.12, select the rsLookup recordset and click OK.
12. Click the Data Bindings tab on the Server Behaviors panel and click the plus sign next to the rsLookup recordset.

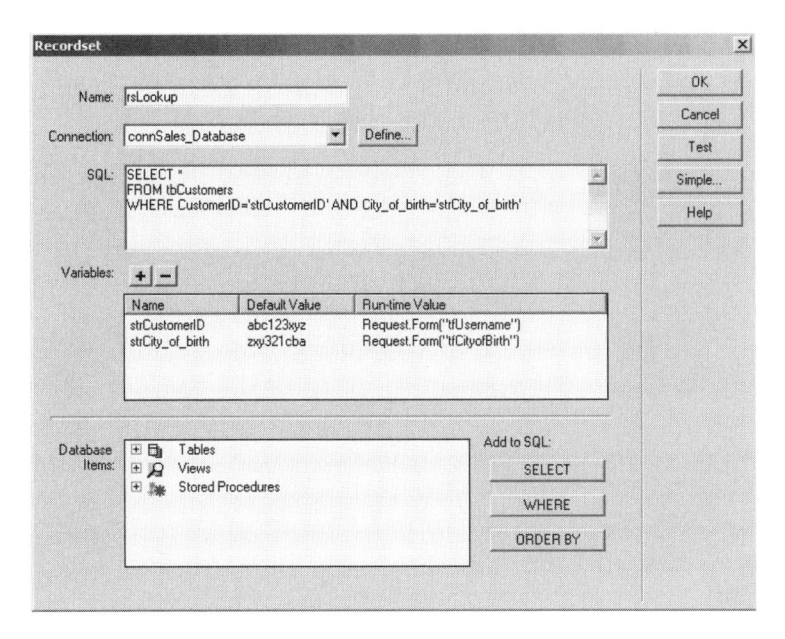

Figure 9.11 Your new recordset should look like this.

> **Note**
>
> **Recordsets and Searches with More than One Parameter** Creating a recordset that searches using only one parameter is easy in UltraDev. The Simple Recordset dialog box allows you to select from a few drop-down menus and fill in a blank or two, and you're off and running.
>
> Creating a recordset with multiple parameters, however, is a whole different ballgame. While UltraDev's advanced view of the Recordset dialog box looks similar to the Simple Recordset dialog box, there are some very big differences.
>
> First, note that you have to build your own SQL query. Although UltraDev does provide you with a clickable tree that displays your database items and the ability to add common SQL commands with the click of a button, it's important that you have at least a basic understanding of SQL queries before you can really take advantage of what the advanced view of the Recordset dialog box can do for you.
>
> If you think you might need to brush up on your SQL skills, take a look at these books. They can get you up to speed relatively quickly:
>
> - Ben Forta's *Teach Yourself SQL in 10 Minutes*, Sams Publishing, 1999.
> - Hernandez, Viescas, Celko, *SQL Queries for Mere Mortals: A Hands-On Guide to Data Manipulation in SQL*, Addison Wesley, 2000.
> - Kline & Kline, *SQL in a Nutshell*, O'Reilly and Associates, 2000.

13. Place the insertion point after the words "Thank You" in the bottom row and drag the CustomerID data source from the Data Bindings panel to the point right before the first period in the text block.

242 Part III Developing a Data-Driven Web Site

14. Drag the Password data source from the Data Bindings panel to the point right before the last period in the text block. As shown in Figure 9.13, your page should now include two dynamic data placeholders.

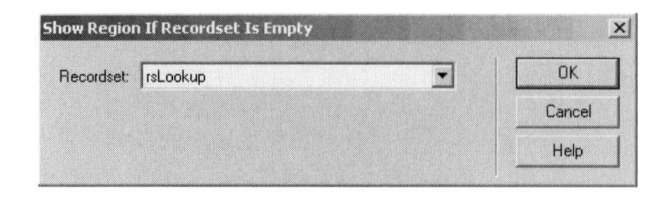

Figure 9.12 Select the rsLookup recordset.

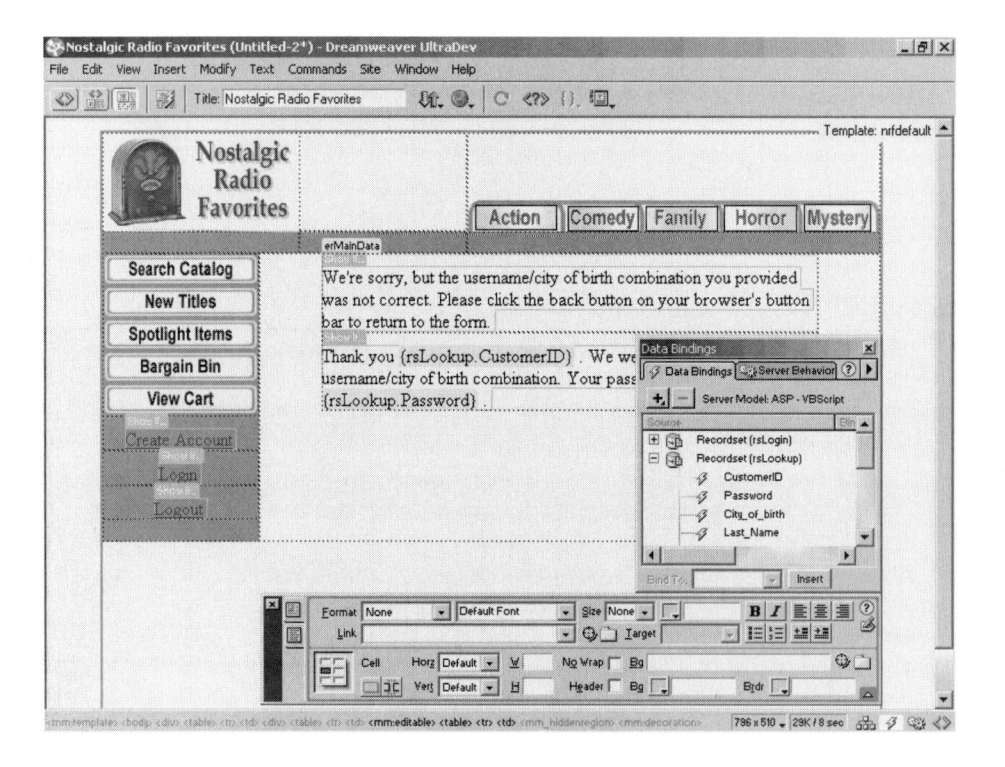

Figure 9.13 The page now includes placeholders for your dynamic data.

15. Click the Server Behaviors tab on the Data Bindings panel.

16. Highlight the contents of the bottom row and click the plus sign on the Server Behaviors panel. Select Show Region/Show Region If Recordset Is Not Empty from the pop-up menu.

17. Select the rsLookup recordset from the Show Region If Recordset Is Not Empty dialog box and click OK.
18. Save this page as **lookupresults.asp** in the root of the InsideUD4 folder.

> **Note**
>
> **Using an Email Application to Send Passwords** In addition to being able to display a visitor's password on the screen, you might consider the option of emailing the password. Although this method provides a little more security since the person must also be able to log in to his mail server, it does require that your server be capable of sending email messages. If you have access to your server, you might consider setting up the Simple Mail Transfer Protocol (SMTP) on your server and using a third-party software package such as AspEmail (http://www.aspemail.com) or w3 JMail (http://www.dimac.net). If you are using Windows NT or Windows 2000 you could also use CDONTS if it has been enabled on your server.
>
> If you don't have direct access to your server, you might contact your Web host or Web master to determine whether there is a viable option installed on your server, such as Sendmail.

Testing the Password Lookup System

Now that the link, the lookup form, and the validation page are present, the only thing left to do is test the system. To ensure that the process functions correctly, you need to be sure that the link, the form validation, and the server behaviors all perform as they should.

Exercise 9.6 Testing the Password Lookup

1. Close UltraDev and open your browser. In the address bar, type **http://localhost/insideud4**.
2. Click the Login link on the left side of the page. As shown in Figure 9.14, there is now a link on the login page that provides a way for visitors to lookup their passwords.
3. Click the link to move to the password lookup page.
4. In the password lookup page, leave the text fields blank and click the Submit button. As shown in Figure 9.15, the browser alerts you that the required fields have not been completed. This means that the form validation behavior is functioning.
5. Click OK to close the alert box.
6. In the Username field, type **test123**.
7. In the City of Birth field type **nowhere**.

244   Part III   Developing a Data-Driven Web Site

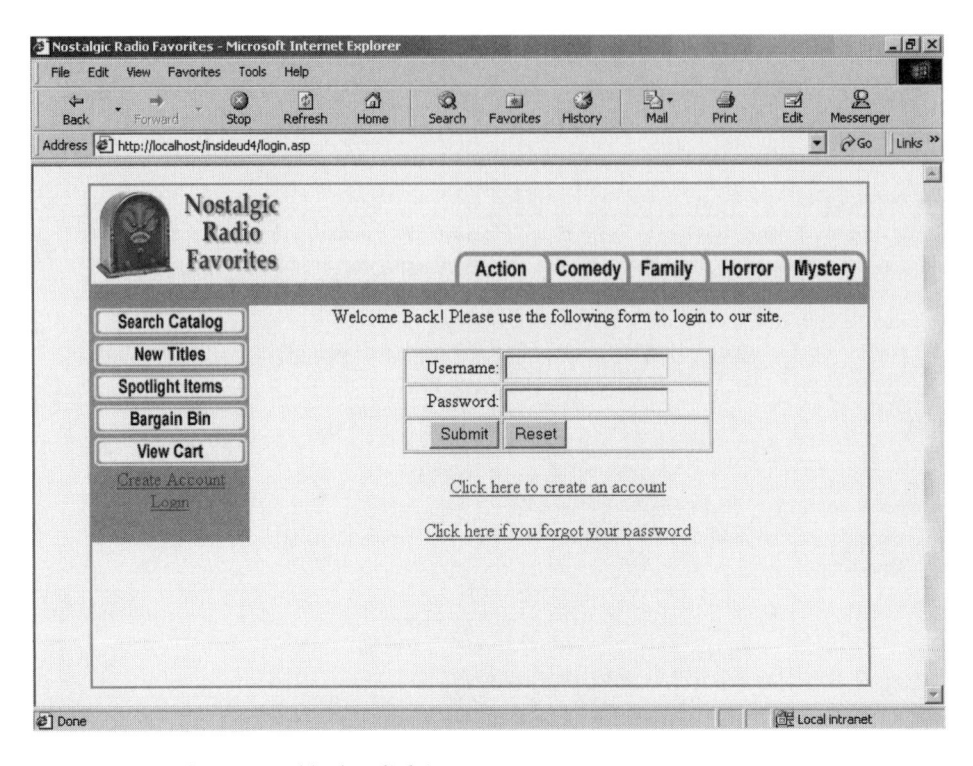

Figure 9.14 The password lookup link is present.

Figure 9.15 The form validation is functioning properly.

8. Click the Submit button. As shown in Figure 9.16, the Show Region dialog box we applied is functioning correctly and the proper region is displayed because there are no records that match the submitted values in the database.
9. Click the Back button on your browser's button bar.
10. In the Username field of the password lookup page, type **traigerj**.
11. In the City of Birth field, type **spokane**.
12. Click the Submit button. As shown in Figure 9.17, the password is displayed because the username/city of birth combination was correct.

Chapter 9 Building Search Capabilities   245

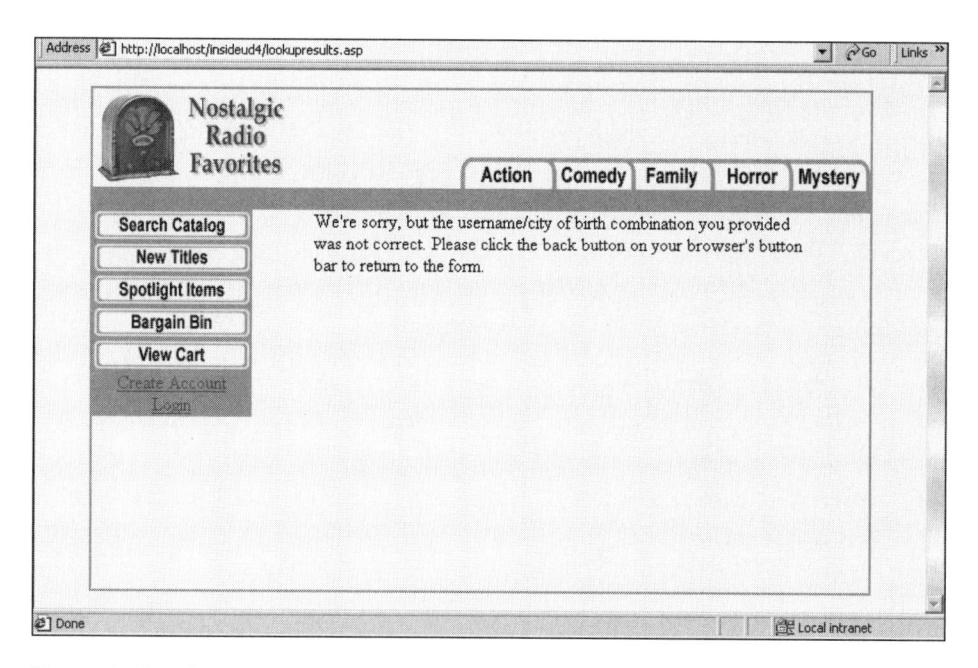

Figure 9.16   The password lookup displays the correct region when the submitted values are not able to be authenticated.

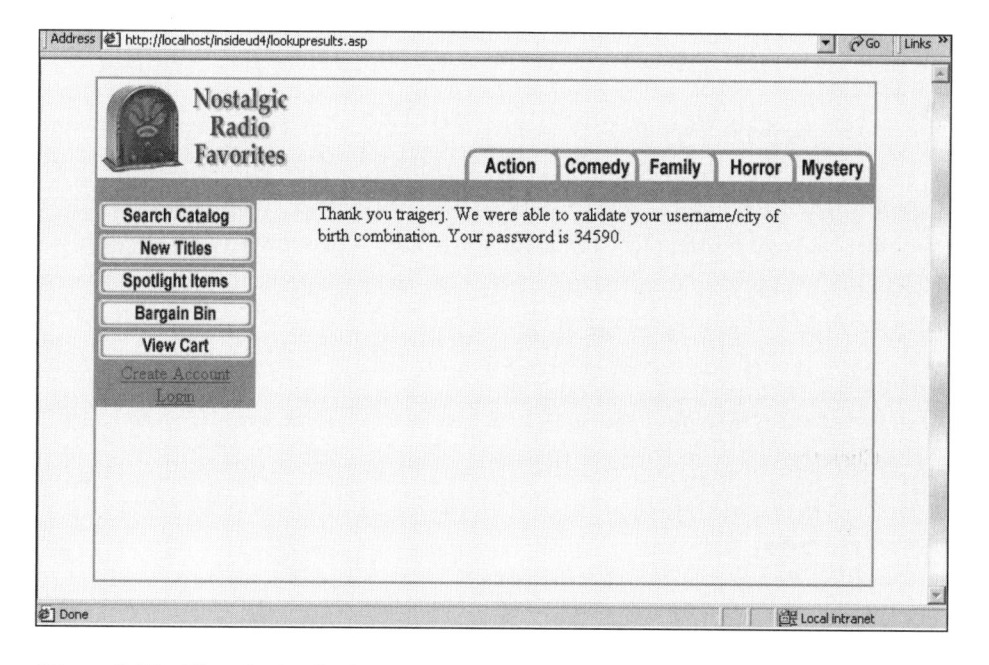

Figure 9.17   The submitted values were correct, so the password is displayed.

Adding Advanced Search Capabilities

Simple searches don't really provide the functionality needed to search a product catalog or an employee directory. In these instances, the visitor may want to filter all the information in a database table by criteria such as product name, type, or cost. She might want to further refine her search by availability or even location of the product. Or if her search doesn't provide the results she was seeking, she might want to broaden the search by reducing the number of restrictions she has entered. For this type of search, visitors need something that provides a great deal of flexibility.

The most flexible search option that you can provide to your visitors is the advanced search. Adding an advanced search to your site offers visitors the opportunity to shape their results by providing a wide variety of search options and allowing visitors to choose which criteria they wish to search by. This allows visitors to make their searches as broad or as narrow as necessary.

Building the Advanced Search Page

Once again, building an advanced search is no problem using UltraDev, although it does require a basic understanding of the mechanics of a simple SQL query. If you haven't brushed up on your SQL terms, this might be a good time to do so since details like the difference between "and" and "or" can cause your search pages to return the wrong results.

To demonstrate the development of an advanced search, you create a form that allows visitors to search the old-time radio show recordings available through the Nostalgic Radio Favorites Web site you've been working with. Because you want visitors to have as much flexibility as possible when searching, a visitor who submits a blank form will retrieve all the records in the database. From there, she will be able to narrow her search using the show title, episode title, genre, and price.

> **Note**
>
> **Understanding How Your Visitors Expect to Search** Once again, it's time to peer into your crystal ball and determine how your visitors will most likely want to search your site. Some Web developers prefer to build forms that, when submitted, return the most results possible. These forms allow the visitor to narrow his search by adding search criteria.
>
> Other Web developers, however, prefer to limit the amount of data a query can return in order to manage resources on the server side and limit the amount of bandwidth that is being consumed. In the end, it's your customers that should influence the decision the most. Analyze how you would want to search the site if you were a visitor, and then build the search form that you think best fits those needs.

Chapter 9 Building Search Capabilities 247

Exercise 9.7 Adding an Advanced Search Page

1. Select File/New from Template from the menu bar. Create a new page from the nrfdefault template. Close any open pages.
2. Delete the {erMainData} text and type **Search Our Catalog** in the editable region. Press the Enter key to move to a new line.
3. From the menu bar, select Insert/Form. Name the form **fmSearchCatalog** and type **searchresults.asp** in the Action field.
4. With the insertion point inside the form, select Insert/Table from the menu bar. Create a table that has **5** rows, **2** columns, and has a width of **60%**. Set the border, cell padding, and cell spacing to **1**. Click OK.
5. Highlight the left column of the table and click the Align Right button on the Property inspector. Set the column width at **50%** by typing the value in the W field of the Property inspector.
6. In the top-left cell, type **Show Title:**. Press the Tab key to move to the next cell.
7. Insert a text field by choosing Insert/Form Objects/Text Field. Name the text field **tfShowTitle**. Place the insertion point after the new text field and press the Tab key to move to the next row.
8. Type **Episode Title:** and press the Tab key. Insert a text field and name it **tfEpisodeTitle**. Press the Tab key to move to the next cell.
9. Type **Genre:** and press the Tab key. Insert a popup menu by selecting Insert/Form Objects/List/Menu from the menu bar.
10. In the Property inspector, name the new menu **mnGenre**. Leave the Type as Menu and click the List Values button.
11. As shown in Figure 9.18, add the Any option and the five genres offered by the site in the List Values dialog box by clicking the plus sign to create a new value. The Item Label refers to the text that the visitor will see when they activate the menu. The Value refers to the actual value that will be used to conduct the search.

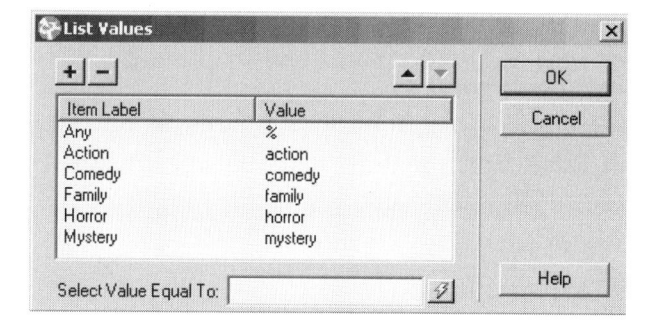

Figure 9.18 The List Values dialog box allows you to create drop-down menus.

12. Click OK to close the List Values dialog box. In the Initially Selected field of the Property Inspector, select Any.
13. Place the insertion point after the new pop-up menu and press the Tab key to move to the next cell.
14. Type **Price:** and press the Tab key. Insert another List/Menu and name it **mnPrice**. Click List Values. Add the Item Labels and Values as shown in Figure 9.19. Click OK.

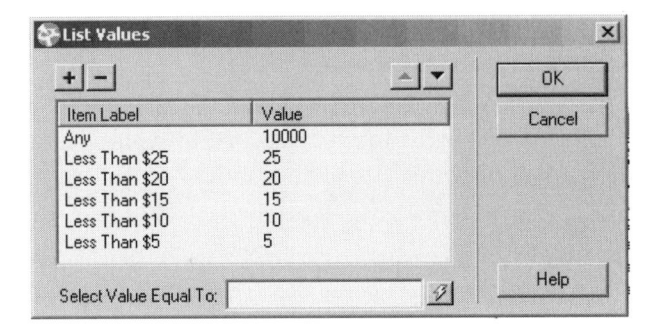

Figure 9.19 The item labels and values for the mnPrice pop-up menu.

15. In the Initially Selected field of the Property inspector, click the Any value. Notice that this label has a value of 10,000. This is to provide the SQL query with an upper limit with which to compare the prices. Essentially, this is saying that every product in your catalog is less than $10,000, so a query of all items under $10,000 would show every item in the catalog.
16. Place the insertion point in the lower-left cell and insert a Submit button. Label the button btSubmit.
17. In the lower-right cell, insert a reset button. Label it btReset. Set the Action to Reset form.
18. Save the page as **search_catalog.asp**.

Building the Results Page

Just as you did with the simple search and the restricted simple search, you now need to build a results page that shows visitors the information that matches their requests. To save time, you can use the results page created for the single parameter search created earlier and make a few modifications to meet our needs.

Exercise 9.8 Adding the Search Results Page

1. Open the genreresults.asp page. Close any open pages.
2. From the menu bar, select File/Save As and save the file as **searchresults.asp**.

3. Open the Data Bindings panel if it is not already open. Double-click the rsSearch recordset. UltraDev opens the Recordset dialog box in the Advanced mode.
4. Delete the SQL Query and the single variable created by UltraDev and modify the recordset so it looks like Figure 9.20.

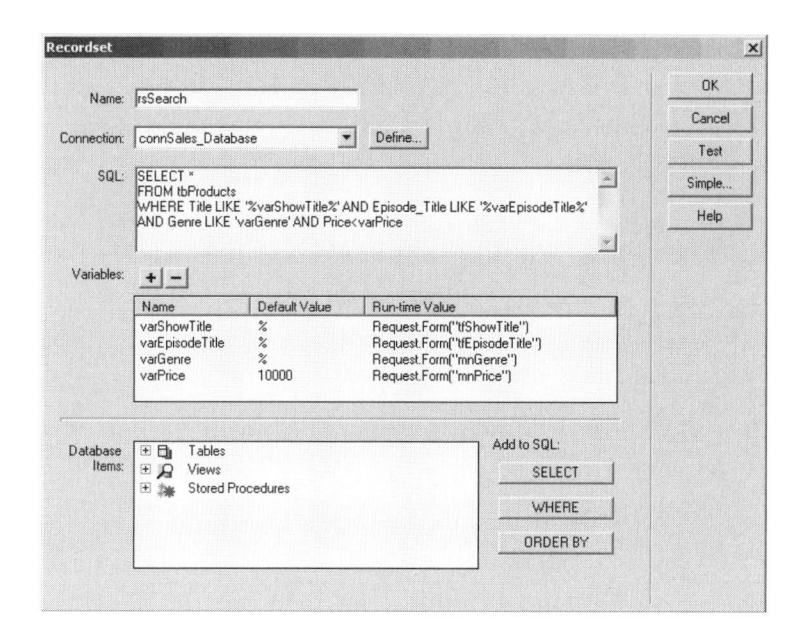

Figure 9.20 Modify the rsSearch recordset to look like this.

> **Note**
>
> **Building a Complex SQL Query** When you use the advanced view of UlraDev's Recordset dialog box, you are able to build a SQL query that compares the input collected from a form with the data in your database tables. By creating variables that represent the empty form fields and filling them with default values, you can test your query prior to making the form available to your visitors.
>
> When building a SQL query, keep in mind that the % sign is a wildcard that means "anything." When used in conjunction with the LIKE command, you can compare the results of a form to see if they match any part of the data stored in the table. For instance, LIKE '%at%' would positively match a database value of "cat" and would also match "attack."

5. Above the results table, change the text that reads Genre Results to **Catalog Results**.
6. Save the page.

Testing the Advanced Search Page

Testing an advanced search page can sometimes be tricky. While the search might appear to be working properly, it's possible that the information being retrieved isn't the information your visitor was looking for.

For instance, suppose your employee directory has two people named John Green, one in Ohio and one in Florida. Next, suppose your search form allows users to type in a first name, a last name, and then select a state from a drop-down list. Finally, suppose a visitor to your Web site submits a form with "John" as the first name, "Green" as the last name, and "CA" for the state.

To see the problems that can arise, imagine that you built a SQL query to display any records where the first name was found in the database AND the last name was found in the database AND the state submitted matched any records in the database. In this case, the visitor's query would correctly display no records because there is no person with the first name "John" and the last name "Green" who is in California.

Suppose, however, that you built your SQL query to display any records where the first name was found in the database OR the last name was found in the database OR the state submitted was found in the database. Now, the visitor's search would return everyone whose first name is John, whose last name is Green, or who is located in California.

Because an advanced search can get a little tricky, it's always a good idea to think about the results you want to provide, and then thoroughly test your form to make sure the results are what you intend.

Exercise 9.9 Testing the Catalog Search

1. Minimize UltraDev and open your Web browser.
2. In the address bar, type **http://localhost/insideud4/** and press Enter.
3. Click the Search Catalog link on the left side of the page. As shown in Figure 9.21, the catalog search is now available.
4. Leave the form with its default settings and click the Submit button. Notice that this returns every record in the database.
5. Click Back to return to the form.
6. In the Show Title field, type **fibber**. Click the Submit button. As shown in Figure 9.22, the results have been filtered and only the Fibber McGee & Molly show is returned.

Chapter 9 Building Search Capabilities 251

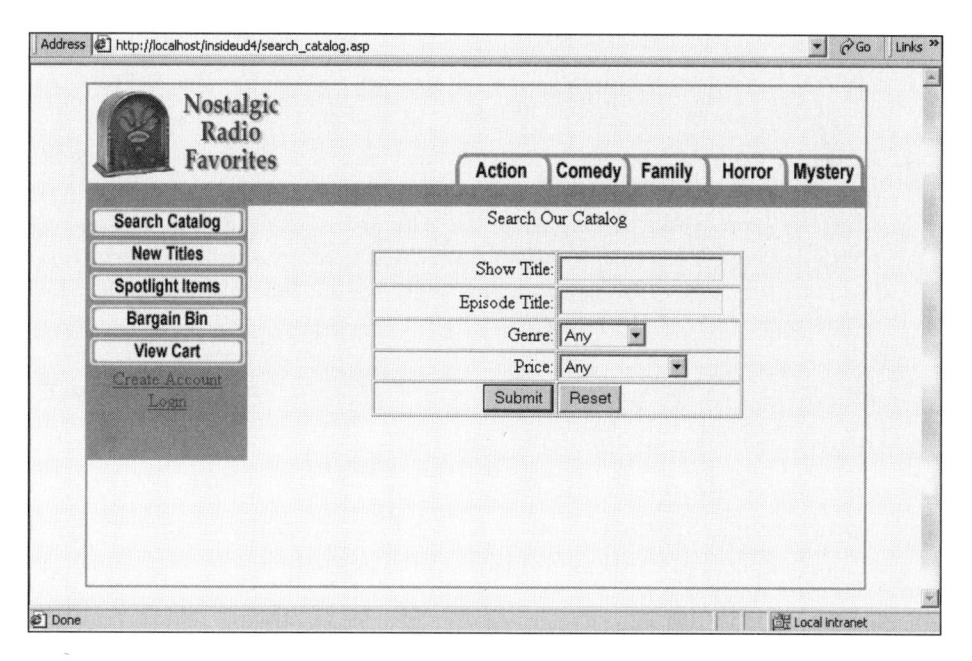

Figure 9.21 The Search Catalog page.

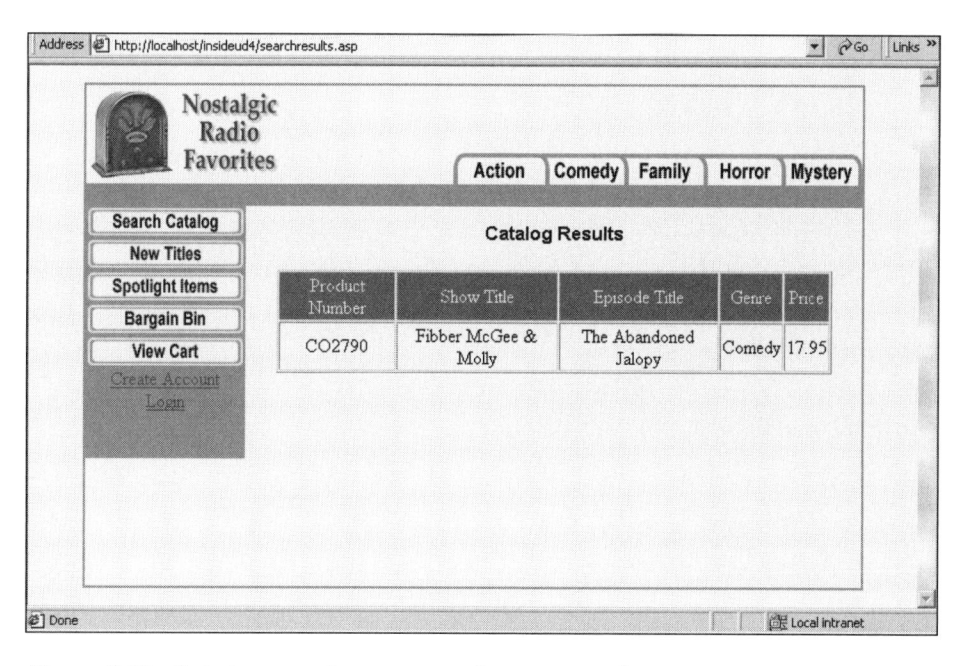

Figure 9.22 Entering a search term returns the correct results.

7. Click Back to return to the form.
8. Click the Reset button. Using the Price dropdown, change the value to **$15**. Click the Submit button. This returns all shows in the catalog under $15.
9. Finally, click the Back button to return to the form. Click the Reset button and type **gunsmoke** in the Show Title field. In the Episode Title field, type **Billy**. Select the Action genre and a price of less than $20. Click the Submit button and notice that the criteria in each field are evaluated to return the proper result, in this case an episode of Gunsmoke called "Billy The Kid" that fits within the Action genre and costs less than $20.

Summary

This chapter showed you three different ways to add search capabilities to your Web site. Using a simple search, a restricted simple search, and an advanced search, you can give your visitors the ability to retrieve information based on their needs.

The next chapter looks at adding dynamic data to your site, including random images or text and time-sensitive information.

Chapter 10

Adding Dynamic Images and Text to Search Results

Imagine what it would be like to maintain and update the content for a high-traffic Web site like Amazon.com. Amazon.com maintains millions of products in their databases, and each product has its own descriptive information and accompanying images. On top of that, the volume of new products that are added to the site's pages on a daily basis must be staggering.

Now, imagine that you had to maintain those pages without the help of a single database. The task of building and maintaining a separate page for each product would be nearly impossible—even for an army of Web developers coding 24 hours a day. Luckily, database-connectivity offers Web developers the ability to simply add the product information to their database and draw upon that data as their Web pages require. UltraDev makes it extremely easy to generate the necessary code.

As you have seen in some of the previous chapters, UltraDev is capable of adding behaviors to your pages that retrieve the location of an image from a database and display that image in a results page. In addition, you've seen how easy it is to extract text from a database field and place it in a page.

As this chapter demonstrates, UltraDev is capable of building code that does more than just display images and text. Using some advanced SQL queries in combination with server behaviors, UltraDev is also capable of adding rotating graphics, recordset navigation links that appear and disappear when necessary, and record counters that allow you and your visitors to track the number of records returned by a recordset.

To highlight these capabilities, this chapter demonstrates some of these features and shows you how to do the following:

- Add rotating images and text to your pages
- Insert time-dependent images and text
- Build dynamic elements that navigate search results
- Add a dynamic record counter to your page

Adding Rotating Images and Text

In Chapter 7, "Connecting Your Web Site to a Database," we briefly demonstrated how to insert a dynamic image into a details page. While it's great to be able to draw images from a database and display them on the page, there may come a time when you don't want the visitor to see the same image every time he loads the page. The answer is dynamic, rotating images.

Probably the most common use for rotating images on the Internet is ad banners. More and more sites are setting aside a little bit of desktop real estate to sell products, promote services, and entice visitors with special deals. Since these banner ads are most often controlled by a database, the site owners are capable of tracking the number of times the banner has been displayed and even the number of times it has been clicked. And the great thing about storing the banner ad information in a database is the fact that the Web developer only need specify which images should be displayed and where the image should go when clicked. The code and database take care of the rest.

Before you can add any dynamic images to your Web site, you first have to add them (or links to them) to your database. The first option you have is to simply include an HTML hyperlink to the image in a field in your database. Then, when you need to display the image dynamically, you can simply have UltraDev draw the link data from the database and insert it into your pages as an image.

The other option is to actually include the entire image in your database. Most of the popular databases on the market support the inclusion of Binary Large Objects (BLOBs) in their tables. When a BLOB is added to a record, the database management software converts the image into binary and stores it in the field as a string of 1s and 0s. Then, when the image is read from the database, the image is converted back into its native format and passed to the Web page. The biggest downside to using BLOBs is the fact that they contain large amounts of data, which rapidly increases the size of your database. This, in turn, can quickly degrade the performance of your server and Web applications.

> **Note**
>
> **BLOBs Versus Links** Links are generally the easiest way to handle dynamic graphics. However, to use a link, you need to know the location and filename of the image. Because of this, the use of links usually lends itself to situations when you are adding graphics that you have created and placed within a folder in your site.
>
> BLOBs, on the other hand, are convenient when you may not know all the information about the image, such as the filename. For instance, suppose you run a Web site that allows your visitors to sell their used boats. One of the features of your site is that you allow each seller to upload a photo of his boat. Although you may be able to control the folder where the files are located, you may not know the actual name of the file they are uploading. In this case, you could upload the file and place it as a BLOB in your database, when the file was placed in the Web page, it would be given a name based on the recordset that called it.

Keep in mind that rotating images are not just for ad banners. Any Web developer who wants to provide visitors with dynamic content could find many useful applications for rotating images. For instance, the following exercise demonstrates how easy it is to rotate between images that have been identified as "Spotlight Items" in the database. Applying this example, the Web developer could quickly change the products in the rotation by opening the database and selecting the items that should by identified as Spotlight Items.

Exercise 10.1 Adding Rotating Images and Text to Your Pages

1. Start UltraDev and open the default.asp page created in Chapter 6, "UltraDev's Graphic and Multimedia Capabilities."
2. Click the flaRadioShow object located in the erMainData editable region. Remove the object from your page by pressing the Delete key on your keyboard.
3. Remove the Play Intro button and the Stop Intro button from the page as well.
4. Place the insertion point in the top cell of the existing table and type **Welcome To Nostalgic Radio Favorites**.
5. Highlight the text and choose the Heading 1 style from the Format drop-down menu on the Property inspector.
6. Choose Arial, Helvetica, sans serif as the font, and set the font size to 3. Click the Bold button on the Property inspector.
7. Press the right-arrow key on your keyboard to move to the end of the line and press the Enter key. Type the following text block on the new line:

    Welcome to Nostalgic Radio Favorites. Our goal is to provide you with high-quality audio recordings of your favorite old-time radio shows in a variety of formats. Feel free to browse our catalog, check out some of our spotlight items, or order an item through our online store.

8. Highlight the text block and select Paragraph from the Format dropdown. Set the font at Arial, Helvetica, sans serif, and the size at 3. On the Property inspector, click the Bold button to turn off the bold formatting. As shown in Figure 10.1, you should now have a heading, a text block, and two empty cells.
9. Place the insertion point in the lower-left cell and click the Align Center button on the Property inspector. Set the cell width to **50%**.
10. From the menu bar, select Insert/Table and create a table that has **4** rows, **1** column, and a width of **95%**. Set the border, cell spacing, and cell padding to **0**. Click OK.
11. Highlight all four cells by clicking in the top cell and dragging your cursor to the bottom cell. Click the Align Center button on the Property inspector.
12. Place the insertion point in the top row of the new table and type **Spotlight Item!**. Press the Tab key to move to the next row.
13. Open the Server Behaviors panel, if it is not already visible, and click the plus sign. From the pop-up menu, choose Recordset (Query).

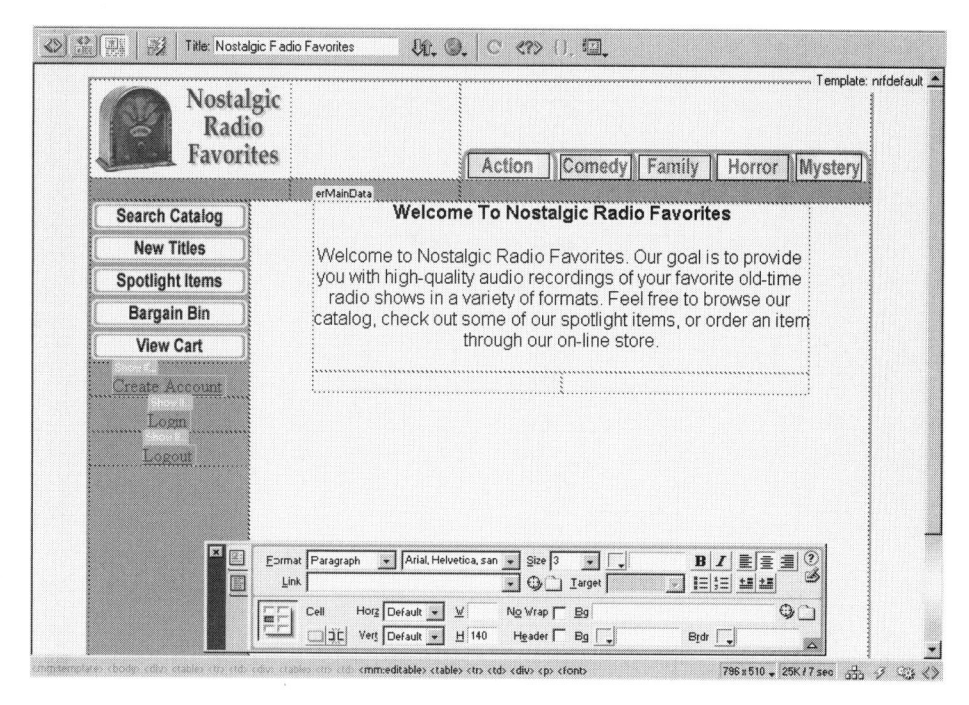

Chapter 10 Adding Dynamic Images and Text to Search Results 259

Figure 10.1 The default.asp page with new text.

14. If the Recordset dialog box is not already in the simple view, click the Simple button. Name the new recordset **rsRandom_Spotlight**. Select connSales_Database as the connection and tbProducts as the Table.

15. In the Columns panel, click the Selected radio button and click Product_No. Press and hold the Ctrl key and click Title, Episode_Title, and Photo_URL.

16. In the Filter panel, set the first field to Spotlight, the second field to =, the third field to Entered Value, and type **YES** in the fourth field. This filters our recordset so that only the records marked as Spotlight Items are retrieved. Your recordset should now look like Figure 10.2.

17. Click the Test button and notice that only four records are retrieved. These are the records that have the Spotlight field set to Yes.

18. Click OK to close the Test SQL Statement dialog box and click OK to close the Recordset dialog box.

19. With your cursor in the cell underneath the Spotlight Item text, choose Insert/Image from the menu bar.

20. In the Select Image Source dialog box, shown in Figure 10.3, click the Data Sources radio button.

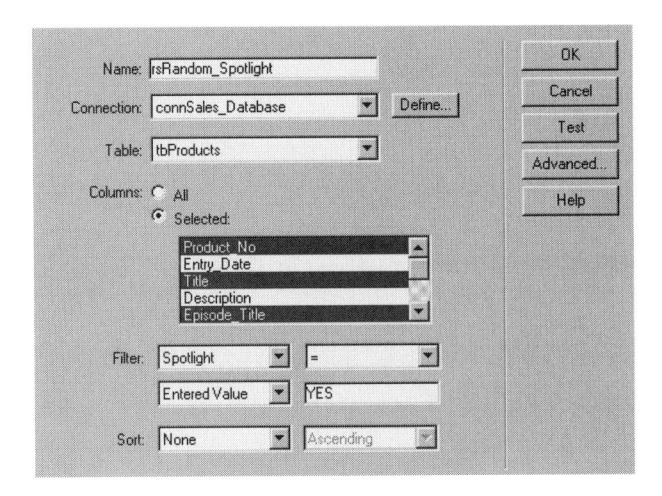

Figure 10.2 Your new rsRandom_Spotlight recordset.

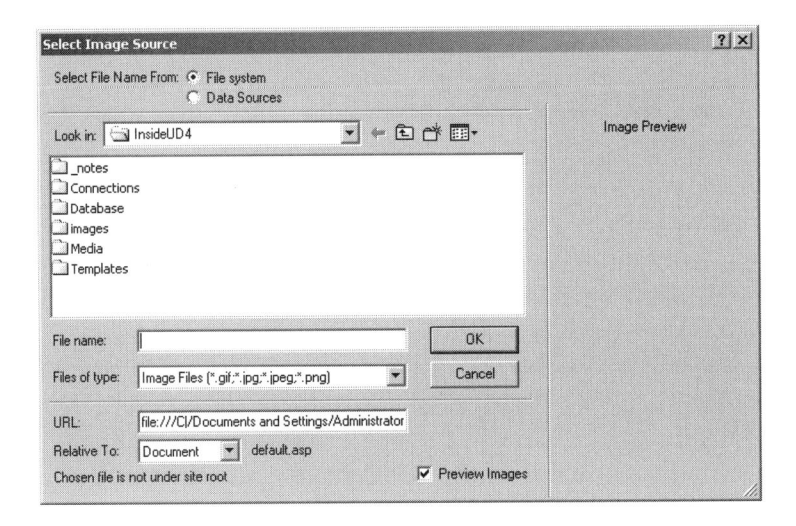

Figure 10.3 The Select Image Source dialog box.

21. Click the plus sign next to the rsRandom_Spotlight recordset to expand its contents.

22. Highlight the Photo_URL column and click OK. Click OK to close the Insert Image dialog box.

23. Press the Tab key to move to the next field and click the Data Bindings tab on the Server Behaviors panel.

24. If the rsRandom_Spotlight recordset is not already expanded, click the plus sign to show its content. From the rsRandom_Spotlight recordset, drag the Title data element into the cell below the newly placed dynamic image.

Chapter 10 Adding Dynamic Images and Text to Search Results 261

> **Note**
>
> **Using Links to Images** There are a couple of things you should consider when creating a database field that contains links to images. First, if you are going to be uploading your site to a different Web server, you might consider using the relative path to the image rather than the complete path. This can help avoid any problems that might arise from Web servers that use different Web roots.
>
> Second, you should be aware that URLs should be stored in your database as text fields. Although some databases like Access and SQL Server have a URL type, the database adds additional coding that UltraDev does not process properly. Therefore, even though the field contents are a URL, leave the field type set to text.

25. Next, drag the Episode_Title data element to the bottom cell of the table. Your page should now look like Figure 10.4.

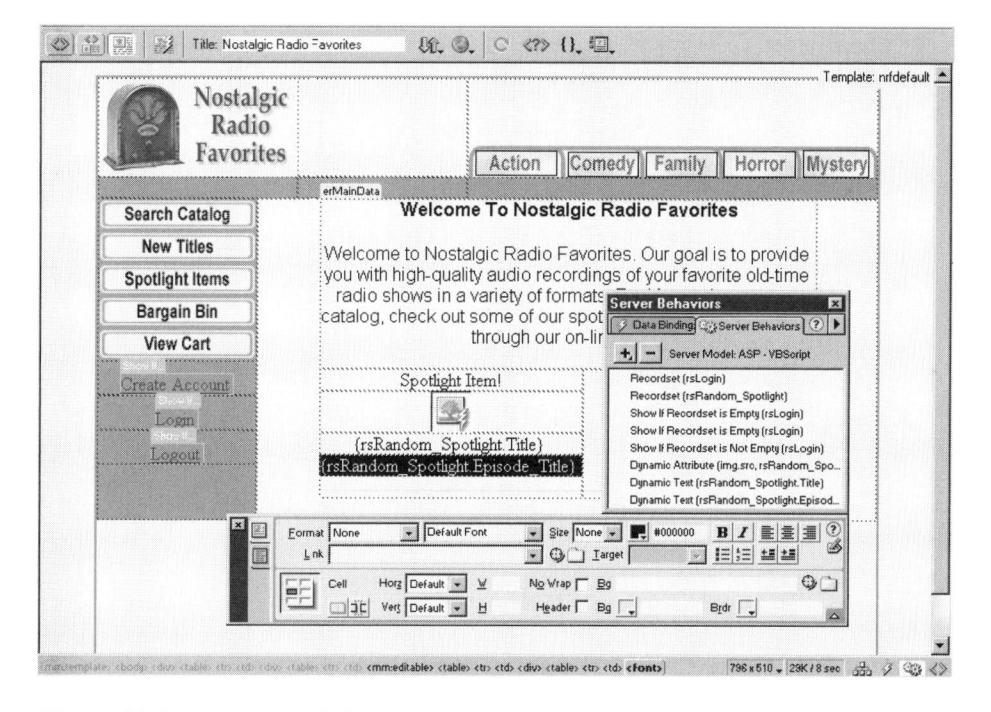

Figure 10.4 Your page with the new elements added.

26. With the {rsRandom_Spotlight.Episode_Title} text highlighted, type **spotlight_items.asp** in the Link field of the Property inspector. Press Enter.

27. Highlight the four cells in the table and set their background color to **#006699** in the Bg field of the Property inspector with the color picker.

28. In the Property inspector, set the Font to Arial, Helvetica, sans serif, set the font size to 2, set the text Color to **#FFFFFF**, and click the Bold button.

29. The final step in making the images random is to add a small piece of code to your page. Click the Show Code View button on the button bar and find the <html> tag (near the top of your page) for your page. Create an empty line above the <html> tag and type the five lines of code shown in Figure 10.5.

```
<%
Randomize
rsRandom_Spotlight.Move Int(Rnd * Cint(rsRandom_Spotlight.RecordCount))
rsRandom_Spotlight.Update
%>
<html>
```

Figure 10.5 Add this code above the <html> tag in your page.

> **Note**
>
> **A Variety of Ways to Create Rotating Images** The method you use to make your images rotate depends on the database you are using and the function used to randomize objects. For instance, an Access database requires that the recordset be built and then a piece of code created using a combination of the Randomize and the Rnd functions. If, however, you are using MySQL for your database, you can simply use the ORDER BY RAND() statement in your SQL query to accomplish the same thing.
>
> Because of the differences between function syntax, it's a good idea to check your database documentation for the correct way to randomize a recordset.

30. In your page's code, find the section of code that creates the rsRandom_Spotlight recordset. It should be 10 lines of code right above the new code you just entered. Find the line that reads

    rsRandom_Spotlight.CursorType = 0

    and change it to read

    rsRandom_Spotlight.CursorType = 3

31. Switch back to the Design view and save the page.

> **Tip**
>
> **Changing the Cursor Type from the Design View** You can also change the cursor type for a recordset by opening the Server Behaviors panel and selecting the recordset. In the Property inspector, select the value you want from the Cursor Type dropdown.

32. Open a Web browser and type **http://localhost/insideud4** in the address bar. Notice that a random spotlight item is present in the home page. Clicking the Refresh button on the browser displays a new random image, and clicking the link takes the visitor to the spotlight_items page.

> **Caution**
>
> **A Different Type of Cursor**   As mentioned earlier, when you connect your page to a database, your page can't talk directly to the database. Instead, you have to build a recordset that then exchanges data between the Web page and the database. In order to effectively maintain communication between the database and Web page, the recordset uses a tool called a cursor. This cursor keeps track of the records in the recordset and enables your pages to move row by row through the data and extract, replace, and add to the recordset.
>
> When you create a new recordset, UltraDev automatically adds some standard variables such as CursorType and CursorLocation. There may come a time, however, when the default value assigned by UltraDev does not function properly, resulting in nasty ODBC errors like the following:
>
> ```
> Microsoft OLE DB Provider for ODBC Drivers error '80040e24'
> Rowset does not support fetching backward.
> /insideud4/default.asp, line 40
> ```
>
> If you are manipulating your recordset and receive errors about fetching backward, take a look at your cursor values and be sure that your current cursor is able to navigate your database as you expect it to. For information on the various cursor settings, check out: http://msdn.microsoft.com/library/psdk/dasdk/pg_a7uwj.htm.

As was mentioned earlier, making changes to the rotation list is extremely easy. New products can be added to the list and old products removed by simply opening the database file and selecting or deselecting the appropriate checkbox. In a matter of seconds, your visitors are provided with fresh, new content that will keep them coming back to see what's new.

Using Time-Dependent Images and Text

The best way to make sure that your visitors keep coming back to your site is to continually offer new and fresh material. Unfortunately, constantly updating information can quickly become a never-ending process. One way to avoid the hassle of updating your pages is to let UltraDev do it for you.

For instance, suppose you could place a newly released product and a link to its details for 30 days and be assured that after 30 days the image would no longer display? To take this idea further, what if you could randomly display all the items that have been added to your product catalog in the last 30 days? Assuming that you continually added products to your catalog, returning customers would always have the opportunity to see what is now being offered by your organization.

Think about it! All you would have to do is enter the products in your database and your page, and the corresponding recordset would automatically draw the new products from the database and display them. That means you get a great-looking, up-to-date site along with more time to work on that putting stroke.

You've just seen that UltraDev can help you add rotating images and text to your pages. Now, you just have to look at how UltraDev can take that one step further and use the date to determine which images should be included in the images that are displayed.

Exercise 10.2 Adding Time-Sensitive, Dynamic Images and Text to Your Pages

1. In the default.asp page, place the insertion point in the empty bottom-right cell of the table and click the Align Center button on the Property inspector.
2. From the menu bar, select Insert/Table and create table with **4** rows, **1** column, and a width of **95%**. Set the border, cell padding, and cell spacing to **0**. Click OK.
3. Highlight the four cells and click the Align Center button on the Property inspector.
4. Place the insertion point in the top cell and type **Look What's New!**. Press the Tab key to move to the next cell.
5. On the Server Behaviors panel, click the plus sign and select Recordset (Query). Name the recordset **rsNew_Items** and select connSales_Database as the connection and tbProducts as the table.
6. In the Columns panel, click the Selected radio button and select the Product_No, Entry_Date, Title, Episode_Title, and Photo_URL fields.
7. Click the Advanced button to switch to the advanced view of the Recordset dialog box. As seen in Figure 10.6, UltraDev has started to build our SQL query for us.
8. In the SQL panel, place the insertion point after the word tbProducts and press Enter to move to a new line.
9. Add the following line to the SQL query:

    ```
    WHERE Datediff('d', [tbProducts.Entry_Date], now()) <=30
    ```

    This line uses the Datediff function to determine the difference in days (indicated by the 'd') between the value stored in the Entry_Date field of each record in the tbProducts table and today's date.

    Keep in mind that more than 30 days have probably gone by since these products were entered into the sample database. If you really want to see how well this exercise works, I recommend that you take a moment to open the database that you are using and change a few of the dates in the Entry_Date field to be less than 30 days from today's date. Otherwise, your recordset will always be empty and your default page won't have any products in the What's New box.

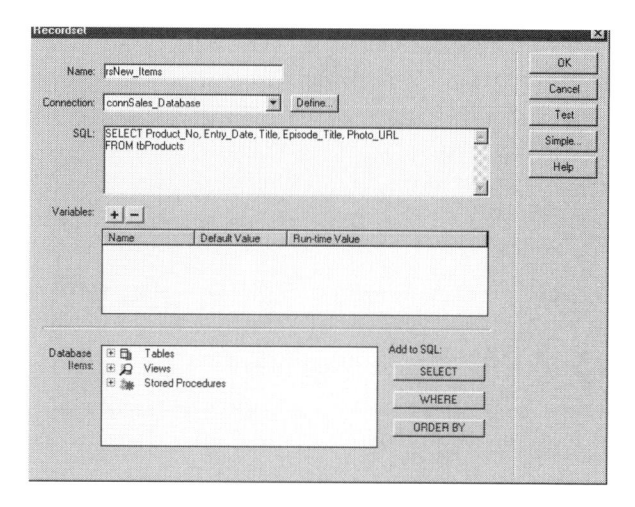

Chapter 10   Adding Dynamic Images and Text to Search Results   265

Figure 10.6   The advanced view of the Recordset dialog box already has the basics of the SQL query built.

10. Your recordset should now look like Figure 10.7. Click OK to close the Recordset dialog box.

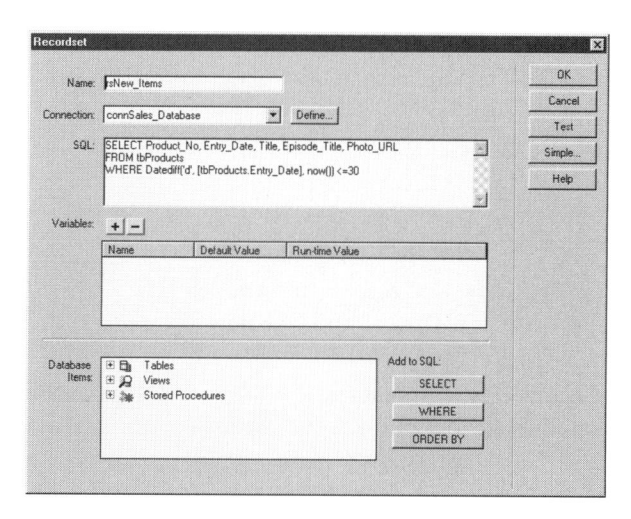

Figure 10.7   The recordset now compares the dates and contains only records less than 30 days old.

11. Place the insertion point in the cell under the "Look What's New!" text and select Insert, Image from the menu bar.

12. In the Select Image Source dialog box, select the Data Sources radio button and click the minus sign next to the rsRandom_Spotlight recordset to hide its elements. Click the plus sign next to the rsNew_Items recordset to display its elements.

13. Select the Photo_URL data element and click OK to close the Select Image Source dialog box.
14. Press the Tab key to move to the next cell and click the Data Bindings tab of the Server Behaviors dialog box.
15. From the rsNew_Items recordset, drag the Title element into the cell directly beneath the new dynamic image. Drag the Episode_Title element into the bottom cell.
16. Again, it is necessary to add a small piece of code to the page to randomize the images. Switch to the Code view and add the code shown in Figure 10.8 to a new line directly above the <html> tag in your page.

```
<%
Randomize
rsNew_Items.Move Int(Rnd * Cint(rsNew_Items.RecordCount))
rsNew_Items.Update
%>
<html>
<!-- #BeginTemplate "/Templates/nrfdefault.dwt" -->
<head>
```

Figure 10.8 Add this code to your page to randomize your images and text.

17. Once again, find the section of code that creates the rsNew_Items recordset and find the line of text that reads

    `rsNew_Items.CursorType = 0`

    and change it to read

    `rsNew_Items.CursorType = 3`

18. Switch back to the Show Design View and highlight the {rsNew_Items.Episode_Title} text and type **new_titles.asp** in the Link field of the Property inspector. Press Enter.
19. Highlight the four cells in this table and set their font to Arial, Helvetica, sans serif. Set the font size to 2 and the Text color to **#006699**. Click the Bold button.
20. Save the page.
21. Open the default.asp page in your Web browser. As you can see in Figure 10.9, the randomized "Look What's New" images are displayed along with their titles and episode titles.

After you have added time-sensitive elements to your pages, it is important that you keep in mind the restrictions that you have placed upon your pages. If no new records are entered into the product catalog, the SQL query will return an empty recordset and your page will have a "Look What's New" section with a blank space. If you know that there will be a time when no new products will be entered, you might consider changing the SQL query to 60 days or whatever suits your needs.

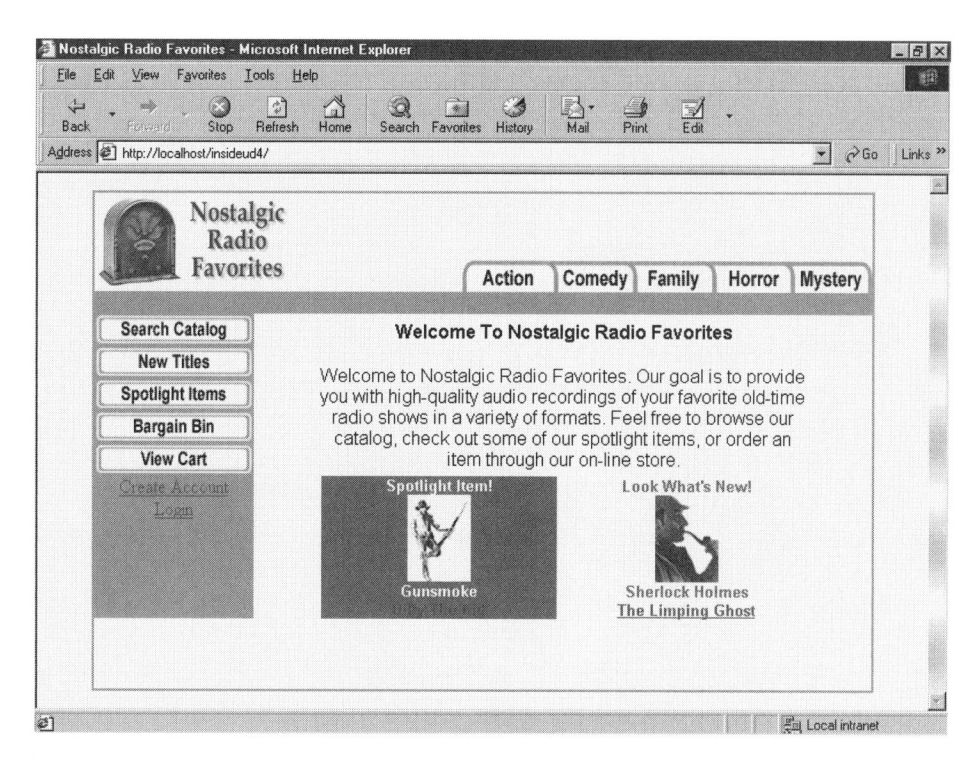

Figure 10.9 The "Look What's New" section now returns random images and text.

> **Note**
>
> **Is It Really Random?** Generating anything random on a computer is a big debate topic among mathematicians and computer scientists. Although no random functions are truly random, the pseudo-random functions they do generate come close enough for us to use for everyday Web applications.
>
> When using images or text that are randomized, don't be concerned if clicking the Refresh button on your browser doesn't display a brand-new image every time. It's possible that the randomization process just picked the same image or text to be served up again. The fewer records that are stored in the recordset, the more likely that the same image will be chosen again to be displayed.

Using Dynamic Links to Navigate Search Results

When you add dynamic results pages to your Web site, it's usually a good idea to provide links that allow your visitors to navigate the results. While you could simply display all 7,365 results that were returned in the recordset, the visitor is probably not going to wait around for that results page to be built, and your Web server might just decide to go on strike.

Instead, you would most likely display five or ten results at a time and allow your visitor to move from page to page to see additional records. This can easily be accomplished using a combination of text or graphics and a few of UltraDev's server behaviors.

Exercise 10.3 Adding a Navigation Bar to a Results Page

1. Open the searchresults.asp page created in Chapter 9, "Building Search Capabilities." Close the default.asp page. Open the Server Behaviors panel, if it is not already visible, and double-click the Repeat Region server behavior that is linked to the rsSearch recordset.
2. Change the settings in the Repeat Region dialog box, shown in Figure 10.10, to display only five records at a time.

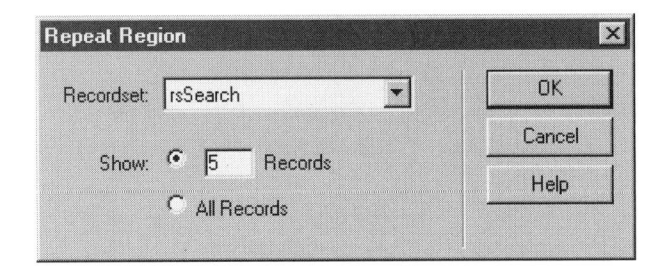

Figure 10.10 Change the server behavior so that only five records at a time are shown.

3. Click OK.
4. Place the cursor on the line below the existing table and choose Insert/Table from the menu bar.
5. In the Insert Table dialog box, create a table that has **1** row, **3** columns, and a width of **25%**. Set the border to **0** and the cell spacing and cell padding to **10**. Click OK.
6. Highlight the three cells by clicking in the left cell and dragging your cursor to the right-most cell. Click the Align Center button on the Property inspector.
7. Place the insertion point in the left cell of the new table and type Previous.
8. Press the Tab key on your keyboard to move to the center cell. Type **New Search**.
9. Press the Tab key to move to the right cell and type **Next**. As shown in Figure 10.11 you should now have a table with navigational text in each cell.
10. Highlight the "Previous" text and click the plus sign on the Server Behaviors panel. From the pop-up menu, select Move To Record/Move To Previous Record.
11. In the Move To Previous Record dialog box, shown in Figure 10.12, choose the Selection "Previous" link and the rsSearch recordset and click OK.

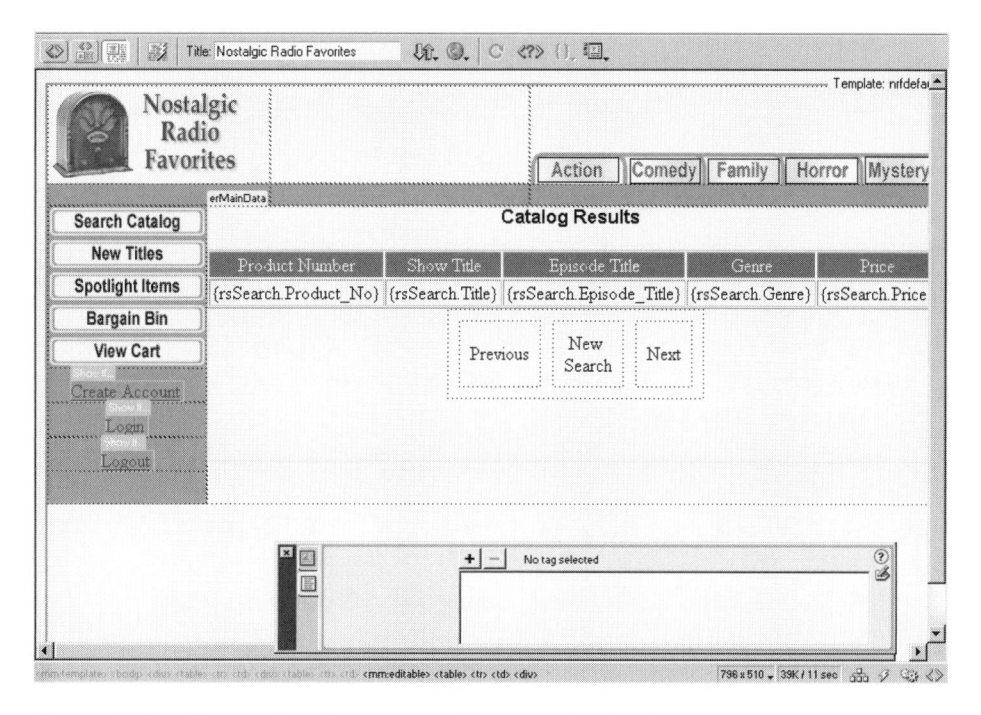

Chapter 10 Adding Dynamic Images and Text to Search Results

Figure 10.11 The searchresults.asp page with new navigational text.

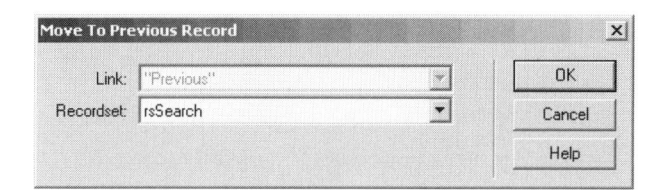

Figure 10.12 Using the Move To Previous Record dialog box, you can build a navigation link that returns to the previous page of results.

12. With the "Previous" text still highlighted, click the plus sign on the Server Behaviors panel and select Show Region/Show Region If Not First Record. In the Show Region If Not First Record dialog box, choose the rsSearch recordset. Click OK.

13. Highlight the "New Search" text and type **search_catalog.asp** in the Link field of the Property inspector. Press Enter.

14. Highlight the "Next" text and click the plus sign on the Server Behaviors panel. From the pop-up menu, choose Move To Record/Move To Next Record.

15. In the Move To Next Record dialog box, shown in Figure 10.13, select the Selection "Next" link and the rsSearch recordset and click OK.

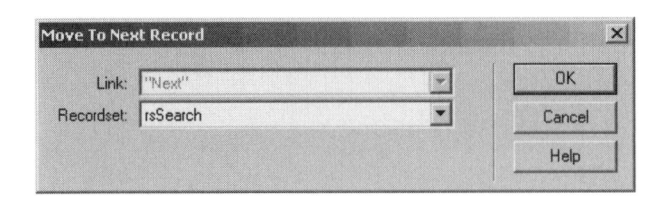

Figure 10.13 The Move To Next Record dialog box allows you to select which recordset you wish to navigate.

16. With the "Next" text still highlighted, click the plus sign on the Server Behaviors panel and select Show Region/Show Region If Not Last Record from the pop-up menu.
17. In the Show Region If Not Last Record dialog box, choose the rsSearch recordset and click OK.
18. Save the document and minimize UltraDev.
19. Open your Web browser and type **http://localhost/insideud4/search_catalog.asp** into the address bar.
20. In the Search Catalog page, leave all the fields blank and click the Submit button. As shown in Figure 10.14, only five records at a time are displayed in the results page. In addition, the "Next" and "New Search" navigation links are now present. The "Previous" navigation link is hidden because this is the first set of records and the link is unnecessary.
21. Click the Next button. As shown in Figure 10.15, the next five results are displayed. Notice that the "Previous" link is now available and the "Next" link is not visible since the last record in the search results is now displayed.
22. Click the Previous link and notice that the original five results are displayed again.
23. Finally, click the New Search link and notice that you have been returned to the Search Catalog page.

> **Note**
>
> **A Quick Way to Add a Navigation Bar** Another easy way to build a navigation bar that contains First, Previous, Next, and Last links is to use UltraDev's Recordset Navigation Bar Live Object. To add this to your page, simply place the insertion point where you want to add the bar and select Insert/Live Objects/Recordset Navigation Bar.
>
> In the Insert Recordset Navigation Bar dialog box, indicate which recordset you want the bar to manipulate and whether you would like text links or images. Then click OK and UltraDev will automatically add the links and appropriate Server Behaviors to your page.
>
> After you have the navigation bar inserted, you can customize it using your own graphics or text or any of the design tools to make it match your pages.

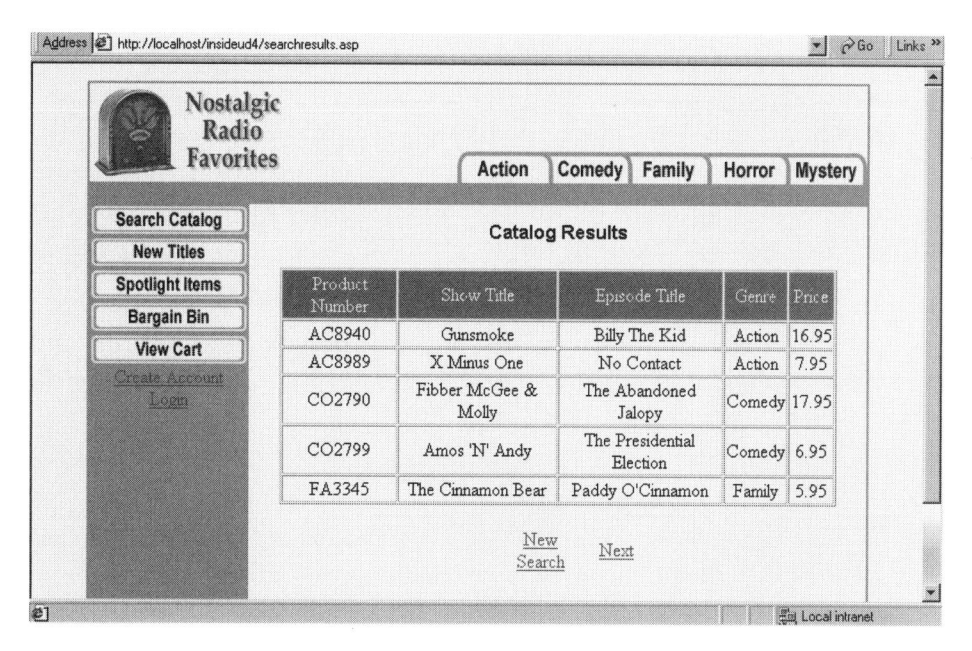

Chapter 10 Adding Dynamic Images and Text to Search Results   271

Figure 10.14 The searchresults.asp page now displays only five records at a time and has new navigation links.

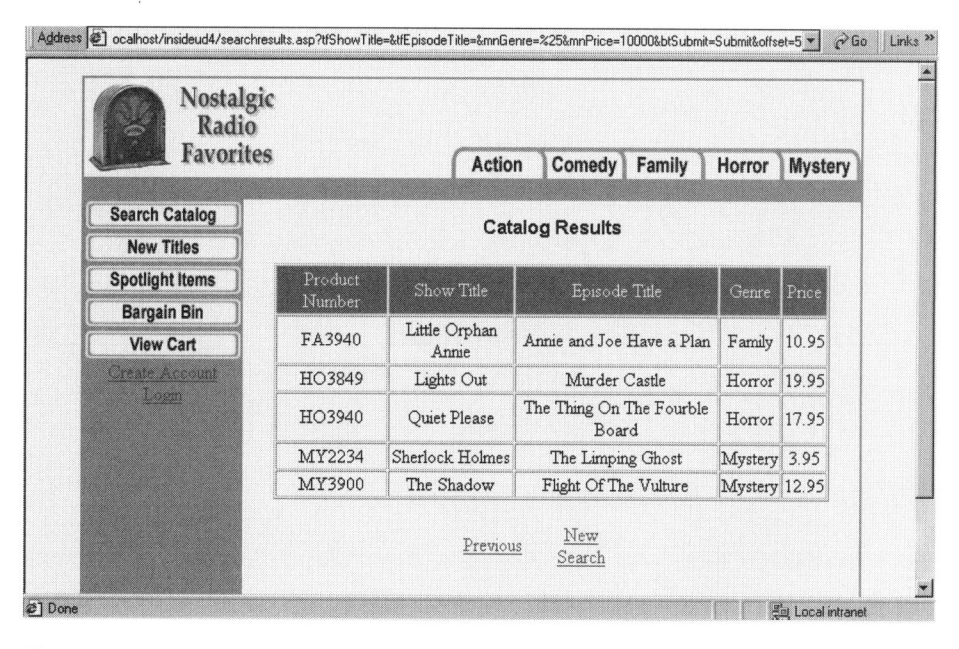

Figure 10.15 The page now displays the next five results in the recordset.

Building a Record Counter

Adding a record counter to your results page is another way to help your visitors navigate the records returned in a search. Because the record counter is simply a combination of text and UltraDev server behaviors, you can build the counter by adding the static text to your page and then adding the First Record Index, Last Record Index, and Total Records server behaviors to the page.

If, however, you would like to create a record counter with just a few clicks of the mouse, you can use the Recordset Navigation Status live object included in UltraDev. The live object automatically adds the necessary text and server behaviors and is fully customizable once it is added.

Exercise 10.4 Adding a Record Counter to Your Page

1. In the searchresults.asp page, place the insertion point before the navigation links table and press Shift+Enter to add a new line between the results table and the navigation links table.
2. Place the insertion point on the new line and press the Align Center button on the Property inspector.
3. From the menu bar, select Insert/Table and create a table that has **1** row, **1** column, and a width of **90%**. Set the border, cell padding, and cell spacing to **0**. Click OK.
4. Place the insertion point inside the new table and select Insert/Live Objects/Recordset Navigation Status from the menu bar.
5. In the Recordset Navigation Status dialog box, shown in Figure 10.16, select the rsSearch recordset and click OK.

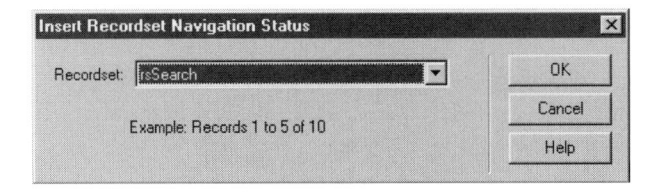

Figure 10.16 The Insert Recordset Navigation Status dialog box.

6. Highlight the newly added text that reads "Records" and press the Delete key on your keyboard.
7. With the insertion point where the "Records" text was, type **Titles**. Be sure to add a space between the Titles text and the {rsSearch_first} text.

Chapter 10 Adding Dynamic Images and Text to Search Results   273

8. Highlight all the newly added text and dynamic elements and type **#006699** in the Text Color field of the Properties inspector located between the size field and the Bold button.

9. Click the Align Left button on the Property inspector. As shown in Figure 10.17, the elements for a customized record counter have been added to the page.

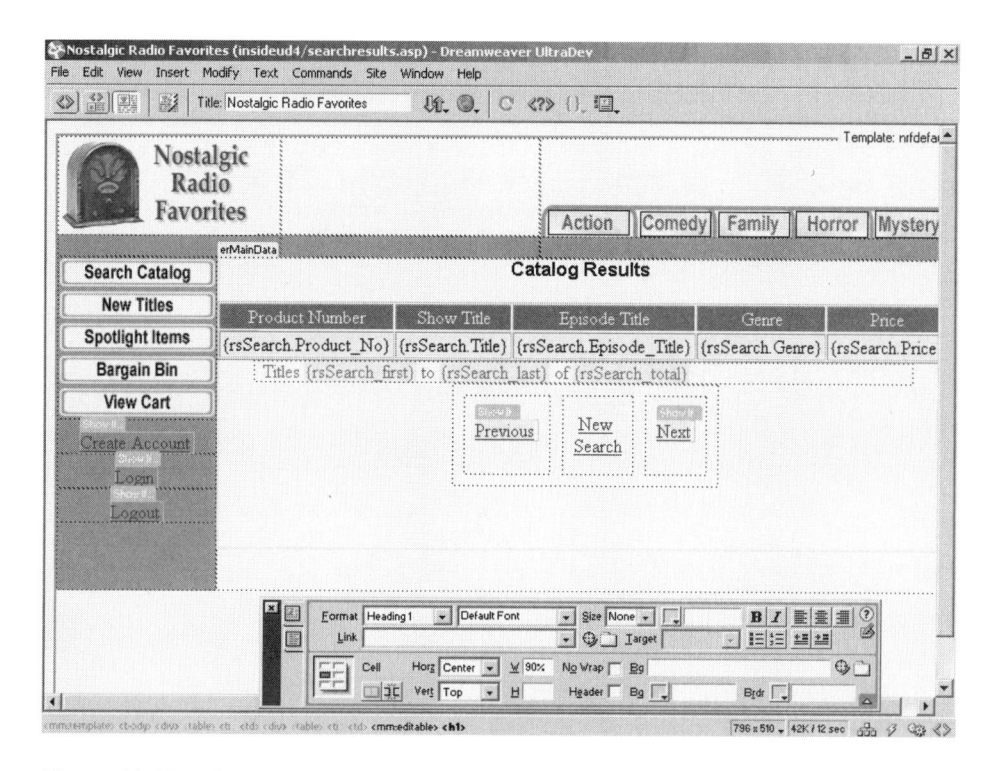

Figure 10.17 The new customized record counter.

10. Save the page.
11. Minimize UltraDev and open your browser.
12. In the address bar, type **http://localhost/insideud4**. In the home page, click the Search Catalog button.
13. In the Search Catalog page, leave the form blank and click the Submit button.
14. As shown in Figure 10.18, the search results page now displays the number of records displayed on the page along with the total number of records returned by the search.

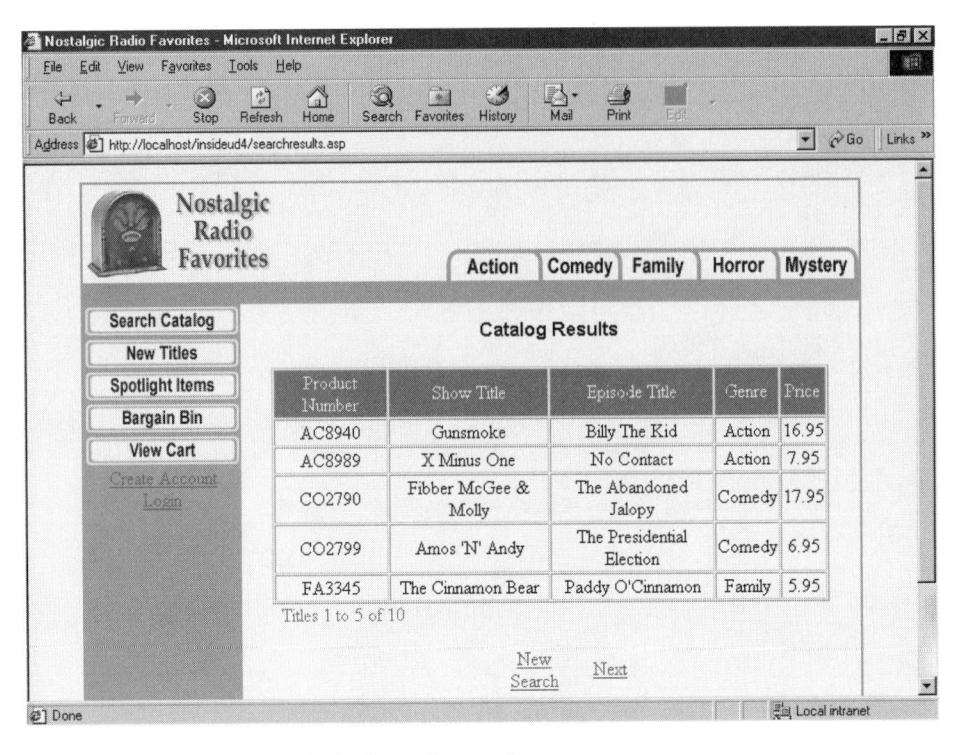

Figure 10.18 Your page with the dynamic record counter.

Summary

This chapter showed you how to take dynamic images and text to a new level. Using UltraDev's server behaviors, advanced SQL queries, and Live Objects, you can add rotating graphics, date-sensitive graphics, navigation bars, and dynamic record counters.

The next chapter looks at combining many of the features demonstrated in the previous chapters with the ability to edit and update database records by building a database administration site. An administration site can provide you and the other members of your organization with an easy way to manage your data using a Web browser.

Part IV

Extending Your Administrative Capabilities

11	Developing a Database Administration Site	279
12	Engaging in eCommerce	313
13	Adding eLearning to Your Site	359
14	Extending UltraDev	389

Chapter 11

Developing a Database Administration Site

One of the organizations that I worked with recently discovered just how convenient a database administration site can be. The organization has a centrally located headquarters building and several satellite offices in different parts of the city. Because of the organization's limited funding and access to technology, for the last few years the employees in the satellite offices have been using modems to dial in to a server in order to update their client records, which were stored in an Access database. Unfortunately, even when they were connecting at 56.6 Kbps, the process was painfully slow because they had to open the entire Access database before they could even begin to manipulate the data. At times, it took 10 to 15 minutes just to open the database, and once the database was open, just scrolling through the records seemed to take forever.

Having worked with Web-based databases before, I suggested to the director of the organization that purchasing a copy of UltraDev, adding Web services to their server, and developing a database administration site could save the outlying offices a lot of time and headaches. After working with the offices for a couple of weeks to determine their needs, I'm pleased to say that, using their new database administration site developed in UltraDev, each office is now able to perform in minutes the same tasks that used to take them hours.

To demonstrate just how quickly you can develop a database administration site using UltraDev, this chapter shows you how to do the following:

- Build the foundation for your administration site
- Add search capabilities
- Add, edit, and delete records from a database
- Test the functionality of the administration site

> **Note**
>
> **Didn't We Do This Another Way Before?** As you read through this chapter and do the exercises, you'll notice that the chapter not only introduces some of UltraDev's database manipulation functions, but also serves as an in-depth review of many of the topics covered in the previous chapters. In some situations, we show you a different way to build a page or add a specific function to a page. We do this to demonstrate that, in many cases, UltraDev offers a variety of ways to accomplish the same result.

Building the Foundation for the Administration Site

Think of the administration site as a completely separate Web site from the site we have been building. Sure, they may share the same logo, the same database connection, and many of the same functions, but access to the administration site will be restricted using different criteria than the main site. In addition, those who do access it may need to see additional information, accessing functions such as adding, editing, and deleting records that the traditional visitor doesn't need to have access to.

As a separate site, you need to build the administration site from the ground up and include functionality such as login and logout pages, a site-wide page template, and a menu to guide authenticated visitors. Although this may sound like a big task, using the connections you have already established along with UltraDev's server behaviors and live objects, you can create a fully functional administration site in no time.

> **Tip**
>
> **Do You Need a Separate UltraDev Site?** Thinking about the administration site as a completely separate Web site may have you wondering if you need to create a new site in UltraDev strictly for the administration site.
>
> If your administration site will be located in a separate folder (rather than a subfolder) or on a different server, it would probably be a good idea to set up a new site that maintains a separate cache. If, however, your administration site will be located in a subfolder of your main site, creating a new site could cause problems.
>
> For instance, in the exercises in this chapter, you will be creating the administration pages in the `http://localhost/insideud4/admin` folder of the site. If you were to attempt to create a site specifically for that subfolder, UltraDev would warn you that creating a new site within an already existing site may lead to problems with the cache used to track your pages.

Beginning with the Login Page

As with your previous login page, you need to verify that username and password combination match data located in the database. One additional restriction, however, lies in the fact that you want only employees of the Nostalgic Radio Favorites company to have access. This means that the database must somehow distinguish between an employee and a non-employee.

Differentiating the employees could be accomplished in several ways. One way would be to create a completely separate table that stored only employee usernames and passwords, which the administrative site would use to authenticate users. The downside to this comes from the fact that an employee would then have to maintain a password in the regular user database and one in the administrative database. As any database administrator will tell you, multiple password systems can often become a nightmare because they require users to change their passwords in more than one place. In these situations, users often forget to update a password and they quickly become "out of synch." Although this issue could be addressed by linking databases and joining tables, it is still a very tricky task that usually requires an advanced understanding of your database management system.

Another way to accomplish the goal would be to create a field in the users table (in your case the tbCustomers table) where you could indicate that a user is an employee by setting the value to 1. Then, you could have the login page check whether the username and password are valid and the employee value is set to 1. If so, the user would be authenticated. Although this is a perfectly acceptable way to solve the problem, we opted to use a different approach to show off the fact that UltraDev can use just about any SQL function to accomplish your goals.

The method we chose was to append a prefix ("nrfemp") to the username of those users who are Nostalgic Radio Favorites employees. The login page then checks to see if the first six characters in the username match "nrfemp" and if so, the page checks whether the username and password combination are valid before authenticating.

Is this the best way to accomplish the task? Probably not. In fact, if I were creating this site for real, I would probably use the first method to ensure the best security with the least inconvenience. I chose, however, to use this method in the exercises because it gives you one more chance to build an advanced SQL query.

> **Warning**
>
> **Don't Connect Your Login Page to the Template** You might be wondering why you don't create your template first and then build the login page from that template. The reason comes from the fact that you will be applying a server behavior to your template that automatically redirects unauthenticated users to the login page. If you were to create this template and then build the login page from that template, you would run into a problem. Because a visitor to the login page is presumably unauthenticated, when the page loads, they would be automatically redirected to the login page. The result would be the loading of the login page over and over.
>
> For this reason, we build the login page first, and then create the template.

Exercise 11.1 Creating a Login Page

1. Open UltraDev. Open a new page if one is not opened automatically.
2. From the menu bar, select File/Save. In the Save As dialog box, navigate to the InsideUD4 folder and click the Create New Folder button on the button bar. Name the folder **admin**. Press Enter.
3. Double-click on the admin folder and save the page as **default.asp**.
4. In the Title field above the page, type **Nostalgic Radio Favorites – Administrative Site**. Press Enter.

Chapter 11 Developing a Database Administration Site   283

5. With the insertion point at the top of the page, click the Align Center button on the Property inspector.

6. Insert a table that has **1** row, **1** column, and a width of **90%**. Set the border to **1** and the cell padding and cell spacing to **0**. Press Enter.

7. With the table selected, type **#999966** into the Border Color field on the Property inspector. Name the table **tbMain**. Set the Height of the table to **100%**.

8. Place the insertion point inside the new table and set the vertical alignment to Top in the Property inspector.

9. In the single cell, insert an additional table. This table should have **3** rows, **1** column, and a width of **70%**. Set the border, cell padding, and cell spacing to **0**. Press Enter.

10. Name the table **tbContainer**.

11. Highlight the three cells in the tbContainer table and click the Align Center button on the Property inspector.

12. With the insertion point in the top cell of the tbContainer table, select Insert/Image and choose the nrf_logo.gif image located in the images subfolder. Click OK. As shown in Figure 11.1, UltraDev warns you that a relative link to the image will be created once you save the page.

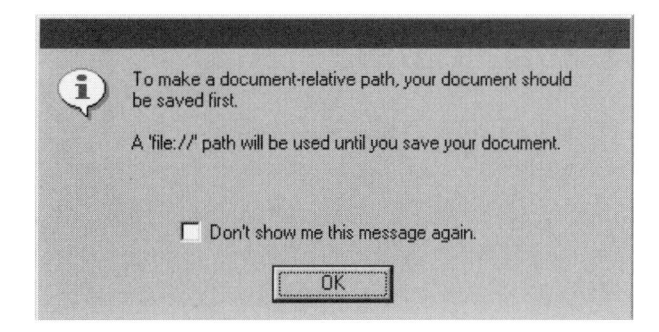

Figure 11.1   Until you save a page, the images placed in it will not have relative links.

13. Click OK to close the alert box.

14. In the second row of the tbContainer table, type **Administrative Site**.

15. Place a form in the bottom row of the tbContainer table by clicking Insert/Form from the menu bar.

16. Name the form **fmAdminLogin**. Press Enter. In the Action field of the Property inspector, type **admin_validation.asp**.

17. With the form highlighted insert a table that has **3** rows, **2** columns, and a width of **60%**. Set the border, cell spacing, and cell padding to **1**.

18. In the Property Inspector, name the table **tbElements**. Press Enter.
19. Highlight the left column and click the Align Right button on the Property Inspector. Set the column width at **50%**.
20. In the top-left cell, type **Username**.
21. In the middle-left cell, type **Password**.
22. In the bottom left cell, insert a submit button. Name the button **btSubmit**.
23. In the top-right cell, insert a text field by choosing Insert/Form Objects/Text Field from the menu bar. Name the text field **tfAdminUsername**.
24. In the middle-right cell, insert a text field and name it **tfAdminPassword**. In the Property inspector, designate this text field as a password field.
25. In the bottom-right cell, insert a reset button and name it **btReset**. Press Enter. As shown in Figure 11.2, you should now have a completed login form.

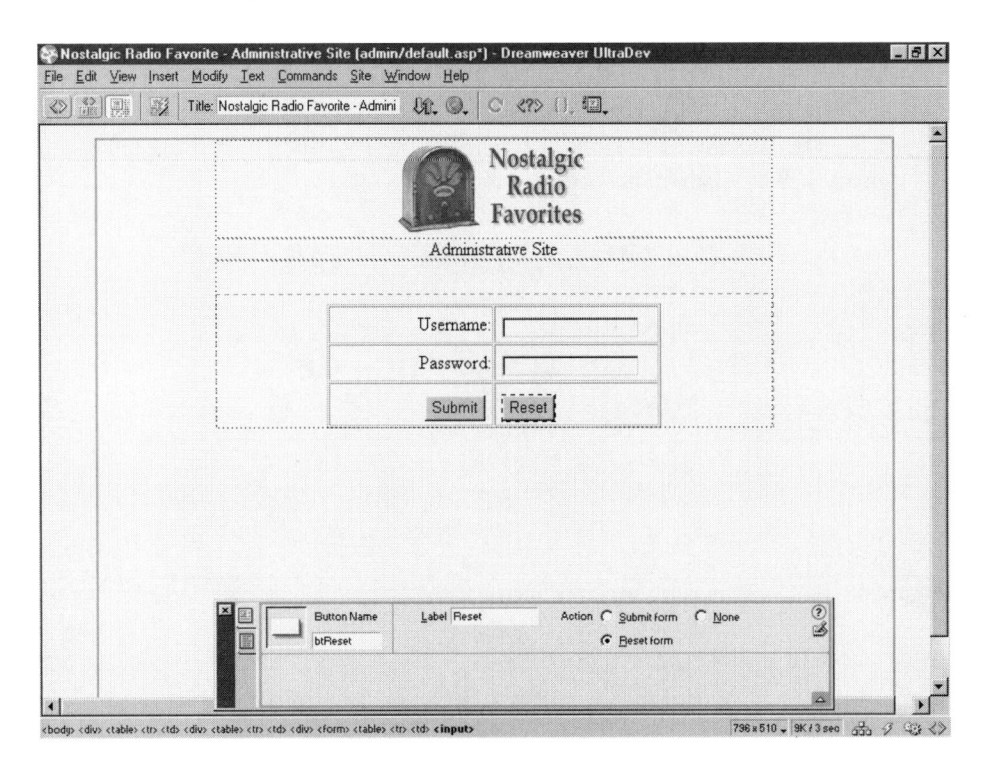

Figure 11.2 The Administrative Site login form.

26. Save the page.
27. From the menu bar, select File/Save As and save the file as **admin_validation.asp**.

28. Select the fmAdminLogin form and press the Delete key on your keyboard. In the bottom cell of the table, type the following text block:

    We're sorry. We were not able to log you in. Please click the Back button in your browser to try again.

29. Replace the "Administrative Site" text with the following text block:

    Thank you. You were successfully logged on to the Administrative Site. Click here to continue.

30. Open the Server Behaviors panel if it is not already open. Click the plus sign and select Recordset (Query) from the pop-up menu.

31. Build a recordset using the parameters shown in Figure 11.3. This recordset looks for usernames that begin with nrfemp. Only users with this prefix will be allowed access to the administrative site. Click OK when finished.

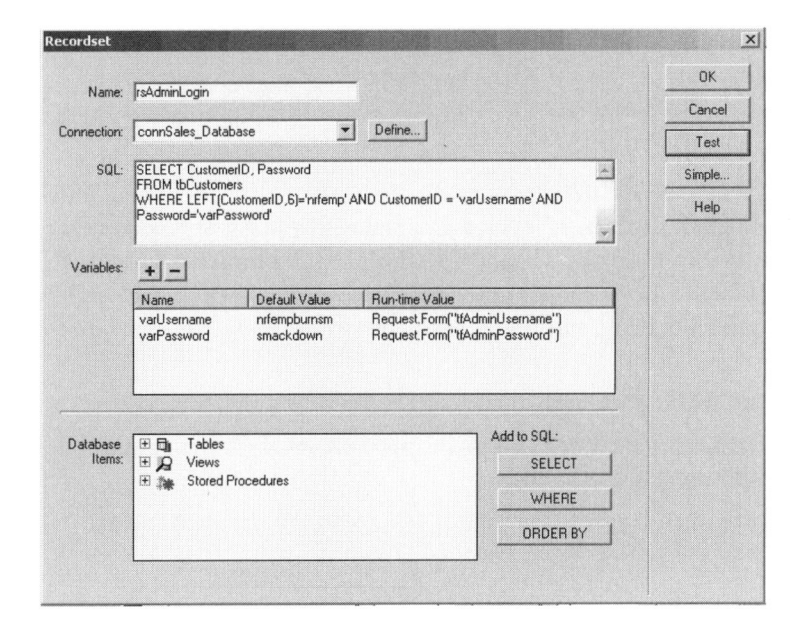

Figure 11.3 Create the rsAdminLogin recordset so that it looks like this.

32. Highlight the text in the middle row and click the plus sign on the Server behaviors panel. Select Show Region/Show Region If Recordset Is Not Empty from the pop-up menu.

33. In the Show Region If Recordset Is Not Empty dialog box, shown in Figure 11.4, select the rsAdminLogin recordset and click OK.

34. Highlight the "Click Here" text in the middle cell and type **admin_menu.asp** in the Link field of the Property inspector. Press Enter.

> **Note**
>
> **Taking Steps to Secure Your Administration Site** For demonstration purposes, the exercises in this chapter use the tbCustomers table to validate the username and password of the user attempting to gain access to the administration site. We designed the exercises this way so we could use the same connection that you have already been using to the Sales_Database.mdb database.
>
> In the "real world" of Web design, however, you would want to keep the usernames and passwords of those having access to the administration site separate from your daily visitors. Doing so minimizes that chance that someone could hack your database and not only retrieve your customer information, but also access your administrative site and add, edit, and delete records.

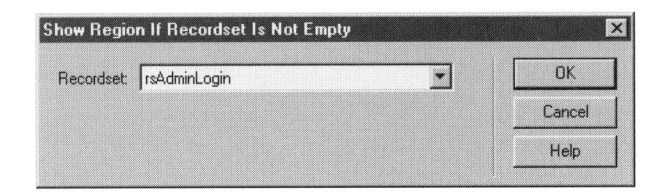

Figure 11.4 The Show Region If Recordset Is Not Empty dialog box.

35. Highlight the text in the bottom row and apply the Show Region If Recordset Is Empty server behavior using the rsAdminLogin recordset. Click OK. As shown in Figure 11.5, you should now have a page that only shows the confirmation text and link to the administrative menu when the username and password are valid.
36. Switch to the Code view by clicking the Show Code View button on the toolbar.
37. Create a new line directly above the opening `<html>` tag in your code and insert the following line of code:

    `<%session("MM_Username")=Request.Form("tfAdminUsername")%>`
38. Switch back to the Design view and save the page.

Creating a Template for Future Commonly Formatted Pages

The next step in developing your administration site is to create a template that you can use to quickly create pages that have the same characteristics. In this particular case, you want to ensure that each page cannot be accessed unless the user's identity has been authenticated by the login page. To accomplish this, use a server behavior that checks for an existing session variable. If the session variable is present, then the user is allowed to view the page.

Chapter 11 Developing a Database Administration Site 287

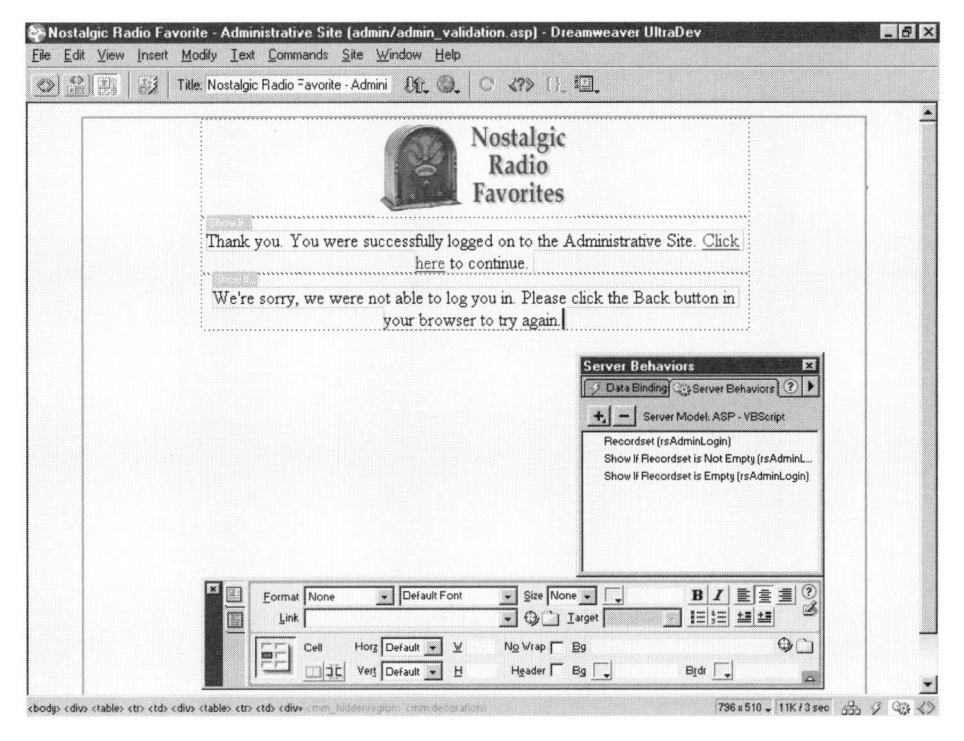

Figure 11.5 The admin_validation.asp page will now display the correct text depending on whether the username and password were authenticated.

By applying both the server behavior and the session variable to the template, you can be sure that every page created from the template will be secure from unauthenticated visitors.

Exercise 11.2 Designing the Administration Site Template

1. In the admin_validation.asp page, click File/Save As Template from the menu bar.
2. In the Save As Template dialog box, select the InsideUD4 site and type **nrfadmin** in the Save As field. Click Save.
3. In the Server Behaviors panel, select the Show If Recordset Is Not Empty behavior and click the minus sign. Remove the Show If Recordset Is Empty server behavior as well. Finally, remove the rsAdminLogin recordset.
4. Highlight the text in the bottom row and press the Delete key.
5. Highlight the text in the middle row and press the Delete key.

288　Part IV　Extending Your Administrative Capabilities

6. Switch to the Code view and delete the code you added in Exercise 11.1, Step 36, located on the line directly above the opening `<html>` tag.
7. Click the Show Design View button to switch back to the Design view.
8. In the Server Behaviors panel, click the Data Bindings tab and click the plus sign. Select Session Variable from the popup menu. In the Session Variable dialog box, shown in Figure 11.6, type **MM_Username** and click OK.

Figure 11.6　The Session Variable dialog box.

9. In the Data Bindings panel, click the plus sign next to Session and drag the MM_Username session variable onto the page underneath the tbContainer table.
10. Place the insertion point in the middle cell of the tbContainer table and select Modify/Templates/New Editable Region from the menu bar. In the New Editable Region dialog box, shown in Figure 11.7, type **erMiddle** and click OK.

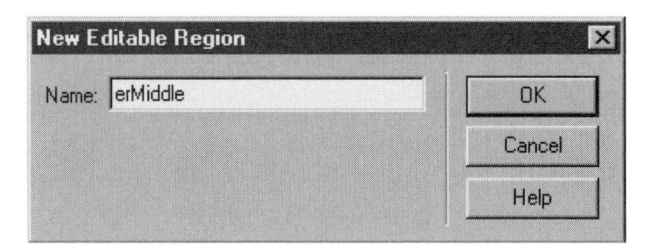

Figure 11.7　The New Editable Region dialog box.

11. Insert an additional editable region in the bottom cell of the tbContainer table and name it **erBottom**.
12. To keep administrators from bookmarking pages and returning without logging in, click the plus sign on the Server Behaviors panel and select User Authentication/Restrict Access To Page.
13. In the Restrict Access To Page dialog box, choose to restrict access based on username and password. In the If Access Denied, Go To field, type **default.asp**. Click OK.

14. Save the page. If you are prompted to update the documents based on the templates, click Yes to update documents. No files are currently associated with this page, so your message will be that no files are updated. As you can see in Figure 11.8, the template now consists of the logo, a couple of editable regions, and the Admin session.

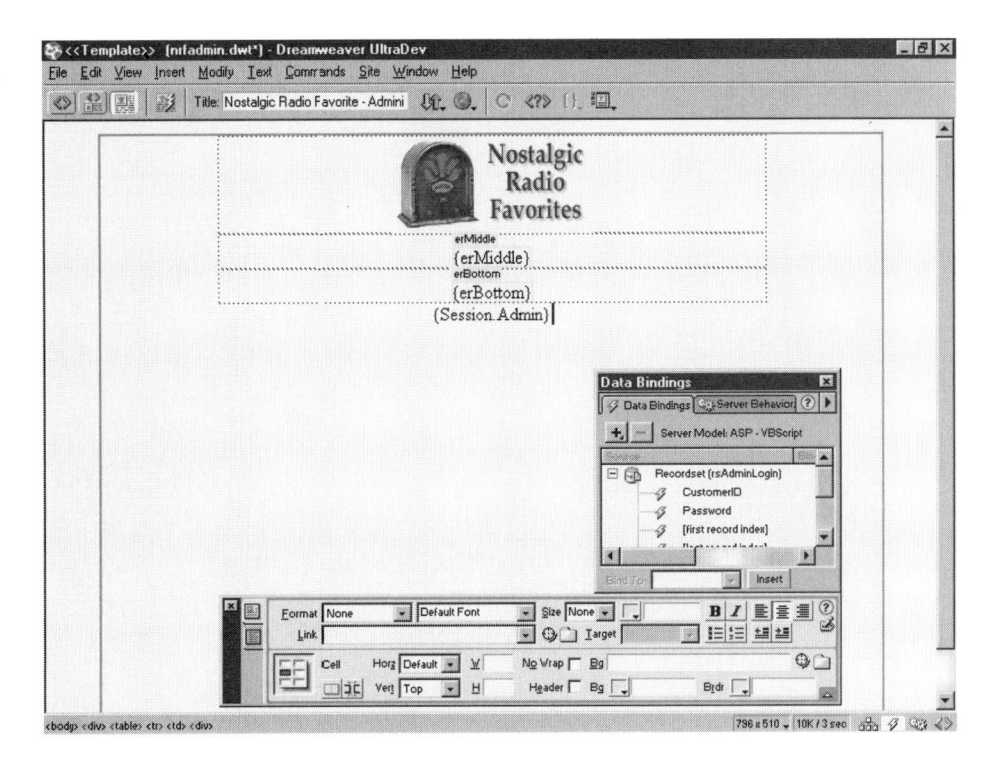

Figure 11.8 The Administrative Site template.

15. Close the template.

Adding a Menu Page to Help Users Navigate the Site

The menu page for the administration site provides authenticated users with links to the various sections of the site. In this case, you will be adding links to add a product to the database or search through the available products where they will be able to update or delete an existing product.

If you want to extend the functionality of the administration site, you could allow employees to administer user accounts or eCommerce transactions or even provide access to database reports. Essentially, the scope of the administration site is up to you, but the menu page is where you let authenticated visitors know what they are able to do.

Exercise 11.3 Creating the Administrative Menu Page

1. From the menu bar, select File/New From Template. In the Select Template dialog box, select the InsideUD4 site and the nrfadmin template. Check the Update Page When Template Changes checkbox and click Select. Close the nrfadmin.dwt page.
2. In the new page, highlight the {erMiddle} text and press the Delete key.
3. Type **Administration Menu** and press the Enter key.
4. Type **Product Search** and press the Enter key.
5. Type **Add A Product** and press the Enter key.
6. Highlight the Product Search text and type **admin_product_search.asp** in the Link field of the Property inspector. Press Enter.
7. Highlight the Add A Product text and type **admin_add_product.asp** in the Link field of the Property inspector. Press Enter.
8. Highlight the {erBottom} text and press the Delete key. In the erBottom editable region, insert a form and name it **fmAdminLogout**. In the Action field of the form, type **admin_logout.asp**.
9. Drop the insertion point in the new form (outlined in red). Place a single button in the form and name it **btLogout**. Change the button label to read **Logout**. Press Enter.
10. Save the page as **admin_menu.asp** in the admin subfolder. As shown in Figure 11.9, the menu page now allows administrators to choose which aspect of the site they would like to administer and to log out if they wish.

> **Note**
> **More than Just Products** Although the exercises in this chapter only cover creating pages to administer the products in the database, you could also create pages that add, update, and delete users or transactions from the database.

Giving Users a Way to Log Out

For every login page you create, it's always a good idea to create a logout page. This allows the user to terminate his session without having to close his Web browser. In the case of an administration site, it's especially important that you provide a logout link and instruct those users with access to be sure to log out. This reduces the risk of unauthorized access, especially from computers that are shared among users in a public setting.

Exercise 11.4 Adding a Logout Page to the Admin Site

1. Create a new page from the nrfadmin template. Close the admin_menu.asp page.
2. Delete the {erMiddle} text and type **Thank you**. You were successfully logged out.

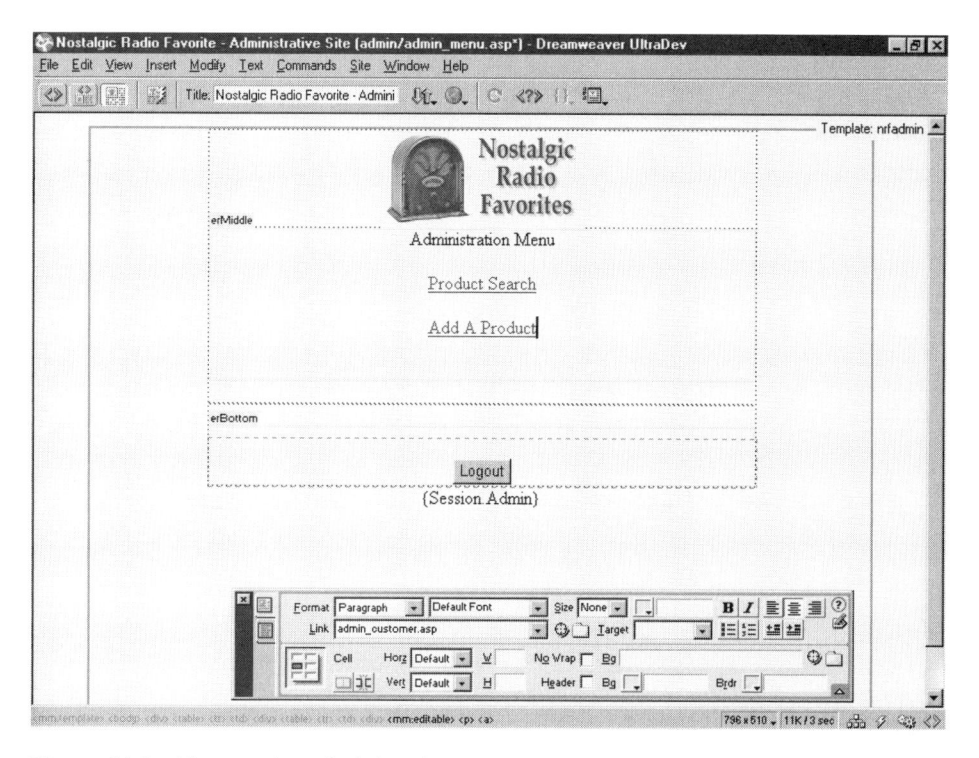

Figure 11.9 The complete administrative menu.

3. Click the plus sign on the Server Behaviors panel and select User Authentication/Log Out User. In the Log Out User dialog box, choose to log the user out when the page loads and click OK.
4. Delete the {erBottom} text.
5. Save the page as **admin_logout.asp**.

Adding Search Capabilities to the Administration Site

After a user has logged on to the administration site, she is obviously going to want to see the records stored in the database. Rather than just dumping every record onto a page, we can provide the user with a search form that allows her to specify which records she wishes to work with. The results page will then display the appropriate records and provide the user with links to edit or delete the record.

Creating a Product Search Page

For the most part, the search page in your administration site is similar to the search page you created in the main site. By combining a form with a variety of text fields and buttons, you can submit the data stored in a form to a results page where the appropriate records will be displayed.

The only differences between the two search pages are the fields able to be searched and the logic used in the relationship between the text fields. In the main site, we created a form that, when left blank, returned every record in the database. We did this because we wanted each text field in the form to work with each other to narrow the results of the query.

In the case of the administrative site, you want your users to be able to find the record they need to work with as quickly as possible. To accomplish this, allow them to either enter the specific product number or enter the title of the show. Then use a SQL query that returns the appropriate record(s) based on whichever field was filled in. If, however, the user doesn't enter any data, the results page interprets this as the user doesn't want any records and returns an empty results page.

> **Tip**
>
> **Searching Different Fields** For the purposes of this chapter, the administrative search offers the ability to search based on Show Title or Product Number. Keep in mind, however, that you could expand this search page to allow administrators to search any field stored in the database.

Exercise 11.5 Building a Product Search Page

1. Create a new page based on the nrfadmin template. Close the admin_logout.asp page.
2. Delete the {erMiddle} text and type **Product Search**. Press Enter.
3. Type **Please enter a product number or show title**. Press Enter.
4. On the new line, insert a form and name it **fmProductSearch**. In the Action field type **admin_product_results.asp**. Press the Enter key.
5. Inside the form, insert a table that has **3** rows, **2** columns, and a width of **60%**. Set the border, cell padding, and cell spacing to **1**.
6. Highlight the left column of the table and click the Align Right button on the Property inspector. Set the column width to **50%**.
7. In the top-left cell, type **Product Number:**.
8. In the middle-left cell, type **Show Title:**.
9. In the bottom-left cell, insert a submit button. Name the button **btSubmit**.
10. In the top-right cell, insert a text field and name it **tfProductNumber**.
11. In the middle-right cell, insert a text field and name it **tfShowTitle**.

12. In the bottom-right cell, insert a reset button. Name the button **btReset** and change the button label to **Reset**. If everything doesn't line up correctly, select the table and set Align to Center in the Property inspector. As shown in Figure 11.10, the search form allows the administrator to search by product number or show title.

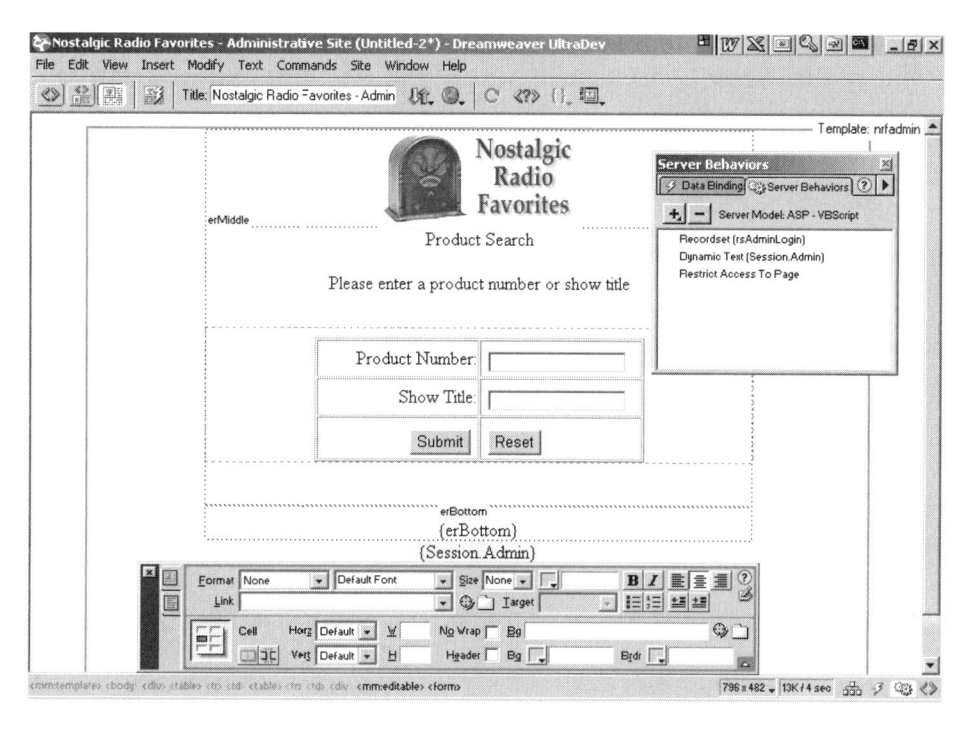

Figure 11.10 The Product Search form.

13. In the erBottom editable region, delete the text and type **Return To Administrative Menu**. Highlight the text and type **admin_menu.asp** in the Link field of the Property inspector. Press Enter.
14. Save the page as **admin_product_search.asp**.

Adding a Results Page to the Administration Site

As I mentioned earlier, the results page in the administration site is based on a different SQL query from the results pages used in the main site. Another difference, however, is the addition of links that allow the user to edit or delete the record. Using a couple of UltraDev's server behaviors, we can quickly build links that will move to the appropriate page and only edit or delete the record whose corresponding link was clicked.

Exercise 11.6 Creating a Product Results Page

1. Create a new page based on the nrfadmin template. Close the admin_product_search.asp page.
2. Delete the {erMiddle} text and type **Product Results**. Press Enter.
3. On the new line, insert a new table with **2** rows, **7** columns, and a width of **100%**. Set the border, cell padding, and cell spacing to **1**. Press Enter.
4. Select the top row of the table and click Align Center on the Property inspector. Set the row's background color to **#006699**. Press Enter.
5. In the top-left cell, type **Product #**. Press Tab.
6. In the next cell, type **Show Title**. Press Tab.
7. In the next cell, type **Episode Title**. Press Tab.
8. In the next cell, type **Genre**. Press Tab.
9. In the next cell, type **Price**. Press Tab.
10. In the next cell, type **Edit**. Press Tab.
11. In the next cell, type **Delete**.
12. Highlight the top row and set the font type to Arial, Helvetica, sans serif, and the font size to **3**. Set the font color to white (**#FFFFFF**) and click the Bold button. As shown in Figure 11.11, the table now has column headings.
13. On the Server Behaviors panel, click the plus sign and select Recordset (Query) from the pop-up menu.
14. Build the rsAdminProducts recordset using the criteria shown in Figure 11.12. This recordset returns the value of either the Product Number text field or the Show Title text field. When you are finished, click OK.
15. Click the Data Bindings tab on the Server Behaviors panel. Click the plus sign next to the rsAdminProducts recordset to expand the available data elements.
16. Click on the Product_No element and drag it to the cell under the Product # heading. Drag the Title element to the cell under Show Title. Continue by dragging the Episode_Title, Genre, and Price elements to the corresponding cells.
17. Place the insertion point in the cell underneath the Edit heading. You may have to scroll the page to the right to see the column.
18. Type **Edit** and highlight the text. Click the plus sign on the Server Behaviors panel and select Go To Detail Page from the pop-up menu.
19. In the Go To Detail Page dialog box, shown in Figure 11.13, type **admin_product_edit.asp** in the Detail Page field. In the Recordset field, select rsAdminProducts and choose Product_No from the Column field. Click OK.

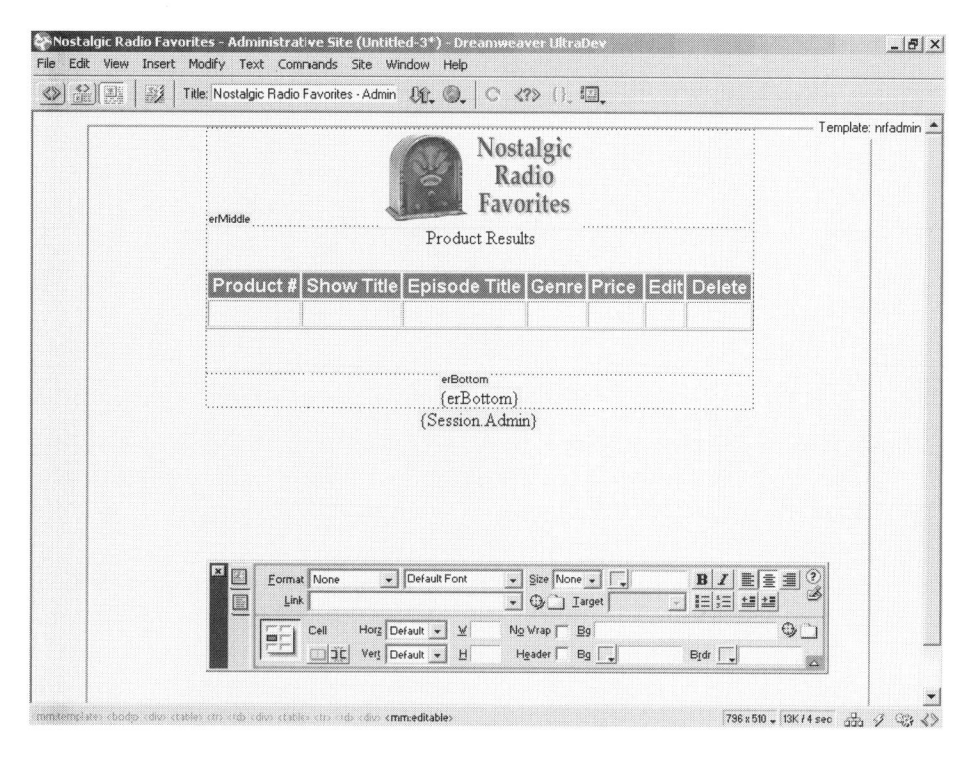

Chapter 11 Developing a Database Administration Site   295

Figure 11.11 The headings for the results page have been created.

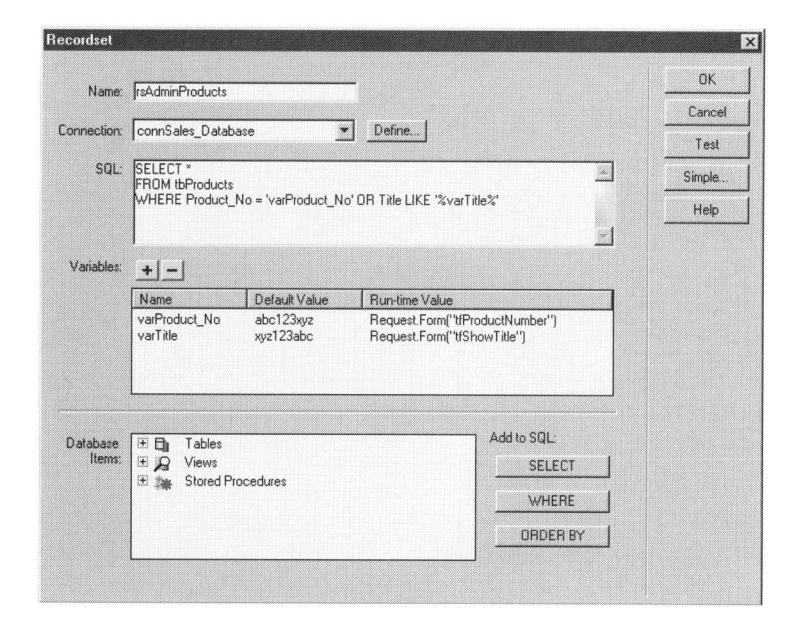

Figure 11.12 The rsAdminProducts recordset.

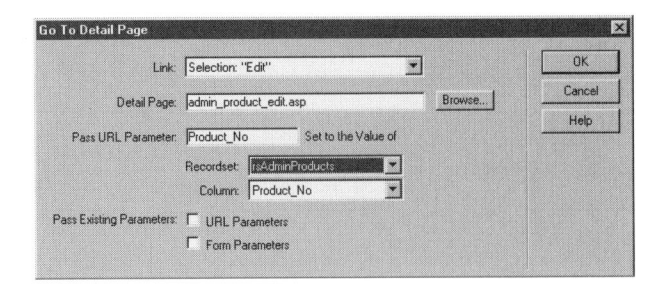

Figure 11.13 The Go To Detail Page dialog box.

20. In the cell below the Delete heading, type **Delete** and highlight the text.
21. Click the plus sign on the Server Behaviors panel and select Go To Detail Page from the pop-up menu. In the Go To Detail Page dialog box, type **admin_product_delete.asp** in the Detail Page field. Choose rsAdminProducts as the recordset and Product_No as the column. Click OK.
22. Highlight the bottom row of the table (beneath the table headings) and click the plus sign on the Server Behaviors panel. Choose Repeat Region from the pop-up menu.
23. In the Repeat Region dialog box, shown in Figure 11.14, select the rsAdminProducts recordset and choose to show **10** records. Click OK.

Figure 11.14 Select the rsAdminProducts recordset in the Repeat Region dialog box.

24. Highlight the text in the erBottom editable region and press the Delete key.
25. From the menu bar, select Insert/Live Objects/Recordset Navigation Bar. In the Insert Recordset Navigation Bar dialog box, shown in Figure 11.15, select the rsAdminProducts recordset and choose to display using text and click OK.
26. Place the insertion point on the line below the new navigation bar and press the Enter key.
27. Type **Return to Administrative Menu**. Highlight the text and type **admin_menu.asp** in the Link field of the Property inspector. Press Enter.
28. Save the page as **admin_product_results.asp**

Chapter 11 Developing a Database Administration Site 297

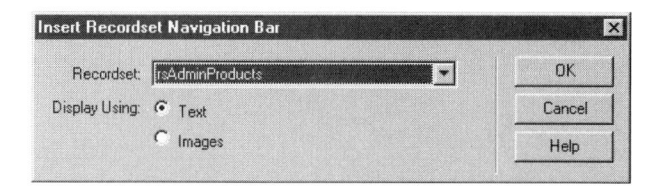

Figure 11.15 Add a navigation bar to your page using UltraDev's Navigation Bar live object.

Adding, Editing, and Deleting Records

As your organization grows and changes, so will your database. Luckily, UltraDev makes it easy to develop pages that allow your administrative users to add, edit, and delete records stored in your database. In fact, using a combination of live objects, server behaviors, forms, and form objects, you can add these common administrative features to your site in a matter of minutes.

> **Note**
>
> **One Operation at a Time** Database administration pages that add, edit, or delete a record can only contain one behavior that interacts with the record. For instance, in your database administration site, you need one page to insert a record, one page to edit a record, and another page to delete a record.

Building a New Product Entry Page

UltraDev makes creating a record entry page extremely easy through the use of the Record Insertion live object feature. Using this, you can skip the step of adding a form, form fields, buttons, and server behaviors to your page. Instead UltraDev asks you into which table you would like to insert the record, and which fields you would like available on the entry form, and then it does the rest.

After the page is loaded, the user can then fill the appropriate fields and click the Submit button and the form contents will automatically be added to a new record in the database.

Exercise 11.7 Creating an Insert Record Page Using UltraDev's Record Insertion Form Live Object.

1. Create a new page from the nrfadmin template. Close the admin_product_results.asp page.
2. Highlight the text in the erMiddle editable region and delete it. Type **Product Addition Page** and press the Enter key.

3. From the menu bar, select Insert/Live Objects/Record Insertion Form.
4. In the Insert Record Insertion Form dialog box, shown in Figure 11.16, select the connSales_Database connection and the tbProducts table.

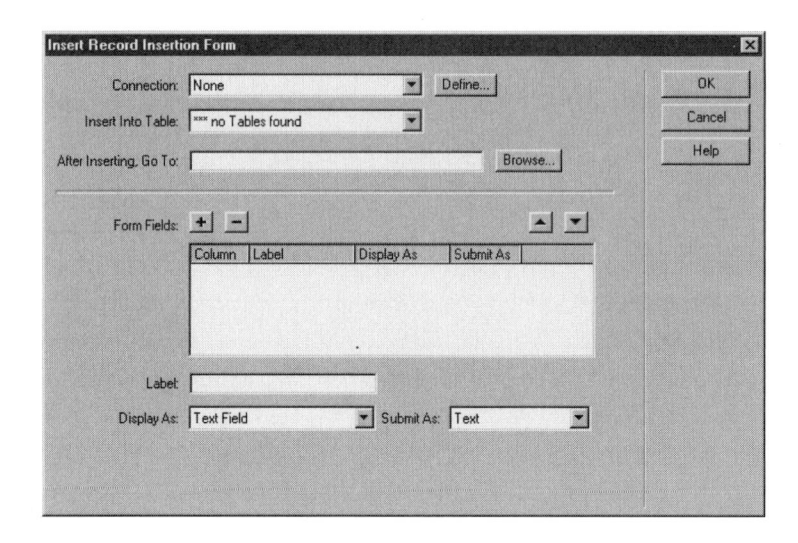

Figure 11.16 Insert a record insertion form using the Insert Record Insertion Form live object.

5. In the After Inserting, Go To field, type **admin_addition_confirmation.asp**.
6. In the Form Fields panel, click the Entry_Date form field and click the minus button to keep it from being displayed. Order the fields according to the following list by highlighting each field and using the up and down arrows to adjust the field's position:

   Product_No

   Title

   Episode_Title

   Air_Date

   Genre

   Price

   Spotlight

   Photo_URL

   Description

7. Click OK. As shown in Figure 11.17, UltraDev has added the appropriate form and form elements to add a product to the database.

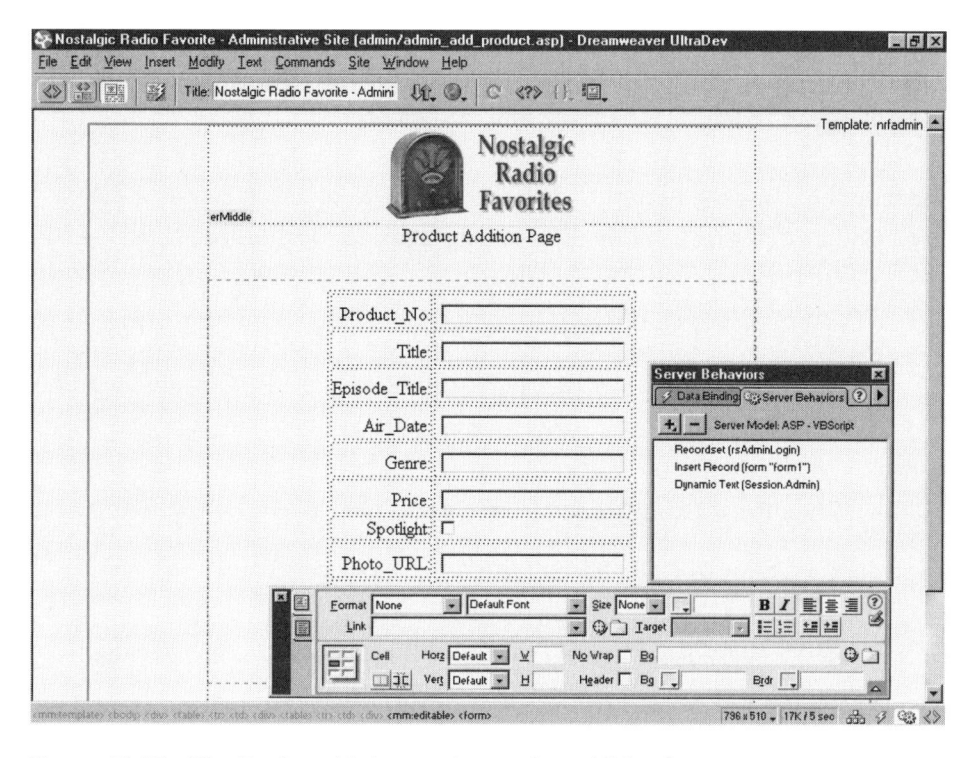

Figure 11.17 UltraDev has added a complete product addition form.

8. Delete the text in the erBottom editable region.
9. Remove the extra line between the Product Addition Page text and the newly created form by pressing the Backspace key.
10. Save the page as **admin_add_product.asp**.

Editing Existing Products

Building a page that allows users to update existing records is extremely easy using UltraDev. Because the results page for your administrative search already contains an edit link, you can simply set that link to pass the record identifier to a new page where you can edit the record.

Using the Record Update live object, UltraDev can easily build the update page that contains a form, the appropriate text fields and labels, and a Submit button. When the page is loaded, the database retrieves the appropriate record from the database and pre-fills the text field with the data currently stored in the record.

After the changes are complete, clicking the Submit button automatically replaces the data in the database with the values stored in the form fields. The user is then redirected to another page, in this case an update confirmation page.

Exercise 11.8 Using the Record Update Form Live Object to Edit Existing Records

1. Create a new page based on the nrfadmin template. Close the admin_add_product.asp page.
2. Delete the {erMiddle} text and type **Edit Record Page**. Press Enter.
3. On the Server Behaviors panel, click the plus sign and select Recordset (Query). In the Recordset dialog box, click the Simple button if you are not already in the simple view.

> **Tip**
>
> **The Update Record Live Object Needs a Recordset** Before you can insert the Update Record live object, you need to be sure that you have a recordset capable of holding the columns that you wish to update. When you conduct a search for a record and then click a link to edit it, the results page passes a variable identifying the product that needs to be updated. The update page then requests that record and houses it in a recordset while you make the updates. Then, when the changes are made, the update page submits the changed record back to the database.

4. Name the recordset **rsProductUpdate** and select the connSales_Database connection and the tbProducts table.
5. In the Columns panel, click Selected and select all the columns except the Entry_Date column.
6. In the Filter panel, set the four fields to Product_No, =, URL Parameter, and Product_No. Your recordset should now look like Figure 11.18.
7. Click OK to close the Recordset dialog box.
8. Place the insertion point on the blank line under the Edit Record Page text.
9. From the menu bar, select Insert/Live Objects/Record Update Form.
10. In the Insert Record Update Form dialog box, shown in Figure 11.19, Select the connSales_Database connection and the tbProducts table.
11. In the Select Record From field, choose the rsProductUpdate recordset.
12. In the Unique Key Column field, select Product_No. When filling this field, make sure you choose the field that contains the unique identifier for the record, in this case the product number.
13. In the After Updating, Go To field, type **admin_update_confirmation.asp**.
14. In the Form Fields panel, remove the Entry_Date field and order the remaining fields in the order previously specified in Table 11.1.

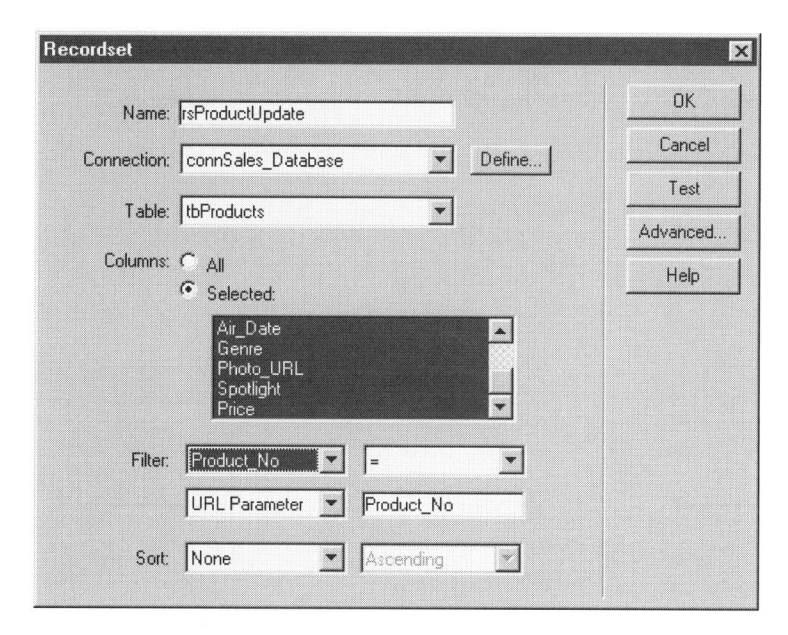

Chapter 11 Developing a Database Administration Site 301

Figure 11.18 Your rsProductUpdate recordset should look like this.

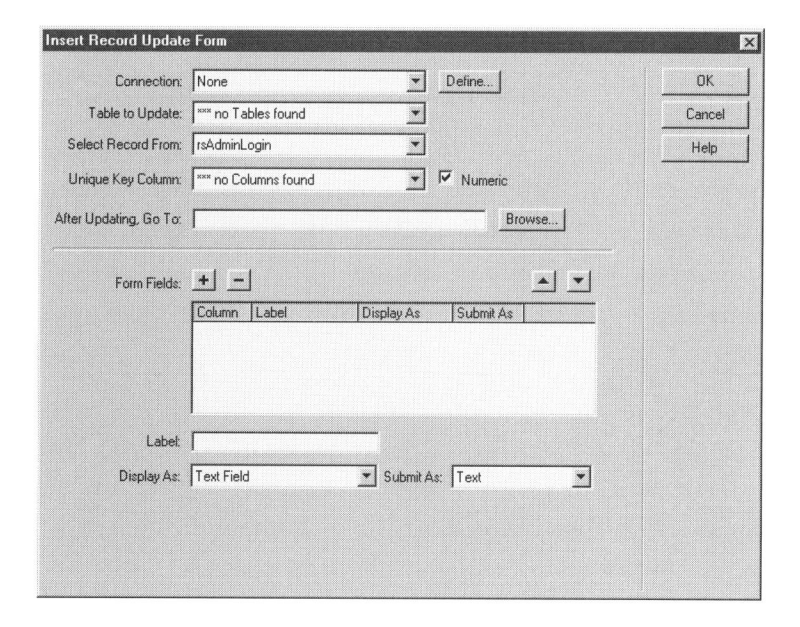

Figure 11.19 The Insert Record Update Form allows you to quickly add a form to update your records.

15. Click OK. As shown in Figure 11.20, UltraDev automatically adds the appropriate fields to your page.

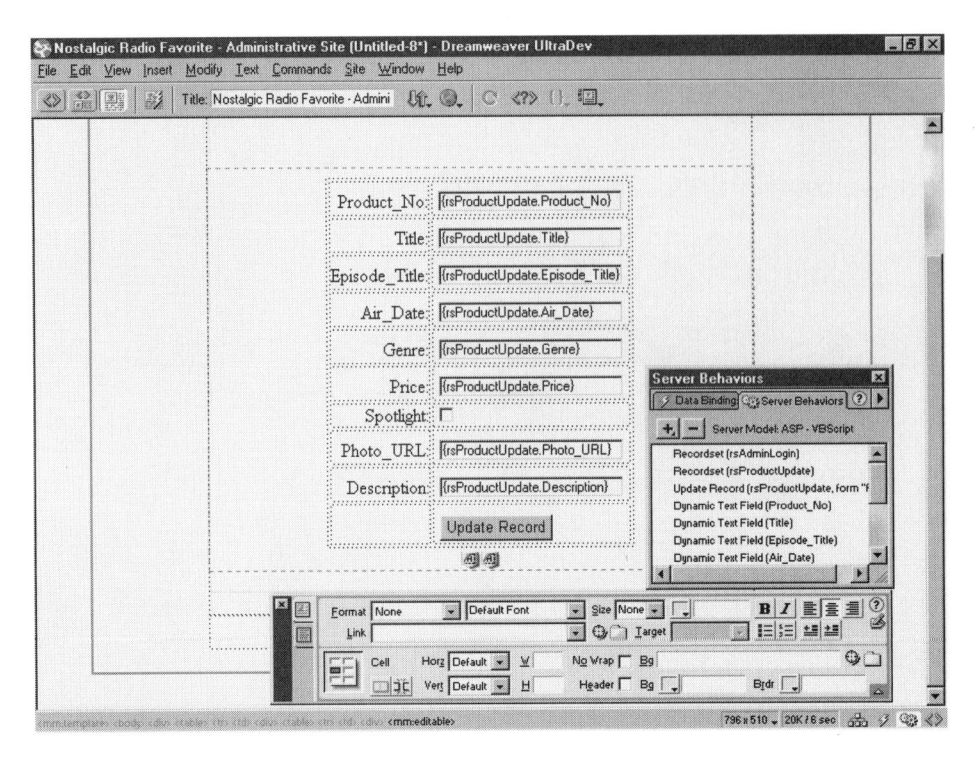

Figure 11.20 UltraDev has added the Update Record form to the page.

16. Remove the extra line between the Edit Record Page text and the Update Record form.
17. Delete the text in the erBottom editable region.
18. Save the page as **admin_product_edit.asp**.
19. Leave the page open.

Removing Products from the Database

Deleting a record from any database is serious business. In most cases, after the data is removed it is not possible to recover it except by reverting to a previously saved version of the database (usually from tape backup). The problem with restoring a database file, however, is that any updates to the database that were made after the backup was done would be lost when the most recent file was overwritten. Because of this, you should take great care in determining whether you actually want to delete the record.

> **Tip**
>
> **Deactivate Rather than Delete** Because of the falling prices of storage space, many organizations are opting to deactivate their records rather than delete them from the database. By adding a column to your table that allows you to specify whether the record is active or inactive, you can set a record to inactive when you no longer want it to be visible to your visitors.
>
> Doing this has the added benefit of saving time if the record needs to become active again. Rather than having to input all the data for the record, you can simply set the record to active and make any necessary updates.

There are times, however, when deleting a record is necessary. To accomplish this, you first need to create a search page and a results page as you have done previously. When the delete link is clicked on the results page, the appropriate record identifier is then passed to the delete confirmation page that contains a form and a button with the Delete Record server behavior applied to it. On this page, the visitor confirms that he wants to delete the record.

Once the button is clicked, the record is removed from the database and the user is redirected to another page—in this case a deletion confirmation page. This page confirms that the record was deleted from the database.

Exercise 11.9 Deleting Records from the Database Using the Delete Record Server Behavior

1. Create a new page from the nrfadmin template.
2. Delete the text in the erMiddle editable region and type **Product Deletion Confirmation Page**. Press Enter.
3. Type the following block of text:

    Product number is about to be deleted. This action cannot be undone. Are you sure you want to delete - ? If so, press the Delete button below the record.

    Notice that there are two spaces between "number" and "is" and there are spaces surrounding the "-". This leaves us placeholders for our dynamic data.
4. Press Shift+Enter.
5. Switch over to the admin_product_edit.asp page. In the Server Behaviors panel, right-click on the rsProductUpdate recordset and choose Copy from the drop-down menu.
6. Switch back to the page created in this exercise and right click in the Server Behaviors panel. Select Paste from the menu. As shown in Figure 11.21, UltraDev has transferred the recordset.

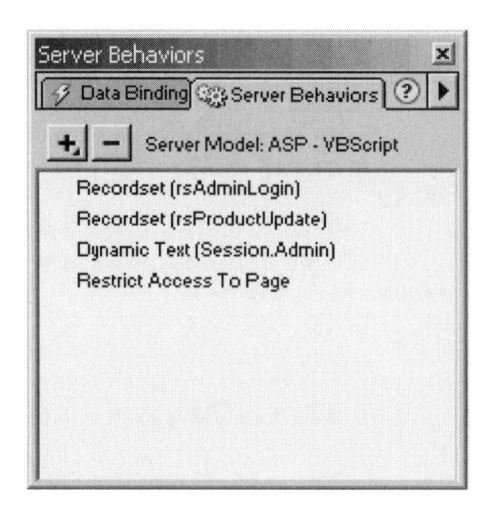

Figure 11.21 UltraDev allows you to easily copy and paste recordsets from one page to another.

7. Click the Data Bindings tab on the Server Behaviors panel and click the plus sign next to the rsProductUpdate recordset.
8. Drag the Product_No element from the Data Bindings panel and place it after the word "number" in the text. In addition, drag the Title element into the text after the word "delete" and before the hyphen and drag the Episode_Title element to the place after the hyphen. Your page should now look like Figure 11.22.
9. Place the insertion point on the line after the text and press Enter.
10. From the menu bar, select Insert/Form Objects/Button. Because a form has not already been created, UltraDev asks if you would like the form tag to be automatically inserted.
11. Click Yes in the pop-up box. As shown in Figure 11.23, UltraDev has added a form and the Submit button to the page.
12. Name the new button **btSubmit**.
13. Click the plus sign on the Server Behaviors panel. From the pop-up menu, select Delete Record.
14. As shown in Figure 11.24, complete the Delete Record dialog box by choosing the connSales_Database connection, the tbProducts table, and the rsProductUpdate recordset. In the After Deleting, Go To field, type **admin_delete_confirmation.asp**. Click OK.
15. Delete the {erBottom} text and save the page as **admin_product_delete.asp**.

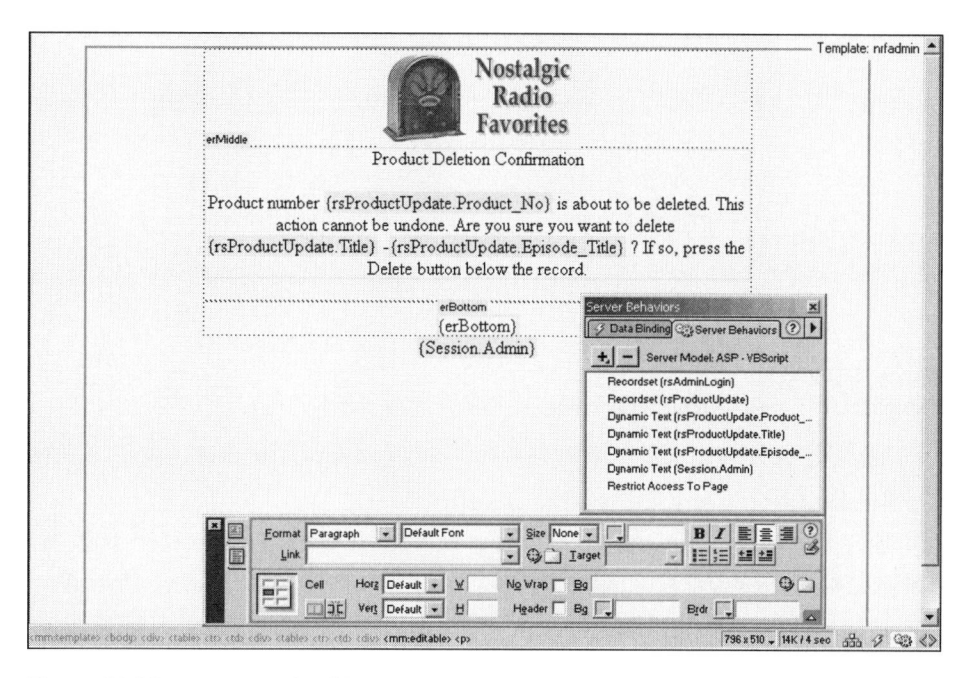

Chapter 11 Developing a Database Administration Site 305

Figure 11.22 Your page should now have dynamic elements placed within the text.

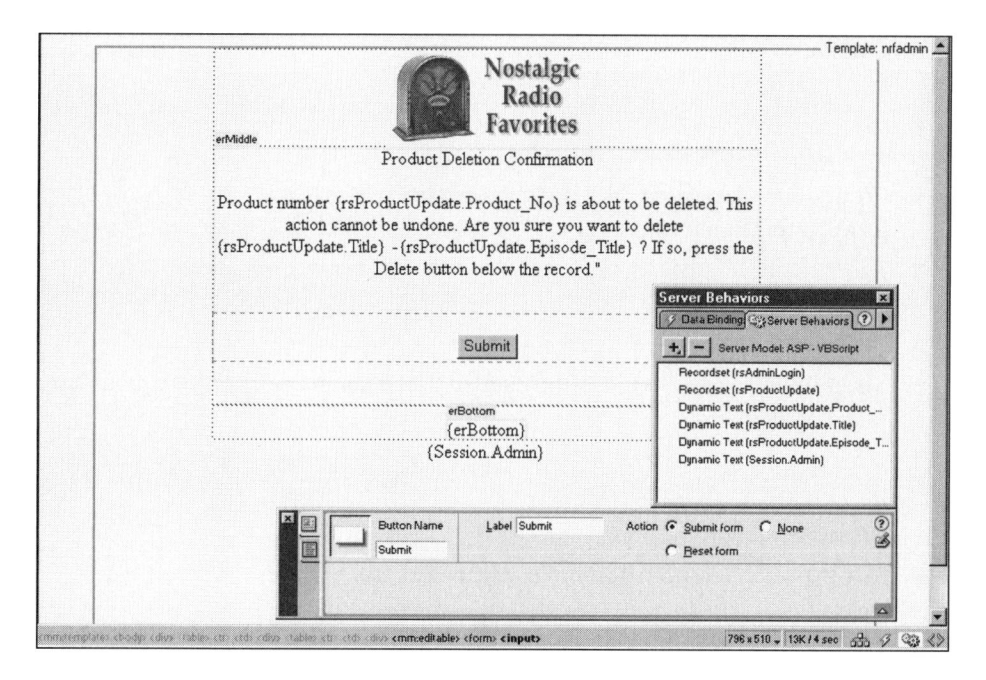

Figure 11.23 A form and Submit button have been added to the page.

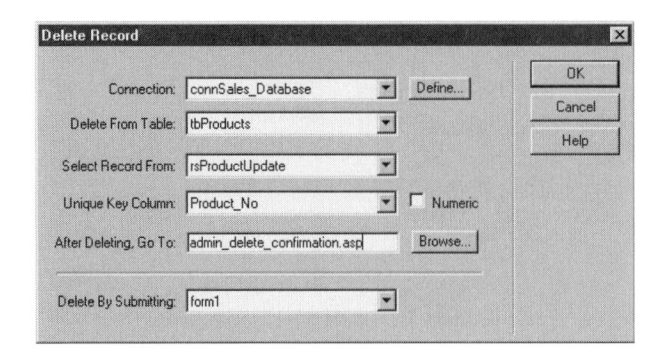

Figure 11.24 Complete the Delete Record dialog box as shown.

Confirming Additions, Edits, and Deletions

Just as every login page should have a logout page, it's a good idea that every page that adds, edits, or deletes a record from your database have a confirmation page. These pages can be as simple or as intricate as you would like, but each page should at least let the user know that the operation was completed successfully and provide a link back to the menu so the user can continue with his administrative activities or logout.

Because your pages will be relatively simple, you can create a single page and then use it as a template for the other confirmation pages.

Exercise 11.10 Creating Confirmation Pages

1. Create a new page from the nrfadmin template. Close the admin_product_edit.asp page and the admin_product_delete.asp page.
2. Delete the {erMiddle} text and type **Product Addition Confirmation**. Press Enter.
3. On the new line type the following text block:

    The product has been successfully added to the database. Click here to return to the main menu.

4. Highlight the "Click Here" text and type **admin_menu.asp** in the Link field of the Property inspector. Press Enter.
5. Delete the {erBotttom} text.
6. Save the file as **admin_addition_confirmation.asp**.
7. Change the heading text to **Product Update Confirmation**.
8. Change the text block to read

    The product has been successfully updated. Click here to return to the main menu.

9. Select File/Save As from the menu bar and save the file as **admin_update_confirmation.asp**.
10. Change the heading text to read **Product Deletion Confirmation**.
11. Change the text block to read

    The product has been successfully deleted. Click here to return to the main menu.

12. Select File/Save As from the menu bar and save the file as **admin_delete_confirmation.asp**.

Testing the Administration Site

The final step in building any Web site is to make sure that it works. In the case of this administration site, you want to ensure that only authenticated users are allowed access. In addition, you want to make sure that each page functions as expected, especially those that add, edit, and update records in the database.

Exercise 11.11 Testing the Administration Site

1. Minimize UltraDev and open a browser window. In the address bar, type **http://localhost/insideud4/admin**.
2. Leaving the logon form blank, click Submit and notice that UltraDev denies access without a proper username and password.
3. In the Username field type **nrfempburnsm** and type **smackdown** in the Password field.
4. Click Submit. As shown in Figure 11.25, the username and password are valid so the login confirmation is displayed.
5. Click the link to continue to the main menu.
6. From the main menu, click the Add A Product link.
7. In the Product Addition Page, fill in the form as shown in Figure 11.26. Note that the full URL for the image is `http://localhost/insideud4/images/theshadow.jpg` and the description is "The very first episode of The Shadow."
8. Click the Insert Record button and notice that UltraDev confirms that the entry was added.
9. Click the link to return to the main menu.
10. From the main menu, click the Product Search link.
11. In the Show Title field, type **Shadow** and click the Submit button. As shown in Figure 11.27, the query returns two records, both with the Show Title "The Shadow." The results include the recently added title.

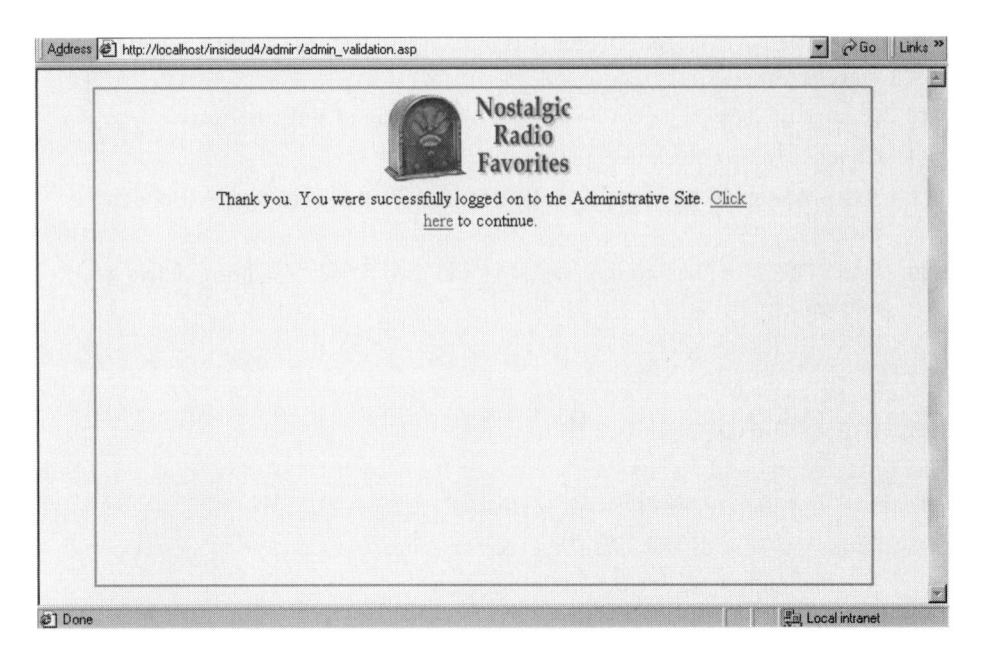

308   Part IV   Extending Your Administrative Capabilities

Figure 11.25   The login was successful!

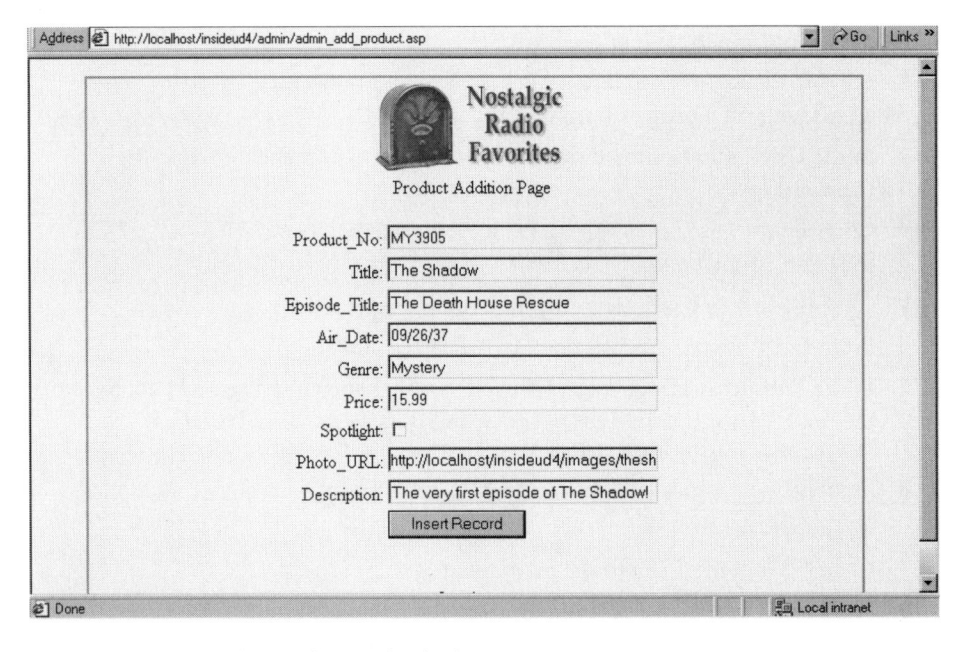

Figure 11.26   Add this product to the database.

Chapter 11 Developing a Database Administration Site   309

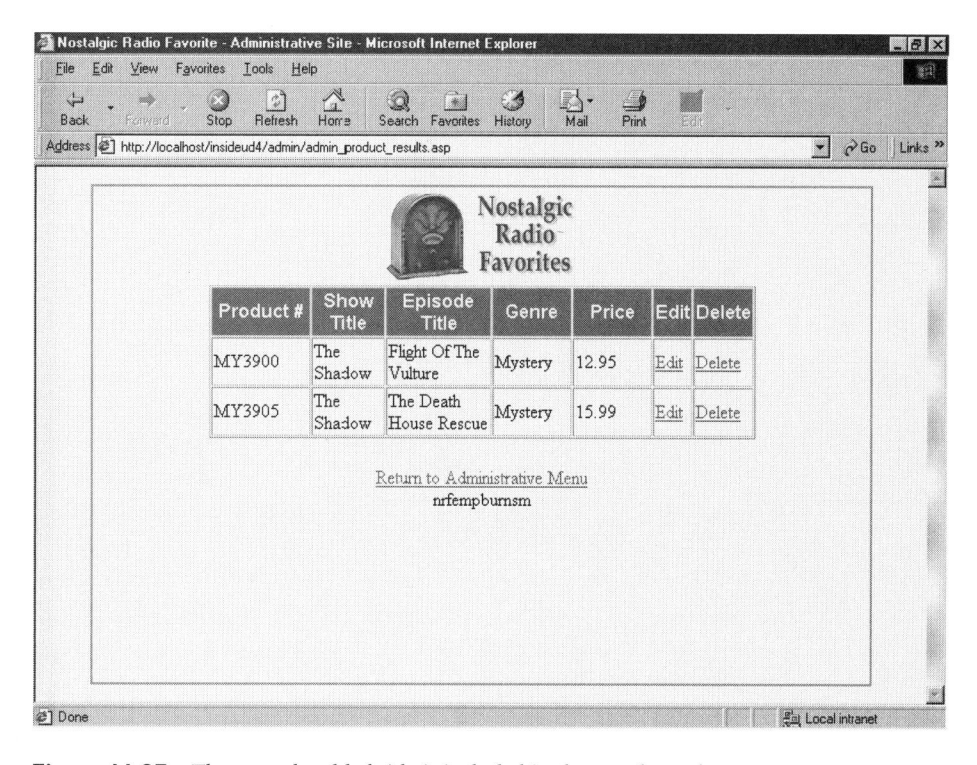

Figure 11.27 The recently added title is included in the search results.

12. Click the Edit button for The Death House Rescue. The Edit Record Page, shown in Figure 11.28, allows you to make changes to the record.
13. Change the price of the episode from 13.99 to **10.99**. Click the Update Record button and notice that the update is confirmed.
14. Click the link to return to the main menu.
15. At the main menu, click the Product Search link and search for product number MY3905. The search returns the recently added record.
16. Click the Delete link. As shown in Figure 11.29, the Record Deletion Confirmation page asks whether you really want to delete the record.
17. Click the Submit button and notice that the product's deletion has been confirmed. Click the link to return to the main menu.
18. Once again, click the Product Search page and search for the title "Shadow." Notice that the recently deleted episode no longer appears in the results.
19. Click the Return To Administrative Menu link.
20. Click the Logout button. The confirmation page successfully logs you out.
21. Click the back button to return to the main menu and then click the Product Search link. The site automatically redirects you to the login page because your session has expired.

Figure 11.28 You can now update the product information.

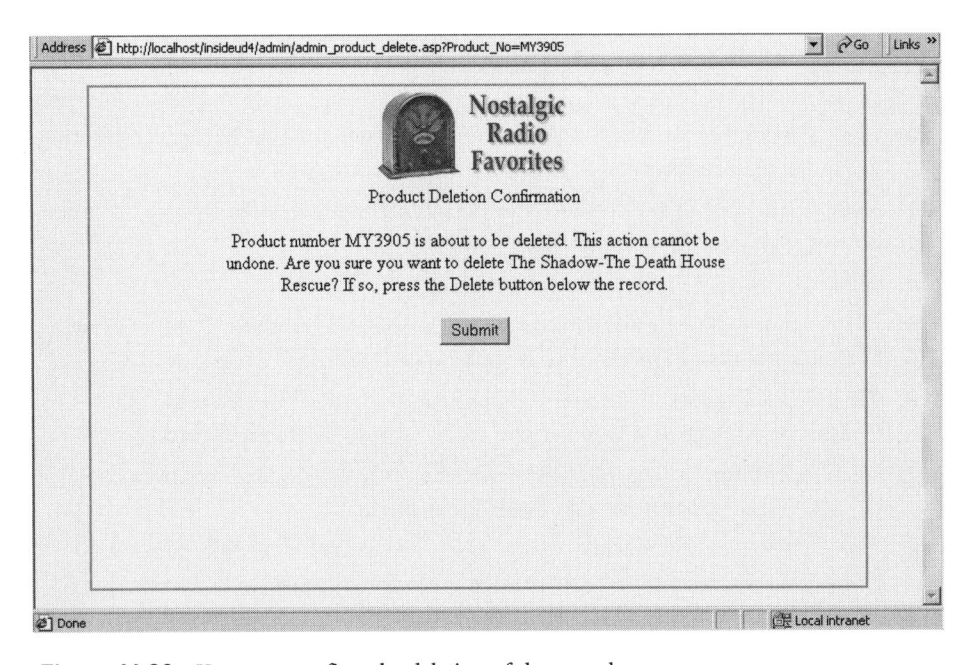

Figure 11.29 You must confirm the deletion of the record.

Summary

In this chapter you reviewed many of the features covered in-depth in the previous chapters and saw how those features can be combined to create an administration site. In addition, you saw how to use UltraDev's live objects in combination with server behaviors to add, edit, and delete records from your database.

In the next chapter we'll take a look at how UltraDev's database connectivity features can be used to add eCommerce capabilities to a site. Also covered are some of the third-party eCommerce solutions that can be used along with UltraDev.

Chapter 12

Engaging in eCommerce

eCommerce is everywhere! Whether you're buying a book, looking for a new car, or just purchasing office supplies, nearly every company that sells a product is now selling on the Web. Along with this rush to sell on the Web comes a need for the ability to create and manage the eCommerce abilities of a Web site.

Although UltraDev does not ship with a very robust set of eCommerce capabilities, it can be used to add simple eCommerce functionality to your Web site. In addition, with the use of a couple of third-party UltraDev extensions, a more powerful shopping cart based system can be implemented.

To demonstrate UltraDev's eCommerce capabilities, this chapter shows you how to create both

- A simple, single transaction site
- A more advanced, shopping cart based site

Building a Single-Transaction eCommerce Site

As I said in the introduction, without any third-party extensions or a significant amount of hand coding, UltraDev's eCommerce capabilities are fairly limited. That does not, however, mean that you can't add eCommerce capabilities to your site using just the UltraDev native server behaviors. What it does mean is that features like calculating tax and using a shopping cart are not available. To include these features, you must find an UltraDev extension that suits your needs or customize the available extensions to include these features. In fact, later in this chapter you'll use a popular shopping cart extension to add to UltraDev's eCommerce functionality.

To start, take a look at what UltraDev can do in the way of eCommerce. The best way to see UltraDev's eCommerce capabilities is to add an eCommerce section to a site. You'll use the Nostalgic Radio Favorites site and add a simple, single-transaction eCommerce system. What this means is that a visitor will be able to browse the product catalog and then purchase a single item. Although this may not sound very functional in the real world of shopping carts and saved profiles, it's a great way to show you one way to build an eCommerce site.

> **Note**
>
> **The Many Faces of eCommerce** There are many different ways to build an eCommerce site. Some people like to walk the customer through steps; others like to conduct the transaction in a single page. Before you begin building an eCommerce section for your site, it's a good idea to look at what information you will be collecting and how your database is designed (if you already have one).

In building the simple site, there are several elements that you need to consider. First, you'll take a look at the sales database and the tables that have been created to accommodate orders. Second, you'll need to build a link that allows visitors to enter the eCommerce section. Third, you will build pages that collect all the appropriate information and submit that information to the database. Finally, you'll test the entire system to ensure that it works.

Setting Up the Database

The first step in setting up the eCommerce section is to take a look at the database and see how each of the appropriate tables is set up and how they will function in the eCommerce system.

Although the tbProducts and tbCustomers tables are important because they control access to the site and give the visitors a catalog to browse, it is the tbOrders and the tbLineitem tables that are most important to the eCommerce ordering system. When an order is completed, the visible and hidden contents of the forms are submitted to these tables and a new order number is generated and assigned to the item or items being ordered. This allows you to track each order through its completion or to look up old orders by the customer's name, the item ordered, or the date of the order.

The tbOrders table is where all the information that is pertinent to the individual order is stored. Each time a new order is taken, a new order ID is assigned and the customer information, date, shipping type, and billing information is entered. No information about the individual products, however, is included in this table. Instead, that information is stored in the tbLineitems table. This table stores the order number, product ID, and quantity of every item ordered through the site.

Because the first eCommerce system you are going to develop is a single-transaction system, every record created in the tbOrders table should then have a corresponding record in the tbLineitem table.

> **Note**
>
> **Consolidating Tables** You might be wondering why we would split these two tables and not include all the information in a single table. For a single-transaction system, this would be appropriate and would actually be a more effective database design. However, later in the chapter, you are going to expand the eCommerce system to include a shopping cart, so the table needs to be separated.
>
> If you know your site will be using a single-transaction system, it would be completely appropriate to consolidate these two tables during your database design.

Providing a Link to Purchase an Item

When a visitor comes across one of the products that he or she would like to buy, you need to give him the opportunity to enter the eCommerce section by clicking a link. This link, however, must provide the following page with a valuable piece of information: the product ID of the item the visitor is ordering. To do this, take advantage of UltraDev's Go To Related Page server behavior that allows the link to not only open a new page, but pass a variable through the URL. After the product ID is passed, you can begin the checkout process.

> **Warning**
>
> **Be Careful with Your Coding!** While building your eCommerce site, you are going to have to do a little hand coding. It's really not that bad, but a missed period or a misspelled variable name can mean the difference between your pages working beautifully and failing miserably. Please be careful when typing the required code. If, when testing the pages, you receive an error page, check the code that you typed for that page and ensure that it is exactly correct. Good luck!

Exercise 12.1 Adding the Purchase Link to a Product Detail Page

1. Open UltraDev and open the bargain_bin_details.asp page created in Chapter 7, "Connecting Your Web Site to a Database."
2. In the bargain_bin_details.asp page, shown in Figure 12.1, place the insertion point below the table in the erMainData editable region.
3. Type the phrase **Purchase This Title**.
4. Open the Server Behaviors panel if it is not already open.
5. Highlight the new text and click the plus sign on the Server Behaviors panel. From the pop-up menu, choose Go To Related Page.
6. In the Go To Related Page dialog box, shown in Figure 12.2, type **purchase_step1.asp** in the Related Page field.
7. Check the box that allows the page to pass existing URL parameters and click OK.

    This link now moves the visitor to the first page in the process of purchasing the product. In addition, the link continues to pass the product number through the URL so that the following pages can automatically know which product is being purchased.

8. Save the page.

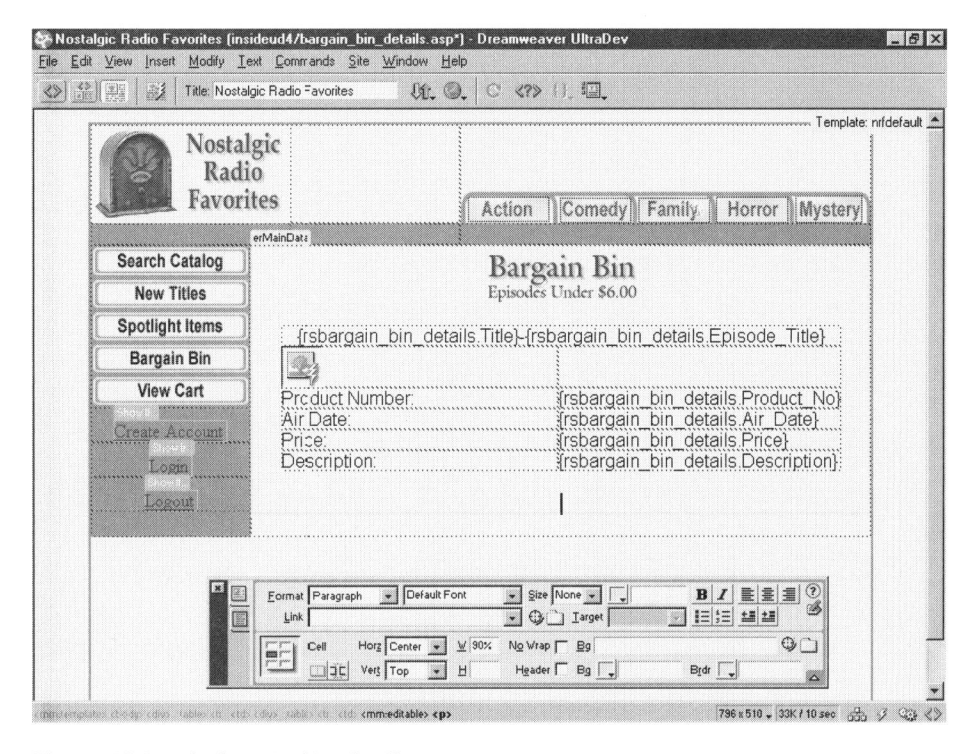

Figure 12.1 The bargain_bin_details.asp page.

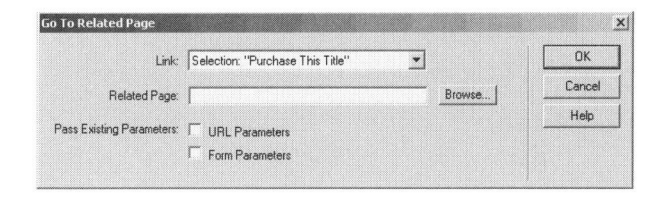

Figure 12.2 The Go To Related Page dialog box.

Allowing Customers to Confirm Their Shipping Information

The first step in your eCommerce system is to ask the visitor to confirm that his shipping information is correct. Although you could just create a page with an empty form and have the visitor fill it out, you can save him a little time by drawing the information from his record in the tbCustomers table. This is the information that the visitor provided when he set up his account to access the password-protected areas of the site.

The additional benefit of doing this comes from the fact that visitors will keep their information up to date. The only downside comes if they want to ship the item to someone else—say, as a gift.

318 Part IV Extending Your Administrative Capabilities

> **Tip**
>
> **Shipping Somewhere Else?** In the following exercise, you're going to assume that the purchaser wants to ship the item to himself. If, however, you wanted to provide your visitors with the opportunity to ship the product to another address, you could set up separate sets of fields in the database. One set would hold the visitor's home address, city, state, and ZIP, whereas the other would hold the shipping address for this specific order.

Exercise 12.2 Building a Shipping Information Page

1. Create a new page based on the nrfdefault template.
2. Highlight and delete the {erMainData} text.
3. In the erMainData editable region, type the following text block:

    Thank you for your interest in this product. Please confirm that your name and address shown below are correct. Feel free to make any changes in the fields and click the Next Step button to move to the next step.

4. Press the Enter key.
5. With the insertion point on the new line, select Insert/Live Objects/Record Update Form from the menu bar.
6. In the Insert Record Update Form dialog box, shown in Figure 12.3, choose the connSales_Database connection.

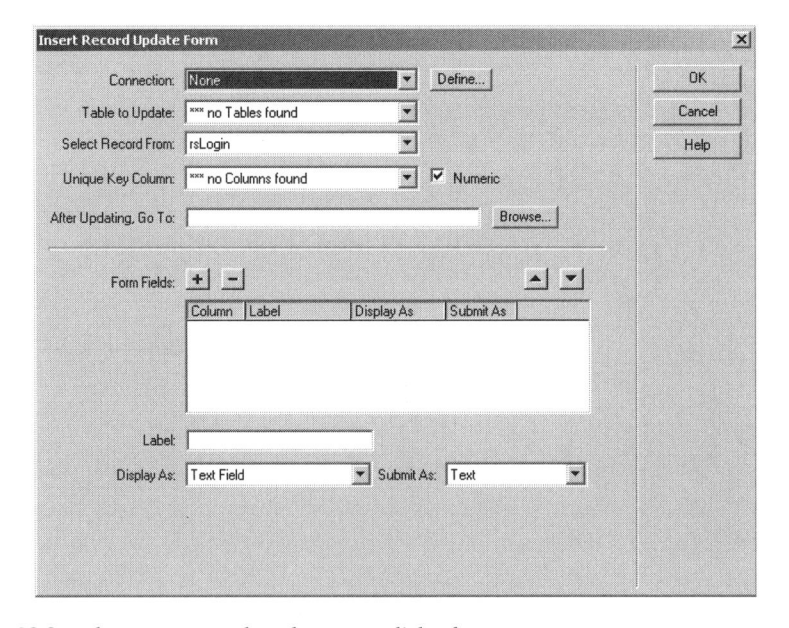

Figure 12.3 The Insert Record Update Form dialog box.

7. In the Table To Update field, select the tbCustomers table. The Select Record From field should automatically be set to rsLogin and the Unique Key Column field should be set to CustomerID.

8. Type **purchase_step2.asp** in the After Updating, Go To field.
9. In the Form Fields panel, use the minus button to remove every field except the following:
   - Last_Name
   - First_Name
   - Address
   - City
   - State
   - Zip
10. Select the First_Name field and click the up arrow to move this field to the top of the available form fields.
11. Click OK to close the Insert Record Update Form dialog box.
12. Place the insertion point on the line above the new form and press the Backspace key on the keyboard. As shown in Figure 12.4, UltraDev has automatically added a form to update the customer's shipping information.

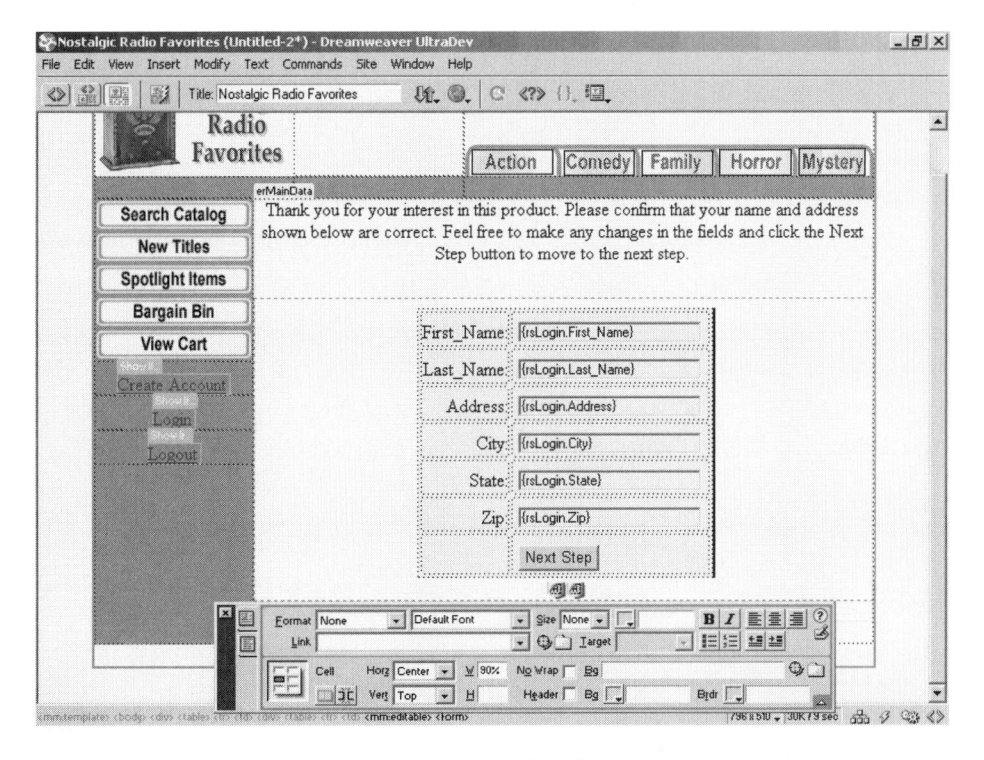

Figure 12.4 A form has been added to the page that allows users to update their shipping information.

320   Part IV   Extending Your Administrative Capabilities

13. Select the Update Record button and change the button label to read **Next Step**. Press Enter.
14. To ensure that the user has properly logged on prior to starting the purchase process, click the plus sign on the Server Behaviors panel and select User Authentication/Restrict Access To Page.
15. In the Restrict Access To Page dialog box, shown in Figure 12.5, select the Username and Password as the restriction basis and type **login.asp** in the If Access Denied, Go To field. Click OK.

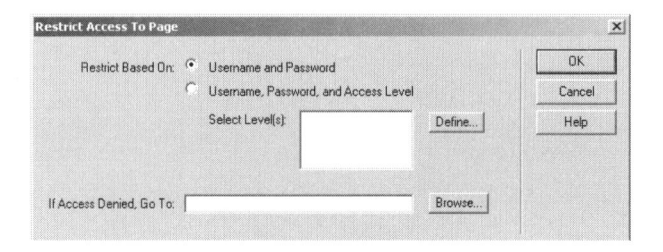

Figure 12.5   The Restrict Access To Page dialog box.

16. Save the page as **purchase_step1.asp** in the root folder of the InsideUD4 site.

Confirming the Order Information

After you have the visitor's shipping information, make sure that the item you are sending him is the item that he ordered. To do this, simply build a table that fills with the information about the product based on the product ID that was passed to the page from the previous page.

In addition, you can ask the visitor to tell how he would like the product shipped. Although you aren't going to build in any extra cost for the different shipping types, it would be relatively easy to do so by assigning a numeric value to the shipping type and then adding that numeric value to the total price at the end of the order.

Exercise 12.3   Confirming the Product Selection and Shipping Method

1. From the nrfdefault template, create another new page.
2. Delete the {erMainData} text and type the following text block:

    Please confirm the product information for the item you are ordering. In addition, please select the shipping type you would like to use. If this is not the item you would like to order, click any button on the left to continue browsing the available products.

3. Press Enter to move to a new line.

4. On the Server Behaviors panel, click the plus button and select Recordset (Query). If the Recordset dialog box is in the advanced mode, click the Simple button.

5. Name the recordset **rsProducts** and complete the fields as shown in Figure 12.6.

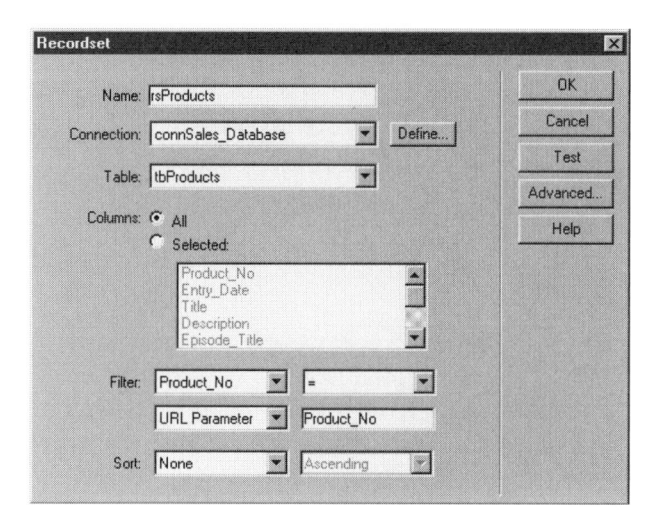

Figure 12.6 Complete the rsProducts recordset so it looks like this.

6. Click the Test button and type **MY2234** in the Please Provide A Test Value dialog box. As shown in Figure 12.7, UltraDev displays the product with the corresponding Product ID.

Figure 12.7 Product number MY2234 is displayed.

7. Click the OK button to close the Test SQL Statement dialog box and click OK to close the Recordset dialog box.

8. Place the insertion point on the line below the text block and select Insert/Form. Name the form **fmOrderInfo** and type **purchase_step3.asp** in the Action field. Press Enter.

9. Inside the fmOrderInfo form, insert a table with **6** rows, 2 columns, and a width of **80%**. Set the border to **0** and the cell padding and cell spacing to **2**. Click OK.

10. Highlight the left column and click the Align Right button on the Property inspector. Set the column width to **50%**. Press Enter.

Part IV   Extending Your Administrative Capabilities

11. Fill in the left cells of the table as shown in Figure 12.8.

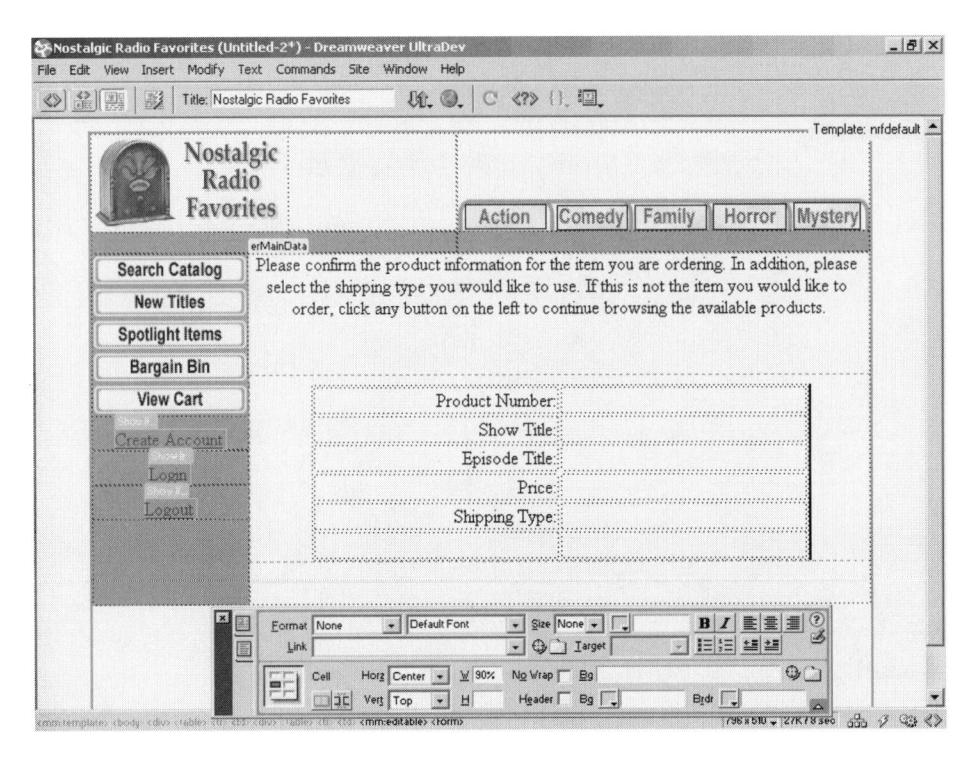

Figure 12.8   Add these text labels to the table.

12. Click the Data Bindings tab on the Server Behaviors panel and click the plus sign next to the rsProducts recordset.

13. Drag the Product_No data element to the top-right cell in the table.

14. Drag the Title data element to the cell next to the Show Title text.

15. Continue by dragging the Episode_Title and Price data elements to cells next to their corresponding text. As shown in Figure 12.9, UltraDev adds dynamic placeholders to the table.

16. Place the insertion point in the field next to the Shipping Type text and choose Insert/Form Objects/List/Menu from the menu bar.

17. Name the new List/Menu object **slShippingType** and click the List Values button on the Property inspector.

18. In the List Values dialog box, shown in Figure 12.10, click the plus sign (if necessary) and **type US Postal Service** in the Item Label field. Press the Tab key and type **US Postal** in the Value field.

Chapter 12 Engaging in eCommerce 323

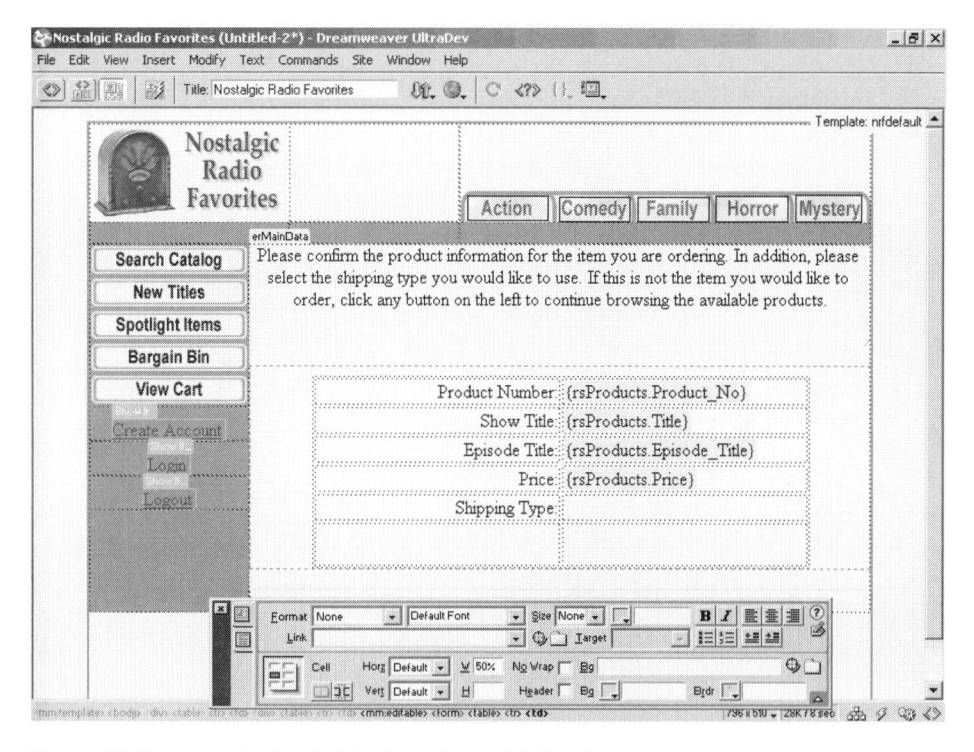

Figure 12.9 Dynamic placeholders have been added to the page.

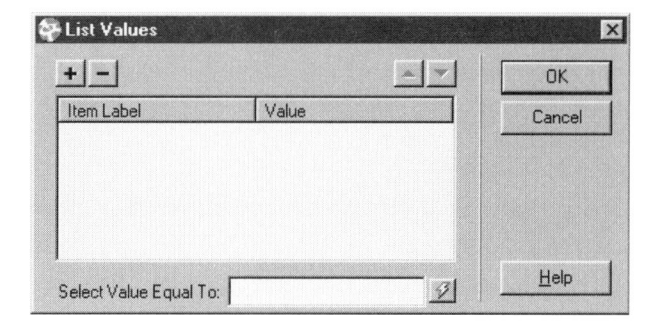

Figure 12.10 The List Values dialog box.

19. Click the plus sign again and type **2-Day Rush** in the Item Label field and type **2-Day** in the Value field.

20. Click the plus sign again and type **Overnight Express** in the Item Label field and type **Overnight** in the Value field. Click OK to close the List Values dialog box.

21. Place the insertion point in the bottom-left cell and choose Insert/Form Objects/Hidden Field. This field will be used to store the Product ID for the specific item that the visitor wants to purchase.

Because of the nature of UltraDev's Insert Record server behavior (which you will be using on the next page), when a visitor submits a form using this behavior, any variables passed in the URL are lost. This means that you won't be able to access the product ID unless you stuff it into a session variable. To do this, simply insert the value of the Product ID querystring variable (the one in the URL) into a hidden form and then pass it to the next page via the form. The next page then assigns the value of this hidden field to the session variable. Although it sounds complex, you'll see just how easy it is to do.

> **Note**
>
> **Problems Passing Variables** For more information on UltraDev's problems passing variables, take a look at the following two articles. The first one outlines the problem and the second one explains how to create a session variable:
>
> http://www.macromedia.com/support/ultradev/ts/documents/passingformdata.htm
>
> http://www.macromedia.com/support/ultradev/ts/documents/session.htm

22. Name the hidden field **hfProdNo** and set the Value field equal to **<%=(Request.QueryString("Product_No"))%>**.

    This grabs the value of the Product_No querystring variable and stores it here. Press Enter.

23. Place the insertion point in the bottom-right cell and choose Insert/Form Objects/Button. Name the button **btSubmit** and change the Label to read **Next Step**. Press Enter.

24. Save the page as **purchase_step2.asp**.

Accepting Payment Information

The last piece of information you need to collect from the visitor is their payment information. In your site, you will allow the user to be billed, pay cash on delivery (C.O.D.), or use a credit card. If the visitor chooses to pay via credit card, then he fills in the credit card type, number, and expiration date. Once these fields are completed, the visitor then clicks a button that submits the information to the database and redirects him to a basic order confirmation page.

Exercise 12.4 Allowing the User to Select a Payment Type

1. Create a new page from the nrfdefault template.
2. In the new page, replace the {erMainData} text with the following text block:
   Please enter the following billing information. If you choose to pay by credit card, please provide the card type, number, and expiration date.

3. Press Enter.
4. With the insertion point on the new line, choose Insert/Form. Name the form **fmNewOrder** and press Enter.
5. Insert a new table into the form. Create a table with **6** rows, **2** columns, and a width of **80%**. Set the border at **0** and the cell padding and cell spacing at **2**.
6. Highlight the left column and click the Align Right button on the Property inspector. Set the column width to **50%**.
7. Place the insertion point in the top-left field and type **Payment Method:**. Press the Tab key.
8. In the next field, select Insert/Form Objects/ List/Menu from the menu bar. Name the new List **slPayment**. Click the List Values button and enter the values shown in Figure 12.11. Click OK to close the List Values dialog box.

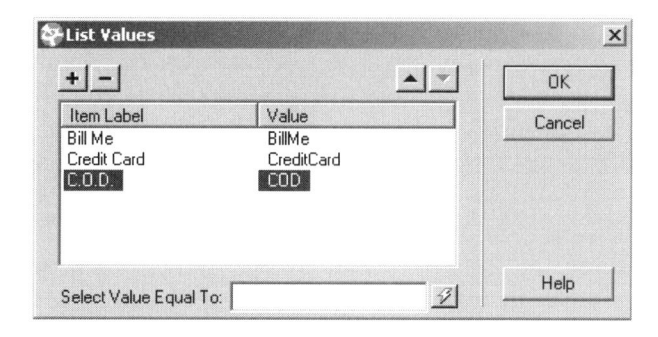

Figure 12.11 Enter these values into the List Values dialog box.

9. In the Property inspector, set the Initially Selected value to **Bill Me**.
10. Place the insertion point in the cell below the Payment Method text and type **Credit Card Type:**. Press the Tab key.
11. In the next field, Insert a List/Menu Form object and name it **lsCardType**. Click the List Values button and enter the values shown in Figure 12.12. Click OK.

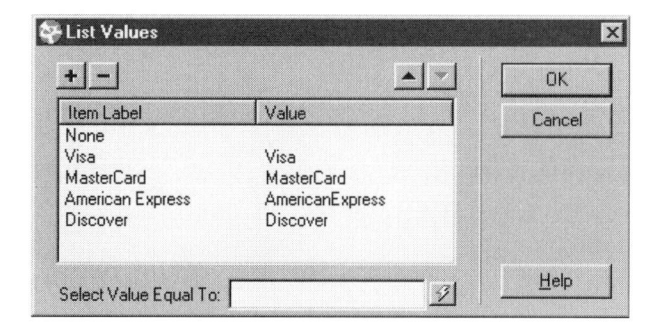

Figure 12.12 Again, enter these values into the List Values dialog box.

12. In the Property inspector, set the Initially Selected value to **None**.
13. Press Enter. Drop the insertion point into the third cell in the left column. Type **Credit Card Number:**. Press the Tab key to move to the next field.
14. Select Insert/Form Objects/Text Field. Name the text field **tfCCNumber**.
15. Place the insertion point in the cell below the Credit Card Number text and type **Credit Card Expiration (mm/yy):**. Press the Tab key.
16. Insert a new text field and name it **tfCCExp**. Set the maximum characters for the field to **5** by typing the value in the Max Chars field in the Property inspector.
17. Place the insertion point in the field below the Credit Card Expiration text. Select Insert/Form Objects/Hidden Field. As shown in Figure 12.13, UltraDev places a yellow tag in the field to signify the hidden element.

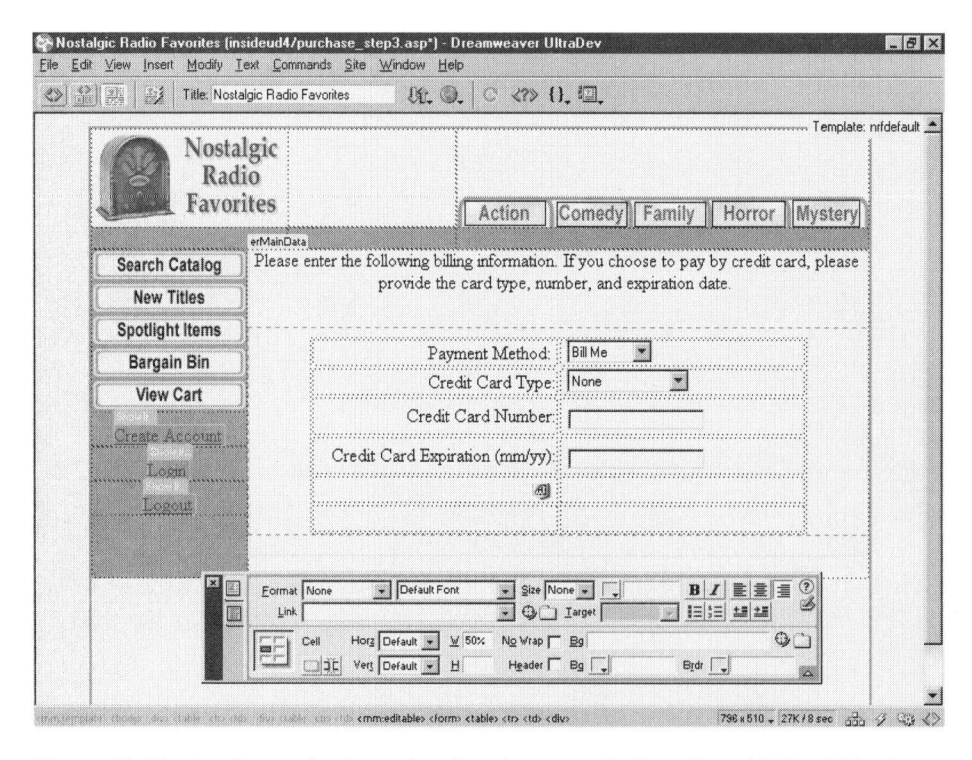

Figure 12.13 A yellow tag has been placed on the page to indicate that a hidden field exists.

18. In the Property inspector, set the name of the hidden field to **hfCustomerID** and type **<%= Session("MM_Username") %>** in the Value field.

    This automatically grabs the visitor's CustomerID from the session variable and inserts it into the hidden field. Because the value is now part of a form, it can then be passed later using the Insert Record behavior. Press Enter. Drop the insertion point in the cell to the right of the current hidden field.

19. Select Insert/Form Objects/Hidden Field. Set the name to **hfShipMeth** and type <%=(**Request.Form**("**slShippingType**"))%> in the Value field. Press Enter.

    This hidden field now grabs the value of the shipping method that was passed from the previous page. Essentially, you are working to get all the values into a single form that can then be inserted into the database.

20. Place the insertion point in the bottom-right cell and insert a submit button. Name the new button **btSubmit** and change the label to read **Final Step**. With the new form complete, your page should now look like Figure 12.14.

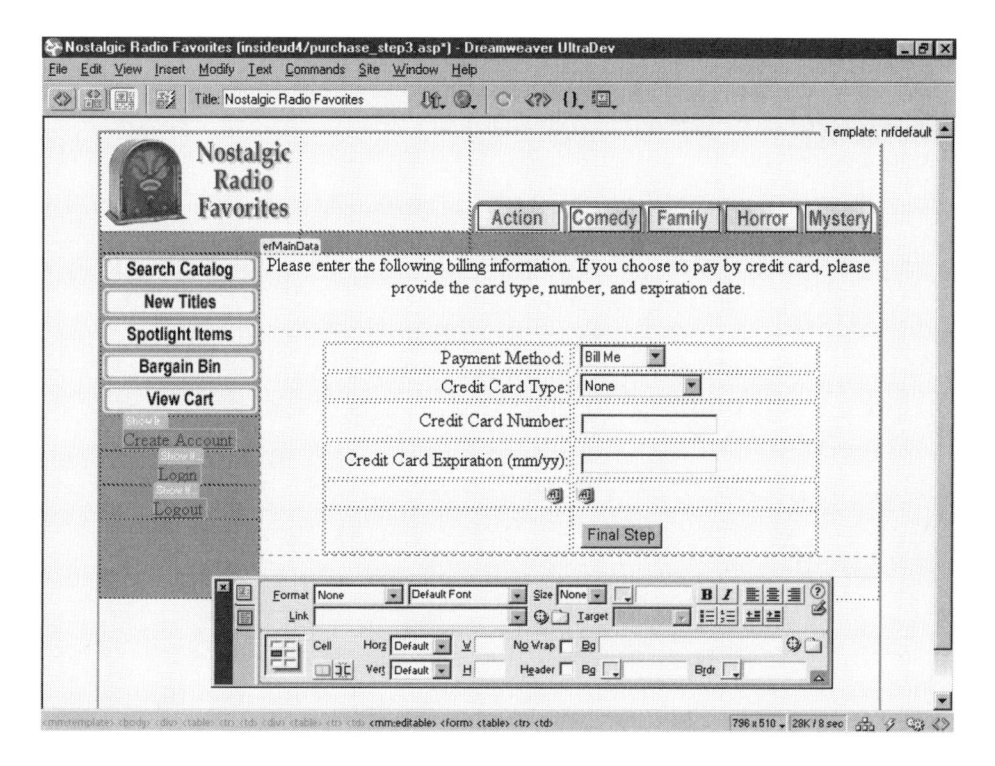

Figure 12.14 Your page should look like this.

21. To add all of the form elements to the database, click the plus sign on the Server Behaviors panel and select Insert Record from the pop-up menu.

22. In the Insert Record dialog box, shown in Figure 12.15, select the connSales_Database connection and the tbOrders table as the destination for the data.

23. Type **purchase_confirmation.asp** in the After Inserting, Go To field.

24. Because there is only one form on this page, the Get Values From dropdown should default to the fmNewOrder form. In the Form Elements panel, highlight slPayment<ignore> and select Payment in the Column dropdown.

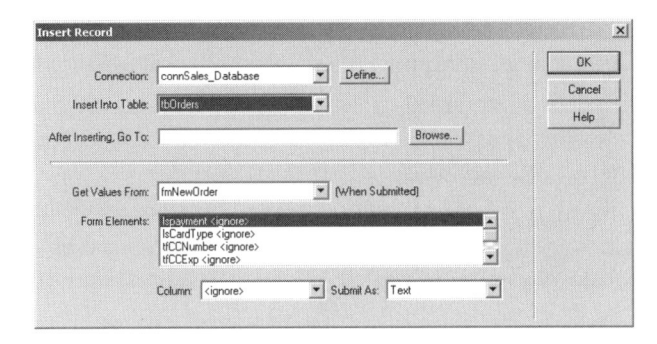

Figure 12.15 The Insert Record dialog box.

25. Highlight the lsCardType element and choose CC_Type from the Column drop-down.
26. Using the same method, link the tfCCNumber element to the CC_Number column, the tfCC_Exp to the CC_Exp column, the hfCustomerID to CustomerID, and the hfShipMeth to the Ship_Meth column. The Insert Record dialog box should now look like Figure 12.16.

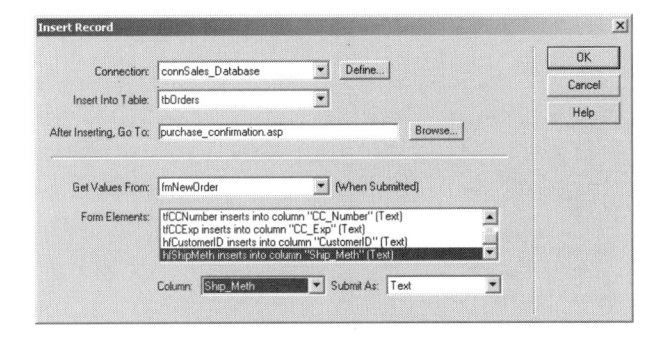

Figure 12.16 Build the Insert Record dialog box so it looks like this.

27. Click OK to close the Insert Record dialog box. UltraDev inserts a yellow tag at the bottom of your page to verify that the Insert Record server behavior has been applied to the page.
28. The last thing you need to do on this page is to create a session variable based on the Product ID that you passed in the previous form. To do this, click the plus sign on the Data Bindings panel and select Session Variable.
29. In the Session Variable dialog box, type **ProductNumber** and click OK.
30. To set the value of the newly created session variable, insert a single line of ASP code. Switch to the Code view and find the <html> tag on your page. Create a new line above the <html> tag and type the following code on that new line:

```
<%session("ProductNumber")=Request.Form("hfProdNo")%>
```

This code gets the value that was submitted in the hfProdNo field in the last page and sets the ProductNumber session variable equal to that value. You can now access the product number on any page within your site.

31. Return to the Show Design View screen.
32. Save the page as **purchase_step3.asp**.

Confirming the Entire Order

The final step in the eCommerce system is the order confirmation page. This page can be as complex or as simple as you would like it to be. Some companies display the entire contents of the order, the total price, and the shipping information. This is handy because it gives the visitor an opportunity to print the page as an invoice. Other sites, however, choose to simply create a page that lets the visitor know that his order was completed. Your page will be somewhere in the middle, demonstrating how to add whatever dynamic information you feel is necessary to the page.

Your page consists of a text block, a table that displays some of the ordering information, and a form. The form contains three hidden form fields, which contain the visitor's user ID, the product ID, and the order number. Once the visitor submits this form, his order will be complete and ready to process.

Exercise 12.5 Adding a Confirmation Page

1. Create a new page from the nrfdefault template.
2. Replace the {erMainData} text with the following text block:

   Thank you for your order. The following information shows your order information including your order number, shipping preference, and total. By clicking on the button below, you will complete the transaction and your order will be processed.

3. Press Enter.
4. On the new line, insert a table that has **4** rows, **2** columns, and a width of **80%**. Set the border at **0** and the cell padding and cell spacing at **2**. Click OK.
5. Highlight the left column and click the Align Right button on the Property inspector. Set the column width to **50%**.
6. Type the values into the cells as shown in Figure 12.17.
7. On the Server Behaviors panel, click the plus sign and select Recordset(Query). In the Recordset dialog box, create a recordset like the one shown in Figure 12.18. This recordset draws all the orders from the tbOrders table for the visitor based on the username stored in the session variable. The results are then sorted in descending order.

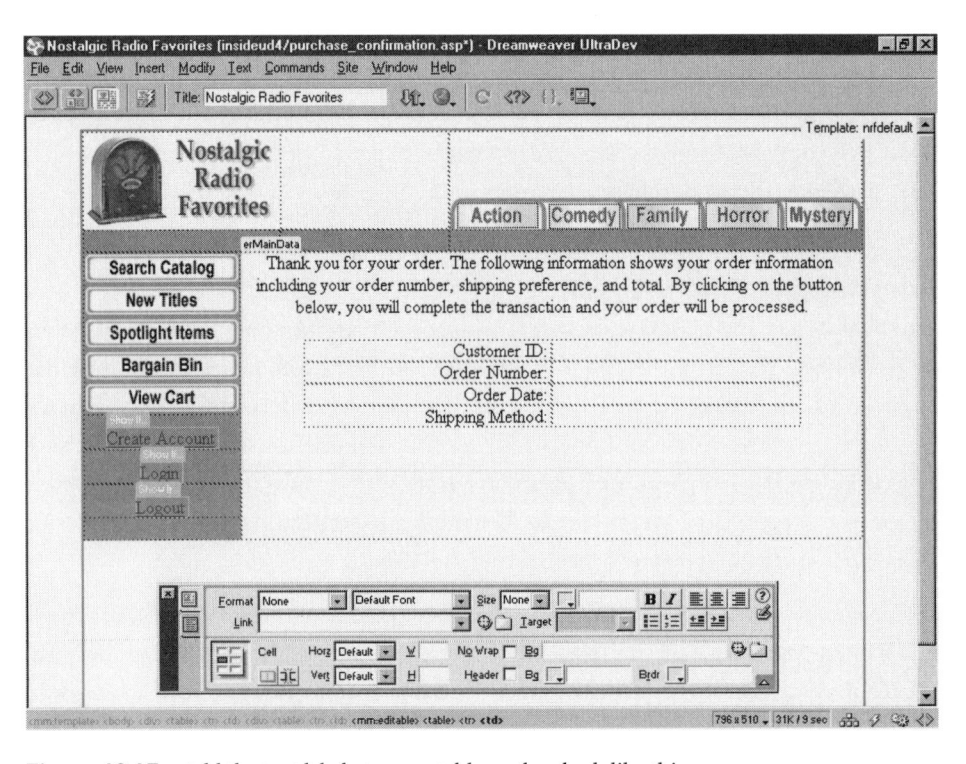

330   Part IV   Extending Your Administrative Capabilities

Figure 12.17   Add the text labels to your table so they look like this.

Figure 12.18   Create a new recordset that looks like this.

8. Click OK to close the Recordset dialog box.
9. Click the Data Bindings tab on the Server Behaviors panel and click the plus sign next to the rsOrders recordset.
10. Drag the CustomerID data element to the top-right cell.
11. Drag the Order_No data element to the cell next to the Order Number text.
12. Drag the Order_Date data element to the cell next to the Order Date text.
13. Drag the Ship_Meth data element to the cell next to the Shipping Method text.

    The next thing you need to do on this page is create a form that includes a button that finalizes the order. When the customer clicks the button, the page submits the order number (which was created in the previous page), product number, and customer ID to the tbLineitem table, which associates the existing order number with the corresponding record in the tbOrders table.

14. Before you can add the form, however, you have to build a recordset that finds the newly created order number. On the Server Behaviors panel, click the plus sign and select Recordset(Query).
15. In the Recordset dialog box, switch to the advanced view if it is not already visible.
16. Name the recordset **rsNewOrder** and set the connection to **connSales_Database**. Type the following lines of code in the SQL field.

    ```
    SELECT max(Order_No)
    FROM tbOrders
    ```

17. Click the OK button.

> **Warning**
>
> **The Possibility of Simultaneous Orders** One potential problem that you should be aware of is the possibility of two customers generating order numbers at the same time. If the first customer does not complete his order before a new order number is issued to a second customer, all the items in the first customer's order will be assigned to the second customer's order number (because it was the highest number in the table).
>
> Because of this possibility, high-traffic Web sites that may have multiple users ordering at the same time should seek other ways to assign order numbers.

18. Place the insertion point on the line below the table where the product information is displayed. From the menu bar, select Insert/Form. Name the new form **fmFinalConf**.
19. Inside the new form, insert a table with **2** rows, **1** column, and a width of **50%**. Set the border, cell padding, and cell spacing to **0**. Click OK.
20. Highlight the two cells and click the Align Center button on the Property inspector.

21. In the top cell, insert a hidden form field and name it **hfProdNo**. Set the value of this field to:

    ```
    <%= Session("ProductNumber") %>
    ```

    This form field now stores the product number that is contained in the session variable.

    > **Tip**
    >
    > **An Easy Way to Set a Form Field Value** Rather than hand-coding the value of a form field every time, an alternative way to have UltraDev insert the code for you is to highlight the form field, click on the Attributes tab of the Property inspector (it's located on the far left of the inspector) and click the plus sign. You can then select the value option from the popup menu.
    >
    > To specify the actual value of that form field at run-time, click the lightning bolt icon and select the session variable or recordset field that you would like the form field to contain.

22. In the top cell, place the insertion point on the right side of the new hidden field and insert a second hidden field. Name this one **hfCustID**.

23. Set the value of the hfCustID field to:

    ```
    <%=(rsOrders.Fields.Item("CustomerID").Value)%>
    ```

    This form field draws the visitor's Customer ID from the rsOrders recordset and stores it.

24. Add an additional hidden form field in the top cell and name it **hfOrderNo**. Set the value of this hidden field to:

    ```
    <%=(rsNewOrder.Fields.Item("Expr1000").Value)%>
    ```

    This field stores the value of the Expr1000 field created in the rsNewOrder recordset. If you'll recall, this recordset simply returns the highest value in the Order_No column of the tbOrders table. Because the only purpose of this recordset is to store the highest value in the Order_No column, UltraDev creates a placeholder column named Expr1000. Even though UltraDev created this placeholder, you can still reference it just like any other database column.

25. In the bottom cell of the table, insert a button and name if **btSubmit**. Change the label of the button to read **Click Here To Complete Your Order**.

26. The final step in developing the eCommerce functionality for your site is to insert the data stored in the hidden form fields into the tbLineitem table. To accomplish this, click the plus sign on the Server Behaviors panel and select Insert Record.
27. In the Insert Record dialog box, select the connSales_Database connection and the tbLineitem table.
28. In the After Inserting, Go To field, type **default.asp**. This sends the customer back to the home page after the transaction is completed.
29. Select the fmFinalConf form as the source of values and highlight the hfProdNo form element. Bind this element to the Product_No field in the database by selecting Product_No from the column dropdown.
30. Using the same process, bind the hfCustID element to the CustomerID field and the hfOrderNo element to the Order_No column.
31. Click OK.
32. Save this page as **purchase_confirmation.asp**.

Testing the Simple eCommerce Functionality

Now that your pages are in place, you need to take your site for a test drive. Essentially, you want to walk through the eCommerce section of your site just as a visitor would by logging on, selecting a product, and completing all the required information. Upon completion of the order, you should see the same confirmation page that any of your customers would see.

Exercise 12.6 Testing the eCommerce Pages

1. Open a browser. Go to http://localhost/insideud4/default.asp.
2. Click the Login link. In the login.asp page, type **testuser** as the username and **testuser** as the password. Click the Submit button. The site should confirm that your account was properly validated.
3. Click the Bargain Bin button on the left side of the page. As shown in Figure 12.19, you should see all items in the database that cost less than $6.00.
4. Click the link to the details page for the episode entitled "The Limping Ghost."

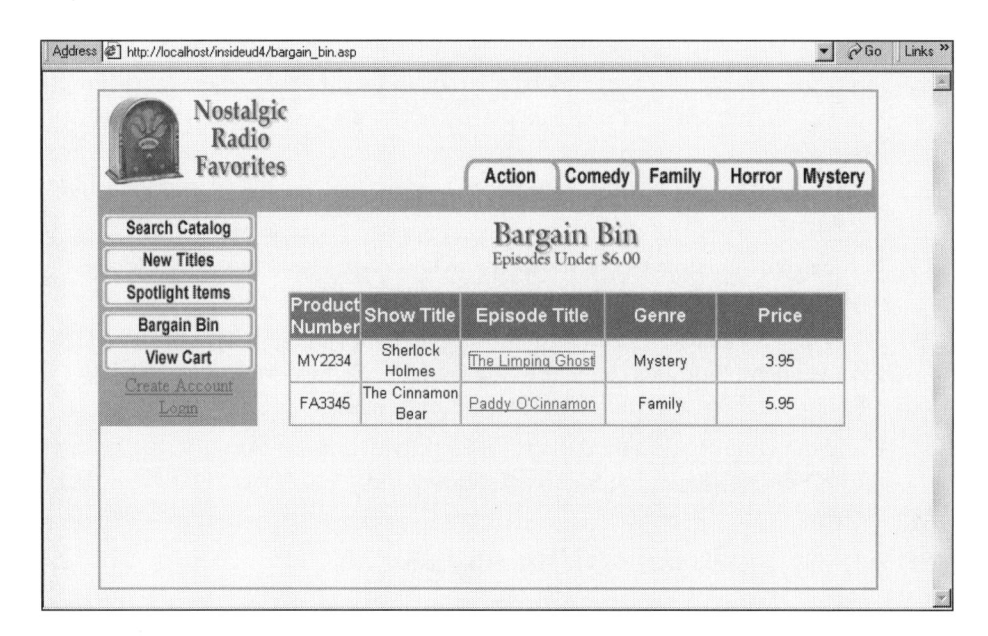

Figure 12.19 The Bargain Bin contains items that are less than $6.00.

5. In the details page, click the "Purchase This Title" link. As shown in Figure 12.20, the visitor's address information is drawn from the database and is able to be updated if necessary.

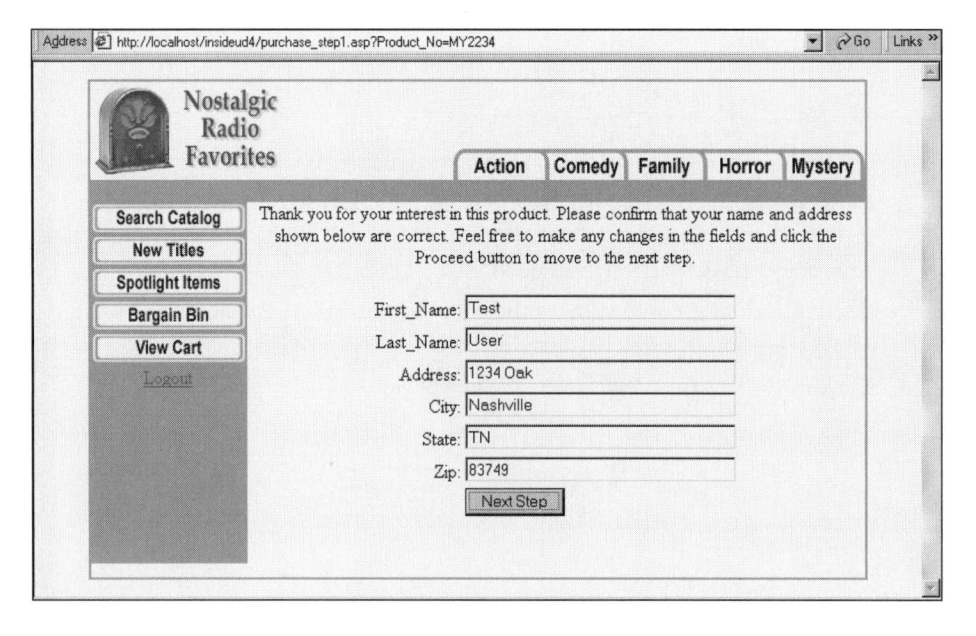

Figure 12.20 The visitor has the opportunity to review his shipping information.

6. Click the Next Step button.
7. In the product confirmation page, shown in Figure 12.21, the visitor is asked to confirm that the product displayed is correct and to select a shipping option.

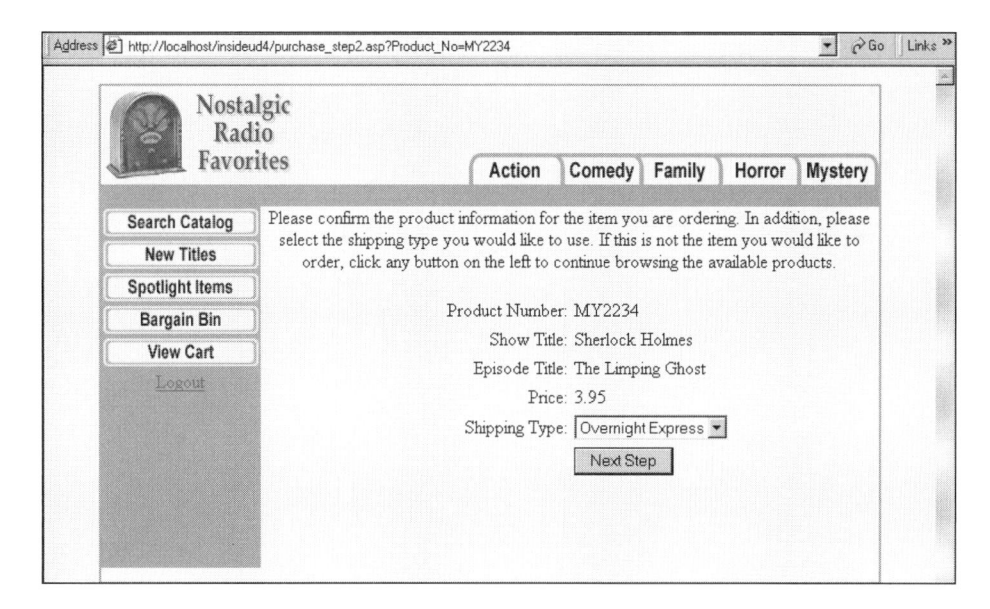

Figure 12.21 The visitor can confirm the product and select a shipping option.

8. In the Shipping Type field, select Overnight Express and click the Next Step button.
9. In the payment information page, select Credit Card as the payment method.
10. In the Credit Card Type field, select Visa.
11. Type **0000000000** (ten zeros) in the Credit Card Number field.
12. In the Credit Card Expiration field, type **01/01**. The page should look like Figure 12.22.
13. Click the Final Step button.
14. As shown in Figure 12.23, the visitor is issued an order number and the order date and shipping method are confirmed.

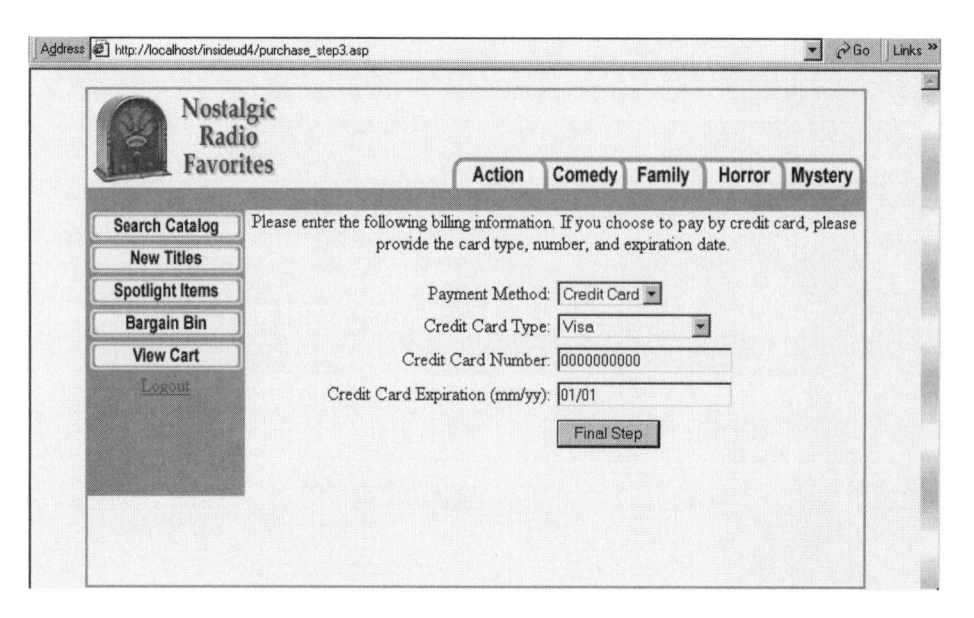

Figure 12.22 Enter this payment information into the form.

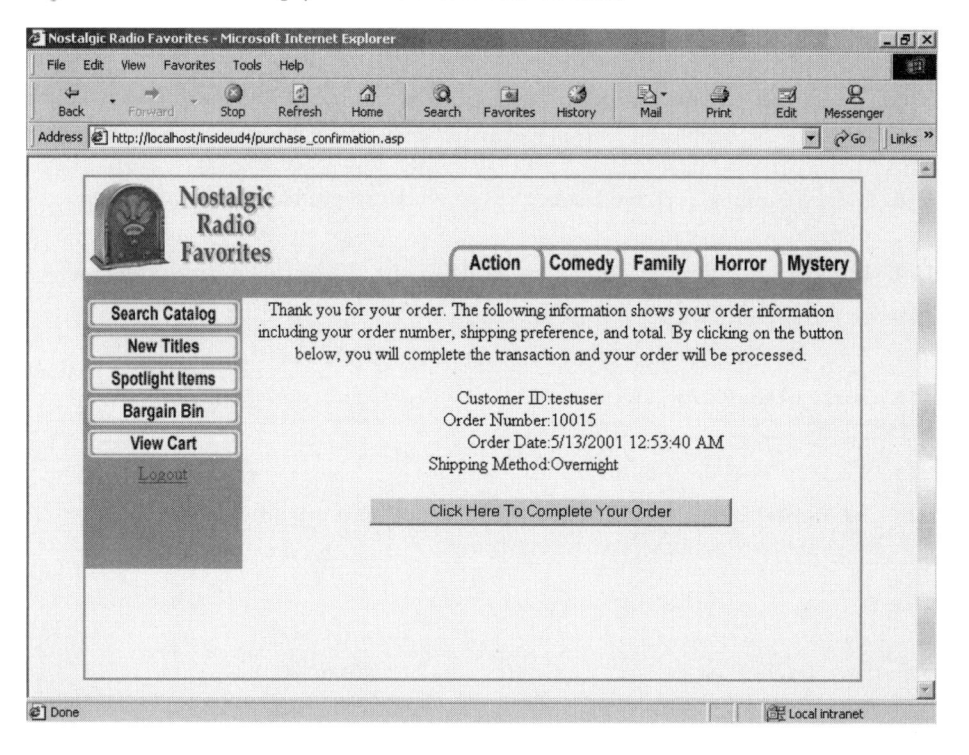

Figure 12.23 The order is complete.

15. Click the button to complete the order.
16. Minimize your browser.

Extending the Model to Include a Shopping Cart

Now that you've seen how to develop a simple single-transaction system, you can extend that system to allow the visitor to order multiple items in the same order session. To accomplish this, you're going to use an UltraDev Extension created by Rick Crawford, President of PowerClimb (www.powerclimb.com) called the UltraDev Shopping Cart. This extension was originally developed for UltraDev 1, but a patch that updates the software to be compatible with UltraDev 4 was developed by Joseph Scavitto, a third-party developer.

Using the patched version of the UltraDev Shopping cart, you can allow your visitors to add items to their shopping carts, where they are stored in session variables until they are ready to check out. When they initiate the checkout process, the visitors follow similar steps to those in the single transaction model. In fact, the only major difference comes when the visitor submits the final form. At this time, one of the shopping cart behaviors inserts each of the items in the shopping cart into the tbLineitem table and associates the previously created order ID with each of the items.

Downloading and Installing the UltraDev Shopping Cart 1.2

The first step in installing the UltraDev Shopping Cart is to download the appropriate version and install the extension using UltraDev's Extension Manager. This is done by downloading a single .mxp file to your local hard drive and double-clicking on the icon. After that, the Extension Manager will take over and insert all the necessary server behaviors and menu items. Once the extension is installed, you can access the UltraDev Shopping Cart's functionality via the Server Behaviors panel.

Exercise 12.7   Installing the UltraDev Shopping Cart

1. Close UltraDev.
2. Open a browser window and visit http://www.powerclimb.com/Behaviors.htm. Download the UltraDev Shopping Cart version 1.2.
3. In the browser, visit http://www.thechocolatestore.com/ultradev/. Download the UltraCart patch for UltraDev 4.
4. Minimize your browser and locate the folder where you downloaded the two extensions.

5. Double click the UC_Cart_V12_Beta2.mxp file to begin the installation process. Read the extension disclaimer, shown in Figure 12.24, and click the Accept button.

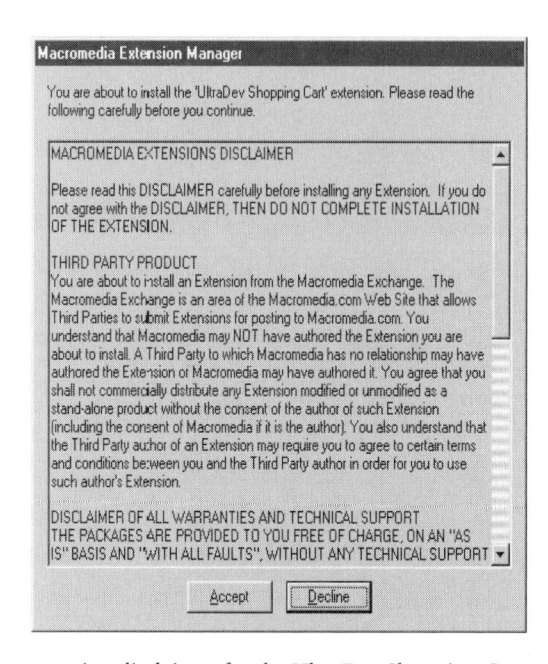

Figure 12.24 The extension disclaimer for the UltraDev Shopping Cart extension.

6. In the pop-up box that alerts you that the extension was installed, click OK.
7. Read through the extension details in the bottom panel of the Macromedia Extension Manager, shown in Figure 12.25, to see which behaviors have been added to UltraDev.
8. Minimize the Macromedia Extension Manager and find the folder where you previously downloaded the extensions. Double-click the UD4CartPatch.mxp file.
9. Click the Accept button to accept the terms of the extension disclaimer. As shown in Figure 12.26, a pop-up box alerts you that new patch is replacing a file that already exists. Be aware that the extension won't replace any of the core UltraDev application files. Click the Yes To All button.

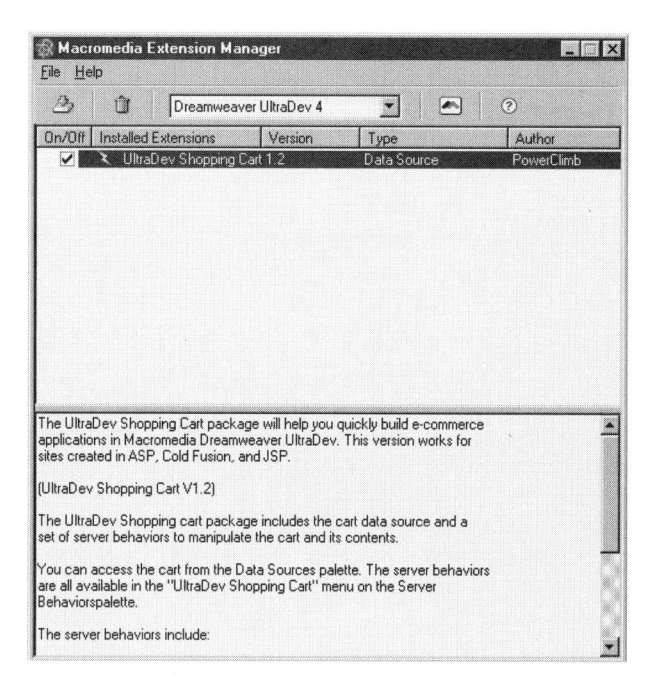

Figure 12.25 The Macromedia Extension Manager.

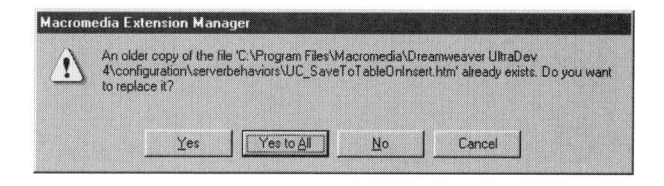

Figure 12.26 The patch is replacing previously existing files.

10. Click OK in the pop-up box that lets you know the extension was installed successfully.
11. Close the Macromedia Extension Manager.

Defining the UltraDev Shopping Cart

With the UltraDev Shopping Cart installed, you now need to define the cart so it will function within your site. When defining the cart, you can choose how long the cart contents will remain in the cart when the visitor leaves the site and what information should be stored within the cart.

Exercise 12.8 Setting Up the Shopping Cart Parameters

1. Open UltraDev.
2. Open the spotlight_items_details.asp page. If you recall, this is the details page that displays information about items that have been designated spotlight items in your database.
3. In the Server Behavior panel, click the plus sign and select UltraDev Shopping Cart/UltraDev Shopping Cart from the pop-up menu. UltraDev displays the UltraDev Shopping Cart dialog box, shown in Figure 12.27.
4. Name the shopping cart **NRFCart** and set the client cookie expiration to **0**.

> **Tip**
>
> **Using Cookies to Save Cart Contents** By default, after a visitor leaves your site or ends his session, the contents of his cart will be lost. If, however, you would like the visitor's cart to remain intact beyond the expiration of his session, you can set the Client Cookie Expiration field in the UltraDev Shopping Cart dialog box to a number other than zero. Whatever number you choose designates the number of days that the shopping cart will remain intact beyond the expiration of the session.

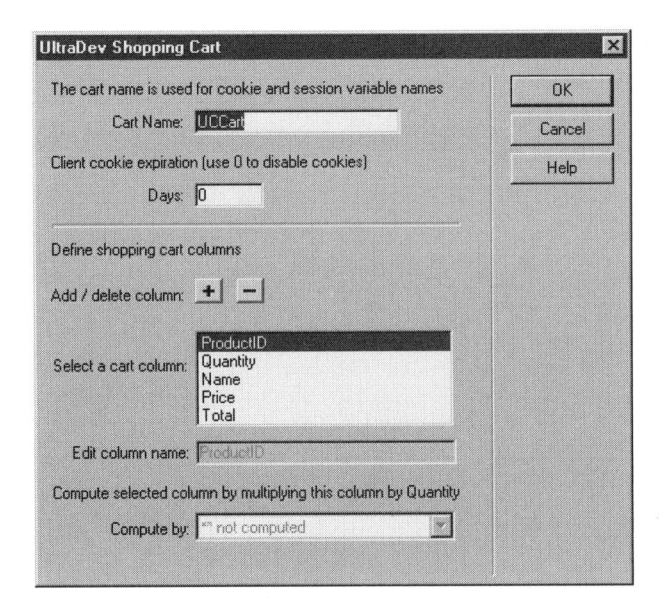

Figure 12.27 The UltraDev Shopping Cart dialog box allows you to define the parameters of your shopping cart.

5. The UltraDev Shopping Cart requires certain columns in order to function properly. Those columns include Product ID, Quantity, Name, Price, and Total. Although the cart requires these columns to be present in the behavior, it is not necessary that you actually use all the columns when adding items to the cart.

6. At this point, leave the default cart columns and click OK to close the dialog box. As shown in Figure 12.28, the Server Behaviors panel should now include the UltraDev Shopping Cart behavior.

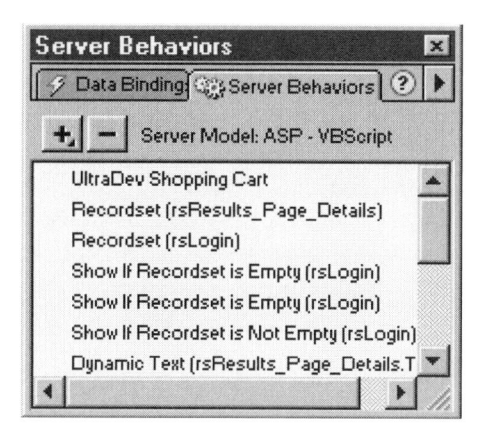

Figure 12.28 The UltraDev Shopping Cart behavior has been added to the page.

Creating a Link to the Cart

To add the shopping cart functionality to the site, give the visitor a way to add a product to his cart. In this case, the best place to do this is on the product details page. This way, when the visitor explores the specifics of each product, he can choose whether he would like to add the item to his cart.

To add this feature to the product details page, you will add a simple form that contains a text field and a submit button. This way, the visitor can type the quantity of the item he would like to order and then submit that form to the shopping cart. The product information and the quantity are then stored in the shopping cart's session variables until they are needed at checkout.

Exercise 12.9 Adding a Shopping Cart Link to a Product Detail Page

1. In the spotlight_items_details.asp page, place the insertion point on the line below the table holding the product information. From the menu bar, select Insert/Form.
2. Name the new form **fmAddToCart**.
3. Select the table containing the product details by right-clicking anywhere in the table and choosing Table/Select Table from the pop-up menu.

4. Click on the dark border in the upper-left corner of the table and drag the table into the fmAddToCart form. Your cursor should turn into a cross-arrow when you are able to drag the table.

5. Click on the {rsResults_Page_Details.Description} text in the lower right cell and press the Tab key. As shown in Figure 12.29, a new row has been added to the table.

6. In the bottom-left cell, type **Quantity:**. Highlight the text and change the font to Arial, Helvetica, sans serif. Press the Tab key.

7. With the insertion point in the lower-right cell, select Insert/Form Objects/Text Field from the menu bar. Name the new text field **tfQuantity**. Set the character width to **2** and the maximum characters to **2**. This limits the number of items that could be added to the cart to 99.

8. Place the insertion point on the right side of the new text field and select Insert/Form Objects/Button from the menu bar.

9. Name the button **btSubmit** and change the button label to **Add To Cart**.

10. In the Server Behaviors panel, click the plus sign and select UltraDev Shopping Cart/Add To Cart Via Form. The Add To Cart Via Form dialog box, shown in Figure 12.30, appears.

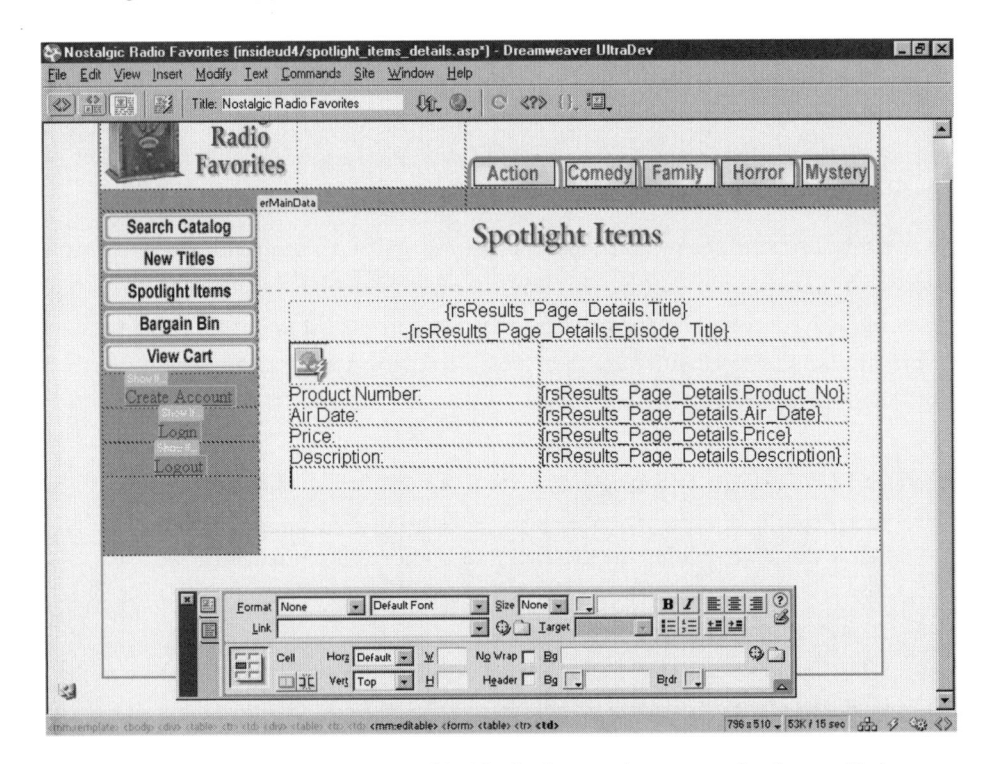

Figure 12.29 The table is now situated inside the form and a new row has been added.

Chapter 12 Engaging in eCommerce 343

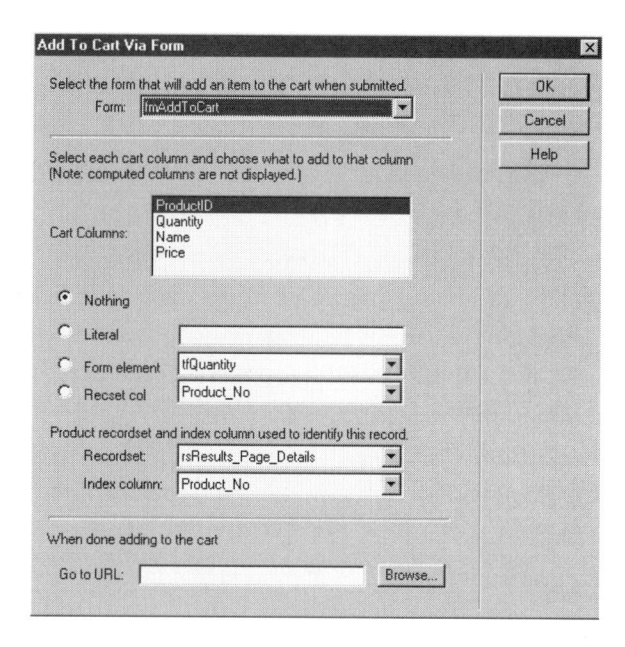

Figure 12.30 The Add To Cart Via Form dialog box allows you to submit the contents of your form directly to the shopping cart.

11. In the dialog box, select the fmAddToCart form and highlight the ProductID cart column. Choose to update the ProductID cart column with the Product_No recordset column by selecting the Recset Col radio button and choosing Product_No from the dropdown.

12. Highlight the Quantity cart column and choose to update it from the form element tfQuantity.

13. Highlight the Name cart column and indicate that it should be updated from the Episode_Title column in the recordset.

14. Highlight the Price cart column and choose to update it from the Price column in the recordset.

15. Be sure that the Product recordset and index column used to identify this record are set to the rsResults_Page_Details recordset and the Product_No recordset column.

16. In the Go To URL field, type **view_cart.asp**.

17. Click OK to close the dialog box.

18. Save the page.

The Shopping Cart Page

Each time the visitor adds something to his cart, you want to show him the contents of the shopping cart. In addition, you have already created a link that exists in each page that allows the visitor to go directly to his cart. The next step is to create that shopping cart page.

In essence, this page is very similar to your spotlight items page, in the fact that it uses a table that includes table headings, dynamic elements, and a repeat region behavior that lists all the items stored in the cart. In addition, the page gives the visitor the opportunity to change the quantity of an item and to remove items from the cart. The final feature is a link that begins the checkout process.

Exercise 12.10 Developing a Page that Displays the Contents of the Cart

1. Open the view_cart.asp page.
2. The first thing you want to do is to make sure that the cart you just created is available here. To do this, switch to the spotlight_items_details.asp page and right-click on the UltraDev Shopping Cart server behavior. From the pop-up menu, choose Copy. Switch back to the view_cart.asp page and right-click inside the Server Behaviors panel and click Paste. The shopping cart should now be present in your page.
3. The next thing you want to do is redirect the visitor to a different page if his cart is empty. To do this, click the plus sign in the Server Behaviors panel and select UltraDev Shopping Cart/Redirect If Empty. In the Redirect If Empty dialog box, shown in Figure 12.31, type **cart_empty.asp**. Click OK.

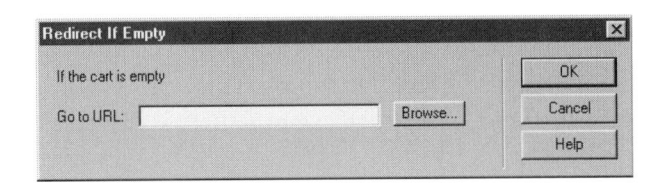

Figure 12.31 The Redirect If Empty dialog box.

4. In the erMainData editable region, replace the existing text with the following textblock:

Thank you for shopping with Nostalgic Radio Favorites! Here are the contents of your cart. Please use the buttons to manage the content of your cart or proceed to the checkout page. If you wish to remove an item from your cart, simply set the quantity to 0 and update the cart.

5. Press Enter.
6. From the menu bar, select Insert/Form. Name the new form **fmManageCart**.
7. Insert a new table inside the form with **2** rows, **5** columns, and a width of **90%**. Set the border, cell padding, and cell spacing for the table to **1**.
8. Highlight the single table row by clicking the <tr> link in the status bar at the bottom of the page. In the Property inspector, click the Align Center button.
9. Place the insertion point in the leftmost cell and type Product Number. Press Tab.
10. In the second cell, type **Episode Name**. Press Tab.
11. In the third cell, type **Quantity**. Press Tab.
12. In the fourth cell, type **Price**. Press Tab.
13. In the fifth cell, type **Total**. Press Tab.
14. Open the Data Bindings panel and click the plus sign next to the UltraDev Shopping Cart. As shown in Figure 12.32, you now have access to all the columns stored in the cart.

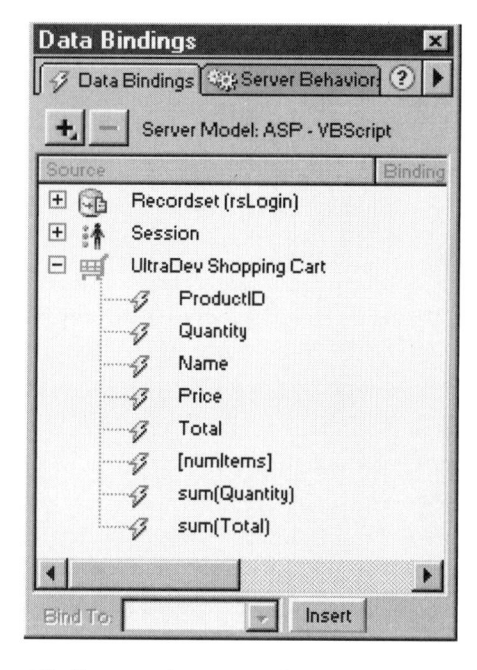

Figure 12.32 The Data Bindings panel now provides access to the columns stored in the cart.

15. Click and drag the ProductID column from the Data Bindings panel to the empty cell below Product Number.
16. Drag the Name column to the cell under Episode Name.

17. In the cell underneath Quantity, insert a text field by choosing Insert/Form Objects/Text Field from the menu bar. Name the text field **tfQuantity** and set the Char Width and Max Chars fields to **2**.

18. From the Data Bindings panel, drag the Quantity column from the UltraDev Shopping Cart into the tfQuantity text field. This displays the quantity of items added to the cart and allows the visitor to update the field by altering the text field and submitting the form.

19. Drag the Price and Total columns to the appropriate cells in the table.

20. Highlight the bottom row of the table and click the Align Center button on the Property inspector. Switch to the Server Behaviors panel and click the plus sign. From the pop-up menu, select UltraDev Shopping Cart/Repeat Cart Region. This displays all the items stored in the cart.

> **Note**
>
> **Repeat Region Versus Repeat Cart Region** In the past, we have always used the Repeat Region server behavior when we wanted to repeat tables. This server behavior, however, requires that a recordset be defined in order to function. Because the shopping cart uses session variables instead of a recordset to maintain its content, the Repeat Region server behavior won't work. Instead, the UltraDev Shopping Cart comes with a built-in Repeat Cart Region behavior that repeats the region until all the entries in the session variables are displayed.

21. Place the insertion point to the right of the new table and press the Enter key.

22. On the new line, type **You have episode title(s) in your cart and your total is .** Be sure to leave an extra space between "have" and "episode" and after "is." Press Enter.

23. In the Data Bindings panel, drag the [numItems] column and drop it between the words "have" and "items."

24. Drag the sum(Total) column onto the page after the word "is."

25. Place the insertion point on the next line and insert a new table. The table should have **1** row, **2** columns, and a width of **50%**. Set the border, cell padding, and cell spacing to **0**.

26. In the left cell of the new table, insert a form button and name the button **btUpdate**. Change the label on the button to read **Update Cart**.

27. In the right cell, type **Go To Checkout**. Highlight the text and click the plus sign on the Server Behaviors panel. From the pop-up menu, select Go To Related Page.

28. In the Go To Related Page dialog box, type **cart_checkout.asp** in the Related Page field and check the URL Parameters checkbox. Click OK.

29. Highlight the Update Cart button and click the plus sign on the Server Behaviors panel. From the pop-up menu, select UltraDev Shopping Cart/Update Cart. In

the Update Cart dialog box, shown in Figure 12.33, make sure that the fmManageCart form is selected and that the Form Element field is set to tfQuantity.

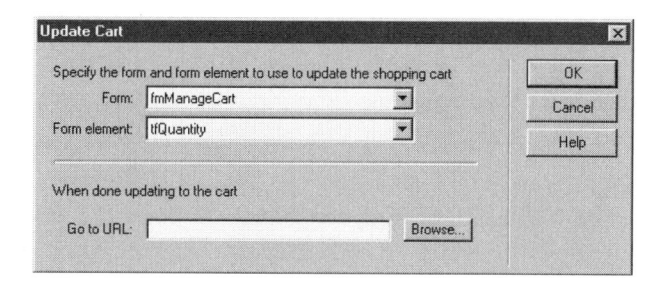

Figure 12.33 The Update Cart dialog box allows you to specify what element of the cart is updated.

30. In the Go To URL field, type **view_cart.asp**. This refreshes the shopping cart page after the cart is updated. Click OK. Your shopping cart page should now look like Figure 12.34.

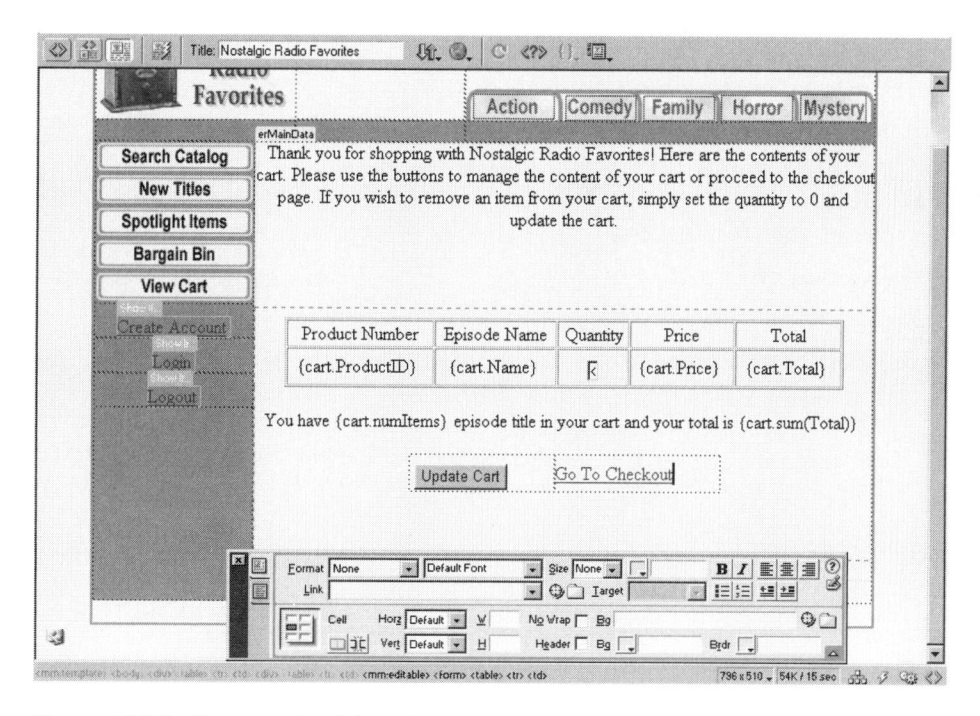

Figure 12.34 Your completed shopping cart page.

31. Save the page.

Checking Out

After the visitor is through adding items to his cart, he can begin the checkout process by clicking the link in the shopping cart page. The only major difference between this checkout system and the single transaction method is the use of a behavior included in the UltraDev Shopping Cart. This behavior loops through the contents in the cart and writes them to the new table, assigning the order number to each of the items. This allows the database to associate one order number with multiple products.

Exercise 12.11 Creating Pages that Verify the Visitor's Shipping and Purchase Information

1. Open the purchase_step1.asp page created earlier. Save this page as **cart_checkout.asp**.

    In the cart_checkout.asp page, double-click the Update Record server behavior and change the After Updating, Go To field to cart_checkout2.asp. Click OK.

2. Save the page.

3. Open the purchase_step2.asp page created earlier and save it as **cart_checkout2.asp**.

4. Highlight the top four rows in the table containing product details and press the Delete button on your keyboard.

5. Highlight the text block at the top of the page and press Delete. Type **Please choose a shipping method**.

6. Highlight the fmOrderInfo form located on the page and change the form action to cart_checkout3.asp.

7. Save the page.

8. Open the purchase_step3.asp page created earlier and save it as **cart_checkout3.asp**.

    The first thing you need to do to make this page work properly is to include the UltraDev Shopping Cart that you have created in this page. To do this, switch to the view_cart.asp page that you created earlier and right-click on the UltraDev Shopping Cart in the Server Behaviors panel and select Copy from the pop-up menu.

9. Switch back to the cart_checkout3.asp page and right-click in the Server Behaviors panel. Select Paste. The UltraDev Shopping Cart should now be visible in the list of Server Behaviors associated with this page.

10. In the Server Behaviors panel, double-click the Insert Record server behavior.

11. In the Insert Record dialog box, remove the text from the After Inserting, Go To field. As shown in Figure 12.35, this field should now be blank. Click OK.

Chapter 12 Engaging in eCommerce 349

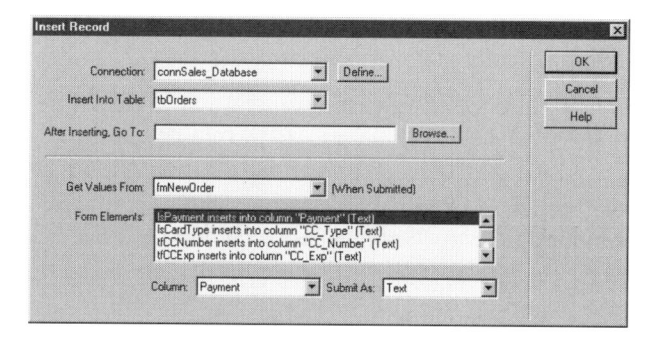

Figure 12.35 Insert Record dialog box.

Before you can insert all the contents of the cart into the tbLineitem table, you need to get the order number that has been generated for this particular order. To do this, build a recordset that contains only the highest order number.

12. On the Server Behaviors panel, click the plus sign and select Recordset (Query).

13. In the Recordset dialog box, switch to the advanced view if is not already visible.

14. Create a recordset identical to the one shown in Figure 12.36. This recordset looks through the tbOrders table and finds the highest order number. Because the Order_No field is set to autoincrement, the highest order number is logically the last order number generated.

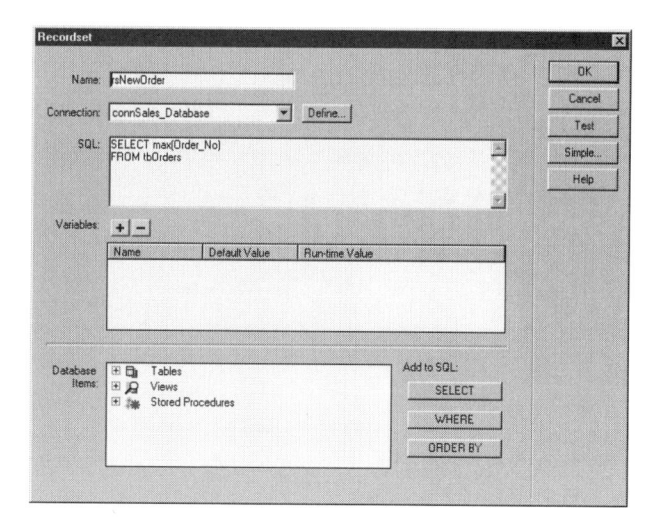

Figure 12.36 This recordset finds the highest value in the Order_No field.

350 Part IV Extending Your Administrative Capabilities

15. After the recordset is created, click the OK button to closest the Recordset dialog box.

    Now that you are able to identify which order number the items in the shopping cart should be associated with, you need to insert each of the ordered items into the tbLineitem table and associate each of the new records in the table with the proper order number. To do this, you can take advantage of a server behavior included with the UltraDev Shopping Cart that does just that.

16. Highlight the Final Step button. In the Server Behaviors panel, click the plus sign and select UltraDev Shopping Cart/Save Cart To Table.

> **Note**
>
> **An Insert Record or Update Record Server Behavior Is Required** Before you can apply the Save Cart To Table server behavior, an Insert Record or Update Record server behavior must be applied. Because your page already contains an Insert Record server behavior, you're in good shape.

17. In the Save Cart To Table dialog box, shown in Figure 12.37, select the connSales_Database connection and the tbLineitem table.

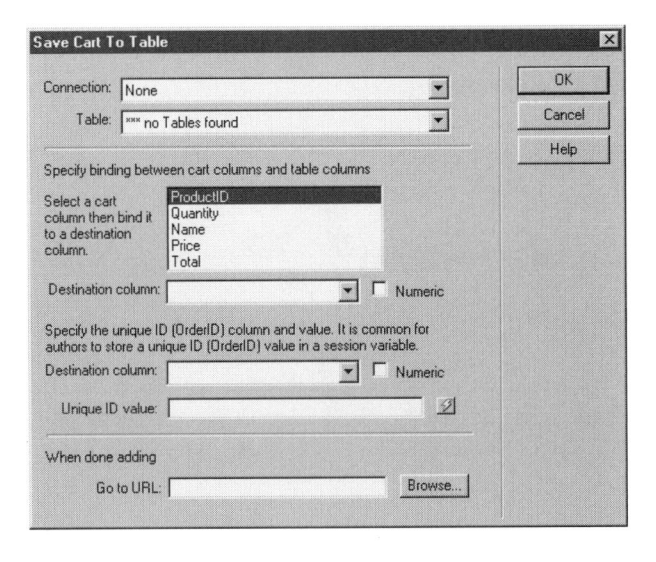

Figure 12.37 The Save Cart To Table dialog box inserts the data stored in the cart into your database.

18. Highlight the ProductID shopping cart column and select Product_No from the Destination Column dropdown. This designates the Product_No column in the tbLineitem table as the recipient of the data stored in the ProductID column of the shopping cart.

19. Using the same procedure, bind the Quantity shopping cart column to the Qty column in the tbLineitem table.

20. When specifying the unique ID (order ID) column and value, select Order_No from the drop-down menu.

21. Click the lightning bolt icon next to the Unique ID Value field. In the Dynamic Data dialog box, shown in Figure 12.38, click the plus sign next to the rsNewOrder recordset. Select the Expr1000 column and click OK.

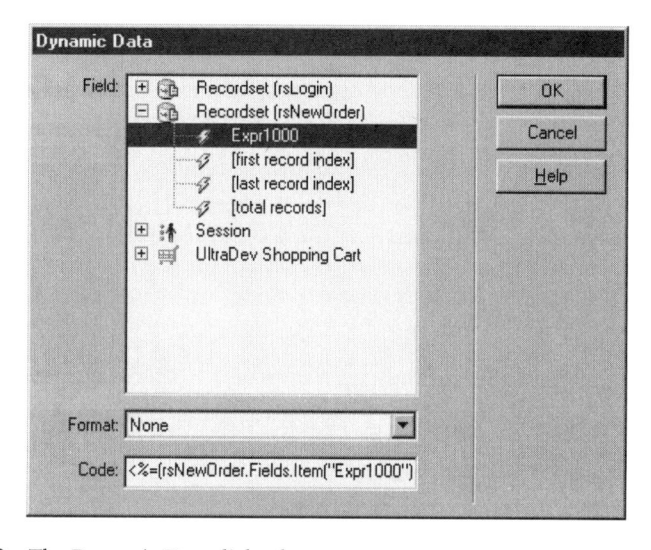

Figure 12.38 The Dynamic Data dialog box.

22. In the Go To URL field, type **cart_checkout_confirmation.asp**. The Save Cart To Table dialog box should now look like Figure 12.39.

23. Click OK.

24. Save the page.

25. Create a new page from the nrfdefault template.

26. Delete the {erMainData} text and type the following text block:

    Thank you for ordering with us. Your order is complete and will be shipped according to your requested shipping method.

27. Save the page as **cart_checkout_confirmation.asp**.

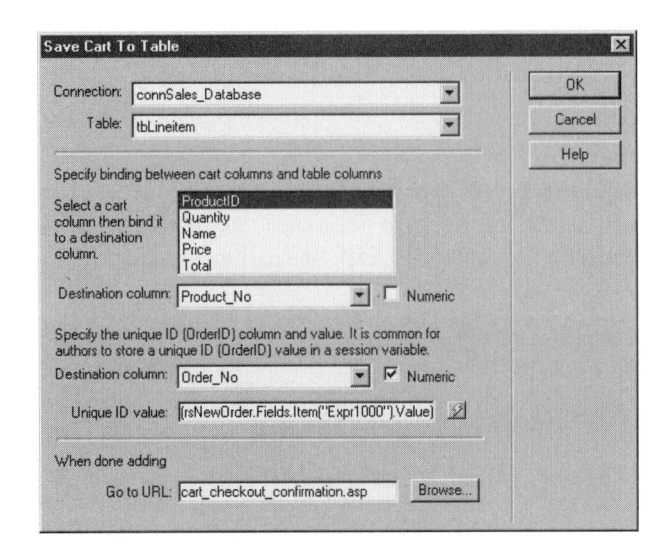

Figure 12.39 Your Save Cart To Table dialog box should look like this.

Alerting Visitors to an Empty Cart

The last page you need to create is a simple one that alerts the visitor that his cart is empty. This page can be as simple or intricate as you want, but the file name must match the one specified when you set up the shopping cart.

Exercise 12.12 Creating a Page that Alerts the Visitor to an Empty Shopping Cart

1. Create a new page from the nrfdefault template.
2. Delete the {erMainData} text and type **Your shopping cart is currently empty**.
3. Save the page as **cart_empty.asp**.

Testing the Shopping Cart

Now that all the pages are in place, you can check to make sure that each feature works correctly. You'll want to be sure that the visitor can add an item to the cart, update the cart, remove items, and then complete the checkout process successfully.

Exercise 12.13 Testing the Shopping Cart Functionality

1. Minimize UltraDev and open a browser window.
2. In the address bar of your browser, type **http://localhost/insideud4**.

3. From the main page, click the Login link.
4. In the login page, type **testuser** for the username and **testuser** for the password. Click the Submit button. The site should confirm that you were authenticated.
5. Click the View Cart button. As shown in Figure 12.40, you are redirected to the page informing us that the cart is empty.

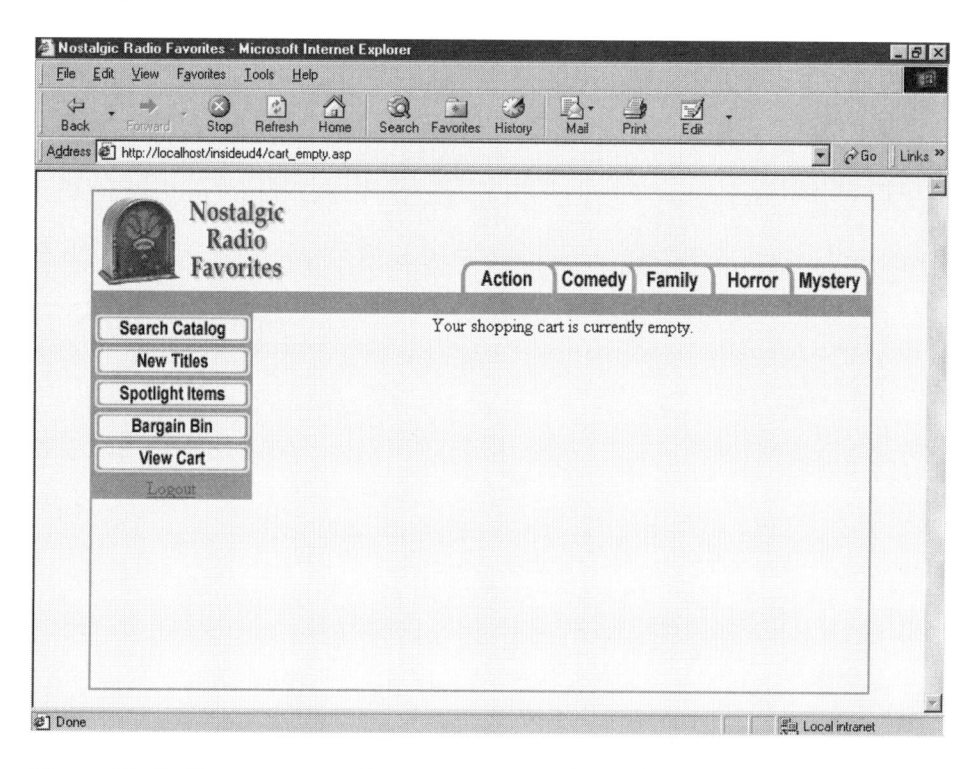

Figure 12.40 Because your cart is empty, you were redirected to this page.

6. Click the Spotlight Items button. In the Spotlight Items results page, click the link to The Presidential Election. As shown in Figure 12.41, you now have the ability to add this item to your shopping cart.
7. In the Quantity field, type **2**. Press the Add To Cart button. As shown in Figure 12.42, your shopping cart now reflects the added items.
8. In the Quantity field, type **1** and click the Update Cart button. The page automatically refreshes and one of the items is removed from the cart.
9. Click the Spotlight Items button again and this time click the link to "The Thing On The Fourble Board." Add two of this title to the shopping cart and press the Add To Cart button.

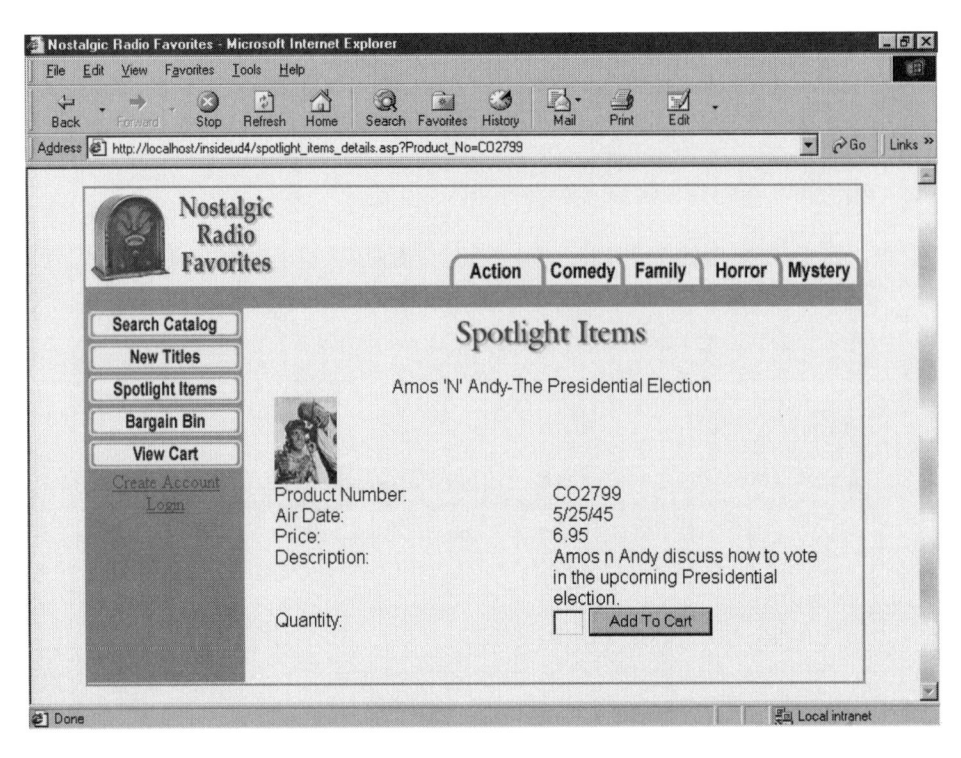

354 Part IV Extending Your Administrative Capabilities

Figure 12.41 The Add To Cart button is now present.

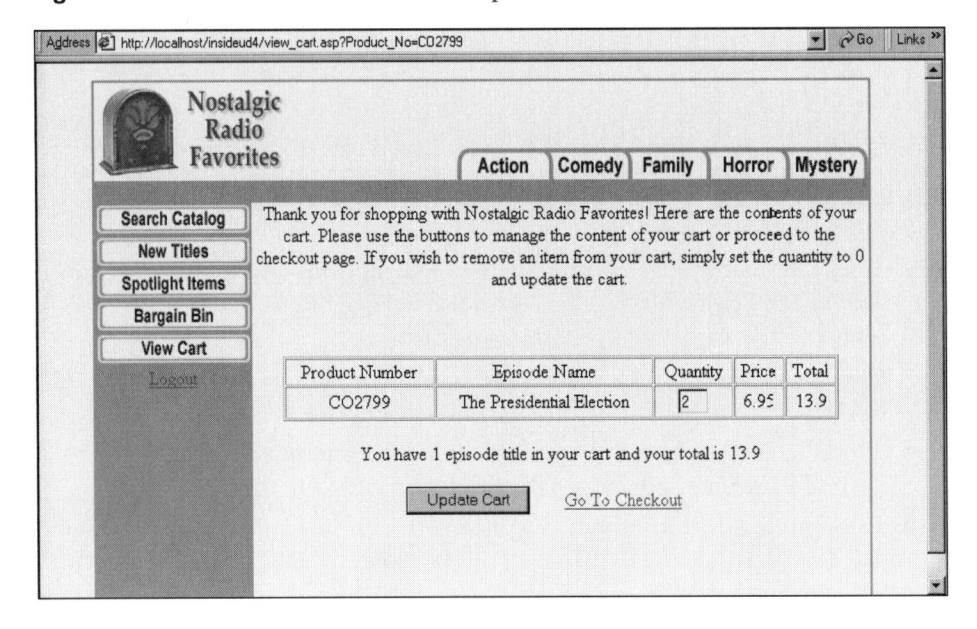

Figure 12.42 You now have items in your shopping cart.

10. In the View Cart page, click the Go To Checkout link. You are taken to the first step in placing your order and are asked to confirm the shipping information that is stored in the tbCustomers table.
11. Click the Next Step button.
12. Choose to ship the order overnight by selecting Overnight Express from the Shipping Type drop-down menu. Click the Next Step button.
13. In the billing information choose to pay by credit card. In the Credit Card Type field, choose MasterCard. Type **0000000000** (ten zeros) as the credit card number and enter an expiration date of **01/01**. Click the Final Step button.
14. As shown in Figure 12.43, your order has been placed.

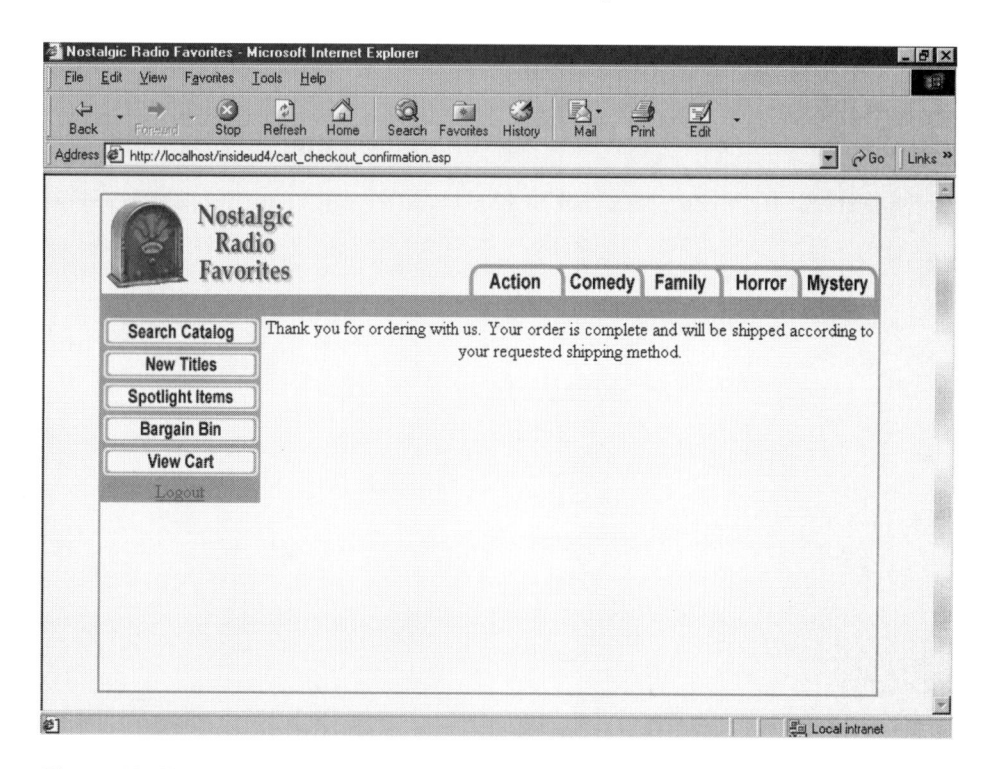

Figure 12.43 The order was successful.

Now that the order has been completed, you can open the database and look at both the tbOrders table and the tbLineitem table. Each one should reflect the appropriate information.

The only other feature you might consider at this point is adding a section to the administrative section that allows you to search all the records in the tbOrders and tbLineitems table. This way you can monitor what orders are made and when they were made. An alternative method would be to set up an email notification system that lets you know when a new order has been created, what items were ordered, and where they should be shipped to.

Summary

This chapter showed you how to implement two different eCommerce models. The first was a single transaction system that allowed the user to purchase one item at a time. The second model expanded the first by adding shopping cart functionality that allowed the user to add multiple items to a shopping cart and then purchase those items using a single order.

In the next chapter, you'll take a look at how UltraDev can be used to add eLearning capabilities to your site. You will see how to create quizzes that are scored and their results recorded in a database.

Chapter 13

Adding eLearning to Your Site

As a Web developer at a university, I am constantly exploring eLearning options that use a variety of technologies to allow professors to expand their course content beyond the classroom. These solutions, however, are often very complex and difficult to maintain, or just don't seem to enhance the learning environment for students. In fact, the most common problem I encounter when evaluating these systems is their complexity.

Fortunately, Macromedia has developed several tools that make my job easier when it comes to developing eLearning applications. Whether it's making class presentations available on the Web, helping professors create interactive test and quizzes, or even developing complete distanced-learning classes, UltraDev and its eLearning extensions make creating and deploying interactive content relatively easy.

To demonstrate just how easily you can develop an eLearning site using UltraDev, this chapter shows you how to do the following:

- Build eLearning applications
- Develop a simple quiz
- Create a complex, database-driven quiz and results-tracking system

As you can see, this chapter is not going to try to cover every aspect of eLearning because entire books could be (and have been) written on that topic. Instead, you're going to look at what UltraDev can to do help you implement Web-based eLearning applications and introduce you to two of the most popular eLearning extensions for UltraDev.

With that said, put on your thinking cap, spit out that gum, and let's do some learning about eLearning.

Why Use eLearning?

Although eLearning applications are obviously appropriate for use in an educational environment, you might be wondering what they can do for your private business, organization, or corporation. The answer is that eLearning applications can add interactivity to your site, train your employees, or even gain valuable feedback from your customers.

All too often, we think of eLearning as a one-way conduit of information where the Web application is teaching the Web site visitor. Whereas this might be appropriate in a virtual classroom setting, we miss the fact that eLearning gives us, as Web developers, managers, and members of the business community, the chance to learn from our visitors. For instance, suppose you want to know the demographics of your Web site visitors. You could accomplish this through the use of a poll created with an eLearning application. Or suppose that you want to see how much your customers know about your product line. Engage them in a 10-question quiz and reward them with a 10% off coupon on their next order. In either instance, it is you who is learning from your visitors.

The other major benefit of eLearning applications is the interactivity they provide your visitors. You see, the more your visitors are able to interact with your site, the more likely they will return, which increases the chance that they'll purchase your products. Think about it for a minute. Suppose you stumbled across the Nostalgic Radio Favorites site via a search engine and were intrigued by the opportunity to test your trivia knowledge of old-time radio shows. In addition, you liked the idea of earning a 10% off coupon just for playing along. By the time you end the quiz, you might be inspired to check out the product catalog and possibly use your coupon to make a purchase that might not otherwise have been made.

When thinking about how eLearning can advance your Web applications, take the time to analyze not only how you can provide information to your visitors, but how your visitors can provide you with feedback about your organization and what effect the interaction with your visitors can have on your site as a whole.

Introducing the CourseBuilder Extension for UltraDev 4

To build the first eLearning application, you will be using the CourseBuilder extension developed by Macromedia. This extension adds a variety of easy to use functions to UltraDev that make it simple to develop interactive pages, including test and quiz questions in a variety of formats.

> **Tip**
> **Frequently Asked Questions About CourseBuilder** A great FAQ on CourseBuilder can be found at http://www.macromedia.com/software/coursebuilder/productinfo/faq/faq.html.

Although CourseBuilder may look a little intimidating at first, you'll be surprised how easy the CourseBuilder interactions are to create and modify and how simple it is to put together a basic eLearning application.

Downloading CourseBuilder

The first step to using the CourseBuilder extension for UltraDev is to download and install it from Macromedia's UltraDev Exchange. Using UltraDev 4's built-in extension manager, adding CourseBuilder's functionality can be done in just a couple minutes.

> **Warning**
>
> **Forget the CourseBuilder Application** If you have been using Macromedia products for a while, you might have purchased the CourseBuilder application that was available for earlier versions of Dreamweaver. Don't be tempted to install that software because it won't work properly with UltraDev 4. Instead, be sure the get the free CourseBuilder extension available for UltraDev 4.
>
> You can use your old CourseBuilder CD as a new coaster for your coffee mug.

Exercise 13.1 Downloading and Installing the CourseBuilder and Learning Site Command Extensions

1. Open your Web browser and visit http://www.macromedia.com/software/coursebuilder/download/.

> **Tip**
>
> **Becoming a Macromedia Partner** Before you can download CourseBuilder, you'll need to sign up as a Macromedia member. One of the great things about signing up for an account is you can have Macromedia alert you to updates and information about their product line through the Macromedia <EDGE> Newsletter.
>
> If you want to be kept up to date on any of UltraDev's products, I highly recommend subscribing to the <EDGE>. The newsletter offers you the ability to indicate which products you are interested in receiving updates about and you can even receive alerts in areas such as training opportunities and upcoming seminars.

2. Download the CourseBuilder extension to a folder on your local hard drive.
3. Close your browser and open the folder where the cb_dw_ud.mxp file was downloaded in Step 2.
4. Double-click the file to start the installation of the extension. Click the Accept button to accept the terms of the User Agreement and UltraDev will begin the installation process. As shown in Figure 13.1, you will be alerted when the process is complete.

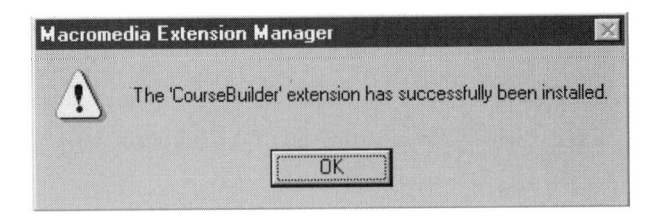

Figure 13.1 The installation of the extension is complete.

5. Click OK to close the alert box. The Macromedia Extension Manager, shown in Figure 13.2, lets you know exactly what new features were installed.

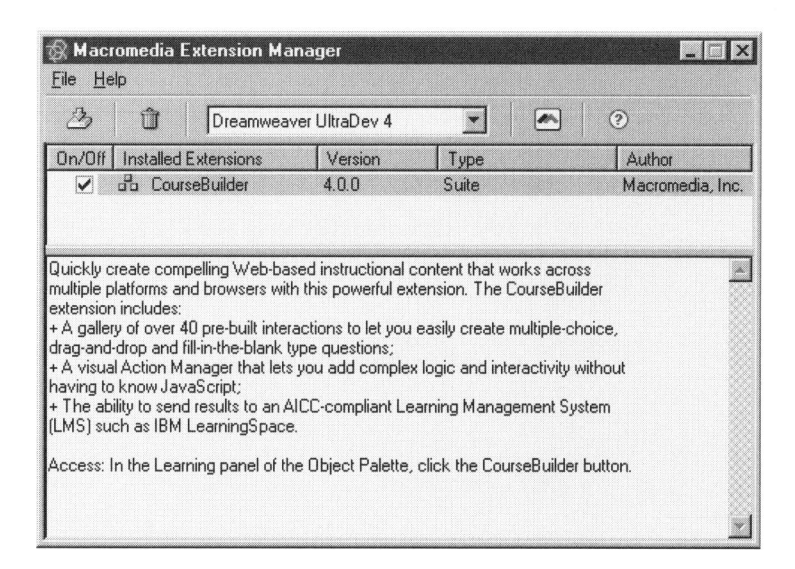

Figure 13.2 The Extension Manager alerts you to what changes were made to your system.

6. Close the Extension Manager.

Taking a Tour of CourseBuilder

Now that CourseBuilder is installed, let's take a minute and explore how to access the eLearning elements that can be added to your pages. In addition, you'll see exactly what types of quizzes, tutorials, and interactions can be created using CourseBuilder.

Exercise 13.2 Exploring the CourseBuilder Extension

> **Tip**
>
> **Close UltraDev Before You Install an Extension** Whenever you install a new extension, it's a good idea to save all your pages and close UltraDev. If you install the extension while UltraDev is still running, the extension won't be accessible until after you restart UltraDev.

1. Open UltraDev. If a new document is not displayed, create one. Save the new document to the root folder of the InsideUD4 site as **tour.asp**.

> **Note**
>
> **Save Your Document First** The scripts and image files used by CourseBuilder all use relative links, so you have to save your new document before you will be allowed to insert any CourseBuilder interactions.

2. From the menu bar, select Window/Objects.

3. In the Objects panel, select the Learning category from the Common dropdown menu. As shown in Figure 13.3, there is now a button for inserting a CourseBuilder interaction.

4. Click the CourseBuilder button on the Objects panel. As shown in Figure 13.4, UltraDev alerts you that certain files need to be copied to your site in order for CourseBuilder to function properly.

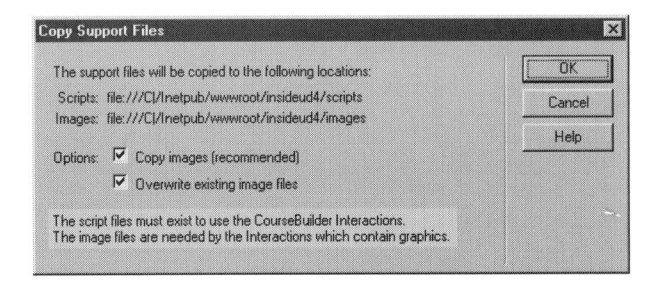

Figure 13.4 UltraDev needs to copy support files to your site in order for CourseBuilder to function.

5. Make sure that both the Options check boxes are checked and click OK. After the files are copied to your site, UltraDev opens the CourseBuilder Interaction dialog box shown in Figure 13.5.

Figure 13.3 A CourseBuilder button has been added to the Learning category of the Objects panel.

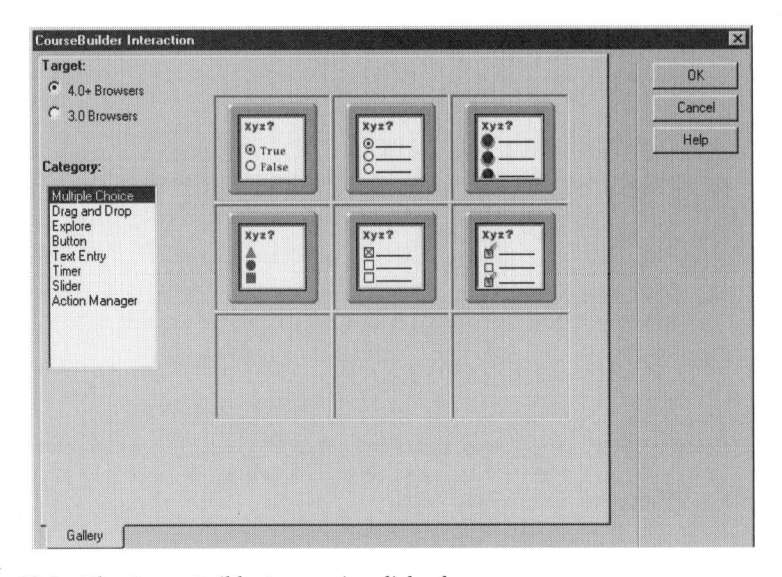

Figure 13.5 The CourseBuilder Interaction dialog box.

6. In the Interaction Gallery, click through each of the available categories and notice that CourseBuilder offers the ability to add many different types of test interactions. Table 13.1 offers a brief description of each of the various categories.

Table 13.1 Explanations for the Gallery Category List

Multiple Choice	Offers visitors a question and then provides answers to choose from. Answers can be either true/false or multiple choice. A multiple-choice quiz can require the visitor to pick a single correct answer or multiple correct answers.
Drag and Drop	Offers users the ability to engage in a matching quiz by dragging one object onto another. If the destination object is correct, then a correct answer is recorded.
Explore	Allows visitors to click on "hotspots" to learn more about the topic of the quiz. When a hotspot is clicked, an HTML layer is activated displaying text or images.
Button	Graphical elements that can be used to control other elements within an interaction. For instance, a toggle switch button might be used to play a sound that the visitor must evaluate.
Text Entry	Interactions such as your typical "fill in the blank" questions. The user is requested to enter a short text response to the question.
Timer	Displays the elapsed time that has passed since the interaction began.
Slider	Allows the visitor to select from a range of numeric values.
Action Manager	Displays all the conditions that have been assigned to the interaction and the behaviors that occur when the conditions are met.

7. Click the Cancel button to close the CourseBuilder Interaction dialog box.
8. Close the tour.asp page. Close UltraDev.

Adding a Simple Quiz to Your Site

Now that you are somewhat familiar with what CourseBuilder looks like, the best way to see how easy it is to add an eLearning element to your site is to build a simple interactive element. To start, you're going to create a very simple, fun quiz that visitors to the Nostalgic Radio Favorites site might enjoy. After this quiz is developed, visitors to the site access the quiz by clicking a link that challenges them to test their old-time radio knowledge.

When the visitor clicks the link, the site spawns a new window, where the first question of the quiz is displayed. As you will see when the quiz is complete, instead of asking the visitor the questions, collecting the answers, and "grading" the visitor's performance, you are going to ask the question and then continually give hints until he gets the answer right. When the visitor gives the correct answer, he will then be moved on to the next question.

Building a Quiz Site

Before you jump into building your new quiz pages, start the process by creating a new UltraDev site. While simple quizzes such as this one can easily be added to an existing site like your InsideUD4 site, more advanced eLearning components like those you are going to create later in the chapter function better when located in a separate UltraDev site. For this reason, you are going to go ahead and create the new site now.

Exercise 13.3 Creating a Separate UltraDev Site for Quizzes

1. Using your operating system's file manager, create a new folder inside the c:\inetpub\wwwroot folder. Name the folder **insideud4quiz**. Close the file manager you are using.
2. Open UltraDev and select Site/Define Sites and create a new site. In the Local Info category of the Site Definition dialog box, name the site **InsideUD4Quiz**.
3. Set the Local Root Folder field to c:\inetpub\wwwroot\insideud4quiz\.
4. In the Application Server category, pick ASP 2.0 from the Server Model dropdown.
5. In the Site Map Layout category, set the Home Page to default.asp. Click OK. When asked if the default.asp should be created, click OK.
6. The Dreamweaver information box may tell you that an initial site cache will be developed. Click OK.
7. Click the Done button to close the Define Sites dialog box.

Adding a Question to the Quiz

Now that you have a site specifically for your quizzes, you're ready to develop your quiz pages. These pages consist of nothing more than a question, a couple of forms, several multiple-choice answers, a submit button, and a few JavaScript behaviors—nothing that you couldn't code by hand if you wanted to.

I'm a big fan, however, of any product that can speed up the development process of my pages without sacrificing quality and the ability to customize the page when necessary—that's why I use UltraDev in the first place. CourseBuilder is a great example of an UltraDev extension that can save you plenty of coding time by asking you to fill in a few fields and creating the pages, JavaScript and all, for you.

After you've added the CourseBuilder elements to your pages, you can then customize each page to fit with the theme of your Web site and still have time left over to work on that golf swing.

Exercise 13.4 Building the First Quiz Question

1. Close the Site window. If necessary, create a new page.
2. Save the page in the insideud4quiz folder as **nrf_quiz.asp**.
3. Click the Insert CourseBuilder Interaction icon on the Objects panel. If the Objects panel has been reset to show the Common interactions, return to the Learning Category, as described in Exercise 13.2, Step 3. CourseBuilder will copy the required support files to the new site. Click OK.
4. In the CourseBuilder Interaction gallery, select the Multiple Choice category and double-click on the MultCh_Radios selection. As shown in Figure 13.6, it is the middle selection in the top row.

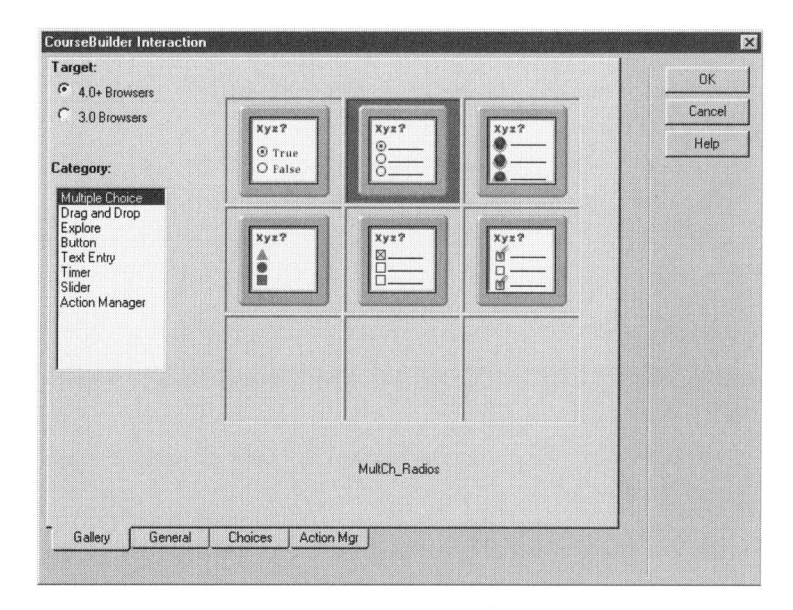

Figure 13.6 Select the MultCh_Radios option.

5. In the General tab of the CourseBuilder Interaction dialog box, name the new interaction **MultCh_NRFQuestion1**. Remember, don't press Enter or click OK.
6. In the Question Text field, type **What was the name of Little Orphan Annie's dog?**

> **Warning**
>
> **Watch that Enter Key!** When creating a new CourseBuilder interaction (a fancy name for a quiz or poll question), be careful not to press the Enter key or click the OK button until you are completely finished filling in each tab. Some people are tempted to press Enter after filling in a field, but this closes the CourseBuilder Interaction dialog box and takes you back to the Design view of the page.
>
> If, however, you do accidentally close the dialog box, you can open it back up by selecting the CourseBuilder interaction icon that was inserted into your page (it looks like an orange ball with a white plus sign on it) and click the Edit button on the Property inspector.

7. Choose to Judge Interaction when the user clicks a button and type **Submit Answer in the labeled field**.

8. The Correct When field should be set to Any Correct and None Incorrect. This requires the user to select the one answer that has been designated as the correct response.

   Choosing All Correct and None Incorrect would allow the visitor to choose an answer that has more than one response designated as the correct answer. An example of this would be a poll where each answer is not necessarily right or wrong.

9. Set the Tries Are field to Limited To and set the number of tries to **4**.

   Because your quiz will only have four possible answers for each question, this will ensure that the visitor has the opportunity to get the correct answer before moving on to the next question.

10. Leave the Time Is field as Unlimited. The General tab should now look like Figure 13.7.

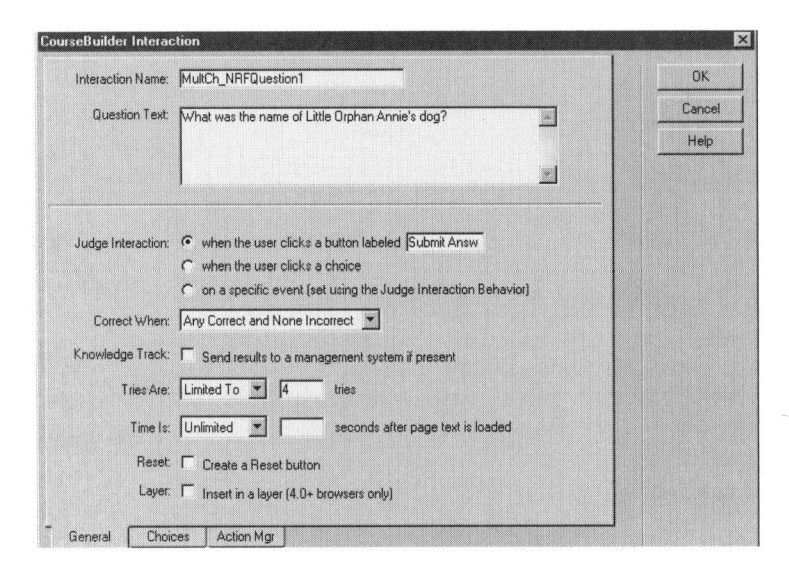

Figure 13.7 The completed General tab for the first question in the quiz.

11. Select the Choices tab at the bottom of the dialog box. Highlight choice1 in the Choices panel and type **Sandy** in the Name field.

12. In the Text (Optional) field, type **Sandy**. Because this choice is designated as the correct answer, be sure that the choice you enter is correct.

13. Select choice2 in the Choice panel and type **Dusty** in the Name field. In the Text field, type **Dusty**.

14. Select choice3 in the Choice panel and type **Bowser** in the Name field. In the Text field, type **Bowser**.

15. Select choice4 in the Choice panel and type **MrFluffles** in the Name field. In the Text field, type **Mr. Fluffles**.

> **Warning**
>
> **No Spaces in the Name Field** Problems can occur if you place a space between words in the Name field, so it's best to avoid using spaces. If you need to separate words, use an underscore instead.
>
> You can, however, use spaces in the Text field with no problems.

16. To mix up the order of where the correct answer is located in the quiz, highlight Sandy in the Choices panel and click the Down button. As shown in Figure 13.8, the Sandy choice should be the third choice in the list.

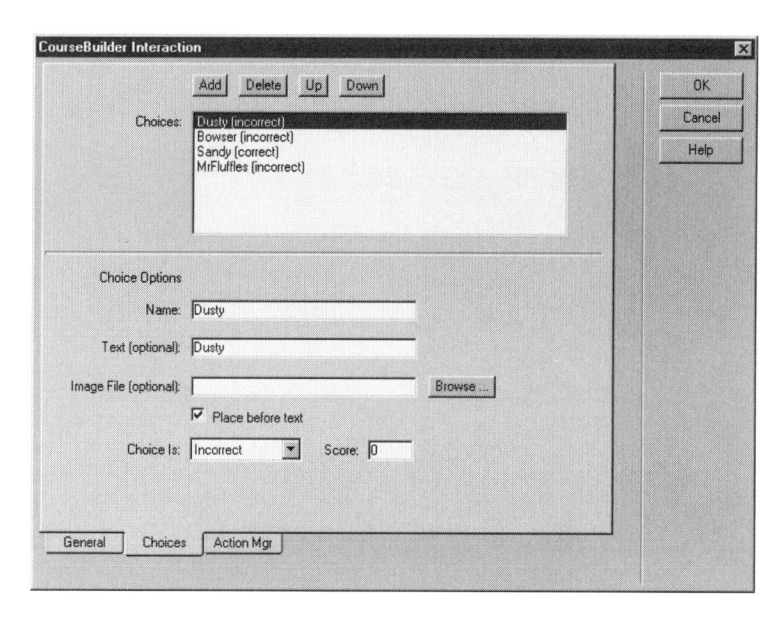

Figure 13.8 The answer "Sandy" has been moved to the third position.

17. Click the Action Mgr tab at the bottom of the CourseBuilder Interaction dialog box.

18. In the Action Manager, shown in Figure 13.9, highlight the Popup Message action below the If Correct condition and click the Edit button.

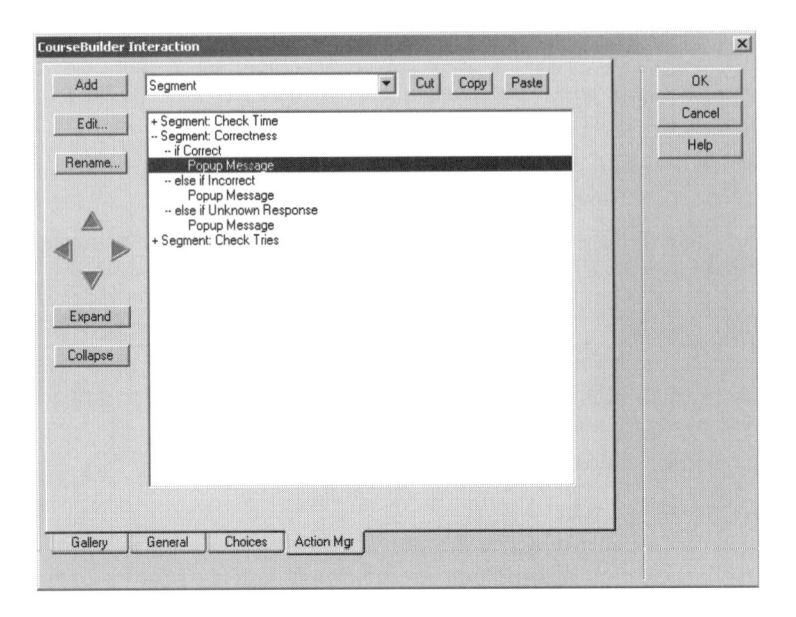

Figure 13.9 CourseBuilder's Action Manager.

19. In the Popup message dialog box, shown in Figure 13.10, delete the Correct text and type **Good Job! Daddy Warbucks would be proud!** Click OK.

Figure 13.10 Visitors see this text when they get the answer correct.

20. In addition to getting a confirmation of the correct answer, you want visitors to be taken to the next question when they answer correctly. To add this behavior, highlight the If Correct condition and select Go To URL from the dropdown menu at the top of the dialog box. Click the Add button.

21. In the Go To URL dialog box, shown in Figure 13.11, type **nrf_quiz2.asp** in the URL field. Click OK.

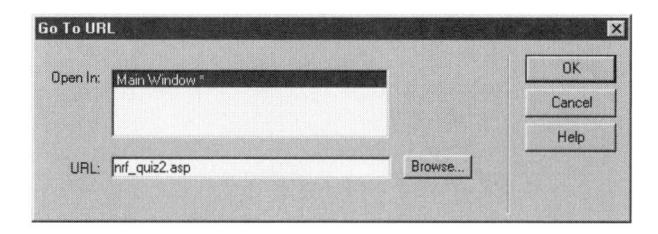

Figure 13.11 The Go To URL dialog box.

Because you want the visitor to be redirected to the new URL after they receive the pop-up message, highlight the new Go To URL behavior and click the down arrow on the left side of the dialog box. This moves the behavior to a position below the Popup message behavior.

22. Next, give UltraDev some text to display when the answer is incorrect. Highlight the Popup Message action below the else if Incorrect condition and click the Edit button.
23. In the Popup Message dialog box, delete the Incorrect text and type **Sorry! Here's a hint: Annie's dog would be happy in the desert**. Click OK.
24. Since you have chosen to allow visitors a specific number of tries at the question, CourseBuilder automatically adds a behavior that spawns a pop-up box that alerts the visitor when he is out of tries. Because you don't want this pop-up box to display (you just want the visitor to be redirected to the next question), remove this behavior.

    To do this, highlight the Segment: Check Tries line and click the Expand button. As shown in Figure 13.12, the conditions and behaviors are visible.
25. Highlight the Popup Message behavior under the if Tries At Limit condition and click the Cut button at the top of the dialog box. This removes the behavior from the CourseBuilder interaction.
26. Click OK to close the CourseBuilder dialog box. As shown in Figure 13.13. The completed quiz question has been added to your page. You may need to move or close the Objects panel.
27. Save the page.

Adding Subsequent Questions

After you have built the initial page for your quiz, adding subsequent pages that are similar in format is relatively easy. All you have to do is save the existing page as the next page in the quiz sequence and make a few modifications.

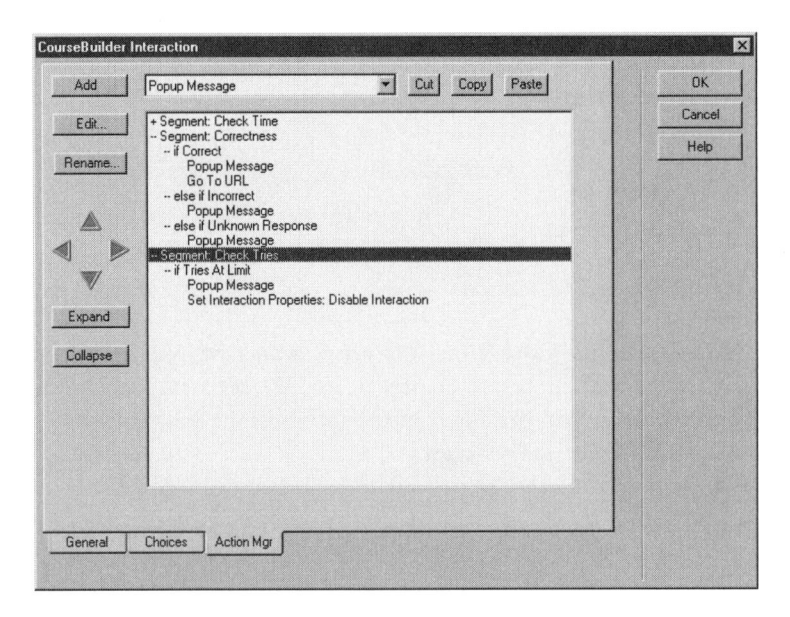

Figure 13.12 The Check Tries conditions and behaviors are now visible.

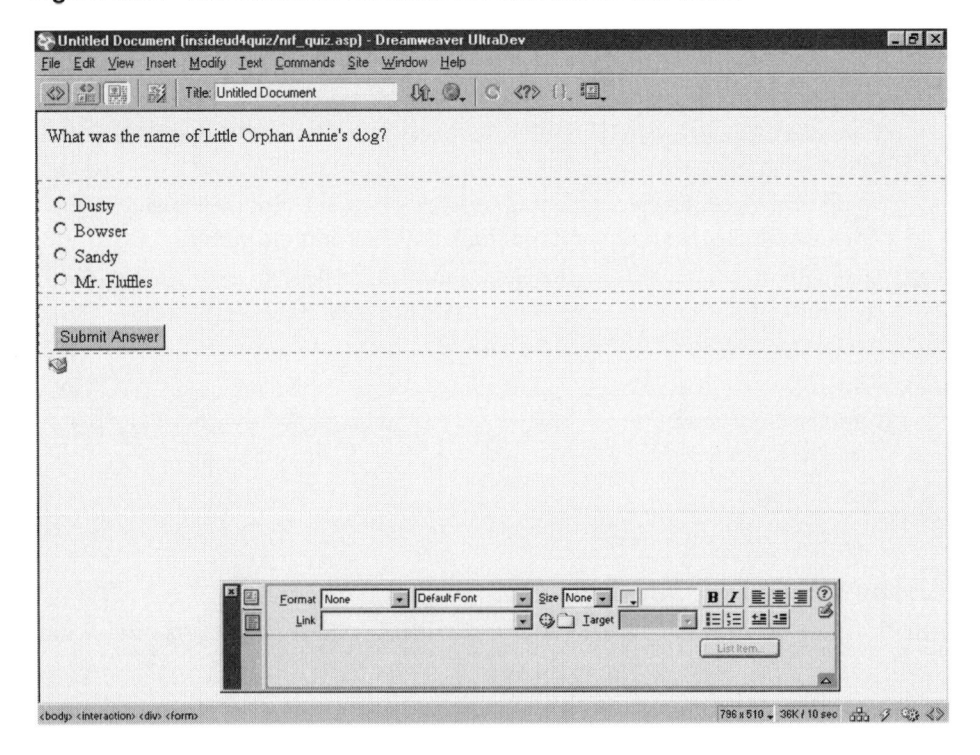

Figure 13.13 Your page now has a new quiz question.

In this case, you want to change the question, the answers, and then customize the pop-up messages that give your visitors the hints necessary to answer the question correctly. After they have completed this question, you'll end the quiz. Keep in mind, however, that you could create another 10 or 20 questions and add them to the quiz in a matter of minutes.

Exercise 13.5 Creating Additional Quiz Pages

1. In the nrf_quiz.asp document, choose File/Save As from the menu. Save the document **as nrf_quiz2.asp** in the root folder of the InsideUD4Quiz site.
2. In the nrf_quiz2.asp document, highlight the "What was the name of Little Orphan Annie's dog?" question and replace it with **Who lived at 79 Wistful Vista?**
3. Highlight the "Dusty" answer and change it to **George Burns and Gracie Allen**.
4. Highlight the "Bowser" answer and change it to **Amos 'n' Andy**.
5. Highlight the "Sandy" answer and change it to **Fibber McGee and Molly**.
6. Highlight the "Mr. Fluffles" answer and change it to **The Shadow**. As you can see in Figure 13.14, the question and answers for the quiz have been changed.

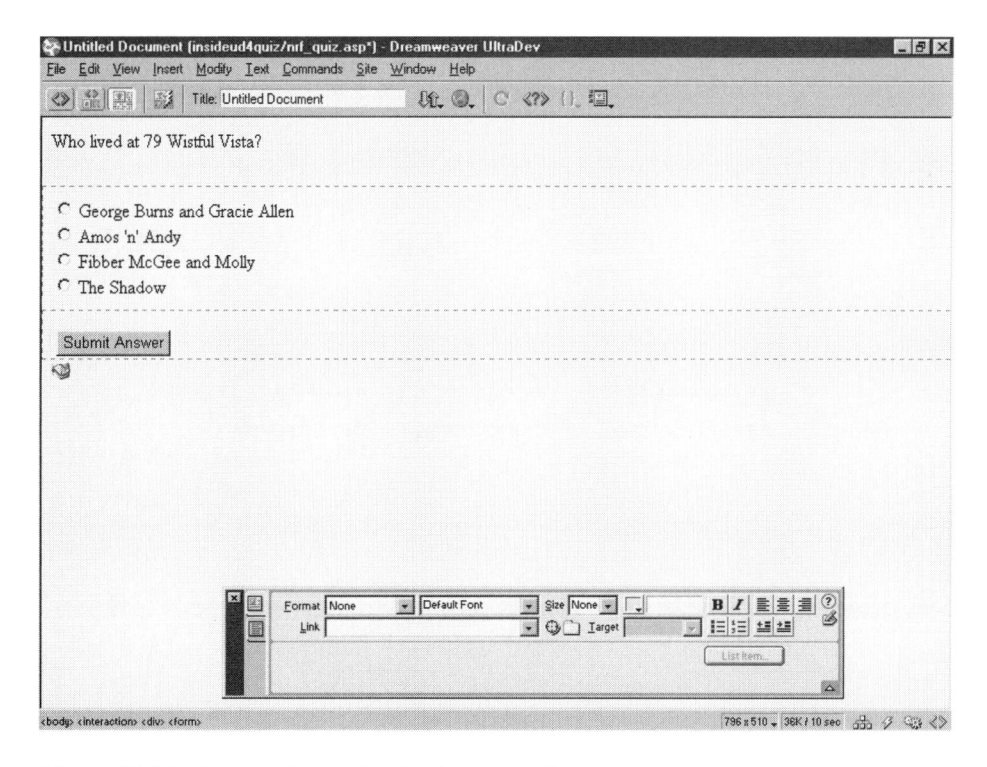

Figure 13.14 A new quiz question has been created.

7. Click the CourseBuilder interaction icon below the Submit Answer button and click the Edit button on the Property inspector.
8. In the General tab of the CourseBuilder Interaction dialog box, change the Interaction name to **MultCh_NRFQuestion2**. Notice that UltraDev has automatically updated the question text based on what was typed in the Design view.
9. Click the Choices tab and change "Dusty" (in the Name field) to **GeorgeAndGracie**.
10. Change "Bowser" to **AmosNAndy**.
11. Change "Sandy" to **FibberMcGee**.
12. Change "MrFluffles" to **TheShadow**.
13. Highlight the FibberMcGee choice and click the down button. This moves the correct answer to the bottom of the list.
14. Click the Action Mgr tab.
15. Under the If Correct condition, highlight the Popup Message interaction and click the Edit button.
16. In the pop-up message dialog box, type **Great Job! You sure know your radio!** Click the OK button.
17. Under the If Correct condition, highlight the Go To URL interaction and click the Edit button.
18. In the Go To URL dialog box, type **nrf_quiz_finished.asp** in the URL field. Click OK.
19. Under the If Incorrect condition, highlight the Popup Message interaction and click the Edit button.
20. In the Popup message dialog box, type **Sorry! Here's a hint: It's a husband and wife team**. Click the OK button.
21. Click OK to close the CourseBuilder Interaction dialog box.
22. Save the page.
23. Create a new page in UltraDev and type **Thank you for taking the Nostalgic Radio Favorites Quiz**. Save the page as **nrf_quiz_finished.asp**.
24. Close UltraDev.

Testing the Quiz

Now that the quiz is complete, take a look at what it looks like in a browser. While testing the quiz, it's always a good idea to answer some questions right and some wrong to ensure that all the JavaScript elements are functioning as expected.

Chapter 13 Adding eLearning to Your Site   375

Exercise 13.6 Interacting with the New Quiz.

1. To see how the quiz works, open a browser window and enter **http://localhost/insideud4quiz/nrf_quiz.asp** in the address bar. As shown in Figure 13.15, the page contains all the elements of a typical multiple-choice question.

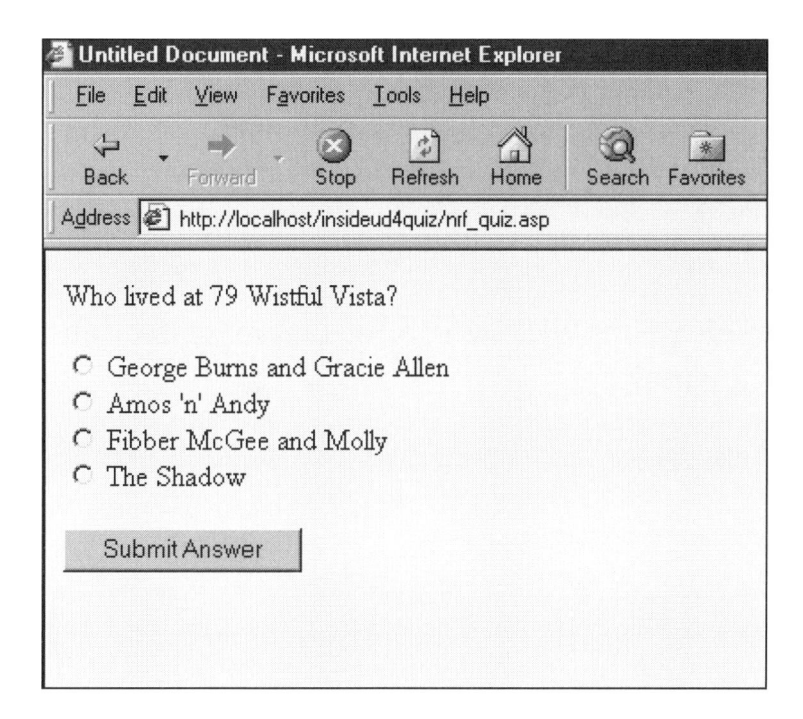

Figure 13.15 The question as viewed in a browser.

2. Select Dusty as the answer to the question and click the Submit Answer button. The browser displays the pop-up box shown in Figure 13.16 letting you know that this is the incorrect answer and giving a hint.

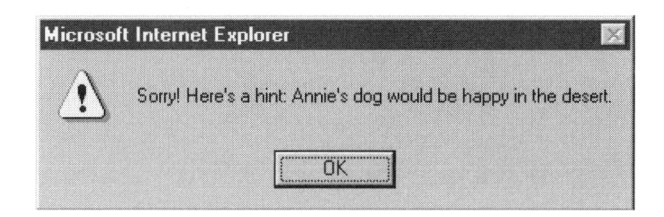

Figure 13.16 This popup is displayed when a wrong answer is given.

3. Click OK to close the pop-up box and choose Sandy as the answer. Click the Submit Answer button. This time, a popup is displayed congratulating you on the correct answer.

4. Click OK to close the pop-up box. You are now redirected to the next page in the quiz, which contains the second question and answer set that you created.

5. Select The Shadow and click the Submit Answer button. Notice that the page displays a custom hint for this page. Click OK.

6. Choose Fibber McGee and Molly and click the Submit Answer button. Because this answer is correct, you receive a congratulations.

7. Click OK and notice that you are directed to the last page in the quiz.

8. Minimize your browser.

Expanding a Simple Quiz to Use Database-Connectivity to Track Results

Now that you've seen how easy it is to develop individual question pages that can be combined into a simple quiz, let's take it up a notch and expand your simple quiz question to a fully-functional eLearning quiz along with a login requirement, grading system, and administrative reporting features.

Although this probably isn't a feature you would add to the Nostalgic Radio Favorites Web site, it would be appropriate in an educational environment where a professor wanted his students to take a quiz online and wanted to provide the most secure method of doing so. Another useful application of a quiz of this sort would be in corporate training, where employees might be required to complete a training module to update their skills. Using this model, administrators can track who has and hasn't taken the quiz and see the results of their participation.

To add the database-connectivity to track the users and quiz results, you will be using another helpful UltraDev extension from Macromedia called the Learning Site Command extension. This extension comes with a built-in database structure that can easily be added to any site for the purpose of grade tracking.

Adding the Learning Site Command Extension

As with the CourseBuilder extension, adding the Learning Site Command extension to UltraDev is just a matter of downloading the extension and double-clicking on the icon. From that point, UltraDev's Extension Manager will take over and do the rest.

Exercise 13.7 Downloading and Installing the Learning Site Command extension

1. Make sure that UltraDev is closed.

   Open a browser window and type **http://www.macromedia.com/exchange/ultradev/** in the address bar.

2. In the Macromedia Exchange for Dreamweaver UltraDev page, type **Learning Site** in the Search Extensions field and click the Go button.

3. In the search results, click the Learning Site Command extension.

4. In the Learning Site Command Extension detail page, download the extension in the appropriate format for your workstation and save it to a folder on your local hard drive.

5. Minimize your browser and browse to the folder where you downloaded the extension. Double-click the MX224665_LearningSite.mxp file that you downloaded in Step 5 to begin the installation.

6. Read the extension disclaimer and click the Accept button to accept the terms of the extension. The Extension Manager will install the new extension and alert you when the installation is complete.

7. Click OK in the alert box that notifies you that the installation is complete. As shown in Figure 13.17, the Learning Site Command extension has now been installed on your system.

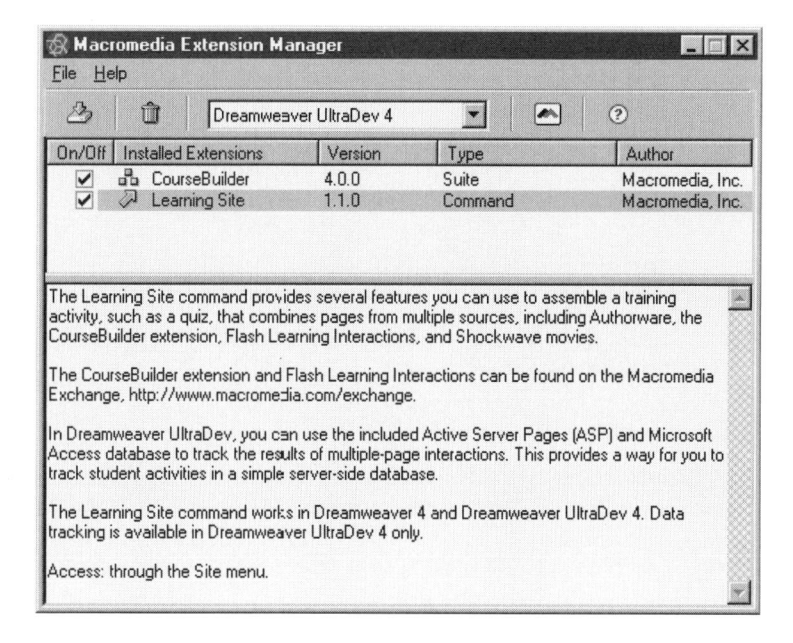

Figure 13.17 The Extension Manager now indicates that the Learning Site Command is installed.

8. Close the Extension Manager.

Setting Up Your Learning Site

Once you have the extension installed, the next step is to create a learning site or convert an existing UltraDev site to a learning site. Essentially, a learning site is very similar to a typical UltraDev site in the fact that UltraDev tracks the relationships between pages and is able to conduct site-wide activities like search and replace or fixing links. The difference, however, is the fact that a learning site contains only the pages that are used in your interactive quiz along with the administrative pages added by the Learning Site Command extension.

As with the previous simple quiz, the Learning Site Command extension creates pages that can be hand-coded if necessary. However, once you configure the learning site you'll see that adding pages and even adding CourseBuilder interactions is simple and can save a lot of time.

Exercise 13.8 Configuring the Learning Site

1. Open UltraDev.
2. From the menu bar, select Site/Learning Site/Create Learning Site. As shown in Figure 13.18, UltraDev alerts you that converting your existing site to a learning site could overwrite some of your existing files.

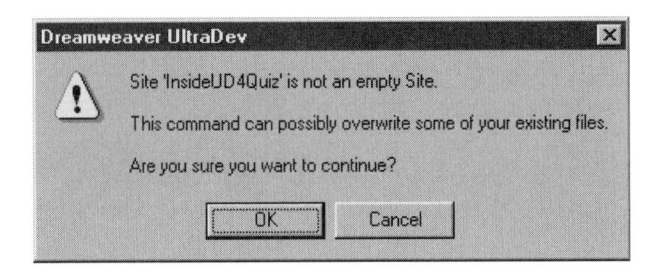

Figure 13.18 UltraDev warns you that converting an existing site to a learning site could overwrite some files.

3. Click OK to continue.
4. In the Learning Site dialog box, shown in Figure 13.19, select InsideUD4Quiz from the Site dropdown. Leave the frameset filename as index.htm. Check the box marked Set as Home Page. Since you want to track the results of the quiz, check the Data Tracking check box as well.

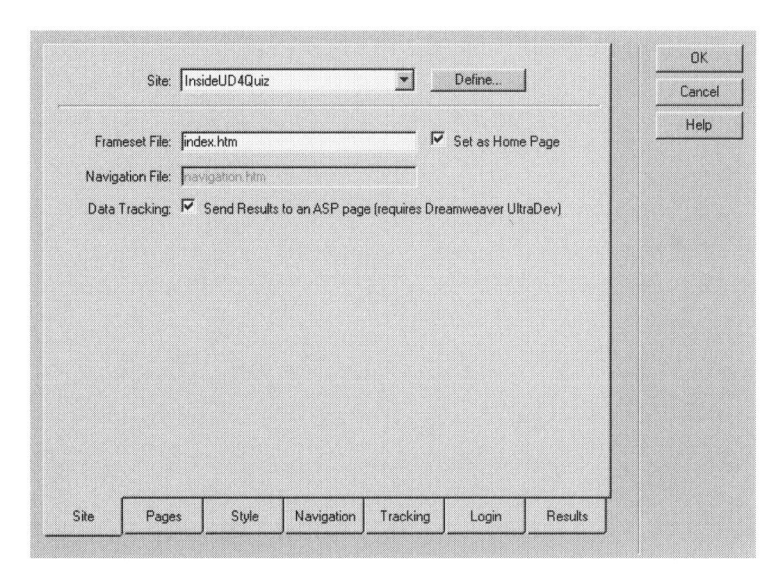

Figure 13.19 The Learning Site dialog box.

> **Warning**
>
> **Check the Box or Don't Check the Box?** When setting up a learning site, if you are working in an existing site and you check the Set as Home Page box, UltraDev automatically assumes that whatever page you specify in the Frameset File field is the home page for your *entire* site. This means that the sitemap of your existing site would be based upon the index.htm page (or whatever page you typed) instead of the home page that you may have created previously for your site.
>
> In this case, it's okay to allow the index.htm to be the home page because you have created a site specifically for the quizzes. Imagine, however, what would have happened if you had turned the InsideUD4 site into your learning site and checked the box. Whenever a visitor loaded the page, instead of getting the home page for your Web site, they would automatically be presented with the home page for the quiz instead.

5. Click the Pages tab at the bottom of the dialog box.
6. Highlight the Untitled-1.htm page in the Pages panel and type **nrf_quiz.asp** in the Page File field.
7. Click the plus sign again and highlight the new Untitled page and type **nrf_quiz2.asp** in the Page File field. Figure 13.20 shows the Pages tab with all the necessary elements.
8. Click the Style tab and select the Simple style from the Layout Style field.

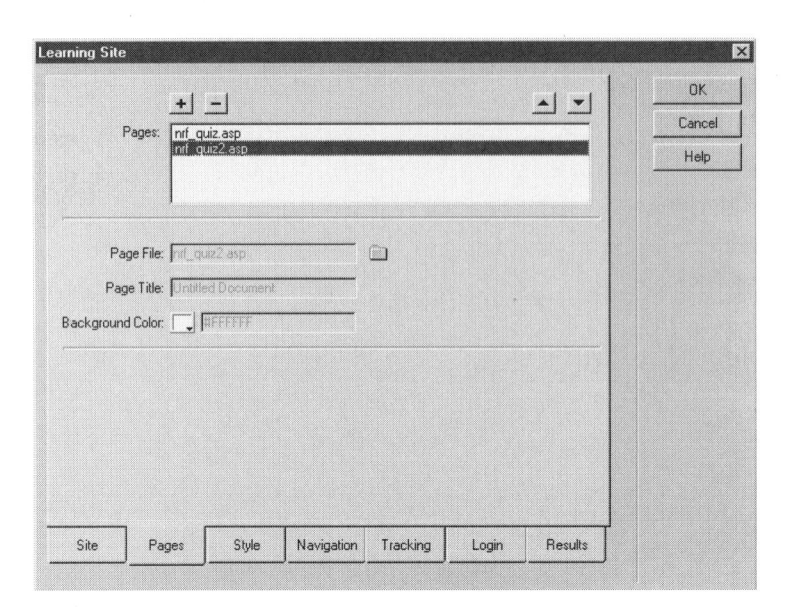

Figure 13.20 Your completed Pages tab should look like this.

> **Tip**
>
> **Making Your Quiz Pages Look Like Your Site** One of the nice things about the Learning Site extension is the fact that using the Custom style, you can use any custom graphics that you have created to make the layout of your learning interactions look like the rest of your site. To customize your pages, just choose the Custom style and specify the location and sizes of each of the required images.

9. Click the Navigation tab. This tab allows you to create custom navigation messages and behaviors depending on whether the visitor is at the beginning of the quiz, end of the quiz, or simply quits the quiz.

10. For your purposes, simply leave the tab at its default settings and click the Tracking tab. This tab, shown in Figure 13.21, allows us to create an Access database where the results of the quiz will be stored. In addition, using this tab you can set up the required DSN connection that allows the pages to send the quiz results back to the database.

> **Note**
>
> **Another DSN?** You might be wondering why you have to create another DSN when you already have a database and a DSN connection for your site. The Learning Site extension has built in behaviors that look for the existence of specific columns in the database. To ensure that your learning site works, it's best to create your database from within the Learning Site panel.

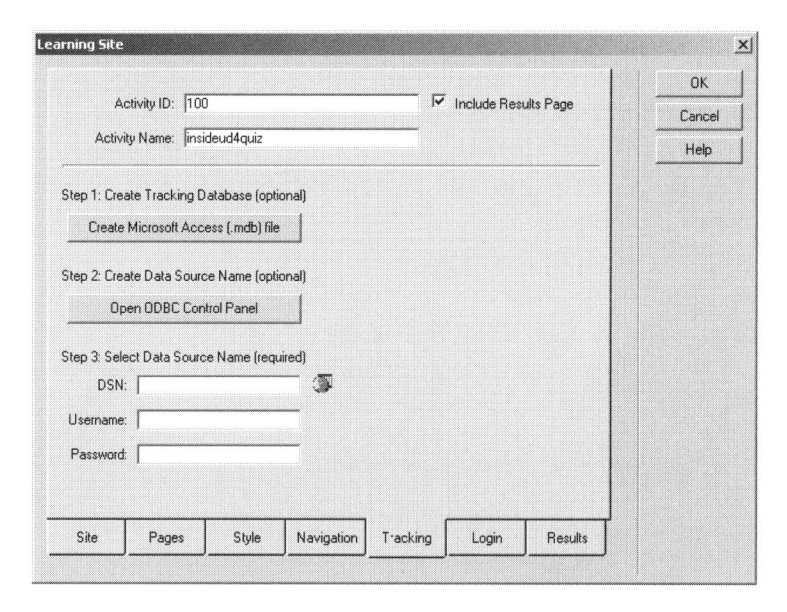

Figure 13.21 The Tracking tab allows you to create the database and connection required to monitor the quiz results.

11. In the Activity ID field, type **100**. Assign this number as a unique ID for this quiz.
12. Click the Create Microsoft Access (.mdb) file button.
13. In the Save Tracking Database As dialog box, browse to the database folder within the InsideUD4 site and name the new database **nrf_quiz.mdb**. Click the Save button.
14. In the Tracking tab, click the Open ODBC Control Panel button. In the ODBC Data Source Administrator, click the System DSN tab and click the Add button.
15. Select the Microsoft Access Driver and click Finish.

> **Warning**
> **Be Sure to Pick the Correct Driver** Some versions of the Microsoft Data Access Components (MDAC) install several different versions of the Microsoft Access Drive in a variety of languages. Be sure that you pick the driver called Microsoft Access Driver(*.mdb).

16. Name the data source **NRF_Quiz** and click the Select button. Browse to the database folder within the InsideUD4 site and select the nrf_quiz.mdb database. Click OK.
17. Click OK to close the ODBC Microsoft Access Setup dialog box. Click OK to close the ODBC Data Source Administrator dialog box.

18. In the DSN field of the Tracking tab, type **NRF_Quiz** or click the globe symbol next to the field and select the correct connection.
19. Click on the Login tab and leave the default values in the first three fields. Select the Simple login logo.
20. Click the Results tab and leave the default values in the first three fields. Select the Simple login logo.
21. Click OK to close the Learning Site dialog box. UltraDev copies the required pages to your site and displays them in the Site window.
22. From the menu bar, choose Site/Learning Site/Copy Admin Files. As shown in Figure 13.22, UltraDev asks you to identify the DSN for the learning site. Make sure that the NRF_Quiz DSN is chosen and click OK.

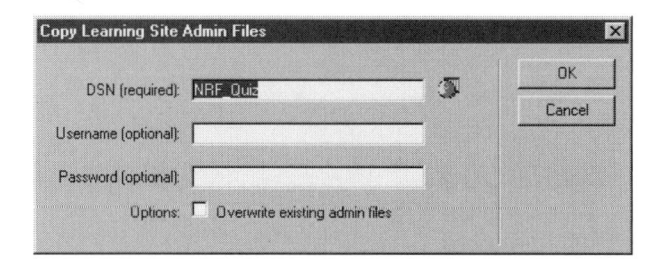

Figure 13.22 Select a DSN for the database where your administrative data will be stored.

Modifying the Quiz Questions to Submit a Score to the Database

When you created the question for your original quiz, you didn't need to assign a value to the question because you weren't grading the visitor's correct and incorrect answers. In this more advanced quiz, however, you want the visitor to get only one try to get the question right and then you want to count how many answers he got right or wrong during the quiz. In addition, you don't want to provide the visitor with hints when he gives the wrong answer.

To accomplish this, you need to make a few adjustments to the CourseBuilder interactions that you created when building your quiz pages. Because the CourseBuilder extension allows us to easily modify any interaction, this is a simple process of making changes to a few fields and removing a couple of behaviors that you previously assigned to specific conditions.

Exercise 13.9 Assigning a Score and Weight to the Questions.

1. Open the nrf_quiz.asp page.
2. Highlight the CourseBuilder Interaction icon below the Submit Answer button and click the Edit button on the Property inspector.
3. On the General tab, place a check in the Knowledge Track check box and limit the number of tries to 1.
4. On the Tracking tab, type **101** in the Interaction ID field and **1** in the Weight field. This tells the Learning Site extension which question to associate the visitor's score with and allows the extension to enter a weight of 1 for a correct answer and 0 for an incorrect answer. If you want one question to count for double points, change the value to **2**.
5. On the Choices tab, select the correct answer (Sandy) and near the bottom of the tab, set the answer to correct, and the score to **1**.
6. In the Action Mgr tab, remove the Pop-up Message and the Go To URL behaviors from the If Correct condition by highlighting each one and clicking the Cut button. In addition, remove the Pop-up Message from the If Incorrect condition.
7. Click OK.
8. Save the page.
9. Open the nrf_quiz2.asp page and follow Steps 2 through 6 to modify the CourseBuilder Interaction. Be sure to set the Interaction ID to **102** so you can tell the difference between question 1 and 2 when the quiz is graded.
10. Save the nrf_quiz2.asp page.

Granting Access and Testing the Quiz

Because the Learning Site Command extension has its own built-in login and password validation system, before you can view the quiz and test the pages you have to log on to the administrative section of the learning site, add a user to the system, and grant them access. Once this is done, you can access the quiz using the user ID and password you created for the account.

Once you are able to view the pages, you'll want to test the functionality of each page including correct and incorrect answers. Finally, after the quiz is completed, you should be given a complete report of your performance on the quiz.

Exercise 13.10 Using the Administration Page to Grant Access

1. Minimize UltraDev. Open a browser window and type **http://localhost/insideud4quiz/adminLogin.asp** in the address bar. The adminLogin.asp page was created automatically for you when you defined the Learning site.

2. As shown in Figure 13.23, the administrative side is password protected. Enter the User ID **admin** and the Password **admin** and click Login. These are the default values established by the Learning Site extension.

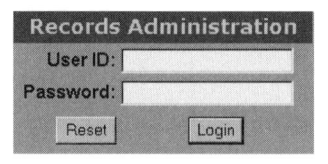

Figure 13.23 Your learning site's administrative login.

3. In the Admin Menu, click the Add User link.
4. Fill in the Add New User form, as shown in Figure 13.24, and click the Add User button.

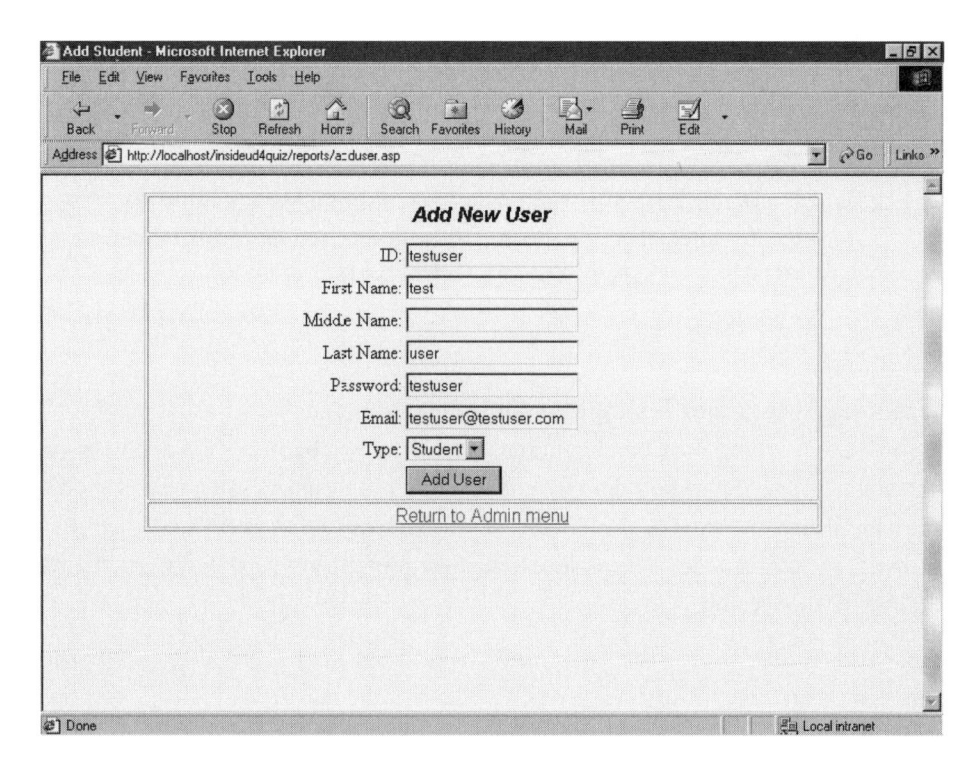

Figure 13.24 Complete the Add New User form with these values.

5. In the confirmation page, click the Return to Admin Menu link.
6. In the Admin menu, click Logout.

7. In the address bar of your browser, type **http://localhost/insideud4quiz/**. As shown in Figure 13.25, you are now asked to provide a valid student User ID and Password.

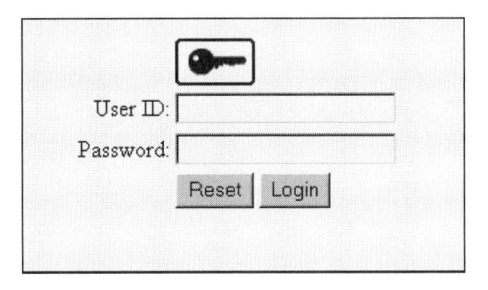

Figure 13.25 You must type a valid student User ID and Password to gain access to the quiz.

8. In the User ID field, type **testuser**. In the Password field, type **testuser**. Click Login.
9. After the password has been validated, you are able to see the first question in the quiz, shown in Figure 13.26.

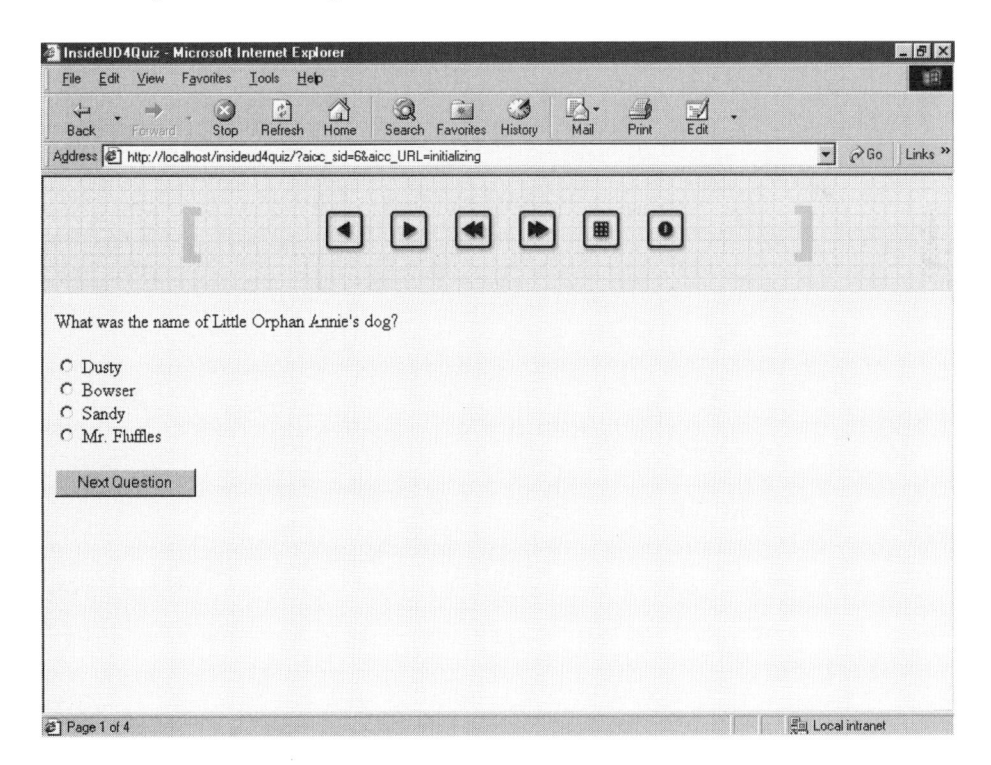

Figure 13.26 The first question in the quiz.

10. In the first question, choose "Dusty" and click the Submit Answer button. After an answer has been entered, click the Next button (second from left) at the top of the page.
11. In the second question, select "Fibber McGee and Molly" and click the Submit Answer button.
12. Click the Finish button (fourth from left) on the button bar at the top of the page. After writing the score to the database, the site now displays the results of the quiz, shown in Figure 13.27.

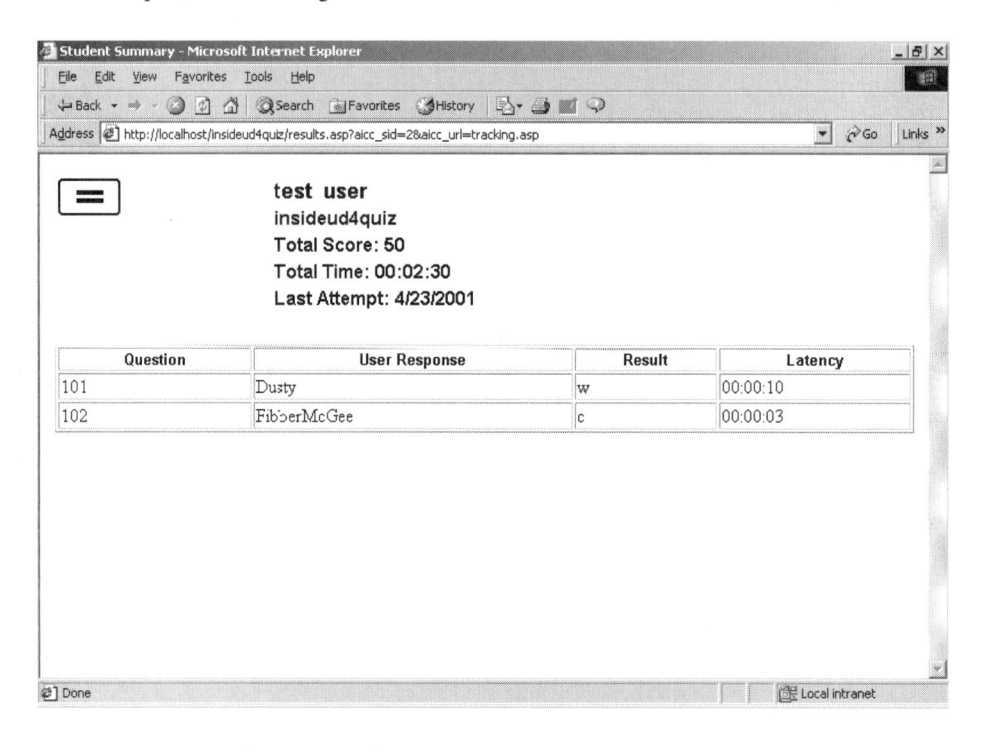

Figure 13.27 The final results of the quiz.

Analyzing Quiz Results

The last feature you'll take a look at is the ability for administrators to view the results of a quiz. Using the administrative pages, you can view an individual's performance on the quiz, or you can look at the quiz itself and see how the group who took the quiz performed as a whole.

This feature is particularly handy for professors who want to look up an individual student's grade or who want to see how the class performed on average.

Exercise 13.11 Viewing Quiz Results from the Administrative Site

1. In your browser window, type **http://localhost/insideud4quiz/adminlogin.asp** in the address bar.
2. Log in using the admin/admin User ID and Password combination.
3. From the Administrative menu, click the Students Overview link.
4. In the Students Overview page, click the link in the UserID field to view testuser's details.
5. Finally, click the InsideUD4Quiz activity to see how the visitor did on the quiz.
6. Close your browser.

Summary

This chapter focused on sample applications of the eLearning extensions available for UltraDev. First, you looked at creating a simple, ungraded quiz that provided the visitor with hints until they answered correctly. Second, you extended that quiz to include a complete administrative system, a password validation procedure, and complete grading results.

In the next chapter, you'll take a look at additional ways to extend UltraDev. With hundreds of extensions available on the Macromedia Exchange, surely there's an extension that can help you complete your project.

Chapter 14

Extending UltraDev

Now that you have seen what UltraDev can do, let's talk about how you can extend UltraDev beyond its current limitations. UltraDev is truly unique in the fact that it is the only dynamic Web application development software that can be extended *by the user* beyond its original programming. You see, Macromedia has made it possible for UltraDev users to create their own custom UltraDev extensions to add functionality to UltraDev that was not included when it shipped.

This makes UltraDev's capabilities virtually limitless for those who are familiar with any of the programming languages supported by UltraDev. Those who are not programmers can also benefit from the hundreds of UltraDev extensions made available via the UltraDev Exchange.

To show you how easy it is to extend UltraDev, this chapter does the following:

- Introduces you to UltraDev extensions
- Demonstrates how to create a new server behavior
- Demonstrates how to edit an existing server behavior
- Shows you how to package an UltraDev extension using the Extension Manager

Introducing UltraDev Extensions

One of my favorite hobbies is working on my motorcycle. My current toy is a 1996 Honda Shadow ACE 1100, and I remember the day that I brought it home from the dealership. Here was this beautiful, shiny motorcycle that seemed to have everything I wanted and needed in a great ride. It looked great, rode like a dream, and (other than the monthly payment) was everything I'd hoped for.

After a couple of months, however, I began to notice things that, although not essential to the operation of the machine, would be nice to have. My wife wanted a backrest for the passenger seat, I wanted a pair of saddlebags for holding items on a ride, and I figured that the number of locusts pounding me in the chest at 55 mph would be significantly reduced with the addition of a windshield.

And so began my addiction with customizing my motorcycle. Soon after I added a new exhaust system, high-flow air filter, tuned the carburetors, and added just about every chrome knick-knack you can think of. Some of the additions improved the functionality of the motorcycle, while others just added to the look and my enjoyment of the riding experience.

So what does this have to do with UltraDev? Well, UltraDev is a lot like a stock motorcycle. Macromedia created a great, easy-to-use program and built in features that provide basic dynamic Web design functionality. Unlike other developers, however, they left the door open for each user to customize UltraDev's abilities to meet his needs. Although you can't chrome out UltraDev or add a cool-looking custom paint job, you can improve on UltraDev's ability to build dynamic Web applications through the addition of UltraDev extensions. And the best thing about UltraDev extensions is that many of them are free.

What Are UltraDev Extensions?

An UltraDev extension is simply an application package that installs new server behaviors and menu items into UltraDev's core program. Some extensions enhance UltraDev's ability to perform functions such as eCommerce, eLearning, or user authentication. Others perform tasks such as updating HTML code or adding dynamic content such as a news ticker to your page. Still others provide patches to previous versions of an extension in order to maintain functionality under new versions of UltraDev.

Just think of an extension as an accessory for UltraDev. Some may be necessary to complete a project, whereas others may make the development process just a little easier. With nearly 500 extensions available at this time, it's likely that there are at least one or two that can assist you in your Web endeavors.

Where Do I Get Them?

UltraDev extensions can be obtained from Macromedia or directly from the third-party developer that designed the extension. Macromedia maintains an exhaustive list of extensions at the UltraDev Exchange at `http://www.macromedia.com/exchange/ultradev`. As shown in Figure 14.1, the UltraDev Exchange allows you to search for extensions that may meet your needs.

If you see an extension that interests you, the UltraDev Exchange offers many details about the origin of the extension. As shown in Figure 14.2, some of these details include who developed the extension and when, what platforms it is approved for, and whether it has been approved by Macromedia.

> **Tip**
>
> **Macromedia-Approved Extensions** If possible, look for extensions that have the Macromedia-approved symbol next to them (it's a black and blue Macromedia "M" with a white oval surrounding). These extensions have been tested by Macromedia's development teams to ensure that the extension functions correctly and meets the design standards of the Dreamweaver or UltraDev graphical user interface.
>
> Those extensions that do not bear the Macromedia-approved symbol have been tested to ensure that they are virus-free, contain no profanity, and are compatible with the Dreamweaver or UltraDev code.

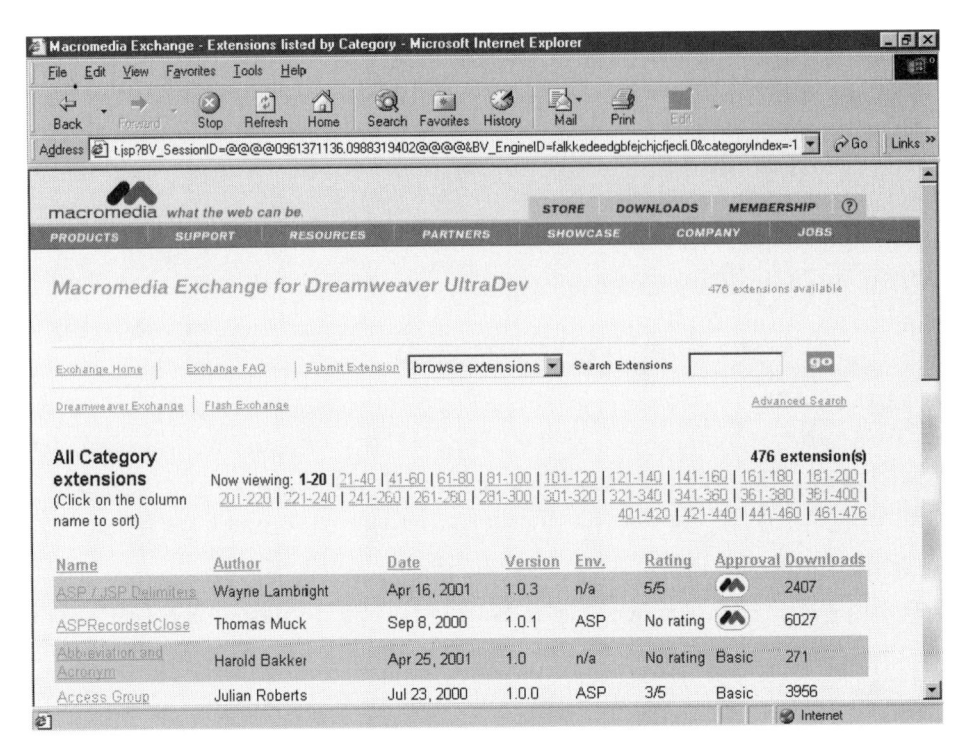

Figure 14.1 The UltraDev Exchange contains a searchable list of extensions currently available.

Figure 14.2 The UltraDev Exchange lists the details for each extension.

If you find an extension that you would like to try, simply click the download button (a green button with a white arrow) for the operating system you are using.

How Do I Install Them?

Now that you've downloaded your new extension, you want to give it a try, right? Fortunately, Macromedia has made installing an extension just as easy as downloading it. Just browse to the folder where you saved the .mxp file and double-click the file. The Macromedia Extension Manager, shown in Figure 14.3, will take over and add the extension.

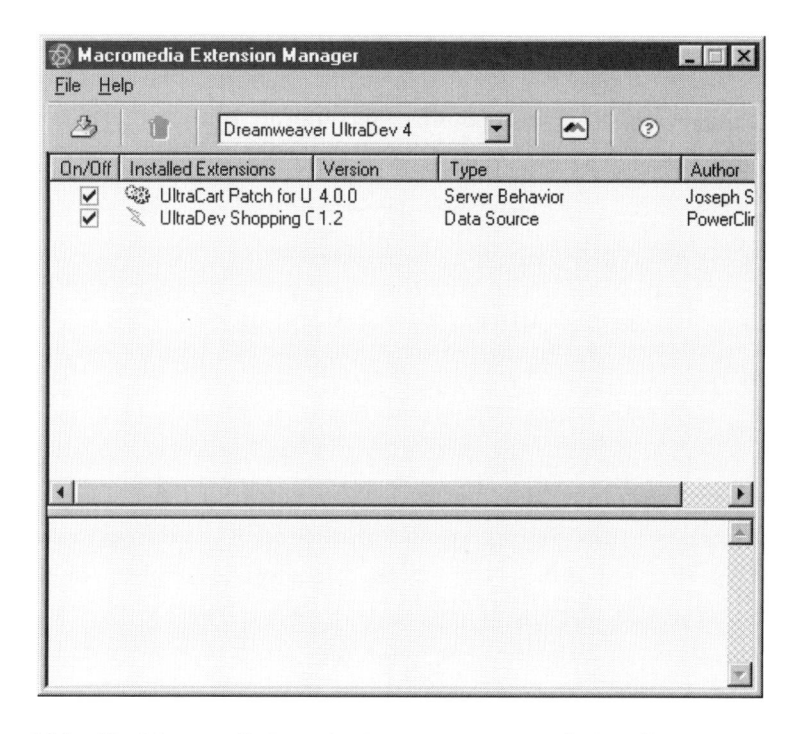

Figure 14.3 The Macromedia Extension Manager automates the installation process.

After the extension is installed, the Extension Manager provides a detailed view of what extensions have been installed and any instructions required to make the extensions function.

Extension Pros and Cons

So far you've looked at the benefits that extensions offer. They allow you to increase the functionality of UltraDev and are easy to download and install. But what about the cons? Are there any downsides to installing an extension, and if there are, what should you look out for?

The first negative aspect to using extensions is that they are often developed by third-party programmers who are creating the server behavior to fit a specific need. Although their need might be similar to yours, the server behavior that they have created still might not do exactly what you need. At this point you have two choices: 1) Stick with the capabilities of the extension and adjust your needs, or 2) Adjust the behavior to meet your needs. If you substantially modify a server behavior to accomplish a task that no other extension has been designed to do, you might consider submitting the modifications to Macromedia as a new extension.

A second detraction associated with extensions is the existence of bugs in UltraDev that make the development of stable extensions more difficult. For instance, many developers have experienced a bug while trying to create new menu entries to access their server behaviors.

An issue that can be seen as a pro in some instances and a con in others is the support system for extensions. Since extensions are often the products of third parties, support for an extension can sometimes be nonexistent. While some developers add a help system to the behaviors themselves, they are usually limited.

Macromedia also hosts a forum for each extension available via the UltraDev Exchange where you can post questions regarding your problem with the extension. Although waiting for a response is not always feasible for a time-sensitive project, I highly recommend that you search through the previous threads to see if someone has already asked a question regarding your difficulty and received an answer. You might also try searching Macromedia's UltraDev forum located at `news://forums.macromedia.com/macromedia.ultradev`. Participants in this forum are very friendly and extremely helpful.

If you still aren't able to find an answer to your issue, you can search the newsgroup archives at `http://groups.google.com`. By typing ***UltraDev*** (with the asterisks) in the advanced search page, you will have access to issues and resolutions that have cycled off the newsgroup.

The final step you can take to get help is to contact the developer directly. Some developers are extremely helpful when it comes to discussing what their extension can and can't do. In other cases, contacting the developer can be a lost cause.

> **Note**
>
> **Rate and Review the Extensions Please!** Macromedia has developed a rating system that enables users of an extension to rate it and leave a review as to how that extension functioned. When I am looking into an extension, I always appreciate it when people leave detailed reviews, since it often alerts me to potential difficulties.
>
> If you use an extension, help others out by leaving a rating and a review. In your review, explain what you were trying to accomplish with the extension and whether the server behaviors served the purpose.

Creating New Server Behaviors

UltraDev has a built-in process for creating your own custom server behaviors. You can create a new server behavior by clicking the plus sign on the Server Behavior panel and selecting New Server Behavior from the menu. In the New Server Behavior dialog box, shown in Figure 14.4, you can select a new name for your server behavior and the server model that it will operate on.

After you have chosen a name and a server model, you can use the Server Behavior Builder, shown in Figure 14.5, to insert blocks of custom code.

Exercise 14.1 Building a New Server Behavior

1. Open UltraDev. Make sure you are in the Design view.
2. Open the Server Behaviors panel.
3. In the Server Behaviors panel, click the plus sign and select New Server Behavior from the pop-up menu. UltraDev displays the New Server Behavior dialog box, shown in Figure 14.4.

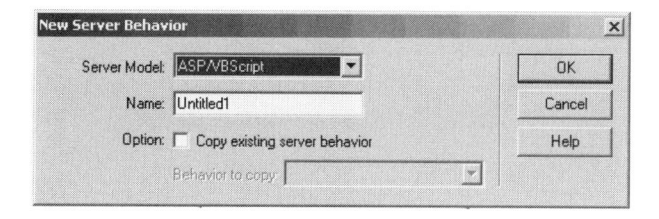

Figure 14.4 The New Server Behavior dialog box.

4. In the Server Model field, select ASP/VBScript.
5. In the Name field, type **SetSessionVariable**. Click OK.
6. In the SetSessionVariable dialog box, click the plus sign.

Part IV   Extending Your Administrative Capabilities

7. In the Create a New Block Code dialog box that follows, shown in Figure 14.5, type **SetSessionVariable_block1**. Click OK.

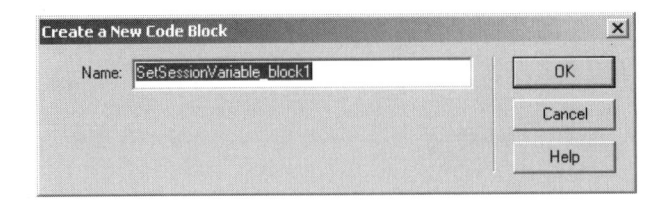

Figure 14.5   The Server Behavior Builder allows you to insert custom code.

> **Note**
> **Text Block Naming Conventions**   Macromedia recommends that developers use a convention such as NameOfBehavior_NameOfCodeBlock when developing extensions.

8. With the new code block highlighted in the SetSessionVariable dialog box, type the following line in the Code Block field:

   `<% Session("@@Session@@") = @@Value@@ %>`

   This code creates a session variable based on the name provided when applying the server behavior. It then sets the value of the session variable equal to whatever parameter the developer designates. Be sure that you include the `@@` markers before and after the session name and the value. These markers allow the Web developer who uses your extension to supply the name and the value of the session variable for his individual pages.

9. Select Above the `<html>` Tag in the Insert Code field and choose Just Above the `<html>` Tag in the Relative Position field. The dialog box should now look like Figure 14.6.

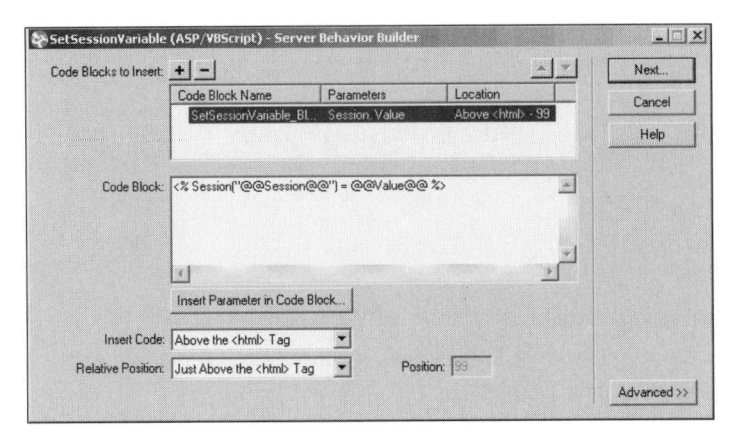

Figure 14.6   The SetSessionVariable dialog box should now look like this.

10. Click Next.
11. In the Generate Behavior Dialog Box dialog box, shown in Figure 14.7, leave both the Session parameter and Value parameter as text fields. Click OK.

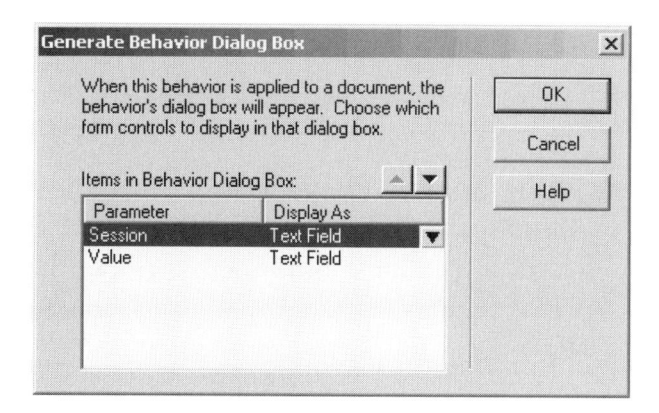

Figure 14.7 The Generate Behavior Dialog Box step lets you control the parameters that will be requested when the server behavior is applied.

12. Open a blank document in UltraDev.
13. In the Server Behaviors panel, click the plus sign and choose SetSessionVariable from the pop-up menu. UltraDev opens the SetSessionVariable dialog box.
14. As shown in Figure 14.8, type **ProductNumber** in the Session field and type **Request.Form("hfProdNo")** in the Value field.

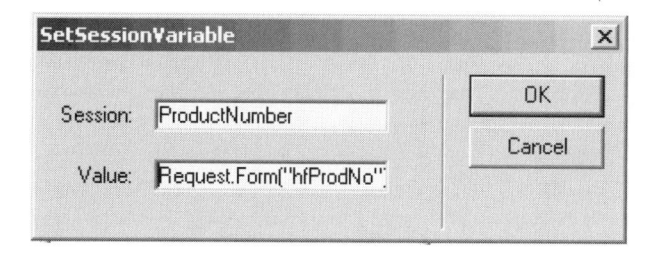

Figure 14.8 Type these values into the SetSessionVariable dialog box.

15. Click OK.
16. Switch to the Code view of the document and notice that UltraDev has added the session variable code to the page, immediately above the <html> tag.

    If you look back at Chapter 12, this code is identical to a piece of code you had to hand-code into one of your documents. Recall the code that you entered in Chapter 12:

```
<%Session("ProductNumber")=Request.Form("hfProdNo")%>
```

As you can see, if your server behavior had been defined in Chapter 12, you would have been able to simply apply the server behavior and then designate a session name and value without ever having to switch to the Code view.

17. Return to the Design view. In the Server Behaviors panel, remove the instance of the SetSessionVariable server behavior that you just added by highlighting the server behavior and clicking the minus button.

Modifying Existing Server Behaviors

The fastest way to create a new server behavior is to simply modify an existing server behavior to fit your needs. If you want to use one of the server behaviors that shipped with UltraDev, you'll need to make a copy of the behavior and then edit the copy. To do this, simply click the plus sign on the Server Behavior panel and choose New Server Behavior from the popup menu. In the New Server Behavior dialog box, choose a name and a server model and check the Copy existing server behavior check box. In the Behavior to copy dropdown, select the server behavior you want to modify.

If, however, you want to modify a custom server behavior that you created or added via an UltraDev extension, just use the Edit Server Behaviors command from the Server Behaviors panel. From this point you can choose which server behavior you would like to modify and make any adjustments necessary.

> **Warning**
>
> **Make Copies Rather than Editing Directly** Editing a custom-designed server behavior is kind of like editing your Web pages on your live server. Sure, it works, but if done improperly, it can have some disastrous results. Just think if you spend an hour or two editing a custom server behavior only to find that it doesn't function as you had hoped. Because you have directly edited the original server behavior, not only is your new version non-functional, but the original has been replaced.
>
> To avoid this circumstance, create a copy of the server behavior and then edit the new server behavior. If the new edited version works, then simply go back and remove the original.

Packaging a Newly Created Extension

After you have finished developing your new server behavior, you can package it as an UltraDev extension by using the UltraDev Extension Manager.

> **Tip**
>
> **Test Your Behaviors First** It is very important that you test your server behavior in a variety of environments before packaging it as an extension. Don't assume that just because it works on your Window 98 SE workstation running Personal Web Server that it will operate on a Window 2000 server running IIS5.

To package your new extension, place all the new server behavior files, which are located in the Macromedia/Dreamweaver UltraDev 4/Configuration/Server Behaviors folder, in a temporary folder. Next, copy the blank extension installation file located in Macromedia/Extension Manager/Samples/Dreamweaver UltraDev/Blank.mxi to your temporary directory. Rename the Blank.mxi file to whatever you would like to name your new extension and modify the file contents to contain the appropriate extension information. Finally, open the UltraDev Extension Manager and select File/Package Extension. Follow the steps to package the extension, and the Extension Manager will pack all the server behaviors into your blank extension file.

> **Tip**
>
> **Use the MXI File Creator Packager to Simplify the Process** Packaging an extension can get tricky fast! If you want to make the process relatively easy, go to the UltraDev Exchange and search for the MXI File Creator Packager extension. This extension walks you through the extension creation process and asks for some simple input regarding the type of extension, its compatibility, and the location of the extension files. From within the packager, you can then package and submit the extension.

After you have created a new extension, you can submit your new creation to Macromedia by selecting File/Submit Extension from the menu bar of the Extension Manager.

Summary

This chapter demonstrated your ability to take UltraDev beyond its original programming through the use of custom behaviors and UltraDev extensions.

Now that you have completed each chapter and the exercises, you should have a fully functional, database-driven Web site that includes features such as the ability for visitors to search a product catalog, create a new user account, and purchase their selection. In addition, you have learned how to implement eLearning modules and add them to the site.

We hope that you have enjoyed this book and the opportunity to explore what UltraDev can do. We have certainly enjoyed taking you through each chapter and explaining just how powerful UltraDev is and how it can be applied in real-world situations. Now, it's up to you to take what you've learned and help make your corner of the Web just a little more dynamic.

Good luck in your development endeavors!

Appendix A

About the Web Site

Additional resource material for this book is located at www.insideultradev.com. You will also find a link to this site from the book title page on www.newriders.com.

This Web site will give you everything you need to complete each of the projects in the book. Just access the figures on the Web site and follow the instructions in the book. To make this more convenient, you will also find all the source code on the Web site. The other links provide added value, so you can expand your digital library of resources. And of course, I'd love your feedback, too! Please access the Web site to send me your comments.

Source Files

This section of the site includes all the source files that are used in the book, listed by chapter. Each chapter has its own folder, and can be accessed by opening the chapters folder found in the Web sites root directory. Please note, however, that you'll not find any folders for Chapters 1 or 3; these chapters contain exercises which do not affect the resulting sample Web site.

Each chapter's folders contain the insideud4 folder that contains the Web site files, connections, and databases that have been created prior to that chapter. If you want to skip to a specific chapter in the book, please copy the insideud4 folder to the root folder of your workstation and establish both and ODBC data source for the database and an UltraDev connection to that data source. You should then be able to walk through the subsequent exercises.

Database Files

This Web site contains the sample database that is used throughout the book in Access 97, Access 2000, and MySQL formats. The database can be downloaded by following the link to the appropriate format.

To access the database via dynamic Web pages, you must create an ODBC data source and an UltraDev connection to that data source. For complete directions on setting up these connections, refer to Chapters 3 and 4.

Third-Party Programs

This Web site also contains links to several third-party programs and demos from leading industry companies. These programs have been carefully selected to assist you in developing your UltraDev skills.

Please note that some of the programs included on this Web site are shareware-"try-before-you-buy"-software. Please support these independent vendors by purchasing or registering any shareware software that you use for more than 30 days. Check the documentation provided with the software on where and how to register the product.

- **Macromedia Dreamweaver UltraDev 4 30-Day Trial.** This is a 30-day free trial of Macromedia Dreamweaver UltraDev 4.
- **Microsoft Personal Web Server.** Personal Web Server is a desktop Web server application designed to serve small Web sites or as a developmental tool for larger sites.
- **UltraDev Shopping Cart.** The UltraDev Shopping Cart extension is an UltraDev extension developed by Rick Crawford of `Powerclimb.com`. This extension adds a series of server behaviors that enable developers to add shopping cart functionality to an eCommerce site.
- **UltraDev Shopping Cart Patch.** The UltraDev Shopping Cart Patch is a software patch, developed by third-party developer Joseph Scavitto, that updates the UltraDev Shopping Cart server behaviors to function with UltraDev 4.
- **Macromedia CourseBuilder Extension For UltraDev.** The CourseBuilder Extension is a free extension, developed by Macromedia for Dreamweaver 4 and UltraDev 4, that allows Web developers to create eLearning Web applications.
- **Macromedia Command Learning Site Command Extension For UltraDev.** The Learning Site Command Extension allows developers to create comprehensive, database-driven, eLearning applications that track test results and provide complete administrative capabilities.

Feedback

I really want to know what you think about the book, so use the feedback form on the site to send me some comments, good or bad! You can always reach me at `sean@insideultradev.com`.

Appendix B

Glossary

Active Server Pages (ASP). Active Server Pages are HTML pages that include scripting code (usually VBScript or JavaScript) that is passed to Microsoft's Personal Web Server, Internet Information Server, or Internet Information Services, where it is processed and sent to the client browser. Active Server Pages are commonly used to add, edit, and update data stored in a database. The ability to process Active Server Pages can also be added to UNIX and Linux servers with additional software such as Chili!Soft.

Apache Web server. Apache is a popular Web server application for UNIX, Linux, and Windows 2000. Apache is available for free under an "open source" license. Details about Apache can be obtained at http://www.apache.org.

Asset. Assets are objects such as images, movies, links, or sounds that are included in a Web page.

Assets panel. The Assets panel, shown in Figure G.1, catalogs the elements available to be added to a page. The Assets panel reads all available assets from the site cache and categorizes the assets for easy access.

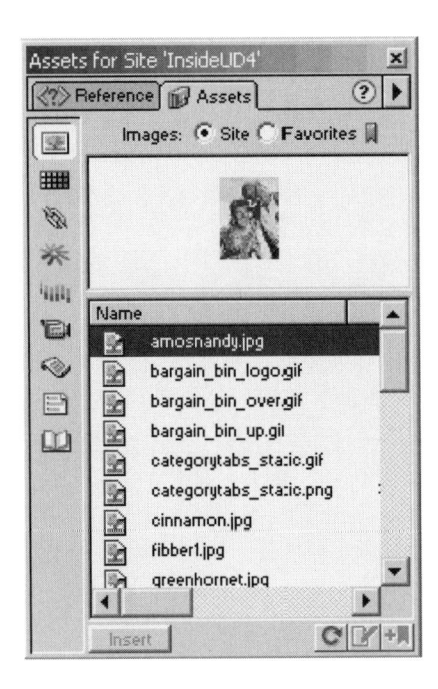

Figure G.1 UltraDev's Assets panel.

Behavior. A behavior is a piece of client-side JavaScript code that performs a task when a specific event occurs. An example of a behavior would be the Swap Image behavior that occurs onMouseOver. This behavior replaces an existing image with an alternate image when the visitor places the mouse cursor over the image.

Behaviors panel. The Behaviors panel, shown in Figure G.2, displays all behaviors currently assigned to a page and provides the ability to add additional behaviors. This panel also allows developers to choose which browsers and versions their pages should be compatible with.

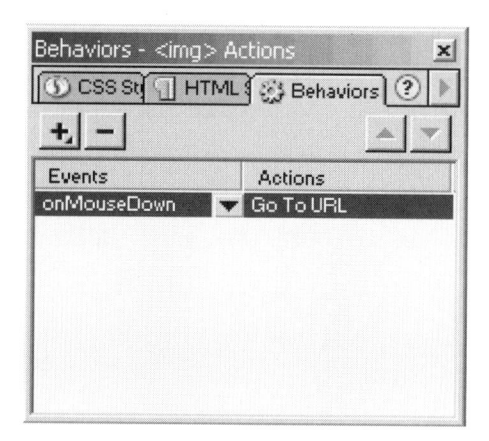

Figure G.2 UltraDev's Behaviors panel.

Binary Large Object (BLOB). A BLOB is usually an image, sound, or other multimedia file that has been encoded due to its large size. Once encoded, these objects can then be stored in a database without hindering its performance. BLOBs are not natively supported by UltraDev.

Chili!Soft ASP. Chili!Soft ASP is a Web application designed by Chili!Soft that allows Web masters to add the ability to process Active Server Pages on a Web server running an operating system other than Windows, such as UNIX or Linux.

Code view. UltraDev's Code view displays the HTML source code and any additional scripting code included in the page.

ColdFusion. ColdFusion is a Web development application suite, developed by Allaire and now owned by Macromedia, that enables users to build complex, database-driven Web sites. ColdFusion applications are driven by the ColdFusion Markup Language (CFML), a language that extends HTML to include dynamic server-side behaviors.

Comanche. The Configuration Manager for Apache (commonly referred to as Comanche) is a graphical user interface being developed and distributed for the Apache

Web server application. Details on Comanche can be viewed at http://www.comanche.org.

Common gateway interface (CGI). The common gateway interface (CGI) is a Web standard that allows a Web application to receive and process data sent from a Web server.

Connection (database). A database connection defines the location of the database and the method used to communicate with it.

Cookie. A cookie is a small file that is placed on a visitor's hard drive by a Web page. The file is used to recall information at a later time. Cookies often store information such as user information, previous searches, and variables that need to be passed from one page to another.

CourseBuilder extension. The CourseBuilder extension is a free extension, developed by Macromedia for Dreamweaver 4 and UltraDev 4, that allows Web developers to create eLearning Web applications.

CourseBuilder interaction. A CourseBuilder interaction describes an eLearning element like a quiz or a poll that can be added to any HTML page using the CourseBuilder extension.

Data Bindings panel. The Data Bindings panel, shown in Figure G.3, displays the data sources that have been added to a specific page. In addition, the Data Bindings panel is used to add new dynamic data sources to a page.

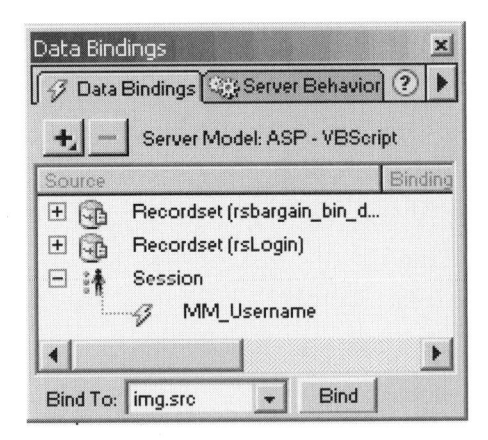

Figure G.3 UltraDev's Data Bindings panel.

Data Source Name (DSN). A Data Source Name (DSN) is used to build a connection between your dynamic Web pages and a database using an ODBC driver.

DB2. DB2 is an enterprise-strength relational database management system developed by IBM. UltraDev is capable of connecting with DB2 databases via an OLE-DB connection.

Delete Record server behavior. The Delete Record server behavior is used to remove a specific record from a database.

Details page. A details page displays the complete information stored in a database record. A details page is often accessed by clicking a link in a search results page.

Drumbeat 2000. Drumbeat 2000, developed by Elemental Software and owned by Macromedia, was the predecessor to UltraDev. Drumbeat 2000 offered Web developers the ability to develop powerful Web applications in both ASP and JSP format. Drumbeat is no longer offered for sale by Macromedia, although limited support is still available.

DSN-less connection. A DSN-less connection describes a connection string that is embedded in a Web application. This connection string dictates the location of the database and what protocol should be used to communicate with it.

Dynamic Web page. A dynamic Web page is one that contains interactive content ranging from animated images and movies to data drawn from a database.

Editable region. An editable region describes a section of a template that can be modified in pages dependent upon the template.

FastCGI. FastCGI is an improvement on the common gateway interface that increases the performance of Web applications that rely on a secondary application to process data.

File Transfer Protocol (FTP). The File Transfer Protocol (FTP) is an Internet protocol that allows users to transfer files between computers. FTP is most commonly used to transfer files from a client computer to a Web server. UltraDev has built-in FTP capabilities that eliminate the need for a third-party FTP application.

Flash. Macromedia Flash is an outstanding Web animation application used to develop everything from rollover buttons to entirely animated Web sites. Flash animations require that the Flash Player be installed in the visitor's browser.

Flash button. Flash buttons are rollover images created using UltraDev's Insert Flash Button command. Flash buttons require that the Flash player be installed in the visitor's browser.

Flash movie. An animation file created using Macromedia Flash.

Flat file. A flat file is a single file that contains unformatted data. In the past, the data in flat files were organized into segments of equal length or divided by a unique character so that the data could be extracted or modified.

Hierarchical Database Model. The Hierarchical Database Model describes a system where child objects are stored and accessed based on their relationship with parent objects. This model is often diagramed using the template of an upside down tree, with each branch storing a data object. In the tree diagram, a single table acts as the "root" of the database from which other tables branch out. Hierarchical databases, although still useful and much more efficient than flat files, are not as effective as relational databases.

Hotspot. A hotspot is a region in an image map assigned a URL link. When a visitor clicks on a hotspot, she is taken to the associated URL. Hotspots can also be used in the creation of rollover images.

HTML. HTML (Hypertext Markup Language) is the set of tags used to develop pages displayed on the World Wide Web. When an HTML page is requested, the Web server sends the page to the Web browser and the browser uses the HTML tags to determine how the page should be displayed.

Insert Record server behavior. The Insert Record server behavior adds a new record to an existing database.

Internet Information Server/Services. Internet Information Server (Windows NT4) and Internet Information Services (Windows 2000) are Microsoft's primary Web server applications. Both versions of IIS offer HTTP and FTP capabilities and are able to process Active Server Pages.

Java Database Connectivity (JDBC). Java Database Connectivity is an application program interface that allows programs written in Java to interact with a database. UltraDev supports the use of JDBC to create database-driven Java Server Pages.

JavaScript. JavaScript is a scripting language developed by Netscape. UltraDev uses JavaScript to enable behaviors and server behaviors that create dynamic elements and interact with databases.

JavaServer Pages (JSP). JavaServer Pages are HTML pages that rely on a small program coded in Java known as a servlet. Servlets are capable of controlling the appearance of the page or interacting with a database. When a JavaServer Page is called, the server executes the servlet that performs a function and then sends a response back to the client browser.

Jrun. JRun is a Java Application Server package developed by Allaire and now owned by Macromedia. JRun provides developers with a J2EE-compliant environment for developing JavaServer Pages.

Keywords. With respect to Web pages, keywords are specific terms defined in a meta tag in the <Head> section of a page that allows some search engines to index the pages. UltraDev enables users to fully customize the keywords on each page.

Launcher bar. The Launcher bar, shown in Figure G.4, provides quick access to several of UltraDev's panels and inspectors.

Figure G.4 UltraDev's Launcher bar.

Layout view. UltraDev's layout view provides an easy way to design a page as it would be viewed in the visitor's browser.

Learning Site Command extension. The Learning Site Command extension is an eLearning extension developed by Macromedia that allows the results of eLearning Web applications to be stored and updated in a database.

Linux. Linux is an inexpensive (and in some cases free) operating system designed to be similar to the UNIX operating system. Linux is often used at the PC level, but can also be used at the server level.

Live Data view. UltraDev's Live Data view displays the page with the dynamic data, usually drawn from a database, in place.

Live objects. Live objects are predefined server behaviors and HTML pages that can be easily added to a page to perform functions such as database navigation and results counting.

Log In User server behavior. The Log In User server behavior compares a submitted username and password with data stored in a database record. Serious security issues have been identified with this behavior and a specific fix must be applied to it for it to function properly. For more information, visit `http://www.macromedia.com/support/ultradev/ts/documents/login_sb_security.htm`.

Macromedia <EDGE> newsletter. The Macromedia <EDGE> newsletter is a monthly newsletter available to Macromedia members. The newsletter contains information on products, seminars, and training offered by Macromedia and is customized for each individual member's preferences. Information about the newsletter can be viewed at http://dynamic.macromedia.com/bin/MM/hub/membershipFAQ.jsp.

Macromedia Extension Manager. Macromedia's Extension Manager, shown in Figure G.5, manages the addition of both Dreamweaver and UltraDev extensions.

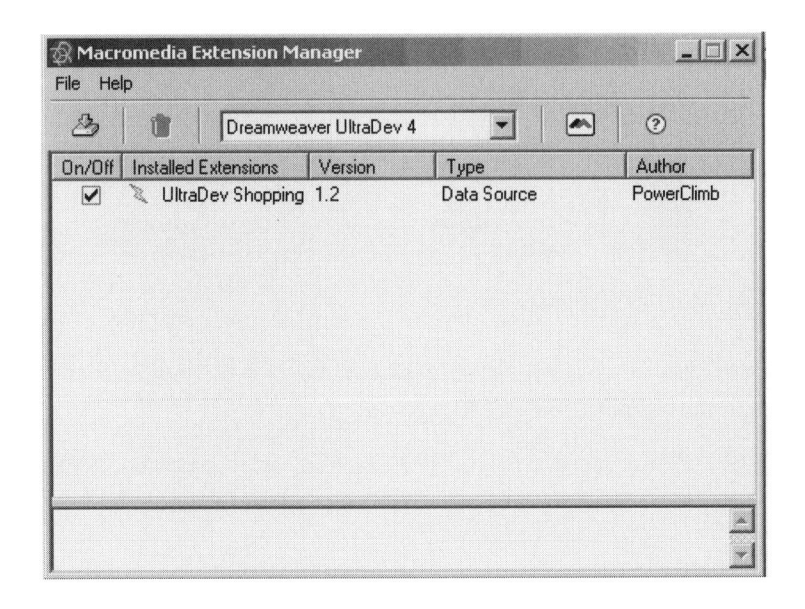

Figure G.5 UltraDev's Extension Manager.

Macromedia Fireworks. Macromedia Fireworks is a graphic design application that focuses primarily on developing high-quality images optimized for the Web.

Meta tag. A meta tag is a piece of code found in an HTML document that describes some aspect of the page. Meta tags often contain a description of the page, keywords used by search engines to index page, or copyright information.

Microsoft Access. Microsoft Access is Microsoft's desktop-level relational database management system. Although Access carries limitations as to concurrent connections and data transfer abilities that hamper its use as a full-blown Web database, it is often used on a development level.

Microsoft SQL Server. Microsoft SQL Server is Microsoft's enterprise-level relational database management system. SQL Server provides a robust set of management tools that make it an attractive choice for developing database-driven Web applications.

MP3. MPEG-1 Audio Layer-3 (commonly known as MP3) is a compression standard used to compress large sound files. MP3 files can be included in a Web page, but are usually downloaded and played using player software included in the user's operating system or from a third-party vendor.

Musical Instrument Digital Interface (MIDI). MIDI is a popular audio protocol used for recording and playing music created using a digital synthesizer. UltraDev supports the inclusion of MIDI files in Web pages.

MyODBC. MyODBC is an ODBC driver developed to connect Web applications to MySQL databases. MyODBC can be downloaded from http://www.mysql.com.

MySQL. MySQL is an open source relational database management system. MySQL uses Structured Query Language to manipulate tables and records. Because of its pricing (free in most cases) and ease of use, MySQL is growing in popularity as the backend choice for database-connected Web sites. MySQL can be downloaded at http:// www.mysql.com.

Network database model. The network database model uses set theory to provide a tree-like hierarchy similar to the architecture used in the hierarchical database model. Using this model, a table can be linked to several other tables in a "many-to-many" relationship rather than just the "one-to-many" relationships allowed in the hierarchical model.

Objects panel. The Objects panel, shown in Figure G.6, contains Web page elements that can be quickly added to a page. Objects are categorized into sections including characters, common elements, forms, frames, head tags, invisible elements, and special items.

Open Database Connectivity (ODBC). Open Database Connectivity is an application-programming interface used for communicating with databases. ODBC drivers are capable of connecting to a wide range of databases, and UltraDev relies on ODBC to communicate with ASP and ColdFusion pages that are connected to a database.

Oracle. Oracle is one of the most powerful relational database management systems available on the market today. Oracle uses the Structured Query Language to manipulate tables and records stored in the database and is capable of communicating with Web

Figure G.6 UltraDev's Objects panel.

pages via both Open Database Connectivity drivers and Java Database Connectivity drivers.

Orphaned page. An orphaned page is one that has no other pages linking to it. Because no links point to it, it is not possible to reach the page except by typing the direct path to the page.

Page properties. When designing a Web page, the page properties refer to unique characteristics for that page, including the page title, page colors, and hyperlink colors. UltraDev provides developers with the ability to update a page's properties in a single dialog box.

Personal Web Server. Personal Web Server is a desktop Web server application designed to serve small Web sites or as a developmental tool for larger sites. Because of limitations on concurrent connections, Personal Web Server does not serve the needs of a high-traffic site, but is ideal for testing pages on a local machine prior to publishing them on the Web. The NT4 Option Pack, which contains Personal Web Server, can be downloaded from Microsoft at `http://www.microsoft.com/ntserver/nts/downloads/recommended/NT4OptPk/default.asp`.

Property inspector. UltraDev's Property inspector, shown in Figure G.7, displays the properties for the selected element. The elements displayed in the Property inspector change depending on the type of element selected.

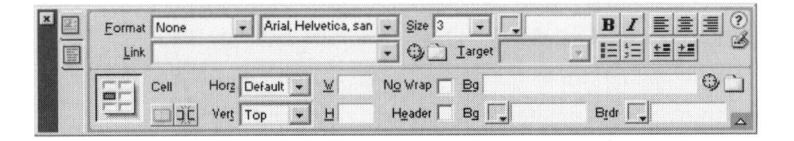

Figure G.7 UltraDev's Property inspector.

Recordset. A recordset is a group of records drawn from a database based upon a SQL query. Recordsets can be used to compare information submitted in a form or to add, edit, and insert records in a database.

Relational database model. The relational database model describes a collection of data objects organized in structured tables. These tables are made up of rows and columns, and the data stored in the tables can be accessed and restructured using queries. Popular databases such as Microsoft's SQL Server and Access, Oracle, and IBM's DB2 are all examples of database management systems based on the relational model.

Repeat Cart Region server behavior. The Repeat Cart Region server behavior is a server behavior included with the UltraDev Shopping Cart extension. This server behavior reads all items stored in the UltraDev Shopping Cart session variables and displays them on the active page.

Repeat Region server behavior. The Repeat Region server behavior reads all records in a recordset and then displays them on the active page in the order they appear in the recordset.

Restrict Access To Page server behavior. The Restrict Access To Page server behavior checks whether a session variable has been created based on username/password authentication. If the session variable does not exist, the visitor is not allowed to view the page and is redirected to another page.

Results page. A Results page displays the records returned from a database search. Often a results page contains links to a details page that displays complete information about the record.

Rollover button. A rollover button is a set of images that are swapped when the visitor places the mouse cursor over it.

Secured Sockets Layer (SSL). Secure Sockets Layer is a protocol used to enable secured transmissions over the Internet. Both Microsoft's Internet Explorer and Netscape's Navigator browsers support SSL transactions on the client side. SSL requires that a digital certificate be installed on the Web server. More information on digital certificates can be found at www.verisign.com.

Server behavior. A server behavior is a piece of code that can be added to a page during the design phase that is executed on the server when the page is loaded.

Server Behaviors panel. The Server Behaviors panel, shown in Figure G.8, displays all server behaviors currently associated with the active page. The Server Behaviors panel also allows you to quickly add new server behaviors to the page.

Session. A session describes the duration of a visitor's time spent exploring a Web site. When a session is created, the Web server maintains information about the user for a period of time or until the visitor ends the session by leaving the site or closing the browser.

Shockwave movie. A Shockwave movie is an animation developed with Macromedia Director. These files require that the visitor have the Shockwave Player installed before the movie can be viewed.

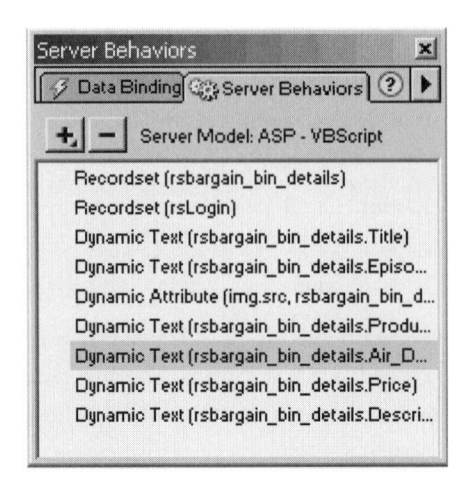

Figure G.8 The Server Behaviors panel.

Shopping Cart. A Shopping Cart system provides visitors to commercial Web sites the opportunity to store products in a temporary state until they begin the purchase process. Shopping Cart systems can be database-driven or rely on cookies to store the items.

Show Region server behavior. The Show Region server behavior examines the contents of a recordset to determine whether or not a specific region of the page should be displayed.

Site window. UltraDev's Site window is used to manage files on both the local workstation and the Web server. The Site window provides developers with site management tools such as search and replace, creating site maps, and adding or removing files from the site.

Split view. UltraDev's Split view displays both the code for the page and the page layout of the elements. The Split view can be customized as to what percentage of the screen is occupied by the Code view and what percentage displays the page layout.

Static Web page. A Static Web page is one that contains no dynamic elements such as database-driven images or text.

Structured Query Language (SQL). The Structured Query Language is the standard programming language used to insert, update, and delete data stored in a database. A variety of SQL "flavors" have been developed by database manufacturers to accommodate the functionality of each database management system.

Template. A template is a document that defines common elements that are displayed on every page based upon that template. UltraDev's templates are divided into editable and non-editable regions. Non-editable regions are those that are inaccessible in pages built upon the template, whereas editable regions are those that are able to be modified.

UltraDev Shopping Cart extension. The UltraDev Shopping Cart extension is an UltraDev extension developed by Rick Crawford of PowerClimb.com. This extension adds a series of server behaviors that enable developers to add shopping cart functionality to an eCommerce site. The UltraDev Shopping Cart extension can be downloaded from `www.powerclimb.com`.

UltraDev Shopping Cart patch. The UltraDev Shopping Cart patch is a software patch, developed by third-party developer Joseph Scavitto, that updates the UltraDev Shopping Cart server behaviors to function with UltraDev 4. The patch can be downloaded from `www.thechocolatestore.com/ultradev`.

UNIX. UNIX is a freeware operating system originally developed by Bell Labs. UNIX is an open source operating system, meaning that anyone is free to develop and modify the operating system code. UNIX's enhanced security and stability make it an attractive operating system for Web servers.

Update Record server behavior. The Update Record server behavior takes the contents of an HTML form and uses them to replace existing data in a database.

Validate Form behavior. The Validate Form behavior checks whether required fields have been filled. If not, the visitor is reminded to fill the fields before they are able to submit the form.

VBScript. VBScript is a scripting language based on Microsoft's Visual Basic language. UltraDev uses VBScript to create Active Server Pages that interact with databases.

Wave file. A Wave file (*.wav) is an audio file that uses the standard PC audio format. Although Wave files are useful for small audio clips, their lack of compression makes them unsuitable for lengthy audio clips.

WYSIWYG. WYSIWYG ("What You See Is What You Get") is a term commonly used to describe a Web page editor that allows the developer to see the page as it will appear when published. In addition, these editors usually allow the developer to construct the page in a graphical format with the application writing all the underlying code. UltraDev is a WYSIWYG editor.

Index

A

accepting payment information, eCommerce sites, 324-329
Access (Microsoft), 60-61
Access 2000, 61
accessing
   pages
      restricting access, 220, 281-282
      with variables, 215
   quizzes, 383-386
   site properties, 90
accounts, user accounts. *See* **user accounts**
Active Server Pages. *See* **ASP**
adding
   additional questions to quizzes, 371-374
   advanced search pages, 247-248
   assets to pages with Assets panel, 143
   audio behavior to pages, 159-160
   confirmation pages, 212, 214
      to eCommerce sites, 329-333
   description tags, 119
   dynamic data, 173-177
   dynamic links, 195-200
   Flash movies, 154-156
   Flash rollover buttons, 148-152
   graphics, 128-130
   header tables, 122-124
   input forms, 204-207
   keywords, 118
   links
      to purchase items, eCommerce sites, 316
      for single parameter searches, 228-230
   logout pages, 290-291
   lost password links, 236
   main data tables, 125-126
   menu pages, 289-291
   meta tags to pages, 117
   movies, 153
   navigation bars to results pages, 267-270
   navigation links tables, 126-127
   page titles, 112
   pages, automatically linked pages, 97-100
   password lookup pages to restricted simple search pages, 237-238
   questions to quizzes, 366-371
   record counters, 272-274
   recordsets, 170-172
      to templates, 198
   results pages to single parameter searches, 230-234
   rotating images, 256-262
   rotating text, 258-262
   search results pages, 248-249
   server behaviors to templates, 198
   sound, 158
   time-dependent images and text, 263-267
   validation pages, 217-218
   video to pages, 158
adjusting links, 129
administration sites, 280-281
   confirmation pages, creating, 306-307
   logout pages, adding, 290-291
   menu pages, adding, 289-291
   new product entry pages, creating, 297-299
   records
      deleting with Delete Record Server behavior, 302-304
      editing with Record Update Form live object, 299-302
      inserting with Record Insertion Form live object, 297-299
   results pages, creating, 293-296
   search pages, creating, 291-293
   security, 286
   templates, designing, 287-289
   testing, 307-309
administrative sites, creating login pages, 282-286
advanced form validation, 208
 advanced search pages
   creating, 246-248
   testing, 250-252

advanced searches, 246
　advanced search pages
　　testing, 250-252
　　advanced search pages, 246-248
　creating results pages, 248-249
advantages
　of eLearning, 360
　of hierachical databases, 56
　of SQL, 73
　of UltraDev, 13-15
　of UltraDev extensions, 394
alerting visitors to empty carts, 352
Allaire, 27
　ColdFusion, 27
　Web sites, 30
analyzing quiz results, 386-387
animated rollover buttons, 145
animations, previewing, 154
Apache Server, 31-32
applying templates to existing pages, 132-134
ASP (Active Server Pages), 32-33
　Chili!Soft, 33
　cost of, 33
　JavaScript, 33-36
　VBScript, 36
Assets panel
　adding assets to pages, 143
　Favorites list, 141-142
　introduction to, 138-139
　refreshing, 140
　viewing images, 140
assigning scores and weights to quiz questions, 382-383
attaching
　Design Notes to pages, 105-106
　Validate Form behavior to objects, 239
audio, 85
　audio behavior, adding to pages, 159-160
automatically linked pages, creating, 97-100
avoiding
　bandwidth thieves, 86
　duplicate usernames, 211-212
　spaces, 369

B

background colors, page properties, 112-115
background images, page properties, 112-115
bandwidth, avoiding bandwidth thieves, 86
base tag, 119
BBEdit 6.0, 6
behaviors
　definition of, 8
　Delete Record Server behavior, 302-304
　Go to Detail Page behavior, 179
　Insert Record, 350
　Log In User Server behavior, 217
　Repeat Cart Region, 346
　Repeat Regions, 346
　server behaviors, 198
　　creating, 395-397
　　modifying, 398
　Show Region behavior, 195, 236
　Update Record, 350
　using without assigning links, 155
　Validate Form behavior, attaching to objects, 239
BLOBs (Binary Large Objects), 257
browsers, previewing pages, 178
building. See also **creating**
　databases for the Web, 64
　　establishing relationships, 68-69
　　tables, 65-68
　　verifying referential integrity, 68-69
　tables, 65-68
buttons
　animated rollover buttons, 145
　creating with Fireworks, 145
　dynamic buttons. *See* dynamic buttons
　My Favorites button, 142

C

cataloging site elements, 83
cells, selecting, 184
CFML (Cold Fusion Markup Language), 40
　code for, 40-41
CGI (Common Gateway Interface), 7
changing
　cursor types, 262
　links, 103
Check In/Check Out feature, enabling, 104
checking for duplicate usernames, 211-212
checking out shopping carts, 348-351
Chili!Soft, 32-33
choosing
　file name extensions, 83
　naming conventions, 122
　page layout view, 120
　page properties, 111
　　background colors and images, 112-115
　　head tags. See head tags
　　link colors, 115
　　titles, 111-112
　platforms for databases, 59-60
　　Access, 60-61
　　IBM DB2, 63
　　MySQL, 62
　　Oracle, 64
　　SQL Server, 61

Web server extensions, 32
    ASP, 33
    CFML, 40
    JSP, 37-39
Web server software, 28
    Apache Server, 31-32
    IIS, 29-30
    Personal Web Server, 28
client-side behaviors versus server-side scripting, JavaScript, 35
code
    for CFML, 40-41
    for JavaScript, 34-35
    for JSP, 38-39
    for VBScript, 36-37
code editors, 6
Cold Fusion Markup Language (CFML), 40
ColdFusion
    Allaire, 27
    using with UltraDev, 41
colors
    background colors, 112-115
    link colors, 115
    Web-safe colors, 115
Column names, 175
commands, Save As, 186
comparing Dreamweaver and UltraDev, 12-13
complex SQL queries, creating, 249
configuring
    FTP connections, 91-92
    Learning Site Command extension, 378-382
    network connections, 89-91
    sites to build dynamic pages, 96-97
    Visual SourceSafe databases, 94
    WebDAV connections, 92-94
    workstations to act as test servers, 41
        Mac workstations, 48-50
        Windows 2000 Profesional, 46-47
        Windows 9x, 42
        Windows NT4, 43-45
confirmation pages
    adding, 212-214
    creating, 306-307
confirming
    order information, eCommerce sites, 320-324
    orders, eCommerce sites, 329-333
connecting databases to the Web, 70
    ODBC, 71-72
connections
    database connections. *See* database connections
    Web servers, 89
        FTP connections, 91-92
        network connections, 89-91
        Visual SourceSafe databases, 94
        WebDAV connections, 92-94

considerations when using Personal Web Server, 30
consolidating tables, 315
controlling Flash movies, 154-156
cookies, 214
    saving contents of shopping carts, 340
cost of ASP, 33
CourseBuilder, 361
    downloading, 361-363
    Enter key, 368
    exploring, 363-365
    FAQs, 361
    installing, 362-363
creating. *See also* **building**
    advanced search pages, 246
    buttons
        with Fireworks, 145
        rollover buttons, 146-148
    confirmation pages, 212-214, 306-307
    database connections, 167-169
    detail pages, 179-185
        from existing pages, 188-189
    dynamic buttons. *See* dynamic buttons
    linked pages, automatically linked pages, 97-100
    links
        for single parameter searches, 229-230
        to detail pages, 178-179
        to password lookup pages, 236-237
    login forms, 214-216
    login pages, 282-286
    logout pages, 219
    main data tables, 125-126
    new product entry pages, 297-299
    pages
        with Site window, 96-97
        from templates, 132
    password lookup results pages, 240-243
    results pages, 248-249, 293-296
        single parameter searches, 230-234
    search pages, 291-293
    server behaviors, 395-397
    signup forms from templates, 201-203
    spotlight items pages, 189-190
    SQL queries, 249
    templates, 131
        for formatted pages, 286-289
    title pages from existing pages, 185-187
    user accounts, visitors creating user accounts, 195
criteria for labels and text fields, 207
cursors, 263
    changing types, 262

D

data bindings, 175
Data Source Name connections, 169
Database Administrator (DBA), 54
database connections, 167
   creating, 167-169
   DSN connections, 169
Database Management System. *See* DBMS
database models, 54
   flat files, 55-56
   hierarchical databases, 56-58
   network databases, 58
   relational databases, 59
database platforms, choosing, 59-60
   Access, 60-61
   IBM DB2, 63
   MySQL, 62
   Oracle, 64
   SQL Server, 61
database-connectivity, tracking users and quiz results, 376
   analyzing results, 386-387
   assigning scores and weights to quiz questions, 382-383
   granting access to quizzes, 383-386
database-connectivity tools, 54
databases, 85
   building for the Web, 64
      establishing relationships, 68-69
      tables, 65-68
      verifying referential integrity, 68-69
   choosing platforms, 59-60
      Access, 60-61
      IBM DB2, 63
      MySQL, 62
      Oracle, 64
      SQL Server, 61
   connecting to the Web, 70
      ODBC, 71-72
   filenames, 66
   for eCommerce, setting up, 315
   recordsets, 170-172
   sample database, familiarizing yourself with, 65-68
DBA (Database Administrator), 54
DBMS (Database Management System), 59
   Access, 60-61
   IBM DB2, 63
   MySQL, 62
   Oracle, 64
   SQL Server, 61
deactivating records, 303
default values, selecting for SQL queries, 197
defining sites, 86-88
Delete Record Server behavior, 302-304
deleting records with Delete Record Server behavior, 302-304
denied permissions, troubleshooting, 176
description tag, 118-119
Design Notes feature, attaching to pages, 105-106
designing
   page layout. *See* page layout
   templates for administration sites, 287-289
detail pages, 178
   creating, 179-185
      from existing pages, 188-189
      links to, 178-179
   displaying, 181
developing site maps, 81
   cataloging site elements, 83
   planning pages and directories, 82
directories, planning, 82
disadvantages of UltraDev extensions, 394
disconnecting pages from templates, 135
displaying
   contents of shopping carts, 344-347
   detail pages, 181
   passwords, 236
Document Design Window, 20
documenting sites, 82
downloading
   CourseBuilder, 361-363
   Learning Site Command extension, 377
   UltraDev Shopping Cart 1.2, 337
dragging selected cells, 184
dragging and dropping files into Site window, 99
Dreamweaver
   comparing with UltraDev, 12-13
   history of UltraDev, 8-9
   upgrading from UltraDev 4, 13
drivers, 70
Drumbeat 2000, history of UltraDev, 9-10
DSN (Data Source Name) connections, 169, 380
duplicate insert entries, 211
duplicate usernames, checking for, 211-212
dynamic buttons, 144
   Flash rollover buttons, adding, 148-152
   rollover buttons, 144-145
      animated rollover buttons, 145
      creating, 146-148
dynamic data, adding to pages, 173-177
dynamic links, adding, 195-200
dynamic pages
   cataloging site elements, 83-84
   configuring
      Mac workstations, 48-50
      Windows 2000 Professional to host, 46-47

forms 425

Windows NT4 to host, 43-45
your site to build dynamic pages with Site
  window, 96-97
identifying, 84
dynamic Web pages, configuring workstations as test servers, 41

E

ECommerce, 314-315
  confirming order information, 320-324
  databases, setting up, 315
  links to purchase items, adding, 316
  orders, confirming, 329-333
  payment information, accepting, 324-329
  shipping information, 317-320
  shopping carts, 337
    alerting visitors to empty carts, 352
    checking out, 348-351
    creating links to, 341-343
    creating shopping cart pages, 344-347
    installing, 337-339
    setting parameters, 339-341
    testing, 352-355
    verifying shipping and purchase information, 348-351
  testing, 333-335, 337
editable regions of templates, selecting, 132
editing
  "live" pages, 42
  pages
    on Web servers, 90
    in workgroup environments, 104-106
  records with Record Update Form live object, 299-302
editors, 6
eLearning
  advantages of, 360
  CourseBuilder. *See* CourseBuilder
  Learning Site command extension
    downloading and installing, 377
    setting up, 378-382
  quizzes. *See* quizzes
  reasons for using, 360-361
  tracking users and quiz results, 376
    analyzing results, 386-387
    assigning scores and weights to quiz questions, 382-383
    granting access to quizzes, 383-386
Elemental Software, Drumbeat 2000, 9
email, sending passwords through, 243
embedding Windows Media Player, 158
Enter key, CourseBuilder, 368

establishing
  ODBC data sources, 71-72
  relationships, 68-69
existing sites, mapping, 89
expanding Property Inspector, 121
explanations for Gallery Category List, 365
exploring CourseBuilder, 363-365
extended site maps, 83
extensions. *See also* **UltraDev extensions**
  CourseBuilder. *See* CourseBuilder
  file names, 83
  Learning Site Command. *See* Learning Site Command extension

F

FAQs (Frequently Asked Questions), CourseBuilder, 361
Favorites list, Assets panel, 141-142
fields
  searching different fields, 292
  verifying required fields are filled, 208-209
file names
  choosing extensions, 83
  lowercase, 82
File Transfer Protocol (FTP), 89
filenames, databases, 66
files
  dragging and dropping into Site window, 99
  site files, viewing, 112
  synchronizing in Site window, 100-102
  templates. *See* templates
finding
  lightning bolt icon, 85
  root folder, 86
  UltraDev extensions, 391
Fireworks, 128
  creating buttons, 145
Flash movies, 153-154
  adding, 154-156
  loops, 157
Flash rollover buttons, adding, 148-152
flat files, database models, 55-56
form fields
  linking to appropriate database fields, 209-211
  values, setting, 332
form validation, 208-209
  JavaScript, 209
formatted pages, creating templates for, 286-289
formatting, 173
forms
  guidelines for creating, 201
  input forms, adding, 204-207

login forms, creating, 214-216
password lookup forms, 237-238
placing insertion points in empty forms, 238
product search forms, 293
signup forms. *See* signup forms
verifying, 208
FrontPage Personal Web Server, 42
FTP (File Transfer Protocol), 89
connections, configuring, 91-92
functions, random functions, 267

G-H

Gallery Category List, explanations for, 365
generating Web pages, 26-27
Go to Detail Page behavior, 179
granting access to quizzes, 383-386
graphical flat file databases, limitations of, 55
graphics. *See also* **images**
adding to pages with Assets panel, 143
inserting, 127-130
linking, 127-130
guidelines for creating forms, 201

head tags, 115-116, 119
base tag, 119
description tag, 118-119
link tag, 119
meta tags, 116
refresh tag, 119
header tables, adding, 122-124
hierarchical databases, database models, 56-58
history
of UltraDev, 8-11
of Web development prior to UltraDev, 6-8
HomeSite 4.5, 6
HTML (HyperText Markup Language), 26
HTTP (Hypertext Transfer Protocol), WebDAV, 92
IBM DB2, 63

I-J

icons, finding lightning bolt icon, 85
identifying
dynamic pages, 84
orphaned pages, 102-103
IIS (Internet Information Server), 29-30
images, 85
avoiding bandwidth thieves, 86
background images, 112-115
BLOBs, 257
links to, 261
rotating images. *See* rotating, images

time-dependent images, adding, 263-267
viewing with Assets panel, 140
input forms, adding, 204-207
insert actions, duplicate entries, 211
Insert Record behavior, 350
insert record pages, creating with Record Insertion Form live object, 297-299
inserting
graphics, 127-130
main tables, 120-122
insertion points, placing in empty forms, 238
installing
CourseBuilder, 362-363
Learning Site Command extension, 377
shopping carts, 337-339
UltraDev extensions, 393
Internet Information Server (IIS), 29-30

J2EE (Java 2 Enterprise Edition), 39
Java Database Connectivity, (JDBC), 16, 70
Java Server Pages. *See* **JSP**
JavaScript, 33
ASP, 33, 35-36
client-side behaviors versus server-side scripting, 35
code, 34-35
form validation, 209
versus JScript, 36
JDBC (Java Database Connectivity), 16, 70
Jscript versus JavaScript, 36
JSP (Java Server Pages), 37-39
code for, 38-39

K-L

keywords, 117-118
trademarked keywords, 118

label fields, criteria for, 207
Launcher toolbar, 22
Learning Site Command extension, 376
downloading, 377
installing, 377
setting up, 378-382
lightning bolt icon, finding, 85
limitations
of graphical flat file databases, 55
of network databases, 58
limiting access to sites, 281-282
link colors, page properties, 115
link tag, 119
linking
form fields to appropriate database fields, 209-211
graphics, 127-130

links
    adding to single parameter searches, 228-230
    adjusting, 129
    changing multiple links, 103
    creating to detail pages, 178-179
    dynamic links, adding, 195-200
    to images, 261
    to password lookup pages, creating, 236-237
    to purchase items, eCommerce sites, 316
    to search results pages, 267-270
    to shopping carts, 341-343
    using behaviors without assigning links, 155
    verifying, 102-103
    versus BLOBs, 257
location of templates, 132
Log In User Server behavior, 217
logging in/out, user accounts, 214
login forms, creating, 214, 216
login pages, 195
    creating, 282-286
    limiting access to, 281-282
    and templates, 282
logout pages
    adding, 290-291
    creating, 219
loops, Flash movies, 157
lost password links, adding, 236
lowercase file names, 82

M

Mac
    setting up Personal Web Server, 49
    versions of Personal Web Server, 48
Mac users, RDBC, 17
Mac workstations, configuring workstations to host dynamic pages, 48-50
Macormedia
    approved extensions, 391
    Fireworks, 128
Macromedia Dreamweaver UltraDev 4.0. *See* UltraDev
main data tables, adding, 125-126
main tables, creating, 120-122
mapping existing sites, 89
MDAC (Microsoft Data Access Components), 381
menu pages, adding, 289-291
meta tags, 116
    adding to pages, 117
Microsoft Access, 60-61
Microsoft Data Access Components (MDAC), 381

Microsoft SQL Server, 61
Microsoft Web site, 29
MIDI files, 159
models of databases. *See* database models
modifying server behaviors, 398
movies
    adding
        to pages, 153
        video to pages, 158
    Flash movies, 153-156
    Shockwave movies, 157
MP3 files, 159
multimedia, 85
multimedia management, 17
multiple parameters, recordsets, 241
multiple selections, 171
multiple views, switching between, 15
MXI File Creator packager extension, 399
My Favorites button, troubleshooting, 142
MySQL, Web sites, 62

N

naming conventions, 82
    choosing, 122
    recordsets, 187
    for rollover buttons, 147
    Save As command, 187
    text block-naming conventions, 396
navigating with menu pages, 289-291
navigation bars, adding to results pages, 267-270
navigation links tables, adding, 126-127
nested tables, selecting with status bar, 234
network connections, configuring, 89-91
network databases, database models, 58
new features
    multimedia management, 17
    RDBC, 16
    switching between multiple views, 15
    syntax coloring, 16
new product entry pages, creating, 297-299

O-P

objects
    Record Insertion Form live object, 297-299
    Record Update Form live object, 299-302
Objects panel, 21-22
obtaining Personal Web Server, 29
ODBC (Open Database Connectivity), 16
    data sources, establishing, 71-72
ODBC data source, DSN connections, 169

Open Database Connectivity Driver, 70
Oracle, 64
order information, confirming, 320-324
orders
    eCommerce sites, confirming, 329-333
    simultaneous orders, 331
orphaned pages, identifying, 102-103

packaging UltraDev extensions, 398-399
page layout, 120
    choosing a view, 120
    creating main tables, 120-122
    graphics, linking and inserting, 127-130
    header tables, adding, 122-124
    main data tables, adding, 125-126
    navigation links tables, adding, 126-127
pages
    accessing with variables, 215
    adding
        assets to, 143
        description tags to pages, 119
        dynamic data to, 173-177
        keywords, 118
        meta tags to, 117
        movies. See *movies*
        recordsets, 170-172
        sound. See *sound*
    advanced search pages. *See* advanced search pages
    applying templates to, 132-134
    attaching Design Notes, 105-106
    confirmation pages
        adding, 212-214
        creating, 306-307
    creating
        detail pages from existing pages, 188-189
        with Site window, 96-97
        from templates, 132
        title pages from existing pages, 185-187
    detail pages, 178
        creating, 179-185
        displaying, 181
    disconnecting from templates, 135
    editing
        on Web servers, 90
        in workgroup environments, 104-106
    insert record pages, creating with Record Insertion Form live object, 297-299
    linked pages, creating automatically linked pages, 97-100
    login pages. *See* login pages
    logout pages
        adding, 290-291
        creating, 219
    menu pages. *See* menu pages
    orphaned pages, identifying, 102-103

    planning, 82
    previewing with browsers, 178
    properties, 111-115
    restricting access to, 220
    results pages. *See* results pages
    search pages. *See* search pages
    signup pages, 195
    spotlight items pages, creating, 189-190
    testing, 220-222
        additions to, 200
    updating pages that are are detached from templates, 230
    validation pages, adding, 217-218
parameters, setting for shopping carts, 339-341
passing variables, 324
password lookup pages
    adding to restricted simple search pages, 237-238
    links to, creating, 236-237
    testing, 243-244
password lookup results pages, creating, 240-243
password lookups, 235
passwords, 235
    displaying, 236
    lost password links, adding, 236
    sending through email, 243
    verifying, 206
payment information, accepting (eCommerce sites), 324-329
permissions, troubleshooting denied permissions, 176
Personal Web Server, 28
    considerations when using, 30
    Mac version, 48
    obtaining, 29
    setting up
        on a Mac, 49
        on Windows 9x machines, 42
    testing, 43
placeholders, 83
placing insertion points in empty forms, 238
planning sites, 80-81
platforms for databases, choosing, 59-60
    Access, 60-61
    IBM DB2, 63
    MySQL, 62
    Oracle, 64
    SQL Server, 61
playing sounds with QuickTime, 160
previewing
    animations, 154
    pages with browsers, 178
primary keys, 67
product search forms, 293

pronouncing SQL, 73
properties of pages. *See* pages, properties
Properties Palette, 21
Property Inspector, 21, 121
purchase information, verifying, 348-351

Q-R

queries, creating SQL queries, 249
questions, adding
    additional questions to quizzes, 371-374
    to quizzes, 366-371
QuickTime, playing sounds, 160
quizzes, 365
    adding questions, 366-374
    analyzing results, 386-387
    assigning scores and weights to questions, 382-383
    creating quiz pages, 366
    granting access to, 383-386
    testing, 374-376

random functions, 267
randomizing recordsets, 262
rating UltraDev extensions, 395
RDBC (remote database connectivity), 16-17
RealNetwork, RealPlayer, 158
RealPlayer, 158
reasons for using, eLearning, 360-361
record counters, adding to results pages, 272-274
Record Insertion Form live object, creating insert record pages, 297-299
Record Update Form live object, editing records, 299-302
records
    deactivating, 303
    deleting with Delete Record Server behavior, 302-304
    editing with Record Update Form live object, 299-302
    showing a certain number of, 186-188
Recordset Navigation Bar Live Object, 270
recordsets
    adding
        to pages, 170-172
        to templates, 198
    creating with multiple recordsets, 241
    naming conventions, 187
    randomizing, 262
    showing a certain number of records, 186-188
    Update Record live object, 300
referential integrity, verifying, 68-69
refresh tag, 119

refreshing Assets panel, 140
relational databases, database models, 59
relationships
    establishing, 68-69
    table relationships, 58
remote database connectivity. *See* RDBC
remote sites, dragging files to, 100
removing. *See* deleting
Repeat Cart Region behavior versus Repeat Regions behavior, 346
Repeat Regions server behavior versus Repeat Cart Region behavior, 346
requirements for Visual SourceSafe, 94
restricted simple search pages, 235-236
    links to password lookup pages, creating, 236-237
    password lookup pages, 235
        adding, 237-238
        testing, 243-244
    password lookup results pages, creating, 240-243
restricting access to pages, 220
results of quizzes, analyzing, 386-387
results pages. *See also* search results pages
    adding record counters, 272-274
    creating, 248-249, 293-296
    links to, 267-270
reusing pages, creating
    detail pages, 188-189
    new title pages, 185-187
reviewing UltraDev extensions, 395
rollover buttons, 144-145
    animated rollover buttons, 145
    creating, 146-148
    Flash rollover buttons, adding, 148-152
    naming conventions, 147
root folder, finding, 86
rotating
    images, 256-262
    text, adding, 258-262

S

sample databases, familiarizing yourself with, 65-68
Save As command, 186
scripting, client-side behaviors versus server-side scripting, 35
search engines
    keywords, 117-118
    spiders, 116
search pages, creating, 291-293
search results pages, 267. *See also* results pages

searches
    advanced search capabilities. *See* advanced searches
    restricted simple search pages. *See* restricted simple search pages
    single parameter searches. *See* single parameter searches
searching different fields, 292
Secure Sockets Layer. *See* **SSL**
security
    administration sites, 286
    SSL, 208
    Web pages, 208
selecting
    cells, 184
    default values for SQL queries, 197
    editable regions of templates, 132
    multiple items, 171
    nested tables with status bar, 234
    payment types, eCommerce sites, 324-329
    tables, 121
sending passwords through email, 243
server behaviors, 17
    adding to templates, 198
    creating, 395-397
    modifying, 398
server-side scripting versus client-side behaviors, 35
serverlets, 37
Set as Home Page box, 379
shipping information
    eCommerce sites, 317-320
    verifying, 348-351
Shockwave movies, 157
shopping carts, 337
    alerting visitors to empty carts, 352
    checking out, 348-351
    creating shopping cart pages, 344-347
    installing, 337-339
    links to, 341-343
    saving contents with cookies, 340
    setting parameters, 339-341
    testing, 352-353, 355
Show Region behavior, 195, 236
signup forms, 201-203
signup pages, 195
Simple Mail Transfer Protocol (SMTP), 243
simultaneous orders, 331
single parameter searches, 228
    adding
        links, 228-230
        results pages, 230-234
site elements, cataloging, 83
site files, viewing, 112

site mapping tools, 82
site maps, 81-83
site properties, accessing, 90
Site window, 95
    adding automatically linked pages, 97-100
    creating new pages, 96-97
    dragging and dropping files, 99
    files, synchronizing, 100-102
sites. *See also* **pages; Web sites**
    administration sites. *See* administration sites
    defining, 86-88
    documenting, 82
    mapping existing sites, 89
SMTP (Simple Mail Transfer Protocol), 243
sound, 158-160
sounds, 85
SourceSafe Updater, 94
spaces, avoiding, 369
speeding up processes, UltraDev, 73
spiders, 116
spotlight items pages, creating, 189-190
SQL (Structured Query Language), 73
    queries, selecting default values for, 197
SQL Server, 61
SSL (Secure Sockets Layer), 208
    passwords, displaying, 236
static pages, cataloging site elements, 83
status bar, selecting nested tables, 234
Structured Query Language. *See* **SQL**
submitting data to databases, 209-211
switching between multiple views, 15
synchronizing files in Site window, 100-102
syntax coloring, 16

T

table relationships, 58
tables
    building, 65-68
    consolidating, 315
    header tables, adding, 122-124
    main data tables, adding, 125-126
    main tables, creating, 120-122
    navigation links tables, adding, 126-127
    nested tables, selecting with status bar, 234
    selecting, 121
tags
    base tags, 119
    description tags, 118-119
    head tags. *See* head tags
    link tags, 119
    meta tags, 116
    refresh tags, 119

templates, 131
    adding recordsets and server behaviors to, 198
    administration sites, designing for, 287-289
    applying to existing pages, 132-134
    creating, 131
        for formatted pages, 286-289
        new pages from, 132
    disconnecting pages from, 135
    editable regions, selecting, 132
    location of, 132
    and login pages, 282
    signup forms, 201-203
    updating, 203
test servers, configuring workstations
    Mac workstations, 48-50
    Windows 2000 Professional, 46-47
    Windows 9x, 42
    Windows NT4, 43-45
testing
    additions to pages, 200
    administration sites, 307-309
    advanced search pages, 250-252
    eCommerce sites, 333-337
    pages, 220-222
    password lookup, 243-244
    Personal Web Server installation, 43
    quizzes, 374-376
    shopping carts, 352-355
text
    rotating text, adding, 258-262
    time-dependent text, adding, 263-267
text block-naming conventions, 396
text fields, criteria for, 207
time-dependent images, adding, 263-267
time-dependent text, adding, 263-267
title pages, creating from existing pages, 185-187
titles, page titles, 111-112
toolbars, Launcher, 22
tools
    database-connectivity tools, 54
    Property Inspector. *See* Property Inspector
    site mapping tools, 82
    Window Size tool, 20
tracking users with database-connectivity, 376
    analyzing results, 386-387
    assigning scores and weights to quiz questions, 382-383
    granting access to quizzes, 383-386
trademarked keywords, 118
troubleshooting
    denied permissions, 176
    My Favorites button, 142

U

UltraDev, comparing with Dreamweaver, 12-13
UltraDev Exchange, 391
UltraDev extensions, 390-391
    advantages of, 394
    disadvantages of, 394
    finding them, 391
    installing, 393
    MXI File Creator Packager, 399
    packaging, 398-399
    reviewing, 395
UltraDev sites, planning, 80
Update Record behavior, 350
Update Record live objects, recordsets, 300
updating
    pages
        that are detached from templates, 230
        with time-dependent images and text, 263-267
    templates, 203
upgrading to UltraDev 4 from Dreamweaver, 13
user accounts
    adding input forms, 204-207
    checking for duplicate usernames, 211-212
    confirmation pages, adding, 212-214
    enabling visitors to create user accounts, 195
    input forms, adding, 204-207
    logging in/out, 214
    login forms, creating, 214-216
    logout pages, creating, 219
    signup forms, creating, 201
    submitting data to database, 209-211
    testing pages, 220-222
    validation pages, adding, 217-218
    verifying required fields are filled, 208-209
usernames, checking for duplicates, 211-212
users, validating credentials, 240-243

V

Validate Form behavior, attaching to objects 239
validating user's credentials, 240-243
validation pages, adding, 217-218
variables
    accessing pages, 215
    passing, 324
VBScript, 36
    code for, 36-37
verifying
    forms, 208
    links, 102-103

passwords, 206
referential integrity, 68-69
required fields are filled, 208-209
shipping and purchase information, 348-351
VeriSign, 236
video, adding to pages, 158
viewing
images with Assets panel, 140
quiz results from administrative sites, 386-387
site files, 112
visitors, enabling visitors to create user accounts, 195
Visual SourceSafe, 94

W-Z

w3 JMail, 243
WAV files, 158
Web
building databases for, 64
establishing relationships, 68-69
tables, 65-68
verifying referential integrity, 68-69
connecting databases to, 70
ODBC, 71-72
Web development, 80-81
prior to UltraDev, 6-8
Web pages
generating, 26-27
security, 208
Web server extensions, choosing, 32
ASP, 33
CFML, 40
JSP, 37, 39
Web server processes, 26
Web servers
editing pages, 90
setting up connections, 89
FTP connections, 91-92
network connections, 89-91
Visual SourceSafe databases, 94
WebDAV connections, 92-94
software, choosing
Apache Server, 31-32
IIS, 29-30
Personal Web Server, 28
Web sites
Allaire, 30
AspEmail, 243
Chili!Soft, 32
eCommerce sites. *See* eCommerce sites
Fireworks, 128
Microsoft Web site, 29
MySQL, 62

quizzes. *See* quizzes
UltraDev Exchange, 391
VBScript, 36
VeriSign, 236
w3 JMail, 243
Web-safe colors, link colors, 115
WebDAV connections, configuring, 92-94
Window Size tool, 20
windows, Document Design Window, 20
Windows 2000 Professional, configuring workstations to host dynamic pages, 46-47
Windows 9x, 42
Windows Media Player, embedding, 158
Windows NT4, configuring workstations to host dynamic pages, 43-45
Windows Sound Recorder, 159
workgroup environments, editing pages, 104-106
workstations, configuring as test servers, 41
Mac workstations, 48-50
Windows 2000 Professional, 46-47
Windows 9x, 42
Windows NT4, 43-45
WYSIWYG editors, 6

Solutions from experts you know and trust.

www.informit.com

- OPERATING SYSTEMS
- WEB DEVELOPMENT
- PROGRAMMING
- NETWORKING
- CERTIFICATION
- AND MORE...

**Expert Access.
Free Content.**

New Riders has partnered with **InformIT.com** to bring technical information to your desktop. Drawing on New Riders authors and reviewers to provide additional information on topics you're interested in, **InformIT.com** has free, in-depth information you won't find anywhere else.

- **Master the skills you need, when you need them**
- **Call on resources from some of the best minds in the industry**
- **Get answers when you need them, using InformIT's comprehensive library or live experts online**
- **Go above and beyond what you find in New Riders books, extending your knowledge**

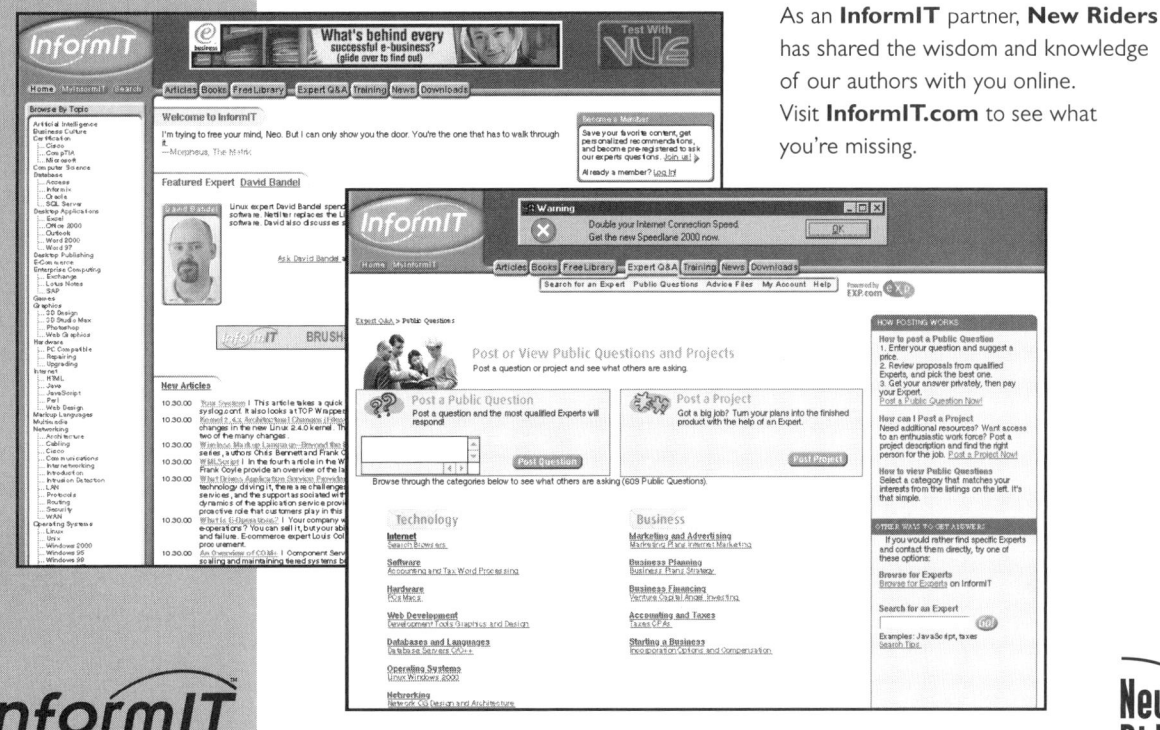

As an **InformIT** partner, **New Riders** has shared the wisdom and knowledge of our authors with you online. Visit **InformIT.com** to see what you're missing.

www.informit.com ▪ www.newriders.com

New Riders

VOICES THAT MATTER

Inside Dreamweaver 4
Anne-Marie Yerks, John Pickett
0735710848
$44.99 (with CD-ROM)
Learn how long-time Dreamweaver users make it really perform! These users share their secrets and give you learning activities that present the new features of Dreamweaver.

Dreamweaver 4 Magic
Al Sparber
0735710465
$45.00 (with CD-ROM)
"If you are serious about Web work, this book will take you to a new level and you won't look back either."
—an online reviewer

**Flash Web Design:
The v5 Remix**
Hillman Curtis
0735710988
$45.00
"The Hillman Curtis deconstruction method of teaching Flash is invaluable. Not only does he teach you the concepts, but by looking at Flash animations in a deconstructive mode you will be able to determine how they were created."
—an online reviewer

**Flash ActionScript
for Designers: Drag,
Slide, Fade**
Brendan Dawes
0735710473
$45.00
In response to the high demand for ActionScripting books! *Drag, Slide, Fade* explains and explores the power of ActionScript for those who design it. The text is supported by four-colored visuals and annotated codes.

**Generator/Flash Web
Development**
Richard Alvarez, Jason Taylor, Matthew Groch
0735710805
$34.99 (with CD-ROM)
"With the publication of Generator/Flash Web Development, the technology world has found a new bible. From conception to completion, this book will take projects to new heights. The knowledge demonstrated by Alvarez, Taylor, and Groch is vast, as are the possibilities that this book will open."
—an online reviewer

Flash to the Core
Joshua Davis
0735711046
$45.00 Coming Soon
Unlike any other Flash book on the market! Joshua Davis shares his cutting-edge techniques and coding secrets. These methods are guaranteed to challenge and inspire all professional readers.

New Riders

W W W . N E W R I D E R S . C O M

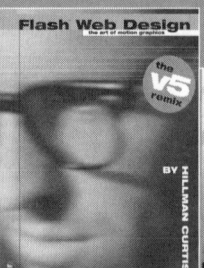